RMY RES
US AR

To Captain Scott Bertinetti -

With best wishes
for continued success.

Jim Currie
23 June 1998

TWICE *the Citizen*

A History of the United States Army Reserve, 1908–1995

(Second Revised and Expanded Edition)

JAMES T. CURRIE
Colonel, USAR

James T. Currie
Colonel, USAR

RICHARD B. CROSSLAND
Colonel, USAR

Department of the Army Pamphlet 140–14

Office of the Chief, Army Reserve
Washington, DC
1997

For sale by the U.S. Government Printing Office
Superintendent of Documents, Mail Stop: SSOP, Washington, DC 20402-9328
ISBN 0-16-048401-4

Acknowledgments

The authors of this study owe debts of gratitude to numerous individuals who helped with what has been by history-writing standards a whirlwind project. Special support was offered from the beginning by Maj. Gen. William R. Berkman, Chief, Army Reserve, and after he joined OCAR, by Brig. Gen. Harry J. Mott, III, Deputy Chief, Army Reserve.

Our immediate supervisor, Lewis C. Brodsky, Director of Public Affairs, Office of the Chief, Army Reserve, has given the entire project his complete and whole-hearted support. We are grateful that amidst the more glamorous fanfare that accompanied the Seventy-fifth Anniversary celebrations for the USAR, he never lost sight of the usefulness and importance of the history project. We owe you a lot, Lew.

The people who helped us locate and collect materials for this study were many. Personnel in the Modern Military Branch of the National Archives were always helpful, particularly Will Mahoney. At the Army's Center of Military History, Hannah Zeidlik and Karl Cocke guided us to documents we might otherwise have missed, and Mr. Cocke and Col. Bettie Morden spent considerable time and effort reviewing the manuscript for us. Within the Army Library at the Pentagon, Patricia Tugwell was always ready to assist us in locating an obscure first name or resolving an inconsistency. Bill Hauser at the US Forest Service's Audio-Visual Archives furnished pictures of the CCC, while the Defense Audiovisual Agency Archives were a treasure trove of old photographs for the book.

Other individual historians who shared with us their knowledge and comments were the Chief of the Joint Chiefs of Staff Historical Office—Willard Webb—and some of his staff members, specifically Walter Poole, Helen Bailey, and Truman Strobridge. Capt. Leonid Kondratiuk, Historian for the National Guard Bureau, was critical, but perceptive in what he had to say. To all of you, we offer our heartfelt gratitude. We absolve you, however, from any remaining differences or errors of fact or interpretation, for we were sometimes too stubborn to take your well-thought suggestions, or our own research led us to different conclusions from yours.

To Lynda Poole, who alone bore the typing load for this project in addition to her many other duties, we give our thanks.

Finally, we want to recognize our families. The spouses of military personnel always put up with so much, and our wives—Maryanna Crossland and Janis Rabbitt Currie—have endured this project with the greatest of patience and understanding. We have enjoyed researching and writing this book, and we hope that it may prove useful and interesting to the reader.

RICHARD B. CROSSLAND
Lieutenant Colonel, USAR
United States Army Training
and Doctrine Command
Fort Monroe, Va.

JAMES T. CURRIE
Major, USAR
Washington, DC

September 1983

Da Pam 140–14

Contents

ACKNOWLEDGMENTS *iii*

LIST OF TABLES *vii*

ACRONYMS AND ABBREVIATIONS *ix*

FOREWORD *xiii*

PREFACE TO THE SECOND EDITION *xvii*

ACKNOWLEDGMENTS FOR THE SECOND EDITION *xix*

A WORD ABOUT FORMAT AND METHODOLOGY *xxi*

DEDICATION *xxiii*

1 Before There Was An Army Reserve *1*

2 The Early Years *17*

3 Between the World Wars, 1919–1939 *33*

4 Mobilization and War, 1940–1945 *63*

5 Peace—And War Again, 1946–1953 *79*

6 The Eisenhower Years, 1953–1961 *115*

7 The Berlin Mobilization *133*

8 Reorganizations Lay the Groundwork for the Total Army Policy *149*

9 The Army Reserve and Vietnam *193*

10 Toward Greater Partnership *211*

11 The Caribbean/Latin America Connection *267*

12 Becoming Part of the Total Force, 1984–1991 *287*

13 Changes in Organizational Structure Create the Modern Army Reserve *317*

14 The Individual Reservist, 1984–1991, Issues of Numbers, Quality, Equality *343*

15 Desert Shield/Desert Storm: Assembling the Force *369*

16 Desert Shield/Desert Storm: USAR Troop Units Respond *383*

17 Desert Shield/Desert Storm: Looking the Enemy in the Eye *407*

18 Desert Shield/Desert Storm: Working with U.S. Soldiers *433*

19 Desert Shield/Desert Storm: Medics and Chaplains—Caring for Body and Soul *457*

20 Desert Shield/Desert Storm: Total Force? *475*

21 Desert Shield/Desert Storm: ARPERCEN and the IRR *493*

22 After the Storm, 1991–1994 *521*

23 Training, Readiness, and Real-World Missions, 1992–1994 *549*

Conclusion *581*

Appendix A Chiefs of the Army Reserve *587*

Appendix B Army Reserve (Organized Reserve Corps) Appropriations *589*

Appendix C Army Reserve Units Mobilized in 1968 *593*

Appendix D Post-Vietnam Emergency Use of the Army Reserve *607*

Appendix E Strength of the Army Reserve Prior to World War II *611*

Appendix F Strength of the Army Reserve after World War II *613*

Appendix G Army Reservists on Active Duty—1948–1982 *615*

Appendix H Western Union Mailgram *617*

Select Bibliography *621*

The Authors *655*

Index *657*

Photographs follow Chapters Three, Five, Eight, Fourteen, and Twenty

List of Tables

Table 2–1 Number of Physicians in the US Army, 1908–1916 *19*

Table 3–1 ROTC Appointments in the ORC, 1920–1937 *39*

Table 3–2 ROTC and CMTC, FY's 1925–1928 *40*

Table 3–3 Active Duty Training (15 Days or Less) of ORC Members, 1924–1930 *41*

Table 3–4 Active Duty Training (14 Days or Less) of ORC Members, 1931–1940 *48*

Table 3–5 Extension Course Enrollment, 1923–1931 *50*

Table 4–1 Percentage of Organized Reservists in Officer Cadres *71*

Table 5–1 ORC Strength, December 31, 1947 *88*

Table 8–1 Comparison of Present and Proposed Reserve Component Structure (1965) *166*

Table 8–2 Force Structure and Organization (Three Brigade Plan—1967) *178*

Table 9–1 Units Mobilized *203*

Table 12–1 Full-Time Support for the Reserve Components *302*

Table 12–2 Army Reserve Components Equipment Funding *304*

Table 12–3 Major Items of Equipment Status (USAR), 1983–91 *305*

Table 14–1 Individual Ready Reserve Screening Results, FY 1987 *350*

Table 14–2 Army Reserve Individual Mobilization Augmentees *352*

Table 14–3 Women in the Army Reserve *354*

Table 14–4 Enlisted Retention Rates *355*

Table 19–1 Medical Units Deployed to the Persian Gulf *459*

Table 21–1 Enlisted IRR—Distribution By Career Management Field *494*

Table 21–2 MOs of Certain IRR Members Activated for Desert Shield/Desert Storm *497–98*

Table 21–3 Army IMA Strength and Rank as of 30 June 1990 *512*

Table 22–1 Organizational Structure of the Army Reserve *546*

Table 23–1 Army Individual Mobilization Augmentees *567*

Table 23–2 Enlisted Retention Rates *574*

Table 23–3 Army Reserve Component Equipment Funding *576*

Table 23–4 Major Items of Equipment Status (USAR), 1992–95 *576*

Acronyms and Abbreviations

ACS	Assistant Chief of Staff (Army)
ADT	Active Duty for Training
AEF	American Expeditionary Force
AGF	Army Ground Forces
AGI	Annual General Inspection
AGR	Active Guard and Reserve
AIT	Advanced Individual Training
Amb	Ambulance
AMOPS	Army Mobilization and Operations Planning System
AMSA	Area Maintenance Support Activities
ARCOM	Army Commendation Medal; Army Reserve Command
ARMC	Army Readiness and Mobilization Command
ARNG	Army National Guard
ARR	Army Readiness Region
ART	Army Reserve Technician
ARTEP	Army Training and Evaluation Program
ATT	Army Training Test
AUS	Army of the United States
AW	Automatic Weapon
AWOL	Absent without leave
Bn	Battalion
Brig. Gen.	Brigadier General
BUT	Basic Unit Training
Capt.	Captain
CAR	Chief, Army Reserve
CASP	Civilian Acquired Skills Program
CCC	Civilian Conservation Corps
Cdr	Commander
CG	Commanding General

C&GSC	US Army Command and General Staff College
CMH	Center of Military History (Army)
CMTC	Citizens' Military Training Camps
CNGB	Chief, National Guard Bureau
Co.	Company
Col.	Colonel
COMUS MACV	Commander, United States Military Assistance Command, Vietnam
CONARC	US Army Continental Army Command
CONUSA	Continental United States Army
DA	Department of the Army
DAMPL	Department of the Army Master Priority List
DCSOPS	Deputy Chief of Staff for Operations
DCSPER	Deputy Chief of Staff for Personnel
Det	Detachment
DMZ	Demilitarized Zone
DoD	Department of Defense
DS	Direct Support
EO	Executive Order
Equip	Equipment
ERC	Enlisted Reserve Corps
ERRA	Executive for Reserve and R.O.T.C. Affairs
Evac	Evacuation
FDR	President Franklin D. Roosevelt
Fin	Finance
Fltg Cft	Floating Craft
FORSCOM	US Army Forces Command
FY	Fiscal Year
G–1	General Staff (Personnel)
G–2	General Staff (Intelligence)
G–3	General Staff (Plans and Operations)
GAO	General Accounting Office
Gen	General
GOCOM	General Officer Command
GPO	Government Printing Office
GS	General Support General Staff
HHC	Headquarters and Headquarters Company
Hosp	Hospital
HQ	Headquarters
H.R.	House of Representatives
IADT	Inactive Duty Training (drill)
IDT	Inactive Duty Training
IMA	Individual Mobilization Augmentee
Inf	Infantry
IRR	Individual Ready Reserve

JCS	Joint Chiefs of Staff
L&LD	Legislation and Liaison Division
Lt.	Lieutenant
Lt. Col.	Lieutenant Colonel
Lt. Gen.	Lieutenant General
M16	Standard Vietnam-era military rifle, caliber 5.56 mm
Maint	Maintenance
Maj.	Major
Maj. Gen.	Major General
MCAR	Military Construction, Army Reserve
M-Day	Mobilization Day
Med	Medical
MI	Military Intelligence
MOBDES	Mobilization Designee
MOBEX	Mobilization Exercise
MOBPERS	Mobilization Personnel Processing System
MOS	Military Occupation Specialty
Msg	Message
MSP	Mutual Support Program
MTCA	Military Training Camps Association
MUSARC	Major United States Army Reserve Command
NG	National Guard
OCAR	Office of the Chief, Army Reserve
OER	Officer Evaluation Report
OERRA	Office of the Executive for Reserve and R.O.T.C. Affairs
OMA	Operations and Maintenance, Army
OMAR	Operations and Maintenance, Army Reserve
OR	Organized Reserve [Corps]
ORC	Office of Reserve Components
	Officers' Reserve Corps
	Organized Reserve Corps
Ord	Ordnance
Ortho	Orthopedic
OSD	Office of the Secretary of Defense
Pers	Personnel
Petr	Petroleum
PIO	Public Information Officer
PL	Public Law
PMP	Protective Mobilization Plan
POL	Petroleum, Oil, and Lubricants
POM	Program Objective Memorandum
PX	Post Exchange
QM	Quartermaster
RA	Regular Army
RAR	Regular Army Reserve
RDF-A	Rapid Deployment Force—Army

RDJTF	Rapid Deployment Joint Task Force
REP-63	Reserve Enlistment Program—1963
RFA	Reserve Forces Act of 1955
RG	Readiness Group
	Record Group (National Archives)
ROA	Reserve Officers Association
ROAD	Reorganization Objective Army Division
ROPA	Reserve Officer Personnel Act of 1954
ROTC	Reserve Officers Training Corps
RPA	Reserve Personnel, Army
RRMRP	Ready Reserve Mobilization Reinforcement Pool
RROTC	Reserve and ROTC Affairs
RTU	Reinforcement Training Unit
RVN	Republic of [South] Vietnam
SARCA	Senior Army Reserve Commanders Association
Sec	Section
SGLI	Servicemen's Group Life Insurance
SP	Self-propelled
Spt	Support
SRF	Selected Reserve Force
SRIP	Selected Reserve Incentive Program
SSAA	Senior Staff Administrative Assistant
STRAF	Strategic Reserve Army Forces
Sup	Supply
Surg	Surgery, Surgical
Svc	Service
TAG	The Adjutant General, US Army
TAGO	The Adjutant General's Office
T/O	Table of Organization
TOA	Total Obligation Authority
TOE	Table of Organization and Equipment
Trans	Transportation
Trk	Truck
USAR	United States Army Reserve
USAREC	US Army Recruiting Command
VHA	Variable Housing Allowance
WAC	Women's Army Corps

Foreword

The United States Army Reserve (USAR) had its official birth on April 23, 1908, in an act "To Increase the Efficiency of the Medical Department of the United States Army." From this modest beginning and limited mission, the Army Reserve has grown into a force of almost a million men and women who are very much a part of today's Total Army. The roots of the Army Reserve go back much further than 1908, however, for the concept of the citizen-soldier was an old one even at the time of the American Revolution.

The idea of writing a history of the Army Reserve originated in November 1982 during the early stages of planning for the USAR's Seventy-fifth Anniversary celebration in 1983. It became evident to Major (now Lieutenant Colonel) Richard B. Crossland and to Lewis C. Brodsky, Director of Public Affairs for the Office of the Chief, Army Reserve, that there was no readily available source of historical data about the Army Reserve. There were bits and pieces of USAR history scattered about, and there were legends enough to fill a file cabinet, but there was no comprehensive, book-length history of the Army Reserve. Major Crossland was thereupon assigned the task of writing such a book. Given the time frame in mind for the project (less than one year), it was soon obvious that this was not a one-person job. Permission was therefore secured to bring in an Army Reserve officer on a special tour of six months or so to work on the book.

The Reserve Components Personnel and Administration Center in St. Louis was given the task of locating an individual to do the job, and the name of James T. Currie popped up. Major Currie was at that time (January 1983) serving in a civilian capacity as Historian for the United States Department of Education, and he accepted the assignment. Lieutenant Colonel Crossland and Major Currie coauthored this volume, which is the only existing history of the Army Reserve. The authors have of necessity worked rapidly, researching and writing a draft manuscript of 450 pages in less than 6 months. The authors realize that in any pioneering study there are almost certainly going to be errors, both of omission and of commission. They have attempted, however, to be as accurate as possible, and every statement of fact is based upon the most credible sources available. They have drawn conclusions from these facts where such seemed justified, but the conclusions are purely their own and do not necessarily reflect the views of the Chief, Army Reserve, the Department of the Army, or the Department of Defense.

The title of the book is taken from Winston Churchill's statement that "The Reservist is twice the citizen," a phrase that also figured in the Seventy-fifth Anniversary High School Essay Contest co-sponsored by the Army Reserve and the Reserve Officers Association. Indeed, since 1908, members of the Army Reserve have taken on responsibilities greater than those required of most citizens, for they have given of their weeknights and weekends and summertime leisure to learn and train and prepare for the day when their country might call upon them in time of war or national emergency. From 1908 until 1948, Army Reservists received no pay except for the time they were on active duty; the many hours devoted to inactive duty drills and training went unrewarded financially. Since 1948 Army Reservists have qualified for an increasing list of benefits, including limited post exchange and commissary privileges and, if they serve long enough and live long enough, for retirement pay. As the citizen-soldier concept has matured and become an integral part of the Army, the United States has gradually given tangible recognition to the value of the Army Reserve. This belated reward does not in any way, however, diminish the fact that the Army Reservist is indeed "twice the citizen."

Within this volume, LTC Crossland was responsible for Chapters I, II, VII, VIII, and X and Appendixes G and H. Major Currie prepared Chapters III, IV, V, VI, and IX and Appendixes A through F. The authors hope that publication of this book will stimulate a greater interest in the United States Army Reserve and that their study will serve as a reference work for persons whose position calls for them to understand the Army Reserve.

Readers who have corrections, suggestions, or additions are urged to send such to the following address:

Headquarters, Department of the Army
Office of the Chief, Army Reserve
Attn: DAAR-PA (History Project)
Washington, DC 20310

Preface to the Second Edition

Colonel Dick Crossland and I began talking about preparing a second edition of *Twice the Citizen* early in 1989. When Desert Shield/Desert Storm came along, we knew that a new edition of the book simply had to be done. In the spring of 1991 we talked seriously about the project, even going so far as to contemplate another active duty tour for me, much as had been done in 1983. Shortly after this conversation, Dick discovered that he had cancer and realized that despite the efforts of the Army's oncology specialists, it would probably prove fatal. We spoke to each other about the book project throughout the spring and summer of 1991 and into the fall. Dick retired from the Active Guard and Reserve (AGR) program on medical disability, and died in the late fall of 1991. I had spoken with him just two days earlier, and almost his last wish was that I complete the second edition of the book. So here it is. The second, revised and updated edition of the official history of the United States Army Reserve, Department of the Army Pamphlet 140–14, *Twice the Citizen*. Chapters 11–23 and Conclusion, represent additions to the first edition.

Acknowledgements for the Second Edition

As with the first edition of this book, I owe thanks to many individuals. Maj. Gen. Roger Sandler, Chief, Army Reserve when I began the revisions, was generous with his funds, allowing me to take several research trips on OCAR money; his successor, Maj. Gen. Max Baratz, has allowed me to continue the project, understanding the difficulty of doing research and writing while holding down a full-time position as a faculty member at one of the senior service colleges. Lt. Col. Steve Anderson, now on the staff of the Reserve Officers Association, backed me on the need for these trips and saw to it that I received the funds as required. Lt. Col. Art House, OCAR public affairs officer, helped with sources and support. 1st Lt. Bruce Kish, historical and public affairs officer with the 99th ARCOM, volunteered his time and efforts and served as a research assistant on the project. Lt. Kish rummaged through back issues of *Army Reserve Magazine* for me and sent me copies of publications he thought would prove useful. They invariably did so.

Thanks also to the following individuals who assisted with research or who read and critiqued parts of the book: Col. Ray Ruppert, Office of the Army Judge Advocate General; Lt. Col. Bernard Horak (Ret.); Col. Tom Damron, Office of the Army Surgeon General; Robert Goldich, Congressional Research Service; Drs. Mickey Schubert and Lorna Jaffe, Joint Staff Historical Office; Lt. Col. Steve Dietrich, U.S. Army Center of Military History; Col. Joseph Schindelholz, Office of the Chief, Army Reserve; Lt. Col. Walter B. Edgar, 360th Civil Affairs Bde.; Myrna Harmon, Kansas State Board of Healing

Arts; Col. Frank Travis, U.S. Army War College; Dr. Susan Canedy, TRADOC; Dr. William Stacy, FORSCOM; Drs. Lee Harford and Kathryn Roe Coker, USARC; Master Sgt. Terrance T. Brown, 94th ARCOM; Lt. Col. Leonid E. Kondratiuk, National Guard Bureau; Donald Lewy, Office of the Chief, Army Reserve; Dr. Richard W. Stewart, U.S. Army Special Operations Command; Sgt. 1st Class Dominick Merced, U.S. Army Medical Department; Lt. Col. Mike Moose, 120th ARCOM; Col. Charles E. Trant, Office of the Army Judge Advocate General; William S. Fulton, Jr., Clerk of Court, U.S. Army Judiciary; Patricia Tugwell, Pentagon Library; Carolyn Turner and Ann Sullivan and especially Tim Renick, superb professionals all at the National Defense University Library.

Many individuals consented to be interviewed during the course of my research. They are cited in the footnotes, but I must give special thanks to Gen. Edwin Burba, then-FORSCOM commander; to Maj. Gen. Max Baratz, then Deputy Commander of the U.S. Army Reserve Command; to Brig. Gen. Thomas Kilmartin, at ARPERCEN, for taking time from their busy schedules to allow my interruption and to Charles Nahlik, also at ARPERCEN. I thank also the many individual Army Reservists who saw the notice in *Army Reserve Magazine* and sent me their stories and their pictures. I could not use them all, but they helped me place the USAR story into context. I attempted to acknowledge everyone with a postcard, but if I missed someone, I apologize profusely. I appreciate the time and effort each of you gave to this endeavor. Thanks also to my bosses at the Industrial College of the Armed Forces, where I practice my trade as a Professor of Political Science. They understood that this research and writing project is useful for the greater knowledge of everyone who is a part of the military establishment of this country.

Finally, I owe a great debt to Al Schilf of Army Reserve Public Affairs, who selected and captioned the photos for the second edition and to Col. James M. Nielsen, Chief of Public Affairs for the Army Reserve. Jim was my prod when I required such, my support when that was called for. He backed the project 100% and took my prose and gave it the benefit of a caring and professional editing job. He also revised all the various appendixes and found the new photographs for this edition. You're good, Jim.

A Word about Format and Methodology

The second edition of this book added to the 1908–1983 period the story of the Army Reserve from the closing months of 1983 to 1995. The level of detail of the added materials is much greater than for the first seventy-five years, and some have questioned the propriety, or even the necessity, of doing so. My response to this criticism is that during the past eleven years the Army Reserve has done much more and been a bigger part of the national defense structure of this country than it was in all of the first seventy-five years of its existence. The Total Army concept gave the Army Reserve more to do and required it to become a more professional force than it had ever been previously. It is my hope that including an increased level of detail will enable the reader to understand just what the Army Reserve role has been during these years and just how much it has matured as a partner in the nation's defense.

Desert Shield and Desert Storm (DS/DS) saw the involvement of the Army Reserve on a scale previously unequalled. There were some 647 USAR units and over 90,000 Army Reservists mobilized for this endeavor (68,000 in troop units and 20,000 from the IRR, plus over 2000 IMAs). I would have liked to have told the individual story of every unit and every Reservist. That was obviously impossible, so what I have attempted to do in the narrative on DS/DS is to tell representative stories about representative units and individuals. In many instances I chose the units at random; in other instances they were the only unit of that type about which I had any information at all. As with any historical project, the historian writes from the material he has available.

Some of the topics covered in the Second Edition of this book are perhaps more controversial than were those in the first edition. Questions of "Total Force" and how well it worked during the Gulf conflict, for example, cannot be ignored, nor can the "Off-site Agreement" that resulted in significant changes in the Army Reserve's size and structure. I have attempted to approach these issues from a historical context, relying on the best documentary sources to guide my narrative. On the sensitive question of why certain Army reserve units commanded by general officers were not called to active duty, I doubt that my narrative will satisfy extremists on either side: those who believe that USAR (and National Guard) general officers cannot be counted on, nor those who believe there was a cabal at Headquarters, Department of the Army level to keep reserve component generals and colonels in their places through what in an earlier time might have been labeled "benign neglect."

The conclusions and opinions expressed in this revised edition are purely my own and do not represent the National Defense University/Industrial College of the Armed Forces, the Chief, Army Reserve, the Department of the Army, or the Department of Defense.

James T. Currie
Colonel, USAR
Alexandria, Virginia
March 1996

Dedication

This second edition is dedicated to the memory of Colonel Richard B. Crossland (1942–1991), USAR. There have been few who loved the Army Reserve as much, and none who understood it better.

1

Before There Was An Army Reserve

The United States Army Reserve, the largest component of the Department of Defense with nearly one million men and women,[1] was officially created in 1908. However, the heritage of the volunteer or "citizen-soldier" goes back to colonial America and has its roots in the enrolled militia of Anglo-Saxon England.

The idea of supplementing Regular or full-time forces with Reserve or part-time forces is even older than the Middle Ages. The Roman Empire of the late fourth and early fifth centuries depended upon the *Comitatus,* a full-time, regular Army that was backed by the *limitanei* of part-time soldiers living on the land along the Empire's long frontiers and charged with defense in time of emergency.[2]

Likewise, the basic 13th century medieval military organization had the standing army of the king or overlord—a highly trained professional army equipped with the finest weapons available—backed by the enrolled militia or select fyrd.[3] While the King's full-time professionals were available for service anywhere, the enrolled militia was a

---

1. As of March 31, 1983, the Office of the Deputy Chief of Staff for Personnel in its DCSPER Report–46 listed the strength of the Army Reserve at 943,396 encompassing the Ready, Standby and Retired Reserves. On December 31, 1982, the active Army, the largest of America's active duty forces, stood at 778,577 men and women.

2. Louis A. Zurcher and Gwyn Harris-Jenkins, editors, *Supplementary Military Forces—Reserves, Militias, Auxiliaries,* (Beverly Hills, Calif.: Sage Publications, 1978), pp. 91–92.

3. Michael Powicke, *Military Obligation in Medieval England, A Study of Liberty & Duty,* (Oxford at the Clarendon Press, 1962), pp. 6–7.

minimally-trained and individually-equipped force of citizen-soldiers normally employed within a few miles of their homes. Except in times of emergency, they carried on their civilian pursuits as farmers, merchants and craftsmen.

Below the enrolled militia was its unenrolled counterpart, the great fyrd or *levees en masse,* which consisted of all reasonably healthy men. This large body of unorganized, undisciplined and generally untrained men was the last-ditch force used to defend the homeland from invasion.[4]

Modified and formalized by the 1181 Assize of Arms, the Statute of Winchester of 1285 and the Instructions for General Muster of 1572, the fyrd became the militia of Elizabethan England. This militia tradition was among the English institutions carried to the American colonies in the early 17th century at a time when militias were falling into disuse in an age of professional armies.

However, in the words of historian Russell F. Weigley, "The American colonies in the seventeenth century were much too poor to permit a class of able-bodied men to devote themselves solely to war and preparation for war."[5] Manpower was scarce, and every colony except Quaker Pennsylvania solved the problem of military protection by turning to the traditional English practice of relying upon a militia.

Even though tradition and the law called upon every able-bodied man to provide his own weapon and be prepared for militia duty, few emergencies required the entire population to rally to arms. As early as 1643, the Massachusetts Bay Colony reorganized its militia by calling for 30 volunteers from each company of the common militia to be ready for service upon 30-minutes notice. The remainder of the company, 65 to 200 men, was exempt from the militia call except under the most dire circumstances.

Other colonies adopted similar provisions, and more or less permanent formations of persons willing to volunteer for duty soon developed. This in effect created an elite, enrolled militia reminiscent of medieval England.

While this arrangement was more than adequate as long as a colonial community remained a frontier community, the prowess of the colonial community militia faded as

---

4. James B. Whisker, *The Citizen-Soldier and U. S. Military Policy,* (North River Press, 1979), pp. 4–5.

5. Russell F. Weigley, *History of the United States Army,* (New York: The Macmillan Company, 1967), pp. 3–4.

the frontier receded. By the time of the French and Indian War, Col. George Washington of the Virginia militia reported that the militia was no longer a match for the Indians.[6] This reality, and the inability of the colonies to muster sufficient forces against the French, led London to send regular British regiments to America.

Although accustomed to European warfare with its highly disciplined maneuvers and point-blank volleys of musketry on open, rolling plains, the British soldiers adapted to the wooded American environment. They did most of the fighting, won the war and set the standard of soldiering for the Americans. Washington was impressed, and his fondest hope was that his militia might pattern themselves after the British regulars.[7]

THE REVOLUTION

A decade later, Washington was fighting a revolution with troops that were essentially the same as his French and Indian War militia. Washington remembered well the weakness of his Virginia militia and urged the Congress to create a large, standing army that he could turn into a professional force. Indeed, Washington wrote that "no Militia will ever acquire the habits necessary to resist a regular force."[8]

Although Washington was able to build an effective force with which victory was ultimately achieved, he was consistently denied a standing army of the size he deemed necessary. Weigley suggests that the Congress was "acutely mindful that the Parliamentary Army of 17th Century England had turned upon its legislative creator and erected the military dictatorship of Oliver Cromwell."[9] On the other hand, it has generally been established that the Revolutionary leadership was by and large conservative and very much inclined to rely upon the traditional militia.

In addition, Revolutionary propagandists had emphasized that a large standing army was an example of tyranny and had used the presence of British regulars in the Colonies to whip up support for the Revolution. This very useful propaganda theme would have been undercut if the Revolu-

6. *Ibid.*, p. 11.

7. *Ibid.*, p. 28.

8. Robert K. Wright, Jr., Army Lineage Series, *The Continental Army*, (Washington: Center of Military History: 1983), p. 156.

9. Weigley, *History of the United States Army*, p. 30.

tionaries had established a large, permanent force of their own.[10]

Eighteenth century military practices also worked against establishing a large, full-time Army. In the 1700's, military campaigns began in the spring and lasted until winter brought a halt to operations. As a rule, the American Revolution followed this pattern, with the battles of Trenton and Quebec being December exceptions to the norm.[11]

It made little sense to the Continental Congress to maintain a large force over the winter with the need to pay, provision and generally care for soldiers who would not be needed until spring. It was far more economical, they thought, to disband most of the Army when the snow started to fall and to later call out the volunteers and militia after the spring planting was done.

Throughout the war, economic factors and the practical impossibility of raising a large, long-term army that Washington wanted caused him to rely upon the militia to build up his forces for major campaigns.[12]

The militia also made the Revolutionary Army ubiquitous. Any victory by the British was immediately diminished because a force of Minutemen seemed always to spring from the countryside and harrass the British columns and in general make life difficult for the British. This added an element of guerrilla warfare to the Revolution that would not have been possible if the Americans had relied totally upon a regular army to prosecute the war.

In *American Military History,* Robert W. Coakley makes the point that both the Continental Army and militia forces

---

10. Wright specifically makes this point, writing that "the rhetoric of protest against British policy had strongly denied the need for a large 'standing army' of regular soldiers in America on the grounds that the colonial militia forces, composed of virtuous citizens-soldiers, were perfectly adequate for local defense. The outbreak of hostilities in Massachusetts did not change this attitude. Lexington, Concord and Bunker Hill only seemed to confirm the validity of that assumption." See Wright *Continental Army,* p. 43. It should also be noted that "quartering of large bodies of armed troops among us" was one of Thomas Jefferson's themes as early as 1774, and this grievance is included in the 1776 Declaration of Independence.

11. Erna Risch, Special Studies Series, *Supplying Washington's Army,* (Washington: Center of Military History, 1981), p. 416.

12. Wright, *Continental Army,* p. 127. The consistent economic woes which plagued the Revolution are detailed in Risch's *Supplying Washington's Army,* particularly on pages 17 and 20. Today's situation where Reserve Components provide an economical means of rounding out regular forces in time of emergency is analogous to the manpower solutions achieved by the Continental Congress during the Revolution.

were necessary to win the Revolution. More importantly, in Coakley's words, "the Revolutionary experience provided ammunition for two diametrically opposed schools of thought on American military policy: one advocating a large Regular Army, the other reliance upon the militia as the bulwark of national defense."[13]

These two schools of thought remain in 1983, even though the issue of large regular forces versus heavy reliance upon reserve or militia forces was apparently resolved with the announcement of the Total Force policy in August 1970. This policy, which states that the Reserve Components would be the principal augmentation of active forces in emergency, has not been proven in wartime, and it is quite likely that the debate will continue after our next mobilization experience.[14]

THE PEACETIME ARMY

The question of the peacetime Army was one of the first issues addressed in 1783 prior to the Sept. 24 signing of the Treaty of Paris that formally ended the Revolution. The handicaps of short enlistments, over-reliance upon volunteers and militia and the lack of standardized training among the part-time forces were recognized by the Revolutionary leadership.[15] A Congressional committee was formed under Alexander Hamilton to study and recommend a military establishment. In the tradition of such committees, witnesses were heard and particular attention was paid to the views of Washington,[16] who recommended a small Regular Army and

13. Robert W. Coakley, "The Winning of Independence," in Maurice Matloff (Gen. Ed.), *American Military History* (Washington: Office of the Chief of Military History, United States Army, 1969), pp. 98–100. See also Wright, *Continental Army,* pp. 3–20.

14. The Total Force policy was not adopted without dissent. Military leaders, including Gen. William C. Westmoreland, thought that the Total Force decision placed too much reliance upon part-time Reserve Component soldiers. This issue is addressed in Chapter 10, and much of this book is devoted to the struggle to develop an effective Reserve Component policy to meet America's world-wide military responsibilities.

15. The lessons learned from the Revolution are summarized in Marvin A. Kreidberg and Merton G. Henry, *History of Military Mobilization in the United States Army, 1775–1945,* (Washington: Department of the Army, 1955), p. 22.

16. Morris J. McGregor, Jr., "The Formative Years, 1783–1812," in Matloff, *American Military History,* pp. 103–105.

a militia of all citizens 18 to 50, modeled after the Swiss militia.[17]

Washington's proposals, however, came to naught, as the Confederation was burdened with war debts and did not have the resources to enact his recommendations. The debate over the military question continued throughout the period of the Articles of Confederation, and the Constitution emerged in 1787 with two military clauses reflecting a compromise on the issues.

Specifically, Article I, Section 8 of the Constitution granted to Congress the power to raise and support armies, to provide for organizing, arming and disciplining the militia and to provide for calling forth the militia to "execute the laws of the union, suppress insurrections and repel invasions." Reserved to the states were the powers to appoint officers and train the militia.[18]

After establishing the Department of War and continuing the small Regular Army in 1789, Congress was faced in 1790 with a detailed proposal for regulating the militia. Drafted by Secretary of War Henry Knox, the plan featured the division of all able-bodied white male citizens, aged 18–60, into three classes:

> Those 18–20 to be called the Advanced Corps and to be trained in state camps for thirty days per year and clothed and fed and armed by the United States at a cost of about $400,000 per year; those 21–45 to be called the Main Corps and to be mustered and trained for four days per year; those 40–60 to be called the Reserve Corps and to be mustered twice a year.[19]

A bill containing the main features of this plan was introduced, debated and tabled in 1790 and again in 1791. Finally, in 1792 a weaker bill passed calling for all able-bodied white male citizens, aged 18–45, to be enrolled in a general militia. This Militia Act of 1792 required each man to furnish his own musket, bayonet, belt, and cartridges. Thus, $400,000 was saved—a considerable amount in that day—and the tradition of underfunding Reserve Components began.

---

17. Russell F. Weigley, *Towards an American Army: Military Thought from Washington to Marshall,* (Westport, Conn.: Greenwood Press, 1962), pp. 10–12.

18. The literal interpretation of these provisions in 1912 by Attorney General George W. Wickersham was a strong argument for a federal reserve force.

19. William H. Riker, *Soldiers of the States,* (Washington: Public Affairs Press, 1957), p. 18.

The 1792 act became the permanent military policy of the United States at a time when European military leaders were turning to massed, conscript armies. While Napoleon was dominating Europe with his conscripts, grand tactics and superior logistics, the United States was rejecting conscripted service and relying upon a militia system obsolete by European standards for 200 years.[20]

THE WAR OF 1812

The American militia system was faced with its first foreign challenge in the War of 1812, and it was found wanting. When Congress voted for war with Great Britian on June 18, 1812, the Regular Army contained fewer than 7,000 men.[21] A call for the states to raise 100,000 men generally went unheeded, and the governors of Massachusetts, Connecticut and Rhode Island opposed the call completely, maintaining that it was unconstitutional and illegal.

During the war itself, militia under Maj. Gen. Henry Dearborn refused to invade Canada, a failure which was remembered a century later when arguments were presented for a federal reserve force.[22] Historically a home defense force, the militia's leaders claimed that the Constitution provided no clear authority for their use outside of the United States. The Madison administration, uncertain of its public support, balked at sending reluctant citizen-soldiers into Canada and skirted the issue.[23] In the future, calling the militia into United States service was handled by regarding militia companies as volunteers for federal duty, serving under the general authority of Congress to raise armies.

THE EXPANSIBLE ARMY

Following the War of 1812, Secretary of War John C. Calhoun produced a pivotal document in the history of American military thought when he prepared his Dec. 12, 1820, "Report on the Reduction of the Army." Building upon ear-

20. Weigley, *Towards an American Army,* pp. 20–24.
21. Kreidberg and Henry, *History of Military Mobilization,* p. 46.
22. Weigley, *History of the United States Army,* pp. 119–20.
23. In fairness to the militia and volunteer forces, McGregor states that the militia fared as well as the Regular Army in victory and defeat. While the refusal of New York and Vermont soldiers to enter Canada scuttled Dearborn's planned 1812 march on Montreal, militia forces served well in the defense of Baltimore and were the key to Jackson's success in the South. See McGregor, "Formative Years," pp. 129–47.

lier proposals, Calhoun emphasized the Regular Army and discounted the militia by calling for an expansible army as the basis for future mobilization. Calhoun wanted to form in peacetime all of the regiments which the Army would require in war. The companies were to be manned at approximately half strength and were to be expanded to full strength for war.[24]

Calhoun thought that the militia might be relied upon to garrison forts and act as skirmishers and raiders if supported by good artillery and some regular infantry; but he wrote, "To rely upon them beyond this, to suppose our militia capable of meeting in the open field the regular troops of Europe, would be to resist the most obvious truth, and the whole of our experience as a nation."[25]

A more obvious truth in Calhoun's time was that the militia had fallen into disrepair. The Militia Act of 1792 had contained no provision for federal enforcement of the militia system, but had relied upon the states to do the job. This did not always occur. In 1816, for example, Delaware abolished fines for men who did not attend "days of parade;" and by 1820, many other states had stopped enforcing annual muster laws. Liberal exemptions from service also abounded, until few states retained an effective militia system on the eve of the War with Mexico.[26]

MEXICO

According to Marvin A. Kreidberg and Merton G. Henry in their *History of Military Mobilization in the United States Army, 1775–1945,* the militia system had so deteriorated by 1846 that many states did not know how to mobilize the militia, and many did not even appoint officers. When President James K. Polk called for volunteers to fight in Mexico, the normal procedure was for governors to issue a proclamation directing militia officers to assemble their men. In cases where militia officers did not exist, county sheriffs called out the militia. Once assembled, the militiamen were asked to volunteer for federal service. Those who volunteered were enrolled into companies, battalions and regiments. In many cases, where the militia system still functioned, entire

24. This cadre concept dominated military thinking until 1912 when the "Report on the Organization of Land Forces of the United States," principally authored by John McAuley Palmer, called for a great army of citizen-soldiers organized into their own units.

25. Weigley, *Towards an American Army,* p. 31.

26. Riker, *Soldiers of the States,* p. 29.

units volunteered;[27] and units such as the First Mississippi Rifles under Col. Jefferson Davis served with distinction.[28]

By the time of the Civil War, the militia was still theoretically in existence, and the Militia Act of 1792 was still the law of the land. However, as a practical matter, the militia did not exist as an effective, well-equipped military force.

CIVIL WAR

Acting under the authority of the 1792 law, President Abraham Lincoln called 75,000 militiamen for three months service on April 15, 1861. When it came time to raise a more permanent army, however, Lincoln called for 42,000 volunteers. Congress subsequently seconded his call on July 22, 1861, by authorizing up to 500,000 volunteers for three years' duty.

As a practical matter during the Civil War, the Secretary of War assigned manpower quotas to states based upon their population, and the governors administered the volunteer system. The individual soldier was drawn from the ranks of volunteers; he was not being mobilized from a previously existing militia unit.[29]

Following the Civil War, the public attitude toward the militia was indifferent. Despite the pride exhibited by veterans' organizations such as the Grand Army of the Republic, this pride was not translated into functioning militia units. Citizen-soldiery, in the opinion of William H. Riker, was at its lowest ebb because the Regular Army was sufficient to control the Indians and because there was no threat of a foreign war.[30] The growing militancy of the labor movement in the 1870s, however, helped revive the state militia. There was a direct relationship between labor unrest[31] in a state and that state's appropriation for the militia which was now more commonly called the National Guard.[32]

---

27. Kreidberg and Henry, *History of Military Mobilization,* pp. 75–82.

28. Lida Mayo, "The Mexican War and After," in Matloff, *American Military History,* pp. 168–72.

29. Kreidberg and Henry, *History of Military Mobilization,* pp. 90–98. The National Guard has a different interpretation of this point, and Civil War unit histories give evidence to both points of view.

30. William H. Riker, *Soldiers of the States,* pp. 41–66.

31. *Ibid.*

32. National Guard Officials were quick to down play the strikebreaking role of the militia. The police function was de-emphasized by

WAR WITH SPAIN

By the time of the Spanish-American War in 1898, the regiments and companies of the National Guard were units of citizen-soldiers available for mobilization, but once again Guard units were not called directly into federal service. Instead, a Volunteer Army was formed. As in the past, the militia provided volunteers for the new army, and National Guard units were encouraged to volunteer en masse. In addition, the Secretary of War was authorized to form 16 special units recruited by the federal government from the nation at large. The 1st Regiment of United States Volunteer Cavalry, the "Rough Riders" of Lt. Col. Theodore Roosevelt, was one of these units.

Even though the National Guard provided most of the manpower for the 125,000-man Volunteer Army, the combat actions of the Spanish-American War were primarily a Regular Army affair. Except for the Rough Riders and two former militia regiments, the 17,000 troops of the Cuban Expeditionary Force were from the old Regular Army. And, when National Guard units performed well in the Philippines, they were characterized as volunteer units by the Army establishment.[33]

The reason for this characterization was that the officers of the Regular Army were in the late 1800's contemptuous of part-time soldiers, whom they considered to be incompetent in military matters. This attitude had been exhibited by many post-Civil War senior officers including Generals Ulysses S. Grant and William T. Sherman, and these attitudes were clearly expressed in Brevet Maj. Gen. Emory Upton's book, *The Military Policy of the United States.*[34]

EMORY UPTON

A West Point graduate who was only 26-years-old at the end of the Civil War, Upton was an innovative thinker who has influenced generations of professional soldiers. After the war he wrote a text on infantry tactics and was subsequently named Commandant of Cadets at West Point. While at West Point, Upton continued to write on tactics, and in

---

promoting the social aspects of the Guard and giving greater attention to military maneuvers.

33. Weigley, *Towards an American Army,* p. 168.

34. Emory Upton, *The Military Policy of the United States,* 4th Edition, (Washington: 1916).

1875 he was sent on a world tour as an official observer for the United States Army. Upon his return in 1876, Upton began writing *The Military Policy of the United States.* He had been impressed by the military achievements of Prussia with its general staff and mass army that was made possible by a federal system of reserve soldiers. To adapt the Prussian system to American military traditions, Upton proposed the maintenance of a Regular Army of not more than 25,000 men.

This army was to be made up of skeletonized battalions that could be expanded in wartime by a federal reserve which Upton called "National Volunteers."[35] Upton advocated leaving the militia to the states to execute the laws of the states and called "the employment of militia and undisciplined troops commanded by generals and officers utterly ignorant of military art" the first and greatest weakness in the American military system.[36]

Upton's disdain for the militia was not unique. Maj. Gen. John A. Logan in his *The Volunteer Soldier of America,* published in 1887, asserted that the West Point system crushed the aspirations of volunteers and that the majority of regular officers would do anything to prevent a volunteer officer from being successful.[37] It should also be pointed out that militia officers often showed great antipathy toward Regulars. It is in light of this animosity that the Army attempted reforms following the Spanish-American War.

Weigley states that the US Army was on the verge of seeking a federally-sponsored volunteer force under Regular Army control on the eve of the Spanish-American War and that following the war Secretary of War Elihu Root was strongly influenced by Upton's writings.[38] Vincent P. Jones seconds Weigley on the latter point, stating that Root took the lead in reorganizing the Army and reforming the National Guard.[39]

---

35. Stephen E. Ambrose, *Upton and the Army,* (Baton Rouge: LSU Press, 1964), pp. 54–135.

36. Upton, *Military Policy,* p. XIII.

37. "The Dangerous West Point Monopoly" by John A. Logan as republished from *The Volunteer Soldier in America* in Russell F. Weigley's *The American Military: Readings in the History of the Military in American Society* (Reading, Mass.: Addison-Wesley Publishing Company, 1969) p. 83.

38. Weigley, *History of the United States Army,* pp. 296, 320.

39. Vincent P. Jones, "Transition and Change, 1902–1917," in Matloff, *American History,* pp. 350–51.

ELIHU ROOT'S PLAN

In his *Report of the Secretary of War* for 1899, Root stated that the regular establishment of the United States would never by itself be the whole machine with which wars would be fought. He further wrote that the Regular Army would form but a part of a great wartime body.[40] Root then proposed that a homogeneous body of regulars and volunteers "using the same arms, familiar with the same drill, answering to the same ideas of discipline, instilled with the same spirit, and capable of equal and even performance" be formed.[41]

By 1901 Root was calling for some means by which young men seeking volunteer commissions might spend their vacations in military study preparing them for commissions in the volunteer army. Root wrote that "it is particularly desirable that a large number of young men should be made competent to perform the duties of volunteer officers in the staff and supply departments. Without such a class at the outbreak of war, with a large volunteer force being called into being, there will always be confusion, waste, delay and suffering . . . ."[42] This creation of a source of volunteer officers was in addition to National Guard officers and was the germ of the idea later espoused by Maj. Gen. Leonard Wood and his allies in the Military Training Camps Association.[43]

In 1902 Root proposed the creation of two categories of Volunteer Reserve to augment the Regular Army and National Guard in wartime. Root's First Volunteer Reserve was to be such companies and regiments of the organized militia as had volunteered for unlimited service during war. The Second Volunteer Reserve was to be composed of men with prior National Guard, Regular Army or Volunteer Army training and would be led by officers whose fitness for commissions had previously been proven.

Root wanted to be able to expand the standing 60,000-man Army to a force of 250,000 well-trained men instantly upon declaration of war. Root asserted that the effectiveness

40. Elihu Root, *Report of the Secretary of War, 1899,* (Washington: War Department, 1899), pp. 45–46, 52.

41. *Ibid.*, p. 53.

42. *Report of the Secretary of War, 1901* (Washington: War Department, 1901), pp. 23–24.

43. The issue of commissioning volunteer officers in reserve is covered in Chapter 2, but credit can certainly be given to Root for recognizing the need to train volunteer officers in advance of hostilities.

of militia or volunteer units depended largely upon the aid which they received from the national government.[44]

As much as Root may have favored Upton's idea of a federally controlled and commanded Reserve,[45] he was a realist. The creation of a federal Reserve force conflicted with the fact that the National Guard already constituted a reserve of manpower, and, to a lesser degree, of equipment. As Weigley puts it, the National Guard "was a force in being, while any other kind of reserve was only hypothetical."[46]

Therefore, Root supported legislation in 1903 to fundamentally upgrade the National Guard while retaining its historical state militia functions. Working with Ohio Congressman Charles W. Dick, a National Guard major general, Root helped draft Public Law 57–33, commonly known as the Dick Act.[47]

THE DICK ACT

This legislation clarified the concept of a universal militia. The militia was divided into two groups. The first was the organized militia, known as the National Guard, which was defined as the regularly enlisted, organized and uniformed active militia of the several states and territories. The second

44. *Report of the Secretary of War, 1902,* (Washington: War Department, 1902), pp. 34–38.

45. In *Upton and the Army,* Ambrose states that Root's reforms of the War Department contain most of Upton's specific proposals. It would appear that Root thought enough of Upton's work to take Upton's unpublished manuscript of *The Military Policy of the United States,* then in the possession of Sen. Henry duPont of Delaware, have it edited by two Army officers and finally published in 1904 under War Department sponsorship. It is clear that Root did read Upton's earlier book, *The Armies of Asia and Europe,* and that Root consistently wrote of the Volunteer Army—not the National Guard per se—as the ultimate Army of the United States. See Root's *Report of the Secretary of War* for the years 1899, 1900, 1901 and 1902. Also, see Ambrose, cited above, pages 151–57 for an assessment of the overall impact of Upton's ideas.

46. Weigley, *History of the United States Army,* p. 321.

47. In "Elihu Root and the National Guard," published in the Spring 1959 issue of *Military Affairs,* Elbridge Colby sets forth the thesis that Root preferred to create a federally-controlled, nationwide Volunteer Army as a Reserve along the European model but that he was compelled for political reasons to upgrade the National Guard as a partial solution to the need for a national reserve force. Colby also contends that Root was strongly influenced by Upton and that Root saw the National Guard as serving state functions and being useful nationally only as a training ground for the Volunteer Army.

group was the Reserve Militia, which consisted of all able-bodied male citizens 18 to 45. Resident aliens who had declared their intent to become citizens were included in the two militias. For the first time, the Dick Act provided that general military stores, as well as arms and equipment, were to be offered to militia units that drilled at least 24 times a year and maintained a summer encampment of not less than five days. The militia units were to be periodically inspected by Regular Army officers, and Regular officers were detailed to the militia. Additionally, National Guard officers were declared eligible to attend Regular Army schools, and Guardsmen were to receive full pay and allowances while on maneuvers with the Regular Army.[48]

In addition, the Dick Act reaffirmed the principles of federal funding, federal inspections, and federal standards for training upon which today's Reserve Components are built.[49] The Act was the first of a series of bills from the establishment of an enlisted Army Reserve in 1912 through the sweeping National Defense Act of 1916 and its 1920 amendments that laid the groundwork for the Army's contemporary Reserve Components.

Following the January 21, 1903, passage of the Dick Act, Root achieved another of his objectives when Congress created the General Staff Corps on February 14, 1903. With the new General Staff of 45 officers, the Army was able to formulate cohesive, continuing military policies for the first time and take those planning steps which are essential for a successful mobilization.[50]

Root's ideas for a reserve corps soon grew into concrete form with a 1908 act "to increase the efficiency of the Medical Department of the United States Army."[51] The new corps was believed necessary to overcome serious wartime shortages of physicians, which had been apparent during the Spanish-American War; and there was no thought at the time that the commissioning of a few hundred Reserve doctors would lead to a force that numbers more than 3,000 units plus an Individual Ready Reserve of almost 250,000. Root's General Staff creation was also important for the Army Reserve, for the General Staff provided a place where John McAuley Palmer could think and write and produce in

48. 32 Stat. 775.

49. *Ibid.*

50. Kreidberg and Henry, *History of Military Mobilization*, pp. 177–79.

51. 35 Stat. 66–69.

1912 a document entitled "The Organization of the Land Forces of the United States." This remarkable work had a considerable influence upon the establishment of a Federal reserve force prior to World War I. The impact of Elihu Root was indeed far-ranging.

2

The Early Years

Behind the regular army must always stand the great reserve army consisting of the able-bodied men of the nation, so trained as to be promptly available for military service if needed, but following their normal occupations in time of peace.

MAJ. GEN. LEONARD WOOD, 1916[1]

THE MEDICAL RESERVE

The passage of Senate Bill 1424 on April 23, 1908, authorized the Army to secure a reserve corps of medical officers who could be ordered to active duty by the Secretary of War during time of emergency. These reserve doctors were to be commissioned as first lieutenants and to rank below all other officers of like grade in the United States. The act also provided for the commissioning of contract physicians in either the Regular Army or the Medical Reserve Corps, depending upon their age.[2] This latter provision generated the only serious opposition to the bill, with Representative

1. Leonard Wood, *Our Military History, Its Facts and Fallacies*, (Chicago: Reilly and Britton, 1916), pp. 226–27.

2. On March 22, 1967, Brig. Gen. Hal C. Pattison, Chief of Military History wrote Maj. Gen. William J. Sutton, Chief, Army Reserve that "although the National Defense Act of 1916 is viewed as providing for the immediate ancestor of our Reserve system in its present form, it is considered appropriate that 23 April 1908 be established as the official birth date of the United States Army Reserve. The Act of Congress on that date which created the Medical Reserve Corps, for the first time in Army history, provided for the establishment of a reservoir of trained officer personnel in a reserve status." Copy in OCAR Historical Files.

James R. Mann of Illinois predicting that it would allow contract surgeons to enter the Army and ultimately flow to the retired list after a short period of time. Mann's objections notwithstanding, the act passed the House 126 to 15, and the nation's first federal military reserve force was established.[3]

The first candidates for reserve commissions were certified on May 4, 1908, and by the end of the fiscal year on June 30, 160 contract physicians had been recommended for commissions in the Medical Reserve Corps. Their commissions would date from July 7, 1908. A year later, Surgeon General R. M. Reilly reported that "in order to build up the Reserve Corps with desirable material, a strong effort has been made to induce prominent physicians, surgeons, hygienists and laboratory workers to head it."[4] By June 30, 1909, 364 men had been commissioned in the Medical Reserve Corps, including 160 former contract physicians, and 184 such men were on active duty.[5]

In his 1909 report, Surgeon General George H. Torney spoke glowingly of his Medical Reserve Corps physicians, noting that "when it was necessary to assemble a board to investigate the important subject of inoculation for typhoid fever, it was possible to do so without going outside of the Medical Reserve Corps."[6] Torney stated that it would have been difficult to find a more qualified board anywhere. He also praised the Reserve doctors for aiding the Army in locating suitable physicians for commissions in the Army Medical Service.

---

3. The full text of Senate Bill 1424, as enacted, can be found on pages 66–69 of Part 1, Volume 35, *The Statutes at Large of the United States of America*. Representative Mann's voluminous objections are recorded on pages 3402–06 of Volume 42 of the *Congressional Record*.

4. R. M. O'Reilly, *Report of the Surgeon General, 1908* (Washington: War Department, 1908), pp. 131–32.

5. According to the *New York Times* of Nov. 30, 1908, the original 364 Medical Reserve Corps doctors included Dr. Roswell Park, the Buffalo, N.Y., surgeon who attended President McKinley after he was shot; Drs. Wyeth and Bryan, ex-Presidents of the American Medical Association; Dr. Souchin, a New Orleans, La., yellow fever expert; and Dr. Frank Billings, a respected surgeon with Johns Hopkins Hospital in Baltimore, Md. The *Times* also reported that the War Department commissioned Drs. William T. Bull and Andrew J. McCosh, "New York surgeons, both of whom are now critically ill in this city." Apparently, the standards for commissioning were somewhat vague.

6. *Report of the Surgeon General, 1909* (Washington: War Department, 1909), p. 173.

Table 2–1 Number of Physicians in the United States Army.

As of June 30 . . .	Medical Reserve Corps: Not On Active Duty	Medical Reserve Corps: On Active Duty	Regular Army Medical Officers
1908	0*	0	301
1909	180	184	283
1910	245	175	345
1911	784	138	381
1912	990	115	414
1913	1,100	105	424
1914	1,163	91	426
1915	1,340	86	433
1916	1,757	146	443

*As of June 30, 1908, 160 surgeons had been recommended for appointment in the Medical Reserve Corps. Their commissions would date from July 7, 1908.

Source: Reports of the War Department (1908–1916).

By June 30, 1910, Torney was pleased to report that the "Medical Reserve Corps has now passed the experimental stage."[7] Within two years, the strength of the Medical Reserve Corps exceeded one thousand; and in 1913, Reserve officers manned the Army's garrisons to allow Regular Army physicians to deploy to the field. In July 1913, Reserve doctors provided medical care to aging Civil War veterans during their Gettysburg encampment, and Torney recommended placing Reserve physicians on active duty at maneuver camps.

In 1914, a number of Medical Reserve Corps officers were appointed as special professors to the Army Medical School to deliver lectures ranging from "prevention and control of infectious diseases" to "cardia arythmia and circulatory efficiency." The Medical Reserve Corps grew to 1,903 officers in 1916 and outnumbered Regular Army doctors four to one.

By virtue of the National Defense Act of 1916, the Medical Reserve Corps ceased to exist on June 3, 1917, when its members were commissioned in the Officers' Reserve Corps as members of the Medical Officer's Reserve Corps. The Act of 1916 also allowed the Surgeon General to appoint officers in the Veterinary Officers' Reserve Corps and

7. *Report of the Surgeon General, 1910* (Washington: War Department, 1910), p. 456.

the Dental Officers' Reserve Corps. Together, these three corps contained 9,223 officers at the end of the 1917 fiscal year—a growth of twenty-five hundred percent in a decade.

While the officers of the Medical Reserve Corps were proving the value and desirability of a federal reserve force, a growing debate over the future of America's citizen-soldiers was beginning. In 1908, Congress had been intent upon clarifying the status of the National Guard and enacted legislation on May 27 to require the War Department to call the organized militia into service ahead of volunteer units when it was necessary to "execute the laws of the Union, suppress insurrection or repel invasion."[8] The Secretary of War was authorized to issue arms, equipment, clothing and military stores in general to the militia—provided that the United States retained title to the property.

When the Army General Staff realized that this act, which amended the Dick Act, required the War Department to use all militia, no matter how poorly organized, equipped or trained, before volunteer units, there was a strong desire to find another alternative reserve force.[9] This desire was expressed by John McAuley Palmer in his 1912 "Report on the Organization of the Land Forces of the United States."

ENTER JOHN MCAULEY PALMER

Palmer was the grandson of Maj. Gen. John M. Palmer, a volunteer Civil War officer who achieved high command with the Army of the Cumberland. A graduate of West Point, the younger Palmer was well acquainted with the capabilities of citizen-soldiers such as his grandfather. He was relatively uninfluenced by the anti-militia views of Emory Upton. Upton's *The Military Policy of the United States* had been posthumously published, and a distrust of the militia was very much in vogue among Regular Army officers in the early 1900s.[10]

---

8. Senate Bill 4316, enacted May 27, 1908, entitled "An Act to Further Amend the Act entitled 'An Act to Promote the Efficiency of the Militia of 1903,'" also divided the militia of the United States into the organized militia, known as the National Guard, and the Reserve Militia, which was otherwise undefined.

9. William H. Riker, *Soldiers of the States*, (Washington: Public Affairs Press, 1957), pp. 74–75.

10. Russell F. Weigley, *Towards an American Army, Military Thought from Washington to Marshall* (Westport, Conn.: Greenwood Press, 1962), pp. 228–29.

Palmer had for some time had the opinion that John C. Calhoun's idea of an expansible army "could have no congenial place in the American political system."[11] When Palmer assumed a peacetime Regular Army nucleus large enough to make a real foundation for effective expansion for war, he realized that the American people would be saddled with a prohibitively expensive standing Army. When he assumed a nucleus small enough to be acceptable to Congress, the expanded wartime force was insufficient for war on the European scale. This dilemma led Palmer to conclude that the only rational alternative was to rely upon the citizen-armies that had served Washington, Grant and Lee so well. He further reasoned that by organizing and training such armies in peacetime, these citizen-soldier armies would be preferable to any expansible army scheme.[12]

In the fall of 1911, Palmer was assigned to the War College Division of the new General Staff. Palmer's desire for a pre-trained reserve of citizen-soldiers coincided with the thoughts of Chief of Staff Leonard Wood. Indeed, Wood had written in his 1910 *Report of the Chief of Staff* that it was "imperatively necessary that steps should be taken to organize a proper reserve from which the regular and militia organizations can be properly filled with instructed men.[13] Palmer was thereupon given the task of drafting a major reorganization of the land forces of the United States. When Palmer was ready to outline his proposals, Wood arranged a meeting with Secretary of War Henry L. Stimson. The meeting took place during a long train ride to Fort Leavenworth, Kan., and Stimson and Wood listened to Palmer's ideas at great length.

Palmer proposed that American military policy should move away from the Regular Army as its central focus. Primary emphasis should be placed instead on "the citizen army and its relation to the permanent establishment." In Palmer's words, the "most important military problem is to devise means of preparing great armies of citizen soldiers to meet the emergency of modern war."[14] Stimson and Wood agreed with Palmer; and once the fundamental principle of a

---

11. John McAuley Palmer, *America in Arms*, (New Haven: Yale University Press, 1941), p. 135.

12. *Ibid.*, pp. 136–37.

13. *Report of the Chief of Staff, 1910*, as found in *War Department Reports, 1910* (Washington: War Department, 1910), Vol. I, p. 131.

14. I. B. Holley, Jr., *General John M. Palmer, Citizen-Soldiers, and the Army of A Democracy* (Westport, Conn.: Greenwood Press, 1982), pp. 200–04.

citizen reserve was agreed upon, Palmer was free to develop the details of the reorganization.[15]

Even though it was late in 1911, Palmer influenced the 1911 Report of the Secretary of War, which Stimson forwarded to the President on December 4. Stimson wrote that "it is absolutely imperative that provision should be made, by an adequate system of regular reserves, to fill up and maintain this first line of defense during the necessary time that must elapse while we are preparing and mobilizing our Militia and Volunteers."[16]

In the same report, Stimson stated that one of the main functions of a modern army is to train citizen-soldiers, who after training go back to their normal lives, ready to be called upon in an emergency.[17] Wood seconded Stimson by writing that "in view of the small size of the Regular Army and the small number of instructed militia, it is imperatively necessary that steps should be taken to organize a reserve of men . . . ."[18] Wood recommended a small monthly pay and 10-days annual maneuver or instruction with full pay for the members of this reserve. Wood also observed that 10 "Reserves" could be maintained for the cost of one Regular Army soldier—a ratio not very different from the cost of Reservists versus Regular Army soldiers in 1983.[19]

The Palmer plan, which was proposed to Congress in detail in 1912, organized the mobile land forces of the United States into three distinct parts. The first was a Regular Army ready for immediate use as an expeditionary force

15. When discussing his memoirs nearly 30 years later, Palmer summarized his beliefs thusly: "A government by the people must rest its defense upon Washington's army of the people and not upon Upton's expansible standing army. We must build strength into the democratic state without creating an exclusive samurai caste. We must have military power without militarism." (Letter of Palmer to Grenville Clark, Sept. 14, 1940.)

16. *Report of the Secretary of War, 1911* (Washington: War Department, 1911), pp. 22–23.

17. *Ibid.*, p. 21.

18. *Report of the Chief of Staff, 1911*, in *War Department Reports, 1911* (Washington: War Department, 1911), Vol. I, pp. 151–52.

19. A Reservist receives approximately one-sixth of the pay of an active-duty soldier, and lower operational and maintenance costs are likewise associated with Reserve units. A member of the Individual Ready Reserve (IRR) frequently receives only two weeks pay a year, or in many cases, no pay at all. Overall, the cost of maintaining the nearly 500,000 Reservists of the Ready Reserve is approximately one-tenth of that of maintaining a like number of men and women on active duty.

or for the first stages of a defensive war while the citizen-soldiery was being mobilized.

The second force was an army of citizen-soldiers organized into units and ready to reinforce the Regular Army in time of war. In 1912 this was the National Guard. Third was the army of volunteers, trained citizen-soldiers. Essentially, the 1912 plan was what the Army finally secured under the National Defense Act of 1920.[20]

The proponents of a federal reserve force were strengthened in February 1912 when Attorney General George W. Wickersham ruled that "the militia while in U.S. service might pursue an invading force beyond the U.S. boundary as part of repelling an invasion, but in general the militia cannot be employed outside of the United States."[21]

In arguing for an Army Reserve, Stimson pointed out that a reserve system was in effect in practically every nation of the world except the United States.[22] He pointed out that when the Spanish-American War broke out, many regiments were "greatly injured by the necessity of throwing into them a large number of perfectly raw recruits."[23] A trained federal reserve force of citizen-soldiers would prevent this problem, Stimson said.

In light of the Wickersham opinion, and persuaded by the exhortations of Stimson and Wood, Congress created an Army Reserve under provisions of Section 2 of the Army Appropriations Act of Aug. 24, 1912. This was accomplished by changing the term of Regular Army enlistment to seven years, with three or four years to be served with the colors and the balance to be a furlough to the Army Reserve.[24] This was the first provision for a federal reserve outside of the Medical Department.

Although pleased by the creation of the Army Reserve through the Act of 1912, Wood continued to press for a

---

20. Palmer, *America in Arms*, pp. 142–43.

21. Letter, Attorney General George W. Wickersham to Secretary of War Henry L. Stimson, Feb. 17, 1912.

22. According to the 1912 War Department *Annual Reports*, the United States had no Army Reserve, while the reserves of Great Britain stood at 215,000, and Japan counted one million reservists. The reserve strength of Italy was 1.5 million; Austria, 2.5 million; France, 3 million; Germany, 4.7 million; and Russia, 5.4 million.

23. *Report of the Secretary of War, 1912* (Washington: War Department, 1912), p. 20.

24. The portion of House Resolution 25531 pertaining to the new Army Reserve can be found on pages 590 and 591 of Part 1, Vol. 37, *Statutes at Large of the United States of America*.

more comprehensive federal reserve force. By August 31, 1913, the Army Reserve consisted of only eight men, and Wood observed that men would not enlist in the Army Reserve under present conditions. He sought pay for Reservists, noting that "we cannot secure valuable service for nothing."[25]

In his 1914 report to the President, Secretary of War Lindley M. Garrison stated that "present legislation with respect to a reserve has proven utterly useless for the purpose."[26] Noting that the Army Reserve had doubled to 16 men, Wood repeated his previous sentiments and asked for authority to commission 400 provisional lieutenants each year. These officers would serve one year in training with the Regular Army and then leave active duty to form a reserve of officers.

Wood's term as Army Chief of Staff ended in 1914, and he was assigned to command the First Military District at Governor's Island, NY. This reduction in responsibility gave him ample time for writing and speech-making. Wood wrote profusely for magazines, and his short books were eloquent and forceful in pleading for an Army Reserve. Wood also became involved in the Plattsburg camps and the Military Training Camps Association.

CIVILIAN TRAINING

As Chief of Staff, Wood had been successful in starting two experimental camps of military instruction for college students during their 1913 summer vacation. The camps had been the idea of Lt. Henry T. Bull, a cavalry officer detailed as professor of military science at Cornell University. Students paid their own transportation to the camps at Pacific Grove, Calif., and Gettysburg, Penn., and paid approximately $27.50 for uniforms and food.

Despite an arduous course of instruction, which began at 5:15 a.m., the 159 young men at the initial camps became so enthusiastic that officers occasionally had to order them to stop drill in order to swim or play ball. Later, 84 of these 159 received Reserve commissions and served in World War I.[27]

---

25. *Report of the Chief of Staff, 1913*, in *War Department Reports, 1913* (Washington: War Department, 1913), pp. 150–51.

26. *Reports of the Secretary of War, 1914* (Washington: War Department, 1914), p. 11.

27. John G. Clifford, *The Citizen Soldiers* (Lexington, Ky.: University Press of Kentucky, 1972), pp. 11–16.

The camps made a strong impression on several college presidents, including Henry Drinker of Lehigh University. Drinker accompanied his son to Gettysburg, and when the students formed the Society of the National Reserve Corps of the United States, Drinker was elected president.[28]

Drinker formed the Advisory Board of University Presidents for the National Reserve Corps and successfully rallied academic support for additional camps in 1914. Wood was able to arrange the detail of additional Army officers to instruct at the camps, and 667 students attended the second summer—again at their own expense.[29]

After the beginning of war in Europe on July 28, 1914, the General Staff began an update of the 1912 "Report on the Organization of the Land Forces in the United States" in order to overcome this country's military weakness. The result was the "Statement of a Proper Military Policy for the United States."

The statement recommended "more than doubling the size of the Regular Army, from 100,000 to 230,000; continued support of the Organized Militia; a Regular Army reserve; a reserve of trained citizen-soldiers; a reserve of officers; and a reserve of essential supplies."[30] To translate the statement into reality, Secretary Garrison devised his Continental Army proposal, which can be reduced to three main points:

1. A Regular Army large enough to meet immediate military needs while training other military forces.
2. A volunteer, trained federal reserve force—the Continental Army—to immediately augment the Regular Army in emergencies.
3. Retain the National Guard under state control, but with increased federal assistance.[31]

Garrison also proposed to recruit officer cadets from the National Guard for his Continental Army, but ruffled National Guard feathers when he said that "strictly speaking,

28. The constitution of the National Reserve Corps is found on page 587 of the Dec. 18, 1913, edition of *Leslie's Illustrated Weekly* as part of an article written by Wood entitled "How to Have a Bigger Army."

29. Clifford, *Citizen Soldiers*, pp. 18–24.

30. Marvin A. Kreidberg and Merton G. Henry, *History of Military Mobilization in the United States Army, 1775–1945* (Washington: Department of the Army, 1955), p. 190.

31. *Report of the Secretary of War, 1915* (Washington: War Department, 1915), pp. 22–27.

nothing less than Regular Army training makes an efficient soldier.[32] Garrison also irritated Guardsmen by writing the 1915 convention of the National Guard Association that Guard units would be "permitted" to transfer from the National Guard to the Continental Army. A speech by Assistant Secretary of War Henry Breckenridge to that same convention left many Guardsmen with the impression that the National Guard would no longer have any federal sanction, and its future would be left up to the states.

Meanwhile, stunned by the sinking of the *Lusitania* in May 1915, law partners Grenville Clark and Elihu Root, Jr., son of the former Secretary of War, determined to do something to demonstrate a firm national policy against Germany. Enlisting the aid of Theodore Roosevelt, Jr.,[33] they approached Wood with the idea of adapting the youth summer camps to camps for men in their twenties and thirties.

The general was supportive. If Clark and the others could sign up at least 100 professional and business men for the camps, Wood would provide the officers and equipment. When recruiting for the businessmen's camps went well, Wood was able to have the adult camp included under War Department General Order No. 38, June 22, 1915, which authorized that summer's college camps.

Approximately 1,200 men assembled at Plattsburg, NY, for the first businessmen's camp. Compressing the five-week student program into four weeks, the men started their day with 5:45 a.m. calisthenics, followed by drill until noon. After lunch, there was specialized instruction in the arms of the service—cavalry, signal, engineering. As with the student camps, the participants at Plattsburg tackled the training with great enthusiasm. Just as the students at Gettysburg organized at camp's end, the men at Plattsburg formed the First Training Regiment.

Determined that Plattsburg should not be a flash-in-the-pan, Clark worked with members of similar busi-

32. *Ibid.*, p. 35.

33. Theodore Roosevelt, Jr., went on to earn a commission before World War I. After a distinguished peace-time public service career, he was recalled to active duty in 1941. He served in the North African, Sicilian and Corsican landings and established a reputation for courage under fire. As a 57-year old brigadier general, he was the only general and the oldest man to go ashore in the first wave of the Normandy assault upon Utah Beach. He was the assistant division commander of the 4th Infantry Division.

nessmen's camps and with the Advisory Board of University Presidents of the National Reserve Corps to form the Military Training Camps Association of the United States (MTCA). The stated purpose of the MTCA was to encourage reasonable military training for citizens through federal training camps, and the group's efforts later played an important role in the "90-day-wonder" commissioning camps of World War I.[34]

In 1915, preparedness was a major issue in America; and the MTCA was an ideal apparatus for spreading the word on preparedness. The MTCA had a number of active committees staffed with well-known personalities, and the movement was national in scope. It was strongly influenced by ex-President Theodore Roosevelt and by Wood,[35] who saw his citizen-army gospel enhanced by the MTCA's enthusiasm for citizen's military training.[36]

In Lindley Garrison's mind, preparedness was his Continental Army plan. To the National Guard and Representative James Hay, Chairman of the House Military Affairs Committee, it was a stronger National Guard with increased federal support. This made for a collection of semi-allies with divergent interests operating under the general banner of increased preparedness.

While these divergent interests agreed that it was necessary to improve the national defense, it was impossible to reach a consensus on what should be done. In fact, in the opinion of historian Russell F. Weigley, the sweeping legislation of the 1916 National Defense Act could never have been achieved except for problems with Mexico.[37]

MEXICO

The United States had been involved in the internal affairs of Mexico following the 1911 overthrow of dictator Porfirio Diaz, the details of which are not relevant to this narrative. It is sufficient that displeasure with U.S. policies led peasant leader Francisco "Pancho" Villa to retaliate by raiding Columbus, New Mexico, on March 9, 1916. Within a week, the War Department sent 5,000 troops under Brig. Gen. John J. Pershing across the border in pursuit of Villa.

34. Clifford, *Citizen Soldiers*, pp. 116–17, 150.
35. Holley, *General John M. Palmer*, pp. 249–50.
36. Russell F. Weigley, *History of the United States Army* (New York: Macmillan Co., 1967), p. 343.
37. *Ibid.*, p. 347.

Villa made a mockery of the campaign, and the Mexican government demanded that Pershing be withdrawn. Villa continued to menace American towns, while war with Mexico seemed almost inevitable. On May 9 the War Department called out the Texas, New Mexico and Arizona National Guards, but this force did not appear to be enough.[38]

On May 17, because of the conditions along the border, all furloughs to the Army Reserve were suspended except for furloughs from the Coast Artillery.[39] On June 28, the War Department ordered the first mobilization of the Army Reserve. The military departments were directed to order Reservists to active duty for service with Regular Army regiments on the Mexican border, and approximately 3,000 Reservists answered the call.[40]

THE NATIONAL DEFENSE ACT OF 1916

Under pressure from events along the border, the Congress acted on compromise legislation proposed by Hay, which passed the Senate on May 17 and the House May 20. This was the comprehensive National Defense Act of 1916 that was signed into law by President Wilson on June 3, 1916.

More than 100 pages long, with 128 sections, the National Defense Act of 1916 defined the Army of the United States as the "Regular Army, the Volunteer Army, the Officers' Reserve Corps, the Enlisted Reserve Corps, the National Guard while in the service of the United States, and such other land forces as are now or may hereafter be authorized by law." As a military omnibus bill, it provided something for everyone.

---

38. *Ibid.*, p. 348; according to the 1917 *Report of the Adjutant General,* approximately 3,000 members of the Regular Army Reserve subsequently responded to a mobilization call of June 28, 1916, and were assigned to Regular Army units along the Mexico border. See page 193, *Report of the Adjutant General, 1917*.

39. Report of the Adjutant General, *War Department Reports, 1916*, (Washington, DC: War Department, 1917), p. 255.

40. *Report of the Adjutant General, War Department Reports, 1917* (Washington: War Department, 1918), p. 193. In contrast to the official War Department reports, the July 7, 1916, *New York Times* reported on page 4 that the War Department was going to summon approximately 5,000 Reservists to the colors. According to The Adjutant General, this would have been impossible, since there were only 4,626 Reservists including the Coast Artillery. According to the National Guard Bureau, 158,664 National Guardsmen were also mobilized.

The National Guard received federal pay for drills,[41] which were set by the act at 48 per year. On the other hand, the carrot of federal pay was used to counterbalance the stick of federal recognition and standards for Guard officers, the authority of the President to prescribe the kind of units to be maintained by the states, and the requirements that enlistment qualifications for the Guard be the same as the Regular Army. Guardsmen were also required to take a dual oath to their State and the United States.

The Regular Army was authorized an increase to 175,000 men over a period of five years, and the number of general officers was increased. The Officers' Reserve Corps, the Enlisted Reserve Corps and the Reserve Officers Training Corps were also established statutorily. The comprehensive federal reserve force so ardently espoused by Root, Wood, Stimson and Garrison was finally authorized.

The MTCA had been instrumental in keeping a training camps provision intact during the legislative process that hammered out the National Defense Act of 1916. The lobbying of Clark and Drinker, with the assistance of Sen. Henry A. duPont of Delaware, resulted in the 16,000 men who took Plattsburg training in the summer of 1916 being the first to do so under federal statute.[42]

According to John G. Clifford in his book, *The Citizen Soldiers,* the 1916 camps were the product of hard work and cooperation between the MTCA and the War Department. The camps gave increased publicity to preparedness and the idea that citizens had a universal military obligation. These camps, called Regular Army Instruction Camps, augmented the country's trained military personnel as MTCA personnel, called Plattsburgers, flocked by the hundreds to join the new Officers' Reserve Corps (ORC) and Reserve Officers Training Corps (ROTC).[43]

By February 1917, approximately 500 Reserve Officers had been commissioned, in addition to nearly 2,000 in the still-separate Medical Reserve Corps. As United States intervention in World War I became more likely, the Army and the MTCA stepped up their recruiting efforts. As of March 1, 939 Reserve Officers had been commissioned and another 565 commissions were pending. The MTCA had 70,000 applicants for the 1917 Regular Instruction Camps. On April 1, 1917, the Regular Army, including the Philippine

41. Riker, *Soldiers of the States,* pp. 76–80.
42. Clifford, *Citizen Soldiers,* pp. 116–17.
43. *Ibid.,* pp. 152–53.

Scouts, had a strength of 133,111. There were 80,446 National Guardsmen in Federal service, plus 101,174 members of the Guard still in State service.[44]

WORLD WAR I

There was an obvious need for more Army officers following US entry into World War I on April 6, 1917, and the MTCA sent Secretary of War Newton D. Baker a telegram proposing to open the instruction camps as early as May to serve as a professional training ground for men being offered commissions in the ORC.

Baker agreed. The staggering task of recruiting 40,000 officer candidates in just three weeks began. The camps opened May 15 using the recently published *Plattsburg Manual*[45] as their basic text. Meanwhile, the commissioning process was accelerated, with 7,957 Reserve Officers appointed by May 15. These officers, as well as the new candidates, were required to attend the training camps in order to retain their commissions.[46]

Including officers transferred from the Medical Reserve Corps when it was merged with the ORC on June 3, 1917, the ORC on June 30, 1917, consisted of 21,543 officers.[47] It was with this nucleus of trained reserve officers and reserve enlisted men with specialized skills that the United States Army entered World War I.

The Enlisted Reserve Corps had been created by the National Defense Act of 1916 for the expressed purpose "of securing an additional reserve of enlisted men for military service with the Engineer, Signal and Quartermaster Corps and the Ordnance and Medical Departments of the Regular Army."[48] The purpose was to obtain a reserve of pretrained specialists who would augment the Regular Army upon call

44. Marvin A. Kriedberg and Merton G. Henry, *History of Military Mobilization in the United States Army, 1775–1945* (Washington: Department of the Army, 1955), p. 374.

45. *The Plattsburg Manual*, first published in March 1917 and indorsed by Wood, was designed to be a first textbook for those who desired an ORC commission. In 336 pages, it covered a wealth of military subjects from physical training to patrolling and trench warfare. It went through 10 printings in 14 months.

46. *Kriedberg, op. cit.*, pp. 224–225.

47. *Report of the Secretary of War, 1917* (Washington: War Department, 1917), pp. 193–94.

48. See Section 55, PL 64–85, 134 U.S.C. 195.

of the President; and this Enlisted Reserve Corps[49] was in addition to the Regular Army Reserve, which had been established in 1912 and continued under the 1916 act.[50]

Furloughs from the active Army to the Regular Army Reserve (RAR) were suspended on April 19, 1917, and virtually all members of the RAR were ordered back to active duty in May. Meanwhile, the Enlisted Reserve Corps was growing rapidly, reaching 35,000 men on June 30, 1917, and 55,000 by October 1 of the same year. According to the Adjutant General, nine Engineer regiments, were organized for railway work abroad, and 27 field Signal battalions, 12 telegraph battalions and six depot companies were formed from this Reserve.

In addition, the Enlisted Reserve Corps provided the men for 235 wagon companies, 106 auto-truck companies, 20 bakery companies and 24 pack-train companies, plus nearly 15,000 men who served in the Medical Department in World War I.[51] In all, approximately 80,000 Enlisted Reserve Corps or Regular Army Reservists served in World War I.[52]

The Officers' Reserve Corps provided a total of 89,476 officers during World War I,[53] of whom 57,307 were commissioned through the 90-day Officers' Training Camps. Included in the larger figure were 639 "colored" officers commissioned at Fort Des Moines, Iowa, in 1917. Two schools in Puerto Rico produced 433 officers.[54]

The Reserve Officers Training Corps produced 3,364 ORC officers, and 23,261 former enlisted men were commissioned through Officers' Training Schools operated by the

---

49. A particularly popular Enlisted Reserve Corps option was in the Aviation Section, Signal Enlisted Reserve Corps. A number of the Army's early aviators came out of this corps including Edward V. "Eddie" Rickenbacker, who won the Medal of Honor and the Distinguished Service Cross with six Oak Leaf Clusters as a World War I flying ace. The Enlisted Reserve Corps was also a holding status for potential officers with special skills such as medical students.

50. The Regular Army Reserve was never a large force. This body of soldiers furloughed from the Regular Army stood at 4,648 on June 30, 1916, and grew to 8,355 before furloughs were suspended on April 19, 1917.

51. *Report of the Secretary of War, 1917.*

52. "Report of the Adjutant General," in *War Department Annual Reports, 1919* (Washington: War Department, 1919), Vol. I, pp. 500–01.

53. *Ibid.*

54. *Report of the Chief of Staff, 1919,* in *War Department Annual Reports, 1919* (Washington: War Department, 1919), pp. 299–301.

various corps and divisions before all distinctions between components were ended on August 7, 1918. After that date, the appellations "Regular Army," "Officers' Reserve Corps," "National Guard," and "National Army" were dropped and all commissions were granted in the Army of the United States.

The American Expeditionary Force (AEF) commander in Europe was General John J. Pershing, a Regular Army man who had previously commanded the US forces on the Mexican border. Pershing was greatly concerned about the short period of training that the American draftees and volunteers received, and he devoted many months to training the men who reached Europe in 1917 and early 1918.[55] Pershing's insistence on additional training was vindicated, for American units gave a good account of themselves in places like St. Mihiel and the Meuse-Argonne,[56] and Pershing himself was apparently convinced that a large standing army was unnecessary in time of peace.

As in subsequent wars, the divisions of World War I did not remain pure Regular Army, National Army or National Guard divisions even prior to August 7. Officers of all components and men from the Enlisted Reserve Corps served in every division, making the Army Reserve's contribution to World War I a contribution to the total war effort.[57]

55. *Report of the Chief of Staff, 1919,* p. 280.

56. Charles B. MacDonald, "World War I: The U.S. Army Overseas," in Maurice Matloff (Gen. Ed.), *American Military History* (Washington: Office of the Chief of Military History, United States Army, 1969), pp. 396–403.

57. *Report of the Chief of Staff, 1919,* p. 280.

3

Between the World War, 1919–1939

Demobilization proceeded rapidly after the war, and by June 30, 1919, 2,608,218 enlisted men and 128,436 officers had been discharged. Six months later the US Army consisted of only 130,000 Regular troops, about the same number as in April 1917.[1] There were no special plans for strengthening the reserve forces of the Army, and in fact Army Chief of Staff Peyton C. March proposed to Congress in 1919 a plan for an expanded Regular Army of over 500,000 men, filled out in time of war by a horde of conscripts backed up by the National Guard.[2]

Congress was in no mood, however, to provide for such a substantial increase in the standing army, and both houses resisted the blandishments of the War Department. Congress sought a reasonable alternative to March's proposal, and in October 1919 it found a man who was willing to offer such. Colonel John McAuley Palmer had been one of Pershing's proteges in the AEF, and he had returned to Washington after the war as a member of the War Plans Division of the General Staff. Palmer's experience in France had strengthened his existing belief in the values of the citizen-soldier, and when Senator James J. Wadsworth invited him to testify before the Committee on Military Affairs, Palmer was ready to offer his opinions.[3]

---

1. Russell F. Weigley, *History of the United States Army* (New York and London: Macmillan Publishing Co., Inc. and Collier Macmillan Publishers, 1967), p. 396.

2. *Ibid.* pp. 396–97.

3. Jonathan M. House, "John McAuley Palmer and the Reserve

By the end of Palmer's two days as an expert witness, Sen. Wadsworth was convinced that the outspoken colonel—who had castigated the proposals of Chief of Staff March—was just the man to work on a Senate proposal for amending the National Defense Act of 1916. Palmer was thereupon loaned to the Committee, and he worked for eight months on the project. After much compromising with the House of Representatives, which had developed its own bill, many of Palmer's ideas (except his plans for universal military training) were enacted into law in 1920.

Usually called the National Defense Act of 1920,[4] this piece of legislation was far-reaching in its impact on the organization of the United States Army. The Army was now defined as consisting of the Regular Army, the National Guard, and the Organized Reserves; and the entire country was divided into corps areas. In each corps was to be at least one division of Organized Reserve troops. The Regular Army reserve was abolished by the 1920 statute, and its members were relieved of further military obligations.[5]

Of primary interest to reservists were a re-statement of the 1916 Defense Act provisions creating the Officers' Reserve Corps, the Reserve Officers' Training Corps, and the Enlisted Reserve Corps and the statutory regulation of the Citizens' Military Training Camps that had developed out of the pre-war Plattsburg movement.[6] Because of the small inter-war size of the Enlisted Reserve Corps, this chapter is restricted almost totally to the Officers' Reserve Corps.

On July 21, 1921, General Pershing succeeded General March as Chief of Staff of the Army, and under him the reserves received greater attention than ever before.[7] The instrument of this attention was none other than Brig. Gen. John McA. Palmer, who was a member of Pershing's personal staff. During Pershing's tenure as Chief of Staff, wrote Palmer, "my principal duty was to advise him in questions of policy relating to reserve and other 'citizen army' affairs." He acted purely in an advisory capacity, said Palmer, and when his advice "pointed to administrative action, he [General Pershing] ordered the proper agency of the War Department to take that action."[8]

Components," *Parameters: Journal of the US Army War College*, Vol. XII (September 1982), pp. 14–15.

4. Public Law 66–242.
5. *Ibid.*, Secs. 3, 30.
6. *Ibid.*, Secs. 37, 40, 47 and 55.
7. Weigley, *History of the United States Army*, p. 560.
8. Letter, John McA. Palmer to Col. E. S. Hartshorn, Executive for

The problems of the Army's Organized Reserve forces after World War I were numerous, even after passage of the National Defense Act of 1920. Lack of an institution for providing guidance at the Army Staff level, poor opportunities for training, and—given these two problems—an unrealistic view of mobilization were endemic. The Army Staff did not have any ready solution in any of these areas, but Chief of Staff Pershing decided that the first priority was to insure that someone at the Army Staff level would have a continuing responsibility for reserve affairs after he and Gen. Palmer were gone.

ESTABLISHMENT OF A RESERVE OFFICE

In a March 1, 1923, memorandum, Pershing directed the Deputy Chief of Staff to study the question of "establishing an agency in the War Department whose express function will be to handle questions pertaining to the Reserves, that is, an agency to which reserve officers seeking information or with recommendations to make, or any business relating to the reserves could go and receive a cordial welcome and thoughtful consideration. I think no such agency now exists in the department."[9]

As a result of Pershing's memorandum, a Reserve Officers' Section was established on June 12, 1923, under the Assistant Chief of Staff, G–2. Maj. C. F. Thompson was given temporary responsibility for the section, as an additional duty. Thompson's tenure, however, lasted only until July 2, at which time he was succeeded by Maj. Walter O. Boswell.[10]

The position of "Chief of the Reserve Section, G–2" did not accord enough importance to the role of the Officers' Reserve Corps during the inter-war period.[11] In March 1927,

---

Reserve Affairs, July 1, 1935, in National Archives, Record Group 319 (Army Staff), Entry #343 (Records for Reserve and ROTC Affairs), Box 100. Hereinafter cited by RG #, Entry #, and Box #.

9. Memorandum, General John J. Pershing to Deputy Chief of Staff, March 1, 1923, RG 319, Entry 343, Box 97.

10. Memorandum, H. C. McCormick to Col. E. S. Hartshorn, June 27, 1935, RG 319, Entry 343, Box 97. Major Thompson returned later as Brig. Gen. Thompson and served as Executive for Reserve Affairs, September 16, 1938–June 9, 1940. A complete listing of the Chiefs of the Army Reserve—by whatever title they were known—is in Appendix A.

11. The Enlisted Reserve Corps, created by the National Defense Act of 1920, was of very minor importance between World Wars I and II. It consisted of only 6000 men in 1928, and by 1936 its ranks num-

therefore, Colonel David L. Stone was transferred to the Army Chief of Staff's Office from the Office of the Assistant Secretary of War and was assigned as "Executive for Reserve Affairs."[12] This reporting relationship lasted only ten days, for on March 15, 1927, The Adjutant General suspended "until further notice" the transfer of the position to the Chief of Staff's Office.[13] Col. Stone's successor, Col. (later Brigadier General) Charles D. Herron, took over the position in May 1930, and he, too, reported to the Assistant Secretary of War. In November 1930, however, Col. Herron was transferred to the Office of the Chief of Staff, where the status of the Executive for Reserve Affairs was "analogous to that of the Legislation Branch." Col. Herron was soon informed that the office, which as late as September 1936 consisted only of the Executive and a secretary, would "be an adjunct to, and will function directly under, the Deputy Chief of Staff."[14]

The Office of the Executive for Reserve Affairs remained at this small staffing level until April 16, 1941, when it was allocated two additional officer positions: a lieutenant colonel and a captain. The title was officially changed at almost the same time to the "Office of the Executive for Reserve and ROTC Affairs," a title that was used until 1954.[15]

---

bered less than 4000. "Organization of the Army, 1928," RG 319, Entry 343, Box 97; "Strength of the O.R.C. and E.R.C., June 30, 1936," RG 319, Entry 343, Box 100.

12. Special Orders No. 53, Par. 24, March 5, 1927, cited in "Digest of War Department Policies," Subject: "Supervision of Reserve Affairs," November 7, 1930, RG 319, Entry 343, Box 98.

13. Letter from TAG, March 15, 1927, cited in "Digest of War Department Policies," Subject: "Supervision of Reserve Affairs," November 7, 1939, RG 319, Entry 343, Box 98.

14. "Digest of War Department Policies," Subject: "Supervision of Reserve Affairs," November 7, 1930, RG 319, Entry 343, Box 98; Memorandum, Gen. C. P. Summerall to The Adjutant General, November 1, 1930, Subject: "Executive for Reserve Affairs," RG 319, Entry 343, Box 98; Memorandum, Brig. Gen. Edwin S. Hartshorn to Mr. Murray, Investigator, Civil Service Commission, September 8, 1936, RG 319, Entry 343, Box 100; Memorandum, Lt. Col. Clement H. Wright, Secretary of the General Staff, to Col. Charles D. Herron, Executive for Reserve Affairs, November 7, 1930, RG 319, Entry 343, Box 98.

15. Letter, TAG to Executive for Reserve Affairs, April 16, 1941, Subject: "Allotment of Additional Officers to the Office, Chief of Staff, War Department Overhead," RG 319, Entry 343, Box 104; Order of the Secretary of War, June 16, 1941, reported in TAG letter, AG 008 ORC (6–11–41), RG 319, Entry 343, Box 104.

The head of the Reserve office during the inter-war period had no direct authority over anyone except his own clerk. Brig. Gen. Palmer, whose position was purely unofficial, had described his role as "solely . . . advisory," and this was the pattern for the men who were later given the title of "Reserve Executive." In 1936, for example, Brig. Gen. E. S. Hartshorn informed an investigator for the Civil Service Commission that "The Chief of Staff retains to himself the supervision and control of the Reserve Component of the Army of the United States. The Executive for Reserve Affairs is the assistant to the Chief of Staff and his immediate adviser in all matters relating to the administration of the Reserve Component. It is the duty of the Executive for Reserve Affairs to maintain contact with the personnel of the Officers' Reserve Corps and, speaking for the Chief of Staff, to render decisions upon such matters as are delegated to him by the Chief of Staff. All instructions issued by the Office of the Executive for Reserve Affairs are given in the name of the Chief of Staff."[16] Though his authority was not very great, the presence of a general officer whose full-time job was that of looking after the interests of Reservists in the Army meant that Gen. Pershing had at least partially succeeded. The Officers' Reserve Corps, the Reserve Officers' Training Corps and the Enlisted Reserve Corps finally had a spokesman, and they would need that and more during the coming year.

BUILDING THE ORC

National defense policy during the years between World Wars I and II was that of maintaining a relatively small Regular Army, supplemented by a much larger force of trained reservists. Philosophically, this was what the nation desired; fiscally, however, it was not prepared to support even this modest level of military activity.

"During the past year," wrote Secretary of War John W. Weeks in 1923, "I have heard a few criticisms of our defensive measures, on the basis of their cost. It is apparently a matter of astonishment for some of our citizens to discover that national defense consumes an appreciable part of the Federal Budget." During Fiscal Year 1923, continued Weeks, the War Department appropriation was

16. Memorandum, Brig. Gen. E. S. Hartshorn, Executive for Reserve Affairs, to Mr. Murray, Investigator for the Civil Service Commission, September 8, 1936, RG 319, Entry 343, Box 100.

$340,884,122, of which $256,415,470 was for "military purposes. These are tremendous sums," he wrote, "but ours is a great nation. The total Federal Budget for this period was over $4,000,000,000. The War and Navy Departments consumed, roughly, 14 percent of the total Federal Budget, and purely military activities 6 percent . . . . The per capita cost is slightly more than $2 annually."[17]

There were two major interrelated problems for the Officers' Reserve Corps during the inter-war years: first, increasing the size of the ORC and second, providing adequate training opportunities for its members. Officers could be commissioned through ROTC and the Citizens' Military Training Camps (CMTC), but unless regular opportunities for training were provided, it would be difficult to sustain motivation, effectiveness, and even membership. Fiscal constraints, however, were a real problem.

World War I had created a large pool of combat veterans from which members of the ORC could be obtained. During the fiscal year that ended on June 30, 1920, there were a total of 35,060 new appointments to the Corps, some 83 percent of which were in the rank of captain and below. Slightly over 12,400 officers left the ORC during the year, so the Officers' Reserve Corps ended FY 1920 with a strength of 68,232.[18] "By means of expert instruction in time of peace," wrote the Secretary of War in 1926, "the Reserve Officers' Training Corps is gradually building up a most valuable complement of junior officers . . . . Without this source of replacement the Officers' Reserve Corps . . . would become ineffective."[19] Indeed, the ROTC was the largest source of new officers for the ORC. Table 3–1 shows the gains from ROTC for the years 1920 through 1937 and indicates for the years 1931–37 the accumulated losses through resignations, dismissals, and other causes. As of 1937 the Army had a goal of 120,000 active members of the Officers' Reserve Corps. The average annual increase in ORC strength was 11,633, of which 6535 came from ROTC. The second largest source of new ORC members was

17. "Report of the Secretary of War to the President, 1923," in *Annual Reports, War Department, Fiscal Year Ended June 30, 1923* (Washington: GPO, 1923), pp. 2–3.

18. "Report of the Adjutant General, 1920" in *War Department Annual Reports, 1920* (Washington: GPO, 1921), p. 257.

19. "Report of the Secretary of War to the President, 1926" in *Annual Reports, War Department, Fiscal Year Ended June 30, 1926* (Washington: GPO, 1926), p. 55.

Table 3–1 ROTC Appointments in the ORC, 1920–1937.[20]

Fiscal Year	# Appointments	Accumulated Total	Accumulated Loss
1920	135	945	
1921	811	2,977	
1922	2,031	5,851	
1924	3,317	9,168	
1925	4,153	13,321	
1926	4,842	18,163	
1927	5,018	23,181	
1928	5,685	28,866	
1929	5,752	34,618	
1930	6,514	41,132	
1931	5,989	47,121	12,935
1932	6,530	53,651	16,935
1933	6,770	60,421	20,179
1934	6,347	66,768	23,649
1935	6,780	73,548	27,410
1936	5,722	79,270	31,927
1937	5,704	84,974	36,601

direct commissioning of civilians, and the third largest source was the Citizens' Military Training Camps.[21]

The CMTC's had grown out of the pre-World War I "Plattsburg idea" promoted by Army Chief of Staff Leonard Wood. The camps were given statutory authority in the National Defense Act of 1920, and they enjoyed the patronage and support of influential members of the political and social hierarchy through the Military Training Camps Association.[22] The CMTC provided a certain amount of military training to the young men who participated, but they consumed a disproportionate share of the War Department's Reserve Officer procurement funds. Table 3–2 compares the appropriations and officer production for the ROTC and the CMTC for the fiscal years from 1925 through 1928.

20. "Analysis of Gains and Losses in ROTC Appointees Since 1920," found in RG 319, Entry 343, Box 102.

21. Memorandum, Lt. Col. J. H. Woodberry, Chief, Statistics Branch, Army General Staff, to Brig. Gen. E. S. Hartshorn, Executive for Reserve Affairs, February 24, 1927, Subject: "Reserve Officer Objective," RG 319, Entry 343, Box 101.

22. Lt. Col. R. A. Hill, "Reserve Policies and National Defense," *Infantry Journal,* XLII (January–February 1935), p. 61; See also Ralph Barton Perry, *The Plattsburg Movement* (New York: Dutton, 1921) and John G. Clifford, *The Citizen Soldiers: The Plattsburg Training Camp Movement, 1913–1920* (Lexington: University Press of Kentucky, 1972).

Table 3-2 ROTC and CMTC, FY's, 1925–1928.[23]

	1925		1926		1927		1928		Total	
	$	#	$	#	$	#	$	#	$	#
ROTC	3.8	4153	3.8	4842	3.9	5018	2.6	5685	14.1	19,698
CMTC	2.3	487	2.8	71	2.8	59	2.8	24	10.7	641

*All dollar figures are in millions; # refers to number commissioned.

Regardless of the source from which the commissions came, the ORC grew too slowly, for projections in 1937 indicated that the Army would not meet its ORC strength objective until sometime in 1944. There was some doubt, moreover, that the training received by this group of officers would prepare them for their wartime roles, because training, indeed, was the Achilles heel of the ORC during the inter-war period.[24]

TRAINING THE ORC

The lessons of World War I, as assimilated by the Army General Staff and the Congress, did not include the necessity for extensive training for members of the Officers' Reserve Corps. From 1920–1940 ORC members were typically under-trained; what training they did receive generally fell into five categories: active duty training with the Regular army, active duty training with Citizens' Military Training Camps, active duty with the Civilian Conservation Corps, inactive duty training with a Reserve unit, and correspondence courses. Many Reservists benefited from several of these methods of training, but few people would maintain that the ORC was ever the recipient of enough training during the inter-war years.

Members of the ORC were lucky if they received a two week active duty training tour every four or five years during the 1920's. Table 3–3 shows the number of individuals

23. Figures are taken from "Reports of the Secretary of War" for Fiscal Years 1925–28 and from "Analysis of Gains and Losses in ROTC. Appointees since 1920," RG 319, Entry 343, Box 102.

24. Memorandum, Lt. Col. J. H. Woodberry, Chief, Statistics Branch, Army General Staff, to Brig. Gen. E. S. Hartshorn, Executive for Reserve Affairs, Subject: "Reserve Officer Objective," RG 319, Entry 343, Box 101. It should be pointed out that producing Reserve officers was not the primary purpose of the CMTC "Instilling citizenship" was its paramount objective.

Table 3–3 Active Duty Training (15 Days or Less) of ORC Members, 1924–1930.[25]

Fiscal Year	# Trained	# Days	Cost of Training (Per Capita)
1924	7,926	15	(*)
1925	10,859	15	(*)
1926	14,883	15	$143.83
1927	16,173	15	$141.27
1928	16,789	14	$123.94
1929	19,608	14	$126.75
1930	21,270	14	$121.89

*Unknown.

who received such training, and the per capita cost of the training.

Table 3–3 does not, however, tell the entire story. In FY 1930, for example, 1,123 Reserve Officers received active duty training in excess of 15 days. The problem from the standpoint of readiness, however, was that there were 79,285 active Reserve Officers at the time, meaning that slightly over 28 percent of the ORC was able to train during that fiscal year.[26]

A member of the 306th Infantry Regiment, 77th Division, recalled that the officers in his unit did not have two weeks of annual training each year. "We went most years," he stated, "to either Fort Dix [New Jersey], or Plattsburg [New York]. Our unit didn't have any vehicles, so we carpooled to camp, or got there on our own. When we got there, they had to issue equipment to us, like rifles and machine guns, because we didn't have anything of our own."[27]

Another ORC member in Chicago remembered monthly meetings during the 1920's. "We had RA [Regular Army] instructors, and we went on occasional field trips. I went to Carlisle Barracks [Pennsylvania], once and spent most of that time studying general military subjects. I

25. Memorandum, Lt. Col. Karl Truesdell, Chief, Budget and Legislative Planning Branch, Army General Staff, to Col. C. D. Herron, Executive for Reserve Affairs, August 14, 1931, RG 319, Entry 343, Box 98.

26. "Report of the Secretary of War to the President, 1930," in *Annual Reports, War Department, Fiscal Year Ended June 30, 1930* (Washington: GPO, 1930), pp. 317, 6.

27. Interview of Capt. Kenneth Carson (USAR—Ret.) by Maj. James T. Currie, April 1, 1983. Notes in OCAR Historical File.

didn't get any pay except for those two weeks." Shortly before World War II, this particular ORC member became commander of a Training Unit of Sanitary Reserve Officers. "We were active, then," he said. "We had monthly dinner meetings, followed by lectures, illustrations, and slide shows. We studied water supply treatment, waste treatment, and field sanitation."

A third ORC Member recalled that "Prior to World War II, reserve training was rather hit or miss, at least in the area of Minneapolis . . . . [We had] space in the Wesley Temple, a church-owned office building. Each fall a schedule of classes was drawn up—September through May—and officers volunteered to instruct one or more sessions. Some subjects were required, and some dates were open for the instructor to pick his own topic. Some officers came well-prepared and gave excellent presentations. Some officers came with no preparation—they spoke 'off the cuff' with no outlines or notes, relying on experience, and these sessions were poor and uninteresting."[28]

Limited funds for Reserve training and the limited number of Regular Army officers available for duty in the CMTC convinced the War Department to use Organized Reserve officers as instructors in the Camps. The individual Organized Reservists showed a high level of competence, and in 1928 the War Department General Staff decided to use some Organized Reserve units to assist with CMTC training.

The Organized Reserve units performed well during the 1928 training year, and in December 1928 Secretary of War Dwight F. Davis directed that Organized Reserve units be used in at least one camp in each of the nine Corps areas. "Reserve organizations assigned to this work," stated Davis, "should be those which are, in the judgement of the Corps Area Commander, best qualified. It should be the objective of Corps Area Commanders to qualify all Reserve units for this work to the end that they may become competent to perform this type of training."[29]

The public reaction was immediate—and unfavorable. The Hearst newspapers editorialized against the use of Orga-

---

28. Interview of Col. A. S. Behrman, (USAR-Ret.) by Maj. James T. Currie, April 11, 1983. Notes in OCAR Historical File; Letter, Col. Stan W. Carlson (USAR-Ret.) to Maj. Dick Crossland, July 4, 1983, OCAR Historical File.

29. Letter, TAG to All Corps Area Commanders, February 9, 1929, Subject: "Training Reserve Regiments through the use of C.M.T.C." RG 319, Entry 343, Box 98.

nized Reserve units at the Camps, and Horace C. Stebbins, a wealthy textile merchant and leader in the Military Training Camps Association, sent a protesting telegram to the Secretary of War. On February 18, 1929, Charles B. Pike, Chief Civilian Aide to War Secretary Davis, forwarded copies of letters protesting the use of Organized Reserve officers in the CMTC.[30] The underlying reason for the protest against the Reserve officers probably was less with doubts of their effectiveness than with a perception that the prestige of the CMTC was diminished by not having a cadre of Regular Army personnel only.

The protests were to no avail, however, and the Army continued to use Organized Reserve officers to train the young men of the CMTC. Considering the small number of men who received their commissions through the Camps, the only way to justify Army expenditures on the CMTC is that the men of the ORC received valuable leadership experience.

The Citizens' Military Training Camps continued to function during the 1930's, and the ORC received just over 4700 new lieutenants from the Camps from 1929 through 1940.[31] As a source of strength for the ORC, the Citizens' Military Training Camps were not terribly important; as a way of providing training for the Reserves, the CMTC was rapidly eclipsed by the Civilian Conservation Corps (CCC).

The New Deal of President Franklin D. Roosevelt began on March 20, 1933, and one of Roosevelt's innovative ways of giving jobs to unemployed men was the Civilian Conservation Corps. The CCC was established almost immediately after FDR took office, and the Army was initially charged only with immunizing the enrollees, issuing them clothing and equipment, and organizing them into companies of 200 men each. The Departments of Interior and Agriculture were given control of all other functions, including that of commanding the camps.[32]

---

30. Telegram, Assistant Secretary of War Charles B. Robbins to Horace C. Stebbins, February 11, 1929 and Letter, Charles B. Pilse to Dwight F. Davis, February 18, 1929, both in RG 319, Entry 343, Box 97; *New York Times*, June 3, 1947, p. 25.

31. Reports of the Secretary of War, 1934–41.

32. "Report of the Secretary of War, 1933," in *Annual Reports, War Department, Fiscal Year Ended June 30, 1933* (Washington: GPO, 1933), p. 4. A recent article on the subject is Terence J. Smith (Col., USAR-Ret.), "The Army's Role in the success of the CCC," *The Retired Officer* (July 1983), pp. 30–34.

The Army handled its role without difficulty, and on April 10, 1933, the President directed the Army to assume "complete and permanent control" of the CCC. To supplement available Regular Army personnel, the President authorized members of the ORC to work in the CCC Camps.

By July 1, 1933, there were a total of 1315 camps in operation. "With few exceptions," stated Secretary of War George H. Dern, "each camp comprised 2 Regular officers, 1 Reserve officer, 4 enlisted men of the Regular Army, and about 200 men of the Civilian Conservation Corps." By the end of the fiscal year a total of 1774 ORC members were on CCC duty, a number that would swell significantly in the next few years.[33]

Thousands of members of the ORC were unemployed during the Great Depression years, and many of these men leaped at the chance for active duty with the CCC. The War Department regarded the CCC as an opportunity for the Reservists to receive some needed training in "practical leadership, "but the main benefit of using the ORC members was that the Regular Army officers could go back to their previous military assignments.[34]

The replacement of Regular Army officers with Organized Reservists continued apace, and by the end of fiscal year 1934 the number of Regulars on duty in the CCC camps had dwindled to 498, while the number of Reservists had risen to 5,035.[35] The number of Officers' Reserve Corps members had reached 5,853 by September 30, 1934, a figure that included 1120 medical officers and 164 chaplains.[36]

A further incentive to the use of ORC members in the CCC Camps was provided by the camp enrollees themselves. The CCC was not intended to be a military experience, and the Regular Army CCC camp commanders were often regarded by the enrollees as "too military" in their attitudes. Relations with the enrollees improved greatly, wrote one student of the CCC experience, once Organized Reservists were placed in command of the camps.[37]

Black ORC members, too, shared the opportunity presented by the CCC, which was racially segregated. There were separate black and white encampments (except for a few camps in California), and the Army initially assigned

33. "Report of the Secretary of War, 1933," p. 6.
34. *Ibid.*, p. 10.
35. "Report of the Secretary of War, 1934," p. 197.
36. "CCC Facts," RG 319, Entry 343, Box 99.
37. John A. Salmond, *The Civilian Conservation Corps, 1933–1945: A New Deal Case Study* (Durham, N.C.: Duke University, 1967), p. 86.

white Regular Army officers as commanders of the all-black camps. This policy changed in 1934, however, and black ORC members thereafter commanded the black CCC camps. This policy was especially encouraged by President Roosevelt until after the 1936 election, following which he apparently lost interest in the matter.[38]

The War Department continued to regard CCC duty as a valuable training experience for the officers in the ORC, and in 1937 it proposed an 18-month limit on the length of a CCC tour, so that more ORC members could benefit from the experience. The outcry from the ORC members, who had come to regard their CCC jobs as permanent, was vociferous, and the War Department quickly backed down on its idea.[39]

Overall, the CCC experience was valuable for the ORC, members of which served on active duty with the camps until December 31, 1939. By that date, "pursuant to Executive directive," all of the ORC members were placed in a civilian status.[40] The total number of Corps members who enjoyed active duty with the CCC was reportedly in excess of 30,000,[41] and it is probable that for many of these men their interest in the Officers' Reserve Corps and their determination to maintain their Reserve status were enhanced by the experience. Given the paucity of incentives for Organized Reserve members during the inter-war period, this was no small accomplishment.

Members of the ORC could not count on two weeks of active duty each year, as could members of the National Guard, and there was no pay at all for inactive duty drills. As was indicated in Table 3–3, the number of Reservists who were given two weeks of active duty training each year varied from under 8,000 in 1924 to over 21,000 in 1930. The strength of the active Reserve grew from 62,000 in the earlier year to 80,000 in the latter, meaning that by 1930 the "average" Reservist had a 1 in 4 chance of getting active duty training in a given year.[42]

---

38. *Ibid.*, p. 190.

39. *Ibid.*, p. 172.

40. "Report of the Secretary of War to the President, 1940," in *Annual Reports, War Department, Fiscal Year Ended June 30, 1940* (Washington: GPO, 1940), p. 66.

41. "How Far We Have Accomplished Our Objectives," in RG 319, Entry 343, Box 101. Although the figure of 30,000 ORC members is given, this seems awfully high.

42. Reports of the Secretary of War for 1924 and 1931.

In actuality, however, the odds were not really as favorable as 1 in 4, because some officers were given training almost every year, to the detriment of others who were forced to wait seven or eight years between tours. Harry S. Truman, for example, a member of the Field Artillery, Officers' Reserve Corps, performed active duty training on ten occasions between 1920 and 1933.[43] Truman was not unique, either, for Secretary of War Patrick J. Hurley reported that during FY 1928, 16 percent of all Reserve officers placed on active duty for training were on their third consecutive tour; during FY 1929 the figure rose to almost 23 percent; and for FY 1930 the figure was 34 percent. Hurley thereupon ordered "that the number of Reserve officers who have been placed on active duty year after year be materially reduced and that effort be made to expend available funds upon Reserve Officers who have had active duty training less recently. A minimum of Reserve officers should be placed on active duty for more than two consecutive years, and where this policy is not adhered to, Corps Area Commanders should be sure that the interests of the Service are being thoroughly considered."[44]

The problem continued, however. As Col. Charles D. Herron, Executive for Reserve Affairs, explained almost a year later, "The argument is between those who believe in a Reserve Corps with a few highly trained officers and a majority practically untrained, as opposed to those who believe that all should have some training. The War Department," stated Herron, "takes the latter stand." The "principal restrictions" in effect at the time, said Herron, were as follows:

"(a) Not more than 10% of the trainees will be field grade officers.

"(b) Not more than 20% will be staff.

"(c) Officers of organizations ordered to unit training are given preference over officers of those not ordered to unit training.

"(d) Officers who have prepared themselves for active duty during the winter through inactive training have preference.

---

43. "Statement of Military Service of Harry S. Truman, 0 129 869," National Archives and Records Service, National Personnel Records Center (Military Personnel Records), St. Louis, Mo.

44. Letter, TAG to Corps Area Commanders, Department Commanders, and Chiefs of Arms and Services, January 10, 1931, Subject: "Training of Organized Reserves," RG 319, Entry 343, Box 98.

"(e) Only key men (regimental commanders, etc.) are placed on duty for more than two consecutive years."[45]

Congressional leaders too, displayed a keen interest in the status of ORC training, though the Congress never apparently considered appropriating enough money to allow yearly training for all ORC members. On April 20, 1934, Sen. Royal S. Copeland and Rep. Ross A. Collins, Chairs of the Senate and House Appropriations Conferees, respectively, sent to the Secretary of War a letter explaining the conference committee's intentions. Trainees, wrote the Congressional leaders, should be a maximum of 45 years old. Ninety percent of them should be company grade officers, and 90 percent should serve in the combat arms. They almost wrote these provisions into the Military Appropriations Bill, said the authors of the letter, but they finally decided against placing an "unconditional age restriction" on Reserve training.[46]

Secretary of War George H. Dern's response, which was prepared by Reserve Executive Herron and revised by a General Staff Major named Eisenhower, informed Copeland and Collins that the War Department's policy in many cases was almost identical to what they were suggesting. Indeed, the policies expressed in Dern's response do not appear to be much different from those enunciated by Col. Herron over two years earlier.[47]

The suggestion that 90 percent of all trainees be combat arms officers, however, rather than the 80 percent specified by War Department policy, met with resistance from the Secretary. "With an appropriation for an annual quota of 20,000, the average staff officer [is] trained once in six years. With adoption of a 90 percent policy and a 16,500 quota, training would occur only once in fifteen years. This means that the trained Reserve staff officer, indispensable to prompt mobilization, would cease to exist." Because of the inadequacy of funds, concluded Dern, "training of the Officers' Reserve Corps has never been carried out on a scale

---

45. Memorandum, Col. Charles D. Herron to Chief of Staff Douglas MacArthur, December 10, 1931, Subject: "Active Duty Training for Reserve Officers," RG 319, Entry 343, Box 98.

46. Letter, Sen. Royal S. Copeland and Rep. Ross A. Collins to Secretary of War George H. Dern, April 20, 1934, RG 319, Entry 343, Box 99.

47. Letter, Secretary of War George H. Dern to Sen. Royal S. Copeland, April 30, 1934 (with pencilled notations indicating authorship), RG 319, Entry 343, Box 99. An identical letter was sent to Rep. Collins.

sufficient to insure requisite efficiency. Aside from inactive instruction, each combat officer should be required to undergo two weeks' training annually, while others should be called out sufficiently often to insure their familiarity with assigned duties. This is the standard that has been fixed by law for the National Guard, and should apply with equal force to the Officers' Reserve Corps."[48]

The number of Reservists who received two weeks of training rose steadily from a low of 14 percent in 1934 to over 30 percent as mobilization neared in 1940, as can be seen in Table 3–4.

Table 3–4 Active Duty Training (14 Days or Less) of ORC Members 1931–1940.[49]

Fiscal Year	# Trained	# Active ORC*	% Trained
1931	20,998	80,399	26
1932	21,527	83,808	26
1933	20,948	86,338	24
1934	11,944	88,107	14
1935	16,785	91,955	18
1936	22,175	95,619	23
1937	22,595	96,545	23
1938	26,089	100,116	26
1939	30,705	104,575	29
1940	31,741	104,228	30

*Includes only those eligible for active duty.

Increasing the number and percentage of ORC members who received two weeks of training each year was only one of the readiness questions facing the War Department during the years prior to World War II. The National Guard had received in the National Defense Act of 1916 a guarantee of Federal pay for 48 drill periods per year for each member, but there was no comparable compensation provision for the members of the Officers' Reserve Corps. "We met once a week," during the 1930's recalled an ORC member of the 306th Infantry Regiment, 77th Division, "and it seems to me that all we ever did was disassemble, clean, and reassemble our machine guns. I did this every week for nine years in a non-pay status."[50] By 1937, mem-

48. *Ibid.*

49. Compiled from "Reports of the Secretary of War" for the fiscal years 1931–1940.

50. Interview of Col. Milton Barall, (USAR-Ret.), by Maj. James T. Currie, February 4, 1983. Notes in OCAR Historical Files.

bers of the ORC, through their lobbying group, the Reserve Officers Association, mounted a campaign to receive pay for inactive duty training (IADT).

H. R. 9503, a bill "To amend the National Defense Act of June 30, 1916, as amended, with respect to the pay and allowances of certain Reserve Officers," was the legislative means through which the inactive duty training change was proposed. The measure contained a $75 per year maximum on the amount of drill pay a member could receive,[51] but the Department of War opposed even this modest proposal. Secretary of War Harry H. Woodring spoke out vigorously against the bill, though he admitted that National Guard officers received pay for inactive duty training. The comparison with the Guard, said Woodring, was "in no sense complete," because the National Guard officers "are required to perform definitely prescribed duties such as armory drills, field exercises, target practice, etc." Why similar duties could not have been required of ORC members as a precondition of receiving IADT pay, the Secretary did not indicate.

Woodring's final argument against IADT pay for the Reservists was a disingenuous statement that the members of the ORC themselves opposed this bill because they maintained their "amateur standing" as a "cherished possession."[52] This specious line of reasoning was repeated from time to time by the War Department, but the issue would not die.

A bill calling for IADT pay and allowances for uniforms and equipment was introduced into the Seventy-Sixth Congress, and it, too, was opposed by the War Department. By the time the bill reached FDR's desk, the IADT provision had been taken out, but Roosevelt vetoed the measure anyway.[53] The level of frustration continued to rise among ORC members, and in March 1940, Col. Edward S. Bres, National President of the Reserve Officers Association, sought to find out why the War Department continued to oppose drill pay for Organized Reservists. Col. Bres was unable to get an official answer to his question, but Brig. Gen. Charles F. Thompson, Executive for Reserve Affairs, told him unofficially that it would simply cost too much—

51. Copy of H. R. 9503 in RG 319, Entry 343, Box 101.

52. Statement of Secretary of War Harry F. Woodring, April 25, 1937, RG 319, Entry 343, Box 101.

53. Message to Congress, August 1, 1939, RG 319, Entry 343, Box 102.

$5 million per year. Furthermore, wrote Thompson, ORC members in the Judge Advocate General, Chaplain, and Medical branches gained their commissions because of their professional qualifications. "It would be of questionable propriety," stated Thompson, "to provide an annual retainer fee . . . " to such officers. Furthermore, said the Reserve Executive, "Many Reserve Officers are concerned with possible detraction from the unselfishness and patriotic motives which heretofore have typified the ORC."[54] The ROA's reaction to Thompson's letter is unknown.

Correspondence courses were an important means of ORC training during the years between the two World Wars. Such courses began in fiscal year 1921, stated Secretary of War John W. Weeks, "to supplement the limited appropriation for the training of the Organized Reserve." Through these courses, wrote Weeks, it was hoped that "much instruction can be given to officers and candidates in the National Guard and Organized Reserve, at the same time meeting the demand for economy in cases when field training is not absolutely necessary."[55]

By 1931 the Secretary of War was able to report that "extension courses continue to be the least expensive means . . . for the dissemination of military knowledge," with a cost per student of approximately $1.85 per year. Table 3–5 shows enrollment data for the years 1923–1931.

Table 3–5 Extension Course Enrollment, 1923–1931.[56]

Year	ORC	ERC	Total Organized Reserves
1923	10,719	613	11,332
1924	10,696	523	11,219
1925	15,939	538	16,477
1926	18,492	639	19,131
1927	22,446	913	23,359
1928	24,204	1,216	25,420
1929	26,356	1,037	27,393
1930	24,120	1,222	25,342
1931	27,505	1,596	29,101

54. Letter, Brig. Gen. Charles F. Thompson to Col. Edward S. Bres, March 11, 1940, RG 319, Entry 343, Box 103. The debate over IADT pay for Reservists did not end until the enactment of Public Law 80–460 on March 25, 1948.

55. "Report of the Secretary of War to the President, 1921," in *Annual Reports, War Department, Fiscal Year Ended June 30, 1921* (Washington: GPO, 1921), p. 26.

56. "Report of the Secretary of War to the President 1931," in

By March 31, 1940, ORC enrollment in extension courses totaled 63,675, while Enlisted Reservists involved in the courses numbered 1,056. The cost per student had dropped to $1.52 per year, and 66,675 students—a figure that includes more than just the Organized Reservists—completed a total of 168,887 subcourses during the year. Mobilization of Organized Reservists and National Guardsmen soon cut into extension course enrollments, but the Army had found a way to keep a sizable number of Reservists active and interested at a very low cost.[57] There were not, however, very many other things the War Department did to reward and encourage the members of the ORC during this period, but two actions do stand out.

REWARDING MEMBERSHIP

By 1932, reported the Secretary of War, "the march of time has so changed the character of the Officers' Reserve Corps that an organization which was in the beginning made up entirely of World War officers has now but one-third of that class." The new officers coming in, reported the Secretary, were almost exclusively the product of the ROTC and CMTC.[58] The need to give additional training to these new officers was obvious, and the Army's way of accomplishing such has already been discussed. What the Army did not anticipate, however, was that these non-war veterans would soon ask for medals and ribbons to dress up their uniforms and reward their service in the ORC.

The Reserve Officers Association first broached the idea to Brig. Gen. Charles D. Herron, Executive for Reserve Affairs, in December 1934. Lt. Col. Frank E. Lowe, ROA President, suggested a ribbon denoting five years of service as a Reserve Officer. Herron was not in favor of the idea, believing that only war-time service should be honored in this manner, but he told Lowe that he would look into the suggestion. Herron's official response was that the War Department did not favor the proposal.[59]

Annual Reports, War Department, Fiscal Year Ended June 30, 1931 (Washington: GPO, 1931), pp. 223–24.

57. "Report of the Secretary of War to the President, 1940," in *Annual Reports, War Department, Fiscal Year Ended June 30, 1940* (Washington: GPO, 1940), p. 64.

58. "Report of the Secretary of War to the President, 1932," in *Annual Reports, War Department, Fiscal Year Ended June 30, 1932* (Washington: GPO, 1932), p. 7.

59. Letter, Brig. Gen. Charles D. Herron to Lt. Col. Frank E. Lowe, January 26, 1935, RG 319, Entry 343, Box 99.

By August 13, 1935, however, the War Department had changed its mind, and on that date it authorized members of the Officers' Reserve Corps to wear as part of their uniform a new "Minute Man" badge. The design was a drawing of Captain John Parker (the Minute Man) superimposed on an eagle and bearing the inscription "Officers' Reserve Corps." A bar showing length of service—five years, ten years, etc.—was to be worn suspended from the badge. ORC members who had received "certificates of capacity" would receive a badge with a red background. The number of ORC members who received this award is unknown, but apparently the ROA was satisfied.[60]

Of considerably more substance and importance to the inter-war Reservists was the passage of Public Law 74–67 on June 15, 1936. This act extended certain benefits to members of the Organized Reserve, National Guard, ROTC and CMTC who were injured in line of duty while undergoing military training. If injured under these circumstances the member was entitled to medical and surgical care, hospitalization, transportation, and pay and benefits during treatment. If the ultimate misfortune occurred, the Army would pay burial expenses.[61]

PREPARING FOR MOBILIZATION

All of the recruitment, training, rewards, and benefits given members of the Officers' Reserve Corps was designed to reach one end: preparation and retention of a trained group of Army officers who could assume leadership roles during any future mobilization and war.

Army planners during the early 1920's envisioned an initial mobilization of 66 divisions: 11 Regular Army, 22 National Guard, and 33 Organized Reserves.[62] By the close of fiscal year 1924, the 27 Organized Reserve infantry divisions were at 73.9 percent of their authorized officer

60. War Department Immediate Release, "Badge for Reserve Officers," August 16, 1935, RG 319, Entry 343, Box 100. Active Reservists are eligible today for both the Army Reserve Components Achievement Medal and the Armed Forces Reserve Medal; the "Minute Man" Badge is no longer awarded. See Army Regulation 672–5–1.

61. Cited in "Report of the Chief of Staff, 1936," in *Annual Reports, War Department, Fiscal Year Ended June 30, 1936* (Washington: GPO, 1936), p. 40.

62. Marvin A. Kreidberg and Merton G. Henry, *History of Military Mobilization in the United States Army, 1775–1945* (Washington: GPO, 1955), pp. 401–402.

strength, and the 6 Organized Reserve cavalry divisions had reached 83.5 percent of their officer strength.[63] Because of the insignificant number of enlisted Reservists, however, these divisions were never more than cadre units during the inter-war period.

By 1933 the Secretary of War reported that there would be 80,000 officer vacancies "in the early weeks of an emergency" in existing Regular Army and National Guard units. Seventy thousand of these vacancies, stated the Secretary, would be filled by Reserve officers, and additional Reservists would be needed for "Reserve units that might be called to the colors during the subsequent stages of a mobilization."[64] By mid-1936 the number of active, eligible members of the Officers' Reserve Corps had reached 95,619, but activation of the first Reserve units was not anticipated until M + 60.[65]

The number of Reserve officers, as has been indicated earlier, grew slowly during the inter-war years, but Organized Reserve units themselves remained only skeletons, having few enlisted personnel and only minimal equipment. The individual members of the ORC were destined to play a major role in any mobilization, but there was some doubt that Organized Reserve units would ever be activated as such.[66] In an article prepared in mid-1939, as threats of war loomed in Europe and war actually raged in the Far East, the Army's Assistant Chief of Staff for Plans and Operations (G–3) wrote that "Many units of the Organized Reserves—most of them in fact—are of late mobilization priority. But the Officers' Reserve Corps is quite another matter." Members of the ORC, stated the ACS/G–3 in a remarkably accurate prediction, would become "inextricably mingled" with

---

63. "Report of the Secretary of War to the President, 1924," in *Annual Reports, War Department, Fiscal Year Ended June 30, 1924* (Washington: GPO, 1924), p. 10.

64. "Report of the Secretary of War to the President, 1933," in *Annual Reports, War Department, Fiscal Year Ending June 30, 1933* (Washington: GPO, 1933), p. 14.

65. "Report of the Secretary of War to the President, 1936," in *Annual Reports, War Department, Fiscal Year Ending June 30, 1936* (Washington: GPO, 1936), p. 72; memorandum, Brig. Gen. John H. Hester to ACS/G–3, November 7, 1940, Subject: "Source of Units for Activation," RG 319, Entry 343, Box 103.

66. The cadre units of the Organized Reserve Corps were not in the Initial Protective Force listed in the Protective Mobilization Plan (PMP). For a discussion of the PMP see Kreidberg and Henry, *History of Military Mobilization*, pp. 476–92.

Regular Army and National Guard personnel in RA and NG units.[67]

As the 1930's drew to a close, it became more and more apparent that the Army would soon be placed into the position of testing its carefully-developed mobilization planning. The question was whether the ORC would be ready, and in enough numbers.

67. Article, untitled, prepared by ACS/G–3, June 20, 1939, in RG 319, Entry 343, Box 102.

Drs. Charles H. (left) and William J. (right) Mayo were among the many prominent physicians who joined the Officers' Reserve Corps. They both achieved the rank of Brigadier General after the First World War. (Photo courtesy of the Mayo Clinic, Rochester, Minnesota)

Members of the 80th Infantry Division receive bayonet training from a British NCO at Boque Maison, France, April 1918. The 80th Division today is an Army Reserve Training Division headquartered in Richmond, Virginia. (Photo courtesy of the National Archives)

Captain Edward V. "Eddie" Rickenbacker was one of the most decorated American flyers during WW I. Rickenbacker joined the Signal Enlisted Reserve Corps on May 25, 1917, and was commissioned a First Lieutenant, Signal Officers' Reserve Corps, on October 4, 1917. Rickenbacker received the Medal of Honor, the Distinguished Service Cross with six Oak Leaf Clusters, the French Legion of Honor, and two Croix de Guerre with Palm. He was appointed a Colonel in the Officers' Reserve Corps in June 1929. (Photo courtesy of the Fort Meade, Maryland Museum)

IDENTIFICATION PASS
1955
ORDNANCE DEPARTMENT
U. S. A.

ADMIT Capt. James S. Smyser, O.R.C

TO Main Office of any Ordnance establishment

FROM May 14 1918 ~~TO~~ ——— 191_

CHIEF OF ORDNANCE

BY William ...

CAPT. ORD R C.

Prior to August 7, 1918, when the distinctions between "Regular Army," "National Guard," and "National Army" were discontinued, Army Reserve officers wore "USR" collar insignia, rather than just "US." The Reserve insignia shows clearly on this identification pass photo of Captain James S. Smyser, ORC. (U.S. Army photo)

Company A, 306th Machine Gun Battalion, 77th Infantry Division, trains with the Vickers gun in France, May 1918. The 77th Division was formed from citizen-soldiers in the New York City area. The 77th U.S. Army Reserve Command, Flushing, NY, is today the inheritor of the 77th Division's heritage. (Photo courtesy of the National Archives)

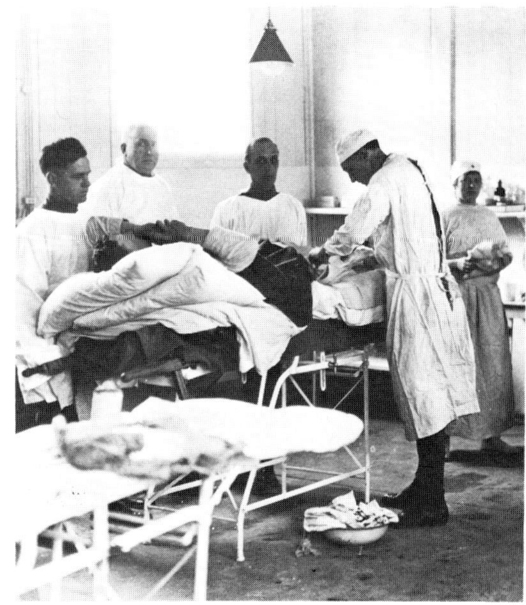

Surgeons attend to shrapnel wounds at Base Hospital No. 6, Sebastopol, France, May 1918. More than 15,000 members of the Enlisted Reserve Corps served in medical units during WW I, and medical officers of the Officer's Reserve Corps numbered 29,299 on November 11, 1918. The number of Regular Army medical officers on that date was 920. (Photo courtesy of the National Archives)

Soldiers from the 78th Division's 305th Machine Gun Battalion fire at German positions near St. Juvin, Ardennes, France, November 1, 1918—just ten days before the Armistice. Today's 78th Division is an Army Reserve Training Division headquartered at Camp Kilmer, NJ. (Photo courtesy of the National Archives)

American Coast Artillerymen pound the German lines opposite Baleycourt Woods, Meuse, France, September 1918. (Signal Corps photograph)

Harry S. Truman was an Army Reservist. Following his active service in the Army during World War I, Truman joined the Organized Reserve Corps and rose to the rank of Colonel as Commander of the 379th Artillery (horse drawn). He also founded the Kansas City, Missouri, chapter of the Reserve Officers Association. Truman's request for active duty at the beginning of World War II was turned down by Army Chief of Staff George C. Marshall, who felt that Truman could be of more use in the U.S. Senate. After stepping down as Commander-in-Chief, Truman retired from the Army Reserve and began drawing his retirement pay of $111.92 per month. (Photo courtesy of the Truman Library, Independence, Missouri)

Charles A. Lindbergh was one of many Army Reservists awarded the Medal of Honor. On December 14, 1927, Congress awarded the medal to Lindbergh for his heroic solo crossing of the Atlantic Ocean. (Photo courtesy of the National Archives)

Drill, chemical mortar, column of squads. These members of the ORC are shown at their training site, Edgewood Arsenal, Maryland, on July 23, 1931. The mortars may well have been a loan from the active Army, since Organized Reserve units had very little equipment of their own. (Signal Corps Photo)

Members of the ORC performed important duty as Commanders of Civilian Conservation Corps camps during the Depression. Some 30,000 ORC members received valuable leadership training through service in the camps. Here, the Commander of the CCC camp in Lassen National Forest (Calif.), presents a meritorious flag to the enrollees with the cleanest barracks. (Photo courtesy US Forest Service)

Training opportunities were limited, and equipment was often primitive for Organized Reserve units during the period between World Wars I and II. ORC members and units trained with the Regular Army whenever possible. Shown is a coordinated infantry-tank assault at Pine Camp, NY, August 1935. (National Archives photo)

Organized Reserve units between the two World Wars usually consisted only of officers. Pictures here is the entire 61st Battalion, 100th Infantry Division during its annual training at Fort Knox, Ky., in July 1934. The battalion commander was Lt. Col. D. Y. Dunn, bottom row, third from left. (Photo courtesy of D.Y. Dunn)

Most members of the Officers' Reserve Corps were called to active duty even before Pearl Harbor, December 7, 1941, and began an intensive training program with Regular Army and National Guard units. Shown here are the 2nd Army maneuvers in Arkansas, September 1941. (Signal Corps photo)

4

Mobilization and War 1940–1945

Hitler's invasion of Poland began on September 1, 1939, and a week later President Roosevelt authorized a 17,000-man increase in the Regular Army, to bring it up to a total of 227,000 men. The Army General Staff did not believe this strength level would suffice for very long, and it began to plan for a Regular Army of, successively, 242,000, 280,000, and 330,000 men. As the Regular Army increased in strength, it became necessary to bring more Organized Reserve officers onto active duty to supplement the 14,000 Regular Officers.[1]

Isolationist sentiment in the Congress was still a powerful force, however, even after the German invasion and conquest of Poland. Throughout the last months of 1939 and on into 1940, there was a marked Congressional reluctance to acknowledge the worsening situation in Europe by appropriating enough funds to modernize the Army and significantly increase its state of readiness. The ORC received very little attention from the Army's planners, and by the time war resumed in Europe the Organized Reserves were little better prepared than they had been a year earlier.[2]

The pace of war in Europe quickened on April 9, 1940, when Germany invaded Denmark and Norway, followed the next day by the NAZI invasion of the

---

1. Marvin A. Kriedberg and Merton G. Henry, *History of Military Mobilization in the United States Army, 1775–1945* (Washington: GPO, 1955), pp. 536–66.

2. Mark S. Watson, *United States Army in World War II, The War Department, Chief of Staff: Prewar Plans and Preparations* (Washington: US Army, 1950), pp. 164–65.

Netherlands, Belgium, and Luxembourg. By June 22 all of these countries, plus France, had fallen before the German onslaught, and public and Congressional opinion in the United States had swung decidedly in the direction of greater defense preparedness.[3]

CALLING-UP THE ORC

War Department planners soon began to realize that there might be a mobilization without an M-day. The Regular Army was gradually expanded, and on August 27, 1940, the 76th Congress, by joint resolution, gave to the President the authority to call the Organized Reserve (officers and enlisted men) and the National Guard to active federal service for a period of twelve months.[4]

The Officers' Reserve Corps consisted in mid-1940 of some 104,228 members who were eligible for active duty, while the ERC consisted of only 3233 men.[5] In a memorandum of September 5, 1940, The Adjutant General directed Corps Commanders to establish rosters for ordering ORC members to active duty, based upon the following priorities:

1. The extent of deferment proposed by the officer and the reasons therefor;
2. The officer's personal obligation to his dependents;
3. The officer's professional attainments and value to the service, together with his age and physical condition;
4. The need for the officer's service in the community as a civilian.

These rosters were confidential, and separate rosters were to be established for medical officers.[6]

The first peace-time conscription in this country's history passed the Congress on September 16, 1940, and draftees began entering the Army in large numbers by the following January. As Kreidberg and Henry expressed it, "The immediate need for large numbers of additional officers was filled by extending the active duty tours of capable Reserve officers already in the service and by calling still more Re-

3. Kriedberg and Henry, *History of Military Mobilization* p. 570.

4. *Ibid.*, pp. 575, 579–80.

5. "Report of the Secretary of War to the President, 1940," *Annual Report, War Department, Fiscal Year Ended June 30, 1940* (Washington: GPO, 1940) p. 95.

6. Memorandum, TAG to Corps Commanders, September 5, 1940, in RG 319, Entry 343, Box 103.

serve officers to active duty." On June 30, 1940, there had been only 2,710 Reserve officers on active duty; by May 15, 1941, there were over 46,000.[7]

Not all ORC members who wanted active duty in 1941, however, were able to obtain such, for field grade officers who were "somewhat old for the grades they hold" were being turned down for active duty by the War Department. This policy drew a sharp protest from Morris Sheppard, Chairman of the Senate Committee on Military Affairs, but Under Secretary of War Robert P. Patterson assured the Senator that "in the event of any enlargement of our present program this age restriction would almost certainly be lifted."[8] Problems of active duty for field grade officers did not end even after Pearl Harbor, but ORC company grade officers never experienced such difficulty. By June 30, 1941, the number of ORC members on extended active duty had reached a total of 57,309, and on that same date more than 90 percent of the company grade officers on duty with the Regular Army were Organized Reservists.[9]

ORC unit members, naturally enough, were more than a little curious about their fate. National Guard units, which contained both officers and enlisted men, had begun entering active federal service in September 1940, but no mention had yet been made of the units of the ORC, skeletal though they were. Brig. Gen. Frank E. Lowe, Executive for Reserve and ROTC Affairs, was on the receiving end of a constant stream of inquiries from members of the ORC, and on July 30, 1941, he asked the ACS/G–3 for a statement as to the War Department's policy on Reserve unit mobilization. The reply from Brig. Gen. Harry L. Twaddle

7. Kreidberg and Henry, *History of Military Mobilization*, p. 605. The Army had a total active strength of 1,320,500 on May 15, including 14,000 RA officers, 20,500 NG officers, and 46,000 ORC officers on active duty. War Department Press Release, May 15, 1941, in RG 319, Entry 343, Box 104.

8. Letter, Under Secretary of War Robert P. Patterson to Senator Morris Sheppard, June 9, 1941, RG 315, Entry 343, Box 104. Commissioned officers are divided into "Company Grade" (lieutenants and captains), "Field Grade" (majors, lieutenant colonels, and colonels) and "General Officers."

9. "Report of the Secretary of War, 1941," p. 95; War Department Study, October 20, 1942, entitled "The Organized Reserve in the War," RG 319, Entry 343, Box 106. Two weeks earlier the percentage of ORC members on active duty, by rank, had been as follows: Col.—31%, Maj.—49%; Capt.—60%, 1Lt.—49%, 2Lt.—43%. Memorandum, Brig. Gen. Harry L. Twaddle, ACS/G–3, to Executive for Reserve and ROTC Affairs, June 19, 1941, RG 319, Entry 343, Box 104.

was unequivocal: "Present plans do not contemplate the mobilization of Organized Reserve units prior to the Declaration by Congress of a national emergency and an attendant authorization for a material augmentation of the Army."[10] The scenario contemplated by Twaddle, however, never did occur, for as a War Department study described it, "The nature of the pre-war mobilization—a state neither of war nor of peace—made it impracticable to activate the units of the Organized Reserve . . . ."[11] Individual Organized Reservists, however, continued to be called to active duty, and the pre-war ORC units themselves, stated Brig. Gen. Edward S. Bres, "were completely disintegrated."[12]

Active duty training tours of 14, 21, and 28 days were largely eliminated during 1941 because there were many opportunities for longer training on an extended active duty basis. Field grade officers were not in as great demand by the regular components, however, as were those of company grade, and in March 1941, the War Department announced plans to give 28-day training tours to 50 colonels, 200 lieutenants colonels, and 250 majors. These officers were attached to Regular Army and National Guard divisions for training.[13]

There were many Organized Reserve officers, however, who received neither orders to active duty nor opportunities for training, and many of them wrote to the Executive for Reserve and ROTC Affairs with their complaints. Brig. Gen. Lowe forwarded these concerns to the Chief of Staff of the Army in early November 1941 and emphasized his opinion that "*first* priority should be given to combat training of all Promotion List Reserve Officers who are eligible, available, and physically qualified for not less than thirty months service with troops . . . ." Lowe's memorandum was never directly answered, however, because by the time it had made its way through the Army's bureaucracy and received a recommendation from the ACS/G–1, the date was December 17, 1941. "In view of the proposed augmentation of the army and the probability that all available Reserve officers

---

10. Memorandum, Brig. Harry L. Twaddle, ACS/–3, to Brig. Gen. Frank E. Lowe, August 16, 1941, RG 319, Entry 343, Box 104.

11. "The Organized Reserve in the War," RG 319, Entry 343, Box 106.

12. Memorandum, Brig. Gen. Edward S. Bres, Executive for Reserve and ROTC Affairs, to ACS/G–3, Subject: "Mobilization Plan," RG 319, Entry 342, Box 9.

13. War Department Press Release, "500 Reserve Field Officers to be Given 28 Days Training," RG 319, Entry 343, Box 104.

will be called to duty within the next few months," wrote Brig. Gen. Wade H. Haislip, "it is believed that no action is necessary on this paper."[14]

By December 1941 over 80,000 ORC members were on active Army duty, and on December 13 Congress removed the pre-war prohibition that restricted the geographical area in which Reservists could be used.[15] On February 6, 1942, President Roosevelt ordered into "active military service of the United States, effective on dates to be hereafter announced by the Secretary of War, for the duration of the present war and for six months after the termination thereof, . . . each of the organizations and units and all of the personnel of the Organized Reserves not already in such service."[16]

President Roosevelt's Executive Order, together with the fact that the Order of Battle list for World War II contains numerous units that were in the Organized Reserve, has led some people to give the Organized Reserve credit for furnishing 26 infantry divisions during the war.[17] This credit is in error, however. "When the decision was taken to activate the divisions and other units of the Organized Reserve early in 1942," explained the War Department, "few of the Reserve officers originally assigned to these units were available for duty with them. Consequently, the units as activated bore small resemblance to those of peacetime . . . ."[18] It would be misleading, then, to allege that Organized Reserve units served during World War II. While it is true that Organized Reserve infantry divisions like the 77th, 79th, 81st, 83d, 90th, 94th, 102d, and others were activated in 1942, very few of the pre-war members of these divisions were available for assignment to them by that time. As a 1965 study of the Army's force structure put it, "The OR divisions of World War II were not reserve divisions in any real sense of the word." This is not to say, of course, that

14. Memorandum, Brig. Gen. Frank E. Lowe, Executive for Reserve and ROTC Affairs, to Chief of Staff, November 4, 1941, Subject: "Extended Active Duty for Reserve Officers," and memorandum, Brig. Gen. Wade H. Haislip, ACS/G–1 to Chief of Staff, December 17, 1941, same subject, both in RG 319, Entry 343, Box 104.

15. "The Organized Reserve in the War," RG 319, Entry 343, Box 106; Public Law 77–338, December 13, 1941.

16. Executive Order No. 9049, February 6, 1942.

17. *Order of Battle, United States Army, World War II, European Theater of Operations, Divisions* (Paris, 1945), p. 571.

18. "The Organized Reserve in the War," RG 319, Entry 343, Box 106.

the Organized Reserve was unimportant during the WW II mobilization. As Chief of Staff George C. Marshall put it in 1941, "The procurement of suitable officer personnel was fortunately solved by the fact that during the lean, post-war years over 100,000 Reserve officers had been continuously trained . . . . These Reserve officers constituted the principal available asset which we possessed at this time. Without their assistance the program could not have been carried out except in a superficial manner, as is evidenced by the fact that today they [Reserve officers] constitute 75% to 90% of the officer strength with Regular Army units."[19]

Even after Pearl Harbor, individual members of the ORC were not always ordered to active duty, even when they requested such. Col. W. R. Frost, the Acting Executive for Reserve and ROTC Affairs, told Col. Porter P. Wiggins in an "informal memorandum" that the chances were "very remote indeed" that any Reserve officers over the age of sixty would be ordered to active duty. "Only in rare cases," wrote Frost, "has an exception been made to [this] . . . policy."[20] By May 1942, the War Department sought to order to active duty all colonels under 53 years old and lieutenant colonels under 51 years old who were physically qualified and who desired active duty.[21]

By the end of 1942 there were over 140,000 Reserve officers on active Army duty, while 12,100 ORC members had not received such orders.[22] Of these Reserve officers who had not been placed on active duty, 1,214 were medical students or interns and 422 were deferred for other academic reasons; 878 were Air Corps Reservists, and 2284 were de-

---

19. See compilation by R. L. Thompson, February 16, 1962, in *Reserve Components History, 1916 to present,* in Center of Military History files; see also memorandum, TAG to Commanding Generals, All Armies, Army Corps and Corps Areas, June 9, 1942, Subject: "Ordering into Active Service Certain Organized Reserve Divisions During August and September, 1942," in AG 320.2 (5–26–42), copy in CMH files. Office, Chief of Military History, Department of the Army, *Historical Resume, Division Force Structure, Active and Reserve, 1935–1963,* copy in CMH Files. *Report on the Army, July 1, 1939 to June 30, 1943, Biennial Reports of General George C. Marshall, Chief of Staff of the United States Army to the Secretary of War* (Washington: *The Infantry Journal,* 1943), pp. 11–12.

20. Letter, Col. W. R. Frost to Col. Porter P. Wiggins, March 26, 1942, RG 319. Entry 343, Box 105.

21. Memorandum, Brig. Gen. J. H. Hilldring, ACS/G–1 to Brig. Gen. Frank E Lowe, May 14, 1942, Subject: "Bringing Reserve Officers to Active Duty," RG 319, Entry 343, Box 105.

22. "The Organized Reserve in the War," RG 319, Entry 343, Box 106.

ferred because of their status with the Veteran's Administration or various branches of the Army. In addition, 92 ORC members had not been called to duty "due to request of G–2;" 46 were "not ordered due to nationality"—"Japs;" 35 were "Congressmen, Judges, Senators, etc.;" and 268 were not available because they were in enemy territory. Other categories included 29 "Colored officers," 7 brigadier generals, 174 colonels, and 427 lieutenant colonels for whom no vacancy could be found. A total of 3,741 Reservists were 59 years old or older, 1962 had over 15 years of service and were considered permanently physically disqualified, and 513 others fit into such categories as "Deferred by Directive G–1," "No Vacancy-Veterinary," and "Resignation Pending."[23]

The war-time files of the Executive for Reserve and ROTC Affairs contain numerous letters from Reserve officers—particularly colonels—who were literally begging for active duty assignments. Many of these men had served fifteen or more years in the ORC, had participated actively in every training opportunity that presented itself, and had been promoted to such a high level that the Army no longer had a place for them on active duty, even in war-time. It was embarrassing, said these officers, to have to explain to their neighbors that they had done everything in their power to get into the active Army. The accusing stares from their fellow citizens were almost more than they could bear, and any attempt by them to justify the Army's policy toward high-ranking Reserve officers only made matters worse.

Brig. Gen. Edward W. Smith, Executive for Reserve and ROTC Affairs, explained the War Department's policy in this area to Col. Philip S. VanCise, an Organized Reservist from Denver who had attempted without success to get active duty orders:

It has been a problem with the War Department to place on duty all of our high-ranking Reserve officers. As you probably know,

23. List signed by Col. H. N. Sumner, Chief, Appointment and Induction Branch, TAGO, December 17, 1942, RG 319, Entry 343, Box 105. According to Maj. Gen. Harry Vaughan, one ORC member whose request for active duty was not granted was Colonel (Senator) Harry S. Truman, commander, 379th Field Artillery Regiment (horse-drawn). When Truman went to Chief of Staff George Marshall and requested active duty, Marshall told him he was too old and said he would be of more value in the Senate The story is recounted in John T. Carlton and John F. Slinkman, *The ROA Story: A Chronicle of the First 60 Years of the Reserve Officers Association of the United States* (Washington: ROA, 1982), pp. 141–42.

the age-in-grade of full colonels is 55 but very few colonels who have passed their fiftieth birthday, either Regular or Reserve, are used with troops for overseas duty. Therefore, officers who have passed their fiftieth birthday are not primarily considered for troop duty but are considered for administrative work. Each Service Command is allotted a certain number of officers of each grade. Naturally, their allotment of full colonels is rather limited and many times the services of these officers cannot be utilized because of the fact that there is no vacancy in their grade existing in the Service Command.[24]

Brig. Gen. Smith went on to say that The Adjutant General's Office was doing its best to put Reserve officers on active duty and that TAGO was "hopeful for results." This effort, reported Smith, was limited to officers who had not reached their fifty-ninth birthday.[25] The effort to put Reserve officers on active duty never met with total success, however, and as late as mid-December 1944 there were almost as many non-active duty Organized Reservists—11,386—as there had been two years earlier.[26] The number of active duty Organized Reserve officers continued to increase throughout the war, reaching a peak of almost 200,000 early in 1945,[27] and ORC members were well-represented in Regular Army and National Guard combat units.

A War Department analysis of officers in an unidentified Regular Army infantry division overseas showed that as of March 31, 1944, the percentage of Organized Reserve officers by rank was as follows:

Colonel—0%
Lieutenant Colonel—42.9%
Major—95.9%
Captain—83.8%
First Lieutenant—56.3%
Second Lieutenant—10.9%

In addition, 62.5 percent of the battalion commanders, 84.5 percent of the company commanders, and 30.3 percent

24. Letter, Brig. Gen. Edward W. Smith to Col. Philip S. Van Cise, January 1, 1943, RG 319, Entry 343, Box 105.

25. *Ibid.*

26. "Reserve and Deferred AUS Officers not on Active Duty," December 15, 1944, RG 319, Entry 343, Box 112. It should be pointed out that the number of Reserve Officers had increased by more than 50 percent during that time. See memorandum, Col. C. M. Boyer to Brig. Gen. Edward W. Smith, October 2, 1944, Subject: "Strength of Reserve Officers as of 31 July 1944," RG 319, Entry 343, Box 112.

27. Letter (drafted, but unsent), Brig. Gen. Edward W. Smith to Cedric Foster, no date, but probably April 1945, RG 319, Entry 343, Box 112.

of the platoon leaders in this particular division were Organized Reserve officers.[28]

In a more extensive study a few months later, the War Department examined the 1st, 4th, and 90th Infantry Division, the 1st and 2d Armored Divisions, and the 29th, 34th and 37th Infantry Divisions (National Guard). The percentage of ORC members of each rank was as given in Table 4–1.

Table 4–1 Percentage of Organized Reservists in Officer Cadres.[29]

1st, 4th, 90th Infantry Divisions 1st and 2d Armored Divisions		29th, 34th, 37th Infantry Divisions (NG)	
BG	12.5%	BG	0
COL	0	COL	0
LTC	52.0%	LTC	21.5%
MAJ	82.5%	MAJ	56.6%
CPT	70.0%	CPT	45.7%
1LT	26.1%	1LT	16.0%
2LT	9.3%	2LT	8.9%
Total	37.4%	Total	22.2%

The number of Organized Reservists who were decorated for heroism is unknown, but it is certain that ORC members were in the forefront of combat activity. From September 1, 1943, to May 31, 1944, 28.7 percent of the officers in the active Army were ORC members. During this same period, ORC officers constituted 52.4% of the officers killed-in-action, 27.7% of those missing-in-action, and 27.4% of officers captured by the enemy.[30]

Reserve officer strength was concentrated in the middle ranks—captain, major and lieutenant colonel—but there were a number of Organized Reservists who achieved general officer rank during the war. As of June 30, 1943, there were 1,065 general officers in the Army. Of these, a total of 18 were from the Officers' Reserve Corps. One Organized Reservist who achieved three-star rank in 1944 was James H. Doolittle, while another well-known ORC general was Maj. Gen. William J. "Wild Bill" Donovan of the Office of Strategic Services—the forerunner of the CIA. Brig. Gen. The-

28. "Chart 3—Infantry Division," RG 319, Entry 342, Box 6.

29. "Composition of Officer Strength," RG 319, Entry 324, Box 9.

30. "Chart 4—Proportion of All Officer Battle Casualties Suffered by Reserve Officers, 1 September 1943–31 May 1944," RG 319, Entry 342, Box 6.

odore Roosevelt, Jr., an ORC member, received a Medal of Honor for his actions in the first assault wave on D-Day as Assistant Commander of the 4th Infantry Division.[31]

INCREASING THE CORPS

In addition to its general officers, the ORC numbered, at its peak in 1945, about 200,000 commissioned officers of lower grades. Almost 100,000 of these individuals had been commissioned in the Reserves after the beginning of the war, mostly through ROTC, Air Corps Cadet School, or by direct appointment from civilian life. This last category had never been a large source of ORC members, because the Army resisted attempts to commission civilians with little or no military training. There had always been a certain number of individuals, however, particularly in the fields of medicine and religion, who received such direct commissions. The Army's desire to avoid politicization of the commissioning process within the ORC was emphasized in a letter that Brig. Gen. Charles D. Herron, Executive for Reserve Affairs, sent to the Reserve Officers Association almost nine years before Pearl Harbor:

> There are undoubtedly many prominent citizens whose appointments in the Officers' Reserve Corps would conduce to the cause of preparedness . . . .But [this] . . . course has the very great disadvantage that in the event of war many of the holders of such commissions would demand, often with great political influence, employment commensurate with their rank. This could only be obtained by wresting such employment from active officers of demonstrated qualifications.[32]

This policy was generally observed until the immediate pre-war period, when many prominent civilians sought Reserve commissions. Secretary of War Henry L. Stimson

---

31. *Biennial Report of the Chief of Staff of the United States Army, July 1, 1941 to June 30, 1943 to the Secretary of War* (Washington: *Infantry Journal*, 1943), p. 111; "General Officer Appointments in the Organized Reserve," *The Officer*, June 1947, *pp. 16–17, 22;* Gordon A. Harrison, *United States in World War II; The European Theater of Operations; Cross-Channel Attack* (Washington: Office of the Chief of Military History, Department of the Army, 1951), p. 304n; Omar N. Bradley (Gen. of the Army) and Clay Blair, *A General's Life: An Autobiography* (New York: Simon and Schuster, 1983), pp. 347–48.

32. Letter, Brig. Gen. Charles D. Herron to Maj. Bennett A. Molter, March 15, 1983, RG 319, Entry 343, Box 99.

thereupon set forth in writing the three criteria that would be applied when considering such requests:

1. No ORC Commission would be given to men who were subject to the draft unless they had completed Army courses leading to a commission;
2. "All political or personal considerations should be rigidly excluded;"
3. A commission was to be given only where the individual had special qualifications required for a particular branch of the service.[33]

Under War Department regulations, officers in the ORC were commissioned for five-year terms. If a Reservist wanted to continue as an active member of the ORC, he had to participate regularly in such training opportunities as were offered, and he had to request reappointment in the ORC at the end of each five-year period. The discouraging lack of training opportunities has already been discussed, and the attrition rate of ORC members, even in the years immediately preceding mobilization in 1940 and 1941, was quite high. During fiscal year 1939, for example, the ORC lost 6,784 active, assignable officers, while 8,956 inactive ORC members had their appointments terminated. By comparison, the ORC gained only 10,682 officers during the year.[34]

This yearly drain of trained Reserve officers meant that when mobilization began in 1940 there were not enough ORC members to fill the Army's needs. By the spring of 1941 the War Department had decided to allow the reappointment of former Reserve officers commissioned after 1933 who had been in an eligible status at the time they had terminated their ORC membership.[35]

The Army, however, rejected the idea of having the ROTC increase its production of lieutenants. With a singular

33. Memorandum from Secretary of War Henry L. Stimson, October 14, 1940, Subject: "Memorandum in Re Appointment of Officers' Reserve Corps from Civil Life," RG 319, Entry 343, Box 103.

34. "Report of the Secretary of War to the President, 1939," *Annual Reports, War Department, Fiscal Year Ended June 30, 1939* (Washington: GPO, 1939), pp. 66–67.

35. Memorandum, Brig. Gen. Wade H. Haislip, ACS/G–1 to Chief of Staff, April 21, 1941, Subject: "Policy with Respect to Reappointment in the Officers' Reserve Corps of Former Reserve Officers, Who are Within the Selective Service Ages (21–36)," RG 319, Entry 343, Box 104.

lack of foresight, Brig. Gen. Harry L. Twaddle, ACS/G–3, scorned the idea of increasing the quota for advanced course ROTC cadets, because he said, the number of lieutenants produced by the ROTC each year "more than meets the contemplated needs of the Army."[36] General Twaddle's thoughts on this subject after December 7, 1941, are not recorded, but a stop-and-go pattern of officer procurement was characteristic of the Army during the war.

On January 12, 1942, Secretary of War Stimson admitted that "there will be a need for the commissioning of a substantial number of men from civil life for administrative and other positions in order to relieve officers qualified for combatant service."[37] A week later minimum age for appointment as an officer was reduced from 21 years old to 18 years old, and a month later the War Department announced the suspension of ROTC summer camps. Cadets would henceforth be sent to basic training courses before commissioning, and the requirement of a college degree could be waived "in special cases."[38]

On February 19, 1942, the Secretary of War announced a more flexible standard for reappointing former ORC members. This policy was more lenient than the previous one in that it applied to officers commissioned after 1931 (as opposed to 1933), and it did not require an officer to have been in an "eligible" status when his appointment in the ORC terminated.[39] This relaxation of policy meant that thousands of officers who had simply let their ORC appointments lapse could now be ordered to active duty in a commissioned status.

---

36. Memorandum, Brig. Gen. Harry L. Twaddle to Chief of Staff, October 23, 1941, Subject: "Increase in Advanced Course Quota, ROTC," RG 319, Entry 343, Box 104.

37. Memorandum, Henry L. Stimson, January 12, 1942, Subject: "In re Appointment of Officers From Civil Life," RG 319, Entry 343, Box 105. Before the war was over, some 100,000 civilians received direct commissions without any military training. Robert R. Palmer, Bell I. Wiley, and William R. Keast, *United States Army in World WAr II, The Army Ground Forces, The Procurement and Training of Ground Combat Troops* (Washington: Historical Division, Department of the Army, 1948), pp. 91–92.

38. War Department Radiogram, January 20, 1942, RG 315, Entry 343, Box 105; War Department Press Release, "Army Suspends R.O.T.C. Camps until Six Months after War Ends," February 12, 1942, RG 319, Entry 343, Box 107.

39. Memorandum, TAG (by order of the Secretary of War), February 19, 1942, Subject: "Appointment of Former Officers in the Army of the United States," RG 319, Entry 343, Box 105.

Even these measures could not meet the Army's needs for commissioned officers during its rapid expansion in 1942, so standards for officer procurement were lowered. By the next year, when mobilization of the ground forces had slowed, the Army had a surplus of junior officers; by 1944 demand exceeded supply again.[40]

WAR-TIME POLICIES

Despite Chief of Staff Marshall's praise of the ORC for providing 100,000 trained officers during the pre-war mobilization,[41] the best interests of Reservists were regarded only lightly—if at all—when personnel policies were implemented during the war.

For example, before May 1942 a Reserve officer who was physically disqualified from active duty was placed in the Inactive Reserve, where he was not subjected to the draft. Beginning in May 1942 the War Department began discharging all physically disqualified Reserve officers who had less than fifteen years of service. These individuals were then subject to being drafted into the Army as enlisted men, because the physical standards for draftees were lower than those for commissioned officers.[42]

Several Reserve officers sent letters of protest to the Executive for Reserve and ROTC Affairs, and on December 4, 1942, he took up the issue with the ACS/G–1. He did not think the policy was fair, stated Col. Edward J. Smith, and he believed that these officers should be reappointed in the ORC or other component if they were physically qualified for even limited service. The next day he discussed the matter in detail with Col. Jenkins of the G–1 staff, and they reached an agreement along the lines that Col. Smith suggested. The physical standards continued to differ for officers and enlisted personnel, however, with the result that men like James P. Chapman continued to be discharged, then drafted. The agreement with Col. Jenkins had not been carried through as War Department policy.[43]

---

40. See Palmer, Wiley and Keast, *Procurement and Training of Ground Combat Troops*, p. 159.

41. "Report of the Secretary of War to the President, 1941," *Annual Reports, War Department, Fiscal Year Ended June 30, 1941* (Washington: GPO, 1941), p. 53.

42. Memorandum, Brig. Gen. Edward W. Smith to Chief of Staff, September 28, 1945, Subject: "Report of Activities of this Office During My Tenure of Office," RG 319, Entry 343, Box 116.

43. Memorandum, Col. Edward W. Smith to ACS/G–1, December

Additional Reserve officers were trapped in this "Catch-22" situation during 1943, and their continuing protests finally led to the announcement of an official change of policy. On October 20, 1943, Maj. Gen. W. G. White, the ACS/G–1, informed the Secretary of War's Personnel Board of the new two-part policy. If a commissioned officer who was discharged for physical reasons after satisfactory active service was subsequently inducted as an enlisted man, he would be reappointed in the grade formerly held. If a commissioned officer who was not serving on active duty was discharged for physical reasons and was later inducted, he would be reappointed to his former grade, *if* a vacancy existed and he was otherwise qualified.[44] This policy still left the possibility that an ORC member could be drafted as an enlisted man, and it was not until May 24, 1944, that War Department Circular 206 eliminated this possibility.[45] The Executive for Reserve and ROTC Affairs had been instrumental in effecting this new policy, but the Army's antipathy toward ORC members was indicated in the time that elapsed after it was brought to the attention of the ACS/G–1 in early December 1942. In disability retirement, too, the Army did not treat the Organized Reserve equitably.

From June 30, 1940, to August 31, 1944, stated the Executive for Reserve and ROTC Affairs, 3864 non-Regular Army officers were relieved from active duty because of physical disability. Of these, only 68 were retired with pay under the Retirement Act, a minuscule percentage that Brig. Gen. Smith thought was evidence of unfair treatment of Organized Reservists. Smith called this discrepancy to the attention of the ACS/G–1, and War Department Circular 205, "Determination of Line of Duty," was changed to make it easier to find "in line of duty" when judging disability.[46]

4, 1942, Subject: "Induction of Former Reserve, National Guard and Other Officers Discharged for Physical Disability" and attached Memorandum for Record, December 5, 1942, RG 319, Entry 343. Box 105; letter, Brig. Gen. Edward Smith to Col. Joseph K. Nicholls, January 1, 1943, RG 319, Entry 343, Box 105.

44. Memorandum, Maj. Gen. W. G. White, ACS/G–1, to Secretary of War's Personnel Board, October 20, 1943, Subject: "Reappointment of Officers Discharged for Physical Disability," RG 319, Entry 343, Box 107.

45. Brig. Gen. Edward W. Smith to Chief of Staff, September 28, 1945, Subject: "Report of Activities of this Office During My Tenure of Office," RG 319, Entry 343, Box 116.

46. "Report on Activities of the Office of the Executive for Reserve

EXECUTIVE OPERATIONS

It is evident that members of the ORC needed someone to represent them—to serve as a sort of ombudsman for them—at the Army Staff level during the war. The Executive for Reserve and ROTC Affairs (ERRA) had long performed this function, and the entrance of the United States into World War II caused no immediate change in the status, activities, or personnel of the office. In March 1942, however, the ERRA was placed under The Adjutant General, and in June it was given independent status under the Chief of Administrative Services, TAG. During that same month the ERRA was designated a member of the "Post-War Planning Board of the War Department."[47]

Brig. Gen. Frank E. Lowe was the first Organized Reserve general officer to serve as ERRA. He had been on the job for a little over one year, and the United States had been at war for some eight months, when he recommended that the office functions "which pertain to the Organized Reserves be suspended for the duration of the present emergency . . . ." He further suggested that the office be transferred to the Legislation and Liaison Branch of the War Department General Staff, a suggestion that was adopted in September, 1942.[48]

The OERRA functioned during the war with a strength of one brigadier general, one colonel, one lieutenant colonel, one major, and four clerical civilians. In addition to aiding individual ORC members with their problems, the ERRA worked with Brig. Gen. John McAuley Palmer, who was putting together a suggested structure for the post-war Reserve components.[49]

By the spring of 1945 the Organized Reserve had become more important, and the OERRA was placed on the War Department Special Staff. The Executive for Reserve

---

and ROTC Affairs for period 1 October 1942 to 31 August 1944," RG 319, Entry 343, Box 111.

47. "Historical Summary," November 9, 1942, RG 319, Entry 343, Box 106.

48. Memorandum, Brig. Gen. Frank E. Lowe to Secretary of the General Staff, August 13, 1942, Subject: "Office of the Executive for Reserve and ROTC Affairs," RG 319, Entry 343, Box 106; Memorandum, Col. Edward W. Smith to Army HQ Commandant, November 5, 1942, Subject: "Transfer of Office of Executive for Reserve and ROTC Affairs to the Pentagon Building," RG 319, Entry 343, Box 107.

49. Memorandum, Brig. Gen. Frank E. Lowe to Secretary of the General Staff, August 13, 1942, Subject: "Office of the Executive for Reserve and ROTC Affairs," RG 319, Entry 343, Box 106.

and ROTC Affairs gave up his additional duties with the Legislation and Liaison Branch and began to devote full-time to the transition to a peace-time reserve force.[50]

CONCLUSION

The officers of the ORC had served well during World War II, furnishing almost one-fourth of the Army's total officer strength during the conflict. Because of pre-war neglect, the units of the Organized Reserve were not prepared to mobilize in 1940 or even 1941, and by the time the units were called to duty after that time, they were ORC in name only.[51]

The future of the Organized Reserve Corps was problematical, for no one knew for sure how many officers had gotten their fill of military duty during the war and whether demobilization would mark the end of their military affiliation. The War Department had been planning the post-war Army for years, but Congress might not accept these plans. The public outcry for a rapid demobilization could not be resisted, but Soviet ambitions loomed large in the minds of the War Department's planners. It was obvious to most military leaders that Reserve forces were going to be needed in years to come and that the neglect of the post-World War I years simply could not be allowed. The question was whether Army plans, Congressional desires, and public will would fit together in a coherent fashion, sufficient for the National defense.

50. War Department General Orders No. 39, May 17, 1945.

51. From July 1, 1940, to June 30, 1946, some 902,000 men served on active duty as commissioned officers. Of this total, 204,000 were members of the ORC; memorandum, TAG to ERRA, November 26, 1946, Subject: "Data on Commissioned Officers, Regular and Non-Regulars for Reserve Officers Association of the United States," RG 319, Entry 343, Box 126 (320.2).

5

Peace—And War Again, 1946–1953

PLANNING FOR THE POST-WAR

Even before Pearl Harbor, the Army had begun planning for the post-war, and the services of Brig. Gen. John McAuley Palmer were a valuable part of that effort. General Palmer's service as a member of the War Plans Division of the General Staff immediately after World War I made him a logical and valuable resource, as did his friendship with George Marshall. "I have some personal knowledge of our government's past experience with this problem," wrote Palmer in November 1942. "Some serious mistakes were made at that time [post-WWI]. If we can avoid them after World War II, in my opinion, the whole problem will be greatly simplified."[1]

Palmer and his committee, formed by Chief of Staff Marshall to develop plans for the post-war, worked diligently, and on August 25, 1944, the War Department issued Circular No. 347, a philosophical blueprint for the post-war military establishment that was developed out of Palmer's life-long study of the Army. The military organization envisioned in this document was based upon two stated assumptions: (1) that the United States would maintain "such temporary military forces . . . as may as necessary . . . to lay the foundations for a peaceful world order" and

1. Letter, Brig. Gen. John McAuley Palmer to Frederic A. Delano, Chairman, National Resources Planning Board, November 9, 1942, RG 319, Entry 343, Box 107. For a good account of Palmer's work see Michael S. Sherry, *Preparing for the Next War: American Plans for Postwar Defense, 1941–45* (New Haven and London: Yale University Press, 1977).

(2) that Congress would provide for universal male military training. The Circular also emphasized—perhaps more than had any official pronouncement in the past—the role of the reserve forces in this nation's military establishment.[2] The "professional peace establishment," stated Circular No. 347, should be "no larger than necessary to meet *normal* [emphasis added] peacetime requirements." The regular army would be reinforced in wartime by a "properly organized citizen army reserve," a proposal described in the circular as a way of "perfecting a traditional national institution to meet modern requirements which no longer permit extemporization after the outbreak of war."[3]

The tradition of the United States had never been that of maintaining a large standing army, or even a large reserve force, in peacetime; mobilization of the untrained civilian community had long been the US response to the need for a large military force. During the two World Wars the United States was given by its allies the luxury of time—time to induct and train men and time to produce the weapons necessary to arm them. At the close of World War II, however, it was evident that the burden of Western defense would fall increasingly on the United States. It was similarly evident—and the authors of Circular No. 347 were quite aware of it—that if a major war were to occur in Europe there would no longer be the luxury of time, for the Soviet Union could overrun Europe long before the first US draftees reached the front lines.

Though the Soviet Union was very much one of the Allies at the time Circular No. 347 was issued, assumptions about Soviet post-war ambitions may well have been on the minds of the War Department's planners. Understood in this light, Circular No. 347 was an ambitious, yet realistic, approach to US military organization. That it did not prove to be an accurate prediction of the future was not so much the fault of the War Department's planners as it was a reflection of the political realities of the time.

The War Department sought a "cautious demobilization" after the defeat of Japan, largely out of respect for the ambitions and military strength of the Soviet Union, as well as in anticipation of worldwide occupation duties. Such a course, however, was politically impossible. The United States Army stood at over 8 million personnel in 1945, and

---

2. War Department Circular No. 347, August 25, 1944.
3. *Ibid.*

most of these individuals demanded nothing less than a prompt and complete release from active service.[4]

Plans for an Army strong enough to deter possible Soviet aggression ran squarely up against powerful opposition: the normal post-war economy moves in the federal Government and an idea that "the bomb"—the atomic weapons monopoly enjoyed by the US—would prove the ultimate deterrent to an aggressor. The United States had not questioned the financial cost of winning World War II, but the immediate post-war political reaction was that of cutting back drastically on the military part of the federal budget.

President Truman himself set the pattern for military spending during the years from 1946–1950 by using a "remainder method" of calculating the military budget. The federal budget would be balanced, he said, by taking total revenues, subtracting from that total all domestic spending, and giving the rest to the military.

This frugality was complemented nicely by the idea that the US monopoly of the atomic bomb was a cheap, effective, and absolutely fail-safe deterrent. The idea that the next major conflict might not be a nuclear one was given some thought by the War Department, but Congress and the President preferred the economy route.

The years between World War II and Korea were characterized by a not-unprecedented desire to achieve national security at the least possible cost, and one cost-effective way of reaching this goal was to build-up a strong reserve force. In theory this idea worked quite well, but in reality the President and the Congress created a military shell and a false sense of security that was nearly as hollow as were the divisions of the Organized Reserve in the years after World War I.

TERMINAL LEAVE PROMOTIONS

Rebuilding the Organized Reserve was an important assumption of War Department Circular No. 347 and of post-war military strength planning. The Army had very little to offer as an inducement, however, to veterans who were invited to join the Corps. One of the few things the Army did in fact offer its veterans was not even tied to their continued membership in the ORC, and this was the "terminal leave

4. Russell F. Weigley, *History of the United States Army* (New York and London: Macmillan Publishing Co., Inc. and Collier Macmillan Publishers, 1967), pp. 486, 569.

promotion" that became such a bone of contention with the Regulars. Reserve promotions had been frozen during the war, while Regular Army promotions had not. The only way an ORC member could receive a promotion during WWII was by being on active duty and in line for a vacancy of the next higher grade. He was then eligible to be considered for an Army of the United States (AUS) promotion. Without the vacancy, there could be no promotion. As Colonel Charles M. Boyer, Executive Director of the Reserve Officers Association, explained it, " . . . Promotions became the luck of assignment, and if a man was lucky in assignment, he went up rapidly, and if he was assigned to a position where there were no vacancies, he stood still."[5] Figures compiled by ROA indicated that by June 1944—over 2 1/2 years after Pearl Harbor—some 21 percent of the ORC members on active duty had not received even one promotion.[6] A plan was therefore devised to correct some of the inequities of the system, and there was some hope that this would encourage continued participation in one of the Reserve components of the Army.

The rules for receiving a terminal promotion were simple and mechanical and applied to all non-Regular Army officers. Any non-Regular Army officer would be given a one-grade promotion effective the day he went on terminal leave, providing he met the following requirements:

1. Below the grade of 0–6 (Colonel);
2. At least two years active duty after September 16, 1940;
3. An efficiency index of at least 35;
4. No promotion while on active duty;
5. Requisite time-in-grade; i.e., 18 months to First Lieutenant or Captain, 24 months to Major or Lieutenant Colonel, and 30 months to Colonel. In computing time-in-grade, overseas service prior to May 1, 1946, counted an additional 50 percent.[7]

There was, of course, no requirement that the officer be promoted into a vacant position, and this was the key to the

5. "Reserve Officer Personnel Act," *Hearings before the Committee on Armed Services, House of Representatives, Eighty-third Congress, First Session,* p. 1676. Hereinafter cited as "ROPA."

6. "Your Association Wins Promotions for Officers Reverting to Inactive Status," *The Reserve Officer* (November 1945), p. 4.

7. Major W. K., Whichard, "Administering the Reserve," *The Reserve Officer* (December 1946), pp. 10–11.

terminal leave promotion. The system was completely inflexible, and an officer who was only a few days short of the required time-in-grade or a few hundredths under the efficiency index level was not promoted.[8] The elimination of the vacancy requirement was the only relaxation of the wartime promotion system, and as a result only about 40,000 officers—not all of whom were ORC members—received a terminal leave promotion.[9] This was only about 5 percent of the 800,000 Army officers on active duty in 1945, but this small percentage was multiplied again and again in the public mind until it was commonly believed that *all* reserve officers had received a promotion upon their release from active duty.[10]

These terminal leave promotions were important, however, to the officers who received them. It is likely that many of these men did join the Officers' Reserve Corps or continue their affiliation with it after their discharge from active service, in part because the terminal leave promotion removed a source of great and continuing frustration for them. It should be clearly understood, however, that the terminal leave promotions were not *per se* connected with either past or future membership in the ORC. These promotions, in all probability, were of value in ORC recruiting, but only in an indirect way.

REBUILDING THE ORGANIZED RESERVE CORPS

The only appeal the Army could actually make, given the paucity of membership benefits in the ORC, was an appeal to patriotism, and when General George C. Marshall addressed a letter to "All members of the Army" in August 1945, that was the heart of his appeal. "We owe it to our country," he wrote, "and to the comrades who have made the great sacrifice, to insure that never again will Americans be drawn into a war unprepared."[11] These were brave and ambitious words from the Army's Chief of Staff, but the next five years did not demonstrate a national commitment to achieving the goal of military preparedness through the

---

8. ROPA, p. 1676.

9. *Ibid.*

10. See, for example, the statements of Rep. Leroy Johnson (R–CA) and Maj. Gen. Boniface Campbell, DCS/G–1, during hearings on the Reserve Officer Personnel Act. ROPA, pp. 1676, 2038.

11. Letter, Chief of Staff George C. Marshall, August 23, 1945, copy in "Office History, 1916 to Present," Center of Military History.

creation of a strong, effective Organized Reserve and National Guard. One example of this was the national response to proposals for universal military training.

Universal military training was an integral part of the planning for the post-war Organized Reserve Corps. "Without it," wrote the Executive for Reserve and ROTC Affairs (ERRA), "it is our considered opinion that the development and maintenance of any material strength within the ORC is improbable."[12] Universal military training was not, however, enacted by the post-war Congress, and recruitment for the Organized Reserve depended entirely upon voluntary enlistments and commissionings.

Given the pre-war participation of men in the Officers' Reserve Corps, it was probably not unexpected that many officers would continue their Army affiliation by joining the post-war ORC. By January 1946 some 52.5 percent of all demobilized officers had accepted commissions in the ORC.[13]

Medical officer recruitment was a problem, however, and even men who had been in the pre-war ORC were refusing any further military affiliation. The war-time experience of Capt. E. H. Phillips is a good illustration of the way the Army alienated ORC doctors. Capt. Phillips had been a member of the Officers' Reserve Corps and had volunteered for active duty in 1942. He was a board certified otolaryngologist—an ear, nose, and throat specialist—but he was never promoted, because there were no higher level vacancies in the command. There were no vacancies, stated Capt. Phillips, because his civilian contemporaries, men who had no military background and no better medical credentials than he had, were commissioned directly from civilian life as majors and lieutenant colonels. Capt. Phillips was angry about the way he had been treated, and Brig. Gen. Edward W. Smith, the Executive for Reserve and ROTC Affairs, sympathized with him. "Civilians could be offered high commissions," stated Smith, "and Reserve Officers

---

12. Memorandum, ERRA to Director of Operations and Training, December 6, 1946, Subject: "Clarification of War Department Policies Pertaining to the National Guard and the Organized Reserve Corps," RG 319, Entry 342, Box 14 (370.01).

13. Memorandum, Lt. Col. J. L. Ballard, Jr., Chief, Strength Accounting and Statistics Office, to Executive for Reserve and ROTC Affairs, February 4, 1946, Subject: "Respective Ratios to Latest Date of (a) New Commissions in Officers Reserve Corps to Total Eligible for Commission, and (b) New Appointments in Enlisted Reserve Corps to Total Eligible for Appointment," RG 319, Entry 343, Box 124 (210.8).

could only be promoted under the slow process of regular promotion."[14]

Despite the problem of medical officer recruitment, the Officers' Reserve Corps reached a strength of 274,839 by June 1947, less than two years after the end of the war. Enlisted recruitment, however, did not go as well. The War Department had anticipated that 10–12 percent of the enlisted personnel would join the Enlisted Reserve Corps (ERC), but only 1.3 percent of those discharged (35,578 of 2,700,000) had joined by November 1945. The percentage of enlisted veterans who joined the ERC had increased to 3.2 percent by January 31, 1946, and the number of enlisted members of the ERC reached 467,608 by June 30, 1948.[15]

MISTER BREGER **—By Dave Breger**

(Reprinted by special permission of King Features Syndicate)

"We just can't simply persuade him that just because he's in the Enlisted Reserve Corps is no reason to be constantly on the alert."

The Organized Reserve was generally a recognizable organization following World War II, as is indicated by this 1946 cartoon by Dave Breger.

14. Letter, Brig. Gen. Edward W. Smith to Capt. E. H. Phillips, September 20, 1945, RG 319, Entry 343, Box 118 (330.14). See confirmation of this policy in memorandum, ACS/G–1 to Chief of Staff, May 14, 1946, Subject: "Officers Separation Point," RG 319, Entry 343, Box 124 (210.8).

15. "Subsection II f—Civilian Components (2)—Organized Reserve Corps," RG 319, Entry 343, Box 127 (326.2).

This latter figure, impressive as it is when compared with the 1941 ERC strength of 2149, was not nearly up to the levels desired by the War Department. One problem was that there were few units of the Organized Reserve to which the men of the ERC could be assigned.

The War Department's initial plans called for a total of twenty-five Organized Reserve Corps divisions and almost 2400 non-divisional units. For the post-war period, there were four classifications of Reserve units: A–1, A–2, B, and C. A–1 units were service units organized with their full complement of officers and enlisted men. Combat units with their full strength of officers and enlisted personnel were designated A–2. Class B consisted of combat and service units that had their full officer strength plus a cadre of enlisted men, and Class C units had only an officer cadre. The War Department's official position was that "All Organized Reserve Corps units will initially be organized as C units, with officers only."[16] This meant that post-World War II Organized Reserve units would, at least initially, resemble the ORC units of the years after World War I. Enlisted men, stated the War Department, would be assigned to an Active Reserve reservoir.[17]

This policy stemmed largely from the fact that in the years of parsimony between World War II and Korea, the Organized Reserve Corps and the National Guard were in competition—conscious or unconscious—for an inadequate pool of dollars. The fact was that the Organized Reserve fared quite badly in this competition. Though the individual members of the Officers' Reserve Corps had achieved an enviable record of service during the war, the Organized Reserve Corps as an organization suffered by comparison with the National Guard. The small number of ORC units that were designated for Class "A" status was a reflection of the Organized Reserve-National Guard competition. This situation did not go unnoticed at the White House, however.

"It has come to the President's attention," wrote President Harry S. Truman's military aide, ORC member Harry Vaughan, to Chief of Staff Dwight D. Eisenhower, "that there is some controversy largely sponsored, I understand, by the National Guard Association against the creation of

16. Memorandum, Lt. Gen. C. P. Hall, Director of Org. and Tng. to Army Chief of Staff, July 10, 1946, Subject: "Inactive Duty Pay for Organized Reserve Corps Units," RG 319, Entry 342, Box 10.

17. "Approved War Department Policies Relating to Postwar National Guard and Organized Reserve Corps," October 13, 1945, RG 319, Entry 343, Box 117 (326.2).

any A–2 Reserve units for the Organized Reserve. The President directed me to advise you that he thinks these units should be created; in fact, he is of the opinion that there is no use in having a Reserve without them."[18] This part of the question of Organized Reserve versus National Guard was quickly resolved, when less than a month later the Secretary of the General Staff informed Vaughan that Chief of Staff Eisenhower "has asked me to advise you now that a decision has been reached, and organization of units of this type is being directed."[19]

The Organized Reserve divisions were not, however, the Reserve units that the War Department had in mind for A–2 status. Priority for divisional organization at the A–2 level of readiness was clearly given to the National Guard. War Department policy, for example, even after the exchange between Vaughan and Eisenhower, was that "until such time as it is clearly demonstrated that requirements cannot be met by the National Guard, Reserve divisions will not be organized beyond class 'B' status."[20] Reserve divisions were to be organized initially as Class "C" units (60 percent of authorized commissioned officer strength) and would advance to "B" status only when they achieved 80 percent of their authorized commissioned and non-commissioned officer strength. To reach Class "A", a unit needed its complete authorized cadre, plus 40 percent of its authorized enlisted strength.[21]

Activation of the first post-war units of the Organized Reserve began on July 1, 1946, and by the end of January 1947 a total of 1141 Organized Reserve units had reached Class C status. The number of such units rose steadily throughout 1947, reaching 3,973 by May 23, 4,479 by June 19, and 6,343 by December 5.[22] By the end of December, the strength of the Organized Reserve Corps was as given in Table 5–1.

---

18. Memorandum, Brig. Gen. Harry H. Vaughan to Gen. Dwight D. Eisenhower, March 29, 1946, RG 319, Entry 342, Box 10.

19. Memorandum, Col. J. W. Bowen to Harry H. Vaughan, April 18, 1946, RG 319, Entry 343, Box 125 (240).

20. Letter, Gen. Jacob L. Devers, CG, Army Ground Forces, to CG's, Armies, May 13, 1947, Subject: "Clarification of War Department Policies Pertaining to the National Guard and the Organized Reserve Corps," RG 319, Entry 343, Box 147 (370.01).

21. "AGF Initiates Reserve Training Mobilization in Six Army Areas," *The Reserve Officer* (August 1946), pp. 7–8.

22. *Ibid.*, p. 7; War Department Press Releases, January 24, May 23, June 6, June 19, and December 5, 1947, RG 319, Entry 343, Box 141 (322).

Table 5–1 Organized Reserve Strength, December 31, 1947.[23]

	Unassigned	Composite Groups	A	B	C	Total
Units			59	887	5,897	6,843
Officers	62,250	167,059	158	6,233	43,133	278,833
Enlisted	325,008	90,717	422	2,382	21,927	450,456

What these figures mean is that fewer than 600 members of the Organized Reserve Corps were in units that would be ready for active duty on M-Day. The implication of these figures had not escaped Brig. Gen. Wendell Westover, the Executive for Reserve and ROTC Affairs. He had earlier informed the Army's Deputy Chief of Staff that "current and mobilization plans are NOT realistic, since they have produced, from 8 May 1945, to date no Reserve force in being. Today, we have in this country less than eighty (80) Class (A) Reserve units, none of which are adequately manned, equipped, and trained; further, most of them are small and of relatively little importance, such as affiliated laundry units, battalion medical sections, and bomb-disposal squads."[24]

The Organized Reserve Corps, wrote Brig. Gen. Westover several months later, only had 355,000 men actually available for use, compared with an authorized strength of 949,000. The "primary difficulties encountered to date," he wrote, "[are a] deficiency of facilities, equipment, and funds . . . traceable to a large degree to the low priorities afforded the ORC and reluctance to accord it requisite support."[25]

The reason for these deficiencies was simple: a lack of determination on the part of the President and the Congress to give the Organized Reserve the financial support it needed. "Economy" was the watch word of the time, and it often seemed as if the legislative and executive branches were trying to outdo each other in cheeseparing. Indeed, the economy measures were so severe that an officer in The Adjutant Gen-

23. Staff Study, Brig. Gen. Wendell Westover, ERRA, to Army Chief of Staff, April 6, 1948, RG 319, Entry 343 (CAR), Box 26 (326.2).

24. Memorandum, Brig. Gen. Wendell Westover, ERRA, to Deputy Chief of Staff, March 17, 1948, Subject: "Immediate Program," RG 319, Entry 342 (CAR), Box 26 (326.2).

25. Memorandum, Brig. Gen. Wendell Westover to Chief of Staff, October 13, 1948, Subject: "Draft of Secretary of Defense Letter Relating to Proposed Presidential Directive," RG 319, Entry 342 (CAR), Box 2 (031.1).

eral's Office indicated that because of a lack of funds, "an adm[inistrative] restriction has been placed on the enlistments auth[orized] in certain Class A units . . . ."[26]

This failure to support the Organized Reserve Corps was nowhere more evident than in the paucity of training opportunities afforded its members during the immediate post-war years. Without proper and continuing training, the members of the Organized Reserve Corps would in the long run be little better than conscripts, though the fact that most of the Corps members from 1945–1950 were World War II veterans was a decided advantage. Proper training, however, was non-existent in the first three years after World War II, and lack of funds was the primary limiting factor. There would be no Organized Reserve Corps unit training until Fiscal Year 1949, wrote Army Under Secretary William H. Draper in late November 1947, because " . . . the unit training of all Battalions would cost more than the entire appropriation in FY 1949 for all Reserve activities . . . ."[27]

Even the training that was provided was often reminiscent of the years between the World Wars, particularly for Class C units of the Organized Reserve. The 98th Infantry Division (ORC) conducted its first post-World War II training during the summer of 1948 at Pine Camp (now Fort Drum), New York. The Division had a summer camp strength of 300 men, of whom 75 percent were officers. In the words of an attached public information officer, "Regiments were of platoon size; battalions and companies were represented by squads, sometimes attenuated . . . . The MOS distribution bore only a faint resemblance to any T/O."

The total divisional artillery consisted of two 105mm howitzers, which were provided to the unit without sights. Not until the Cornell University ROTC—150 miles away—agreed to loan sights for the weapons were the howitzers anything more than decorative. The division had no organic vehicles, so "the Division walked to work." Lt. Col. George F. Havell, the PIO who wrote about the 98th Division's training, concluded his account with the following observation: "To point out that the 98th Division has a long way to go before it can be welded into an effective fighting unit is

26. Memorandum for the Record, Maj. Frey, July 23, 1948, RG 407, Box 1613 (353-Org Res Corps 4/1/48–12/31/48). See Appendix B for a tabulation of ORC funding during this time.

27. Letter, William H. Draper, Jr., to Lt. Col. Robert B. Fentress, November 21, 1947, RG 319, Entry 343, Box 127 (326.2).

to state the obvious. That will take more manpower, equipment, long training, and—above all—time."[28]

CHANGES IN THE DEFENSE ESTABLISHMENT

The Organized Reserve Corps, of course, operated in neither a political nor an organizational vacuum, and in fact the future of the Corps was intimately related to the post-war organization of the military establishment of this country. War-time proposals for unification of the military services resulted in the National Security Act of 1947, which created the National Military Establishment headed by a Secretary of Defense. There were also created three military Departments: Army, Navy and Air Force.[29]

Following the passage of this act, Secretary of Defense James Forrestal appointed on November 20, 1947, a Committee on Civilian Components, headed by Army Assistant Secretary Gordon Gray, to make a "comprehensive, objective and impartial study" of the Organized Reserve and the National Guard.[30] President Harry S. Truman supported the unification of the Organized Reserve and the National Guard, and his military aide, Maj. Gen. Harry H. Vaughan, had previously published an article arguing that military efficiency would be enhanced by unification of the Guard and Reserve and suggesting that there was no longer any real need for a federally-supported state militia.[31]

The "objective and impartial study" required of the Committee was submitted to the Secretary of Defense on June 30, 1948, and its recommendations stirred immediate controversy. The "Gray Board Report," as the study came to be known, proposed that the Organized Reserve and the National Guard be transformed into a federal "National Guard of the United States." The National Guard should remain in existence, suggested the Gray Board, but it "must be directly under Federal control." The Committee members were "convinced that the same forces can no longer be expected to perform both local and national functions and that a

28. Lt. Col. George F. Havell, "A Fighting 98th Division Will Be Built," *The Reserve Officer* (November 1948), pp. 14–15, 22.

29. Weigley, *History of the United States Army,* p. 493.

30. Eilene Galloway, *History of United States Military Policy on Reserve Forces, 1775–1957.* Prepared for the use of the Committees on Armed Services, (Washington: GPO, 1957), p. 465.

31. Harry H. Vaughan, "National Guard and Reserve Must Be Unified," *The Reserve Officer* (October 1947), pp. 4–5.

modern Federal striking force cannot be prepared adequately under State control."[32]

The lengthy report drew immediate opposition from the National Guard Association, which labeled the unification proposal as "just another effort over a long period of time by the War Department and the Regular establishment to supplant the National Guard system with a Federal Reserve or Militia."[33] Despite the support of President Truman, the idea of merging or unifying the Guard and Reserve was dropped for the time, and it did not surface again as a serious proposal until the 1960's. In another area, however, the Organized Reserve finally caught up with the Guard, and that was in the matter of compensation for inactive duty training (IADT).

The War Department had long been opposed to inactive duty pay for members of the Organized Reserve, for reasons that were explained in Chapter Four. The post-war need to encourage Organized Reserve membership, however, finally caused a change in the attitude of the War Department. It is quite likely, too, that the Executive for Reserve and ROTC Affairs was instrumental in effecting this change. Col. John V. Rathbone, for example, wrote to the ACS/G–1 on behalf of the ERRA in mid-April 1946. Without pay for IADT, he stated, "It will be impossible to provide the units and personnel in the desired quantity and quality." A month later, Lt. Col. Jay W. Doverspike, Acting Executive Officer of the OERRA, advised that it was "not considered possible to develop the required units within the Organized Reserve Corps unless some provision is made for pay to members of these units, for training other than active duty."[34]

With Defense Department support, the provision of inactive duty pay for members of the Organized Reserve Corps became law on March 25, 1948, though the first payments under this statute were not made until October 1, 1948.[35] Because of limitations on funds, the Department of the Army established four priorities for payment of IADT:

---

32. *Report of the Committee on Civilian Components,* pp. 10–11.

33. Maj. Gen. Ellard A. Walsh, "One Federal Force? No," *The Reserve Officer* (June 1949), p. 6.

34. Memorandum, Col. John V. Rathbone to ACS/G–1, April 17, 1946, Subject: "Legislation for the Organized Reserve Corps," RG 319, Entry 343, Box 117 (326.2); memorandum, Lt. Col. Jay W. Doverspike to Chief, L & LD, May 14, 1946, no subject, RG 319, Entry 343, Box 125 (240).

35. Public Law 80–460; Department of the Army Press Release, October 23, 1948, "Drill Pay Regulations Issued for Army Reserve," RG 319, Entry 343 (CAR), Box 37 (240).

1. Organized Reserve Corps personnel in units that were in direct support of the 18-division Army;
2. Individuals with mobilization assignments as "filler personnel" for Regular Army and National Guard divisions;
3. Members of the Class B Organized Reserve Corps divisions; and
4. Remaining Organized Reserve Corps personnel.[36]

Another legislative battle that was fought and won by the Organized Reserve during the years immediately following World War II was that of retired pay. Pre-World War II proposals for such had run into solid opposition from the War Department, including the Office of the Executive for Reserve and ROTC Affairs. Even late in the war, Brig. Gen. Edward W. Smith, the ERRA, wrote that "The military is an avocation of the Reserve officer, prompted by patriotic motives while employed in a gainful civilian pursuit which, presumably, provides for his own retirement from the active business world."[37]

The difference that a change in Organized Reserve leadership can make is exemplified by the response of Brig. Gen. Edward S. Bres, successor to Brig. Gen. Smith as ERRA. When asked to comment on a similar piece of retirement legislation, the response was quite positive—but for officers only. "This office is firmly of the opinion," wrote Bres, "that provision for retirement pay in some form should be made for Reserve officers. Retirement pay should include credit for both active Federal service as well as inactive duty service. It is believed retirement pay will insure the continued interest of future officers."[38]

The proposal for non-disability retirement pay for reservists—both officers and enlisted personnel—was finally enacted by the provisions of Public Law 80–810 (June 29, 1948). The law provided for payment beginning at the age of 60 to reservists who had served at least twenty years in the reserve and active components. Retired reservists were not yet, however, permitted to use the commissaries or post

36. Department of the Army Press Release, "Drill Pay Regulations Issued for Army Reserve," RG 319, Entry 343 (CAR), Box 37 (240).

37. Memorandum, Brig. Gen. Edward W. Smith to ACS/G–1, January 18, 1944, Subject: "Comments on H. R. 3946, providing for 'retirement pay for certain members of the armed forces,'" RG 319, Entry 343, Box 115.

38. Memorandum, Brig. Gen. Edward S. Bres, ERRA, to Chief, Legislation and Liaison Division, March 4, 1946, Subject: "H. R. 5204, 79th Congress," RG 319, Entry 343, Box 124 (210.85).

exchanges, despite a concerted campaign by the Reserve Officers Association.[39]

WOMEN IN THE RESERVES

The question of how to increase the strength of the Organized Reserve Corps had plagued War Department planners since the end of World War II. The same questions, of course, had confronted the active Army during the war, and one source of high quality personnel had been the women of this country. Women had served in American armies, sometimes clandestinely, at least as early as the Revolutionary War. There had been no women in the Organized Reserves, however, before World War II, and there was no legal authority for them to join the Organized Reserves after the war.

This situation changed in 1947 when Congress authorized members of the Army Nurse Corps and Women's Medical Specialist Corps to serve in the Regular Army and the Officers' Reserve Corps.[40] The following year it authorized Women's Army Corps (WAC) members to serve in the Regular Army and the Organized Reserves under the provisions of the "Women's Armed Services Integration Act of 1948."[41]

A restriction, however, was that only prior service personnel were eligible to join the Organized Reserve Corps. This proviso meant that only members of the World War II Women's Army Corps, the Army Nurse Corps, or the female component of one of the other services, could join the Organized Reserves. Despite this restriction, within two years after passage of PL 80–625 the number of women in the Organized Reserve Corps had reached 4000. By May 1950 membership in the Organized Reserve Corps was opened to non-prior service women between the ages of 18 and 34, and a waiver to age 45 was allowed.[42] Women, of

39. Letter, Maj. Gen. Edward F. Witsell, The Adjutant General, to Brig. Gen. E. A. Evans, Reserve Officers Association, December 3, 1947, RG 319, Entry 343, Box 137 (210.85).

40. Public Law, 36–80, April 1947.

41. Public Law 80–625, June 12, 1948.

42. Department of Defense Press Release, May 25, 1950, Subject: "Women Without Prior Military Service now Eligible for WAC Reserve," RG 319, Entry 343, Box 2 (000.7); for a good account of the Women's Army Corps during World War II, see Mattie E. Treadwell, *The Women's Army Corps* (Washington: Department of the Army, 1954). The restriction that only veterans could join the Organized Reserves was partially lifted in 1947, when enlistment of a non-veteran was permitted if

course, formed only a small percentage of the active Army during World War II, and by law they could not be used in combat. This combat restriction on women also applied to the Organized Reserve Corps, so what the Army and the Organized Reserves really needed was a large and steady source of men.

SELECTIVE SERVICE AND RESERVE ORGANIZATION

Universal military training would provide a source of manpower, but UMT had been rejected immediately after the war. It was revived, however, in the Gray Board Report in 1948. Congress was still unwilling to embrace the idea completely, but the 80th Congress did pass a new selective service act, which became law on June 24, 1948. This statute provided that men from 19 to 26 years old could be inducted for up to 21 months of active service. They would thereafter serve in a Reserve component for five years, an obligation that could be reduced to three years by service in a unit of the Organized Reserve Corps or the National Guard.[43]

Individuals who were members of Organized Reserve Corps or National Guard units as of the date of the act were exempt from the draft for as long as they continued to participate satisfactorily, as were World War II veterans with more than 90 days of active service. This legislation was of little immediate value in Organized Reserve Corps recruiting, but it did hold forth the promise of funneling men into the Reserves and Guard once they had performed their active duty.[44] As a practical matter, however, the Selective Service Act of 1948 was not immediately effective even at providing soldiers for the active Army, for only 300,000 men were drafted in the first two years after its passage.[45]

President Truman was dissatisfied with the progress—or lack of progress—being made in putting together an effective Army reserve organization, and he undoubtedly realized that the Selective Service Act of 1948 would have only a minimal immediate effect on the Organized Reserve Corps and the National Guard. In October 1948, not quite four months after the Gray Board had submitted its report, he

---

the individual agreed to assignment to and training with a troop program unit. AR 150–5, Ch.3, December 11, 1947.

43. Public Law 80–759, June 24, 1948.

44. *Ibid.*

45. Weigley, *History of the United States Army,* p. 501.

issued an Executive Order calling upon the Secretaries of the Army, Navy, and Air Force to "proceed without delay, utilizing every practicable resource of the regular components of the armed forces, to organize all reserve component units, and to train such additional individuals . . . as may be required for the national security; and to establish vigorous and progressive programs of appropriate instruction and training for all elements of the reserve components . . . ."[46]

Under the provisions of the Executive Order, Army Secretary Kenneth C. Royall asked the Committee on Civilian Components, headed by former Secretary of State James F. Byrnes, for a report of recommendations for the Organized Reserve and the National Guard.

The Byrnes Committee submitted its report to the Secretary on February 21, 1949, and recommended that the strength of the Organized Reserve be set at 579,300. Included in this total would be 96,900 members of 25 Class "B" Organized Reserve divisions (1,876 officers and 2,000 enlisted men per division); 149,400 members of combat support units; 242,000 members of combat service support units; and 91,000 officers and enlisted men who would be used as fillers during the early phases of mobilization. The Committee also recommended that paid administrative assistants be provided for units of the Organized Reserve Corps.[47]

KOREA

The Organized Reserve Corps did not, however, achieve the strength goals outlined by the Byrnes Committee prior to the Korean War. On June 30, 1950, the Corps consisted of 217,435 officers and 291,182 enlisted men, of whom only 68,785 officers and 117,756 enlisted men were participating in paid drills.[48]

The parsimony of the years after World War II was not, of course, restricted to the reserve components of the Army, for the active forces had not fared much better. Some efforts were made in 1948 and 1949 to improve Army readiness and to make the Organized Reserve a force upon which the

---

46. Executive Order 10007, October 15, 1948. It should be noted that fiscal frugality was not thereafter abandoned by the President.

47. Department of the Army Press Release, February 21, 1949.

48. *Study of the Functions, Organization, and Procedures of the Department of the Army; OSD Project 80 (Army), Part VII, Reserve Components* (Washington: Department of the Army, 1961), p. VII–B–7.

United States could depend, but it was a case of too little, too late.

The official history of the Joint Chiefs of Staff puts it this way:

> The outbreak of the war was to reveal that these forces were suffering from severe defects, largely stemming from the Administration's efforts to hold military expenditures to a minimum. President Truman had laid down this economy objective in 1948 [there really was not much of a change from earlier], and had held to it in the preparation of the budgets for fiscal years 1950 and 1951. Its effect was to force the services to abandon the plans they had drawn, following the hasty and ill-considered demobilization at the end of World War II, to expand their forces to levels judged necessary for the 'cold war.' Thus the Army, which in 1947 had set a goal of 25 divisions, cut this back to 10 and maintained the lower figure only with some difficulty.[49]

When the North Koreans struck across the 38th parallel on June 25, 1950 the US Army was not in any condition to resist. Five years of neglect had taken its toll, and the weakness of depending for security upon an atomic umbrella was demonstrated by the inability of the Army to respond to anything short of all-out mobilization. General Douglas MacArthur had an immediate need for additional American combat forces for Korea, and it soon became obvious that the active Army was not prepared to offer the required level of support. President Truman quickly received Congressional authorization to order members and units of the Organized Reserve Corps to active service. A call for volunteers had yielded few positive results, so in July 1950 the Army turned to what Army Secretary Frank Pace described as "our sole immediate source of manpower"—that is, to the members of the Organized Reserve Corps and the National Guard.[50]

The first members of the Organized Reserve Corps to be called to active duty were 7,862 captains and lieutenants who were not assigned to units of the ORC. By the end of August 1950 a total of 404 units of the Organized Reserve, plus 10,584 individual Organized Reserve officers, had been

49. James F. Schnabel and Robert J. Watson, *The History of the Joint Chiefs of Staff: The Joint Chiefs of Staff and National Policy, Volume III—The Korean War, Part I* (unpublished, 1978), p. 45.

50. Frank Pace, Jr., "The Reserve Forces of the Army," *The Reserve Officer* (March 1952), p. 7.

called to active duty.[51] Unlike World War II, the Army's policy for Korea was that officers and enlisted personnel would not be stripped out of organized units and sent to Korea as replacements.[52] The justification for this policy was that coherent units of the Organized Reserve would be needed in the event that a more general war broke out elsewhere in the world.

A tremendous problem of equity ensued from this decision, however, for two reasons. First, non-unit members of the Organized Reserve Corps had not been receiving inactive duty pay, and might well have received no active duty training, either, since their demobilization after World War II. Since they had received few benefits from their Organized Reserve Corps membership, they felt they should not receive the first call to duty. Second, there were by 1950 many millions of young men who had never served in the military at all. Since most Organized Reserve Corps members were also World War II veterans, the ORC men did not think this double jeopardy call-up was fair.[53]

In September 1951 the ACS/G–1 suggested six priorities for ordering reservists to active duty:

1. Qualified volunteers from the Organized Reserve Corps and the National Guard;
2. Members of Organized Reserve Corps units;
3. Members of the active reserve with less than 12 months of WW II service;
4. Members of the inactive reserve with less than 12 months WW II service;
5. Other members of the active reserve;
6. Other members of the inactive reserve.

The Executive for Reserve and ROTC Affairs non-concurred in the proposed list and suggested that the number 2

51. Msg, G–1, WCL 37558, August 10, 1950, RG 319, Entry 343 (CAR), Box 35 (210.4); letter, Hubert E. Howard, Chairman, Munitions Board, to Secretary of Defense, August 28, 1950, Subject: "Recall Requirements of Reservists," RG 319, Entry 342, Box 15 (CAR) (210.4); Office, Chief of Military History, Department of the Army, *Problems Encountered in Bringing Units Up to Strength and Condition of Readiness for Korea*, p. 2.

52. Presentation by Col. George E. Butler before the Section 5 Committee, September 25, 1950, RG 319, Entry 342 (CAR), Box 38 (334).

53. *Study of the Functions, Organization, and Procedures of the Department of the Army; OSD Project 80 (Army), Part VII, Reserve Components*, p. VII–B–5.

priority—members of units—be moved to the bottom of the list. "To order into the active military service members of Organized Reserve Corps units," wrote Brig. Gen. Hugh M. Milton, echoing a familiar line, "would seriously affect the capabilities of these units to perform their training mission and to assume their planned role in the event of full mobilization."[54]

By the next month—barely a year after the United States had gotten into the fighting in Korea—the ACS/G–1, Lt. Gen. Anthony C. McAuliffe, announced the officer recall program for Fiscal Years 1952 and 1953. Because the active Army had a shortage of some 11,000 officers, wrote McAuliffe, it would be necessary to call additional men to active duty. These men, he stated, would be those who had been in a pay status in the reserve. He recognized the danger this posed to overall US readiness, but he said, "This calculated risk is necessary since it is not politically, nor militarily, practical to order additional members of the Inactive and Volunteer Reserve into active service."[55]

Secretary of the Army Frank Pace soon expanded upon McAuliffe's statements in a memorandum to the Army Chief of Staff. "The Department is limited in its ability," wrote Pace, "to utilize the Volunteer and Inactive Reserve in that it is the desire of Congress that paid reservists be utilized in lieu of those who have not received pay for reserve activity. However, in implementing this Congressional intent, reservists who at any time since the beginning of the Korean conflict have been paid for reserve activity will be considered as available for recall and will be utilized to the maximum extent practicable. This will be without regard to the length of time in pay status," concluded Pace, "whether currently in a pay status, or whether currently in the Organized, Volunteer, or Inactive Reserve."[56]

Although the priority and liability for service varied somewhat among the different groups of the organized Reserve Corps, the fact remains that large numbers of ORC

54. Memorandum, ACS/G–1 to RROTC, September 26, 1951, Subject: "Involuntary Ordering into Active Service of Reservists," RG 319, Entry 342 (CAR), Box 15 (210.4); and memorandum, RROTC to ACS/G–1, October 1, 1951, same subject, *ibid.*

55. Memorandum, Lt. Gen. A. C. McAuliffe to addressees, October 26, 1951, Subject: "Recall Program, FY 52 and FY 53," RG 319, Entry 342 (CAR), Box 15 (210.4).

56. Memorandum, Frank Pace, Jr., to Chief of Staff, January 14, 1952, Subject: "Ordering into the Active Military Service Officers of the Organized Reserve Corps," RG 319, Entry 342 (CAR), Box 15 (210.4).

members were called to active Army service. By the end of the first full year of fighting in Korea, more than 200,000 members of the Organized Reserve and 95,000 National Guardsmen had been called to duty. During this same period, the Army received 550,000 draftees and 175,000 volunteers.[57]

The number of Organized Reserve Corps members who served in Korea has not been determined, though 240,500 ORC members were called to active duty. Fourteen separate ORC battalions and 40 separate ORC companies, plus an unknown number of individuals, actually went to Korea. Many ORC members were in combat units, and with the general lack of combat preparedness on the part of the United States Army, opportunities for heroism were far too numerous. Members of the Organized Reserve received a fair share of recognition for their actions against the enemy. Seven Medals of Honor—five posthumously—were awarded to ORC members, as were approximately 10 percent of the other top combat decorations.[58]

Even reservists who were not called to active duty were subjected to the inequities of the Korean mobilization. Unlike World War II, when the entire country, broadly speaking, was involved in and united behind the war effort, Korea was never even dignified by being a declared war. It was a "police action," and the conduct of the war was not of intimate concern to a large percentage of the American population. Only a fraction of the 2,500,000 members of the reserve components was ever called to active duty, but all Reservists lived, and worked under the daily threat of mobilization.

Although membership in the Reserves carried with it the ultimate responsibility and hardship of responding to a mobilization order, Reservists discovered in 1950 that hardship could occur without their being mobilized. Indeed, within two months of the initial outbreak of war in Korea,

---

57. Dr. Robert W. Coakley, "Highlights of Mobilization, Korean War, Prepared in Office of the Chief of Military History, Department of the Army, 10 March 1959," p. 2 (copy in CMH files).

58. *Semiannual Report of the Secretary of Defense, January 1 to June 30, 1953* (Washington: GPO, 1953), pp. 67–68. The 40 ORC units contained 8651 enlisted personnel. The number of Organized Reserve officers in Korea was undoubtedly substantial, because only 15% of the officers in the Eighth Army were Regulars. For a good discussion see Office, Chief of Military History, *Problems Encountered*, pp. 1–4. Statistics on combat decorations were compiled from Department of the Army General Orders. The percentage is based on a sample.

reports were reaching the Department of the Army that Organized Reserve and National Guard members, because of the uncertainty surrounding their possible mobilization, were having trouble finding permanent employment. This situation did not improve, and in October 1950, Rear Adm. I. M. McQuiston, a member of the Secretary of Defense's Civilian Components Policy Board, addressed the matter in a memorandum to the Secretaries of the Army, Navy, and Air Force:

> There is evidence of serious deterioration in the morale of reservists—a deterioration that is progressive and is expanding at an alarming rate. Indications are prevalent that a growing attitude in a large proportion of the members of the Civilian Components is their intent to resign their commissions or terminate their enlisted status at the first opportunity. This is not because of any unwillingness to serve their country in time of war, but because the reservist finds himself unduly penalized in time of limited mobilization.[59]

ARMED FORCES RESERVE ACT OF 1952

The lessons learned from the Korean War mobilization led to renewed Congressional interest in the reserve components, the result being the Armed Forces Reserve Act of 1952.[60] This statute brought together in one place many of the existing laws that related to the reserve components, and it established in much greater detail than ever before the composition, responsibilities, and regulation of the reserves. The reserve components were redefined by this law, which provided that each of the seven reserve components would have a Ready Reserve, a Standby Reserve, and a Retired Reserve. The Officers' Reserve Corps and the Enlisted Reserve Corps were legally eliminated, and the Organized Reserve Corps was renamed the Army Reserve.[61]

---

59. Memorandum, Rear Adm. I. M. McQuiston to the Secretaries of the Army, Navy, and Air Force, October 1950, Subject: "Employer-Employee Relationship under Current Expansion Program," RG 319, Entry 342 (CAR), Box 15 (210.4). Some twenty years after Korea the Department of Defense established the National Committee for Employer Support of the Guard and Reserve in an effort to prevent problems similar to those of the Korean War era. This committee has been of immense help to reservists, but there are continuing instances of employer discrimination. For a recent discussion of this question see Capt. Art House, "Defense Honors Four-Decade Backer of Reserve and Guard," *Army Reserve Magazine* (Spring 1983), pp. 33–34.

60. Public Law 82–476.

61. *Ibid.*, Secs, 202 and 302.

A ceiling of 1,500,000 was set for the Ready Reserve, the members of which would be liable for active duty during wartime or any national emergency declared by Congress or the President. Members of the Standby and Ready Reserves were only liable for active duty under a Congressional declaration.[62] One useful change effected by the act was that reserve commissions would henceforth be given for an indefinite term, rather than for five years.[63] By the end of fiscal year 1953 a total of 247,500 Army Reserve officers had accepted the indefinite-term commissions, while 68,000 had declined them.[64]

Another provision of the Armed Forces Reserve Act of 1952 established within the Office of the Secretary of Defense a Reserve Forces Policy Board of eighteen members. This board provided advice at the Department of Defense level similar to the way the "Section 5" committees did for the Department of the Army.[65]

The Korean War mobilization experience was not ignored by the Armed Forces Reserve Act of 1952. In a strongly-worded section of the act, Congress required that consideration be given to the "duration and nature of previous service, with the objective of assuring such sharing of hazardous exposure as the national security and the military requirement will reasonably permit . . . ."[66] The law further required that "Insofar as practicable, in any expansion of the active Armed Forces of the United States which requires that units and members of the reserve components be ordered into the active military service of the United States, members of units organized and trained for the purpose of serving with a unit shall be ordered involuntarily into active duty only with their units."[67]

As practical matter, neither this law nor any law since 1952 has completely addressed the question of equity. Members of the USAR serve with the idea that they may be called to fight if this country goes to war, and only a political decision—to be discussed in Chapter Nine—kept the Army Reserve from having a large presence in Vietnam.

62. *Ibid.*, Secs. 205–207.

63. *Ibid.*, Sec. 224.

64. *Semiannual Report of the Secretary of Defense, January 1 to June 30, 1953*, p. 71.

65. PL 82–476, Sec. 257.

66. *Ibid.*, Sec. 233 (b)(2).

67. *Ibid.*, Sec. 233 (g).

CONCLUSION

The Korean War Armistice was signed in July 1953, just six months after Dwight D. Eisenhower had assumed the Presidency. Korea was over, though the country remained divided. Its legacy, however, would be an important one. The most comprehensive Congressional history of the reserve forces of the United States concluded that the Korean War had caught the Department of Defense largely unprepared.[68] Indeed, the belated efforts to strengthen the Army's reserve components that began in 1948 had barely begun to show results two years later. The extreme frugality of the post-World War II period—a historically typical US reaction—had created what to any reasonable observer was not even an illusion of military strength. The idea that any future war would be an unlimited one, with an exchange of nuclear firepower, had led inexorably to the belief that conventional armed forces were not as important as they once had been. Korea had revealed the flaws in this line of reasoning, and the first American fighting men in that conflict had suffered too certainly the deadly results of this error. Research and development had been neglected; equipment modernization had been delayed; active military strength had been drawn down below safe levels; and the Army's neglect of its own Organized Reserve Corps had created not only inequities and injustices, but also deadly inefficiency. The United States finally achieved a sort of peace in Korea, but the fighting men there paid a terrible price for the parsimony and neglect of the post-war years. Talleyrand was not speaking of military matters when he said it, but he could well have been describing this period in American history: "It [was] . . . worse than a crime; it [was] . . . a blunder."

68. Galloway, *History of the United States Military Policy on Reserve Forces, 1775–1957.*

Brig. Gen. Theodore Roosevelt, Jr., was the only general officer who stormed ashore with the first wave on D-Day, June 6, 1944. Shown here with his ever-present cane, Brig. Gen. Roosevelt was awarded the Medal of Honor for his actions that day. The citation read as follows: "After two verbal requests to accompany the leading assault elements in the Normandy invasion had been denied, General ROOSEVELT'S written request for this mission was approved and he landed with the first wave of the forces assaulting the enemy-held beaches. He repeatedly led groups from the beach over the sea wall and established them inland. His valor, courage, and presence in the very front of the attack and his complete unconcern at being under heavy fire inspired the troops to the heights of enthusiasm and self-sacrifice. Although the enemy had the beach under constant direct fire, General ROOSEVELT moved from one locality to another and rallying men around him, directed and personally led them against the enemy. Under his seasoned, precise, calm, and unfaltering leadership, assault troops reduced beach strong points and rapidly moved inland with minimum casualties. He thus contributed substantially to the successful establishment of the beach-head in France." Brig. Gen. Roosevelt, who was serving as Assistant Commander of the Fourth Infantry Division, died of a heart attack the day this photograph was taken, July 12, 1944. (Signal Corps photo #ETO–HQ–44–7576–A)

Army infantrymen hit an unidentified beach in Italy in 1944. The Officers' Reserve Corps furnished almost one-fourth of the Army's officers during WW II, mostly in the middle grades (captain, major, and lieutenant colonel). (Signal Corps photo, #229080)

Tank crew members of the 2nd Armored Division await the signal to move out in pursuit of retreating Germans near Champ Du Bouet, France, August 10, 1944. Some 37 percent of the officers in this division were ORC members at this time. (Signal Corps photo)

Pictured here is Maj. Gen. William J. "Wild Bill" Donovan, member of the ORC and head of the Office of Strategic Services (forerunner of the Central Intelligence Agency) during WW II. Donovan had received the Medal of Honor for his heroism during World War I. (Photo courtesy of Veterans of the OSS)

Sergeant Hiroshi H. Miyamura is shown here receiving a Medal of Honor from President Eisenhower in 1953. Miyamura, who entered the active Army from the Enlisted Reserve Corps early in the Korean War, was serving as squad leader of a machine gun platoon in Korea when the Chinese attacked his position in April 1951. According to the citation for his award, Miyamura "killed more than 50 of the enemy before his ammunition was depleted and he was severely wounded. He maintained his magnificent stand despite his painful wounds, continuing to repel the attack until his position was overrun. When last seen he was fighting ferociously against an overwhelming number of enemy soldiers." Miyamura spent over two years in a Chinese POW camp and was released in August 1953. At least six other Army Reservists received Medals of Honor for their heroism in Korea. (Signal Corps photo #427741–S)

Members of the Eighth Army move across a Chinese-made bridge in the Chugyong-san area of Korea, March 1951. Members of the Organized Reserve were very much in the thick of fighting in Korea, especially during the first year of the war. (Signal Corps photo)

Summer training continued for members of the Organized Reserves, even as the first ORC members were on their way to Korea. Shown here firing the .50 caliber machine gun at Fort Sill, Oklahoma, are members of the 18th FA Battalion in August 1950. (Signal Corps photo)

Members of the 240th Port Co. (ORC), from Miami, Florida, review the proper handling of the carbine. They are undergoing their summer training at Camp Leroy Johnson, New Orleans, Louisiana, in July 1950. (Signal Corps photo)

Crouched beside a tank at Fort Ord, California, members of the 418th Military Police Escort Guard Company plan their attack in June 1951. (Signal Corps photo)

Enlisted reservists undergo the same basic training as members of the active Army. These men of the ERC are completing the final part of the confidence course at Fort Hood, Texas, in November 1950. (Signal Corps photo)

Learning to climb poles is a necessary part of learning to be a lineman. These ORC members from the 494th Signal Construction Company of Birmingham, Alabama, are at their training site at Fort Gordon, Georgia, in August 1951. (Signal Corps photo)

On their second day of summer training at Camp Leroy Johnson, Louisiana, members of the 817th Transportation Truck Battalion of Albuquerque, New Mexico, learn about the assembly of a vehicle engine. (Signal Corps photo, July 12, 1950)

Officers of the 3027th ASU, Organized Reserve Corps, are shown the latest model flame thrower by instructors from the Army's Chemical Corps Training Center, Fort McClellan, Alabama, June 1951. (Signal Corps photo)

"A smart, well-groomed appearance and esprit de corps influence each other. . . . Today's uniform, sold in war surplus stores as work clothes and worn by a legion of displaced persons and ex-prisoners of war, hardly achieves this purpose."—Sec. of the Army Robert T. Stevens, introducing the new Army uniforms in 1954. These members of the 808th Engr. Petr. Distr. Co. (ORC), shown here with a Bailey bridge panel during their 1951 annual training at Camp Polk, La., bear eloquent testimony to the truth of the Secretary's remarks. The ORC received hand-me-downs in virtually every category. (Signal Corps photo, #381379)

The crew of a 90 mm anti-aircraft gun prepares to fire during summer training at Yakima, Washington, Training Center in June 1954. These men are members of the 405th AAA Bn, USAR. (Signal Corps photo)

The Army Reserve today has about one-tenth of the Army's field artillery strength. Shown here twenty-five years ago is a crew of the 446th Field Artillery Battalion, an Army Reserve unit from Lakeland, Fla., firing their 8-inch howitzer during a field problem. (Signal Corps photo, #529549)

Armies have to be fed, and the USAR has a lot to do with feeding of the US Army. Members of the 394th QM Recovery and Disposition Co. are preparing food during two weeks of training at Fort Knox, Ky., during the summer of 1959. (Signal Corps photo, #566606)

Learning the proper techniques for deactivating a land mine are members of the 308th QM Salvage Co. of Chattanooga, Tenn., during their summer training at Fort Campbell, Ky., 1959. (Signal Corps photo, #566601)

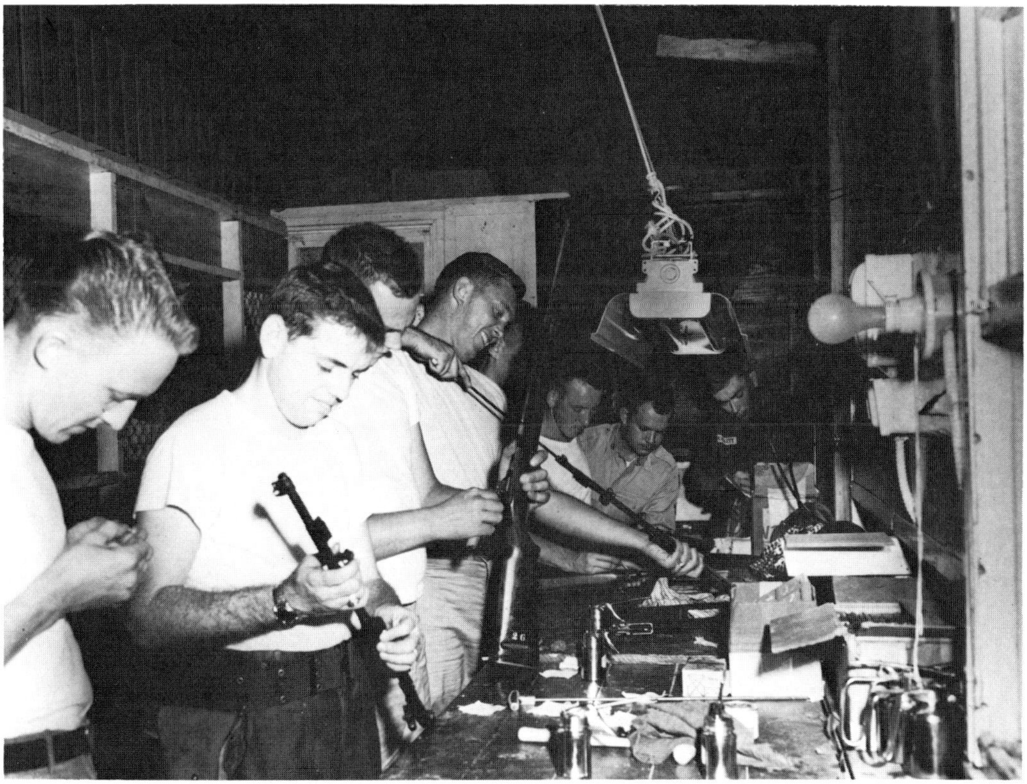

Learning to keep one's weapon clean is an important part of soldiering. These men from an Army Reserve unit seem to be having fun as they clean .30 caliber carbines at Fort McClellan, Ala. (Signal Corps photo, #589772)

Waiting for the green light. Members of the Army Reserve's 12th Special Forces Group prepare to jump during an exercise near Chicago on November 11, 1961. (Signal Corps photo, #588714)

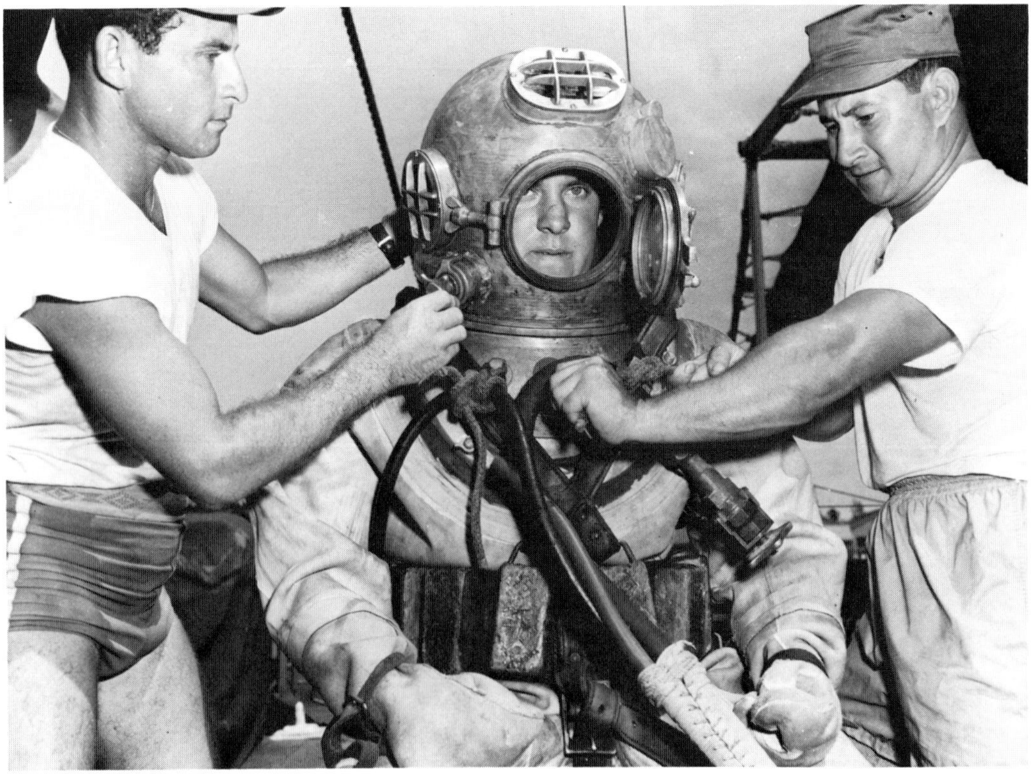

Army Reservists also plunge beneath the surface of the sea. Here getting ready for a dive at the San Juan, P.R., Naval Station is SP5 Jesus Peres Felix, a member of the 428th Engr. Diving Det., USAR, on June 17, 1960. (Signal Corps photo, #591126)

6

The Eisenhower Years: 1953–1961

The Organized Reserve Corps emerged from the Korean War with a new name—the Army Reserve—and a significantly enhanced reputation. Thousands of individual members of the Organized Reserve (or Army Reserve) served with distinction in non-Reserve units, and the 14 separate USAR battalions and 40 separate USAR companies that fought with the Eighth Army were described by the Secretary of Defense as "uniformly excellent."[1]

There were, however, significant problems that were highlighted by the war. Certain problems such as the creation of a statutory system of promotion consideration for reserve officers were dealt with through the legislative process. Others, such as the number of organized units, drill participation, quantity of equipment on hand in the units, physical facilities, and the number of full-time personnel were affected both by new statutes and by the new administration's policies toward the Army Reserve. The verbal support was tremendous.

"Confronted with the possibility of direct attack," wrote Eisenhower's Secretary of Defense Charles E. Wilson, "our Nation faces the alternative of either maintaining over the years ahead substantially larger active forces than at present or supplementing existing forces with a well-trained, readily available reserve of adequate size. It is the latter course which has been approved by both the President and

---

1. *Semiannual Report of the Secretary of Defense, January 1 to June 30, 1953* (Washington: GPO, 1953), p. 68.

the Congress."[2] Despite this rhetoric, however, the Eisenhower administration's main reliance was on a strategic policy of "massive retaliation," which was simply an updated version of Truman's reliance on "the bomb."[3]

This policy combined quite well with the President's fiscal conservatism, and as a result the Army Reserve was never given support sufficient to correct the neglect of earlier years. Largely because of Congressional support, however, the USAR proportion of the Army budget rose from 0.93 percent in 1953 and again in 1954 to 1.7 percent in 1955. It then rose to 2.9 percent ($211 million) in 1956 and jumped to 4.5 percent ($344 million) in 1957. The percentage and the dollars declined slightly in 1958, dropped significantly in 1959, and rose again in 1960. Compared with the 1960's, the Eisenhower years saw a larger percentage of the Army budget going to the USAR than was the case during the tenure of either John F. Kennedy or Lyndon B. Johnson. It was not until 1965, for example, that the 1960 USAR budget total was surpassed, even though dollars were certainly cheaper by the latter year.[4]

Congress, too, showed an increased interest in the Army Reserve and the other reserve components in the years after Korea. One direct result of this interest was the Reserve Officer Personnel Act of 1954 (ROPA), which is the basic law on the subject today.[5]

ROPA

The existing statutory provisions pertaining to reserve officers prior to ROPA were largely contained in the Armed Forces Reserve Act of 1952. This law required the various service Secretaries to establish "an adequate and equitable system for the promotion of members of the reserve components in an active status."[6] The Army, in fact, had issued

---

2. *Semiannual Report of the Secretary of Defense, January 1 to June 30, 1955* (Washington: GPO, 1956), pp. 18–19.

3. James E. Hewes, Jr., *From Root to McNamara: Army Organization and Administration, 1900–1963* (Washington: Center of Military History, 1975), p. 216; Russell F. Weigley, *History of the United States Army* (New York and London: Macmillan Publishing Co., Inc. and Collier Macmillan Publishers, 1967), pp. 525–26.

4. See Appendix B for budget data.

5. Public Law 83–773; "Address by Senator Margaret Chase Smith to the 29th National Convention, Reserve Officers Association," *The Reserve Officer* (August, 1955), p. 13.

6. Public Law 82–476, Sec. 216.

the required regulations within six months of the passage of this act, but Army Reserve officers were not satisfied.[7]

The Reserve Officers Association lobbied hard for new legislation, and ROA representatives spent a great deal of time testifying before the House Armed Services Committee. The principal witness for ROA was Maj. Gen. Melvin Maas a Marine Corps Reserve officer, former Congressman, and Chairman of the association's Legislative Committee. Maas pointed out the primary difference between the desires of reserve officers and the official position of the Department of the Army. Reserve officers, stated Maas, would "no longer . . . be satisfied with merely saying it is in the regulations. They know regulations can get changed. We know that for years now, every time they come up with a new plan this is going to be fine. This is going to give you a fair break. But they have not found it so. They no longer believe in the regulations. They want to see it in the law now."[8]

This was the very issue on which the Department of the army opposed the bill. "The Army view," stated Lt. Col. A. H. Parker, Office of the Assistant Chief of Staff, G–1, "is that regulations, which have only recently gone into effect and have not yet been thoroughly tested by operating experience, should provide the basis for drafting appropriate legislation on this subject when all the 'bugs' have been worked out of the new system."[9] Reserve officers, however, were not willing to be left to the tender mercies of the regulatory process of the Department of the Army, and their lobbying groups pushed the legislation through the Congress over the objections of the Pentagon.

ROPA was of tremendous importance to officers in the Army Reserve, because it gave to them and other Reservists a statutory basis for promotion and service comparable to that given Regulars by the Officers Personnel Act of 1947. Under ROPA, for example, Reserve officers were not subject to mandatory removal until they had reached a certain number of years of service. For officers in the grades of 0–2 through 0–5, the cut-off was twenty-eight years; for 0–6 and 0–7 it was thirty years; and for Reserve 0–8's it was thirty-five years.[10] The top three grades could, however, re-

---

7. See Army Regulations 135–155, 135–156, and 135–157.

8. *Hearings before the Committee on Armed Services, House of Representatives, Eighty-third Congress, First Session, Pursuant to H. R. 122. Reserve Officers Personnel Act* (Washington: GPO, 1953), p. 1616. Hereinafter cited as "ROPA Hearings."

9. *Ibid.*, p. 1559.

10. Public Law 83–773, Section 327.

main active until they had five years time-in-grade. The maximum age for active Reservists was set at sixty-two years for major generals and sixty years for all those of lower rank.[11]

Mandatory consideration for promotion was also statutorily guaranteed by ROPA. First lieutenants had to go before a promotion board their fourth year in grade, while captains and majors had to be considered for promotion by their seventh year. All of these officers also had to meet time-in-service criteria. Unit members of the reserve components were given an additional promotion possibility through "unit vacancy" promotions.[12]

Female Army Reserve officers were subject to the same promotion procedures as were male officers, with one important exception: promotion opportunities for women were considerably more limited than were those for men. Women's Medical Specialist Corps officers could not be promoted above the rank of major, while Women's Army Corps and Army Nurse Corps officers could only make it to lieutenant colonel.[13]

ROPA authorized 275,000 active Army Reserve officers, a total well above the 145,382 who were actually members of the Ready Reserve on June 30, 1955.[14] The number of active Reserve officers, however, could not exceed the following percentages in each grade:[15]

Colonel. . . . . 2 percent
Lieutenant Colonel. . . . . 6 percent
Major . . . . 13 percent
Captain . . . . 35 percent

One of the most important provisions of ROPA was its correction of an anomaly that had plagued the Army Reserve since 1920. Under the National Defense Act of 1920, the time-in-grade of a commissioned officer was determined by taking his date of rank and adding to it his total active duty service. Inactive duty Reserve participation did not count for precedence purposes, and discussion of proposals to change this system for the Army Reserve, Air Force Reserve, and

11. *Ibid.*, Sec. 326.
12. *Ibid.*, Secs. 310 and 309.
13. *Ibid.*, Sec. 304.
14. Public Law 83–773, Sec. 304.
15. Public Law 83–773, Sec. 307; *Semiannual Report of the Secretary of Defense, January 1 to June 30, 1955* (Washington: GPO, 1956), p. 68.

the National Guard occupied a considerable portion of the time devoted to hearings on the proposed legislation.

Col. Charles M. Boyer, the Executive Director of the Reserve Officers Association who worked closely with the members of the House committee as they considered H.R. 1222, delivered the sentiments of ROA on the question. "The Reserve Officers Association," he stated, "strongly recommends that date of rank and date of commission be the same." Former South Carolina Governor (and colonel in the Army Reserve) Strom Thurmond sent a letter to the Committee echoing the same conclusion. "Under the present Army and Air Force policy," wrote Thurmond, "a competent, experienced Reserve officer may, upon mobilization, become junior to a Regular officer who is actually junior in age, experience, and judgement. The sheer inefficiency of a system which requires wholesale revising of dates of rank for thousands of Reserve officers each time they serve a tour of active duty (for as little as two weeks in most cases) is deplorable."[16] Maj. Gen. Melvin Maas, also representing the ROA, called the existing date of rank system "an unworkable monstrosity." "There is not an IBM machine conceived," stated Maas with no small amount of hyperbole, "that could tell you the relative seniority of a Reserve officer at any time, let alone when he is mobilized."[17]

The Navy and the Marine Corps had long since adopted for their reserve components a system like the one proposed by the ROA; the Army and Air Force Reserves and the National Guard, however, used only active duty in determining seniority. Although the Navy and Marine Corps experience had been a positive one, both the Army and the Air Force resisted any change in their own procedures, and the National Guard was ambivalent.[18]

The ranking Army witness was Maj. Gen. Boniface Campbell, Assistant Chief of Staff, G–1, who testified that "The Department of the Army favors continuation of its present concept that seniority on active duty be based on active military experience. It is of the firm opinion," continued Campbell, "that the Reserve Officers Association proposal that seniority on active duty be based on date of appointment is not in the best interest of the Reserve Officers themselves, and certainly not of the service as a whole."[19]

---

16. Public Law 83–773, Sec. 307.
16. ROPA Hearings, pp. 1600–1602.
17. *Ibid.*, pp. 1613–14.
18. *Ibid.*, *passim.*
19. *Ibid.*, p. 2037.

Campbell then raised the spectre of thousands of inexperienced Army Reserve officers being mobilized and assuming their places on active duty. "The impact," stated Campbell, would be " . . . overwhelming under the most favorable conditions. If thousands of the least experienced officers must assume command of and responsibility for the training of our new forces," he warned, "inefficiency would almost certainly result. And the results might be extremely serious, if not disastrous."[20]

Maj. Gen. Campbell was, of course, using the most extreme scare tactics with the committee and was completely ignoring the fine combat record established by reserve officers during World War II and Korea. He was "not familiar with the detailed working" of the Navy and Marine Corps system, stated Campbell, but he speculated that "had the Navy followed the system currently used and advocated by the Army, . . . it is conceivable that they might be as happy with it as they are said to be with their present system."[21]

The original of the bill under consideration—H.R. 1222—proposed to give one day of precedence for each retirement point earned through inactive duty training and each point earned through correspondence course completion. The Department of the Army favored this proposal, as did the Department of the Air Force.[22]

The members of the House Committee adopted in large part, however, the ROA proposal. Under the new formula for computing date of rank, Army Reserve officers received a year's credit for each good retirement year, plus one day for each point earned in a year that was not credited for retirement.[23] ROPA was quite a significant step for the Army Reserve, but it did not purport to address every problem confronting the USAR.

THE RESERVE FORCES ACT OF 1955

On January 12, 1954, President Eisenhower asked Arthur Flemming, Director of Defense Mobilization, to prepare a plan for the development of an improved reserve system. Even before Flemming made his recommendation,

20. *Ibid.*, p. 2039.

21. *Ibid.*, p. 2040; see Chapter Four for an account of the Army's reserve officers during WW II.

22. *Ibid.*, pp. 2047–52.

23. Public Law 83–773, Sec. 702.

Eisenhower pledged that the "establishment of an adequate reserve . . . will be a number one item submitted to the Congress next year."[24]

Eisenhower, like many American Presidents before him, had long expressed support for a strong Army Reserve. Writing as Army Chief of Staff, he had stated: "There is no component of more importance to the security establishment than the Organized Reserve Corps . . . . The new Reserve Corps can and must become the well-trained citizen Army Reserve required to supplement immediately, in an emergency, our small Regular Army and our National Guard."[25] Eisenhower as President realized that the creation of a strong Army Reserve was both politically and fiscally desirable, and he quickly adopted the recommendations of the Flemming study, which became known as the National Reserve Plan. Eisenhower submitted his National Reserve Plan to Congress in a special message on January 13, 1955. He pointed out the need for an improved Reserve force and suggested five areas for legislative attention.

First, he recommended that a Reserve group of unspecified size be maintained at a high state of readiness to meet immediate mobilization requirements.

Second, he proposed that young men from 17 to 19 years old be permitted to volunteer for 6 months of basic training, to be followed by 9 1/2 years of service with the Reserves. He also proposed a Reserve forces draft, if there were not enough volunteers.

Third, Eisenhower proposed that enlistees in the National Guard be required to undergo six months of training before joining their units. Additionally, he requested the authority to assign prior-service personnel to National Guard units, if these units were unable to recruit enough personnel.

Fourth, he asked Congress to accept the concept that honorable military service included both active duty and statutory Reserve participation, the idea being that men

24. *Study of the Functions, Organization and Procedures of the Department of the Army, OSD Project 80 (Army), Part VII, Reserve Components* (Washington: Department of the Army, 1961), p. VII–B–6; "Strong Reserve to Be Number One Item for Next Congress-Eisenhower," *The Army Reservist* (November 1954), p. 15.

25. General Dwight D. Eisenhower, "The Reserve Component and Our Future Security," *The Reserve Officer* (July 1946), pp. 9–10; *Semiannual Report of the Secretary of Defense, January 1 to June 30, 1955* (Washington: GPO, 1956), pp. 20–21.

who failed to complete their Reserve requirements would be given less than an Honorable discharge.

Fifth, Eisenhower suggested that the States be permitted to organize militia forces in addition to their National Guard units, so that there would be someone to take over local security missions when the National Guard was federalized.[25]

Both the House and the Senate conducted extensive hearings on the Administration's proposal. Secretary of Defense Charles E. Wilson, Joint Chiefs Chairman Adm. Arthur Radford, Army Chief of Staff Gen. Matthew Ridgway and others—a veritable who's who among the DoD hierarchy—all testified in favor of the President's plan.

Witness after witness told the Subcommittee about the need for a stronger reserve system, and Secretary of the Army Robert T. Stevens hit particularly hard on the need for changes in the status quo. "Our Reserve at the present," stated Stevens, "is inadequate to meet our needs. Its inadequacy is due primarily—yes, I can say almost solely—to the failure to procure the participation of enlisted personnel in adequate numbers in organized units. All other problems associated with the Reserve," concluded Stevens, "are subordinate thereto. Therefore the keystone to a truly Ready Reserve is the procurement of the basically trained personnel who can be integrated, further trained, and retained for a reasonable period of time."[26]

During World Wars I and II, stated Stevens, "we were fortunate in having friends who were able to hold the enemy in check until our forces could be mobilized, trained, and deployed . . . ." The Administration's proposal for the Army Reserve, said Stevens, "is designed to fill the gap between the commitment of the Active Army, and the time when the rawest recruit can be trained to confront the aggressor."[27]

Carter Burgess, Assistant Secretary of Defense for Manpower and Personnel, then told the House Subcommittee that "The plain fact is that our Reserve Forces are not in line with current conditions and requirements." There were not adequate provisions under the current law, stated Burgess, to rectify the situation, and he recommended the Pres-

26. "National Reserve Plan," Hearings before Subcommittee No. 1 of the Committee on Armed Services, House of Representatives, Eighty-fourth Congress, First Session, p. 1282; hereinafter cited as "National Reserve Plan Hearings."

27. National Reserve Plan Hearings, pp. 1282–83.

ident's plan as a comprehensive system for supplying men to the Ready Reserve.[28]

Despite the vehement opposition of temperance organizations that did not want the young men of America subjected to the temptations of beer drinking in the Army[29] and of religious and quasi-religious groups that feared the universal military training implications of the National Reserve Plan,[30] the Congress finally enacted a modified version of Eisenhower's proposal. As signed on August 9, 1955, it differed somewhat from the Administration's proposal, but it did hold out the promise of substantial improvements in the Army Reserve.

The Reserve Forces Act of 1955 (RFA) took the form of amendments to the Armed Forces Reserve Act of 1952, just as the National Defense Act of 1920 was written as amendments to the National Defense Act of 1916. The RFA first raised the Ready Reserve ceiling from 1,500,000 to 2,900,000, then it set forth provisions by which these additional reservists would be forthcoming.[31]

After enactment of the RFA, a man had four ways in which he could fulfill his military obligation through some form of service in the Army Reserve:

1. Enlist in the active Army for three, four, or five years, then go into the Ready Reserve. There was a total of five years active duty and Ready Reserve obligation, with an additional year in the Standby Reserve.
2. Enlist in the Army Reserve for six years, two years of which would be spent on active duty. The obligation after that two years was three years in the Ready Reserve and one year in the Standby Reserve. This option was only available before receiving induction orders.
3. Wait for induction into the Army. This would entail two years of active duty, three years in the Ready Reserve, and one year in the Standby Reserve.
4. Enlist prior to age 18½ in a unit of the Army Reserve. This would result in an eight-year military obligation, six months of which would be spent on active duty for training (ADT). Payment during the ADT phase was set

28. *Ibid.*, pp. 1407–10.
29. *Ibid.*, pp. 1856–73.
30. *Ibid.*, pp. 1876–86, 1941–46, 1949–62, and *passim*.
31. Public Law 84–305, Sec. 2(a).

at $50 per month, which was $28 per month less than a draftee received.[32]

Option four was the immediate hope for increasing the strength of the Army Reserve, though in the long run the USAR stood to gain considerable numbers of men who had completed their active duty obligation under one of the other options. The Army Reserve was once again at a disadvantage when competing with the National Guard, however, because enlistees in the Guard had to perform *no* active duty or active duty for training, though the Guardsman was required to participate satisfactorily in unit training to age 28.[33]

President Eisenhower did not approve of this feature of the RFA, because it impaired the readiness of the National Guard. The President was also disturbed that members of the National Guard who volunteered for six months ADT would receive $78 per month for their efforts, compared with the $50 that Army Reservists were paid during the same training. He approved, however, of the provision of the RFA that gave him the authority to order to active duty up to 1,000,000 Ready Reservists—not just Army Reservists—in any Presidentially-proclaimed emergency.[34] The RFA also provided that Army Reserve units would have forty-eight drill periods (inactive duty training) per year and up to seventeen days of active duty for training.[35]

USAR MEMBERSHIP PROBLEMS

One of the long-term problems of the Army Reserve, however, was that it always looked much stronger on paper than it was in reality. As the Reserve Forces Policy Board had put it, "The Ready Reserve as a whole is not ready in fact or by statutory definition."[36] There were entirely too many mem-

32. "Choices Available to Fulfill Enlisted Service Obligation," *Army Information Digest* (February 1956), pp. 36–37.

33. *Ibid.* New National Guard enlistees after April 1, 1957, had to take the six months of ADT.

34. "President Eisenhower's Reserve Statement, August 9, 1955," *The Reserve Officer* (August 1955), p. 2; In April 1956 Congress amended the Reserve Forces Act to provide the same pay and disability and death benefits for both Army Reservists and National Guardsmen taking the six months of training. *Semiannual Report of the Secretary of Defense, January 1 to June 30, 1956* (Washington: GPO, 1957), p. 19.

35. Public Law 84–305, Sec. 2(b).

36. *Semiannual Report of the Secretary of Defense, July 1 to December 31, 1954* (Washington: GPO, 1955), p. 13.

bers of the USAR who did not take part in inactive duty training, particularly enlisted men with prior service. There was not much incentive for them to devote their weekends to Army Reserve duty, because military pay at the time was hardly enough to serve as a motivator. The non-participation problem was truly substantial. As of June 30, 1953, only 117,323 of 798,026 members of the Army Reserve (14.7 percent) were in a drill-pay status, and a year later the percentage had fallen even further (136,918 of 1,108,967 or 12.3 percent). By June 30, 1955, shortly before passage of the RFA, membership in the Army Reserve had grown to 1,648,626, and drill participation had risen to 163,137. These figures meant, however, that participation in inactive duty training had fallen to less than 10 percent of the total Army Reserve strength.[37]

There was not in the mid-1950's—and, in fact, there is not today—any particularly effective way to compel Army Reserve participation among men who have completed their military obligation. For men who chose one of the RFA options involving a specified term in the Ready Reserve, however, Public Law 84–305 provided a tool for enforcing the Reserve obligation. Participation in forty-eight inactive duty training drill periods and up to seventeen days annual training was required of all obligated members of the Ready Reserve. Failure to participate satisfactorily could result in an obligated Reservist's being ordered to active duty for training for up to forty-five days. If he attempted to slack off in his last year in the Ready Reserve, his time could be extended for up to six months.[38]

Although the Reserve Forces Act of 1955 did eventually prove beneficial to Army Reserve recruitment, there was initial disappointment with its lack of effect. From August 10, 1955, to June 30, 1956, only 13,012 men chose the two year active duty—three year Ready Reserve—one year Standby Reserve option, and only twice that number—27,272—chose the six months ADT—7½ year Ready Reserve program. According to Defense Department estimates, the latter program was expected to produce some 90,000 enlistments per year, so it was evident that the

37. *Semiannual Report of the Secretary of Defense, January 1 to June 30, 1954* (Washington: GPO, 1955), pp. 64, 333; *Semiannual Report of the Secretary of Defense, January 1 to June 30, 1955* (Washington: GPO, 1956), p. 296.

38. Public Law 84–305, Sec. 2(b).

young men of America were not exactly falling over each other trying to join the Army Reserve.[39]

For the next six months recruits under the 2–3–1 and 6-month ADT options numbered only 12,850 and 17,934, respectively. The Reserve Forces Policy Board offered its analysis of the problem: "Experience has shown that voluntary enlistments in reserve components have been high when the draft rate is high and conversely low when the draft rate is low."[40] This reasoning has become almost a truism in Army Reserve recruiting, for during the Vietnam War, the young men of America *were* falling over each other trying to join the USAR. The Defense Department, however, rejected the solution recommended by the Board, which was to draft men directly into the Reserve components. It decided to conduct instead "an unprecedented peacetime recruiting campaign . . . to secure voluntary enlistments under Section 262 [the six-month ADT option] of the [Reserve Forces] Act . . . ." Despite the recruiting campaign, the number of men who chose the six-month ADT option grew very slowly. Not until the recession of 1957–58, in fact, did enlistments begin to pick up at all. By the end of fiscal year 1960 only 177,712 men had enlisted under Section 262, and paid drill strength in the Army Reserve had only reached 276,992.[41]

The disappointing lack of enlistments in the Army Reserve was reflected, naturally enough, in the organizational status of USAR units. Of some 7200 company-size units authorized for the Army Reserve on June 30, 1956, only 5284 were in an active status; of the 618,000 personnel required for these units, only 180,000 (29 percent of requirements) were actually assigned. Six months later the Army Reserve had activated 5439 units, to which 210,679 Reservists belonged (32 percent of requirements).[42] The Army Reserve, as discussed later in this chapter, soon re-

---

39. *Semiannual Report of the Secretary of Defense, January 1 to June 30, 1956* (Washington: GPO, 1957), p. 66.

40. *Semiannual Report of the Secretary of Defense, July 1 to December 31, 1956* (Washington: GPO, 1957), p. 11.

41. *Semiannual Report of the Secretary of Defense, January 1 to June 30, 1957* (Washington: GPO, 1958), p. 69; *Annual Report of the Secretary of Defense, July 1, 1959, to June 30, 1960* (Washington: GPO, 1961), p. 101. Recessions always seem beneficial to Army recruiting generally.

42. *Semiannual Report of the Secretary of Defense, January 1 to June 30, 1956* (Washington: GPO, 1957), pp. 66–67; *Semiannual Report of the Secretary of Defense, July 1 to December 31, 1956* (Washington: GPO, 1957), p. 13.

duced the number of units to 4350 under the Pentomic division structure. Accurate comparisons of unit strength and numbers are therefore impossible to make. It can be said, however, that although Army Reserve units in the mid-1950's were more fully-manned than were the ORC units of twenty years earlier, they still did not possess the degree of readiness that would allow them to fulfill their role in the event of a sudden mobilization of the US Army.[43]

MATERIEL READINESS AND TECHNICIAN SUPPORT

Questions about personnel strength, however, were only one of the issues that faced the post-Korea Army Reserve. There were significant problems, for example, in the area of materiel readiness. The Organized Reserve units had never had much equipment, and equipping Army Reserve units was a slow process. Although the Reserve Forces Policy Board was able to say in July 1954 that "The Reserve forces are perhaps the best equipped that they have been in their history," this statement does not really mean much. The Board went on to say, however, that "The chief limitation at present lies not in the unavailability of equipment but rather in the lack of facilities and storage space in which to adequately safeguard the equipment."[44]

The extent of the facilities problems in the USAR was indicated a year later when the Board reported that of the 2570 locations where Army Reserve facilities were needed, only 355 were considered "adequate." Over the preceding four years the Army had spent only $33 million on USAR training centers, and there was a shortfall of some $400 million. As an idea of the priority attached to correcting this deficit, the Army requested for FY 1956 a total of only $31,611,000, to be used for 17 Army Reserve Training Centers, 243 National Guard Armories, and 124 non-armory projects for the National Guard.[45] By the end of fiscal year 1957 the Army Reserve had received facilities appropriations totaling $70 million; the Reserve Forces Policy Board estimated a need for an additional $348 million in the future.[46]

---

43. *Annual Report of the Secretary of Defense, July 1, 1959, to June 30, 1960* (Washington: GPO, 1961), p. 103.

44. *Semiannual Report of the Secretary of Defense, January 1 to June 30, 1954* (Washington: GPO, 1955), p. 66.

45. *Semiannual Report of the Secretary of Defense, January 1 to June 30, 1955* (Washington: GPO, 1956), pp. 74–75.

46. *Semiannual Report of the Secretary of Defense, July 1 to December 31, 1956* (Washington: GPO, 1957), p. 17.

The question of adequate facilities was tied closely with questions relating to equipment issue and full-time USAR maintenance personnel. Until June 1956 equipment pools served all of the Army Reserve units in a given area. This policy changed at the end of FY '56, and USAR units began to receive their own equipment. "This new policy," wrote the Reserve Forces Policy Board, "is being implemented as rapidly as storage and maintenance facilities and the necessary personnel can be provided."[47] The immensity of the problem confronting the Army Reserve is shown in the fact that by June 30, 1957, USAR units had only about 4 percent of their authorized Table of Organization and Equipment (TOE) allowances on hand. "Most of the equipment issued to Army reserves," reported the Secretary of Defense, "is standard, limited standard, or serviceable substitute type items and is adequate, along with equipment available in Army Reserve equipment pools, for training purposes."[48]

By the end of Fiscal Year 1960 the units of the USAR had received 41 percent of their overall TOE equipment allowances. "The majority of the US Army Reserve units," stated the Reserve Forces Policy Board, "can now conduct platoon-level basic unit training with the quantities of equipment on hand." The Board concluded, however, that "Maintenance of all levels continues to be a pressing problem." The primary cause of the maintenance problem in 1960 was the same one as in 1953—too few full-time personnel in the units.

The Army Reserve Technician Program was established in 1950, but it did not experience rapid growth during its first decade. Although President Eisenhower gave lip-service to the need for increasing the readiness of the Army Reserve, his administration was unwilling to give the USAR the number of full-time support personnel required to overcome the maintenance deficit. Eisenhower prided himself on his prudent fiscal management, and part of this management was that of cutting back on the number of civilian employees of the Department of the Army.[49] By fiscal year 1960 the USAR had a requirement for 5,100 technicians,

47. *Semiannual Report of the Secretary of Defense, July 1 to December 31, 1956* (Washington: GPO, 1957), p. 18. The Army reinstituted equipment pools for the USAR in the mid-1970's.

48. *Semiannual Report of the Secretary of Defense, January 1 to June 30, 1957* (Washington: GPO, 1958), p. 81.

49. See, for example, the proud statement of how he reduced DA Civilian employment by 13 percent during his first full year in office.

but only 3,046 were authorized by the Department of the Army.[50]

REORGANIZATION

One of the other things that made it difficult for the Army Reserve to attain a high state of readiness was a major structural reorganization, comparable in scope to the pre-World War II change from square to triangular divisions. This time the change was brought about by theories as to the effects of nuclear weapons on the battlefield. In 1957 the Army decided to reorganize and re-equip its combat units into a "Pentomic" divisional structure, an awkward arrangement that combined the latest in nuclear weaponry with the "circle the wagons" mentality of Indian Wars days. The three brigades of the triangular division were replaced under this doctrine by five "highly mobile combat groups organically supported by 5 batteries of light artillery and 1 battery of HONEST JOHN rockets . . . ."[51] The task of reorganizing the active Army's infantry, airborne, and armored divisions into the Pentomic configuration was completed by the end of calendar year 1957, and the number of active divisions was reduced from 18 to 15.[52]

Reorganization of the ten USAR combat divisions to the Pentomic structure was completed by the end of December 1959, one year ahead of schedule.[53] The irony of this accelerated conversion was that the active Army was ready to abandon the configuration because it simply did not work. By fiscal year 1961 the Army, in an attempt "to make our combat divisions more flexible and mobile," embraced the Reorganization Objective Army Division (ROAD). Under the ROAD concept the Army's combat divisions could be tailored to meet a specific battlefield need by adding and subtracting different types of battalions.[54] Conversion of the

---

Semiannual Report of the Secretary of Defense, January 1 to June 30, 1954 (Washington: GPO, 1955), p. 97.

50. *Annual Report of the Secretary of Defense, July 1, 1959, to June 30, 1960* (Washington: GPO, 1961), p. 104.

51. *Semiannual Report of the Secretary of Defense, January 1 to June 30, 1957* (Washington: GPO, 1958), pp. 3–4.

52. *Semiannual Report of the Secretary of Defense, July 1 to December 31, 1957* (Washington: GPO, 1958), p. 23.

53. *Annual Report of the Secretary of Defense, July 1, 1959, to June 30, 1960* (Washington: GPO, 1961), p. 103.

54. *Annual Report of the Secretary of Defense for Fiscal Year 1961* (Washington: GPO, 1962), p. 60.

Army Reserve to the ROAD division structure would wait, however, until the 1960's.

Other organizational changes during the Eisenhower years were not detrimental to Army Reserve readiness. On December 7, 1954, for example, the Executive for Reserve and ROTC Affairs became the Chief, Army Reserve and ROTC Affairs. This title change, however, had little effect on the operations of the office, though it held out a promise that the CAR would assume more responsibility for the USAR. In July 1956 the Headquarters, Continental Army Command, (CONARC) established the office of Deputy Commanding General for Reserve Forces. This person had the mission of coordinating and supervising the CONARC General Staff in the development of plans and directives for Reserve Component programs in the Zone of Interior Armies. Then on November 1, 1956, the Office of the Assistant Chief of Staff for Reserve components was established at the DA Staff level.[55]

CONGRESSIONAL INTERVENTION

The Eisenhower years were in many ways a time of tremendous growth for the Army Reserve, but in most instances the progress of the USAR was achieved despite the President's policies instead of because of them. In each year from 1958 through 1960 the Eisenhower administration put forth budget proposals calling for a 10 percent reduction in the paid drill strength of both the Army Reserve and the Army National Guard. The first of these proposed reductions was announced on March 31, 1958, by Army Secretary Wilber M. Brucker, who coupled the reductions to the Pentomic structure conversion. Under this proposal the number of Army Reserve combat divisions would be reduced from 10 to 6 by converting 4 infantry divisions to training divisions. The National Guard under this proposal would drop from 27 divisions to 21.[56] Concurrently, the paid drill strength of the Army Reserve was to be reduced from 300,000 to

55. James E. Hewes, Jr., *From Root to McNamara: Army Organization and Administration, 1900–1963* (Washington: Center of Military History, United States Army, 1975), p. 400; *Semiannual Report of the Secretary of Defense, July 1 to December 31, 1956*, p. 12.

56. William F. Levantrosser, *Congress and the Citizen-Soldier: Legislative Policy-making for the Federal Armed Forces Reserve* (Columbus: Ohio State University press, 1967), p. 97; Department of Defense News Release, "Fact Sheet on Reorganization of U. S. Army Reserve Components," July 8, 1958, copy in Center of Military History files.

270,000, while the National Guard was to be reduced from 400,000 to 360,000.[57]

Congressional reaction to these plans was immediately unfavorable, and the outraged cries from the Congress caused the Department of Defense to back down quickly. "The Secretary of Defense has modified his previous guidance," said a DoD News Release, "so that the Army has been authorized to develop a plan looking toward the retention of the present 37 divisions in the Reserve Forces Structure . . . provided that this troop structure is maintained with no increase of cost or personnel beyond current programmed levels."[58] Under the "revised guidance," the Army Reserve would consist of 10 Pentomic infantry divisions, 13 training divisions, 2 maneuver area commands, and several hundred supporting companies. Simultaneously, the Army consolidated 46 military districts into 13 US Army Corps (Reserve) Headquarters.[59]

Additional Eisenhower administration attempts to reduce the Army Reserve's budget and paid drill strength in 1959 and 1960 met with similar opposition in the Congress. The primary impetus for cutting the budget of the USAR seems to have come from the Department of Defense level, and not from the Department of the Army. Congressional lobbyists for the Reserve Officers Association attempted in both the House and the Senate to put into the DoD appropriations bill language placing a floor on paid drill strength for the Army Reserve. The move was unsuccessful in the House, but Strom Thurmond was able to accomplish this maneuver on the floor of the Senate. As a result, funds for both the Army Reserve and the National Guard were increased, and a minimum paid drill strength was established.[60]

President Eisenhower was not pleased with this turn of events, which he labeled "an unprecedented departure from past policy." Though he was technically correct, the President was not apparently willing to admit that this latest action on the part of Congress was simply the next logical step in the progression of Congressional oversight of the Reserve Components.[61]

---

57. *Annual Report of the Secretary of Defense, July 1, 1959, to June 30, 1960* (Washington: GPO, 1961), pp. 100, 62.

58. *Ibid.*

59. *Annual Report of the Secretary of Defense, July 1, 1958, to June 30, 1959* (Washington: GPO, 1960), p. 57.

60. Levantrosser, *Congress and the Citizen Soldier*, pp. 110–11.

61. *Ibid.*, pp. 111, 98.

What the President did not realize—or perhaps did not plan for—was that the Army Reserve had developed into a potent political force and that the Reserve Officers Association had honed its political clout with the Congress. The Executive branch had on many occasions surrendered to Congress the initiative on the National Guard's budget, and by the 1950's the same thing was happening with respect to the Army Reserve.[62]

CONCLUSION

The entire Eisenhower era was one of tremendous importance to the Army Reserve. Largely because of the influence and leadership of the Congress, the Army Reserve was strengthened immeasurably by the Reserve Officer Personnel Act of 1954 and the Reserve Forces Act of 1955. Reserve officers finally had a statutory guarantee of promotion consideration paralleling that of the Regulars, and the Army Reserve was provided with a dependable source of manpower for as long as the draft was in operation.

President Eisenhower, though a distinguished soldier and verbal supporter of the reserve components, was overcome by his own fiscal conservatism. The reserves were a convenient concomitant of this conservatism because they were cheaper than active forces, but when he turned to a policy of massive retaliation to the near-exclusion of all other levels of deterrence, the reserves, as well as the active forces, were a logical and convenient place to reduce. That he failed in his efforts to reduce the reserves was not so much a measure of his weakness or lack of resolve as they were an indication of the increasing role of the Congress. The Army Reserve was getting stronger in every way, and the Kennedy and Johnson eras would provide it with the opportunities to demonstrate whether it was a paper tiger or a responsive, effective part of this country's defense.

62. For a good discussion of this entire period see *Ibid.*, pp. 97–124, *passim*.

7

The Berlin Mobilization

The 1960's were a decade of major accomplishments for the Army Reserve. More than 60,000 Army Reservists were called to active duty for the 1961 Berlin Crisis in what has generally been termed the most efficient American mobilization up to that time,[1] and nearly 6,000 Army Reservists were mobilized for Vietnam in 1968.

The Berlin Crisis, which lasted roughly from June 1961 to June 1962, occurred at a time when American defense policy was undergoing a fundamental change. The 1950's strategy of massive retaliation had been severely criticized by Gen. Maxwell D. Taylor in his 1960 book *The Uncertain Trumpet*, and Presidential hopeful John F. Kennedy adopted Taylor's thesis of flexible response as a major campaign issue.

Kennedy campaigned hard upon the theme that the Eisenhower Administration had neglected national defense by placing undue reliance upon massive retaliation. Shortly after assuming office, Kennedy set the theme for his administration when he directed Secretary of Defense Robert S. McNamara to reorganize the Defense Department to create a more flexible deterrent.

Early on, McNamara concluded that the Army's Reserve Components were improperly structured and burdened with hundreds of unnecessary units. His conclusions led him to propose a succession of reorganization plans for the Army Reserve, plans that met considerable opposition within and without the Congress.

---

1. *Department of Defense Annual Report, 1962*, p. 66.

Nevertheless, McNamara won a partial victory. The Army Reserve was reorganized along the Army Reserve Command (ARCOM) structure found today, and major changes were made in the force structure. For the first time, Reserve requirements were tied directly to contingency plans,[2] and equipment and manning levels were increased for Army Reserve units. The groundwork was thus laid for the "Total Army" concept of the 1970's.

Army Reserve units were deliberately understrength, based upon the planning assumption that three-quarters of all Reserve Component divisions would have six months or more to build up and train after mobilization.[3] The 10 Army Reserve infantry divisions were manned at 53 to 60 percent of combat strength, and the 4,353 company-sized units of the Army Reserve were manned at 53 percent or less, even though the majority of them would be needed in the early stages of mobilization.[4]

Across the board, Army Reserve units were equipped at less than 50 percent of full combat requirements, and the equipment that was available was generally obsolete material of Korean War or even World War II vintage.[5] Readiness was further hampered by a shortage of full-time employees, and the Army Reserve had only one-third of its required 1,103 reserve centers.[6]

Even so, Maj. Gen. Frederick M. Warren, the Chief, Army Reserve and ROTC Affairs, testified before Congress on May 10, 1960, that the Army Reserve was at its highest state of readiness ever and was basically sound and ready to complement existing ground forces. In less than 18 months, the accuracy of Warren's testimony was tested in the Berlin Crisis call-up.

---

2. On page 114 of his 1968 testimony before the Senate Armed Services Committee regarding the 1969 Defense budget, McNamara stated that for the first time the materiel and personnel requirements of the reserve components necessary to support contingency plans had been included in Defense programs. Also, units for which no military requirement existed in contingency plans had been eliminated and other units which were needed had been added to the force structure.

3. Karl Cocke, *The Reserve Components*, undated manuscript, Center of Military History, p. VIII–4.

4. Maj. Gen. Frederick M. Warren, Posture Statement Presentation before House Armed Services Committee, May 10, 1960. Copy in OCAR Historical File.

5. *Annual Report of the Reserve Forces Policy Board*, June 30, 1961, p. 4.

6. *Annual Historical Supplement*, Office of the Chief U.S. Army Reserve and ROTC Affairs, 1960, pp. 13, 28.

BACKGROUND OF THE CRISIS

The Berlin Crisis was not an isolated incident, but was instead part of a challenge to the position of the United States as a world power.[7] Since World War II, US-Soviet relations had been tense; and the Kennedy Administration came to office during a period of wary maneuvering for advantage.[8] By 1961, recent Soviet space successes had bolstered Soviet confidence, and US failure to support the Cuban Freedom Fighters following their Bay of Pigs landing on April 17, 1961, cast doubt upon the willingness of the United States to employ arms against communist forces.

These circumstances tempted Soviet Premier Nikita S. Khrushchev to pressure the United States to accept a longstanding Soviet proposal for turning Berlin into a "free city." The city had remained under Four Power control following World War II, and the Western sector of Berlin under French, British and US rule had become an island of democracy in East Germany. This island was a haven for refugees fleeing from East Germany and had thereby become an uncomfortable thorn in the sides of the Soviet Union and its allies.

Meeting with Kennedy in Vienna, Austria, on June 3 and 4, Khrushchev told the President that the status of Berlin would be resolved during 1961 with or without the cooperation of the United States. Khrushchev's remarks to Kennedy included a clear implication that the Soviets were prepared to employ military force to achieve their end.[9]

Kennedy was unprepared to give in to such an ultimatum. He had come to office pledging to strengthen American military power to the point where no aggressor would dare challenge US interests. On May 25, he had delivered an address on "Urgent National Needs" to Congress and requested a Defense budget increase of $237 million to expand America's conventional war capability. Kennedy had also directed a realignment of active and reserve forces to improve responsiveness and combat readiness. The Khrushchev ultimatum stimulated an urgent review of American military capabilities in Europe.

7. Henry L. Trewhitt, *McNamara* (New York: Harper and Row, 1971), p. 101.

8. Robert W. Coakley, *et al.*, *U.S. Army Expansion, 1961–62*, undated manuscript, Center of Military History, p. I–11.

9. Richard P. Stebbins, *The United States in World Affairs, 1961* (New York: Harper and Brothers, 1962), pp. 22, 35, 37–38.

On June 27, McNamara requested a Joint Chiefs of Staff study to improve the force structure under conditions of a partial mobilization. His guidance was that the active services were to be increased by approximately 500,000 men, with initial emphasis placed upon the use of Ready Reserve personnel and Reserve Component units.

On July 6, the Joint Chiefs of Staff recommended a declaration of national emergency and a mobilization of 559,000 men. The active forces were to be increased by four divisions, and Reserve combat support units were to be mobilized to provide a logistics back-up to the Active Army.[10] Two days later, Khrushchev asserted that the bellicose attitude of the United States over Berlin was forcing the Soviet Union to increase its military expenditures.[11] By July 12, the Joint Chiefs of Staff recommendations had been pared down to a mobilization of 285,500 men, and on July 19 the President decided on a more limited call-up without the declaration of national emergency. The plan was to send six additional divisions to Europe from the stateside strategic reserve by early 1962 while ordering a partial mobilization to reconstitute the depleted strategic reserve.[12]

With his basic plan decided, Kennedy appealed to the nation in a special televised address on the evening of July 25. Citing Khrushchev's grim warnings about the future of the world, Kennedy asserted that "the immediate threat to free men is in West Berlin." He reminded the American people that the fortunes of war and diplomacy had left West Berlin an island of free people 110 miles behind the Iron Curtain and that the United States had a basic right to be in Berlin as a result of victory over NAZI Germany. As 50 million Americans watched, Kennedy called West Berlin the "great testing place of Western courage" and asked for sacrifice on the part of all citizens. He firmly announced his intention to fight over Berlin if necessary.[13]

MOBILIZING THE RESERVES

The next day, Kennedy requested Congressional authority to order to active duty up to 250,000 Ready Reservists—units and individuals. The Congress responded quickly, and Public Law 87–117 was enacted on August 1 by a vote 403 to

10. Coakley, *U.S. Army Expansion 1961–62*, pp. II–1 through II–4.

11. Stebbins, *United States in World Affairs, 1961*, p. 40.

12. Coakley, *U.S. Army Expansion, 1961–62*.

13. *New York Times*, July 26, 1961, p. 10.

2 in the House and 75 to 0 in the Senate. The authority was in effect until July 1, 1962, and allowed the President to call the Reservists to duty for up to 12 months. The President could also extend all terms of active military service.

On August 13, communist forces sealed the borders to West Berlin, halting the flow of refugees which had reached thousands a day. As construction on the Berlin Wall started, there was a renewed sense of urgency in the Pentagon. McNamara pushed for an earlier reinforcement of Europe, and on August 15, he accepted the idea of sending regular units to Europe while replacing them stateside with Reserve units.[14]

The next day, the Army alerted 113 Guard and Reserve units for possible active duty and extended 84,000 active duty enlisted men beyond their normal release date. Secretary of the Army Elvis J. Stahr, Jr. then announced a 12-month extension for Reserve officers presently on active duty for six-month training tours. Ready Reserve obligations were also extended for one year. In all, a dozen measures were taken to allow the United States to reinforce its units in Europe while doubling from three to six the number of combat-ready divisions in the Strategic Reserve of the stateside active forces.[15]

On August 23, the Army staff proposed calling 46,519 Reserve Component soldiers to active duty—the 23,626 in the units previously alerted, 4,396 members of the USAR's 100th Training Division who would open a training center at Fort Polk, La., and 18,497 soldiers to man non-divisional units for the Strategic Reserve Army Forces (STRAF). McNamara obtained Kennedy's approval and on August 25 announced a call-up of 210 units, including the 100th Training Division. All except the 100th were to report for duty on October 1. The 100th was ordered into service on September 25.[16]

Intensified combat readiness training was ordered for 479 units of the Army National Guard and Army Reserve on September 6, with four Guard divisions and 146 smaller units being told to add another weekend drill to their monthly training schedules. These units were alerted for possible call-up. Meanwhile, Stahr told an Association of the

---

14. Coakley, *U.S. Army Expansion, 1961–62*, p. II–27.
15. Press Release 57, Army News Service, August 17, 1961.
16. Coakley, *U.S. Army Expansion, 1961–62*, p. II–37.

US Army convention that the build-up would soon permit reinforcement of Army units in Europe.[17]

In less than two weeks, the warning order had become an active duty call as the Army told two National Guard divisions—the 32nd Infantry Division from Wisconsin and the 49th Armored Division from Texas—and 248 non-divisional Reserve Component units to report by October 15. The 49th was sent to Fort Polk, which in turn forced the 100th Training Division to mobilize at Fort Chaffee, Ark., and establish a new training center there. The 4009th US Army Garrison was told to help the 100th get ready for its first shipment of 1,000 trainees on October 17. The 100th Training Division's mission was to turn out 60,000 new soldiers over the next year.[18]

Morale appeared to be high among the recalled Reservists. According the the *New York Times,* attitudes ranged from a patriotic sense of duty to eagerness to engage the Russians, the latter feeling personified by Sgt. Nikolai Klinkowski. Klinkowski, a member of New York's Company B, 101st Signal Battalion, was a 25-year-old refugee from communist-controlled Poland, and he wanted very much to "go right now, fight right now and even die right now" to free his country.[19]

A week later, the *Times* reported that a Yankee Stadium souvenir vendor, PFC Marvin Belsky would be losing a small fortune—$35 to $50 a day—by missing the World Series. In Belsky's words, he was now earning peanuts—$99.10 a month—instead of selling them. Other members of the Bronx, N.Y., 920th Transportation Company gave the call-up mixed reviews.[20]

PROBLEMS OF THE CALL-UP

Most reserve units reported to active duty without all of the equipment authorized by their Tables of Organization and Equipment (TOE). This was due in part to the reduced allowances authorized for training purposes. More importantly,

17. *New York Times*, Sept. 7, 1961, p. 1.

18. *Army Information Digest*, July 1962, pp. 2–14. The 100th Training Division was warmly praised by the Army leadership for doing an outstanding job. Special mention is made of the 100th in 1961 and 1962 annual historical supplements, and Chief of Staff Gen. George H. Decker made special mention of the 100th as well as the 301st Logistical Command in a March 1962 article in *Officer* magazine.

19. *New York Times*, Sept. 24, 1961, p. VI–32.

20. *New York Times*, Oct. 2, 1961, p. 16.

many items were in short supply nationally, highlighting the common complaint that the Army had been neglected during the later Eisenhower years.

For years, austere funding had not kept pace with the consumption of Army equipment through wearout and obsolescence. For four of the six years prior to 1961, the appropriation for Army materiel did not cover day-to-day losses and likewise failed to provide for modernization. Consequently, by June 30, 1961, the materiel readiness of the Army was substantially below that required for a modern, combat-ready force.[21]

In addition, much of the equipment on hand was approaching the end of its useful military life and was of little value except in training new soldiers. The unsatisfactory situation was made worse by the fact that Operation and Maintenance (OMA) appropriations had been constrained in the 1950's, leading to an impressive maintenance and rebuild backlog. The result was that the Army entered the Berlin build-up handicapped by past neglect and forced to take expedient measures.

Among the measures quickly adopted by the Army was to withdraw equipment from those Army Reserve units not mobilized. Mobilized units did receive additional equipment to aid in training, but the bulk of the equipment efforts were directed toward Europe in support of the planned build-up there.[22]

Equipment was not the only problem. Guard and Reserve units were deliberately undermanned and required the recall of some 38,827 individual Reservists to bring them to full strength. Of these, 15,734 were sent to the 444 mobilized Army Reserve units, and 23,053 filled out Army National Guard units.[23]

The selection and call-up of individual Reservists was not fully satisfactory either. According to McNamara, "The lack of adequate information on the status of individual Reservists recalled as 'fillers' and the urgent requirement for men with special skills requiring long training combined to produce some inequities and some misassignments."[24] The Army was in the midst of a changeover from manual to

---

21. Coakley, *U.S. Army Expansion, 1961–62*, pp. VII–1 and VII–2.

22. *Ibid.*, pp. VII–2 through VII–4.

23. *Summary of Major Events and Problems*, Office of the Chief, Army Reserve and ROTC Affairs, 1 July 1961 to 30 June 1962, p. I–2.

24. *Department of Defense Annual Report, 1962*, p. 22.

machine-processed Reserve personnel records, and the recently reorganized command structure for the Army Reserve magnified the problems associated with a rapid call-up of individuals.[25] The objective of the call-up was to produce additional operational units as quickly as possible. Although the lack of equipment and the infusion of filler personnel delayed the start of training in some cases, Reserve units began an intensified, five-phased training program.

Phase One, lasting three weeks, was devoted to a general shakedown, receipt of filler personnel, and cadre training. During the next two-week phase, units concentrated on squad, section and crew training. Weeks six and seven, comprising Phase Three, were for small unit and team training. The fourth phase, weeks eight through ten, covered platoon and company training, essentially basic unit training. The final phase lasted another three weeks. This was for battalion, battle group and division field exercises. Units also participated in command post and logistical exercises.[26]

The last of the 68,883 Army Reservists mobilized for the crisis had hardly been on duty two weeks when McNamara gave indications that additional recalls would not be necessary. In a November 17 press conference, McNamara expressed confidence in the build-up and said that 300,000 men had been added to the armed forces in recent months while 45,000 had been sent to Europe to reinforce combat units there. He said that the build-up was ahead of schedule and that there was no need to call additional Reservists.[27]

DISCONTENT AMONG RESERVISTS

This announcement cheered those Reservists alerted for additional recalls, but it did little for the rapidly growing mood of discontent among some mobilized Reservists. The honeymoon of the first few weeks was coming to a close, and by the end of November the press was questioning Kennedy about the rumors of discontent and low morale among Reservists.

Kennedy responded that the stories were "wholly wrong" and that it should be clearly explained to all Reservists that they were performing valuable service. Kennedy

25. Irving Heymont, *Review and Analysis of Recent Mobilization, U.S. Reserve Components* (General Research Corporation, 1972), pp. 4–5.
26. *Summary of Major Events and Problems*, p. I–3.
27. *New York Times*, Nov. 18, 1961, p. 1.

added that he intended to release the Reservists from active duty as soon as possible.[28]

Four days later, the front page of the *New York Times* proclaimed "Why Us?". It appears that Kennedy's effort to explain to Reservists why they were in uniform again had about the same effect as a peashooter on a tank.

Aside from classic gripes about food and housekeeping details, Reservists were questioning the call-up procedures. Some, called as individual fillers, wanted to know why they were recalled when men who had never served were not being drafted. Others complained about a lack of work; and one young man, SP5 Willard M. Miller, wrote a letter of complaint to the Boston *Herald,* receiving an Article 15 (non-judicial punishment) for being so bold as to complain about being recalled from his college classes. He had violated a standing order about writing for publication without prior approval, and he also stirred up quite a bit of controversy.[29]

Army Secretary Stahr immediately cancelled Miller's punishment of two weeks' restriction and extra duty, but the Secretary had to answer to the Pentagon press corps. Stahr called a December 4 news conference to explain the Miller situation and to counter the impression fostered by newspaper articles that the Army had received a landslide of complaints from Reservists and National Guardsmen. Stahr explained that the regulation was misapplied to Miller and was meant to cover speeches and articles, not letters to editors. He also said that letters of complaint represented less than one percent of the Reserve Component soldiers recalled, which was about the normal complaint rate for the Active Army.[30]

In his prepared statement, Stahr said that "It is recognized that many individual reservists were not happy to leave families and civilian pursuits and opportunities for military service. However, the individual obligor and volunteer, with rare exception, had accepted the call of his country and has displayed admirable spirit, willingness and 'can do' attitude."

While admitting to equipment shortages and problems in identifying individual replacements, Stahr said that the call-up had proven that the Reserve system would work and work very well. He referred to a special investigation made

28. Transcript of Nov. 29, 1961, news conference as reported in the *New York Times*, Nov. 30, 1961, p. 14.

29. *New York Times*, Dec. 4, 1961, pp. 1 and 19.

30. *New York Times*, Dec. 5, 1961, pp. 1 and 29.

by Gen. James A. Van Fleet on behalf of the Chief of Staff. Van Fleet reported that the spirit of the citizen-soldier was truly magnificent and reflected the readiness of America to answer the call of the President. In short, Stahr concluded that the 1961 call-up was "far superior to any previous mobilization in this country."[31]

Stahr's opinion was seconded by seasoned journalist Hanson W. Baldwin, who called many of the complaints "cry-baby" and recalled the far more serious problems of the Korean War when many who fought in Korea had undergone the "double jeopardy" of serving in two hot wars. The inconveniences of a cold war were minor by comparison.[32]

Nevertheless, in a move to reduce complaints from the field, the Army issued on December 15 a pamphlet entitled "Why Me." More than two months after recalling Reservists to active duty, the Army finally explained to the troops that a call-up was the only way to immediately increase strength and that larger draft calls would not provide the needed strength in time. In general, the pamphlet answered the most serious questions on Reservists' minds, but it did not end the controversy surrounding some aspects of the call-up.[33]

MCNAMARA AND THE ROA

The issues of mobilization and recall had become entangled in a debate over the future of the Army's Reserve Components. Early in his administration, Kennedy had directed McNamara to reorganize the Defense Department to maximize capabilities while increasing flexibility. This reorganization naturally affected the Reserve Components when McNamara concluded that "not only did the reserve structure make very little sense in terms of size, [but that] its mission was obscure to say the least."

McNamara wanted the reserve components to be ready to replenish the strategic reserve in a timely manner, and he set about to reorganize the Reserves with this thought in mind.[34] The serious discussion of alternative Army National

31. Secretary Stahr's remarks are reported in *Army News Service* Release, No. 100, dated Dec. 5, 1961.

32. *New York Times*, Dec. 5, 1961, p. 8.

33. The text of the pamphlet is contained in *Army News Service* Release, No. 107, dated Dec. 15, 1961, as well as several major newspapers.

34. William W. Kaufman, *The McNamara Strategy* (New York: Harper and Row, 1964), p. 65.

Guard and Army Reserve force structures was underway when the Berlin Crisis overwhelmed all other planning. The crisis and subsequent mobilization put reorganization plans on hold, but in some quarters any discussion of the 1961 mobilization was inextricably linked with the threat of Reserve reorganization.[35]

The matter was made worse by the perception within the Reserve Officers Association (ROA) that McNamara had deliberately failed to defend Reserve Component honor against criticism in the press. The organization's membership also concluded that the Pentagon hierarchy didn't know very much about its Reserve Components.[36] On December 21, these smoldering feelings broke into the open when the ROA accused McNamara of "a national libel" against the Reserves. The Association charged that McNamara had failed to heed Congressional advice on how to carry out a mobilization.[37]

The ROA claimed that "there is no secret about the desire on the part of some authorities in the Defense Department to undermine and eliminate from the National Defense complex the Reserve programs . . . . [This has been] reflected in the continuing efforts during the post-Korea period to substantially reduce—and actually to phase out over a period of several years—the Reserve Forces."[38]

It would be difficult to fully substantiate the ROA charges, but the Association's outburst stimulated Congressional interest in the 1961 mobilization. Subsequently, Rep. Carl Vinson (D–Ga.), Chairman of the House Armed Services Committee, directed Rep. F. Edward Hebert (D–La.), to head a comprehensive inquiry into the defense posture of the Reserve Components. Vinson wrote Hebert that the "desirability of such an inquiry was significantly heightened by the recent partial mobilization of Reserve Components under PL 97–117."[39]

The newspaper reports of poor use of Reservists and the accusations by the ROA coincided with demobilization plan-

35. The McNamara reorganization plans will be discussed in detail in the next chapter.

36. John T. Carlton and John F. Slinkman, *The ROA Story: A Chronicle of the First 60 Years of the Reserve Officers Association of the United States* (Washington: ROA, 1982), pp. 455–62.

37. *New York Times*, Dec. 22, 1961, p. 1. Additional details are also found in the *Army-Navy-Air Force Register*, Jan. 13, 1962, pp. 14–15, and the *Officer*, Feb. 1962, Vol. 38, pp. 12–13.

38. *Army-Navy-Air Force Register, op. cit.*

39. Letter, Vinson to Hebert, reprinted in *Military Reserve Posture*, House Committee on Armed Services, Aug. 17, 1962.

ning and served to make the national leadership sensitive to the public relations impact of demobilization.[40]

DEMOBILIZATION

Once the Reservists had been called to active duty, the balance of staff planning actions for the call-up shifted from the problem of getting Reservists into uniform to that of returning them to civilian status. As early as the first week of December, the Army Deputy Chief of Staff for Operations (DCSOPS) proposed releasing some individual fillers by January 6, 1962, with a proposed release schedule for mobilized Army Reserve units later in the month. The two Army National Guard divisions would be released in March and May.

On December 28 and 29, the Army proposed releasing 32 units with 7,426 personnel because they could not be used effectively, mainly because of equipment shortages. Emphasis was placed upon having enough time to develop an effective public relations plan to explain the demobilization.

The President was reluctant to release units until two new active Army divisions could be organized and trained, and McNamara was unwilling to accept shortages of equipment, lack of useful mission or long lead-time training requirements as reasons to release Reserve units. It would be difficult to explain why the units had been mobilized if they had no mission or could not be trained.[41]

Later, potentially adverse public reaction and the unpredictable reaction of Reservists themselves influenced a decision not to deploy Reserve units overseas. When the rumblings of discontent by some Reservists continued, Army Chief of Staff Gen. George H. Decker recommended on March 2 that overseas deployment of the Reserve Components should not be considered unless there were overriding changes in the situation.[42]

---

40. This particular aspect of demobilization planning is covered in historical context in DA Pamphlet 20–210, *History of Personnel Demobilization in the United States Army* and is cited in Marvin A. Kreidberg and Merton G. Henry, *History of Military Mobilization in the United States Army, 1775–1945* (Washington: Dept. of the Army, 1955), p. 377.

41. Coakley, *U.S. Army Expansion, 1961–62*, pp. VIII–67 through VIII–81.

42. Memorandum, Decker to Under Secretary of the Army, March 2, 1962, Subject: "Overseas Utilization of RC Units/Personnel."

Decker took the discontent seriously. Artillerymen at Fort Bragg, NC, had boycotted their mess hall March 1–4 demanding an early release. Approximately 30 wives had demonstrated in front of the main gate of Fort Devens, Mass., calling for their husbands' release; and members of the 49th Armored Division at Fort Polk, La., had held a two-hour demonstration on March 5.

On March 13, Decker sent a message to the field emphasizing that commanders down to the company and battery level must fully explain the problems facing the United States and emphasize the need to retain Guardsmen and Reservists on active duty. In part, Decker stated that the United States was in a very real sense at war and that the threat against Berlin had not disappeared.[43]

The memo was made public on March 21, and on March 22, Kennedy told a news conference that he would release Reserve Component soldiers "at the first possible date consistent with national security." He noted that the two new Regular Army divisions intended to replace the Army National Guard divisions would be ready in August or September.[44]

By early April, McNamara was ready to release Reserve units as the US military posture improved. On April 6, he proposed to the President that the Reserve Components should be released about August 1 and that a minor degree of risk could be accepted while the two new divisions achieved full combat capability.

Kennedy agreed. His decision was made public on April 12.[45] The next step was to plan the release.

Detailed demobilization instructions were issued by Department of the Army and supplemented by a Continental Army Command (CONARC) letter of instruction. Units could be released from readiness mission as early as July 15, but none could depart for home until August 1. All units had to leave their mobilization station by August 11, and all mobilized Reservists had to return to civilian status by August 31.

The demobilization was not accomplished very smoothly. For example, Army Reserve garrison commands had to outprocess other Reserve Component units while try-

43. Coakley, *U.S. Army Expansion, 1961–62*, pp. VIII–81 through VIII–83.

44. *Army News Service*, Release No. 25, March 22, 1962.

45. *Army News Service*, Release No. 30, April 12, 1962.

ing to clear post themselves.[46] Also, as the Reserve units were released, critical items of equipment such as generators, trucks and communications equipment had to be turned in before departure for home station.[47]

ANALYSES OF THE MOBILIZATION

The last Reservist had barely left for home when the first official post-mortem of the 1961 mobilization was published. For months, the Hebert subcommittee had been delving into the problems and accomplishments of the call-up. On August 17, the subcommittee made its findings public, and these findings were not very complimentary.

The subcommittee zeroed in on the chronic problems of the Reserve Components—not enough equipment, not enough men and not enough training. The Army was scored for allowing Reserve policy matters to "rock and stumble along without any imaginative or aggressive effort to resolve them."[48]

However, the subcommittee saved its greatest concern for the Army's lack of information about the Reserve Components. Specifically, "for reasons the subcommittee was unable to ascertain, the Department of the Army did not have available to it records and reports which should have reflected the essential facts relating to the readiness of Reserve units".[49] Additionally, the Congressmen pointed out that the "military departments had not prepared contingency plans which contemplated a partial mobilization and hence were unable to properly select units for recall."[50] This was a major lesson that the Army should have learned from the confused Korean War mobilization.

The lack of knowledge and inability to partially mobilize was highlighted by the problems faced by the individual Ready Reserve members who had to fill out the understrength Guard and Reserve units. The overwhelming majority of these Reservists were veterans who the Army said had "hard skills" not found in the Reserve units. Nevertheless, the subcommittee estimated that less than half of these for-

---

46. Fifth US Army, after-action report: Subject: "Release of Reserve Component Units."

47. Coakley, *U.S. Army Expansion, 1961–62*, p. VIII–92.

48. *Report of Subcommittee No. 3 on Military Posture*, p. 6640.

49. *Ibid.*, p. 6657.

50. *Ibid.*

mer Active Army soldiers served in their primary Military Occupation Specialty (MOS) during the call-up. Clearly, in the subcommittee's opinion, the Army didn't know whom to recall and where to send them once they were recalled.

The Defense Department seconded the subcommittee's findings when McNamara wrote in his 1962 Annual Report that "equipment shortages existed in many units and had to be met by redistribution from other Army assets. The assigned personnel strengths of the recalled units averaged 70 percent of full active duty strength, making it necessary to fill existing vacancies with individual reservists".[51]

McNamara promised to prevent future inequities and misassignment of individual Reservists and asked for increased procurement in his 1962 and 1963 budgets to improve Army Reserve readiness. He also promised to raise the authorized manning level of Reserve units and stated his intent to match units with current contingency plans.

In summary, he said that the recall of Reservists during the summer of 1961 made it possible to meet urgent readiness requirements. Despite their problems, "Army Reserve units and individuals were in a higher state of readiness than ever before."[52] McNamara's conclusion begs the question: Did the mobilization of 1961 achieve its purpose?

CONCLUSION

The 1961 mobilization was a demonstration of national will (or more likely, a demonstration of Presidential will) and was intended to prevent a war rather than fight one. Because the Berlin Crisis did not deteriorate into a hot war and because Berlin was saved as a democratic symbol in the heart of East Germany, the mobilization has to be rated as a qualified success.

On the other hand, the active forces were not much strengthened by the call-up. In his contemporary *SECRET* report, Robert W. Coakley concluded that the mobilization bought time for the Army to add two divisions to its strategic reserve while increasing the number of combat ready divisions in the United States.[53]

---

51. *Department of Defense Annual Report, 1962*, pp. 22–23.
52. *Ibid.*
53. Coakley, *U.S. Army Expansion, 1961–62*, pp. VIII–199 through VIII–200.

In 1972, a Research Analysis Corporation study concluded that the mobilization had achieved its purpose but that the greatest failings were severe weakness in the management of the individual Reservists and the lack of planning for partial mobilization. The study argued that the Reserve system in effect in 1961 was inadequate.[54]

McNamara had made the same argument in 1961 when he first proposed a revamping of the Army's Reserve Components. The Berlin mobilization experience strengthened his resolve and placed him in direct conflict with the Congress and the professional associations of the Reserve Components. The battle over Reserve reorganization was ready to begin in earnest—a battle which did not end until 1967.

54. Heymont, *Review and Analysis*, pp. 4–10 and 4–11. Heymont's criticism of the Berlin mobilization is essentially the same as for the Korean War call-up. This opinion is also evident in the Hebert report as well as Coakley's analysis. A review of previous chapters in his work will show that the Berlin and Korean mobilizations suffered from nearly identical problems—haphazard recall of individuals, undermanned and underequipped units, lack of partial mobilization plans and the misuse of mobilized units. Essentially, if the Army had learned anything at all from the Korean effort, those lessons had yet to be effectively applied by the time of the Berlin mobilization nearly a decade later.

8

Reorganizations Lay the Groundwork for the Total Army Policy

For a full decade, from the announcement of the One Army concept in 1958 to the establishment of the two-star US Army Reserve Commands (ARCOMs) in 1968, the Army Reserve was in a constant state of turmoil and reorganization. As previously discussed, the USAR changed from the triangular division structure to the Pentomic structure to the ROAD structure.[1]

Likewise, it was a time for new strategic choices, with the massive retaliation policy of the Eisenhower era giving way to the Kennedy emphasis on counterinsurgency and limited, "brush fire" wars. More importantly, the national leadership recognized that the Reserve Components must be linked to specific contingency plans in order to be a cost-effective military asset.

To increase flexibility and reduce costs, the Army's Reserve Components were weaned from an outdated, inflexible, full-mobilization mission and given discrete responsibilities in support of specific war plans. However, this was not accomplished easily. Although the Kennedy administration was determined to streamline the Army Reserve, their efforts were initially blocked by a Congress jealously protecting its Defense prerogatives.

The reorganization tactics of Secretary of Defense Robert S. McNamara were heavy-handed and angered the Congress as well as the politically powerful Reserve Officers Association. The result was seven years of vicious in-fighting, during which the Army Reserve was left to muddle

---

1. See Chapter Six for a discussion of these changes.

along without firm guidance or clear prospects for the future.

A reasonable compromise was reached in 1967, and the Army's Reserve Components achieved a mix of units that has remained substantially unchanged into the 1980's. The reorganizations of the 1960's eliminated low-priority units from the Army Reserve and gave the Army Reserve a clearer role in national defense. The stage was thus set for the Total Force policy of the 1970's and 1980's.

As stated previously in Chapter Seven, Kennedy had campaigned upon the theme that the Eisenhower Administration had neglected national defense by placing undue reliance upon the nuclear strategy of massive retaliation. Like Truman before him, Eisenhower subordinated military needs to a conservative fiscal policy that placed first priority upon balancing the federal budget.

Because it was impossible to be ready for a wide range of conflicts and still balance the budget, the nuclear deterrent was given first priority as a cost-effective way of achieving more bang for the buck. Even so, the United States did retain a conventional, non-nuclear capability and was able to project its power when inclined to do so—such as during the 1958 intervention in Lebanon.

THE KENNEDY STRATEGY

What Kennedy did was to remove the fiscal strait jacket of the Truman and Eisenhower administrations. By placing defense needs ahead of a balanced budget, Kennedy allowed Defense planners to seek flexible solutions to potential threats.

In keeping with his desire to be able to respond to a wide range of threats, Kennedy directed McNamara to reappraise America's entire defense strategy. McNamara was told to develop the force structure necessary to meet foreign policy objectives without regard to budget ceilings. Once the force structure was decided upon, McNamara was told to produce it at the lowest practical cost.[2]

McNamara in turn emphasized America's ability to respond in the "gray areas" of the world—the Far East, Southeast Asia and Latin America. This emphasis led to the increased importance of conventional forces, with the Reserve Components being responsible for significantly augmenting

2. William W. Kaufmann, *The McNamara Strategy* (New York: Harper and Row, 1964), p. 47.

the Active Army. The Reserves were also to provide a base for large-scale mobilization in the event of general war.[3]

Consistent with its desire to strengthen conventional forces, the Kennedy administration moved swiftly to improve readiness by reorganizing the Reserve Components. The groundwork for the 1962 Army Reserve reorganization was laid in mid-May 1961 when the Assistant Secretary of Defense for Manpower, Personnel and Reserves, Carlisle P. Runge, directed the Secretary of the Army to submit a plan to streamline the Army's Reserve Components.

The Army was given ten days to propose a reorganization that would significantly improve the Reserves' responsiveness and combat readiness for conventional, limited-war contingencies. Runge imposed no restrictions on the composition or size of the Reserve force structure. However, an earlier review in March 1961 indicated a need for a total Army force of 42 divisions, with 14 or 15 divisions in the active Army.[4]

Based upon the March review, the Army proposed a reduction in the Reserve Component combat force from the existing 37 divisions to 29 divisions. While the number of divisions was being reduced, the manning levels for the remaining divisions and their support units were to be increased. The remaining divisions were to be reorganized along ROAD lines, and the amount of equipment procured for training would be increased. There would also be an increase in the number of technicians, and provisions were made for up to 100,000 men of the Ready Reserve Reinforcement Pool (today's Individual Ready Reserve) to receive two weeks of Annual Training a year.

Overall, the proposal would increase the Army's Reserve Component budget by 43 percent, to $1.1 billion in 1962. The intent was to have two high-priority Reserve divisions available for emergency combat operations on three-week's notice, with two more Reserve Component divisions available with five-weeks' notice. Six additional divisions and their support forces were to be ready to fight on eight-weeks' notice or less.

On May 22 and 23, this ten-division plan was presented to the General Staff Committees on Army National Guard and Army Reserve Policy (otherwise known as the Section 5 Committees, from their authorization by Section 5

---

3. *Ibid.*, pp. 97–98.

4. Karl Cocke, *The Reserve Components* (undated manuscript, Center of Military History), pp. VIII–3 through VIII–4.

of the 1920 amendments to the National Defense Act of 1916).[5] The Committees agreed with the plan in principle, and McNamara concurred on May 25.[6] That evening, Kennedy made a special address to Congress in which the ten-division plan was made public. Kennedy announced a complete reorganization of the Army's division structure to increase its non-nuclear firepower while improving flexibility and tactical mobility.

With regard to the Reserve Components, Kennedy said, "The Army is developing plans to make possible a much more rapid deployment of a major portion of its highly-trained reserve forces. When these plans are completed, and the reserve is strengthened, two combat-equipped divisions, plus their supporting forces, a total of 89,000 men, could be ready in an emergency for operations with but three weeks' notice." He explained that "these new plans will allow us to almost double the combat power of the Army in less than two months, compared to the nine months hithertofore required."[7]

Kennedy's statement was expanded upon on June 13 when the Army issued a fact sheet saying that a realignment of the Reserve Component structure was necessary to make the Reserve Components more responsive to strategic plans. Although the Army National Guard and the Army Reserve had achieved the best readiness posture in the peacetime history of the nation, the fact sheet said that it was necessary to close the gap between the readiness posture of active Army units and top-priority reserve units.[8]

On June 21, Secretary of the Army Elvis J. Stahr, Jr. explained the reorganization in an address to the 35th Annual Conference of the Reserve Officers Association (ROA) in San Antonio, Tex. Stahr, who was a former Reserve Officer and an ROA member, said that the Kennedy defense policy was geared to the belief that American forces were more likely to have to fight limited wars than a "no-holds-barred" global war.

Stahr emphasized that the Reserve Components would assume an increasingly important role in the 1960's. He illustrated his point by noting that the "forward strategy" of the United States placed seven Army divisions overseas—

5. 10 U.S.C. 3033.

6. Cocke, *Reserve Components,* pp.VIII–5 through VIII–8.

7. *New York Times,* May 26, 1961, p. 12.

8. Army News Service Fact Sheet, "Army Plan for Realignment of Reserve Component Structure," Release No. 40, June 13, 1961.

five in Europe and two in Korea. This left six active divisions in the United States, three—including the two airborne divisions—in the Strategic Army Corps, and three devoted to training new soldiers. The fourteenth Army division on active duty was split between Hawaii and Okinawa. According to Stahr, the three training divisions could not be deployed without the extensive use of Reserve Component combat and combat support units.

Beyond this augmentation role, the Reserve Components maintained seven divisions for strategic Army forces, and the Army Reserve itself had 10 divisions to meet the deployment requirements of a truly major war. In addition, the Army Reserve had 13 training divisions, for a total USAR force structure of 4,338 company-sized units and an average paid drill strength of approximately 300,000. In all, the reinforcement echelon of the Ready Reserve was 748,000 strong, with 330,000 of these men dedicated to bringing the active duty divisions to full strength.[9]

Stahr said that the Reserves were organized, trained and equipped on the assumption that units would have up to six months to be prepared for combat. However, this assumption was no longer valid as the United States and the Soviet Union moved toward conflict over Berlin. In Stahr's words, "in view of the critical world situation, it is imperative that measures be taken promptly to improve the deployment readiness posture of our Reserve Components and make them more responsive to strategic plans. The pace and nature of modern warfare require that reaction time be measured in weeks rather than months."[10]

Summarizing the argument for Reserve Component reorganization, Stahr said that "the proposed realignment of the Reserve Component structure was developed to meet a changed world situation. Unless such a realignment is accomplished, it is difficult to justify reliance on Reserve Forces, most of which could not be used until several months after an emergency arose."

The implication was that the Reserve Components had to reorganize in order to justify their existence. As Stahr put it, the Army staff was enthusiastic about the reorganization,

9. Strength figures cited in Stahr's text can be confirmed in *Summary of Major Events and Problems*, Office of the Chief, U.S. Army Reserve and ROTC Affairs, 1 July 1960, to 30 June 1961, pp. 12–16.

10. To place Stahr's remarks into perspective, the Vienna summit between Kennedy and Khrushchev was June 3 and 4. See the previous chapter for the details of increasing international tensions.

and it was up to the individual Reservists to assume an overriding personal responsibility to make it work.[11]

The groundwork had been laid for the first McNamara reorganization of the Reserve Components, but the reorganization did not occur because the Berlin Crisis, as described in the previous chapter, diverted attention from reorganization to partial mobilization. The crisis and mobilization also changed the Administration's attitude toward the Reserve Components.

The Berlin call-up had raised questions in the minds of President Kennedy and Secretary McNamara over the value of Reserve Components. Defense officials decided on September 22 to hold Reserve Component drill strength at 700,000, while reducing previously planned Reserve budget increases.[12] The reorganization plan had been through 19 revisions by November 1961,[13] and the Army staff had to make further revisions as DoD reduced the combined Guard and Reserve paid drill strength by 30,000, to 670,000. Finally, by mid-November, the action was shifted to the Office of the Assistant Secretary of Defense, Comptroller, where Dr. Merton J. Peck took the lead.

THE PECK PLAN

The resulting "Peck Plan" called for 670,000 Ready Reservists (Guard and Army Reserve) in a paid drill status—a 27 division force. Ten excess divisions would be reduced to operational headquarters. Six new ROAD combat brigades would be formed, and 100,000 members of the Ready Reserve Reinforcement Pool would receive two weeks' training annually. The plan also called for a 4,000-man increase in the number of Army Reserve technicians, a cost which was to be offset by converting 160,000 paid drill slots to 24 paid drills a year status, a decrease from the customary 48 paid drills.[14]

Before the Peck Plan could win final Administration approval, the *New York Times* reported on the plan to cut the Army's Reserve Components. Citing unhappy experiences with the Berlin call-up, the *Times* said that "the Pentagon

11. The Stahr address is quoted extensively in *The Army Reservist,* Sept.–Oct. 1961, pp. 3–6.

12. Cocke, *Reserve Components,* p.VIII–8.

13. *Ibid.,* p. VIII–9.

14. *Ibid.,* p. VIII–10.

has all but abandoned plans to place increased reliance upon the Reserve forces for emergency use."[15]

The *Times* article recalled the Eisenhower attempts to cut 70,000 slots from the combined Army Guard and Army Reserve strength, thus reducing the total to 630,000, and predicted that the latest idea to reduce the Army's Reserve Components would mean political trouble for the Administration. A key stumbling block was predicted to be a law which required the consent of a state's Governor before a National Guard unit could be transferred.

On December 14, Hanson W. Baldwin reported in the *New York Times* that Defense officials thought that expenditures for Reserve Forces were too high and that the existing troop basis was too large. Baldwin pointed out that Defense thinking had reversed itself since the Berlin Crisis. Prior to the Crisis, the idea was to increase Reserve Component strength while keeping the active Army strength steady.[16] Now, wrote Baldwin, the Army was going to increase its active force to 16 divisions, a gain of two divisions.[17]

On December 17, the *New York Times* quoted Deputy Defense Secretary Roswell L. Gilpatric as saying that the President had profound second thoughts about the call-up of Reservists. According to the *Times,* the move to reduce the strength of the Army's Reserves was caused by a reluctance to support sizeable reserve forces in an era of possible nuclear war. The argument was that hostilities might well be over before Reserve units could be brought into combat service.[18] On the other hand, the hostilities over the Army's Reserve Component reorganization were just beginning.

As was discussed in Chapter Seven, the Reserve Officers Association objected strenuously to McNamara's reorganization attempts.[19] It was evident that the issues of the Berlin call-up and the reorganization of the Army's Reserve Compo-

15. "Pentagon Maps Cut In Army's Reserves," *New York Times,* Dec. 3, 1961, pp. 1 and 11.

16. "Reserves Facing Ten-Division Cut," *New York Times,* Dec. 14, 1961, p. 1.

17. This is, of course, exactly what happened. The active Army was increased by two divisions during 1962, and the two mobilized Army National Guard divisions—the 32nd Infantry Division and the 49th Armored Division—were released from active duty along with all of the other mobilized Army Reserve Component units by Aug. 31, 1962.

18. "Fight Is Brewing On Reserve Role," *New York Times,* Dec. 17, 1961, p. 17.

19. "Reserve Officers Accuse Pentagon of Call-Up Libel," *New York Times,* Dec. 22, 1961, pp. 1 and 11.

nents were intertwined,[20] and on January 13, 1962, *The Army-Navy-Air Force Register* called for a "dispassionate survey of what has been gained or lost by the recent emergency call-up."[21]

The result of this call was the Hebert committee, also discussed in the preceding chapter. This subcommittee's August 17, 1962, report devoted most of its attention to the Peck reorganization plan which had eclipsed the readiness posture issue by the summer of 1962.

The General Staff Committees on Army National Guard and Army Reserve Policy, the Section 5 committees, were briefed on the Peck Plan on January 26, and they objected to it. The Section 5 committees endorsed a counterproposal calling for the retention of all 37 Reserve Component divisions and an increase in paid drill strength to 716,000—a net gain of 16,000 instead of the loss of 30,000 under Peck. The Reserve Forces Policy Board concurred with the Section 5 committees on February 1, 1962. Ignoring the proposals of these two statutory bodies charged with advising the Secretary of the Army and the Secretary of Defense, respectively, on reserve matters, the Army moved ahead with its realignment plans.[22]

On April 4, 1962, the Army announced its plans for Reserve Component realignment. These included reducing four National Guard and four Army Reserve divisions to headquarters status, with the simultaneous activation of eight brigades as non-divisional units. The brigades were to be formed under the ROAD concept using the personnel of the "realigned" divisions. At the same time, the top-priority Reserve Component divisions would be maintained at 75 to 80 percent of TOE strength as compared with 52 to 78 percent in the past.[23]

The realignment also cut 58,000 paid drill positions from the Army's Reserve Components, reducing them to a

---

20. Jonn T. Carlton and John F. Slinkman, *The ROA Story, A History of the Reserve Officers Association of the United States*, (Washington: ROA, 1982) pp. 456–63. This work sheds considerable light upon ROA attitudes during this period, but it is unfortunately without footnotes and frequently omits dates from its narrative.

21. "Reserve and Guard Hassle," *Army-Navy-Air Force Register*, Jan. 13, 1962, p. 14.

22. Cocke, *Reserve Components,* VIII–11 to VIII–13. An excellent contemporary explanation of the organization, responsibilities and authority of the Section 5 committees can be found in the Nov. 1963 issue of *Army Reservist,* pp. 8 & 9.

23. "Army Announces Plan for Reorganization of Reserve Components," *Army News Service,* Release No. 29, April 5, 1962.

total drill strength of 642,000—a level 28,000 below the 670,000-man force proposed in the Kennedy fiscal year 1963 budget.[24] The reduction would allow a savings of $53.1 million that year, according to testimony before the Hebert subcommittee on May 11.

In addition to the divisional realignment, the 1962 reorganization plan called for the modernization of non-divisional Reserve Component units. In the words of a May 21, 1962, press release, the reorganization was "the result of a thorough study of the actual needs of the Army." The goal was to make the Reserve Components "more responsive to the needs of the Army in the event of rapid mobilization."

Among the changes proposed were the elimination of 90 mm anti-aircraft gun battalions, air observation detachments, and special services companies, the latter being the units designed to provide entertainment and recreation programs for troops overseas. In turn, the reorganization proposed to add corps and army-level aviation companies, armored cavalry squadrons, and armored medical companies to the Reserve Components. There was also to be an increase in Nike-Hercules air defense battalions at the expense of the older Nike-Ajax units, an increase in self-propelled artillery, and a reduction in towed artillery.[25] In all, approximately 800 units would be eliminated from the Army's force structure.

REACTIONS TO THE PLAN

The reorganization plan was not well received outside of the Pentagon. According to one study, "The Army plan for realigning the Army National Guard and the Army Reserve received a cool reception on Capitol Hill, where it came under the close scrutiny of the Armed Service and Appropriations Committees of both the Senate and House of Repre-

---

24. "Pentagon Revamps Reserves: 58,000 Pay Spaces, 8 Divisions Go," *Armed Forces Register,* April 7, 1962, pp. 1 and 46.

25. "Fact Sheet on Reserve Realignment," *Army News Service,* Release No. 34, May 21, 1962. It should be noted that while some of these force structure decisions have stood the test of time, such as increasing the ratio of self-propelled artillery to towed artillery, the decision to abandon air defense guns in favor of complex missile systems can be faulted. Lessons learned from Vietnam combat showed that a combination of conventional air defense artillery and missile systems to be more effective against jet aircraft than either system alone. Also, the Army invested heavily in the Nike-Ajax and Nike-Hercules missile systems only to abandon stateside missile defense sites in the early 1970's.

sentatives." Congressional resistance forced a compromise on the number of ready reservists to be maintained in a paid status, and the fiscal year 1963 appropriations act established a paid drill strength of 700,000 for the Army Reserve Components.[26]

The Reserve Officers Association and the National Guard Association opposed the reorganization. Articles in *The National Guardsman* derided the idea that a 58,000 cut in strength could actually result in greater readiness,[27] and the Stackpole Company rushed into print a volume entitled *Reserve Forces and the Kennedy Strategy,* which plainly stated that it was impossible to grow stronger by cutting muscle. This book made the observation that "in any case, money is the key to more readiness. If we want a truly ready reserve, keyed to forseeable requirements of a strategy of freedom of action and adaptable either to general or limited emergencies, we are going to have to pay for it. More drill-pay spaces, more full-time technicians, higher schedules of annual drills, higher levels of equipment, speed-up of weapons procurement, an increased flow of six month trainees—all these things cost money."[28] All of these solutions have been applied with success since the advent of the Total Force policy in 1970, but McNamara was not prepared in 1962 to accept solutions that *increased* the cost of the Army's Reserve Components.[29]

More important than the opposition of the Reserve Component professional associations was the reluctance of state governors to accept any cutback in National Guard strength. In an attempt to win support for his reorganization plan, McNamara spoke before the July 2, 1962, National Governor's Conference at Hershey, Penn. McNamara stated that the revised structure would increase readiness by matching the Reserve Component structure to the "detailed, time-phased, unit requirements established by our military

26. Cocke, *Reserve Components,* pp. VIII–16 and VIII–17.

27. See "The Big Slice," *The National Guardsman,* May 1962, pp. 6–7 among others.

28. George F. Eliot, *Reserve Forces and the Kennedy Strategy,* (Harrisburg, Penn.: Stackpole Co., 1962), pp. 39–52 and 68–69.

29. For FY 1961, the Army Reserve's share of the Army's Total Obligation Authority (TOA) was 3.1 percent. McNamara reduced this share to 2.4 percent in 1964, 2.0 percent in 1966 and 1.6 percent for FY's 1967 and 1968. Under the later Total Force concept, the Army Reserve's share of the Army's TOA rose to 2.6 percent in 1971 and 2.8 percent in 1972 and then stabilized in the 3.2 to 3.5 percent range for the fiscal years 1973 through 1983.

planners." Even though 1,700 obsolete units would be eliminated, more than 1,000 other units would be added to the force structure. The result, McNamara promised the governors, would leave approximately the same dispersion of units as before the reorganization. He claimed that only 16 National Guard armories would lose all of their units and that the Guard would be left with 4041 units, which he contended was sufficient to meet state responsibilities.[30] McNamara did not succeed, however, in winning the state chief executives to his side, and their opposition was seconded by the August 17 report of the Hebert subcommittee.

The subcommittee came down four-square against the McNamara reorganization, finding it "difficult to comprehend how a reduction of 58,000 men in Reserve drilling units would result in an increased mobilization capability." The subcommittee unanimously opposed the Peck plan because it would lower morale, would not increase readiness, would hurt retention of trained enlisted personnel, and would offer no solution to the Reserve Component equipment shortages.[31] Unable to win Congressional or statehouse support, Defense planners went back to the drawing boards.[32]

By mid-November, a reorganization plan which retained a drill strength of 700,000 was developed, and on December 3, after a personal briefing, Hebert informed McNamara that the plan was acceptable. Although Defense spokesmen had denied as recently as November 30 that any concessions would be made on reorganization,[33] the Army announced that it would go ahead with a 700,000-man reorganization on December 4 and dropped any hint of reducing paid drill strength.[34]

Gov. Albert D. Rosellini of Washington, Chairman of the National Governor's Conference, immediately announced his opposition to the December 4 plan, while the Reserve Officers Association quickly withdrew its opposition. Not-

---

30. "Proposed Army Reserve Component Reorganization," *Speech File Service,* No. 7–2–62.

31. See report on "Military Reserve Posture," Aug. 17, 1962, (Washington: GPO), pp. 6644 and 6667–76.

32. The extent of the governors' opposition is chronicled on pages 3–5 of the Aug. 1962 issue of *The National Guardsman.* Additional details are found in the Oct. 1962 issue of *The National Guardsman.*

33. See *New York Times,* Nov. 30, 1962, p. 30.

34. "Army's Revision of Reserve Units and Guard Begins," *New York Times,* Dec. 5, 1962, pp. 1 and 25.

ing that the December plan contained many concessions to the positions maintained by Congress and the ROA, the association's spokesman, Col. John T. Carlton, summed up the ROA position by saying that "it's hard to be against proposals for modernization."[35]

COMPROMISE

The Pentagon immediately set about to convince Gov. Rosellini and several other governors who were still opposed to the December plan. By early January 1963, a Defense concession to convert Army National Guard divisions to the ROAD organization was apparently sufficient to obtain the necessary state-level support, and the reorganization moved ahead.

Approximately 1,850 company or detachment size units were dropped from the force structure, and approximately 1,000 new units added. This represented a 10 percent drop in the 8,807 unit structure of the Army's Reserve Components. The 700,000 drill strength—400,000 for Army National Guard and 300,000 for Army Reserve—was retained, while McNamara was able to drop four divisions each from the Guard and Reserve and replace them with separate brigades. Meanwhile, higher recruiting standards were set for the Reserve Components to bring them up to active Army levels. The civilian full-time technician force was expanded, and the manning levels for top-priority Reserve units were increased.[36]

McNamara did achieve his basic goal of bringing the Army's Reserve Components into closer alignment with mobilization requirements. The remaining 23 Army National Guard divisions and the six Army Reserve divisions were reorganized at higher levels of authorization, and the entire process was completed by May 1, 1963.[37] The important point is that the Army Reserve ended the 1963 fiscal year better able to support the new Kennedy strategy of flexible response. There was also increased emphasis upon the development of early-deploying Reserve forces in accordance with contingency plans.[38]

---

35. "Reserve Drop Fight on Revision," *New York Times,* Dec. 6, 1962, p. 25.
36. Cocke, *Reserve Components,* VIII–20; also, see *Army Reservist,* Jan. 1963, pp. 3–4.
37. "Army Reserve Components Complete Reorganization," *DOD News Release,* No. 665–63. May 10, 1963.
38. Cocke, *Reserve Components,* p. VIII–22.

Along with the reorganization, the Reserve Component priority system was changed to reflect a dichotomy within the force structure. Those units which would be needed promptly for reinforcing the active Army, deploying overseas or expanding the mobilization base were designated as Priority I and Priority II and were called the Immediate Reserve. The remaining Reserve units, Priority III, were needed for full mobilization and were identified as the Reinforcing Reserve. The Immediate Reserve met the requirements for rapid response and flexibility. The Reinforcing Reserve met the needs of a broad-based mobilization. In addition to dividing Reserve Component units into an Immediate and Reinforcing Reserve, the reorganization subdivided the Ready Reserve Mobilization Reinforcement Pool (RRMRP) of individual Ready Reservists.

The higher priority individual pool of the RRMRP was preassigned to the units of the Immediate Reserve—both Army National Guard and Army Reserve. The Army National Guard was given the authority to recruit volunteers for an Inactive National Guard, while the Priority III units of the Army Reserve were prohibited from recruiting men who had a Ready Reserve obligation. The idea was to channel obligated Reservists into the Immediate Reserve while staffing Reinforcement Reserve units with non-obligated volunteers. The result was to reduce the need for fillers in high-priority units. This would reduce one of the glaring problems of the Berlin mobilization when large numbers of filler personnel created problems for mobilized units.

REORGANIZATION AND REALIGNMENT

At the same time, the Army staff was being reorganized. The change having the greatest influence upon the Army Reserve was the creation on January 2, 1963, of the Office of Reserve Components. For the first time, the responsibility for policy, direction and the control of the Reserve Components was under a single three-star officer. The Chief, National Guard Bureau and the Chief, Army Reserve were placed under the general supervision of the Chief, Office of Reserve Components (CORC). This ended the situation where the Chief, National Guard Bureau was essentially independent while the Chief, Army Reserve was a relatively minor official on the Army staff.[39]

39. Details of the reorganization of the Immediate Reserve and the Reinforcing Reserve may be found in the *Annual Historical Supplement,*

ing levels with the force required. The 45-division requirement for waging general war could be ignored on the assumption that such a general war would require total mobilization on the level achieved for World War II. In such an all-out war, peacetime budget restraints would be abandoned, and the issue of Defense costs would become moot. This intellectual drill was nothing more nor less than balancing the benefits and costs of a limited war capability versus the risks and costs of an extensive conventional capability short of general war.

Although the risk analysis technique is routine today, it created considerable anxiety in 1964 when individuals refused to believe that there was ever justification for reducing the size of forces.[43] Realizing this, it is easier to understand why the December 12, 1964, proposal to reduce again the Army's Reserve Components raised so much furor—a situation which created much heat of controversy without shedding much light upon the problem.

The impetus for the 1964 proposals came when Secretary of the Army Stephen Ailes recommended to McNamara in July that consideration be given to "bringing manpower, equipment and war plans into consonance," and that a single management system be developed for the Reserve Components. Responding to McNamara's request to expand upon his recommendation, Ailes appointed a small group under Brig. Gen. Thomas A. Kenan on October 6, 1964, to find ways the Reserve Components could achieve better balance, readiness and management.[44]

MERGER PROPOSED

The Kenan committee studied the deficiencies of the Reserve Components, the costs of maintaining two separate Reserve systems, the impact reorganization would have upon the states, and the related political ramifications. Despite the

43. A consistent argument made by opponents of the reorganization and merger plans announced on Dec. 12, 1964, was that any reduction in forces automatically reduced America's defense capability. These individuals failed to see that maintenance of undeployable and ineffective units was actually a drain upon resources which in turn lowered the capability of the rest of the force. Maintenance of a large force, which appears stronger on paper than it actually is in reality, creates a false sense of security. This is akin to the pre-World War II days when the 27 ORC divisions represented very little real military power.

44. *Hearings, ibid.*, pp. 3601, 3628 and 4158.

political hazards involved, the committee recommended the merger of all Army Reserve units into the National Guard, while the Army Reserve would consist solely of individual Reservists.[45]

Two weeks later the recommendations were tentatively approved by Ailes and sent to the Army Staff for comment. The staff coordination was completed in approximately three weeks, with Maj. Gen. William J. Sutton, the Chief, Army Reserve (CAR) first learning of the plan on November 4. The Section 5 committees had not yet been consulted on Ailes' proposal, and this fact, combined with the late involvement of the CAR, gave Reservists the impression that the plan to abolish Army Reserve units was being concocted in secret.[46]

The failure to include the CAR and the Section 5 committees in the planning process subsequently angered many Congressmen who were more upset over the failure to follow the policies enacted by Congress than by the particulars of the merger plan. The Section 5 committees had been specifically created by Congress to insure that Reserve Component interests were fully considered before the Army took any action affecting the Reserves.

On December 11, McNamara approved the merger plan to transfer all Army Reserve units to the National Guard while reducing the Army's Reserve Component drill strength by 150,000. By this time, reports were appearing in the newspapers of a forthcoming merger, and Defense officials later contended that "leaks" had forced a premature announcement on December 12, 1964. This was one day before the planned December 13 meeting of the Section 5 committees—a date when they were supposed to be informed of the merger.[47]

MCNAMARA AND THE CONGRESS

McNamara's December 12 press conference contained some tactical errors which in all probability contributed to Congress' ultimate rejection of the merger. When asked if the merger could be handled without Congressional approval,

---

45. Cocke, *Reserve Components,* p. VIII–25.

46. *Hearings,* pp. 3678 and 4058.

47. *Hearings,* pp. 3632 and 4234. For an example of articles in the press, see "Plan to shift Reservists Faces a Fight at Capitol," *New York Times,* Dec. 11, 1964.

Table 8–1 Comparison of Present and Proposed Reserve Component Structure.

	Present Structure				Realigned Structure	
Unit Category	Army National Guard	US Army Reserve	Total	Manning Level(%)	Army National Guard	Manning Level(%)
UNITS FOR WHICH THERE IS A MILITARY REQUIREMENT:						
Air Defense	7,400	—	7,400	85	7,400	85
Units to Round Out Active Army & Reserve (units will be added)	76,500	78,600	155,100	80	160,020	80
Bdes (now 11 to be increased to 16 bdes)	25,000	16,300	41,300	75–80	69,614	80
Mobilization Base	2,600	66,600	69,200	75–100	69,200	75–100
6 Div Forces	118,000	64,100	182,100	75–80	189,860	80
2 Special Purpose Div. Forces	25,600	2,600	28,200	70	33,520	80
Support to Other Svc	1,900	9,300	11,200	70	11,200	70
State HQ	4,000	—	4,000	100	8,500	100
Total	261,000	237,500	498,500		549,314	
UNITS FOR WHICH THERE IS NO MILITARY REQUIREMENT:						
Other Div. (21 div—15 Guard & 6 Reserve)	122,800	45,600	168,400	55–60	—	
Non Divisional Units	15,450	16,300	31,750	55	—	
Comd Hq's, Divisional	750	600	1,350		—	
Total	139,000	62,500	201,500		—	
TOTAL	400,000	300,000	700,000		549,314	

* Equipment procurement now authorized for on site Air Defense; Round Out units; support to other SVCS; Part of Mobilization Base; 6 Div Forces; and 11 Bdes. Equipment will be authorized for these forces plus 2 Special Purpose Divs and 5 Bdes.

† Unit composition will change in a number of instances.

Source: *The Army Reserve Magazine*, January 1965, p. 12.

McNamara replied "Yes, it can be." He also announced that he was ending the practice of offering Reserve commissions to Congressmen, and he hurt his case when he said that he intended to transfer to the Standby Reserve the 100 or so Congressmen who were Reservists. This was in addition to an earlier McNamara decision to abolish the special Congressional training detachments where Congressmen were able to earn enough retirement points to give them a "good" year toward retirement.[48]

The merger proposal was also prejudiced by being presented as a *fait accompli.* A December 12 memorandum from the Secretary of the Army to Army Reserve commanders told the Reservists that their positions were being abolished because the Army needed a "quick reaction force." Ailes explained that he couldn't abolish the National Guard because it was needed on the state level for natural disaster and civil disturbance missions. Since he was determined to have only one Armed Reserve Component, he was left with no choice but to abolish the Army Reserve units.

The arguments about economy, simplified command, and faster reaction time did little to assuage Reservists who would have to join the National Guard if they wanted to continue in a troop unit. The problem was particularly acute for senior Army Reserve officers who had understandable doubts about their ability to obtain corresponding positions within the National Guard structure.

ROA AND OTHER OBJECTIONS

The reaction by senior Reservists and their professional association, the Reserve Officers Association, was swift and predictable. They had suspected that the merger plan was forthcoming,[49] and McNamara had no sooner made the merger public than the ROA fired off a telegram to President Johnson asking him to hold off any action on the merger until public hearings could be held. Johnson refused the ROA requests, citing the need to take Defense economies wherever possible.

As the organization most actively opposed to the merger, the ROA encouraged its membership and friends to express opposition to the plan. While the ROA drew up a 30-point rebuttal to the merits of the merger, the basic strategy

---

48. In order to count a year toward the 20-year requirement for a Reserve Component retirement at age 60, a Reservist must earn 50 retirement points a year. Retirement points are earned at the rate of one point for every day of active duty and one point for every drill (of at least 2 hours length) attended. Reservists may also earn points by taking correspondence courses and by performing certain specific equivalent duties. By far the easiest way to earn points is by attendance at drills or meetings with a unit, and the abolition of the Congressional detachments made it much harder for Congressmen with their busy schedules to earn points. The "good" year term applies to any year in which 50 points are earned.

49. See the *New York Times*, Nov. 25, 1964, Section C, p. 10.

was to agitate for Congressional hearings. This was a sound strategy, because McNamara had strained relations with several key Congressional committees. Furthermore, his attitude and the unfortunate handling of the merger announcement gave the impression that McNamara was being contemptuous of Congress.[50]

While the political storm clouds gathered, the Army moved ahead on the merger proposal. A steering committee was formed in the Office of Reserve Components, and representatives of the National Guard and Army Reserve were asked to compile troop lists for the merger. At the Department of Defense level, the Reserve Forces Policy Board voted 6 to 6 on the merger; and at the Army level, the General Staff Committee on the National Guard and Reserve Affairs approved of the merger,[51] over the unanimous dissent of its Army Reserve members. The USAR members prepared several alternative plans, which were rejected out-of-hand by the Army staff because they all called for the retention of both Army Reserve and Army National Guard units.[52] The assumption apparently made by the Army staff was that the Army Reserve and the Army National Guard would have to contain identical units to be independent of each other and totally self-sufficient. The concept of mutually supporting and mutually dependent components making up a Total Army as we have it today was totally incomprehensible to the Army in early 1965.

Meanwhile, ROA had been effective in mounting a grass roots movement against the merger. ROA chapters and individual members had been vigorous in contacting their Congressmen to demand public hearings on the merger. Their efforts were also having an impact upon editorial opinion. Although initial reporting had been generally favorable to the merger, the attitude changed in January and February.

Probably one of the more damaging articles to appear was Brig. Gen. S. L. A. Marshall's piece in the January 23, 1965, *New Republic* entitled, "McNamara's Latest Reform: Why His National Guard Merger Scheme Won't Work." Marshall referred to the unsuccessful 1948 attempt by the Gray Board to merge the Reserve Components, a move

---

50. William F. Levantrosser, "Army Reserve Merger Proposal," *Military Affairs*, Fall, 1966, pp. 137–39.

51. *Ibid.*, p. 139.

52. Details of the alternative plans are found in pages 3714 to 3784 of the *Hearings* cited above.

which floundered when the Guard opposed tighter federal control over its operations. Marshall exhumed every traditional criticism of the National Guard, from incompetent training and political generals to the interference of governors in national defense matters. He argued that only a federal reserve could attract the specialists and uniquely skilled individuals needed on a standby basis. Whether Marshall was right or wrong, his opinions received national circulation and were later quoted in hearings against the merger.[53]

CONGRESSIONAL HEARINGS

A significant factor in the debate over the merger was the attitude of Congress. In general, veteran lawmakers sensed a challenge to Congressional prerogatives in Defense matters. The new chairman of the House Armed Services Committee, Rep. L. Mendel Rivers (D–S.C.), felt a need to assert Congressional authority over Defense policy; and Sen. John Stennis (D–Miss.) led opposition to the merger. Another outspoken critic was Sen. Strom Thurmond (R–S.C.), who was a retired Army Reserve major general and a former president of the Reserve Officers Association.[54]

Hearings were called by subcommittees of both the House and Senate Armed Services Committees, with the hearings before an Hebert House subcommittee being particularly hostile toward McNamara and Army Secretary Ailes. What was developing was a confrontation between the Executive and Legislative Branches over authority to merge the Reserves.

McNamara refused to concede a need for Congressional approval, except that he would require an increased appropriation for a larger National Guard. Hebert directly challenged this contention. Another key point in the hearings was whether the Defense Department had made proper use of the statutory groups created to advise on Reserve Component matters. Considerable time and effort were expended to

---

53. *Hearings,* p. 3642.

54. Thurmond was not the only Reserve general in Congress. Sen. Barry Goldwater, R–Ariz., was an Air Force Reserve major general; and Sen. Howard W. Cannon, D–Nev., was an Air Force one-star. In all, 83 members of Congress were members of the Ready Reserve; and the ROA counted 170 members on the Hill. See page 84 of the Dec. 13, 1964, *New York Times* for a complete listing of Congressional Ready Reservists by grade and service.

establish the fact that these committees had not been consulted until after McNamara had decided to move ahead with a merger.

Defense officials were hard pressed to deny that they had circumvented the intent of Congress. One particularly notable verbal blunder was made by Ailes when pressed by Hebert on authority of the Section 5 committees. Ailes conceded that legislative language gave the committees the authority to oversee Reserve-related matters. In Ailes' words, "That is what the language literally says, but I never assumed it means that."[55]

The Army was also embarrassed to admit that on October 22, 1964, Army General Counsel Alfred B. Fitt had rendered the legal opinion that the Secretary of the Army was utterly lacking in authority to compel the merger. Fitt opined that Army policy would be thrown upon the mercies of the governors.[56]

Hearings on the merger, which continued through March and April, temporarily ended with a joint press conference May 15, 1965, between Hebert and McNamara. The conference announced a face-saving compromise in which McNamara indicated that he would seek legislation to clarify some of the aspects of the merger, and Hebert expressed satisfaction that the Congress had reached full partnership with the administration in discussing the merits of the merger.[57]

The merits of the merger from the Department of Defense point of view can be summarized as follows:

1. The merger would create a single chain of command through the National Guard Bureau, as opposed to separate Army Reserve and National Guard chains.
2. Approximately 200,000 paid drill spaces in unnecessary units would be eliminated with a concurrent cost savings.
3. The manning level of the remaining units would be increased, with these units going from 498,500 troops prior to the merger to 549,314 troops afterwards.
4. Because of reduced drill strength, future retirement costs would be reduced. McNamara made this point at his December 12, 1964, press conference.

55. *Hearings*, p. 3697.
56. *Hearings*, pp. 4320–36.
57. Levantrosser, "Army Reserve Merger Proposal," p. 142.

5. Equipment levels in the retained units would be increased as equipment was transferred from abolished units.
6. Concurrently, personnel assets in the full-time support force of the Reserve Components would be redistributed among fewer units, thereby increasing Reserve readiness.[58]

The case against the merger was made by ROA's Carlton in testimony on April 8, 1965, before the Hebert subcommittee. Describing the plan as "not militarily sound," Carlton's lengthy arguments can be summarized thusly:

1. The claim of increased manning levels is false. Most units would not receive increased manning levels, while the strength of state *headquarters* would be doubled.
2. The command structure would not be simplified. Instead of having the units of the Army Reserve under a single commander, the merger would place these assets under 50 different commanders—state governors.
3. Readiness would be decreased while the Reserve Components go through the transition from one chain of command to another and while new senior personnel are assigned under National Guard leadership. Carlton contended that this readiness loss would take several years to reverse.
4. A 29 division-equivalent force would be inadequate to meet the threat. According to the ROA, the fact is that our mobilization base should be structured to counter enemy capabilities, and not what some economy-minded comptrollers may conceive the enemy's intentions to be.[59]
5. It is imprudent to reduce the strength of our Reserve Components at a time of increased troop commitments in Vietnam.[60]

---

58. The entire DoD position is found in the January 1965 issue of *The Army Reservist* which reprints Ailes' letter to commanders of Dec. 12, 1964, the DoD press release on the merger, the press' questions and answers from that date and a detailed chart showing how the force structure would change. The plan for the execution of the merger is found on pages 7 and 8 of the March 1965 issue of *The Army Reservist*.

59. This particular argument is found on page 11, March 1965 issue of *The Officer*.

60. For Carlton's entire testimony, see *Hearings, ibid.*, pp. 4189–4219. The ROA's case for the Army Reserve is explained in detail in the May 1965 issue of *The Officer* and runs nearly 30 pages.

The issue of Vietnam was a serious one. By mid-April 1965, the United States had 33,500 troops in Vietnam, with the combat role of 5,000 Marines there openly acknowledged. In late April, McNamara obtained a strength increase to 75,000 Americans; and the United States forces in Vietnam reached 50,000 by the end of May.[61]

Gen. William C. Westmoreland has since written that he had come to the conclusion that some sort of a national mobilization would be required.[62] In any case, the decision to commit a larger segment of the active forces to Vietnam made clear the need to maintain a continental reserve. Even though the President subsequently chose to bolster manpower levels through the draft rather than by calling up Reserve units, the very fact that a call-up of Reserve forces had been under consideration was instrumental in convincing many Congressmen that the merger and reduction in Reserve Component strength was unwise.

Amidst signs of increasing Congressional opposition to the merger, the Hebert subcommittee resumed House hearings in early August. Deputy Secretary of Defense Cyrus R. Vance, the principal pro-merger witness, restated the same arguments previously made before the committee. He insisted that the merger would strengthen the national defense, but most of the subcommittee remained highly critical of the plan. The subcommittee shelved the merger by a vote of 8 to 1 on August 12 with Rep. Lucien N. Nedzi (D–Mich.), being the sole McNamara supporter.

In announcing the subcommittee decision, Hebert said that the full committee would oppose any effort to destroy the Army Reserve by merging it with the National Guard. Committee Chairman Russell supported Hebert's position; and the ranking minority member of the House Armed Services Committee, Rep. William H. Bates (R–Mass.), seconded the chairman. However, the committee held open the door for compromise by saying that it would not rule out a reorganization of the Reserves as long as an Army Reserve structure was retained.[63]

---

61. Donald C. Odegard, *Non-Mobilization and Mobilization in the Vietnam War,* (Carlisle Barracks, Penn.: Army War College, 1980), pp. 11–13.

62. William C. Westmoreland, *A Soldier Reports* (Garden City, NY: Doubleday and Co., 1976), pp. 140–141. The subject of Reserve Component mobilization for Vietnam will be covered in detail in the next chapter.

63. Cocke, *Reserve Components,* pp. VIII–39 & VIII–40.

The House Appropriations Committee and its Senate counterpart had already recommended separate funding for the Army Reserve and Army National Guard. The Senate committee had even inserted restrictive language into the 1966 Department of Defense Appropriations bill to prohibit the merger. The language was modified in conference committee, with the subsequent September 29 appropriations act stating that a realignment of reorganization of the Army Reserve Components could take place only with the approval of the Congress.[64] This act also had a proviso that the Army Reserve be programmed for a paid drill strength of 270,000 and that the Army National Guard attain an end strength of 380,000. This was 50,000 less than previous legislation.

MCNAMARA ACTS

On November 13, McNamara ignored the Congressional rebuff of the merger and announced that he would inactivate 751 Army Reserve units containing 55,000 Reservists. He contended that there was no further use for these units. The directive to the Chief, Army Reserve to abolish the units was accompanied by an authority to establish Reinforcement Training Units (RTU) to replace deactivated units.[65] The RTUs allowed Reservists to earn retirement points in a non-paid status through weekly meetings or work on special projects. Within a year, the number of RTUs rose from 364 to 526, and their membership increased from 6,675 to 11,346. Altogether six divisions, 19 battalions and 126 smaller units were chosen for a December 31, 1965, phase-out.

At the same time, McNamara announced the formation of a Selected Reserve Force (SRF). Consisting of 976 Army Reserve and Army National Guard units, the SRF would be a 150,000-man force to quickly back up active forces in case of disturbances outside of Vietnam. The SRF consisted of three divisions and six independent brigades from the National Guard and 232 combat support and combat service support units of 31,519 men from the Army Reserve.

The SRF units were authorized 100 percent of their combat strength instead of their former 70 to 80 percent manning levels, and the number of unit training assemblies was increased by 50 percent, to 72 a year. All of these as-

64. Sec. 639, 79 U.S.C. 879. (Public Law 89–213).

65. *Army Reserve Magazine,* Dec. 1965, p. 27; Levantrosser, "Army Reserve Merger Proposal," p. 143.

semblies had to be four hours long, as compared with the two-hour minimum then allowed other Reserve Component units.

In addition, battalion-sized units and larger commands were authorized up to 96 drills a year to update plans and SOPs as well as to conduct exercises. The SRF units received top priority on active duty training quotas for new enlistees, and they were alerted for a special, more rigorous period of active duty during 1966.[66] Although the formation of the SRF was said to be only precautionary, there were ample reasons to be concerned about Reserve Component Readiness at this time.

The proposed merger had thrown the Army Reserve into turmoil. The Army Reserve had just begun to recover from the Berlin Mobilization, which had resulted in a severe post-mobilization personnel loss. When its future was placed in doubt, all Army Reserve construction was terminated and the recruitment of non-prior service personnel virtually stopped in early 1965. The number one concern of the Army Reserve leadership was for its own future.[67]

The uncertain Army Reserve situation was made worse by developments within the active force. The build-up of active forces for Vietnam taxed the training base to the extreme, making it virtually impossible for even SRF units to obtain training. Despite increased priority for equipment, SRF units did not see substantial gains in their equipment posture, and some SRF units even lost equipment to active forces.[68] A drawdown of Army Reserve equipment for Vietnam had begun.

CONGRESS AND THE MERGER

Meanwhile, the main battle between McNamara and the Congress over the future of the Army's Reserve Components continued. Several reasons, which also seem to have currency today, help explain why such a clash of wills occurred between the Executive and Legislative branches.

According to one study, the merger was an attractive arena for Congress to exert its prerogatives in Defense policy-making, because force levels and organization charts are easily understood in layman's terms. Many Congressmen had

66. *Army Reserve Magazine,* Dec. 1965, pp. 4–6.
67. Odegard, *Non-Mobilization and Mobilization,* pp. 9 and 10.
68. Based on author's own observations while assigned to the 198th Artillery, Delaware Army National Guard.

first-hand knowledge of the military through active or Reserve service, and quite a few were members of military professional organizations. There was no widespread organized opposition among the general public to Reserve forces, and the citizen-soldier tradition allowed legislators to discard any worry about offending constituents. On the contrary, because the Reservists were only part-time soldiers, their unrestricted political activity was a very positive political benefit to their Congressional supporters.[69]

When McNamara submitted his 1967 budget to Congress in January 1966, he kept the merger issue alive by again proposing no expenditures for Army Reserve units. Once more, Congress opposed McNamara's plans, and the Senate Preparedness Investigating Subcommittee unanimously recommended against the merger. The subcommittee was piqued by the December 31, 1965, deactivation of 751 Army Reserve units, including all six of the Army Reserve's remaining combat divisions.

The full Armed Services Committee declared that any future Army Reserve or Army National Guard deactivations of the 1965 magnitude should be taken only after consultation with the Congress.[70] In response, Defense officials countered that there was no military requirement for the 751 units and that it made no sense to spend money on them. Officials said that 25,400 of the 55,000 men affected did transfer to other units and that nearly all of the remaining men were assigned to the Ready Reserve Mobilization Reinforcement Pool (RRMRP). A Defense statement also said that the Reserve Components were in excellent condition and that the merger proposal of the previous year was still valid.[71]

The protests of Defense officials notwithstanding, Congress once more blocked the merger. The 1967 Defense Appropriations Act required a minimum Army Reserve paid drill strength of 260,000, and the House went so far as to pass a bill requiring a permanent Army Reserve unit strength of at least 260,000.[72]

It was rapidly becoming evident that the merger would never gain Congressional approval, and the latest House ac-

69. Levantrosser, "Army Reserve Merger Proposal" p. 143.

70. "Senate Preparedness Committee Blasts Merger," *The Officer*, June 1966, pp. 5 and 6.

71. DOD News Release, No. 417–66, May 14, 1966.

72. The bill passed the House by a 332 to 6 vote on Sept. 21, 1966.

tion implied that Congress would legislate strict strength and organization guidelines unless McNamara dropped his proposal to abolish all Army Reserve units. Without formally conceding the fight, McNamara announced that alternative approaches were being taken to alleviate the Army's Reserve Component problems.

The moderation of McNamara's stance came in his January 23, 1967, statement on the 1968 budget before a joint session of the Senate Armed Services Committee and the Senate Preparedness Subcommittee. It was the only rational option open to him, because declining Army Reserve readiness demanded an end to the struggle between McNamara and Congress.

While the merger debate had raged, the condition of the Army Reserve deteriorated. Because the future was uncertain, the Army had not converted the Army Reserve units to the more modern Tables of Organization and Equipment (TOE) then in the active Army. The Army also deferred reorganizing Reserve combat service support units to the new COSTAR (Combat Support to the Army) concept, where the old technical service units were functionalized into combat service support units. Active Army and Army Reserve units were no longer compatible. They were not organized and equipped in such a manner as to allow rapid integration into the active Army upon mobilization, and this defeated the "One Army" concept and reduced readiness.[73]

MCNAMARA ACQUIESCES

McNamara accommodated Congressional desires by proposing a 1968 end strength of 400,000 drilling Army National Guardsmen and 260,000 Army Reservists. He contended that there were still unnecessary units in the force structure but that it would be possible to bring the Reserve Components into line with Defense needs.[74]

The decision by Defense leaders to work within Congressional guidelines rather than trying to push a merger past Congress lessened the conflict over policy prerogatives.

---

73. These points were made in a February address to the ROA Midwinter Conference, 1967, by Lt. Gen. C. W. G. Rich, Chief, Office of Reserve Components. The address is reprinted on pages 4–6 of the April 1967 issue of *The Army Reserve Magazine*.

74. McNamara's address is reprinted in the March 1967 issue of *The Army Reserve Magazine*.

Army planners were finally able to draft a proposal to bring the Reserve Components in line with mobilization requirements.

On May 24, 1967, Lt. Gen. C. W. G. Rich, Chief of the Office of Reserve Components, signed a plan to realign the Reserve force structure. The plan had been approved by the Chief of Staff on April 21 and endorsed in an 11–10 vote by the Section 5 committees on May 4. Despite the non-concurrence of the Chief, Army Reserve, the plan was approved by Secretary of the Army Stanley R. Resor on May 31.

NEW RESERVE COMPONENTS PLAN

Basically, the plan called for a Reserve Component of 698,100 men in eight divisions and 16 independent brigades complete with the appropriate support increments. In addition, the Reserve Components would include 6⅓ support increments (Combat Support and Combat Service Support) to round out active Army organizations. The command structure of the Army Reserve would be modified. Although Army Reserve units would still be commanded through the Continental Army Command (CONARC), the 14 corps would be eliminated. The Reserve units would be commanded by new two-star Army Reserve Commands (ARCOMs) that would answer to CONARC through the numbered Continental US Armies (CONUSAs). The goal was to convert Reserve units to the new "G" series TOEs and the COSTAR organization starting Sept. 30, 1967, and to have the entire process, including the creation of the ARCOMs, finished in time for Annual Training in the summer of 1968.[74]

On June 2, 1967, McNamara announced the approval of the above plan with the only major difference being a reduced paid drill strength of 640,000—400,000 in the Army National Guard and 240,000 in the Army Reserve. According to McNamara, 92 percent of the units in the new structure would come from the old structure with little or no change in unit organization.

The Army National Guard would be composed of mostly combat units while the Army Reserve would have only combat support and combat service support units. The Army Reserve would retain its 13 training divisions.

This latest plan met little opposition in Congress, except that the Committee on Armed Services insisted that some combat units be retained in the Army Reserve. The result was a compromise by Army officials and the develop-

Table 8–2 Force Structure and Organization—Three Brigade Plan.

	Structure, End FY1967			Future Structure[2]		
Units	ARNG IR/RR[1]	USAR IR	Total	ARNG	USAR	Total
Combat Divisions	8/15	0	23	8	0	8
Training Division	0	13	13	0	13	13
Command Hq Divisional	0/5	0	5	0	0	0
Combat Brigades	7/0	4	11	18	3	21
Maneuver Area Cmds	0	2	2	0	2	2
Air Defense Bns	44/0	0	44	31	0	31
Field Army Supt Comd	0	0	0	0	1	1
Support Brigades	0	3	3	1	4	5
Adjutant General Units	36/0	96	132	40	120	160
Civil Affairs Units	0	77	77	0	51	51
COSTAR Units	0	38	38	122	134	256
Finance Units	1/0	18	19	1	26	27
JAG Units	0	196	196	0	226	226
Hospital Units	15/0	107	122	15	106	121
Military Police Bns	6/0	4	10	7	4	11
Public Info Units	34/0	25	59	34	24	58
PSYOPS Units	0	8	8	0	6	6
Garrison Units	0	18	18	0	9	9
Terminal Units	0	19	19	0	19	19
Total Companies and Detachments	2,520/1,480	3,575	7,575	2,900	3,450	6,350
Paid Drill Strength (000)	307.9/110.6	260.0	678.5	400	260	660

[1] IR—Immediate Reserve: Manned at 80% or higher of full wartime strength; necessary equipment being procured. RR—Reinforcing Reserve: Manned at 50% of full wartime strength; no equipment being procured.

[2] Manned at 90% or higher of full wartime strength; to be fully supported with equipment, technicians, spare parts.

ment of the "three brigade" plan whose unit structure is shown in Table 8–2.

The three brigade plan was outlined by Resor in a July 12, 1967, letter to Sen. Richard B. Russell (D–Ga.), Chairman of the Senate Committee on Armed Services. Three separate brigades would be dropped from the National Guard and given to the Army Reserve. The Army Reserve would also have 10 infantry battalions, 15 separate artillery battalions and 16 combat engineer battalions, while increasing in strength from 240,000 to 260,000.

To balance this, units originally planned for the Army Reserve were placed in the National Guard. These included 13 hospitals, 52 composite service companies, 6 construction engineer battalions and 8 ordnance companies. The National Guard paid drill strength would stay at 400,000. There was a net decrease in the number of Reserve Component units, but this loss was offset by increasing the manning levels to an average of 92 percent of full wartime strength—up from the former average of 75 percent.[75]

The acceptance of the three brigade plan allowed the Army to finally reorganize the Army Reserve. The concept for the new ARCOM organization was made public in July 1967, with the target date for the change-over from the corps structure being December 1968.

The locations of the 18 new ARCOMs were announced on December 21, 1967. Their mission was to insure attainment and maintenance of mobilization readiness of attached and assigned units. By commanding units within their geographical area of responsibility, the ARCOMs were to supervise and coordinate training, supervise materiel readiness, coordinate public and troop information programs and supervise the preparation of unit mobilization plans.[76] This is essentially the mission performed by the ARCOMs today.

The reorganization was completed by May, 1968. The elimination of the Corps, which had been staffed by active Army personnel, was a basic revision in the command concept for the Army Reserve. For the first time, all Army Reserve units were under the command of an Army Reserve general officer, and this implied substantially greater responsibility for Reserve commanders.[77]

RESERVE FORCES BILL OF RIGHTS AND VITALIZATION ACT

Army Reservists also gained a formal voice at the Department of the Army level as a result of the reorganization controversy. Although there had been a full-time officer on the Army Staff responsible for Army Reserve matters since 1927, this position, known today as the Chief, Army Reserve, was not statutory until the passage of Public law 90–168.

This law resulted ultimately from the 1965 hearings on McNamara's reorganization proposals. At that time, the

75. See CORC, 24 May 1967, "Proposed Plan for Reorganizing the Army's Reserve Components," signed by Lt. Gen. Rich. Copies are in the possession of US Army Center of Military History and the Public Affairs Office, Office of the Chief, Army Reserve.

76. Testimony, Army Secretary Stanley R. Resor, Senate Committee on Appropriations, July 12, 1967.

77. *Annual Report of the Secretary of Defense on Reserve Forces, 1968*, p. 9.

House Committee on Armed Services expressed serious reservations about Reserve readiness. On October 23, 1965, the Committee announced its intention to prepare comprehensive legislation early in the next Congressional session to clarify and resolve the future status of the Reserve Components.

This legislation, H.R. 16435, the "Reserve Forces Bill of Rights and Vitalization Act," was introduced in July 1966. In addition to setting minimum drill strengths for the Reserves, the bill provided for statutory Chiefs of the Army Reserve and Air Force Reserve. The bill passed the House 322 to 6 on September 21, 1966, but the Senate was unable to act on the legislation because it was too late in the session. Meanwhile, one of the objectives of H.R. 16435 was temporarily achieved in the 1967 Department of Defense Appropriation Act, which established a minimum drill strength for the Army National Guard and Army Reserve.

Subsequently, Hebert introduced substantially the same legislation into the 90th Congress on January 10, 1967, with H.R. 2. The bill moved quickly through the House, receiving passage February 20, 1967, by a vote of 324 to 13. The Senate began hearings in June and passed an amended version on November 8, 1967. After a conference committee reconciled differences, the two chambers agreed to the conference committee report on November 16, and the measure became Public Law 90–168 on December 1, 1967.

Also entitled the "Reserve Forces Bill of Rights and Vitalization Act," H.R. 2 and the debates surrounding it reflected the very essence of the struggle between the legislative and executive branches over defense policy prerogatives. The House, according to Hebert, had a fundamental responsibility for raising armies and supporting a Navy, and this responsibility extended to the Reserve Components.

While the Defense Department agreed that the Congress had prerogatives in the defense arena, the executive branch contended that Congressional prerogatives were limited to broad oversight responsibilities. These responsibilities, in the eyes of DoD officials, did not include setting exact requirements for the force structure or dictating the internal organization within an agency of the Army.[78]

78. Report No. 13, House of Representatives, 90th Congress, 1st Session, Feb. 13, 1967, p. 2. Levantrosser suggests that the extreme interest in the Reserve Components was a departure from the norm and

The House version of the legislation was far more detailed than the final Senate version and reflected a distrust of the Defense Department. The House bill established a minimum drill strength for each of the seven Reserve Components and established the Chief, Army Reserve as the commander of the Army Reserve. The legislation even went so far as to describe how the Office of the Chief, Army Reserve was to be organized. Similar guidance was given for the Air Force.

The House also wanted to create an Assistant Secretary of Defense for Reserve Affairs, while the Senate preferred to have a Deputy Assistant Secretary of Defense for Reserve Affairs to serve within the Office of the Assistant Secretary of Defense for Manpower and Reserve Affairs. The House acceded to the Senate's desires on this point.

Both bodies were concerned about the role of the Reserve Forces Policy Board. The purview of the board was expanded by allowing any member of the board to bring matters forward for consideration. Previously the board could consider only matters referred to it. The individual service secretaries were given the authority to appoint board members, a right which formerly belonged to the Secretary of Defense. Some modifications were also made in the Army Reserve Forces Policy Committee—the Section 5 Committee—and its Air Force counterpart.

The final legislation also contained benefits for National Guard technicians and an authority for the Air Force Reserve and the Air National Guard to exceed temporarily former limitations on field grade officers.

The final version of the bill resolved House–Senate differences over drill strength policy by providing that authorized personnel strength of the Selected Reserve of each Reserve Component would be set by Congress each year as part of the appropriations process. This satisfied the desire of House members to include some minimum strength provision or other language which would prevent the Secretary of Defense from making drastic cuts in the Reserve Components without Congressional consent. The role of the Chief, Army Reserve was subject to somewhat more debate.

Testifying before the Senate Committee on Armed Services, Secretary of the Army Stanley R. Resor said on September 27, 1967, that the Army had no objection to creating a statutory Chief of an Office of Reserves since it

---

was more of a reaction to McNamara's perceived arrogance than a desire to dictate detailed policy. See Levantrosser, *ibid.*, p. 144.

paralleled the present law which had established the National Guard Bureau. Resor did object, however, to provisions which set forth that office's organization in great detail. He felt that such matters were properly the responsibility of his office or the Army Chief of Staff.

Resor also objected to language which made the Reserve office an operating agency responsible for preserving the integrity of the Reserve Component. He believed that this would establish two chains of command. The Defense Department objected to the provision which made it mandatory for the Chief, Army Reserve to be a Reserve officer. Defense officials believed that such a requirement would restrict them from appointing the best possible officer to the position.[79]

In the end, the Senate Committee on Armed Services agreed with Resor that the Chief, Army Reserve (CAR) should be an advisor to the Chief of Staff on Army Reserve matters. But, the CAR was to come from the officers of the Army Reserve and had to have at least 10 years commissioned service in the Army Reserve. The CAR was to be appointed by the President to a four-year term, with the advice and consent of the Senate. The Chief was to be a major general and was eligible to succeed himself.

Maj. Gen. William J. Sutton, who was already serving as the Chief, Army Reserve under the Chief, Office of Reserve Components, became the first statutory Chief, Army Reserve. Subsequently, the CAR became the appropriations director for the Reserve Personnel Army (RPA) and Military Construction Army Reserve (MCAR) appropriations[80] with responsibility for testifying annually before Congress. This in effect gave the Army Reserve a national spokesman.

Although the Congress has retained a high degree of interest in the Reserve Components, the passage of Public Law 90–168 put an end to the acrimonious debate over Reserve Component policy. The Army was able to turn its attention to the 1968 reorganization. Assured that their component would continue to exist, Army Reservists were able

---

79. Resor's testimony is found on pp. 124–137 of "Reserve Components of the Armed Forces and National Guard Technicians," Hearings, Committee on Armed Services, United States Senate, June 26 to Oct. 3, 1967.

80. At this time Army Reserve Operations and Maintenance funds were a sub-account of the Operations and Maintenance Army (OMA) appropriation. The Operations and Maintenance Army Reserve (OMAR) appropriation was not created until 1973.

to concentrate on repairing the damage inflicted by years of uncertainty; and the Army Reserve began to make real progress toward readiness goals.

While the 1968 reorganization was taking place, forty-two Army Reserve units were mobilized in April. Most were sent to Vietnam, but a few reinforced the strategic reserve forces on active duty in the United States.

A second Selected Reserve Force (SRF) was organized on May 1, 1968, allowing the first SRF to be relieved of its expanded mobilization responsibilities. Experience with the first SRF showed that Reserve units could achieve full TOE strength with notable increases in readiness. On the negative side, officials learned that drills at the rate of 72 per year over a sustained period would cause drop-outs by non-obligated Reservists.[81]

The SRF continued until August 1, 1969, when it was relieved of its mission. Personnel pressures had forced the number of drills to be reduced to 58, 10 more than required for other Reserve units; and equipment shortages remained until the end. It was easy to assign higher priorities to Reserve Component units, but it was not always so easy to sustain them or to provide adequate training facilities. The active Army came first.[82]

CONCLUSION

In summary, the Army Reserve changed significantly from 1960 to 1969. The Army Reserve began the decade with 4,338 company-sized units with a drill strength of approximately 300,000. By 1970, the Army Reserve had 3,478 company-sized units with a membership of 260,000. The number of Individual Ready Reservists increased from 748,000 in 1960 to 931,000 in 1970.

The manning levels of Army Reserve units increased from the 55–70 percent level in 1960 to 93–100 percent as the decade ended. Despite the equipment drains of Vietnam, the Army Reserve did make modest equipment gains. Unit TOEs were modernized, and Reserve units were able to replace their World War II rifles and trucks.[83]

81. *Annual Report of the Secretary of Defense on Reserve Forces, 1968,* p. 13.

82. Cocke, *Reserve Components,* p. VIII–55.

83. When the author enlisted in the early 1960's, his Reserve Component unit was firing M1 rifles, two generations behind the active force. These weapons were collected and M14s were issued in 1965. The older M1s were eventually issued to irregular forces in Vietnam.

More important, the Army Reserve force structure was modified to meet contingency plans. Low-priority units were abolished, and the three components were no longer a mirror image of each other. They had started to take on today's structure of mutually dependent and mutually supporting parts of the Total Army.

Army Reservists gained greater control of their component. Reserve generals took command of all Army Reserve units under the supervision of the Continental US Armies (CONUSAs); and the Army Reserve gained a national focus and spokesman in the person of the Chief, Army Reserve. These events did not occur without considerable debate and anguish along the way, but these birth pains were necessary to set the stage and make possible the Total Army concept of the 1970's and 1980's.

The third and final tier of a 3000 barrel water tank is put into place by the 461st Pipeline Co. of Cody, Wyo. This USAR unit built the water tank during two weeks of training in June 1961. (Signal Corps photo, #591581)

Most of the Army's smoke generator units are in the USAR. Reservists from the 375th Chemical Co., 472nd Chemical Bn (USAR), create a smoke screen during summer training at Camp McCoy, Wisc., in 1961. (Signal Corps photo, # 585646)

The Army Reserve contains all of the Army's railroad assets. This USAR maintenance team is working on the boiler of a steam locomotive at Fort Eustis, Va., in 1962. (Signal Corps photo, #596511)

Army Reservists also learn to destroy things. Shown here is a member of an Army Reserve Special Forces Group as he instructs a class in demolition at Fort McClellan, Ala., in 1966. (Signal Corps photo)

When Hurricane Agnes swept through Pennsylvania in the summer of 1972, over 1000 Army Reservists were called to duty to help with rescue and clean-up operations. Shown here are members of the 469th Engr. Bn, of Caven Point, NJ, who are constructing a Bailey bridge in Schickshinny, Penn. (US Army photo)

Women have helped defend this country since before the American Revolution. It was not until after World War II, however, that women were allowed to join the Army Reserve. In 1982, women comprised approximately 14 per cent of the Ready Reserve of the USAR. Shown here is the change of command ceremony (September 1973) by which Capt. Ruth Glaspey, WAC, became the first woman to take command of an Army Reserve Transportation Unit. (US Army photo)

Thirty-five USAR units were sent to Vietnam in 1968, including the 513th Maintenance Bn, from Boston, Mass. Members of the Direct Support Platoon of the 513th are shown here as they work on a 5-ton truck. (US Army photo)

US soldiers on patrol near Hue, South Vietnam, 1971. Over 100,000 individual members of the USAR served on active duty each year from 1967 through 1971, and many of these men and women did serve in Southeast Asia. (US Army photo)

Long Binh, Republic of Vietnam, was an incredible complex built up by the United States to support its effort in Southeast Asia. Several of the USAR units that went to Vietnam in 1968 operated out of Long Binh. (US Army photo)

Army Reservists of the 737th Transportation Co. present arms during welcome home ceremony on August 13, 1969, in their home town of Yakima, Wash. This USAR unit was one of 35 that was sent to Vietnam in 1968. It served with the 1st Log. Command near Chu Lai and was awarded the Meritorious Unit Commendation for its service. (US Army photo)

A public affairs specialist with the 1209th US Army Garrison, Mattydale, NY, conducts a field interview during her unit's annual training at Fort Drum, NY, May 1982. (US Army photo)

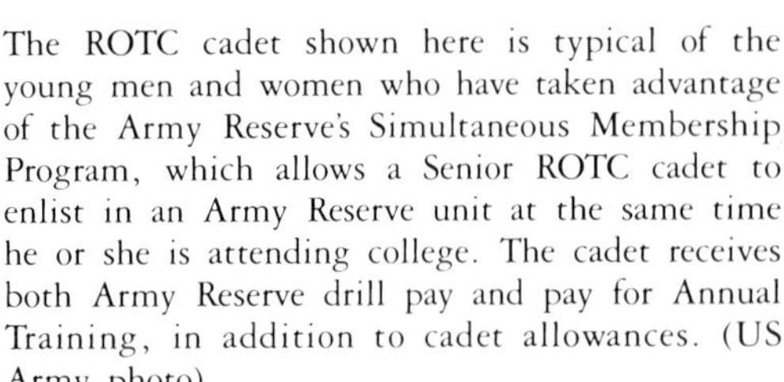

The ROTC cadet shown here is typical of the young men and women who have taken advantage of the Army Reserve's Simultaneous Membership Program, which allows a Senior ROTC cadet to enlist in an Army Reserve unit at the same time he or she is attending college. The cadet receives both Army Reserve drill pay and pay for Annual Training, in addition to cadet allowances. (US Army photo)

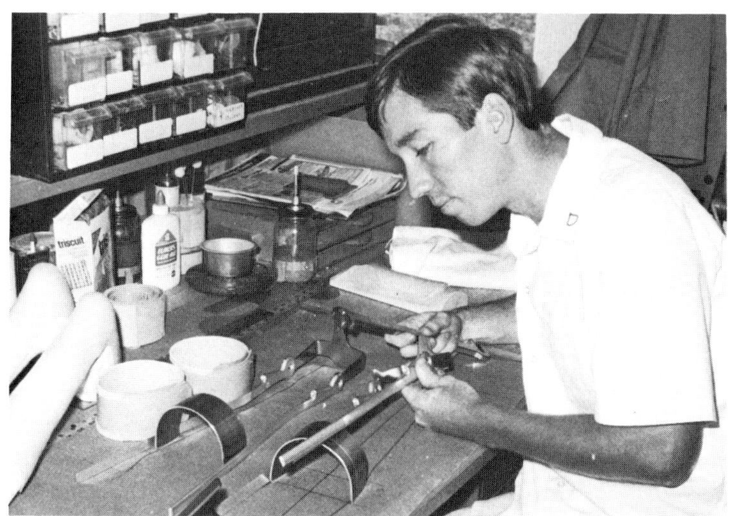

An Army Reserve orthopedic specialist assembles a leg brace during training at Walter Reed Army Medical Center, Washington, DC. Many of the skills taught to Army Reservists are directly transferrable to civilian employment opportunities. (US Army photo)

While other crew members watch, the section chief repairs the firing mechanism of an 8-inch self-propelled howitzer during his unit's annual training at Fort Drum, NY, in 1982. (US Army photo)

The Army Reserve celebrated its 75th Birthday on April 23, 1983, with a cake-cutting ceremony at the Pentagon. Shown here is Lt. Col. D. Y. Dunn, 92-year old retired Army Reservist, who represented the oldest group of those who have served in the USAR. Behind Dunn is Eric Heginbotham, whose swearing-in at the ceremony made him the newest Army Reservist. (US Army photo)

9

The Army Reserve and Vietnam

THE 1965 DECISION

The 1968 decision to mobilize units of the Army Reserve came three years after Secretary of Defense Robert McNamara first raised the idea with President Lyndon Johnson. In May and June of 1965 South Vietnamese forces suffered a string of defeats, and in July the Defense Secretary went to Vietnam on a fact-finding mission. McNamara returned with a recommendation that the number of US personnel in Vietnam be raised immediately from 75,000 to 175,000, with an increase to 275,000 early in 1966. A large part of this increased strength in Vietnam would come from the Army's Reserve Components, from which McNamara wanted to call up 125,000 men.[1]

The question of calling up the reserves was only a part of the much broader debate that went on with the Johnson administration. Indeed, the critical decision in July 1965 was whether to pull out of Vietnam entirely, to maintain the current level of involvement, or to "give our commanders in the field the men and supplies they say they need."[2]

In examining the various options, wrote Lyndon Johnson in his autobiographical account of his Presidency, "I realized what a major undertaking it [McNamara's proposal] would be. The call-up of a large number of reserves was part

---

1. Col. Donald C. Odegard, *Non-Mobilization and Mobilization in the Vietnam War (Draft Report of the Study Group) 10 January 1980* (Carlisle Barracks, Penn.: Strategic Studies Institute, US Army War College), pp. 13–15.

2. *Ibid.*, p. 16.

of the package. This would require a great deal of money and a huge sacrifice for the American people."[3] Johnson thereupon summoned a group of what he called his "top advisors" to the White House on July 21, 1965, the day after McNamara's return from Vietnam.[4] After a series of meetings that included General Earl C. Wheeler, Chairman of the Joint Chiefs of Staff, President Johnson had made his decision.

> I had concluded that the last course [expanding the number of men and amount of materiel in Vietnam] was the right one. I had listened to and weighed all the arguments and counter-arguments for each of the possible lines of action. I believed that we should do what was necessary to resist aggression but that we would not be provoked into a major war. We would get the required appropriation in the new budget, and we would not boast about what we were doing. We would not make threatening noises to the Chinese or the Russians by calling up reserves in large numbers.[5]

After what amounted to a perfunctory discussion with Congressional leaders, Johnson made part of his decision public in a July 28 press conference at the White House. "I had asked the Commanding General, General [William C.] Westmoreland, what more he needs to meet this mounting aggression. He has told me. We will meet his needs." Johnson went on to say that he was increasing the number of troops in Vietnam from 75,000 to 125,000. "Additional forces will be needed later," he said, "and they will be sent as requested." He was raising the monthly draft calls from 17,000 to 35,000 men, stated the President, but he had concluded that it was "not essential to order Reserve units into service now. If that necessity should later be indicated, I will give the matter most careful consideration and I will give the country—you—an adequate notice before taking such action, but only after full preparations."[6]

Johnson was doing everything he could to minimize the impact of his decision, even to the extent of not revealing the full measure of it. He said he had rejected the idea

---

3. Lyndon B. Johnson, *The Vantage Point: Perspectives of the Presidency, 1963–1969* (New York, Chicago, and San Francisco: Holt, Rinehart, and Winston, 1971), pp. 146–47.

4. *Ibid.*, p. 147.

5. *Ibid.*, p. 149.

6. *Public Papers of the Presidents of the United States. Lyndon B. Johnson, Containing the Public Messages, Speeches, and Statements of the President, 1965, II* (Washington: GPO, 1966), p. 795.

of declaring a national emergency—which was a necessary prerequisite to calling up the Reserves—because he saw no reason for it. In answer to a question from the press, the President indicated that he did not want to choose between guns and butter, but would have the government do all it could to continue the "unparalleled period of prosperity."[7]

There was at the press conference no discussion of why the Reserve components were not being called up for Vietnam, and Johnson did not mention the subject in his autobiography. As mentioned previously, General Earl C. Wheeler, Chairman of the Joint Chiefs of Staff, was present for at least one of the White House meetings in late July. Research conducted by the Historical Division of the Joint Chiefs has not, however, discovered any evidence that the topic of Reserve mobilization was discussed at the July meeting from the standpoint of military efficacy.[8]

The best historical judgment of the decision not to employ Reserve Component units—particularly the Army Reserve and the Army National Guard—in Vietnam is that Johnson had made an almost purely political decision. Lyndon Johnson was gradually involving the United States in a land war in Asia, yet he was disguising his every move. The short-range success with which he accomplished this goal was exemplified by a front page headline in the next day's *New York Times:* "Most in Congress Relieved by the President's Course."[9] There was "general satisfaction" in the Congress, reported E. W. Kenworthy for the *Times,* "that the President had decided to increase the draft and postpone a decision on calling up reserve units." The President had become "increasingly sensitive," reported the *Times,* "to the possible political effects of a reserve call-up." Thirty-three House Democrats confirmed the political repercussions of Reserve forces mobilization, saying that they had been getting "'heavy flak' from families that would be affected by a reserve call-up."[10]

Calling-up the Reserve Components, stated one study of this period, would not have been consistent with John-

---

7. *Ibid.,* p. 800.

8. *The History of the Joint Chiefs of Staff. The Joint Chiefs of Staff and the War in Vietnam, 1960–1968,* Part II. (Top Secret). (Unpublished work: Historical Division, Joint Secretariat. Joint Chiefs of Staff, 1 July 1970). See especially Chapter 22, "Growth of Forces in RVN to End of 1965."

9. *New York Times,* July 29, 1965, p. 1.

10. *Ibid.,* pp. 1, 11.

son's attempts to portray Vietnam as "a limited war of short duration which could be fought with little domestic dislocation and without interfering with his administration's war on poverty."[11] Another author described the process somewhat more cynically:

> He was using force but using it discreetly, and he was also handling the military. They were moving toward war, but in such imperceptible degrees that neither the Congress nor the press could ever show a quantum jump. All the decisions were being cleverly hidden; he was cutting it thin to hold off opposition. If there were no decisions which were crystallized and hard, then they could not leak, and if they could not leak, then the opposition could not point to them. Which was why he was not about to call up the reserves, because the use of the reserves would blow it all. It would be self-evident that we were really going to war, and that we would in fact have to pay a price. Which went against all the Administration planning: this would be a war without a price, a silent, politically invisible war.[12]

Whether a substantial mobilization of the Army Reserve and Army National Guard—McNamara had suggested 125,000 men—in 1965 would have made any difference in Vietnam is certainly open to debate. McNamara's attempt to merge the two components had been squelched by the Congress, but the Army Reserve was still in a state of McNamara-induced turmoil; the Army National Guard was undoubtedly in better condition for mobilization.[13] From a purely military point of view, 125,000 men could have been sent to Vietnam much quicker by mobilizing the Army Reserve and the Army National Guard than was possible through the long, slow process of the draft. No one knows whether this would have made any significant difference in the military outcome in Vietnam, but a Reserve forces call-up would almost certainly have precipitated a closer public and Congressional scrutiny of the war itself. As Baskir and Strauss put it, "Reservists and guardsmen were better connected, better educated, more affluent, and whiter than their peers in the active forces, and the administration

11. Lawrence M. Baskir and William A. Strauss, *Chance and Circumstance: The Draft, the War, and the Vietnam Generation* (New York: Alfred A. Knopf, 1978), p. 50.

12. David Halberstam, *The Best and The Brightest* (New York: Random House, 1969, 1971, 1972), p. 593.

13. Odegard, *Non-Mobilization and Mobilization*, pp. 9–10, 15.

feared that mobilizing them would heighten public opposition to the war."[14]

The US role in Vietnam grew ever-broader in the 2½ years following the July 28, 1965, announcement. The number of Army troops in Vietnam rose steadily all during this period, but the increase in active duty strength came almost exclusively from draftees and draft-motivated volunteers. In 1966 and 1967—as in 1965—the Johnson administration was unwilling to admit publicly that Vietnam was anything other than a limited war of short duration. That it had been going on for years before the US ever thought of getting involved was not considered relevant by Johnson and his advisors.

In the years from 1965 to 1968 it became even more politically difficult to consider a Reserve call-up, because the Reserve components had become havens for those who wanted to avoid active military duty—and Vietnam. According to Baskir and Strauss, who wrote what is perhaps the most comprehensive book on the draft and its effects during this time, "A 1966 Pentagon study found that 71 percent of all reservists were draft-motivated," and anyone who was associated with any of the Reserve Components during those years can remember the long lists of men who wanted to join the unit.[15]

THE RUSSELL AMENDMENT

Even as it became more politically difficult to call-up the Reserves, however, it became legally easier. Under the Armed Forces Reserve Act of 1952, a Presidential declaration of emergency was required before Reserve components could be ordered to active duty. To the Fiscal Year 1967 Department of Defense Appropriation Act, however, Senator Richard B. Russell (D–Ga) added the "Russell Amendment," which gave the President the authority, until June 30, 1968, to "order to active duty any unit of the Ready Reserve of an armed force for a period of not to exceed twenty-four months."[16] A June 1967 amendment to the Universal Military Training and Service Act gave the President authority to order non-unit members of the Ready Re-

14. Baskir and Strauss, *Chance and Circumstance*, p. 50.
15. *Ibid.*, p. 51.
16. Public Law 89–687, October 15, 1966.

serve to active duty until they had completed a total of twenty-four months service.[17]

This expanded legal authority for the President did not make the political decision any more palatable, however, so all through 1965, 1966, and 1967 Reservists sat at home and draftees went to Vietnam. This was almost the exact opposite of the first year in Korea, when Army Reservists and National Guardsmen had borne the burden with the members of the active components. This is not to imply that Army Reservists were not fighting in Vietnam during these three years, because most of the officers on active duty with the Army held Reserve commissions, the product of the Army's ROTC programs. Members of Army Reserve units, however, as well as members of the Individual Ready Reserve, were not sent to Vietnam during these three years.[18]

PUEBLO AND TET

The next year—1968—was to prove different, however, though not as different as it might have been. The year began most inauspiciously for the United States when the North Koreans seized the *U.S.S. Pueblo,* a Navy spy ship, off the coast of North Korea on January 23. Two days later President Johnson used the authority given him by the Russell Amendment (Public Law 89–687) to mobilize twenty-eight units of the Air Force Reserve, Air National Guard, and Naval Reserve. This mobilization had nothing directly to do with Vietnam, though some of these men were eventually sent to Southeast Asia.[19]

Less than a week after the *Pueblo* incident the North Vietnamese launched their Tet Offensive. Tet was a military defeat for the North Vietnamese, but it was a psychological

---

17. Public Law 90–40, June 30, 1967.

18. In a unique exception to the usual pattern, thirteen second lieutenants with USAR commissions were called to active duty in 1966 from the 4th Bn, 198th Artillery (AW) (SP), Delaware National Guard. These individuals had incurred an active duty obligation as a result of their ROTC commissioning, and they were called-up as individual Army Reservists, despite their being in the National Guard. One of these men was 2Lt. Richard B. Crossland, co-author of this study.

19. Odegard, *Non-Mobilization and Mobilization,* pp. 43–44; "Where Are They Now? Activated Reservists Just Waiting Around," *Wall Street Journal,* March 15, 1968, p. 1; Major John D. Williams, "Public Affairs Aspects of the 1968 Reserve Mobilization," *Air University Review/Air Force Review,* November-December 1971, pp. 59, 63.

defeat for the United States, coming as it did when US officials were proclaiming that the Viet Cong and North Vietnamese were on the verge of military collapse.[20]

According to General William C. Westmoreland, the US Commander in Vietnam, the Tet Offensive "had at last presented the right opportunity" for calling-up the Reserves. Westmoreland, who states in his autobiography that he had earlier opposed a Reserve mobilization, now felt that "with additional strength and removal of the old restrictive policy, we could deal telling blows—physically and psychologically—well within the time frame of the reservists' one-year tour. The time had come to prepare and commit the Reserve."[21]

PLANNING FOR MOBILIZATION

US forces in Vietnam at the time numbered about 500,000 of the 525,000 approved to that point by the President. General Westmoreland wanted 10,000 more troops sent to Vietnam immediately. In response to a request from Secretary of Defense McNamara, the Joint Chiefs of Staff began to look at various possibilities for reinforcing Westmoreland, including Army, Navy, Air Force and Marine Corps assets in their deliberations. The Army Staff worked feverishly to develop force structure packages in support of overall JCS goals, but the Army planners were severely handicapped by several factors. First, time pressures were enormous. During the eleven-week planning period the Assistant Chief of Staff for Force Development (ACSFOR) issued some seventy-five different force packages, generally under such short suspenses that there was often no time to coordinate them with anyone outside the DA staff.[22]

Coordination was effected, however, with the Office of Reserve Components (ORC), the Chief, Army Reserve (CAR), and the Chief, National Guard Bureau (CNGB). Because of what was described as "the need to maintain security," however, ORC was not allowed to contact the Continental United States Armies, US Army Reserve Commanders, or State Adjutants General. Data on which to base the various force packages, then, had to be compiled from information on hand in

20. Odegard, *Non-Mobilization and Mobilization*, p. 44.

21. General William C. Westmoreland, *A Soldier Reports* (Garden City, NY: Doubleday Co., Inc., 1976), pp. 193, 354.

22. Department of the Army, *After Action Report: Mobilization of Reserve Forces, 1968* (Declassified from Secret), pp. 1–1, 1–2.

the Army Staff offices. A further problem, which aggravated the situation at the Department of the Army level, was that the Army's Reserve Components had begun a major reorganization on December 1, 1967, a reorganization that was not completed until May 31, 1968.[23]

All of this frenetic activity at the Army Staff level was in turn being driven by political and other decisions being made higher up. The Joint Chiefs of Staff, for example, was busily considering three different overall plans for the mobilization, with a total strength mix ranging from 90,000 to 126,000 men.[24]

The question of mobilizing the Reserve Components was top-most in the minds of the JCS, because only through such a mobilization could the United States maintain any sort of strategic reserve, if additional active forces were sent to Vietnam. The JCS had long been urging a Reserve forces mobilization, and the JCS recommendation, which General Wheeler offered in a February 12 meeting with the President, was that "Deployment of emergency reinforcements to Vietnam should not be made without concomitant call up of Reserves sufficient at least to replace those deployed and provide for the increased sustaining base requirements of all services."[25]

Defense Secretary McNamara, however, had done a turnaround from his 1965 advocacy of a Reserve call-up. McNamara had gotten his knuckles rapped for his earlier position, and he now opposed mobilization of the Reserves for Vietnam duty. President Johnson asked McNamara and Wheeler to "study the problem further and to agree on a recommendation."[26] The Secretary of Defense was not prepared to wait for JCS agreement with his position. Instead, he immediately recommended, and President Johnson ordered, the deployment to Vietnam of one brigade of the 82nd Airborne Division and a Marine regimental landing team—a total of 10,500 men.[27] The Joint Chiefs thereupon urged on February 13 the call-up of 32,000 Army Reserve

23. *Ibid.*, p. 1–2.

24. *Ibid.*, p. 1–5.

25. Quoted in *United States-Vietnam Relations, 1945–1967*, Vol 5, Printed for the use of the House Committee on Armed Services (Washington: GPO, 1971), iv.c.6.(c), p.3. The twelve volumes of this set comprise the "Pentagon Papers."

26. Johnson, *Vantage Point*, p. 386.

27. JCS Msg 9926, 130218Z Feb 68, Subject: "Deployment of Brigade Task Force of 82nd Airborne Division to SVN (S)," cited in *United States-Vietnam Relations*, Vol. 5, iv.c.6.(c), p.6.

Component, 12,000 Marine Corps Reserve, and 2,300 Naval Reserve personnel. The Army personnel were needed, stated the JCS, "to replace the forces deployed from the strategic reserve, to provide support units to meet anticipation requirements in I CTZ and to provide a wider rotation base of requisite ranks and skills."[28]

According to President Johnson's account, McNamara and Wheeler continued to disagree on the question of a Reserve forces call-up.[29] McNamara's tenure ended on February 28, however, and he was replaced by Clark Clifford, who was believed at the time to be more inclined to mobilize the Reserves. At the same time, General Wheeler returned from a trip to Vietnam and presented Westmoreland's request for 206,000 additional troops.[30]

For the next month the President and his advisors considered various levels of reinforcement for Vietnam, and with every change of nuance a new force structure package had to be developed by the Army Staff. On March 31, President Johnson announced in a nation-wide television address that he would not run for re-election.[31] The last real political obstacle to a Reserve-forces call-up for Vietnam had now been removed. The final troop list was submitted to the JCS on April 2 and was based on the mobilization of 54,000 men in three increments, a total far short of the number Westmoreland had said he needed. The total of 54,000 men was modest enough in itself, but even this figure would not stand for long. Just two days later, Secretary of Defense Clifford stated that this option was too expensive, and he pared the call-up to only the first increment. A final revised troop list was prepared by April 8, calling for the mobilization of seventy-six Army Reserve Component units with a total of 20,034 personnel, not all of whom would go to Vietnam. It was this list that the Secretary of Defense announced in an April 11 press conference.[32]

---

28. JCSM 96–68, 13 Feb 68, Subject: "Emergency Reinforcement of COMUSMACV (C)." quoted in *United States-Vietnam Relations*. Vol.5, iv.c.6.(c), pp. 7–8.

29. Johnson, *Vantage Point*, p. 387.

30. Odegard, *Non-Mobilization and Mobilization*, pp. 44–45.

31. *Public Papers of the Presidents of the United States, Lyndon B. Johnson, Containing the Public Messages, Speeches, and Statements of the President, 1968–69, Book I* (Washington: GPO, 1970), p. 476.

32. *After Action Report: Mobilization of Reserve Forces, 1968*, p. 1–5; OSD Memorandum for Secretaries of the Military Departments and Chairman of the Joint Chiefs of Staff, April 4, 1968, Subject: "Reserve Recall," cited n Odegard, *Non-Mobilization and Mobilization*, p. 46.

The final selection of types of Reserve units was based on specific requirements set forth by the US commander in Vietnam, plus units needed to reconstitute the Strategic Army Forces. The threat of civil disturbances was a major factor in the elimination of particular National Guard units from consideration, though it had no bearing at all on the units of the Army Reserve. The DA goal was to select Army Reserve and National Guard units based upon the proportional strengths of the two components, and the final mixture of 31.9 percent USAR to 68.1 percent ARNG compared with actual force percentages of 40 percent to 60 percent. Units were spread geographically as much as possible, the final troop list representing thirty-four states. Every attempt was made at Department of the Army level to select the most operationally ready units of each type required, but a lack of up-to-date information hindered this effort. Of the seventy-six Army Reserve Component units in the final troop list, fifty-nine were current or former members of the Selected Reserve Force (SRF); two units had no SRF counterpart. The other fifteen units were selected after considering such factors as readiness status, location (for geographic balance), civil disturbance role, command and control requirements, and length of time the unit had been organized.[33]

The irony was that after all the planning and changing and revising and considering of the proper mix of units needed for support of the war in Vietnam, the total of seventy units mobilized was decided in the end by financial considerations. "The major factor governing the final decision on the size of the force in the 1968 Partial Mobilization," concluded the Army's official after action report, "was . . . the financial support required for such a force and not operational requirements for additional forces to cope with a worsening world military situation."[34] Lyndon Johnson had apparently concluded that the American people could not continue to have both guns and butter, and he was therefore cutting back on the rate of procuring the guns.

THE USAR MOBILIZATION

Regardless of the reasons that went into their selection, forty-two units of the Army Reserve were mobilized in this relatively-small call-up. The types of units are shown in Table 9–1.

33. *After Action Report: Mobilization of Reserve Forces, 1968*, pp. 1–6 to 1–8.

34. *Ibid.*, p. 1–5.

Table 9–1 USAR Units Mobilized.[35]

Type Unit	Number	Total Auth Strength
Inf Bn	1	782
MI Det	2	64
AG Units	4	190
Composite Svc Units	8	1,552
Med Units	11	667
Fin Units	1	40
Ord Units	2	313
QM Units	3	457
Trans Units	10	1,814
Total	42	5,869

Most of the members of these units first learned of their call to duty through the media, rather than through official Army notification channels. According to the Army's after action report, the Department of Defense had prohibited DA from following the procedures developed and prescribed after the 1961 mobilization. "This action," concluded the report, "caused confusion, embarrassed field commanders and contributed to a general feeling of consternation among many reservists."[36]

Nevertheless, over 5000 Army Reservists reported to their home stations (see Appendix C) on May 13, 1968, and within a week they were on their way to active Army mobilization stations. There was considerable local publicity given the mobilized units, and in at least one instance there were special ceremonies to mark the mobilization. When the 737th Transportation Co (Med Truck Petr) left Yakima, Washington, for Fort Lewis on the morning of May 14, the town of Yakima was ready. From 8:30 a.m. to 9:00 a.m. the men of the 737th were treated to a special "send-off" party by the Greater Yakima Chamber of Commerce, attended by "mothers, wives, children, relatives, girl friends, and citizens." Music was provided by the Davis High School Band.[37] Other Army Reserve units may not have received

35. *Annual Historical Summary, RCS–CSHIS–6 (RZ), Office of the Chief, Army Reserve, 1 July 1967 to 30 June 1968,* Part I, p. 3. A complete listing of these units, with their home stations, is at Appendix C. The figure of forty-five USAR units mobilized is sometimes seen. This figure refers to "company/detachment" size units and as such counts the 100th Bn, 442nd Inf as four units (HHC and three line companies).

36. *After Action Report: Mobilization of Reserve Forces, 1968,* p. 2–1.

37. "737th Mobilizes at Center" and "737th Earns Proud Sendoff from Yakima," both in *Yakima Herald-Republic,* May 14 and 15, 1968.

such fanfare, but they convoyed to their mobilization stations nevertheless, and for the next three to seven months underwent the training needed to make them of maximum value in Vietnam.

Few of these Army Reserve units had 100 percent of their authorized strength, so the Department of the Army had to find filler personnel for them. There had been no national emergency declared in conjunction with the call-up, so there were in reality few options within the Army Reserve system. One primary source of fillers for the mobilized units was to be found among certain Reserve Enlistment Program—1963 (REP–63) personnel in the Individual Ready Reserve (IRR). Some 4,132 of these men had enlisted for a six-year hitch in the Army Reserve, and after their initial active duty for training, they were obligated for 5½ years of satisfactory unit membership. For one reason or another, however, they had been transferred to the IRR, and they were fair game for a call-up.[38]

Of the 4,132 REP–63 personnel who were screened for active duty orders, 1,380 were exempted from call-up for reasons ranging from hardship and dependency (371) to inability to locate them (325). Eventually, 1,692 IRR personnel were assigned to the mobilized USAR units, and 1,060 were given assignments with the active Army. Over 1,800 enlisted vacancies in the Army Reserve units were filled with active Army personnel, as were any officer vacancies.[39]

Army Reserve units—even those in the SRF—had never received all of the equipment required by their TOE, and the forty-two mobilized units were no exception. By July 12, however, all mobilized units had received equipment necessary to bring them to a C–1 Readiness Condition. According to the after action report, "No significant [equipment] problems occurred after that date."[40]

The standard training week for the mobilized units was forty-four hours long. General training guidance was provided by DA for all units, while the thirty-five Vietnam-bound units were given additional training, including a minimum of sixteen hours with the M16 rifle.[41] There were few complaints from Army Reservists who claimed they were not being given meaningful training or things to do,

38. *After Action Report: Mobilization of Reserve Forces, 1968*, p. 3–10.
39. *Ibid.*, pp. 3–11, 3–3, 4–7.
40. *Ibid.*, p. 3–4.
41. *Ibid.*, p. 3–6.

in marked contrast to many such complaints from the Air Force and Navy Reservists who had been mobilized earlier in the year.

CHALLENGES TO MOBILIZATION

This is not to say, however, that there were *no* complaints from the Army Reservists. When Rep. Charles A. Vanik visited the Fort Meade, Maryland, training site of the 1002d Supply and Service Company from Cleveland, Ohio, members of the unit complained to him about "the lack of combat training, pass policies, laxity in the conduct of physical training tests, and low morale."[42]

Other major Congressional interest in the mobilization came from the Senate delegation from Massachusetts, composed of Edward Kennedy and Edward Brooke. As early as May 27, barely two weeks after reporting for duty, eighty-eight enlisted members of the HHC, 513th Maintenance Battalion, signed a letter of complaint to Sen. Brooke. These men charged that the 513th was not prepared for active duty, much less for deployment to Vietnam, and should not have been mobilized. The Army response was that "At the time of selection the 513th was the best qualified unit of the six available in the US Army Reserve."[43]

Controversy surrounding the 513th continued later, however, when sixteen members of the unit filed suit in US District Court in Baltimore charging that they had not received all of their mandatory training.[44] Senator Kennedy asked the Army to postpone the 513th's deployment after sixty-seven additional unit members corroborated the complaints of the sixteen men who had filed the suit. Kennedy asked Secretary of the Army Stanley R. Resor to "conduct a full and prompt investigation" of the claims and to "keep this unit available until an appropriate inquiry is satisfactorily completed." Resor declined Kennedy's request, and a spokesman stated that the Army had investigated "as far as

---

42. *Ibid.*, p. 3–16.

43. DF, CAR to CORC, June 12, 1968, Subject: "Mobilization of the 513 CS Bn," with enclosures, found in Records of the Chief, Army Reserve, Washington National Records Center, Suitland, Maryland, Accession No. 71A–3109, 402–05, "Congressional Correspondence, 68, A–G."

44. "Boston Reservists Fight Viet Duty," *Boston Herald-Traveler*, October 4, 1968, p. 1.

they're going to and as far as they are concerned, it's a closed case."[45]

Both political and legal challenges failed, however, as the US Supreme Court, in an 8–1 decision from which Justice William O. Douglas dissented, turned down the plea from members of the 513th and five other Army Reserve units. A total of 256 plaintiffs had joined in the suit, which had two major claims: (1) that in being called-up for twenty-four months they were not given credit for active duty time already served and (2) that they could only be called up after a declaration of national emergency. The plaintiffs were thus challenging the constitutionality of the Russell Amendment.[46]

THE VIETNAM EXPERIENCE

The 513th—all 251 members of it—did go to Vietnam, as did the members of thirty-four other units of the Army Reserve. In December 1982 Lewis C. Brodsky, Chief of Public Affairs for the Office of the Chief, Army Reserve, sent letters to each of these units, asking for their help in compiling the story of the Army Reserve in Vietnam.[47] Many units responded to this request with newspaper clippings, letters of commendation, general orders, unit lineages, after action reports and other documents generated during or immediately after their tour of duty in 1968–69. Together with information gleaned from other sources, this material has allowed at least a paragraph or two to be written about many of the Army Reserve units that went to Vietnam, and these narratives are contained in Appendix C. There are many common threads of experience that run throughout the record of these units, and the author does not believe that focusing on the particularly units about which information could be obtained will lead to an erroneous impression

---

45. "Ted Pleads for Boston Reservists," *Boston Herald-Traveler,* October 8, 1968, p. 1.

46. "Dissidents in Uniform: Supreme Court Rejects Challenge," *Boston Herald-Traveler,* October 8, 1968, p. 1; other units which had members who joined the suit were the 1002d Sup and Svc Co. (Cleveland, Oh), 448th Army Postal Unit (New York, NY), 1018th Sup and Svc Co. (Schenectady, NY), 74th Field Hospital (New York, NY), and the 173d Petr Co (Greenwood, Miss.). These cases were styled *Morse et al.* v. *Boswell et al.; Berke et al.* v. *MacLaughlin; Felberbaum et al.* v. *MacLaughlin;* and *Looney et al.* v. *MacLaughlin* (393 U.S. 802) (1968).

47. Letter, Lewis C. Brodsky, Chief, Public Affairs Office, to thirty-five addressees, December 10, 1982, Subject: "Request for Historical Information," copies in OCAR Historical Files.

of the role and performance of the Army Reserve in Vietnam.

The stories of the Army Reserve units in Vietnam are varied, but they offer a number of common elements. First, the units themselves were not nearly ready for active participation in the Vietnam War when they were mobilized in May 1968. It required months—sometimes up to six or seven months—of intensive training before the thirty-five units were ready to go to Vietnam. Many of the Army Reserve units that were chosen for the 1968 mobilization had only recently undergone TOE changes, and some of them had changed from one branch of the Army to another.

The maturity of the individuals in the USAR units and the esprit of the unit personnel were major factors in making up for the lack of long-term technical expertise. Most of the men and women in the Army Reserve were older than the typical draftee, and the Army Reservist, if the fragmentary statistics on discipline, AWOL, and courts martial are representative, was less likely to become involved in criminal activities than was the draftee. The personnel of the Army Reserve units were likewise determined to prove to the active Army—and perhaps to themselves as well—that they were as good as anyone in uniform. And they did just that in Vietnam, for Army Reserve units were constantly being lauded and decorated by the men under whom they served.

Members of the thirty-five USAR units in Vietnam received 277 Certificates of Achievement and the following other awards:

Silver Star	1
Legion of Merit	5
Bronze Star	384
Air Medal	7
Army Commendation Medal	779
Purple Heart	20

Additionally, the 231st Transportation Company, Fltg Cft, from St. Petersburg, Florida, was selected as the Army's outstanding transportation unit in Vietnam and received the National Defense Transportation Award. Two Army Reserve units were recommended for the Presidential Unit Citation, thirteen for the Meritorious Unit Citation, and one for the Unit Cross of Gallantry (Vietnam).[48]

48. "Awards for Vietnam Service," *The Army Reserve Magazine*, January 1970, p. 7.

There were some problems with Army Reserve units in Vietnam, but they were not problems caused by the units themselves. The biggest gripe from unit personnel was the Army's policy of "infusion," i.e., of taking members out of USAR units and replacing them with non-unit personnel.

As the French military thinker Ardant Du Picq stated:

> Four brave men who do not know each other will not dare to attack a lion. Four less brave, but knowing each other well, sure of their reliability and consequently of mutual aid will attack resolutely. There is the science of the organization of armies in a nutshell.[49]

One of the primary strengths of the Army Reserve units in Vietnam was that the men and women in the units knew each other well. Indeed, through years of training together they had developed the highest possible level of esprit, and they were not afraid to "attack a lion" once they got to Vietnam. "Fusion," however, whatever its merits as a means of distributing the individuals with particular Special Skill Identifiers among units or of preventing home-town tragedies, was a destroyer of the esprit built up among the Army Reservists.

The US Army could well have learned a lesson from the British in this regard, for the British Army has long recognized the value of unit integrity and unit identification as a motivator, and even as a means of enhancing combat effectiveness. The US Army now seems with its active Army unit identification system to have taken a step in this direction. The Army Reserve's experiences in Vietnam should serve to confirm and strengthen this trend.

CONCLUSION

The final question that can be asked about the Army Reserve's role in Vietnam is whether it made any difference or not. The individuals and the units mobilized did an "outstanding" job, to use that over-worn Army phrase. The Army Reservists in Vietnam, however, were only a small fraction—less than 5 percent—of the total Army force involved there. They did their jobs, and they did them well.

---

49. Col. Ardant Du Picq, *Battle Studies: Ancient and Modern Battle.* Translated by Col. John N. Greely and Maj. Robert C. Cotton (New York: Macmillan Company, 1921), p. 110.

But whether they made any *real* difference in the war is debatable.

As this chapter is being written (1983), the United States has just passed through a major transition period on the subject of Vietnam. The Vietnam Memorial has become one of the must-see places on the Mall in Washington, and Vietnam veterans are getting some belated recognition and attention and help. Although the individual members of the Army Reserve who went to Vietnam may have done their duty in anonymity, the men and women of the units mobilized in 1968 and returned from Vietnam in 1969 generally experienced a reception much more akin to that following World War II, when Johnny and Jane came marching home to a hero's or heroine's reception.

If some Army Reservists were subjected to scorn and hostility, most received welcomes like those in Yakima, Washington, or Provo, Utah. Their communities greeted their return as American towns and cities have long greeted returning veterans: with bands and flags and parades. If the public had turned against the war in Vietnam by 1969, the communities where there were Army Reserve units had not turned against their men and women in uniform, just because the War was an unpopular one. It had been a long time in happening, but the Army Reserve unit had become an integral part of the community in much of small-town America, and these true citizen-soldiers were very much in the mainstream of community life and consciousness.

Indeed, the growing involvement of the Army Reserve could well have been the key to what might have been a different course for the Vietnam War. Hindsight is always speculative, of course, but if in 1965 President Johnson had decided to fight the Vietnam War with Reserve Component forces, rather than draftees, he would have been forced to ask for explicit Congressional authorization. The Gulf of Tonkin Resolution, which provided the legal basis for Johnson's actions on Vietnam, would not have given him sufficient authority to call up the Reserve Components without declaring a national emergency. The whole question of our involvement in Vietnam might have been subjected to the sort of public and Congressional debate that never really occurred. Such a debate might well have revealed the painfully learned truth that there was not a deep and enduring national resolve on the question of Vietnam, and it might have foreshortened the US involvement in the war. It would not have been as easy to call up the Reserves as it was to increase the draft calls, and in the history of the Vietnam War, the decision not to mobilize the Army's Reserve Components in 1965 may have been Lyndon Johnson's key decision. Indeed, the Army Reserve ought not to be too easy to mobilize, lest it be used before the crisis has been properly considered. Once a national consensus is reached, however, and the Congress and the President agree on US objectives, the Army Reserve should be ready and able to do its part. Vietnam proves both the truth and the tragedy of this thesis.

10

Toward Greater Partnership

The Army's ability to fight a war without the Reserves is zero. This sums up Lt. Gen. William R. Richardson's remarks to the Association of the United States Army in October 1982 and illustrates the vital role of the Army Reserve in the early 1980's.[1] Only a few years earlier, in spite of the fine performance of duty in Vietnam by the 35 Army Reserve units that were sent to Southeast Asia in 1968, it would have been more accurate to say that the Army Reserve's ability to go to war was near zero.

The Army Reserve ended the 1960's in disrepair and disarray. The Reserve leadership, with the substantial aid of the Reserve Officers Association (ROA), had just fought off Secretary of Defense Robert S. McNamara's attempt to merge the Army Reserve with the National Guard. The Reserve had been stripped of essential materiel for the Vietnam War, and Reservists were characterized as summer soldiers—draft-dodgers in the eyes of some Regulars—who had avoided Vietnam combat through Reserve membership. This innuendo was directed at the Army Reserve even though more than 130,000 Army Reservists were serving on active duty in 1969 at the peak of America's involvement in Vietnam.[2]

---

1. Faith Faircloth, "AUSA Panelists Focus on Reserve Readiness," *ARNEWS*, Release No. 407, Department of the Army, Washington, DC, 1982.

2. *Department of Defense Selected Manpower Statistics, Fiscal Year 1982*, (Washington, DC: Department of Defense, 1983), pp. 199–200.

In addition, more than 70 percent of the Army's Reserve Centers were inadequate,[3] and proper facilities for field training were few and far between. The Army Reserve's share of the Army's budget had fallen to 1.6 percent in 1967 and 1968, the lowest share since the Korean War.[4]

In little more than a decade, from 1969 until today, the Army Reserve underwent a major transformation and emerged as an essential partner in the Total Army. The precipitating event for this transformation was the decision to end of the draft in favor of an all-volunteer force, while the events leading up to the formation of the Rapid Deployment Joint Task Force (RDJTF) hammered home the need for a strong Army Reserve.[5]

The policy responsible for the recent enhancement of the Army Reserve—the Total Force Policy—was publicly announced on September 8, 1970, but the genesis of the Total Force Policy came earlier from the decision to achieve an all-volunteer military force. According to a comprehensive study of this subject, "The failure of Congress and the Johnson Administration to reform the draft in 1967 was important to the evolution of the All Volunteer Force. That failure, continued high draft calls, and increased opposition to the war and draft assured that the draft would be a major issue during the 1968 presidential campaign."[6]

Sensing a winning issue, Richard M. Nixon campaigned on the theme of ending the draft, and Nixon's election brought to the White House a man who favored draft reform and a volunteer military.[7] On March 27,1969, two months after assuming office, President Nixon appointed an Advisory Commission on an All-Volunteer Armed Force under the chairmanship of Thomas S. Gates, Jr., a former Secretary of Defense.

Nixon directed the commission to develop a comprehensive plan to eliminate conscription and move toward an

3. *Annual Report of the Secretary of Defense on Reserve Forces, Fiscal Year 1970,* (Washington, DC: Department of Defense), p. 20.

4. *Annual Historical Supplements,* Chief Office of Reserve Components (CORC) for 1967 and 1968. Also, *OSD Project 80 Report,* Chart 10.

5. For an expansion upon this point, see "RDJTF: Can It Get There Without the USAR?", *Army Reserve Magazine,* (Spring 1982), pp. 8–10.

6. Gus C. Lee and Geoffrey Y. Parker, *Ending the Draft: The Story of the All Volunteer Force,* (Alexandria, Va.: Human Resources Research Organization), p. 29.

7. *Ibid.,* p. 31.

all-volunteer force. The commission was asked to study a broad range of incentives to make military careers more attractive, and the entire issue of a voluntary military was given a high priority within the Nixon administration.[8]

One important point to remember is that Nixon directed the commission to study *how* the All-Volunteer Force was to be achieved, and not *whether* it should be achieved. On February 20, 1970, Gates reported to the President that the commission unanimously believed that the nation's interests would be better served by an All-Volunteer Force than by a mixed force of conscripts and volunteers. The commission was satisfied that such a volunteer force would not jeopardize national security.[9]

In making detailed recommendations to the President, the commission made little mention of the Reserve Components. The emphasis was upon the active forces, where substantially increased pay for junior members was supposed to make the military competitive with civilian industry. The commission recommended that the draft authority be terminated by July 1, 1971, and that $3.3 billion in military pay increases be placed in the 1971 Defense budget.[10]

In its February 1970 report, the commission recognized that the Reserve Components would need special attention in an all-volunteer era but that a lack of data made it difficult to assess the impact of the volunteer army upon the Reserves. The general problem of future Reserve Component strength was dismissed by the committee when it concluded that pre Vietnam strength levels would not have to be required in the future.[11] The committee thought that the Reserves would be substantially enhanced by the large flow of active duty servicemen being separated between 1970 and 1973.[12] While the move toward an All-Volunteer Force was a political decision stimulated by the civil unrest of the late 1960's, the Total Force policy developed more in response to fiscal realities.

8. Statement by the President, March 27, 1969, included on page vii in *Report, The President's Commission on an All-Volunteer Armed Force,* (Washington, DC, 1970).

9. Letter, Gates to Nixon, Feb. 20, 1970, in *Report, President's Commission.*

10. Recommendations summarized by Lee and Parker, *Ending the Draft,* p. 59.

11. *Report, President's Commission,* p. 99.

12. *Ibid.,* p. 117.

DOLLARS DICTATE TOTAL FORCE POLICY

By mid-1969, with the Nixon emphasis upon Vietnamization, it was obvious to the military leadership that the post-Vietnam Army would be reduced in size. Because the Vietnam build-up had been accomplished by adding to the active forces instead of mobilizing the Reserves, there was a redundancy between the active force and Reserve force in certain types of units. As the Army scaled down upon withdrawal from Vietnam, the attractive solution to the force structure duplication was to remove units from the active force. By placing support capabilities in the Reserve Components, money could be saved for the modernization of the active force—a modernization that had been postponed when Vietnam placed a heavy strain upon the Defense budget.

With the visibility of the Reserve Components expected to increase in the near future, the Army's Chief of the Office of Reserve Components initiated a ten point improvement program for the Army National Guard and Army Reserve in August 1969, and in November 1969 he directed a special study of resource allocations to the Reserve Components.[13]

On December 22, 1969, the Chief of Staff of the Army presaged Secretary of Defense Melvin Laird's Total Force Policy by issuing a memorandum establishing that the Reserve Components must be considered the initial and primary source of additional units and individuals in any future rapid mobilization. He directed that Army planning be predicated on this concept.[14]

Laird's Total Force Policy simply formalized what Army leaders had already anticipated. The economic link between the need to hold down Defense costs and the cost effectiveness of the Reserve Components was very clearly made by Laird. This policy was enunciated in an August 21, 1970, memorandum to the service Secretaries in which Laird wrote that the Selected Reserves of the Guard and Reserve, rather than draftees, would in the future be the initial and primary source of augmentation in any emergency requiring rapid

13. Army Chief of Staff General William C. Westmoreland claims that he foresaw Laird's shift in emphasis to the Reserve Component problems in 1969. Westmoreland states that despite the reduction in active forces, the Army's basic responsibilities did not change. This required increased emphasis upon Reserve Components. See Westmoreland's *Report of the Chief of Staff of the United States Army, July 1, 1968, to June 30, 1972.* (Washington, DC: Department of the Army), pp. 35–39.

14. *Annual Report of the Secretary of Defense on Reserve Forces, Fiscal Year* 1970, p. 6.

and substantial expansion of the active forces. The military departments were directed to consider the Reserve Components as part of the Total Force available to meet security needs.[15] This was a return to traditional reliance on the Reserve Components and a forceful renunciation of the Johnson Administration's failure to mobilize the Reserves in 1965.

SUPPORT WAS NOT UNANIMOUS

The memorandum was made public on September 8 and generated front page stories in major newspapers.[16] The *Washington Post* quoted Laird as saying that "in many instances the lower peacetime sustaining costs of reserve units, compared to similar active units, can result in a larger total force for a given budget, or the same size force for a lesser budget."[17] The *New York Times* pointed out that continued reduction in defense budgets would mean fewer troops on active duty and that an Army Reserve unit could be maintained for one-sixth to one-half of the cost of an active duty unit.[18] The Associated Press said that Laird was reversing President Lyndon B. Johnson's policy on the use of Reserve forces, and that the Total Force Policy was directly linked to Nixon's goal to reduce the budget.[19]

Laird said as much himself on March 9, 1971, while testifying on the 1972 Defense Budget before the House Armed Services Committee:

> Lower sustaining costs of non-active duty forces, as compared to the cost of maintaining larger active duty forces, make possible a greater flexibility in planning the Total Force structure. This lower cost of non-active forces allows more force units to be provided for the same cost as an all-active force structure, or the same number of force units to be maintained for lesser cost.

Despite the economic advantages associated with the Total Force Policy, support for the Policy was not unan-

---

15. *Annual Report of the Secretary of Defense on Reserve Forces, Fiscal Year 1971*, p. 1.

16. Ironically, the *Army Times* did not address the Total Force issue in the weeks immediately following Laird's announcement, and internal Army publications such as *Soldiers* were likewise mute on the subject.

17. "Reserves, Guard Get Buildup Role," *Washington Post*, September 9, 1970, p. 1.

18. "Pentagon to Cut Use of Draftees in Fast Build-ups," *New York Times*, September 9, 1970, p. 1.

19. The Associated Press Story, "Laird Reverses Johnson Policy on Reserve Use," was carried in the September 9, 1970, issue of the *European Stars and Stripes*.

imous. On June 30, 1972, in his final report to the President on the status of the US Army, Gen. William C. Westmoreland wrote that "only Regular Army forces in being can achieve the levels of readiness required." Westmoreland recommended that the Regular Army be considered a cadre that could be expanded rapidly in an emergency. This expansible army would "serve as a hedge against the high risk associated with the heavy reliance on the Reserve Components."[20] The expansible army of John C. Calhoun had been rejected in 1916 and 1920 when the Army took firm steps toward establishing a federal reserve force as a means of expanding the active establishment, but the cadre concept still seemed to enjoy some popularity.

Writing in the August 1972 issue of *Army,* Gen. Hamilton H. Howze proposed that the U.S. Army follow the Israeli Army and establish a 25 percent cadre of Regular Army troops to hold key positions in Reserve Component units.[21] On September 4, 1972, David R. Boldt disputed the value of the Total Force in a *Washington Post* article entitled "Reserve: Force or Farce?" Boldt questioned the value of spending so much on Army Reservists when their training was disorganized, their equipment inadequate, and their cooperation with the active component only minimal.[22]

On February 27, 1973, Col. David R. Hampton concluded that "today's Army Reserve cannot fulfill the requirements imposed by the total force concept." Hampton believed that using Regular Army officers and noncommissioned officers as a cadre for Reserve units was the first change to be made in a system desperately in need of change.[23]

---

20. Letter, Westmoreland to President Nixon, dated June 30, 1972, and included as Appendix D to *Report of the Chief of Staff of the United States Army, July 1, 1968, to June 30, 1972.* It should be noted that Gen. Westmoreland's knowledge of the Reserve Components may be somewhat confused. In his 1976 book, *A Soldier Reports*, he consistently refers to being able to mobilize Reservists for only one year during the Vietnam era, when the operative act of the time, Public Law 69–305 carried no such restriction. Westmoreland also refers to the Army Reserve as US Army Organized Reserves—a term that went out of official use in 1952.

21. Hamilton H. Howze, "Toward Real Reserve Readiness: The Case for the Cadre System," *Army* (August 1972), pp. 12–16.

22. David R. Boldt, "Reserve: Force or Farce," *Washington Post,* September 4, 1972, p. 1.

23. David R. Hampton, *Society and the Army Reserve,* (Army War College, Carlisle Barracks, Pa., 1973), pp. ii and 39.

The cadre concept proposed by Hampton, Howze and Westmoreland is inherently attractive to some individuals because a cadre provides the essential nucleus of an organization without the costs of maintaining the full combat strength of a unit in peacetime. The cadre concept was successful for Prussia in the 19th century, and to a large degree the American divisions of World War I and World War II were built upon cadres of Regulars and previously-trained Organized Reservists and Guardsmen. Following World War II, many US divisions were in effect cadre units, a fact that became evident when they were suddenly thrust into combat at the start of the Korean War. The same situation applied to Vietnam when new units were built around a cadre of veterans and fleshed out with new recruits recently graduated from Advanced Individual Training.

TECHNICIANS FORM A CADRE

As attractive and logical as they are to some, the cadre proposals for the Reserve Components overlooked the fact that a cadre system was already in effect for the part-time forces. This cadre system consisted of technicians and advisors to Reserve units. The role of these technicians and active component advisors, their numbers, and how they were to be organized were greatly debated in the 1970's and early 1980's. The expansion of the full-time support force behind the Army Reserve has been one of the major changes of the last 15 years.

The technician programs as they exist today had their beginnings in the National Defense Act of 1916, which provided for caretakers to feed the Federally owned horses issued to the National Guard. When the Guard became motor-drawn, maintenance personnel were added to the caretaker force and clerks were added to the force just before World War II. After World War II, Reserve Component units became larger and more complex. There was a great emphasis upon training and property accountability, and as a result, administrative personnel were authorized down to the company level. Staff assistant positions were established at battalion and higher.

During the 1950's and 1960's the technician program expanded, and the concept of having technicians carry out essential functions between weekly or weekend training assemblies (drills) became firmly established. By 1971, the Army Reserve was authorized more than 6,400 technicians. By the mid-1970's the whole concept of a technician workforce was under review as greater reliance was being placed upon the Reserve Components.

The October 1976 "ART Study" by the US Army Forces Command (FORSCOM), for example, concluded that the technician force was necessary and that the force should be expanded.[24] Two years later, however, the civilian technician program was under fire. In a May 24, 1978, memorandum to the Deputy Secretary of Defense, Assistant Secretary for Manpower, Reserve Affairs and Logistics John P. White stated that the Army Reserve had the least effective full-time force of any Reserve Component. White criticized the management of the technician program and the fact that many technicians were not mobilization assets because they could not deploy with their units.[25] White contended that readiness is directly linked to the percentage of full-time personnel in a Reserve Component and noted that the Army Reserve's technician force represented only four percent of USAR strength, while the Air Force Reserve had 22 percent full-time personnel. He recommended that the percentage of full-time personnel in the Army Reserve be increased to improve readiness.[26]

The next month, White's office issued an even more critical report on the full-time training and administration of the Reserve Components. The report concluded that the civilian technician force of the Army Reserve was almost unmanageable, mainly because it was administered under competitive civil service rules. White wanted the technician

24. *Army Reserve Technician Study (ART),* (Fort McPherson, Ga.: Headquarters, U.S. Army Forces Command, 1976), p. 2.

25. Since 1960, Army Reserve Technicians (ART) had been required to be members of the unit which they supported. If a technician lost his or her Reserve status he had to be placed in a non-technician civil service position. This requirement to meet both civil service and Army Reserve standards became known as dual-status, and dual-status was deemed essential if a technician were to be able to mobilize with a unit and help ease the unit through its transition to active duty. The flaw in this system was that a technician did not lose his or her job if the Selected Reserve status was lost through no fault of the technician. Examples of no-fault loss of military status include retirement from the Ready Reserve upon 20 years of qualifying service or denial of continued military status because of medical disqualification. By 1978, 20 percent of the Army Reserve's technicians had lost their dual status through no fault of their own. They were no longer mobilization assets and were referred to as "status quo" technicians.

26. Memorandum, Assistant Secretary of Defense to Deputy Secretary of Defense, May 24, 1978, p. 4.

force to be either all military or administered under excepted civil service rules.[27]

Although there was no cost saving in converting the technician force from civilian to military, White recommended that this conversion be considered. His argument was that the civil service status of the technician force did not recognize its essentially military nature.[28] He noted that a full-time military force would be available 24 hours a day and that the military considerations of the job must be paramount. White's report and memorandum seconded the December 1977 "Stroud Study", which had recommended excepted status for civilian technicians.[29] However, White went further in suggesting a conversion of the technician force to military status, thereby raising an issue which is unresolved today.

As early as 1975, the United States Defense Manpower Commission had recommended creating a special category of full-time Guardsmen and Reservists on active duty to replace civilian technicians,[30] but the idea of such an active duty force did not gain support until 1978.

In June 1978, the House Armed Services Committee asked the Army to begin a 15-month "Technician Conversion Test" to see if it was desirable to phase out the Army Reserve's civilian technician program. During the test, which ended in June 1980, the Army Reserve brought 1,276 Army Reservists on active duty in an Active

---

27. Under excepted service rules, a civil service employee serves at the pleasure of his employer and literally accepts the requirements laid down by the employer as a condition of continued employment. This is the status of Army National Guard technicians. A civil servant hired under competitive rules has formal, relatively immutable requirements for hire and promotion and a relatively fixed job description. It is also impossible under competitive service to make a military rank and occupation specialty a prerequisite for promotion or selection.

28. *Report on the Study of the Full-Time Training and Administration of the Selected Reserve,* (Washington, D.C.: Department of Defense, 1978), p. 11.

29. Ansel M. Stroud, *Study on the Full Time Personnel Requirements of the Reserve Components,* (Washington, D.C.: Department of the Army, 1977), p. III–37. Stroud also concluded that the Army Reserve had insufficient full-time personnel to meet the workload at the company level and that assigning active duty personnel to augment the civilian force was the least desirable option open to the Army.

30. United States Defense Manpower Commission, *The Total Force and Its Manpower Requirements, Including Overviews of Each Service,* Volume II, (Washington, DC: Government Printing Office, 1976), p. G–11.

Guard–Reserve (AGR) status to fill vacant civilian technician positions. In December 1980, even though the conversion test caused considerable distress among the civilian force, the Army concluded that conversions should continue through attrition and that nearly 3,000 more positions should be converted to AGR status in the next few years.[31]

As a result of the discontentment, however, the conversion program was slowed considerably. By the end of the 1982 fiscal year, only 1,540 civilian positions had been converted to AGR status,[32] and action on the 1983 Defense Budget restricted further conversion. Specifically, the House Appropriations Committee objected to FORSCOM plans to convert the 43 Senior Staff Administrative Assistant (SSAA)[33] positions to full-time colonel positions; and that same committee insured that the continuing resolution which funded the Defense Department for 1983 contained language prohibiting the SSAA conversion. It also limited the total number of converted positions to the number already converted. This put a temporary halt to Army plans to phase out civilian technicians.

FULL-TIME SUPPORT EXPANDS

The Congressional action did not halt, however, the expansion of full-time support to the Army Reserve provided under the AGR program. This expansion, which began in the 1970's and which is projected to increase in the years ahead, is one of the most important steps taken by the Army in the Total Force era to improve Army Reserve readiness.

Historically, there have always been a limited number of Reservists on active duty in support of Reserve Component programs and interests. Starting with the June 4, 1920, amendments to the National Defense Act of 1916, Congress has authorized a minimum of five Reserve officers

---

31. Office of the Chief, Army Reserve, Press Release 81–3, "Technician Conversion Report," January 12, 1981.

32. Maj. Gen. William R. Berkman, Chief, Army Reserve, *The Posture of the U.S. Army Reserve,* (Washington, DC: Department of the Army, 1983), p. 25.

33. The Senior Staff Administrative Assistant, GS–13, is the highest Army Reserve technician position. As the senior technician for an Army Reserve general officer command (GOCOM), the SSAA supervises the daily operations of a command of up to 12,000 men and women. The SSAA has ultimate supervision over hundreds of technicians and is frequently called upon to make important decisions on urgent matters when the commanding general cannot be reached. It is a position of considerable responsibility.

to be on duty with the Army's General Staff to insure the proper consideration of Reserve-related matters.

Subsequently, Section 265, Chapter 11, Title 10 US Code, authorized each service to have reserve officers on active duty in a status other than training, for the purpose of preparing and administering policies and regulations affecting the Reserve Components.[34] These positions are primarily in Washington, DC, and at major headquarters having responsibility over Reservists. Until the early 1970's, the number of such officers on active duty was limited.[35]

The first major expansion of the 265 program occurred with the Army's 1973 reorganization, known as the STEADFAST program. Under STEADFAST, 200 Reserve Officers were to be brought on active duty to assist in improving Army Reserve readiness, although the Commander of the Continental Army Command (CONARC) doubted that such a large number of qualified Reserve officers could be found.

On the enlisted side, the first move toward an increase in Reservists on active duty came in January 1972. At that time 27 in-service recruiters were stationed at active Army installations to recruit active duty soldiers for Army Reserve units before they were automatically transferred to the Individual Ready Reserve upon separation from active duty. In 1973, 64 Reserve non-commissioned officers were placed at US Army Recruiting Command main stations as liaison NCOs to help with referral of prospective soldiers between the active component and the Army Reserve. Further expansion of efforts took place in 1976, when 654 Army Reserve non-commissioned officers were called to active duty to expand the Army Reserve's recruiting force that had been composed of civil service, dual-status technicians. In July 1977, the recruiting force was expanded to 1,030; and on January 1, 1978, 97 non-commissioned officers were called to active duty to serve as full-time unit training managers.

With the use of full-time enlisted and commissioned Reservists showing positive results, the Army planned a major increase in Reservists on active duty. Reservists were to be added at the company level in maintenance, supply and training, while at battalion level and above, the emphasis

34. 10 U.S.C. 265.

35. According to the *1971 Annual Historical Supplement of Office of the Chief, Army Reserve,* as of June 30, 1971, there were 26 Chapter 265 officers on active duty with the Army. This was an increase from 17 the year before.

was on management and planning. The Department of the Army, FORSCOM, and the Continental US Armies (CONUSAs) were authorized additional mobilization planners and coordinators, and active duty installations and service schools were to be assigned full-time Reservists to coordinate Reserve Component support and to support the Total Force concept.

On February 26, 1980, Maj. Gen. William R. Berkman, the Chief, Army Reserve, testified to the Senate Armed Services Committee that the "assignment of full-time military to positions in Army Reserve units has the greatest potential for improving unit readiness." He pointed out that the Army Reserve had historically the lowest percentage of full-time personnel of all of the Reserve Components, and he requested funds to bring the number of full-time Reservists to 5,400 by September 30, 1981.

What had begun as a very minor program was first expanded to solve urgent recruiting problems and to assist with mobilization planning. The divergent active duty statutes for Reservists were combined in February 1979 into a career program commonly known as the Active Guard-Reserve (AGR) Program. Reservists in the AGR program are competitively selected for active duty after a minimum number of years in Reserve status, selectively retained and promoted, reassigned under centralized personnel management and offered an opportunity for retirement after 20 years active duty. The number of Army Reserve AGR personnel is expected to surpass 7,400 by 1984,[36] and a special Army Deputy Chief of Staff for Personnel (DCSPER) study group is expected to make recommendations for additional AGR and full-time support positions in late 1983. In addition to AGR personnel and civilian technicians, the full-time support to the Army Reserve includes active component soldiers. Traditionally, this has been in the form of advisors, evaluators and trainers.

ADVISOR QUALITY QUESTIONED

Regular Army officers were assigned as a skeleton full-time staff to the Organized Reserve divisions prior to World War II. After World War II, full-time advisors were assigned to Reserve Component units down to the battalion level. Although some of the officers assigned to Reserve Component

36. *Ibid.*, pp. 24–27.

duty before and after World War II were outstanding professionals,[37] a general feeling developed in the 1960's that Reserve Component duty was not career-enhancing.

By 1970, the CONARC had become concerned about the quality of officers assigned as Reserve Component advisors. Although CONARC determined that the advisor program was sound in concept, it published an advisor handbook in June that year and instituted a 40-hour course for advisors to familiarize them with their duties. The command also recommended to DA that all advisors in the grades of lieutenant colonel and colonel be Command and General Staff College graduates.[38]

The next year, CONARC continued to complain about the quality of advisors and the lack of Army guidance in their use. On July 31,1970, CONARC recommended changes in the advisor chain of command and higher standards for advisors. In December the Army approved more stringent criteria for assignment to Reserve advisor positions and raised the priority of advisor assignments, thus increasing the advisor fill from 74 percent to 92 percent of authorized strength.[39]

A few months later, Lt. Gen. Walter T. Kerwin, Jr., the DCSPER, admitted to the Under Secretary of the Army that the advisor program had problems. Not only were the Reserve Components lacking in advisors, but it was common for officers to be assigned to positions requiring an officer two or more grades higher. It was not unusual for first lieutenants to be advising Reserve Component colonels.

In addition, Kerwin admitted to educational deficiencies in the advisor force. For example, only 29 percent of the captains assigned to Reserve Component duty were college graduates, while 49 percent of captains on active duty possessed a college degree. For colonels assigned to the Re-

---

37. Future General-of-the-Army and Chief of Staff George C. Marshall was assigned to Reserve Component duty in the 1930's by Chief of Staff Douglas MacArthur. The assigning of full-time RA advisors to Reserve units was confirmed in an interview with D. Y. Dunn (Lt. Col., USAR-Ret.) on April 22, 1983.

38. *Continental Army Command Annual Historical Summary, Fiscal Year 1970,* (Fort Monroe, Va.: CONARC, 1971), pp. 226–29. By contrast, in 1983, an Army Reserve officer is required to have completed Command and General Staff College for promotion to colonel, and half of the Command and General Staff Officer Course must be completed for promotion to lieutenant colonel.

39. *Continental Army Command Annual Historical Summary, Fiscal Year 1971,* (Fort Monroe, Va.: CONARC, 1972), pp. 188–92.

serve Components, less than half had college degrees at a time when 97 percent of all active Army colonels were college graduates. Another indicator was that 37 percent of lieutenant colonels in Reserve assignments were Command and General Staff College graduates. Army-wide, 59 percent of the lieutenant colonels were C&GSC graduates in 1971.[40] For senior officers, Reserve Component assignments were terminal assignments and a transition to the civilian world upon retirement.

In December, under pressure from the Army's civilian leadership, Maj. Gen. George W. Putnam, Jr., the Director of Military Personnel Policies, conceded that the demand for quality officers exceeded the supply. Rather than assign command credit for senior advisor duty as was done for advisors to the Vietnamese, Putnam suggested better housing as a way to induce high quality officers to apply for Reserve Component duty. He suggested that Reserve Component tours be stabilized at 30 months, but he resisted the idea that Reserve Component duty was equal in any way to overseas service.[41] The opportunity to upgrade the advisor program came in the Army reorganization that was pending in 1972.

By January 1972, the Army had concluded that outside pressures, particularly from the Department of Defense and the Congress, made a reorganization of CONARC particularly inevitable. The octopus-like CONARC span of control had to be reduced.

A March 31, 1972, Army staff study concluded that the only reasonable course of action was to divide CONARC into a training and doctrine command and a forces command. A project group was appointed under Maj. Gen. J. G. Kalergis to work out the details of the reorganization, and by July 19, 1972, they had accomplished their task.

The principal impact upon the Army Reserve was a complete revision in the manner by which the active Army advised, evaluated and assisted the Army Reserve. While the Army Reserve Commands (ARCOMs) established in the 1968 reorganization remained unchanged, the relationship between the ARCOMs and Continental U.S. Armies (CONUSAs) was strengthened. The CONUSAs would be relieved

40. Letter, Lt. Gen. Walter T. Kerwin, Jr., Army Deputy Chief of Staff for Personnel, to the Under Secretary of the Army, July 16, 1971.

41. Letter, Maj. Gen. George W. Putnam, Jr., Director of Military Personnel Policies, to the Under Secretary of the Army, December 9, 1971.

of all responsibility for active forces and installations and would concentrate upon command of the Army Reserve and the readiness of both the Army Reserve and the Army National Guard.

A series of seminars between August 8 and August 15, 1972, refined the concept, which called for three CONUSAs assisted by nine Readiness Assistance Regions. The Regions were not in the Army Reserve chain of command, but instead consisted of branch teams to assist Reserve units. The Regions would command the advisors dedicated to Army Reserve general officer commands and the National Guard State Adjutants General, and the dedicated advisors at the battalion level would be eliminated to provide the manpower for the regions and their subordinate Readiness Group (RG). The regions and the Readiness Groups were the doers—hands-on workers who were responsible for improving Reserve Component readiness.[42] On August 21, 1972, the Chief, Army Reserve strongly endorsed the region and Readiness Group concept,[43] and on September 21, Chief of Staff Gen. Creighton W. Abrams approved the Readiness Regions and Groups as part of the CONARC reorganization.[44]

The Readiness Assistance Region concept changed slightly before the Regions were finally formed on July 1, 1973. They were renamed Army Readiness Regions (ARRs), and the advisory/assistance functions of the ARR were organized in three echelons:

1. Dedicated advisors at major levels such as Army Reserve Commands, divisions and brigades;
2. Readiness Groups with mobile teams to assist units within specific geographical areas; and
3. Readiness Coordinators who coordinate ARR-wide assistance efforts and who act as a staff for the ARR Commander.

It became Army policy that the best qualified personnel available were assigned to the ARRs and RGs. Such

42. *Continental Army Command Annual Historical Summary, Fiscal Year 1972,* (Fort Monroe, Va.: CONARC: 1973), pp. 57–87. See also, *U.S. Army Forces Command Annual Report of Major Activities, Fiscal Year 1974,* (Fort McPherson, Ga.: FORSCOM: 1976), pp. 1–75.

43. Letter, Maj. Gen. D. V. Rattan, Deputy Chief, Office of Reserve Components, to Lt. Gen. Harris W. Hollis, Chief, Office of Reserve Components, September 20, 1972.

44. Memorandum for Record, Lt. Gen. Harris W. Hollis, Chief, Office of Reserve Components, September 27, 1972.

role of the ARRs. The FORSCOM alternative was approved in late 1979, and the transition from ARRs to ARMRs was completed in the summer of 1980.

Meanwhile, the issue of excess levels of management did not go away. On December 11, 1979, the Senate Appropriations Committee and House Appropriations Committee conference report on the 1980 Defense Appropriations Act stated that "the Conferees agree that significant savings should be available beginning in FY 81 from eliminating unproductive management layers in the Army Reserve Component support structure."[52] The conferees requested a realignment to reduce excess levels of management be started by September 30, 1980. The Army did not meet the deadline requested by the Congress, but it did continue to work on the problem.

After the Reagan Administration took office, Kenneth P. Bergquist, the new Deputy Assistant Secretary of the Army for Reserve Affairs and Mobilization, proposed sweeping revisions in the Army Reserve's command and control structure. An Army Reservist with a background as a Senate staffer, Bergquist wanted to organize the Army Reserve in peacetime for the way it would fight in wartime. He also wanted to upgrade the management of the Individual Ready Reserve, which he characterized as inadequate and ineffective. Specifically, Bergquist proposed transferring Reservists in the Training Divisions, Reception Stations and Army Reserve Schools to the US Army Training and Doctrine Command (TRADOC) and transferring non-deploying Army Reserve medical units to the Health Services command—moves that would affect 75,000 drilling Reservists.

Bergquist wanted to place Army Reserve units under the peacetime command of the ARMRs. Some ARCOMs would be merged with ARMRs, while others would be given post-mobilization missions. The Bergquist ideas were opposed by the Senior Army Reserve Commanders Association (SARCA) and were little supported by the Army staff. They did, however, stimulate additional thought on the organization of the Army Reserve.[53]

---

52. Point Paper, DAAR–OT.

53. Interview between the author and Secretary Bergquist at the time of the proposal. See also *Washington Update*, Senior Army Reserve Commanders Association, Riverdale, Md., December 1981 issue. The issue of placing training divisions, reception stations, and Army Reserve schools under TRADOC remained alive and was still being pursued by TRADOC in September 1983.

Meanwhile, the Congress continued to press the Army to eliminate one level of the Army Reserve's management structure. There were also particular concerns over the fact that the Chief, Army Reserve did not command the Army Reserve in the manner that his Air Force counterpart enjoyed authority over the Air Force Reserve. In latter 1981, the Senate Preparedness Subcommittee asked the Army to take action to enhance the authority of the Chief, Army Reserve and indicated that legislation to that end would be proposed if the Army failed to act.

A year later, the Army announced that the Army Reserve command and control structure was being reorganized. The ARMRs would be eliminated, and the role of the ARCOMs would be enhanced. The FORSCOM span of control would be increased from three armies to five, and the CONUSAs would assume many of the responsibilities of the disbanded ARMRs. Concurrently, the Army promised to enhance the role of the Chief, Army Reserve.[54]

In March 1983, the Army announced that the Chief, Army Reserve would soon establish an Army Reserve Personnel Center as a field operating agency of OCAR. This center would provide career management to AGR, IRR and Individual Mobilization Augmentee (IMA) personnel. On May 2, came a report that the Army had told FORSCOM to increase the responsibility of major Army Reserve Commands over training force modernization and mobilization planning. According to a story in *Army Times,* FORSCOM was told to give the ARCOMs significant, well-defined, meaningful, post-mobilization missions.[55]

The published plans were explained to the Executive Committee of the Senior Army Reserve Commanders Association on May 5 and 6. Following the briefing, Brig. Gen. Raymond M. Jacobson, SARCA's Executive Director, wrote Army Chief of Staff Gen. Edward Meyer, expressing concern that the ARCOMs would not be given sufficient additional assets to carry out additional responsibilities under the planned reorganization.[56] Meyer's June 8, 1983, reply to Jacobson emphasized that "a key objective of this reorganiza-

54. "Reorganization Planned," *CARNotes,* Office of the Chief, Army Reserve, Washington, DC (Jan.–Feb. 1983), pp. 1 and 6.

55. Larry Carney, "FORSCOM Told to Increase Reserve Command's Control," *Army Times,* May 2, 1983, p. 3.

56. Letter, Brig. Gen. Raymond M. Jacobson to Gen. Edward C. Meyer, May 25, 1983, as reprinted in the June 1983 issue of *Washington Update,* Senior Army Reserve Commanders Association, Washington, DC.

tion is to invest Major US Army Reserve Commands (MUSARCs) with more responsibility and authority for their own management. This is appropriate recognition of both the increasingly critical role of the Army Reserve in the national defense, and its increased capability."

Meyer also wrote, however, that the need to reduce overall Army manpower spaces, and the need to add two new CONUSAs to the command structure meant that no additional resources would be given to the ARCOMs to carry out their added responsibilities. Meyer suggested that ARCOMs should re-evaluate the manner in which they intended to employ the added full-time personnel planned for them in 1984 under the AGR program.[57] The emphasis upon reducing manpower requirements was seconded in July 1983 when *CARNotes* announced that the elimination of the ARMRs would mean a reduction of 125 military and 75 civilian spaces. According to *CARNotes,* the changes were designed to increase the efficiency of the Total Army.[58] The implication is that the reorganization has more to do with saving dollars and manpower spaces that it does with enhancing the authority of the Chief, Army Reserve or the ARCOMs.[59] However, with the final decision not firm by mid-1983, the net effect of the announced reorganization cannot be predicted.

As important as the full-time support structure is to the Army Reserve, the cadre and support forces and their organization was but one of several major issues facing the Army Reserve in the post-1968 timeframe. Immediately after the 1968 reorganization, the principal Reserve Component concern was materiel readiness. Once the Army entered the All-Volunteer Force era, the concern shifted to personnel strength. After the strength picture improved in the 1980's, the principal concern became materiel readiness and the potential block obsolescence of Army Reserve equipment.

---

57. Letter, Gen. Edward C. Meyer to Brig. Gen. Raymond M. Jacobson, June 8, 1983, as reprinted in the June 1983 issue of *Washington Update,* Senior Army Reserve Commanders Association, Washington, DC.

58. "Army Trims Command Structure," *CARNotes,* Office of the Chief, Army Reserve, Washington, DC, (July–August 1983), p. 1.

59. The reorganization is expected to produce annual savings of $5.5 million. See *Army News Service Release No. 103,* "Reserve Component Command and Control," Department of the Army, Washington, DC, May 26, 1983.

THE AVF BRINGS STRENGTH PROBLEMS

One of the first effects of the All-Volunteer Force policy and the ending of the draft was a drastic reduction in Ready Reserve strength. The paid drill strength of the Army Reserve fell from 263,299 on June 30, 1971, to 239,715 on June 30, 1973. The next year Army Reserve units had a net loss of 14,000 members and the paid drill strength dropped to 191,919 on June 30, 1976. By September 30, 1978, the drill strength was down to 185,753 and it stayed around that total until a steady increase began in 1981.

Concurrently with the unit losses, the Individual Ready Reserve dropped from 1,059,064 on June 30, 1972, to 143,882 on January 30, 1978. The combined effect was that the Ready Reserve, which stood at 1,192,453 men and women when the Total Force Policy was announced in 1970, was down to 338,847 seven years later. The Standby Reserve, which consisted mostly of soldiers in the last year of their six-year military obligation, dropped by more than 300,000 between 1970 and 1977.

The precipitous decline in the Army's Ready and Standby Reserves was a cold, hard reality that threatened the success of the Total Force Policy. Improvements in materiel readiness, training, and mobilization planning were hollow accomplishments when the Army Reserve simply lacked the manpower necessary to carry out its responsibilities to the Total Force.

One of the great ironies of the All-Volunteer Force era and the Total Force Policy is that the net effect of ending the draft was increased Reserve Component responsibilities, and hence greater numerical strength requirements, while the capability to fill the Reserve Component ranks was decreased.[60] This inherent conflict between personnel requirements and the ability of the Reserve Components to obtain volunteers gave rise to a decade of handwringing as the Army attempted to make the Volunteer Army concept work for the Army Reserve.[61]

---

60. This paradox is one of the conclusions drawn by a National War College research group in April 1982. See: James W. Browning II, *et al.*, *The U.S. Reserve System: Attitudes, Perceptions, and Realities*, (Washington, DC: The National War College, 1982), p. 40.

61. Much of what is said here about the Army Reserve applies equally to the Army National Guard. However, the history of the Army National Guard is not the main thrust of this book, and specific policies and examples will be addressed to how they affect the Army Reserve.

The Volunteer Army concept was based upon the assumption that if soldiers were paid a competitive wage the military could attract enough manpower to sustain a volunteer active Army in the range of 800,000 to 1,000,000 men and women. The incentive of higher wages worked reasonably well for the active force, especially when coupled with relaxed personnel policies. The wage incentives, however, failed to maintain Reserve Component strength in the 1970's.

The wage incentives failed because the motivation for joining the Reserve Components was not the same as for joining the active forces. The active components offered a complete benefit package that the Reserve could not offer. The benefits ranged from travel and medical care to paid vacations and a change of lifestyle. This was in addition to providing a wage that allowed a young person to quickly satisfy material wants. Although both the active and Reserve forces could offer initial job training and work experience, the Reserve Components could not meet a young person's day-to-day needs. The fact that the Reserve Components were essentially viewed as a part-time job by their junior personnel and potential enlistees was not recognized until the *Reserve Compensation System Study* was complete in June 1978. In addition to the Defense Department's belated recognition that the Reserve Components required unique incentives to maintain strength without the inducement of a draft, the Reserves entered the 1970's with several handicaps.

THE LEGACY OF VIETNAM HURTS THE ARMY RESERVE

The greatest handicap faced by the Army Reserve in 1970 was the failure of the Johnson Administration to mobilize the Reserve Components to an appreciable degree for Vietnam. This allowed the Reserves to become a haven for individuals seeking to avoid combat duty. While this situation may have allowed the Reserves the luxury of waiting lists and the ability to choose whom they wanted, it also created a Reserve peopled with over-educated and affluent junior enlisted men who had absolutely no motivation to reenlist once their initial tour was over. As a result, there was a mass exodus of first-term Reservists in the early and mid-1970's, and waiting lists disappeared as draft calls were reduced in 1970 and 1971.

Second, the Army Reserve was handicapped by a lack of equipment and adequate training facilities. Because of equipment drawdowns, the supply of equipment to Reserve units was so diminished that it became impossible to train. As a result, Reserve commanders were forced to turn to movies and classroom lectures to fill inactive duty training time. It was quite common for NCOs to read lesson plans to masses of sleepy, bored, college-educated first-termers while the officers and full-time technicians wrestled with administration—which incidentally included drafting detailed lesson plans.[62]

Third, the surfeit of potential enlistees and the practical restraints against realistic training made the Reserve leadership lazy. Commanders, who were responsible for their own recruiting, forgot how to recruit; training officers, who were responsible to their commanders for realistic training, forgot how to plan field training; and the active Army leaders responsible for overseeing or advising Reserve training came to accept poor performance as the norm.[63]

These handicaps created in the public's mind an impression that the Army Reserve could offer very little to prospective enlistees and that there was little to be proud of

---

62. The author's own experience followed this pattern.

63. In May 1973, Maj. Gen. Edward Bautz, Jr., described Army Reserve training this way during an Army and Army Readiness Region Commanders conference:

One of my first IDT visits was to a thousand-bed fixed hospital. When I asked where they stood in their training program I was advised, 'the fourth week of BUT'. When I asked what this really meant for a thousand-bed fixed hospital, there was a fair amount of conjecture among the commander and his principal staff officers. Investigation showed that there was no precise ATP for a thousand-bed fixed hospital . . . . I observed a POL company engaged in a week-long exercise hauling empty 5,000-gallon tankers on a 150-mile turn-around. The men obviously were not getting much out of it . . . . On observing an infantry company ATT, I learned that the company had attacked, withdrawn, and attacked over the same 4 to 5 kilometer stretch of ground—and this was soon to be followed by a helicopter extraction. According to the tactical scenario, a helicopter extraction would have been disastrous . . . . (but) the CONARC Infantry Company Test required a helicopter extraction as the last event.. . . In visiting a POL supply point during AT, I found a very well laid out arrangement. In talking to three men—all college graduates—their primary mission for two weeks was to pump gas into a vehicle fuel tanker whenever one rolled up. The skill level required is equal to that needed in a self-service gasoline station. . . . If this gives you the impression that most Reserve Component units do not know how to train properly, I would have to agree—*but I hasten to point out that in almost every instance I was accompanied by a senior Active Army officer who bore some responsibility for this training. In at least half of these examples the Active Army officer was a general officer.* Quoted from a cleared transcript of remarks in possession of the First US Army Historian.

in Army Reserve membership. This created a difficult hurdle to overcome at a time when the Army Reserve had to compete against the active forces and the civilian employment and education market for volunteers. The Army Reserve has had a difficult time overcoming this hurdle.[64]

THE ARMY TACKLES STRENGTH PROBLEMS

In spite of the handicaps and a negative public perception of the Army Reserve, the Army took a four-pronged approach to solving Army Reserve strength problems in the 1970's:

1. Establish and then increase the size of the recruiter force.
2. Add low-cost incentives to the Reserve benefits package.
3. Take administrative actions to include changing Individual Ready Reserve (IRR) regulations while offering a variety of Reserve enlistment options.
4. Institute a Selected reserve Incentive Program (SRIP).

The first three approaches, which were relatively low cost, were started as soon as it became apparent that the Army Reserve's strength problems were not going to be solved by wishful thinking. Bonuses, with their relatively high cost, were tried last, even though the Army has continued with low-cost initiatives such as asking Congress to extend the total military obligation to eight years.

With enlisted strength dropping rapidly and waiting lists all but gone, 1972 marked the start of Army initiatives to maintain Army Reserve strength. A separate recruiting and retention branch was established within the Office of the Chief, Army Reserve to coordinate the recruiting and retention programs. On January 3, 1972, a 42-man, in-service recruiting force was established at 27 active Army installations to encourage soldiers to join Reserve Component units upon release from active duty.

Aided by an early release program for those joining a Reserve Component unit, the in-service recruiters signed up

64. After the Iranian Crisis began in the fall of 1979, Reserve recruiters received a large number of calls from parents wanting to know if their sons could join the Army Reserve so that they would not have to serve in the Army. It appears that the Vietnam legacy of the Army Reserve as a refuge from combat service died slowly. A major finding of the November 1974 Gilbert Youth Survey was that only 13 percent of young men were at that time favorably disposed toward Army Reserve service. See *Attitudes of Male Civilian Youth Toward Military Service* Manpower Research and Data Analysis Center, 1975, p. ii.

25,000 active duty soldiers for the Army Reserve by March 29, 1972.[65] The Army Reserve backed unit recruiters and in-service recruiters with a national print media advertising campaign starting in January; and unit recruiters were given full-time help starting on July 1, 1972, when the Army Reserve started hiring 365 GS–7 Recruiting Specialists.

In 1973, 64 Army Reserve liaison non-commissioned officers were placed in active Army recruiting main stations to coordinate referrals between the components, and in 1976 the dual-status technician recruiting force was augmented by 654 Reserve non-commissioned officers in an active duty status. In July 1977, the number of Army Reserve Recruiters on active duty was expanded to 1,030, marking a 300 percent increase in the full-time recruiting force in a little over four years.[66]

In August 1978, the Vice Chief of Staff decided to make Army Reserve Recruiting a responsibility of the US Army Recruiting Command (USAREC). The transition of the recruiting mission from FORSCOM to USAREC began October 1, 1978, and was completed in May 1979. Meanwhile, the advertising budget in support of recruiting grew from $2 million in 1972 to $11.1 million in 1979.

Today, USAREC remains responsible for the Army Reserve's recruiting mission, although Reserve unit members are still an important source of leads for recruiters. Army Reserve recruiters and active Army recruiters share recruiting station space. They have similar incentive programs for high production and parallel management structures under the District Recruiting Commands. Recruiters commonly share referrals, but proposals to give active Army recruiters full credit toward their monthly enlistment quotas for Army Reserve accessions and vice versa have not been accepted.

BENEFITS ARE INCREASED

No-cost and low-cost benefits to improve recruiting and retention were tried as early as 1972. In that year, the active duty retiree's Survivor Benefit Plan was extended to retirees from the Army Reserve, and drilling Reservists were ex-

65. *Department of the Army Annual Historical Summary, FY 1972,* (Washington, DC: Department of the Army, 1976), p. 108.

66. Prior to the second expansion of the full-time recruiting force, units were still responsible for recruiting. They were assisted by the full-time recruiters, but units still had to have trained recruiting teams. A considerable share of the Army Reserve's discretionary active duty for training funds were expended for training and subsequent recruiting duties.

vidual Training. In between the two training phases, the Reservist earns IDT pay.[69]

When it became obvious that low-cost enhancements were not effective in increasing Army Reserve unit strength, Congress took the initiative and passed Public Law 95–79 on July 30, 1977. This act authorized enlistment bonuses of up to $1,800, or educational assistance of up to $4,000, for soldiers enlisting in selected critical skills or designated units after October 1, 1977. In 1978, Congress dropped the education assistance part of the program, but it included reenlistment bonuses.

The educational assistance provisions were reinstated in 1980, and the present program (1983) pays up to $1,000 per year for books, fees and tuition for postsecondary education. There is, however, a $4,000 maximum payment for a six-year enlistment. The present enlistment bonus ranges from $1,500 to $2,000, and the reenlistment bonus is $900 to $1,800, depending upon the length of the reenlistment.

Between October 1, 1978, and September 30, 1982, the Army Reserve spent $37 million on the bonuses and educational assistance incentives for the 43,000 USAR members who took advantage of the Selected Reserve Incentive Program (SRIP). Congress has extended the program through 1985, and it is estimated that the program will cost over $15 million in 1983.[70] According to Maj. Gen. William R. Berkman, the Chief, Army Reserve, "the incentives have a two-fold effect: an increase in Army Reserve paid drill strength each year since initiation in FY 79; and the channeling of new members into high priority units."[71] Berkman stated that the SRIP has contributed substantially to Army Reserve strength improvement.[72] Berkman's enthusiasm for SRIP is not shared by the GAO, but it is sup-

69. When combined with the Simultaneous Membership program, the split-training option provides a way for a young person to receive up to six years of part-time employment and four summers of paid training while in high school and college. In 1983, this package was estimated to be worth $14,000 to an enlistee who goes on later to take ROTC and receive a commission after his or her sophomore year in college.

70. Data is taken from official questions and answers prepared for the press on Dec. 9, 1982, regarding the SRIP. Memoranda supporting these data are on file in the Public Affairs Office, Office of the Chief, Army Reserve.

71. Testimony, Maj. Gen. William R. Berkman, Chief, Army Reserve, before the Subcommittee on Manpower and Personnel, Committee on Armed Services, US Senate, Mar. 11, 1982.

72. Berkman, *Posture of the U.S. Army Reserve*, FY 1984, p. 12.

ported by the 1981 tracking study of Reserve Component attitudes. This study found that bonuses such as SRIP double the propensity of middle class youths to join the Army Reserve and that the educational assistance aspect of the SRIP is a strong incentive for high school graduates to enlist.[73]

Beginning October 1, 1980, the Army added an Affiliation Bonus to the Reserve Component's incentive arsenal. This bonus pays members of the Individual Ready Reserve and soldiers leaving active duty $25 a month to complete the remainder of their military obligation in a Reserve Component Unit. By the end of 1982, more than 3,000 soldiers had taken advantage of the bonus, receiving an average of $325 each. The benefit of this program is that it creates immediately available troop unit mobilization assets rather than more theoretical assets for Ready Reserve.[74]

The Army also took action, however, to strengthen the Individual Ready Reserve (IRR). The IRR is the primary source of pretrained individuals which the Army depends upon to augment the active forces and Reserve Component units in the event of war or national emergency. As such, the IRR figures prominently in mobilization planning. The number and mix of specialities required early in a mobilization has been the subject of considerable debate both inside and outside the Defense Department. Estimates of IRR needs during the first 90 to 180 days of a conflict range from 200,000 to over a half-million. The latest unclassified figures estimate a need for 400,000 IRR soldiers to flesh out units and to replace casualties during the first 90 days

73. In the fall of 1982, the General Accounting Office prepared a draft report on the Selected Reserve Incentive Program (SRIP). The GAO made three basic findings: the Army allowed overstrength Military Occupation Specialities (MOS) to benefit from the program, some low-priority units were allowed to award the bonuses, and the Army failed to manage SRIP. Because the GAO was working with data over a year old, the report was overcome by events prior to its final publication in January 1983. Beginning October 12, 1982, the Army paid SRIP bonuses by MOS instead of the broader career field, which allowed a few individuals in overstrength MOSs to receive bonuses. Also, the unit priority for SRIP payments was tied directly to a unit's resource priority—which in turn is almost directly linked to its mobilization priority. *Reserve Component Attitude Study, 1981 Tracking Study*, (Philadelphia, Penn.: Associates for Research in Behavior, Inc., 1982), pp. vi and vii.

74. Data is taken from official questions and answers prepared for the press on December 9, 1982, regarding the SRIP. Memoranda supporting these data are on file in the Public Affairs Office, Office of the Chief, Army Reserve.

after mobilization.[75] It should be pointed out that this figure is consistent with the manpower needs that were projected in the mid-1970's.

Manpower for the IRR comes from individuals with prior service in the active and Reserve Components who have a remaining service obligation. IRR strength is therefore almost totally dependent upon the number of soldiers leaving active duty or Reserve Component units. As long as a draft was in effect, there was a constant source of manpower for the IRR as draftees left the active force following their two years of active duty. They were then available to the IRR for three years before being transferred to the Standby Reserve for the last year of their six-year military obligation. When the United States scaled down its involvement in Vietnam in the early 1970's and reduced the size of the active Army, the IRR shrank. With fewer men entering the active force, there were fewer men to be transferred to the IRR following their initial period of service.

The IRR, which stood at 1,059,064 on June 30, 1972, had dropped to a low of 143,882 by January 31, 1978. It had fallen below the critical 400,000 figure as early as 1975, and IRR strength suddenly became a matter of serious concern within DoD.[76] The Army did little, however, to enhance the IRR until 1978.

On February 1, 1978, the Army extended the six-year military obligation to women who joined the military. Previously, women could join the active force or a Reserve unit for three years and then be discharged. The new policy required women to remain in the IRR for three years following their active duty or Reserve Component service. A few months later, the Army stopped transferring soldiers to the Standby Reserve during the sixth year of their military obligation. This policy became law on October 20, 1978, with the signing of Public Law 95–485. In May 1979, the Army began to enlist soldiers directly into the IRR, where they would remain mobilization assets for six years following a short period of active duty for training. Since the IRR direct enlistment option carried few benefits with it, very few young men and women chose this option.

---

75. *Fiscal Year 1984 Defense Manpower Requirements Report*, (Washington, DC: Department of Defense, 1983), p. III–31.

76. By 1976, the projected IRR shortfall was 321,000, and this shortage was considered critical. *See Secretary of Defense's Annual Report on Reserve Forces, FY 1976*, (Washington, DC: Department of Defense, 1976), p. 24.

On October 1, 1979, the Army stopped discharging soldiers for hardship, pregnancy or dependency. Instead, individuals qualifying under these categories were released from active duty or Reserve units and placed in the IRR until the end of their six-year obligation. Members of the Trainee Discharge Program and Expeditious Discharge Program were also sent to the IRR if their command thought they might be of value in a full mobilization.[77]

In 1981, the Army tested an IRR reenlistment bonus which paid soldiers in selected skills $600 to reenlist in the IRR for three years following the end of their six-year obligation. This was a modest success, with 3,815 soldiers reenlisting in the IRR in 1981, but the Congress declined to continue the bonus in 1982.[78] The Army is again proposing direct IRR enlistment and has also sought legislation to extend the basic military obligation of all service personnel to eight years instead of six. Another step to increase IRR strength was taken in 1983 when the Army tacked a two-year IRR obligation on the end of all reenlistments, even if the soldier had already served more than six years.

Faced with severe IRR shortages, the Army has turned to its retirees as a source of mobilization manpower. Soldiers who retire from the active Army after 20 years of service become members of the Retired Reserve and remain mobilization assets. Starting in October 1981, the Army began issuing pre-mobilization orders to selected members of the Retired Reserve. These individuals would be ordered to stateside duty in case of mobilization. These older soldiers have typically been given training, planning, and administrative assignments which would free younger servicemen for field duty.

The Army has assumed that 100,000 recent retirees could be recalled promptly. The use of retirees and an assumed increase in IRR strength over the next few years has enabled the Army to reduce its predicted IRR shortfall to 15,000 by the mid-1980's.[79] These assumptions have not been universally accepted.

---

77. The Trainee Discharge Program permitted the discharge, without bias, of enlistees during Basic Training and Advanced Individual Training if it appeared that they would be unable to succeed in the active force. The Expeditious Discharge Program allowed for quick release of individuals who were unable to adapt to military life following the successful completion of their initial training.

78. Berkman, *Posture of the U.S. Army Reserve, FY 1984*, p. 20.

79. A change of planning assumptions has also enabled the Army to reduce its IRR requirements. The peak demand for IRR members is

The General Accounting Office has been critical of the Retiree Recall Program and the overall status of the IRR. On October 15, 1982, the GAO called the Army's plan for recalling retirees unreliable;[80] and on January 31, 1983, a GAO report stated that the Army has less than one-half of the IRR members needed in wartime.[81] Additionally, the 1982 Military Manpower Task Force Report to the President on the Status and Prospects of the All-Volunteer Force also expressed reservations about the Retiree Recall Program and the IRR.[82] It would appear that current incentives may not be adequate to meet the Army's IRR needs.

WOMAN-POWER INCREASE

As effective as incentives and administrative enhancements have been in building Army Reserve unit manpower in the 1970's and early 1980's, a key to Army Reserve strength improvement has been womanpower.

Women won a permanent place in the American military through the Women's Armed Services Integration Act of 1948 and other legislation at about the same time, but the former act restricted the number of women to two percent of the enlisted force and the number of female officers to 10 percent of female enlisted strength. The strength limitations were removed by Congress in 1967, but female strength in the Army Reserve remained low throughout the early 1970's.

On July 1, 1972, there were 483 members of the Women's Army Corps (WAC) in Army Reserve units and 281 in the IRR. There were also a number of women in a Reserve status in the Medical Corps, Army Nurse Corps, Medical Service Corps, and Medical Specialist Service Corps. At the urging of Maj. Gen. William J. Sutton, then Chief, Army Reserve, Reserve recruiters began a drive to substantially increase the number of women in the Army Reserve. In the first year of that drive, nearly a thousand women

---

now assumed to occur at M+120 instead of M+90. See *Fiscal Year 1984 Defense Manpower Requirements Report, p. III–31.*

80. *The Army's Ability to Mobilize and Use Retirees as Planned is Doubtful,* Report FPCD–83–6, (Washington, DC: General Accounting Office, 1982).

81. *Personnel Problems May Hamper Army's Individual Ready Reserve in Wartime,* Report FPCD–83–12, (Washington, DC: General Accounting Office, 1983).

82. Casper W. Weinberger, *Report to the President on the Status and Prospects of the All-Volunteer Force,* (Washington, DC: Military Manpower Task Force, 1982).

were added to the Army Reserve's rolls, and the number of women in Army Reserve units skyrocketed to 6,669 by June 30, 1974.[83]

To a substantial degree, the rapid increase in female numbers was made possible by the previously-mentioned Civilian Acquired Skills Program (CASP), which allowed an individual to enlist for three years in a civilian-related skill at an advanced grade.[84] A liberal policy allowed the appointment to grade E4 or E5 after completion of a two-week familiarization course, which was supposed to be the equivalent of basic training. (Men, as mentioned, had to undergo eight weeks of training.) Reserve units were supposed to augment the two-week training with a series of mandatory classes, but units frequently skipped these classes and put women to work immediately.

Specialities in the administrative and medical fields were the most popular areas for women joining the Army Reserve under the CASP program as well as under other enlistment options. The CASP criteria were gradually made more strict over the years, and the two-week basic training option was eliminated. Nevertheless, CASP gave the USAR a substantial boost and helped it recruit a substantial number of women in rapid fashion. The program remains on the books today.

After 1974, female membership in the USAR grew steadily, reaching 38,961—16.4 percent of unit strength—by June 30, 1982. The opening of the Reserve Officers Training Corps to women in 1972 dramatically increased the number of female Reserve officers, and there are approximately 5,000 female officers—exclusive of the medical specialities—in Army Reserve units in 1983.

Recruiting statistics released on October 8, 1982,[85] show that women accounted for 28 percent of first-time Army Reserve enlistments during the 1982 fiscal year end-

83. These figures and subsequent personnel figures, unless otherwise noted, are from the Office of the Chief, Army Reserve, *Annual Historical Summary* for the year indicated. Prior to 1972, the Office of the Chief, Army Reserve did not record female and minority strength figures.

84. The provisions of the CASP program are outlined in AR 140–111. The criteria for awarding grade changed over the years, but initially a person was given E4 rank for one year's experience and E5 rank for two year's civilian experience. In some specialities, such as Social Worker, post-high school education could be substituted for work experience. Men were also eligible for CASP enlistments, but had to take eight-weeks of training before being granted accelerated rank.

85. *Selected Reserve Manpower Strength Assessment and Recruiting Results*, News Release 443–82, Department of Defense, Oct. 8, 1982.

ing September 30, 1982. The Army Reserve had 64,388 women in the IRR and Army Reserve units on August 31, 1982, and Army Reserve units are expected to add another 1,000–12,000 women in the next few years.[86]

THE ARMY RESERVE SEEKS MINORITIES

In addition to recruiting more women in the 1970's, the Army Reserve turned to another almost untouched source of manpower—minority group members. Although minorities had been part of the Army Reserve since the first World War, the percentage of black and Hispanic soldiers in the Army Reserve was small. In the mainland United States, the overwhelming majority of Army Reserve units were overwhelmingly white. This practice of de facto segregation abruptly changed in 1973.

In 1973 the Army Reserve's official policy became one of recruiting minority groups so that units would reflect the ethnic characteristics of the community. As a result, the number of blacks in Army Reserve units doubled from 6,869 to 13,099 during fiscal year 1973, and the number of black unit members reached 24,998 two years later. The number of blacks in the Selected Reserve of the Army Reserve (unit strength plus Individual Mobilization Augmentees) was 59,216—23 percent of the force on June 1, 1983. Other minorities accounted for 5.8 percent of the force at that time. Blacks accounted for 26 percent of 1982 enlistments but remain underrepresented in the Army Reserve commissioned ranks, for only 6.2 percent of Selected Reserve officers are black.[87]

In a final effort to improve unit strength, the Army Reserve relocated units. Between July 1, 1975, and September 30, 1976, the Army Reserve relocated 88 units to improve their recruiting base. Every major metropolitan area was carefully examined, and there was a deliberate effort to match unit types to the interests and skills of potential enlistees in the area.[88] Today, the ability of an area to sustain a Reserve unit is one of the principal criteria considered when the Army looks at potential unit locations.

---

86. Source: Maj. Margaret Novak, Human Resources Action Officer, Office of the Chief, Army Reserve. Women equalled 16.7 percent of the Selected Reserve on June 1, 1983, and are expected to increase to 18.1 percent by 1988.

87. *Ibid.*

88. *USAR Paid Drill Strength Capped at 237,000,* Press Release 82–88, Office of the Chief, Army Reserve, July 12, 1982.

Army Reserve unit strength problems are minimal in 1983. Although there are some units which are understrength enough to affect their readiness, seriously understrength units are few.

The principal constraint on Army Reserve unit strength is money. On July 12, 1982, the Army Reserve announced that it was holding unit strength at 237,000 for the rest of fiscal year 1982 because there was not enough money to pay for any more members.[89]

On April 6, 1983, Maj. Gen. William R. Berkman testified to the Subcommittee on Preparedness of the Senate Armed Services Committee that the 1984 Army Reserve budget request reflects the Army's decision to hold down personnel costs. According to Berkman, the 1984 paid drill strength of the Army Reserve is being held to the 1983 level and the fiscal year 1983 end strength of 251,500 represents an increase of only four percent over the previous year's authorization. Berkman also testified that Army Reserve unit strength was approximately 50,000 short of wartime requirements.

EQUIPMENT SHORTAGES CONTINUE

Fiscal constraints are also evident in the Army Reserve's equipment posture. As satisfying as recent strength improvements have been, personnel cannot fight effectively if they lack weapons and support equipment. The Army Reserve has traditionally had equipment problems. This was clearly recognized under Secretary of Defense Robert S. McNamara when he decided to abolish the ten Army Reserve divisions which he could not equip. The issue of insufficient equipment for low-priority divisions could be dismissed as *de minimis* in 1964, but a lack of Reserve Component equipment is serious in the Total Force era.

The equipment status of the Army's Reserve Components had been allowed to deteriorate under McNamara, as first priority went to Vietnam and second priority went to NATO. The Reserves were not permitted to requisition major items of equipment in the late 1960's because these requisitions were not going to be filled and the paperwork would only clog the requisition system.[90]

---

89. *Ibid.*

90. Study: *Resource Allocations to Reserve Components,* Chief, Office of Reserve Components (CORC), Washington, DC, 1969, p. 54.

Major items remained unavailable to the Army Reserve through 1970, but an unprecedented issue of equipment was begun in 1971. Issuing $134 million worth of equipment to the Army Reserve that year was made possible when the active Army withdrew from Vietnam. It was made necessary by the Total Force policy.[91]

Considering the technology available and the state of the art of military equipment in 1971, the 1971 equipment issue only serves to underscore the woeful neglect of the Army Reserve under McNamara. Reservists, for example, were still training with M–1 rifles and older weapons that were two or three generations behind the active force. These venerable weapons, veterans of World War II and Korea, were replaced with M14s and M16s. The slush box M211 2½ ton trucks were replaced with M35s, and the Army Reserve started receiving the M151 quarter-ton truck to replace the Korean War-era M38 jeeps. The Army Reserve was issued M60 machine guns to replace the Browning 1919A1 .30 calibre machine guns, and M48A3 tanks began to replace the M48A1 tanks in Army Reserve armor battalions. The Army also started to replace the vacuum tube radios in Army Reserve units.[92]

In 1972, the equipment issue was also $134 million, and in 1973, $105 million was given to the USAR. As a result, the Chief, Army Reserve reported that USAR units had on hand 56 percent of the equipment they needed in wartime.[93] Issues of $71 million, $79 million, and $64 million in the three following years brought the Army Reserve to 71.1 percent of its wartime equipment requirements by 1976.[94]

However, starting in 1978, equipment intended for the Army Reserve was diverted to Europe to build up NATO stocks. As a result, the Army Reserve equipment availability fell to 61 percent of peacetime authorization and only 50 percent of wartime requirements by September 30, 1979. The lack of sufficient modern equipment prevented a substantial number of Army Reserve units from meeting their

---

91. Melvin R. Laird, *Annual Report of the Secretary of Defense on Reserve Forces, Fiscal Year 1971*, (Washington, DC: Department of Defense, 1972), p. 40.

92. *Ibid.*

93. *Annual Historical Summary, 1973, Office of the Chief, Army Reserve*, (Washington, DC, 1974), p. 6.

94. *Annual Historical Summary, 1976, Office of the Chief, Army Reserve*, (Washington, DC, 1977), p. 18.

readiness objectives. These problems were particularly acute for Army Security Agency, Data Processing, and Engineer units. Equipment shortages delayed force structure actions at a time when the Army was trying to align more closely its mix of Reserve units and its war plans.[95] On February 1, 1980, the Chief, Army Reserve reported to the Reserve Components Coordinating Council that 48 percent of Army Reserve units could not meet their mobilization objectives because of a lack of mission-essential equipment. More than 60 percent of Army Reserve units were rated as not combat ready (C4) as of October 15, 1979.[96]

Admittedly, personnel shortages were also a major readiness problem at this time. The Army Reserve was turning the corner on meeting its strength requirements, however, much faster than it was in the equipment area. A 1980 issue of $44 million in equipment improved the situation slightly to 52 percent of wartime requirements,[97] but the over-riding problem was a lack of money for Army Reserve equipment. Army Chief of Staff Gen. Edward C. Meyer spoke of this on February 3, 1981, when he told the Senate Armed Services Committee that the lack of equipment in the Reserve Components was not being addressed as rapidly as necessary because of a lack of money.[98]

The equipment issue cannot be ignored if Army Reserve units are to meet their mobilization objectives as a vital part of the Total Force. The Association of the United States Army expressed the urgent equipment needs of the Reserve Components this way in 1980:

> There must be a major increase in early acquisition of current generation equipment right off of the production lines for the Guard and Reserve if our early deploying units are to be compati-

95. *Annual Historical Summary, 1979, Office of the Chief, Army Reserve,* (Washington, DC, 1980), pp. 14 and 46.

96. Information Paper, *Overview of USAR Readiness Ratings and Trends,* (Office of the Chief, Army Reserve, DAAR–OT, Washington, DC, February 1, 1980).

97. Information Paper, *USAR Equipment Status,* (Office of the Chief, Army Reserve, DAAR–LO, Washington, DC, December 18, 1980). The information paper stated that "lack of sufficient quantities of modern, first-line equipment continues to prevent the Army Reserve units from attaining their prescribed readiness objectives. Acute major item shortages continue to exist in data processing, heavy engineer, cryptologic and communications and electronic equipment."

98. Transcript of Authorization Hearings on Army Programs, reprinted as Speech File Service, No. 5, Office of the Chief Public Affairs, Department of the Army, 1981. p. 23.

ble with the Active force already deployed or currently deployable.[99]

Citing the House Armed Services Committee report on the Fiscal Year 1981 Defense Authorization Act, the Association explained the cause of the Reserve Component equipment shortages as follows:

> Over the years, the political requirements of budget-making have overruled the real needs of the military. We now find ourselves with a backlog of requirements that are essential to national defense and security. Each requirement is urgent in a world becoming more dangerous each day. This backlog of requirements is, itself, a product of the claim of "unaffordability" in past years.[100]

In 1981, the US Army Forces Command reported favorable increases in Army Reserve deployability because of an increase in personnel and improved training. Equipment improvements did not keep pace, however, and FORSCOM reported that "it was obvious that if DA could match growing personnel strengths with increased issues of now short items of equipment, there could be a major improvement recorded over the next several years."[101]

On December 1, 1981, Deputy Assistant Secretary of Defense (Reserve Affairs) Edward J. Philbin testified before the Senate Armed Services Committee that the shortages of Reserve Component equipment were a reflection of overall shortages of equipment in the Total Force. He admitted that Reserve forces had obsolete equipment and that much of it was not deployable, but Philbin stressed that Reserve units could still effectively perform a variety of missions.[102]

On February 8, 1982, Secretary of the Army John O. Marsh, Jr., told the House Armed Services Committee that he intended to place special emphasis upon the Army National Guard and the Army Reserve and that the committee would see the results of this emphasis in the current and

---

99. *A Status Report on the Army National Guard and the United States Army Reserve,* Association of the United States Army, Arlington, VA, 1980, p. 19.

100. *Ibid.,* pp. 18–19.

101. *Annual Historical Review, Oct. 1, 1980–Sept. 30, 1981,* U.S. Army Forces Command, Fort McPherson, GA, 1982, pp. 305–330.

102. Testimony, Hon. Edward J. Philbin, Deputy Assistant Secretary of Defense (Reserve Affairs), Preparedness Subcommittee, Senate Armed Services Committee, December 1, 1981, pp. 10 and 18.

coming years.[103] The Army Secretary's 1982 emphasis may produce some materiel gains in future years. On February 25, 1983, Chief of Staff Meyer testified that $750 million worth of equipment would be delivered to Guard and Army Reserve units in 1984, and he projected that $1 billion of the active Army's 1984 procurement would be distributed to the Reserve Components in the years ahead.[104] Shortly thereafter, Lt. Gen. Richard H. Thompson, Army Deputy Chief of Staff for Logistics, gave the following data for the Army's Reserve Component share of future procurement dollars:

FY 1984	$ 906,900,000
FY 1985	885,000,000
FY 1986	769,400,000
FY 1987	1,885,200,000
FY 1988	2,461,700,000[105]

This is a total of $6.9 billion over the next five years. When it is considered that estimates of the Army Reserve's equipment shortages ranged from $3.9 to $5.6 billion[106] early in 1983, it would appear that even $6.9 billion will not cure all Army National Guard and Army Reserve equipment problems. Such a sum, however, would be a major step toward achieving materiel readiness.

There are, however, two problems in anticipating major real gains in Army Reserve equipment status by 1990. First, two-thirds of the billions shown above are planned for the "Out" years of the budget cycle. Procurements planned that far ahead are often revised downward when budget priorities are developed.

Second, the 1983 Army Reserve shortage figures do not consider potential force structure changes. As the Total Force structure is refined each year to meet evolving contingencies, it is quite likely that new units will be added to the Army Reserve and lower priority Reserve units dropped

103. Testimony on the Posture of the Army, reprinted as Speech File Service, No. 3, Office of the Chief Public Affairs, Department of the Army, Washington, DC, 1982, p. 1.

104. Statement, Gen. Edward C. Meyer, before the Committee on Armed Services, United States Senate, February 25, 1983, p. 7.

105. Memorandum for the Secretary of the Army, *Project ALARM*, DALO-PLM, Department of the Army, Washington, DC, 1983, p. 2.

106. Berkman, *Posture of the U.S. Army Reserve*, p. 20. The difference of $1.7 billion between the two figures depends on whether Army Reserve armored battalions are issued the M–1 Abrams tank. If Army Reserve units are equipped with the M60 tank, the value of 1983's equipment shortage is $3.9 billion.

from the force structure. The new units will require equipment that is not on hand today and which cannot be anticipated today. This will add to overall Army Reserve equipment needs as we approach 1990.

As severe as some equipment shortages may be, the clear facts remain that the Army leadership is well aware of the Army Reserve's equipment deficiencies and is attempting to solve the most serious deficiencies within the limits imposed by the Army budget. Equally important is the very substantial progress made in the quality and quantity of equipment on hand between the beginning of the Total Force policy in 1970 and today—1983.

MAINTENANCE IMPROVES

Two subjects closely related to equipment on hand and strongly influenced by the quantity of Army Reserve equipment are maintenance facilities and programs in general and the overall adequacy of Army Reserve facilities. The increased issue of equipment to the Army Reserve in the early 1970's presented problems of maintenance, storage, and training. At the beginning of the decade, units were responsible for their own maintenance, and upper echelon maintenance for Army Reserve equipment was performed by active Army facilities on a space-available and time-available basis. This system worked when Reserve units possessed only a few of their major pieces of equipment, but it broke down under increased equipment issue.

The solution was to increase the number of maintenance facilities operated directly by the Army Reserve. By June 30, 1972, the Army Reserve was reaching maintenance self-sufficiency with 203 maintenance shops and 2,175 maintenance technicians. These shops were known as Area Maintenance Support Activities (AMSAs), and their work was supplemented by assigning Army Reserve direct support units the mission of supporting other Army Reserve units.

In 1977, the Chief, Army Reserve reported that the 212 AMSAs were keeping Army Reserve materiel readiness up to active component standards. In general, the Army Reserve's maintenance capability has not been a negative factor on unit training or readiness. There is still, however, a maintenance backlog for Army Reserve units estimated at $61.2 million in 1981.[107]

107. *Annual Historical Review, Oct. 1, 1980–Sept. 30, 1981,* U.S. Army Forces Command, p. 451.

INADEQUATE FACILITIES

The chronic nature of inadequate facilities was evident in 1969 when a resource allocation study determined that at the current rate of construction—$25 million a year—the construction requirements could be met by the year 2016.[108] In 1971, only 287 of 1019 centers were considered adequate, generating total construction requirements of $338,400,000. The unfinanced construction requirement had expanded to $399 million by 1974, at which time the Army declared a 10-year Army Reserve Construction Program to eliminate most of the major problems by 1980.

This plan called for spending $54 million a year on Military Construction Army Reserve (the MCAR appropriation). This figure was approached only once in the next decade—$53.8 million in 1977—and fell to $30 million in 1980. By the time $65 million was available in 1982 and $53 million was requested for 1984, inflation had halved the value of such a sum. As a result, the Army Reserve's construction backlog stood at $848 million in 1982.[109] Even though the Army Reserve possesses many fine, modern Reserve Centers well-equipped with maintenance facilities and training areas, the majority of Army Reserve centers are inadequate. Some centers are inadequate because they are old or too small, while others are inadequate because they are rented facilities that were not designed to house Army Reserve units. There has not been enough money appropriated to replace or upgrade all of the inadequate facilities, and there are Army Reserve units in 1983 training in former automobile showrooms and unused portions of bowling alleys.

The USAR must also build and maintain maintenance facilities and certain training areas. The Army Reserve is responsible in part for the training areas of a number of installations such as Fort Indiantown Gap, Pa. and Fort Pickett, Va., where MCAR monies have been spent on training ranges and other facilities used by Reserve units.[110]

---

108. *Resource Allocation to Reserve Components,* p. 68.

109. The $848 million dollar backlog figure comes from *The Posture of the Army and Department of the Army Budget Estimates for Fiscal Year 1983,* p. 55; other construction figures are found in the Annual Historical Summaries of the Office of the Chief, Army Reserve and *The Posture of the U.S. Army Reserve,* previously cited.

110. Sometimes the planned use of facilities by Reservists can lead to some decisions of dubious long-term value. For example, when the Army Reserve funded the construction of an encampment area on Fort

The adequacy of training areas has a direct impact upon the ability of a unit to train for its mobilization mission, and when a unit must travel several hours to reach a suitable facility for field training, the amount of time remaining for training is seriously reduced. Although there has been an upgrading of training areas in recent years, many units cannot meet their full potential because of a lack of ranges or maneuver areas.

Despite budget constraints which have placed limits on training facilities, equipment issues and personnel strength, the Army Reserve has made considerable progress since 1970 in the critical area of training. In the past 10–12 years, training has become more imaginative, training has become better managed, training–support personnel have been increased, training flexibility has been achieved, and training standards have been upgraded. In addition, the Army has instituted affiliation programs between the active and Reserve Components, and the long-standing Mutual Support Program has enhanced training and readiness.

In 1970, the Army Reserve had two major training problems. The first was an extensive backlog of new Reserve enlistees who had been unable to obtain their initial active duty training. Since the establishment of the REP–63 enlistment program on September 3, 1963, Army Reserve enlistees were guaranteed as much initial active duty as was necessary to complete basic training and become qualified in their military occupation specialty. When the Army was expanded in the mid-1960's, priority for training went to active Army draftees, and Army Reservists were unable to obtain basic training and technical schooling.

Basic training delays of up to two years were not uncommon in the 1960's. By July 1, 1969, 21,652 Reservists—approximately 10 percent of the USAR enlisted force—were awaiting training. The inability to obtain initial training was particularly acute in medical specialities,[111] and this problem was not alleviated until 1971. As the number of new soldiers entering the active Army decreased,

Pickett in 1982, the Army denied funds to install heating in the barracks and administrative areas. The rationale was that these facilities would only be used by Reservists on weekends and in the summer during Annual Training. The Fort Pickett commander's entreaties that there just might be a winter mobilization someday were rejected so that a relatively few dollars could be saved.

111. *Annual Historical Summary, July 1, 1970 to June 30, 1971*, Office of the Chief, Army Reserve, Washington, D.C., pp. 7–8.

Reservists were able to obtain training. The REP–63 backlog was down to 1,904 by June 30, 1972, and it ceased to be a problem the next year.

The second major problem in 1970 was that the entire Army Reserve training philosophy and approach seemed to be inadequate. Ever since the Korean War, Reserve units had concentrated on basic unit training (BUT), with the attainment of company-level proficiency as the objective. Once the unit had achieved company-level proficiency, it would take the standard Army Training Test (ATT). Once all of the companies of a battalion passed their ATT, the battalion would start on battalion-level training. This, however, rarely occurred.[112]

In theory, units were supposed to be able to progress three weeks along the training cycle toward battalion and higher level proficiency each year. Such progress was in reality almost impossible, because units would have a 20 percent turn-over among their junior enlisted personnel each year. After two or three years, it became necessary to stop company-level training and start over on squad and platoon-level training.

This endless cycle of training was exacerbated in the 1960's by inadequate training facilities, curtailment of Reserve operations and maintenance funds, reduction in advisor support, and the REP–63 backlog. Something had to be done.

In January 1970, following the Chief of Staff's December 22, 1969, memo reaffirming the Reserve Components as the principal source of mobilization expansion, the Department of the Army directed the Continental Army Command (CONARC) to improve Reserve Component training and readiness.[113] After studying the problem, CONARC determined that improvements in the advisor system, an affiliation between active and Reserve units and more mutual support between the components would lead to major improvements in training and readiness.

---

112. In 1970, 31 percent of Army Reserve companies had achieved company-level training. There was little progress though. That year, 11 percent of Army Reserve battalions reported that they had moved from squad-level to platoon-level training and seven percent reported progress from platoon-level to company-level training. See *Annual Historical Summary, Fiscal Year 1971,* Continental U.S. Army Command, Fort Monroe, Va, 1972, p. 187.

113. *Annual Historical Summary, Fiscal Year 1970,* Continental U.S. Army Command, Fort Monroe, Va, 1971, pp. 226–29.

CAPSTONE created a training and planning relationship that focused upon wartime missions and left no doubt as to the wartime organization of every unit in the total peacetime force. CAPSTONE thereby became the basis for much mobilization planning. This planning is an extraordinarily complex task involving manning, equipping, training and deploying more than 4,000 separate military units to more than 50 different installations.[119]

Mutual Support Programs have proven beneficial, and Roundout and Affiliation solved an Army force structure problem. Roundout and Affiliation led to CAPSTONE, but Roundout and Affiliation did not alter the fact that Army Reserve unit training did not seem to progress very quickly.

Unit commanders were given more flexibility in training in 1972 when the number of mandatory and general subjects was reduced to allow more emphasis upon mission-related training. In 1974, the Army started to move away from the Army Training Test and began to develop the Army Training and Evaluation Programs—ARTEPs. The ARTEPs defined unit training status by the ability of a unit to perform a number of mission-related tasks. The ARTEP was different for each type of unit and gave the commander a guide by which to tailor his training program. More importantly, the ARTEP concept made it easier to define training readiness. The ARTEP concept abolished the practice of estimating how many weeks a unit had progressed during the year. Instead, a unit's training readiness was measured by the proportion of major and minor training tasks the unit could or did accomplish. Thus, the training portion of the overall readiness equation became more objective and less subjective.

FORSCOM EMPHASIZES REALISTIC TRAINING

At the same time the Army was developing the ARTEPs, the Steadfast reorganization was having an effect upon Army Reserve training and readiness. The new FORSCOM emphasized field exercises, the use of aggressor forces for realistic training, field skills such as camouflage, cover and conceal-

119. Testimony, Maj. Gen. William R. Berkman, Chief, Army Reserve, before the Committee on Armed Services, U.S. Senate, Feb. 26, 1980. See also, *Department of the Army Historical Summary, FY 1980,* (Draft), Department of the Army, Washington, DC, pp. II–6 and VIII–28.

ment, adventure training, and the realistic use of training aids. In 1974, FORSCOM's second year, the new command emphasized mission-related training for Army Reserve units during weekend IDT. Reserve combat support and combat service support units were urged to perform actual support missions on weekends. The next year, FORSCOM required Army Reserve units to conduct at least two weekend field training exercises, and units were told to minimize parades, details and fatigue work during IDT. Looking carefully at typical Reserve unit training, FORSCOM personnel concluded that half of IDT was not directed toward mission training. Two weekends each year were devoted to preparation for the Annual General Inspection (AGI); two went into recruiting; one was lost to ceremonies and parades; and one was spent in MOS testing. Annual Training (AT) time was also lost to administration, weekend passes, parties, PX visits, issue and turn-in of equipment and travel. It was estimated that only 8 to 9 days of useful training were being accomplished during the 14-day AT period.[120]

The problem was that many of the diversions from mission-related training were either justifiable or desirable. In the mid-1970's, the Army Reserve was having tremendous recruiting and retention problems. Reserve commanders recognized that benefits such as making use of the PX and active Army recreation facilities during AT were inducements for Reservists to remain in the Army Reserve. Commanders realized that having the middle weekend off reduced family objections to Annual Training, and a final night party was good for morale.

The administrative problems were a fact of life. This was before the Army Reserve started to receive additional help under the full-time manning program. Paperwork requirements—generated by the active Army—had exploded, and the increased administrative workload was a direct result of the Total Force policy. With the increased reliance upon the Reserve Components, Reserve units were subjected to the full weight of active Army requirements with little or no change in the full-time manpower to support this workload.[121]

---

120. *Annual Report of Major Activities, Fiscal Year 1975,* U.S. Army Forces Command, Fort McPherson, GA, 1976, pp. 423 and 424.

121. C. F. Briggs, *1980 Reduction of Administrative Workload at the Reserve Component Unit Level,* final report, RCCC Task Force, Department of the Army, Washington, DC, 1980, p. 4–2.

There simply was not time enough in 280 training hours a year to achieve all desirable training objectives while accomplishing all *required* administrative tasks. When faced with a choice between looking good on an AGI, which concentrated on administration, or improving training readiness, which was still very subjective, unit commanders chose to pass their AGIs.[122]

Although recognizing the dilemma that strict training policies created, FORSCOM continued to demand more realistic training. In 1978, Reserve commanders were required to conduct 88 hours of mission-related training during AT. This mission-related time could not include travel, equipment issue and turn-in, pay call, physical training testing, marksmanship, or even clearing of post at the end of AT. As a result, unit commanders began to schedule evening and overnight training to achieve the mandatory 88 hours. The increased night-time training was what the Reserve units needed, and the end result was an improvement in field training.

In 1979, Reserve units were told to emphasize night training and to concentrate upon mission essential training—those tasks which had to be done to perform the wartime mission. Since then, mission-essential training has been the watchword, and units have concentrated on likely wartime missions, in contrast to achieving every capability identified for their type of unit. Army Reserve training readiness thus made major improvements between 1970 and 1983 because of stricter standards, increased active Army assistance, the adoption of the ARTEP system, and a clearer identification of wartime responsibilities as defined by CAPSTONE relationships. An increase in the number of full-time personnel has helped reduce the administrative problems faced by commanders, and advances in mobilization planning have more clearly identified the tasks that units need to accomplish in peacetime.

---

122. The Briggs report urged the army to reduce the administrative workload at the unit level. A watchdog organization was set up within The Adjutant General's (TAG) Office, but by 1983 its accomplishments have been more form than substance. Probably the two biggest changes which have slightly reduced unit administrative requirements are the lengthening of the minimum Officer Evaluation Report (OER) time to 120 days and dropping the monthly serial number check of weapons. Weapons are now counted monthly, and the serial number check is done quarterly.

MOBILIZATION

Estimates of readiness aside, the key to Army Reserve unit usefulness is the ability to mobilize. At least one-half of the Army's war-making capability is in the Ready Reserve, and the entire Total Force policy is predicated upon the ability of the Reserve Components to mobilize quickly. Mobilization is a complex process requiring that people and equipment be brought together in the right proportions at the right time. Mobilizing a Reserve unit means assembling all of its members, separating them from their families and civilian jobs, gathering all of their personal gear and unit equipment, moving this assemblage in a few days to a mobilization station, performing last minute training, perhaps going overseas, and, finally, arriving at the wartime destination able to perform the unit mission. Obviously, much can go wrong with this process.[123] It is an undertaking fraught with opportunities for failure and confusion. Experience with Reserve Component mobilization for World War II, Korea,

---

123. The stark necessity for mobilization exercises is vividly illustrated by the experience of the 3397th US Army Garrison during MOBEX 78. This Chattanooga, Tenn., Army Reserve unit was assigned to operate Camp Shelby, Miss. At the time, the press described Camp Shelby as a swampy, mosquito-ridden camp, some 45 miles north of Biloxi, Miss., which had not been used by active units since the end of World War II. It was one of some 15 semi-active or state-operated installations which would have to be used for mobilization purposes in cases of full mobilization.

The garrison's mission in MOBEX 78 was to prepare Camp Shelby to receive five Reserve Component combat brigades that were coming to Shelby for final training before overseas deployment. The garrison's first problem was that Camp Shelby had only enough barracks for one brigade, and even these were wooden, temporary World War II buildings. The garrison attempted to requisition tents, but the requisition was cancelled by an improperly-programmed computer. The computer problems proved meaningless anyway, because the Army did not have enough tents for four mechanized brigades. Actually, however, the garrison didn't need tentage for four brigades, because the units coming to Shelby were 4,000 men understrength.

The garrison tried to requisition trained men to flesh out the brigades. However, at the time, the Army had three different personnel requisitioning systems in effect—one each for active Army, National Guard and Army Reserve. These systems could not be made compatible. In the end, there was a 40 percent error rate on the personnel assigned as fillers.

According to outside observers at the time, it was difficult to see how the troops could have been given final training at Camp Shelby. There was no ammunition available for firing, and Shelby had no place to store the diesel fuel needed for maneuvers. There was no way to get the M60 tanks and armored personnel carriers to Camp Shelby because of

Berlin, and Vietnam has shown that it is very easy for the process to break down.

Though each mobilization has gone more smoothly than the previous one, even the small Vietnam mobilization was far from perfect. This tendency was recognized in the early 1970's, so the Army decided to practice mobilization. The result has been a series of mobilization exercises (MOBEXs) in 1976, 1978, 1980 and 1982 which have led to changes in Army Reserve administration and training while fine-tuning mobilization planning.

The first exercise, MOBEX 76, was the first large-scale test of mobilization plans since the Berlin mobilization provided a real world practical exercise in 1961. The 1976 exercise was a free-play command post exercise representing a deliberate full mobilization for general war in Europe. Nearly 300 Army Reserve units participated in the exercise, which simulated alert, mobilization at home station, and movement to the mobilization stations. Even though MOBEX 76 was only a paper exercise, the Army learned from it. As a result, mobilization and deployment plans were revised, and the Army took steps to correct the deficiencies it revealed.

MOBEX 78 was code-named "Nifty Nugget". The crisis situation portrayed in Nifty Nugget involved a short warning, fast breaking attack on NATO forces in Europe. In such a crisis, the United States would have to use the forces in being, and there would be little time to improve the readiness of the Reserve Components. This exercise was DoD wide and involved several other departments of the federal government. As in 1976, Reserve personnel and equipment did not actually move, but took part through representative player cells who provided real-world data for the exercise. As in 1976, Nifty Nugget showed that the United States had severe mobilization problems. First, existing mobilization plans were a hodgepodge of old and unconnected Presidential emergency orders, policies, regulations and procedures. Second, although contingency plans as-

---

a shortage of flatcars. Further, even if the necessary 300 heavy-duty flat cars could be found, the one decrepit rail line leading to Shelby was incapable of handling them. In addition, the telephone system at Camp Shelby did not work. The entire mobilization at Shelby would have been a disaster.

In the end, FORSCOM concluded that there was nothing grievously wrong at Camp Shelby that couldn't have been cured by the efficient application of sufficient resources. (Adapted from pp. 402–404 of FORSCOM's *Annual Historical Review, Oct. 1, 1980 to September 30, 1981*).

sumed that units would be at their desired levels of personnel and equipment, Reserve Component units were seriously short of personnel and equipment in 1978. On the civil side, the federal government was in disarray. Civil emergency planning had concentrated only upon natural disasters and nuclear attack. There was no coordination on the industrial base, and the public health sector was unprepared for mobilization.[124] Following Nifty Nugget, the Federal Emergency Management Agency was formed to coordinate government-wide emergency planning.

The next MOBEX, in 1980, was known as "Proud Spirit". Like its predecessors, Proud Spirit revealed that the mobilization preparation of the United States was woefully inadequate.[125] From the Army Reserve's point of view, Proud Spirit confirmed the inability of active Army installations to support a rapid influx of Reserve units. The exercise did identify problems to be attacked by the Army Readiness and Mobilization Regions (ARMRs). The exercise was carried out during the Iranian Crisis and after the decision to form the Rapid Deployment Joint Task Force (RDJTF). As a result, the exercise gave valuable clues as to the steps required to make the RDJTF a true rapidly-deployable force.[126]

The most recent such exercise, MOBEX 83, took place in the fall of 1982, and was actually three exercises in one. Three different warplans were played in successive weeks, and officials reported very extensive improvements in mobilization capabilities. The exercise focused on the Army's Reserve and National Guard and found them able to deploy despite continued equipment shortages.[127]

MOBEX–83, moreover, confirmed the results of an earlier exercise that dealt with accessions. This exercise, Grand Payload, indicated that TRADOC would have difficulties in

---

124. July 23, 1980, the Department of Defense released an unclassified 24-page report on Nifty Nugget. The findings of this report are summarized in "Exercise Reveals Defense Problems," *Pentagram News*, Washington, DC, July 31, 1980, pp. 1–4.

125. See John J. Fialka, "The Pentagon's Exercise Proud Spirit: Little Cause for Pride," *Parameters, Journal of the U.S. Army War College,* Vol. XI, No. 1, pp. 38–41. See also, Maj. Richard B. Crossland, "Suppose the Balloon Goes Up: Then What," *Army Reserve Magazine* (Winter 1981), pp. 24–27.

126. See John J. Fialka, "U.S. Again Fails Test of Ability to Mobilize," *Washington Star,* Dec. 21, 1980, pp. A–1 and A–6.

127. "U.S. Crisis Exercise Reports Major Gains in Ability to Mobilize," *New York Times,* Dec. 12, 1982. Also, Capt. Robert Pratt, "Mobilization: No Straight A Report Card," *Army Reserve Magazine* (Summer, 1983), pp. 22–23.

expanding the training base upon mobilization. For example, Army Reserve reception stations did not possess the automatic data processing equipment required to rapidly process new soldiers into the Army. The Army Reserve training divisions were not fully prepared to expand the training base because of a lack of equipment, and the Army's training requirements and resourcing systems were unable to cope with a partial mobilization.[128]

By taking part in these exercises, Reservists gained valuable experience in the mobilization process. On a larger scale, the federal Government gained an appreciation of the need for better mobilization planning. Although changes have come slowly, the federal Government in general and the military departments in particular have placed greater emphasis upon mobilization planning in recent years. For the Army Reserve, the increased emphasis upon mobilization has made mobilization capabilities a top consideration in day-to-day decisions. Training activities and administration are now being conducted in light of how these actions will enhance mobilization.

On the practical level, mobilization planning was clearly defined for Army Reservists with the August 1982 publication of the *Reserve Component Commanders Handbook for Mobilization.* For the first time, every peacetime action that a unit commander must take to prepare for mobilization is indicated.

The Mobilization Personnel Processing System (MOBPERS) has been compiled out of the experiences of the MOBEXs. These exercises have finally helped the Army achieve the ability to swiftly and smoothly mobilize the Reserve Component, including the Retired Reserve. The Army has also established the Army Mobilization and Operations Planning System (AMOPS) as the single, integrated mobilization and deployment planning system for the Army.

The new systems and procedures they represent have been a quantum leap ahead for Army Reserve readiness. Because a sturdy framework of mobilization concepts has been established and because additional personnel assets have been devoted to mobilization planning in recent years, the Army Reserve is better able to mobilize in 1983 than at any other time in its history.

128. For the results of Grand Payload, see *Evaluation Report, Exercise Grand Payload* (Arlington, Va.: Systems Research and Applications, Corp., 1982). Proud Saber Reports are outlined in After Action Reports, HQ, TRADOC, MOBEX 83.

THE IMPACT OF THE IRANIAN CRISIS

Finally, any history of the Army Reserve in the 1970's and early 1980's would be incomplete without an overview of the impact caused by the Iranian Crisis and the Soviet invasion of Afghanistan. The November 4, 1979, seizure of the American embassy in Tehran underscored this country's inability to project conventional forces into the Middle East, while the December 27, 1979, Soviet invasion of Afghanistan raised the issue of American capability to counter Russian threats in the Persian Gulf region. President Jimmy Carter committed the United States to the defense of the Persian Gulf in his January 23, 1980, State of the Union Address. The RDJTF was officially established on March 1, 1980, with the mission of executing that commitment.

As soon as planners began to draw up contingency plans, it became obvious that Reserve units were going to be key elements of the Rapid Deployment Force—Army (RFD–A) troop list. A decision to employ the task force would require a call-up of Reserve units in excess of the 50,000-man authority that had been in the law since May, 1976.[129] Defense officials immediately sought an increase in the 90-day call-up authority. Congress responded quickly, and in December 1980, Carter signed Public Law 96–584 giving him authority to mobilize up to 100,000 members of the Selected Reserve without a declaration of war or national emergency. Concurrently, the Army revised its former Mobilization Designee (MOBDES) program and instituted the Individual Mobilization Augmentee (IMA) program. These individuals were included in the Selected Reserve, thus making them eligible for the 100,000 call-up.

The 100,000 figure had a direct relationship to the number of Reservists of all services that would be needed to sustain the RDJTF. In answering questions from the floor during the convention of the Association of the US Army in October 1981, Lt. Gen. Robert C. Kingston, the RDJTF commander, said that he would need almost the entire call-up authority to move and sustain a corps-sized RDJTF in the Middle East.

129. On May 14, 1976, the Reserve Forces Call-Up Authority, became Public Law 94–286. It permitted the President to mobilize a maximum of 50,000 Selected Reservists for a period of up to 90 days without declaring a national emergency. This authority was necessary to add teeth to the Total Force policy of heavy reliance upon the Reserve Components.

A few months later, Kingston told the midwinter conference of the Reserve Officers Association that "the Rapid Deployment Joint Task Force is one of the foremost 'customers' of the Reserve Components. If this force is ever deployed in anger, a sizable portion of my forces—particularly combat support and combat service support forces—will come from the Reserve and the National Guard."

Kingston stated that the Army Reserve was absolutely critical to the success of the RDJTF, pointing out that 80 percent of his psychological operations capability came from the Army Reserve. He told the ROA that Army Reserve units would be among the first of those deployed with the RDJTF and that Reserve commanders had to do everything within their capability to get their units ready for immediate deployment.[130]

The exact number of Army Reserve units earmarked for the RDJTF—now called the US Central Command—in 1983 is classified. However, in March 1981, Maj. Gen. Berkman testified before Congress that "the importance of the Army Reserve continues to grow. An increasing number of reserve units have been assigned high priority because of the essential combat service and logistical support needed early upon mobilization and deployment, and for support of the Rapid Deployment Force. Recently, 83 Army Reserve units have been identified for inclusion in the Army's portion of the Rapid Deployment Force because of the essential combat support and combat service support they represent."[131]

Following their inclusion in the RDJTF, Army Reserve units came under intensified management. The RDJTF units went to the top of FORSCOM's Intensified Management Force List, which had previously been led by Roundout units. These USAR RDJTF units had their mobilization plans updated and their equipment priority adjusted upward.[132]

---

130. Prepared remarks, Lt. Gen. Robert C. Kingston, for delivery to the Reserve Officers Association Midwinter Conference, Feb. 15, 1982.

131. Testimony, Maj. Gen. William R. Berkman, Chief, Army Reserve, before Subcommittee on Military Personnel and Compensation, House Armed Services Committee, March 11, 1981.

132. For details on the increased priority of USAR units and cross-leveling of assets, see Maj. Richard B. Crossland, "RDJTF: Can It Get There Without the USAR?," *Army Reserve Magazine*, (Spring 1982), pp. 8–10.

Despite the fact that Army Reserve units moved higher on the Army's resource list, it would be naive to assume that all of the Army Reserve's RDJTF–identified units are at full readiness. Many of these units are in doubtful condition for immediate deployment because of severe equipment shortages.

There is a hard core of shortage items for these priority units, and many of these pieces of equipment will not be available until at least 1985. There are unique units with unique equipment needs for which equipment has not even been type-standardized, let alone procured. In other cases, funds are not available to buy needed items such as landing craft and lighterage.[133]

Defense guidance and projections reveal that equipment problems will continue in future years. Unclassified portions of the 1983–87 Program Objective Memorandum (POM) state that a significant portion of the RDJTF combat support package will remain in the Reserve Components, even while those components remain underequipped. The Army leadership has consistently testified that the Reserve Components will remain a vital part of the Army for the foreseeable future, and there has been no mention of a diminished RDJTF role for the Army Reserve. It would appear that the Army Reserve will have high-priority contingency missions for a long time to come.

In summary,the Army Reserve's integration into immediate deployment plans is an indication of how far the Total Force policy progressed between 1970 and 1983. In this short span of time, the Army's Reserve Components have changed from being back-up forces to be deployed 90–150 days into a crisis, to being a part of the first units to deploy in case of an emergency. Since 1970, the training and equipping of the Army Reserve have improved more than in any similar period of American history. The citizen-soldier concept has matured in late 20th century America, and the blending of the traditional American reliance upon Reserve Components with the practical military needs of today's risky world represents an evolution of the citizen-soldier concept and a triumph for American democracy.

---

133. The problem of lighterage and watercraft is discussed in the November–December issue of *Army Logistician* and is included in Secretary of the Army John O. Marsh, Jr.'s 1983 Army posture statement.

11

The Caribbean/Latin America Connection

The Army Reserve had barely celebrated its seventy-fifth anniversary when it found its skills needed on a small Caribbean island that few Americans had ever heard of prior to October 1983. The island was Grenada, and its invasion by U.S.-led forces was an outgrowth of the Cold War and the continuing attempt by Fidel Castro's Cuba to extend its influence in the hemisphere.

The internal politics of Grenada and the pros and cons of the U.S. intervention there are irrelevant to the role the Army Reserve played in Urgent Fury, as the military operation was called. It is sufficient to say that Grenada had become a Cuban-influenced outpost in the eastern Caribbean and was widely regarded by its neighbors as a threat to the peace and tranquility of the region.

The immediate causes of the U.S.-led effort to free the island from its Marxist government were a bloody coup, a subsequent plea from the Organization of Eastern Caribbean States (OECS) for assistance in bringing order to one of its member states, and a fear—well-founded or not—that U.S. citizens resident at a medical college in Grenada were in danger.[1]

A hastily-organized task force of U.S. and OECS forces landed in Grenada during the early hours of October 25,

---

1. General information on the Grenada operation, code named Urgent Fury, is based on accounts in Lt. Col. Ronald H. Spector, *U.S. Marines in Grenada, 1983* (Washington: Headquarters, U.S. Marine Corps, 1987) and Maj. Mark Adkins, *Urgent Fury: The Battle for Grenada* (Lexington, Mass.: Lexington Books, 1989).

1983, and secured the island after several days of heavy fighting.[2] No reserve component forces were included in the assault, but the follow-up operation required the Army Reserve.

In 1983 as now, the vast majority of United States Army's civil affairs expertise resided in the Army Reserve. Indeed, of the thirty-seven civil affairs units in the Army in 1983, thirty-six were USAR assets.[3] On October 28, just three days after the invasion, Col. Gabriel Zinni, commander of the 358th Civil Affairs Brigade, USAR, was called by the CINCLANT J–5 and told to begin planning for a deployment to Grenada.[4] It was entirely appropriate for the 360th to receive the first call, as they were affiliated with the Atlantic Command (LANTCOM) through the Army's CAPSTONE program. This meant that LANTCOM staff officers knew the members of the 358th and were confident of their ability to perform the mission.[5]

The first Army Reservist into Grenada, however, was not affiliated with one of the civil affairs units. Maj. Tony Lawton, an active reservist assigned to the staff of the 79th U.S. Army Reserve Command (ARCOM) in Willow Grove, Pa., was sent to Grenada on November 2 to assess the situation there. His task was to determine whether Army Reserve civil affairs specialists would be helpful in restoring the civil government of the island nation.

Lawton, who commented that Grenada was the "first time I've been sent into a hostile fire zone and put up at a motel," arrived in country before the fighting had completely ended. He inspected the situation, made his assessment, and returned to LANTCOM headquarters in Norfolk, Va., on November 5. He concluded that Army Reservists would be of use in Grenada, and the call went out for volunteers.[6]

Thirty members of the Army Reserve's 358th Civil Affairs Brigade, headquartered in Norristown, Pa., the 416th Civil Affairs Company, also of Norristown, and the 304th Civil Affairs Group from Philadelphia were the first to answer the call. They were joined by a reservist from the Individual Ready Reserve

2. Adkins, pp. 167ff.

3. Maj. Art House, "Grenada: Army Reserve Goes into Action," *Army Reserve Magazine*, Vol. 30, No. 2 (1984), p. 19.

4. Lt. Col. Willard B. Fenstermacher, "CAPSTONE Relationship Put to Test in Grenada," *The Officer*, February 1984, pp. 21–24. CINCLANT is the Commander-in-Chief, Atlantic Command.

5. *Ibid.*, p. 21.

6. "Full-Timer Spearheads USAR Role," *Army Reserve Magazine*, Vol. 30, No. 2 (1984), p. 21; Fenstermacher, "Capstone Relationship Put to Test in Grenada," pp. 21–22.

(IRR).[7] Some of the volunteer Reservists remained in CONUS headquarters, but others left immediately for Grenada.

The first seven civil affairs volunteers arrived in Grenada on November 9, only twelve days after the initial alert had been issued. The team was headed by Lt. Col. Bill O'Brien, a Princeton University administrator.[8] The breadth of their experience was extraordinary, but it was not atypical of the civilian skills brought to the military by members of the reserve components.

O'Brien, for example, assumed responsibility for coordinating efforts to restore the island's public facilities and utilities. Maj. David Henderson was a senior official in the government of Philadelphia, Pa. Sgts. 1st Class Gordon Funk and Raymond G. "Buddy" Webb were, respectively, vice president of a water treatment company and a supervisory iron worker. Maj. Paul Decker—the IRR member—was vice president for tourism for the city of Philadelphia, Maj. Frank Vecchiarello was an airline pilot, and Maj. Mike Radbill was an engineer at a nuclear power plant. The mix was unusual, but the results were not. According to Ted Morse, the head of the U.S. Agency for International Development mission in Grenada, the Grenada experience was "the smoothest civilian-military interface I've experienced in 23 years."[9]

Members of the Army Reserve civil affairs community remained in Grenada through August 1985, continuing their mission of restoring and improving government services on the island, including the public school system there.[10] Members of the USAR's 360th Civil Affairs Brigade, headquartered in Columbia, S.C., had landed in Grenada in July 1984, and were given the mission of rehabilitating twenty of the sixty-four schools on the island. Working in three-week increments, the reservists coordinated their activities with personnel of the Agency for International Development (USAID) and spent more than a year on the project.[11] USAID applauded the

7. House, "Grenada: Army Reserve Goes into Action," p. 19; Larry Carney, "20 Reservists Serving in Grenada," *Army Times*, December 19, 1983, p. 37. CAPSTONE is a program wherein a reserve component unit affiliates with an active headquarters or unit and trains with it on a regular basis. The 358th had such a relationship with Headquarters, CINCLANT, and the members of the 358th were well known to the staff at the unified command headquarters.

8. House, "Grenada: Army Reserve Goes into Action," pp. 19–20; Fenstermacher, "Capstone Relationship Put to Test in Grenada," pp. 21–22.

9. Fenstermacher, "Capstone Relationship Put to Test in Grenada," pp. 21–22.

10. Lew Brodsky and Tim Miller, "Grenada: USAR Takes on Vital Schools Mission," *Army Reserve Magazine*, Vol. 31, No. 3 (1985), p. 14.

11. Maj. Rudolph C. Barnes, "Grenada Revisited," *The Officer*, July 1985, pp. 14–17.

work of the reservists and asked repeatedly for their continued involvement in Grenadian improvement efforts.[12]

Not only did the Army Reservists repair the schools' physical facilities, but members of the reserve civil affairs teams on the island quickly identified another pressing need: textbooks. Maj. Larry Ochalek, an Army Reservist in Southfield, Mich., heard about the textbook shortage and realized that the "obsolete" books that his school system had little use for would go a long way toward meeting the needs of the Grenadians. Ochalek collected 20,000 pounds of textbooks which were transported to Grenada by a private charitable organization.[13] They were met there by an eight member team from the 360th CA Bde. According to Grenada's Minister of Education, George McGuire, "We have gotten rid of all those books that can be regarded as political propaganda and [will] replace them with books that have relevance to democracy."[14]

Civil affairs specialists were not the only USAR soldiers deployed to Grenada. Indeed, the Grenada operation seemed to set a pattern for overseas deployment of Army Reservists that was expanded and repeated throughout the remaining years of the decade. The 149th Judge Advocate General Detachment from Norfolk, Va., for example, served an annual training rotation in Grenada during the spring of 1984 working on claims against the United States government arising out of the invasion of the previous year. The 149th, like the 358th Civil Affairs Brigade, had a CAPSTONE relationship with an active component headquarters. In the case of the 149th, that unit was the 18th Airborne Corps. This established relationship undoubtedly smoothed the meshing of active and reserve component forces and allowed the 149th to function efficiently during its tour in Grenada. Of the 300 claims outstanding against the United States, the members of the 149th settled some 50 during their brief time in Grenada.[15]

It would be stretching the evidence to suggest that the successful—if limited—involvement of the Army Reserve in Grenada and the subsequrnt training opportunities led directly to the increase in overseas training during the remain-

12. Letter, James W. Habron, USAID Representative, Grenada, to Lt. Col. Earl Horan, U.S. Military Support Element, Grenada, July 19, 1984; letter, same author, to Lt. Col. Arthur Graves, U.S. Military Support Element, Grenada, August 3, 1984; copies of both letters in possession of the author.

13. Brodsky and Miller, "Grenada: USAR Takes on Vital Schools Mission," p. 18.

14. *Ibid.*, pp. 14, 18.

15. Donna Bolinger, "Grenada: The Mission Continues," *The Voice* (1st Army newspaper), June 1984, p. 3.

ing years of the decade. It is a fact, however, that the late 1980s saw a growing number of Army Reserve units deployed to Central and South America for annual training.

The overseas involvement of the Army Reserve in the hemisphere peaked at the end of the decade, when Army Reservists were intimately involved in the aftermath of Operation Just Cause—the removal of General Manuel Antonio Noriega from power in Panama. Between Grenada and Panama, however, and even after that time, the Army Reserve made its presence known in areas south of the U.S. border.

Before relations between the United States government and the Panamanian government headed by General Noriega worsened, Army Reserve units were regular visitors to Panama. Generally engineers and medical specialists, they went to Panama to train under conditions different from any they would encounter in the United States, building roads in areas where there had never been any roads and treating diseases they had only seen in textbooks.

These road-building exercises, called by different names in different countries, were superb training, and provided significant benefits to villagers whose only means of access to the world outside was a long trek through the jungle or a canoe ride down a river.

PANAMA ROAD BUILDING

"Costa Abajo '86" ("lower coast 1986") was one of these exercises, sponsored by the United States Southern Command (USSOUTHCOM). Army Reserve engineers from units in Alabama, Georgia, Mississippi, Texas, and Kentucky joined with units from the Army National Guard and members of the Panama Defense Forces in a road-building exercise that began in early January 1986 and ran through May. During this five-month period a total of 5000 reserve component soldiers—visiting Panama 900 at a time—constructed a nine-mile road along the Caribbean coast of Panama, connecting the villages of Rio Indio and Miguel de la Borda. In addition to the engineer involvement, public affairs specialists from sixteen states went to Panama and practiced their trade by preparing press releases and stories about what their compatriots were doing.[16]

Elsewhere in Panama, Army Reservists from C Company, 448th Engineers, Ponce, Puerto Rico, engaged in a bit of civic

16. Diane Dove, "Costa Abajo '86," *Army Reserve Magazine*, Vol. 32, No. 4 (1986), pp. 23–26; Capt. Kenneth W. Moore, "First Person Reflections on Panama," *Army Reserve Magazine*, Vol. 33, No. 1, 1986), pp. 18–19.

action of their own, constructing a steeple for a local church, repairing the roof of a schoolhouse, and building a latrine with septic tank. Working both with members of the Panama Defense Forces and soldiers from the U.S. active component, these Reservists were part of an Exercise named Kindle Liberty '87.[17]

It should be added parenthetically that at the same time as Exercise Kindle Liberty '87, members of Puerto Rico's 369th Station Hospital, USAR, were dispensing medical assistance to residents of the island of Vieques, seven miles off the coast of Puerto Rico. These medical personnel were assisted in accomplishing their mission by Reservists from the 448th Engineers, the 346th Transportation Battalion, and the 399th Port Construction Co.[18]

FUERTES CAMINOS

The Central American country of Honduras saw active USAR involvement in the 1980s, begun largely because of U.S. interest in the communist government of Nicaragua, located immediately south of Honduras.

Named "*Fuertes Caminos*"—"strong roads"—the exercises were designed to do many of the same things as the road-building in Panama: to provide unusual training opportunities for reserve soldiers, to increase the accessibility of Honduran villages that were isolated from other areas of their own country, and to serve as an instrument of United States foreign policy. The primary benefit for the Army Reserve was training: real, tough, no-nonsense practicing of soldier skills in a harsh and demanding environment.

In addition to the Army Reserve engineer and other construction personnel who were given the chance to improve their MOS skills during *Fuertes Caminos* or Blazing Trails exercises, Army Reserve cooks, launderers, medics, military police, and civil affairs specialists also trained under real-life conditions. The 1001st Field Service Company, from Chillicothe, Oh., for example, supported Blazing Trails '87 with fresh biscuits, clean clothes, and hot showers.[19]

Meanwhile, soldiers from the 377th Military Police Company from Cincinnati, Oh., and the 428th MP Co. from Niles,

17. Maj. Ernesto Fonseca and Lt. Col. Luis M. Garcia, "It's Back to School for 448th Engineers," *Army Reserve Magazine*, Vol. 33, No. 3 (1987), p. 18.

18. "Puerto Rican Reservists Assist Isolated Islanders," *Army Reserve Magazine*, Vol. 33, No. 4 (1987), p.15.

19. Pvt.2 Ed Meier, "The Supporting Cast: It Takes More than Engineers to Build a Road," *Army Reserve Magazine*, Vol. 33, No. 2 (1987), p. 16.

Mich., provided security for the Army Reservists and others who were in Honduras for the exercise. Army Reserve medical personnel treated tropical diseases that U.S. forces might encounter in a deployment to any number of countries in Central or South America, Africa, or Southeast Asia. As in the case of the engineer road-builders, the first-rate training enjoyed by these Reservists was magnified by the good that was done in helping Honduran civilians whose medical needs were not being met.[20]

MEDRETES

Medical readiness training exercises, or MEDRETEs, were a superb opportunity for the surgeons, general practitioner physicians, dentists, veterinarians, nurses, and other Army Reserve medical specialists. Medical teams deployed to Honduras throughout the last half of the 1980s. In 1986, for example, thirty Reservists from the 44th Evacuation Hospital in Oklahoma City, the 337th Dental Detachment from New Orleans, and the 565th Dental Detachment from Mesquite, Tex., spent their annual training in that Central American country.[21]

Many of the procedures were quick and relatively easy, such as pulling diseased teeth, but other surgical procedures such as correction of cleft-palate and cleft-lip deformities were more involved. In one short period in the summer of 1990, an Army Reserve medical team deployed to Honduras and in only two weeks operated on 37 individuals.[22]

FUERTES CAMINOS AGAIN

Fuertes Caminos '87, '88, and '89 were much like their counterpart in 1986, except that in some instances the road-

---

20. Capt. John R. Kachenmeister, "MP's Provide Security," *Army Reserve Magazine*, Vol. 33, No. 2 (1987), p. 17.

21. Maj. Bob Pratt, "Honduras: Reservists Practice Medicine in the Third World," *Army Reserve Magazine*, Vol. 32, No. 1 (1986), p. 20.

22. Sgt. Dave Olsen, "Blazing Trails Medics Make a Difference," *Army Reserve Magazine*, Vol. 33, No. 2 (1987), p. 18; Van D. Hipp, "An Emerging Role," *The Officer*, April 1991, p. 17. The author was in Honduras on numerous occasions during the years 1985–1991 and often met with Army Reserve physicians and nurses who were there on MEDRETEs. To a person, these Reservists were convinced that the experience they received treating patients in this small Central American country was both professionally rewarding and militarily beneficial. Several of the physicians indicated that some of the skin diseases they encountered there were found only in textbooks in the U.S. and that the opportunity to observe these pathologies firsthand was of tremendous medical value.

builders and medical personnel were joined by USAR civil affairs specialists who distributed used clothing that had been shipped down from the United States. Aviators also practiced their flying skills in support of the exercises, which operated from base camps with names ranging from *Oso Grande* (Big Bear) to Camp Powder Horn.[23]

412TH ENGINEER COMMAND

Engineers trained in other Central American countries at the same time, though in a slightly different context. Soldiers from the 412th Engineer Command, Vicksburg, Miss., one of the Army Reserve's two major engineer commands, went to Costa Rica and Guatemala—not to mention Bolivia, Colombia, Ecuador, Guyana, Peru, Uruguay, and Venezuela in South America—as an extension of the SOUTHCOM engineering staff, primarily to conduct project assessments and develop engineer work estimates.[24]

The 412th, experienced in South American deployments, took on the mission of supporting SOUTHCOM in the early part of the 1990s. The mission offered the benefits of realistic training for the unit and augmentation of its engineer staff for the unified command.[25]

In Costa Rica the 412th looked at projects ranging from road construction to a ferryboat terminal; in Guatemala, it examined sites for military headquarters, evaluated possible airport runway extensions, and considered the feasibility of constructing seawalls and drilling wells. Providing advice to SOUTHCOM on the Cano Blanco Road project, a proposal to construct and improve a road from Maryland, Costa Rica, to Parismina, Costa Rica, was typical of the work estimates prepared by these Army Reservists.[26]

---

23. ARNEWS, "U.S., Honduran Engineers Work Together in Latest Road-Building Exercise," *Army Reserve Magazine*, Vol. 34, No. 1 (1988), p. 25; Mst. Sgt. Nick Grand, "Saddling Up for Blazing Trails," *Army Reserve Magazine*, Vol. 33, No. 1 (1987), p. 22. See also, Rohloff, "A Day at 'Big Bear,'" p. 14; SSgt. Joyce Darwin, "*Fuertes Caminos* '88," *Army Reserve Magazine*, Vol. 34, No. 3 (1988), pp. 14–17 and Capt. Mark Zimmer, "Fuertes Caminos '89," *Army Reserve Magazine*, Vol. 35, No. 2 (1989), pp. 22–25.

24. Capt. Bruce R. Moore, "Reservists Pave Way in Costa Rica," *Engineer Update*, July 1991, p. 11 and Maj. Robert R. Bottin, Jr., "412th Engineers Train in South and Central America," *Open Channels*, Spring 1991, pp. 12–13; Maj. Robert R. Bottin, Jr. and Maj. Jimmy E. Fowler, "Reserve Engineer Command: Helping Latin America," *Engineer*, November 1992, p. 6.

25. Bottin, "412th Engineers Train in South and Central America," p. 12 and SSGt. Phil Hearn and Spec.4 Karen Magruder, "412th Engineers Assure Quality Work," *Army Reserve Magazine*, Vol. 33, No. 3 (1987), p. 26.

26. Bottin and Fowler, "Reserve Engineer Command," pp. 8–10.

A typical project statement, as epitomized by the Cano Blanco project, detailed the location and scope of the work proposed; analyzed the terrain and expected weather and the type of soil in the area through which the road would be built, and included such details as the location of local roadbuilding materials; a listing of the materials, manpower, and equipment required for the project; a time estimate; and a recommendation as to what parts of the project could be used as training opportunities by U.S. engineer soldiers.[27]

ECUADOR

As mentioned previously, Army Reservists also trained in South America during this period, with much of that activity taking place in Ecuador. "*Abriendo Rutas*" ("Open Roads"), the Ecuadoran equivalent of *Fuertes Caminos* or Blazing Trails, consisted of building a road through the eastern part of the country where the only other road had been destroyed by earthquakes in March 1987.[28]

Abriendo Rutas achieved its two major goals: (1) providing access to an oil pipeline that had been damaged by the quake so Ecuadoran engineers could get in and repair it and (2) opening a road to the outside for the 75,000 Ecuadorans who had been cut off from the other parts of their country. The pipeline, which carried Ecuadoran crude oil, was vital to the economy of the small South American country, and as in Honduras, Costa Rica, and Panama, the work of the Reservists served both their own training needs and U.S. national security interests.[29]

The reserve component soldiers worked under the aegis of Task Force 1169, headquartered near the small Ecuadoran town of Archidona. Several soldiers from the 478th Civil Affairs Company of Coral Gables, Fla., were fluent in Spanish, and their linguistic skills, proved invaluable during the roadbuilding exercise.[30] According to Col. Bruce E. Moats, Jr., a member of the 412th Engineer Command, the experience in Ecuador was a valuable lesson. "We are learning new engineering techniques," said Moats, "and we are experiencing the problems associated with deployment to an area with a

27. *Ibid.*

28. "Action Shifts to Ecuador for 'Abriendo Rutas,'" *Army Reserve Magazine*, Vol. 33, No. 3 (1987), p. 25.

29. Jim Haas, "Army Reservists to Help Repair Earthquake Damage in Ecuador," *Army Reserve Magazine*, Vol. 33, No. 2 (1987), p. 23.

30. SSgt. Will Sullivan, "Army Reserve Interpreters Essential to Success," *Army Reserve Magazine*, Vol. 33, No. 3 (1987), p. 27.

different language and culture."[31] The difficulties of deploying to a country with a different culture would be experienced just a few years later by many Army Reserve units, though the locale would be far from South America.

BOLIVIA

Bolivia is a land-locked country in South America that may best be known to Americans as a source of cocaine. The Army Reserve visited there in 1993 as part of a medical readiness training exercise: a MEDRETE. Members of the Army Reserve, the Army National Guard and the active component, traveled to the Beni Valley to provide medical assistance to villagers there. Thirty-two Reservists from the 305th Field Hospital in Gulfport, Miss., were part of this group.[32]

These men and women—medical doctors, dentists, and nurses, and other medical personnel—saw 3300 medical patients and 357 dental patients (extracting some 1,029 teeth) over the eight-day training period. The veterinarian saw 567 animals and performed over 1600 procedures, from vaccinating to treating intestinal parasites. The soldiers also distributed clothing and toys collected in the Gulfport area, leaving the villagers in better health and better clad than when they arrived.[33]

JUST CAUSE

None of the Army Reserve's involvement in Latin America and the Caribbean during the period 1983–1993 was as exciting as its participation in Operation Just Cause, the U.S. invasion that ousted Panamanian General Manuel Antonio Noriega Moreno from power. Panama had been of special interest to the United States for most of the twentieth century, primarily because of the canal that sliced the country in half. The United States had been instrumental in securing Panamanian independence from Colombia in 1903, and then had secured rights to a "Panama Canal Zone" and built the canal through it.[34]

A 1977 treaty, which went into effect in 1979, transferred control of the Zone to Panama and contained a provision re-

31. Hearn and Magruder, "412th Engineers Assure Quality Work," pp. 26–27.

32. Lt. Col. Paul Adams, "Bolivian Smiles," *Army Reserve Magazine*, Vol. 403, No. 1 (1993), p. 24.

33. *Ibid.*, p. 25.

34. Sandra W. Meditz and Dennis M. Hanratty (Eds.), *Panama: A Country Study* (Washington: GPO, 1989), pp. xxiii–xxvi and 22–24.

quiring complete U.S. departure from the country by the year 2000. General Noriega, an officer in the Panama National Guard and the defacto head of state, had been at the same time our intelligence source for U.S. drug enforcement agents and a valued conduit for the cocaine cartels that shipped the illegal drug out of Colombia to the United States and Europe.[35]

The U.S. relationship with Noriega was schizophrenic at best, with rumors of his being on the payroll of the Central Intelligence Agency competing with other rumors that he had stashed millions of drug cartel dollars in bank accounts in Switzerland. In 1987 the United States began to squeeze Noriega by cutting off all economic and military assistance to Panama, and in 1988 two separate federal grand juries in Florida indicted him on racketeering and drug trafficking charges. Noriega responded by becoming cozier with Fidel Castro, and the Panamanian strongman blustered and threatened the United States and its personnel in Panama.[36]

ARMY RESERVISTS IN THE PLANNING PROCESS

Military planning for the ouster of Noriega began in 1988, went through several plans code-named ELABORATE MAZE, FISSURES and BLUE SPOON, and ended in Noriega's defeat and capture under Operation JUST CAUSE in December 1989. The military operation was executed largely without difficulty. What was more problematical was the end-state to be achieved after the military victory: the restoration of democracy.[37]

Consideration of the requirements needed for a post-Noriega transition to democracy had begun at the same time as serious operational planning for his removal from power. SOUTHCOM was not without its civil affairs assets, but they were few in number. The civil affairs portion of the J–5 staff consisted of four Army Reserve officers serving in the Active

35. *Ibid.*, pp. xxix–xxx and 48–57.

36. The author was Chief of the Latin America Division and press spokesman for the United States Senate's Select Committee on Intelligence during this period. He was constantly questioned by the news media about alleged ties between Noriega and the CIA. Meditz and Hanratty, *Panama*, pp. xxx and xxxiv.

37. John T. Fishel, *The Fog of Peace: Planning and Executing the Restoration of Panama* (Carlisle Barracks, Pa.: Strategic Studies Institute, U.S. Army War College, 1992), pp. 5, 7, 28–29. For good accounts of Operation JUST CAUSE, see Thomas Donnelly, Margaret Roth, and Caleb Baker, *Operation Just Cause: The Storming of Panama* (New York: Macmillan, Inc., 1991) and Rod Lenahan, *Operation JUST CAUSE: The U.S. Intervention in Panama* (Washington: National Defense University Press, 1995).

Guard and Reserve (AGR) program and assigned to the headquarters there.[38]

Realizing that civil affairs would be a significant part of the requirement once Noriega was removed, the SOUTHCOM J–5 requested volunteers from the 361st Civil Affairs Brigade, headquartered in Pensacola, Fla. This unit had a CAPSTONE relationship with the command in Panama and had been working with the J–5 section since 1983. As result of its affiliation, the Reservists had devoted many annual training periods to Panama and many of the members of the unit had first-hand experience in the country.[39]

As might be expected, the exact nature of the assignment could not be revealed to the Reservists until they were actually on-board in Panama and "read-in" to the plan. Despite the uncertain nature of the call, however, members of the 361st volunteered for thirty-one day Temporary Tours of Active Duty (TTAD) in Panama. Once these initial volunteers from the 361st had reported for duty and been briefed on the government-restoration plan as it existed at that time, they developed a draft plan which would be refined by members of the 361st who performed later tours at SOUTHCOM.[40]

The Reservists completed their planning in August 1988, by which time relations between the United States and General Noriega had deteriorated considerably. According to one assessment of the planning process, the use of the Army Reservists from the 361st Civil Affairs Brigade had been a success. "This support [from the 361st]," wrote John T. Fishel of the U.S. Army War College's Strategic Studies Institute, "not only was forthcoming in a rapid and timely fashion, but also brought with it regional, functional, and country expertise that was not to be found in all of USSOUTHCOM. This expertise included individuals who had conducted civic action seminars with the PDF [Panama Defense Forces] over the previous 5 years, knew many of the players, knew members of the U.S. Embassy staff, and knew how government and non-governmental institutions worked in Panama."[41] Another advantage to using the members of the 361st, suggested Fishel, was that these Reservists were ready and able to deploy for 31 day tours on short notice. A disadvantage encountered by the Reservists was that the level of classification of BLUE SPOON, the name given the operational plan, meant that they

38. Fishel, *Fog of Peace*, p. 8.
39. *Ibid.*, pp. 9–10.
40. *Ibid.*, p. 10.
41. *Ibid.*, p. 14.

had to operate without knowledge of other aspects of the effort to oust Noriega. One aspect of the plan that was not satisfactorily resolved prior to the invasion was its assumption that Army Reserve units would be involuntarily activated to support the Panama operation. Shortly after the plans were completed, the situation in Panama calmed down, and the focus on Noriega's removal from power became less intense among the U.S. military planners in Panama.[42]

A series of incidents in early 1989 changed the situation. One of these was the seizure of several busloads of U.S. dependent school children by members of the PDF in March. Following this incident, SOUTHCOM Commander-in-Chief General Fred Woerner directed that the BLUE SPOON plans, including the civil affairs plan code-named BLIND LOGIC, be reexamined and updated.[43] Members of the 361st were brought back to Panama, and one of the determinations by those who reviewed the plan at this point, including members of the active component 96th Civil Affairs Battalion, was that without a Reserve civil affairs call-up there would be a shortage of command and control headquarters in the civil affairs area as well as a shortage of expertise on what would be required to restore democracy to Panama by establishing a post-Noriega government there.[44]

On December 15, 1989, Noriega committed a significant mistake by having the Panamanian Chamber of Peoples Deputies declare that "a state of war existed in Panama because of the North American aggression." The next day, U.S. Marine Corps Lt. Robert Paz was killed at a checkpoint by members of the Panama National Guard, and on December 17 President George Bush ordered the execution of Operation JUST CAUSE—the name finally given to BLUE SPOON—a military endeavor designed to remove Noriega from power.[45]

JUST CAUSE commenced at 0100 hours on December 20, 1989, with nearly-simultaneous attacks on the centers of power of the Panama Defense Forces. JUST CAUSE was an unqualified success. Yet to come was the execution of BLIND LOGIC, the civil affairs plan that accompanied it. The first casualty was the name: the SOUTHCOM J–5, Brig. Gen. Benard Gann, decided that BLIND LOGIC was simply not appropriate, and PROMOTE LIBERTY became the name of the operation in which the Army Reserve took part.[46]

42. *Ibid.*, pp. 14–15, 11, 17.
43. *Ibid.*, pp. 17–18.
44. *Ibid.*, p. 19.
45. Meditz and Hanratty, *Panama*, p. xxxiv; Fishel, *Fog of Peace*, pp. 1, 4.
46. Fishel, *Fog of Peace*, pp. 31–32.

The Joint Chiefs of Staff approved the concept for PROMOTE LIBERTY on December 21, except for the part of the plan which called for the activation of Army Reserve civil affairs units. Instead, the JCS guidance provided only for individual volunteer Army Reservists—not Reserve units—with a Temporary Tour of Active Duty (TTAD) length of 139 days. This tour length played havoc with the planning done by the 361st Civil Affairs Brigade, which had contemplated either a unit activation or 31 day TTADs, as had been the routine during the planning phase.[47]

One problem caused by this lengthy tour requirement was that of the 25 members of the 361st who had been identified for service in Panama on a voluntary basis, only 3 were able to accept a tour of 139 days. The financial hardships visited upon someone whose livelihood does not lie in active military service were just too great for many of the members of the unit, a situation that too many members of the reserve components would discover less than two years later when they were involuntarily activated for Desert Shield/Desert Storm.[48]

Within a few days after the shooting phase of the exercise was over, however, SOUTHCOM had sent a message to the U.S. Army Reserve Special Operations Command (USARSOC) and the U.S. Army Reserve Personnel Center (ARPERCEN) asking for additional volunteer Reserve civil affairs specialists to serve Temporary Tours of Active Duty of 31–139 days length.[49] Army Reserve civil affairs units received the tasking on December 22, and by December 23, USARSOC had sent ARPERCEN a request for orders for the initial twenty-five volunteers. By the following day, the first group of Reservists was on their way to Fort Bragg for deployment processing and then on to Pope Air Force Base, S.C., for the flight to Panama.[50]

The requirement for Army Reserve civil affairs personnel did not stop with the first request. On December 26 SOUTHCOM again asked for volunteers, identifying specific skills needed in Panama at that time. This amounted to virtually every specialty needed to run a country or a city: hospital and public health administrators, engineers who were familiar with municipal utility systems (electrical, water, natural

47. *Ibid.*, p. 32.

48. *Ibid.*, pp. 34–35.

49. The JCS guidance of 139 day tours was for the initial contingent of 25 Reservists.

50. Lt. Col. Courtenay S. Welton, II, "Army Reservists Serve in Panama Operation," *Army Reserve Magazine*, Vol. 36, No. 2 (1990), pp. 10–11.

gas distribution, solid waste disposal, and sewerage), prison administrators, law enforcement professionals, drug enforcement and customs experts, telephone system experts, radio and television station repair persons, veterinarians, international lawyers, agronomists, bankers, civil engineers, and experts in state, local and national government.[51]

By December 29, an additional 122 Reserve volunteers had arrived at Fort Bragg. Like the first group who processed through the North Carolina post, these Reservists devoted two days to processing and preparation for deployment. They left Fort Bragg on December 31, and arrived in Panama on January 1, 1990.[52]

In addition to unit members of the USAR; 63 Individual Mobilization Augmentees (IMAs)—60 of whom were from outside the civil affairs ranks—and 11 members of the Individual Ready Reserve (IRR) with civil affairs backgrounds deployed in support of PROMOTE LIBERTY. In all, 146 Army Reservists had deployed within ten days after the first request for assistance had gone out from SOUTHCOM, and by early March 1990, 311 Army Reservists had served in Panama.[53]

Many of the non-unit Reservists had been identified by the U.S. Army Personnel Center (ARPERCEN) and its Total Army Personnel Data Base-Reserve (TAPDB–R). Using the information in TAPDB–R, members of ARPERCEN'S Officer Personnel Directorate could locate Reservists who were already on active duty, and who might then be sent to Panama, as

---

51. Theresa L. Kraus, U.S. Army Center of Military History Information Paper, DAMH–RAM, March 27, 1991, Subject: "The Army's Role in the Nation-Building Process in Post-Noriega Panama," unpaginated; copy in possession of the author; statement of Stephen M. Duncan, Assistant Secretary of Defense for Reserve Affairs, before the Readiness Subcommittee, House Armed Services Committee, on H.R. 4739, National Defense Authorization Act for Fiscal Year 1991, Title III, Operations and Maintenance, p. 1593; hereinafter cited as "Duncan statement, FY 1991 Defense Authorization Act."

52. Welton, "Army Reservists Serve in Panama Operation," pp. 11–12, 15. See also letter to the editor from Capt. Jack L. Skidmore, "Forgotten in 'Just Cause,'" *Army Reserve Magazine*, Vol. 36, No. 4 (1990), p. 29. Units represented were as follows: 354th CA Bde., Riverdale, Md;, 431st CA Co., N. Little Rock, Ark.; 416th CA Co., Norristown, Pa.; 478th CA Co., Miami, Fla.; 426th CA Co., Upton, Calif.; 489th CA Co., Knoxville, Tenn.; 490th CA Bn., Abilene, Tex.; 413th CA Co., Lubbock, Tex.; 411th CA Co., Danbury, Conn.; 364th CA Bde., Portland, Ore.; 445th CA Co., Oakland, Calif.; 15th Psyops Co., Ft. Thomas, Ky.; 24th Psyops Co., Aurora, Colo.; 402d CA Co., Tonawanda, NY; and the 448th CA Co., Ft. Lewis, Wa.

53. Welton, "Army Reservists Serve in Panama Operation," p.15; Kraus, "The Army's Role in the Nation-Building Process in Post-Noriega Panama." Over 2000 civil affairs Army Reservists volunteered for service in Panama. See Lenahan, *Operation JUST CAUSE*, p. 232.

was being prepared to go to war without the train-up time that had been a traditional part of the reserve planning scheme. The next conflict, in the words so often spoken in Reserve centers across the country, was to be a "come as you are" war.

As the reserve components grew larger and received increased emphasis and attention during the 1980s, policymakers asked more penetrating questions about the readiness of these forces to play the role expected of them in national defense. James H. Webb, Jr., Assistant Secretary of Defense for Reserve Affairs,[3] for example, suggested in 1986 that the Army Reserve—as well as other parts of the reserve component structure—had significant problems with training and readiness; problems that could not be ignored.

Webb singled out the Army Reserve because of the increasing reliance the Army was putting on it. More combat service support was being forced into the Army Reserve, said Webb, while at the same time Reserve units were receiving soldiers who were not qualified in the basic Military Occupation Specialty (MOS) of the unit to which they are assigned. As a result, suggested the assistant secretary, "commanders complain that they spend all their training time teaching soldiers new specialties and thus are not adequately preparing their units for war."[4]

MOS QUALIFICATION

The situation among individual members of the Army Reserve did not look so bad on the surface. As of the end of FY 1987, only 12 percent (29,000) of Army Reservists in the Selected Reserve were not MOS-qualified. An additional 22 percent (54,000), however, were identified as "MOS-qualified," but not working in the job for which they were trained. At the end of that training year, over one-third of Reservists did not possess the qualifications required for their job.[5]

By the next year the numbers had improved significantly. As of September 30, 1988, only 6.1 percent (19,127) of Re-

3. As proof that the reserve components were receiving more attention, Congress mandated in 1984 (Section 1212 of the Department of Defense Authorization Act of 1984—Public Law 98–94) that there be the position of Assistant Secretary of Defense for Reserve Affairs.

4. Paul Smith, "Reserve Training Troubles May Force Missions on Army," *Army Times*, June 23, 1986, p. 3.

5. *Reserve Component Programs, Fiscal Year 1987: Annual Report of the Reserve Forces Policy Board* (Washington: OSD, 1988), p. 39; hereinafter cited as *Annual Report, RFPB, FY87.* In comparison, the comparable figures for the ARNG were 9% not MOS qualified and 20% not working in their MOS.

servists were reported as not MOS qualified, and only 16.1 percent (50,307) were said not to be working in their MOS.[6] This represented a startling increase in the number of qualified Reservists, a trend which did not carry forward to the next year.

By the close of FY 1990, the Army Reserve reported that 11 percent of its soldiers were not MOS qualified, and 27 percent were not qualified in their duty MOS.[7] This significant decrease in qualification percentage even from two years earlier makes one question the accuracy of the FY 1989 figures.

Unit readiness was another matter, for it was measured both by the qualifications of the unit members and by the equipment the unit possessed. Both unit and individual readiness were questioned and questionable. The way to overcome deficiencies was with training and with procurement of equipment for the Army Reserve.

THE TRAINING DILEMMA

The deployments of the Army Reserve to Latin America and the Caribbean were important for what they taught these units about packing up and moving overseas, in addition to the training itself. A majority of the Army Reserve's overseas training during this period, however, consisted of sending units to Europe and the Pacific region, with European training predominating. Important as they were, however, short overseas training periods were not what the Army Reserve as a whole was doing during those years. Indeed, most of the training conducted by Army Reserve units from 1984–1990 was simply basic unit training of the kind that would pay off if a mass mobilization ever became a reality.

The problem faced by Reservists in the 1980s was the same one that has confounded them from the beginning of the reserve concept: how to prepare on a parttime basis to do the same job as those who are members of the full-time force. This dilemma was laid out in 1984 in a fine article in *Military Review* written by two active component officers.[8] The article provides a useful framework for examining the history of

6. *Reserve Component Programs, Fiscal Year 1988: Annual Report of the Reserve Forces Policy Board* (Washington: OSD, 1989), p. 46; hereinafter cited as *Annual Report, RFPB, FY 88.*

7. *Reserve Component Programs, Fiscal Year 1990: Report of the Reserve Forces Policy Board* (Washington: OSD, 1991), p. 66; hereinafter cited as *Annual Report, RFPB, FY 90.*

8. Col. Benjamin F. Sharp, Jr. (USA-Ret.) and Maj. Donald B. Skipper, "The Reserve Component Dilemma: Mission Versus Time," *Military Review* (November 1984), pp. 63–79.

Army Reserve training during this period, though this author does not suggest that it was in any way instrumental in shaping such training.

In their article, Col. Benjamin F. Sharp and Maj. Donald B. Skipper suggested that one of the primary reasons for the attractiveness of the reserve components is cost: reservists are a bargain compared with members of the active force. Moreover, suggested Sharp and Skipper, by 1984 the Army had come to depend upon its reserve components for part of its go-to-war capability. This concept—the Total Army—was discussed in some detail in Chapter Ten and remains the heart of Army philosophy today (1996). Furthermore, the authors found that the dependence on the reserves is predicated upon a near-zero period of post-mobilization training, an assumption whose accuracy they questioned. Nevertheless, said the authors, despite the increased resources directed at the reserves, "... the one resource that has not been substantially increased is time."[9]

The authors pointed out ways in which reserve training was being beefed-up to assist readiness and enhance training, an attempt to "increase time," as it were. These methods, which were used in the mid-1980s and for the next ten years, included having reserve units participate in overseas exercises that exceeded the 13–15 days normally devoted to annual training, providing Additional Training Assemblies (ATAs), Readiness Management Assemblies (RMAs), and for reserve aviators, Aircrew Flight Training Periods (AFTPs), extending annual training beyond 13–15 days and providing fulltime personnel to perform administrative tasks at the unit level.[10] The difficulty inherent in all of these fixes was that they cost money, and even in during the years of the Reagan defense build-up, funding for the reserve components never equalled the need.

TRAINING DETRACTORS

The Reserve Forces Policy Board, a mixed group of military officers and civilian political appointees within the Department of Defense, indicated in its report for FY 1984 that ". . . despite its vital importance, training remains the most difficult and elusive aspect of Reserve Component readiness to measure." The Board went on to suggest, however, that several factors influenced training readiness. Among these were the availability of

9. *Ibid.*, pp. 63–64.
10. *Ibid.*, pp. 71–72.

an adequate number of trainers, training areas, and equipment; realistic missions and goals; budget resources for training; and service school opportunities to train the trainers.[11]

Despite the problem engendered by the lack of full-time support which forced a myriad of administrative tasks that seemingly consumed every moment of every weekend drill, the Army Reserve conducted a significant amount of meaningful training during this seven-year period, particularly during the two week annual training periods. The general type of training depended on a unit's mission, but the specifics of mission training were limited only by the imagination of those responsible for its planning. What follows are three examples of widely-varying multi-unit Army Reserve unit training during the period 1984–1990.[12]

FIREX '88

Army Reservists from eleven states representing thirty-five separate units participated in a training exercise called "FIREX '88," a huge artillery live-fire exercise conducted in the Utah desert in June 1988. Army Reservists represented about one-fourth of the total of 14,000 soldiers involved in the exercise.[13]

Reserve units in the exercise included a 155mm howitzer battalion (6/83 from Ogden, Utah) and a real cross-section of combat support units in the Reserve inventory. These included supply and service units like the 155th Supply and Service Battalion from El Monte, Calif.; truck companies such as the 180th Transportation Co. (Medium Truck) from Grand Rapids, Mich.; and ammo suppliers like the 841st Ordnance Co. (Ammo) from Butte, Mont. Even combat service support outfits were allowed to play, including the 335th Data Processing Unit from Los Angeles and the 358th Public Affairs Detachment from Ft. Douglas, Utah.[14]

---

11. *Annual Report, RFPB, FY 84*, p. 5–1.

12. In addition to the specific examples described below, see also "Infantry Training at Fort McCoy," *Army Reserve Magazine*, Vol. 34, No. 4 (1988), p. 17; Sgt. Terry L. Conder, "Reserve Signallers Take Part in Natural Team IV," *Army Reserve Magazine*, Vol. 34, No. 4 (1988), p. 21; Reed Hildreth, "Army's Lumberman on Cutting Edge," *Army* (February 1987), pp. 36–39; Cdr. O.D. Briggs and Sgt. Doug Rowley, "USAR Artillery Unit Trains with Navy Attack Fighters," *Army Reserve Magazine*, Vol. 34, No. 1 (1988), pp. 16–17; Col. Benjamin W. Covington, III, "Reserves and Active Army: Mission is the Same, Challenges Different," *Army* (July 1988), pp. 39–42.

13. "Thunder Over Utah," *Army Reserve Magazine*, Vol. 34, No. 4 (1988), p. 14.

14. *Ibid.*, pp. 14–15.

ONAWAY EAGLE: A TRAINING DIVISION AT WORK

Other Reserve units generated their own training opportunities. The 76th Division (Training), for example, devoted the summer of 1985 to conducting a "Mobilization-Army Training Center" (M–ATC) at Fort Campbell, Ky. During the June–August time period, Reservists from the 76th put 600 recruits through a complete basic training cycle—precisely the mission the division would perform if it were mobilized.[15]

The actual conduct of the training was delegated to the 4th Brigade of the 76th Division, headquartered in Rhode Island. This training could not have been accomplished within the normal 15 or so days of annual training time allotted to a Reservist each year. Fifty-three members of the brigade accordingly volunteered for Special Active Duty for Training (SADT) tours of 10–12 weeks length to provide the necessary continuity for the assignment. In addition, another seven brigade members volunteered for 179 day tours at Fort Campbell.[16]

Reserve units that supported the training in addition to those in the 76th Division included the 80th Division Logistics Group from Richmond, Va., the 377th Combat Support Hospital from Chattanooga, Tenn., the 478th Engineer Battalion of Ft. Thomas, Ky., the 623d and 629th Transportation Companies of Dubois, Pa., and Ft. Totten, N.Y., and the 356th and 362d Public Affairs Detachments from Ft. Meade, Md., and Manchester, N.H.[17]

The idea of allowing a Reserve unit to train new soldiers, rather than sending them through a program conducted by active component personnel was a novel one, so the commander of the 76th Division, Maj. Gen. John Ricotilli, had been forced to persuade both Forces Command (FORSCOM) and Training and Doctrine Command (TRADOC) to allow this experiment.[18]

When the training cycle was done, both the FORSCOM commander, Gen. Robert W. Sennewald, and the TRADOC commander, Gen. William R. Richardson, pronounced the work of the Reservists a success. Sennewald commented that the 76th had ". . . set a new standard for the way all Army Reserve training divisions may train in the future." Richardson suggested that the 76th represented "a leap ahead in training." What may have impressed these two active component gen-

15. "'Good Feeling Inside': 'Onaway-Eagle Training First for 76th Division," *The Officer*, Vol. LXI, No. 11 (November 1985), p. 20.

16. *Ibid.*

17. *Ibid.*

18. *Ibid.*, pp. 21–22.

eral officers was one particular result achieved by the Reservists: rifle marksmanship scores that averaged ten percent higher than those achieved by basic trainees at other posts.[19]

ORCHID SAGE

Units of the Army Reserve participated in a number of other training and mobilization exercises during this period. One of these, Exercise Orchid Sage, involved over 6000 medical specialists from the Army Reserve, Army National Guard, and Air Force Reserve. Described as "one of the largest medical exercises in modern times," Orchid Sage took place at Fort Drum, N.Y.[20]

Twenty-five of the units participating in Orchid Sage were from the 77th Army Reserve Command (ARCOM), headquartered at Fort Totten, N.Y. The exercise was directed by the Army Reserve's 8th Medical Brigade, from Brooklyn, N.Y. The 241st and 331st General Hospitals, from Utica, N.Y., assisted with command and control by providing training and operations personnel for the Patient Operations Center.[21]

Patients—soldiers with elaborate simulated wounds, called "moulage"—were treated by units like the 320th Evacuation Hospital of Newburgh, N.Y., which tested the Deployable Medical Systems, or DEPMEDS. The training on DEPMEDS was invaluable, for this was one of the systems sent to the Persian Gulf in 1990 and 1991. Without the up-to-date training such as was provided in Orchid Sage and other exercises, the Reservists would not have been as well prepared as they were when the real thing came along.[22]

In addition to those who actually treated the "patients," Reserve units like the 423d Medical Ambulance Detachment (Air Ambulance) of Syracuse, N.Y., practiced their airborne evacuation and patient delivery, refining their skills at flying while wearing night vision goggles. Working the ground evacuation side of the exercise was the 646th Medical Company (Ground Ambulance) which transported patients to the hospital units.[23]

Orchid Sage, said Brig. Gen. Francis Donohue, commander of the 77th ARCOM, provided an opportunity for these 6000 soldiers to prove "not only that they were individually professional, but that as members of a team they can

19. *Ibid.*, pp. 22–23.

20. Capt. Ann Freed, "Exercise Orchid Sage 1989: USAR Holds One of the Largest Medical Exercises Ever," *Army Reserve Magazine*, Vol. 36, No. 1 (1990), p. 16.

21. *Ibid.*, p. 17.

22. *Ibid.*, p. 18.

23. *Ibid.*, p. 19.

mesh with other units under battlefield conditions in an effective and cooperative way."[24]

CAPSTONE

One way the Army attempted to enhance Reserve training and readiness was through the CAPSTONE program. The precursors to CAPSTONE had been in existence since 1975, and in 1979 CAPSTONE took on the form it would keep through the 1980s.[25]

What CAPSTONE meant for the Army Reserve was that each USAR unit was to have a wartime chain of command and an affiliation with an active component unit with which it would train. In the words of the regulation, it ". . . aligns Reserve units with their gaining wartime commanders for the purpose of premobilization planning."[26] CAPSTONE consisted of four alignment packages: Europe, Pacific, Central Command, and the Continental United States (CONUS).[27] The idea, as related by FORSCOM planner John Scott, was that "For the first time in the history of the Army all the components are planning together and training together in peacetime with the units they'd be fighting alongside in wartime."[28] In fact, not all Army Reserve units had a CAPSTONE trace, but for those that did, it could be rewarding.[29]

Much of the CAPSTONE training was conducted in conjunction with exercises directed by the Joint Chiefs of Staff or another high level entity within the Department of Defense. REFORGER, sponsored by the European Command (EUCOM), and Bright Star, sponsored by the Central Command (CENTCOM) saw regular Army Reserve participation, as did other JCS and unified command training.

There were two significant benefits of CAPSTONE training of this type. First, the active component units became familiar with the personnel and capabilities of the reserve units affiliated with them and second, the reservists benefited from

24. *Ibid.*

25. Elizabeth Tabb, "CAPSTONE—A Peacetime Partnership Pays Off," *Army Reserve Magazine*, Vol. 30, No. 2, (1984) p. 24.

26. Army Regulation 11–30, p. 4.

27. Maj. Gen. William J. Berkman, "The Posture of the U.S. Army Reserve," testimony given to Congress in March 1984, p. 26.

28. Tabb, "CAPSTONE—A Peacetime Partnership Pays Off," p. 24.

29. Kathryn Roe Coker, *The United States Army Reserve Command (USARC): The First Years, USARC Command History, 1 January 1989 to 31 December 1992* (Atlanta: USARC, 1994), p. 7. This is the definitive, official history of the first three years of the USARC's existence and is hereinafter cited as Coker, *The U.S. Army Reserve Command.*

familiarization with the country to which they would deploy upon mobilization. As in the case of the members of the 361st Civil Affairs Brigade in Panama, discussed in Chapter Eleven, such familiarity could be significant.

BRIGHT STAR

Both REFORGER and Bright Star, as well as countless other smaller exercises, allowed Reservists to work with active component and Army National Guard units in a realistic scenario and setting. Bright Star '87, for example, afforded a superb training opportunity to some of the transportation terminal units (TTU) of the USAR.

These units, which work as part of the Military Traffic Management Command (MTMC), saw to the loading of 2500 pieces of cargo shipped to Egypt for Bright Star. The 1174th TTU of Fort Totten, N.Y., and the 1185th of Lancaster, Pa., as well as the 1302d Military Police Detachment from Orangeburg, N.Y., practiced exactly what they would do in a wartime situation.[30] Barely three years later, these same units would be called upon to load nearly-identical cargo for shipment to the Persian Gulf region. The training was not only invaluable, it was irreplaceable.

Meanwhile, the 332d Medical Brigade of Nashville, Tenn., was participating in Bright Star '87 from an Egyptian location. Members of the 332d furnished medical care to the thousands of Reservists and others who took part in the exercise, learning a great deal about the twin dangers of diarrhea and dehydration that would prove invaluable when they, too, were mobilized and sent to Saudi Arabia during Operation Desert Shield.[31] Army Reserve units of other types also participated in similar exercises in other parts of the world ranging from Canada to Christmas Island, Republic of Kiribati.[32]

CAPSTONE AND THE 361ST CIVIL AFFAIRS BRIGADE

The benefit of a CAPSTONE affiliation was that it was meant to be a continuing relationship. One that was forged during

30. Maury Peerenboom, "U.S. Army Reserve Terminals Move Cargo for Bright Star '87," *Army Reserve Magazine*, Vol. 33, No. 4 (1987), p. 11.

31. Capt. Michael L. McGurl, "Medical Support Vital in Rugged Desert Climate," *Army Reserve Magazine*, Vol. 34, No. 1 (1988), p. 20.

32. See, for example, *Annual Report, RFPB, FY 87*, p. 106 and 1st Lt. Dan Smith and Bill Peoples, "Kiribati's a long way from the Great Smokies," *Army Reserve Magazine*, Vol. 36, No. 3 (1990), pp. 8, 10. The Reserve Forces Policy Board reports each year on the various locations where overseas training took place.

this period existed between the United States Southern Command (SOUTHCOM), one of the unified commands, and the 361st Civil Affairs Brigade from Pensacola, Fla. The Reservists worked closely with SOUTHCOM throughout the 1980s and when the time came to formulate plans to implement democracy following the ouster of Panamanian strongman Manuel Antonio Noriega, members of the 361st were called upon to do the planning.[33]

Even the CAPSTONE affiliation of the 361st did not result in its being mobilized when the anti-Noriega operation—code-named JUST CAUSE—began. The Pentagon planners relied instead upon volunteer Army Reservists to accomplish the mission contemplated for the 361st, a decision that was contrary to the intention of the CAPSTONE program.[34]

Desert Shield/Desert Storm offered additional examples where the CAPSTONE affiliation was ignored, causing some to question its efficacy as a part of the doctrinal basis for Army training in the 1980s. CAPSTONE was not meant to be applied inflexibly, though some of the Reserve units involved in it may have thought that they were joined to the active component by a kevlar umbilical cord. The program may actually have increased the training opportunities for Army Reserve units, but political realities—both inside and outside the Army—meant that CAPSTONE would never result in an absolute imperative to activate reserve units and send them wherever their affiliated active component units were sent.[35]

OVERSEAS TRAINING

Over the first years of the CAPSTONE program the extent of participation by the Army Reserve in overseas training—much of which was CAPSTONE related—increased significantly. From 12 units or cells in FY 1976, the number of participating Reservists increased to 1035 units/cells[36] with 10,840 soldiers in FY 1985, to 1447 units/cells with 19,175 soldiers in FY 1988. In FYs 1989 and 1990, the number of Reservists training over-

33. *Ibid.*, p. 27.

34. The full story of the 361st and its Panamanian involvement is recounted in Chapter Eleven.

35. See also the analysis of CAPSTONE in "The Posture of the U.S. Army Reserve," a statement submitted to Congress by Maj. Gen. William R. Berkman, Chief, Army Reserve, in March 1984, pp. 26–28.

36. "Unit" is a self-evident term; a "cell" is a portion of a unit split out from it for some purpose such as training. Cells were often sent to Europe to participate in exercises such as REFORGER.

seas actually went down slightly. In FY 1989, for example, the numbers were 1341 units/cells and 18,401 individuals; while in FY 1990 it was 1343 units/cells and 18,492 individuals.[37]

Overseas training had its place, but it was expensive and time-consuming. The percentage of troop program members of the Army Reserve who experienced overseas training was fairly small throughout this period. Of the 310,000 soldiers assigned to the Selected Reserve[38] at the end of FY 1990, for example, only 18,492 (6 percent) had undergone overseas training during the fiscal year. This was slightly better than the 4.8 percent of Army National Guard soldiers who had experienced such training, but even as Desert Shield began, it demonstrated the difficulties of funding and carrying-out such an ambitious training program, beneficial as it was for readiness.[39]

EUROPEAN RESERVISTS

Not all Reservists who trained overseas had to be sent there to do so. In both Europe and the Far East were Army Reservists who were counted as members of the force. By 1985 there were some 3500 Army Reservists in Europe, spread throughout the continent. The eight Reserve units included the 2d Hospital Center (Forward) in Bury St. Edmonds, England, and seven units in Germany: the 8th Medical Brigade (Forward), headquartered Heidelberg; 310th Theater Army Area Command (Forward) in Rheinberg; 454th Replacement Detachment, in Offenbach; USAR Military Detachment, Europe, also in Heidelberg; 3745th USAR School in Munich; 3747th USAR School in Offenbach, 412th Engineer Command (Forward) in Mannheim. The 412th was the only one of the units not under supervision of U.S. Army Reserve-Europe, which was commanded by Col. Carl G. Sica. Only 280 Reservists were in paid drill slots, the remainder being Individual Mobilization Augmentees and members of the Individual Ready Reserve. U.S. Army Reserve-Europe was headquartered at McGraw Kaserne, Munich.[40]

37. *Annual Report, RFPB, FY 88*, p. 89; *Annual Report, RFPB, FY 90*, p. 96. Not all overseas training was CAPSTONE affiliated. Much of the training in Latin America discussed in the preceding chapter, for example, was not conducted under the auspices of a CAPSTONE relationship.

38. The "Selected Reserve" portion of the Army Reserve consists of USAR unit members and Reservists serving in IMA and AGR positions.

39. *Annual Report, RFPB, FY 90*, pp. 45, 89.

40. Larry Carney, "Reserve Strength in Europe to Increase to 4000," *Army Times*, August 5, 1985, p. 25; SSgt. Frank Cox, "USAR-Europe Unique," *The Officer* (March 1985), pp. 21–24.

Most of the Reservists were civilian employees of U.S. firms or dependents of U.S. military personnel or civil service workers stationed in Europe, and their numbers increased to the point where an Army Reserve Command could be justified. The 7th Army Reserve Command (ARCOM) was activated in Europe on February 15, 1986, to manage the 4200 Reservists in Europe at that time. It was responsible for 19 subordinate units.[41]

Its headquarters was in Heidelberg, Germany, and it was commanded by a colonel. By 1988 the number of Army Reservists in Europe had reached 5000, with some 350 participating as drilling members of the troop units there.[42] In recognition of the increased number of Army Reservists serving in Europe, the top position in the ARCOM was elevated in April 1990 to general officer level, and Col. Richard J. Dirgins, the ARCOM's commander, received a promotion to brigadier general.[43]

RESERVISTS IN KOREA

Army Reservists in Korea did not have the option of joining a Reserve unit while living there. In June 1990 the Army finally acceded to desires of Reservists who lived there and activated the 343d Rear Tactical Operations Center (RTOC) under the command of Eighth Army and manned by in-country members of the Army Reserve.[44]

THREE WEEK ANNUAL TRAINING

One answer to the problem of not having enough training time is to increase the time devoted to training. During FY 1986 the Army Reserve allowed certain units to engage in three-week annual training periods, "on an exception basis when there were unique training opportunities," such as a JCS-sponsored exercise. On the surface, such an expansion of

41. Interview, Lt. Col. James T. Currie with Col. John A. Topper, Senior USAR Advisor, Headquarters FORSCOM, June 30, 1992. Notes in possession of the author.

42. Maj. David T. Zabecki, "Why Doesn't One Army Concept Reach Reservists in Europe?" *Army* (November 1986), p. 14.

43. "European ARCOM gets first general officer," *Army Reserve Magazine*, Vol. 36, No. 3 (1990), p. 7.

44. Msg., HQDA (DAAR–CO) to Cdr, Eighth Army (RMJ/CJ–RC/EAFC), dtg: 152100Z Jun 90 (June 15, 1990), Subject: Funding New U.S. Army Reserve (USAR) Unit in Korea. Copy in possession of the author.

annual training from 13 days to 21 days might not seem difficult. In practice, it caused significant problems.[45]

According to the Reserve Forces Policy Board, one of the problems with such expanded training is that many employers did not support it. As a result, some Reservists were forced illegally to use vacation time for their active duty beyond the normal two week period. Furthermore, the Assistant Secretary of Defense for Reserve Affairs studied the idea of mandatory three-week annual training during the FY 86 test and concluded that such would not be desirable,[46] a conclusion that had previously been reached by the members of the Army Reserve Forces Policy Committee.[47]

Three-week training for members of the Army Reserve has been a reality since that time, but it is clearly the exception. In part, the decision not to require a longer annual training period, whatever its benefits for readiness, foundered upon the twin pillars of opposition from employers (and from Reservists themselves in some instances) and from the reality of the increased cost that would be associated with such an initiative.

INACTIVE DUTY TRAINING

If there was one significant weakness in Army Reserve training during this period, it was in the inactive duty part, the weekend drills that form the basis of so much of what a Reservist does with his or her time. When one examines the training time available to a Reserve unit commander, a calendar year translates into 24 days of inactive duty training per year (weekend drills) and another 13–15 days of active duty training, including travel time, for a total of only 37–39 possible days of training per year.

A study at the United States Army Missile and Munitions Center and School cited by the authors of a study published in *Military Review* found that "Reserve component commanders . . . were fortunate if they could set aside 15 of the 38 pos-

45. *Annual Report of The Reserve Forces Policy Board, Fiscal Year 1986* (Washington: OSD, 1987), pp. 69–70; hereinafter cited as *Annual Report, RFPB, FY 86.*

46. *Ibid.*, p. 70.

47. Memorandum for the Secretary of the Army and Chief of Staff of the Army from Maj. Gen. Louis H. Ginn, III, Chairman, Army Reserve Forces Policy Committee, 25 February 1985, Subject: Army Reserve Forces Policy Committee (ARFPC) Quarterly Meeting, 13–15 February 1985 — Information Memorandum, p. 3. Copy in possession of the author.

sible training days for MOS type training. . . . The other 23 days were normally used for such things as inspections, and other administrative requirements and activities."[48]

This frustration was evident in the yearly reports of the Reserve Forces Policy Board, reflecting the data supplied to them by the various reserve components. For the Army's reserve components, the comments are almost duplicative from one year to the next. During FY 1987, for example, the Board found that "Unfortunately, significant time is spent on administrative functions and other activities that do not contribute to readiness."[49] The Board identified some such functions as "reporting requirements," "redundant inspections," and lack of flexibility of "active component and full-time support personnel, who manage and maintain bases and facilities used by National Guard and Reserve units."[50]

The same types of problems were noted with Army Reserve inactive duty training in 1988, 1989, 1990 and 1991. In this latter year, the Board noted that "In the Army National Guard and Army Reserve, administrative burdens continued to be the major detractors to unit training."[51] One way the Department of Defense and the Congress attempted to resolve this problem, which was both evident and thoroughly acknowledged, was through the provision of full-time manning for Reserve units. Such full-time support for the reserve components was certainly not new. The increased attention paid to it was significant, however.

FULL-TIME SUPPORT

Members of reserve units, including commanders and senior NCOs, were constantly pulled from high-priority training to take care of such matters as inspections, roll calls and reports. Some of these items might demand the attention of the drilling Reservist, but other training detractors could well be taken care of by full-time Reservists (Active Guard and Reserve—AGR) personnel or by civilian unit technicians.

The Army Reserve realized during this period that using an increasing number of AGR and full-time civilian personnel

48. Sharp and Skipper, "The Reserve Component Dilemma: Mission Versus Time," p. 71.

49. *Annual Report, RFPB, FY 87*, p. 98.

50. *Ibid.*

51. Office of the Secretary of Defense, *Reserve Component Programs, Fiscal Year 1991: Report of the Reserve Forces Policy Board* (Washington: OSD, 1992), p. 109; hereinafter cited as *Annual Report, RFPB, FY 91.*

(competitive civil service and military technicians)[52] would free the commander and staff to pursue activities during weekend drills that would result in more appropriate training and a better-prepared unit. During FY 1985, the Army Reserve had 24,700 such persons assigned, plus some 5393 active component soldiers assigned to USAR support. Of the AGR soldiers supporting the Army Reserve, some 93% were in direct or general support of Reserve units.[53]

In 1985 the Reserve Forces Policy Board projected that full-time support for the reserve components as a whole would increase by 38% as of FY 1991. In the case of the Army Reserve this would have meant a total of 41,528 full-time support personnel serving at the end of FY 1991.[54]

The actual number of full-time support personnel assigned to the Army Reserve by this date actually decreased, however, from the 1985 figure, primarily because of a significant drop in the number of active component soldiers assigned to the duty. At the end of FY 1991, the USAR had 13,704 AGR soldiers (compared with 10,751 in 1985); 8,463 military technicians (compared with 7,857 in 1985); 5,155 civil service employees (compared with 6,099 in 1985); and 1,124 active component soldiers (compared with 5,393 in FY 1985).[55]

As of the end of FY 1991, the Army Reserve had the lowest percentage of fill of its authorized full-time support of any components of any of the services. The USAR had an assigned:authorized fill rate of 63%, compared with an ARNG fill rate of 73%, a USNR fill rate of 103%, a USMCR rate of 106%, an ANG rate of 90% and a USAFR rate of 96%.[56] This meant that even as the Army Reserve was being given increased responsibility, and training was emphasized even more than previously, the administrative support available to the commander was decreasing. It was decreasing even relative to the support given other reserve components.

52. One difference between these two categories is that technicians are generally members of the unit they support, while the competitive civil service civilians do not have to be members of the Army Reserve. Membership in the USAR is a condition of employment for technicians.

53. *Army Reserve Forces Policy Committee, Annual Report 1985* (Washington: OSA, 1986), p. 9; hereinafter cited as *Annual Report ARFPC, FY 85*; *Annual Report, RFPB, FY 85*, p. 13.

54. *Annual Report, RFPB, FY 85*, p. 11.

55. *Ibid*., p. 13; *Annual Report, RFPB, FY 91*, p. 61.

56. *Annual Report, RFPB, FY 91*, p. 61.

CONGRESSIONAL INTEREST IN RESERVE EQUIPMENT SHORTAGES

Congress, meanwhile, had been making its own decisions about reserve component equipment needs since 1981. In that year Congress had added funding for reserve equipment despite—or perhaps because of—its not being included in the President's budget. Congress, in fact, had added funding each year during the decade of the 1980s under a category called National Guard and Reserve Equipment Appropriations (NGREA). The following table shows the amount of equipment funding Congress provided for the Army Reserve and National Guard in this special account during the period 1982–1991.

Table 12-2 Army Reserve Components Equipment Funding National Guard and Reserve Equipment Appropriations (NGREA) (Millions of Dollars)

	Army Reserve	Army National Guard
1982	$ 0.0	$ 50.0
1983	15.0	50.0
1984	0.0	100.0
1985	150.0	150.0
1986	365.0	532.0
1987	90.0	146.0
1988	85.0	273.0
1989	30.0	256.0
1990	89.0	315.0
1991	71.0	796.0
Total	$895.0	$2,668.0

Source: *Annual Reports of the Reserve Force Policy Board for FY 1987* (p. 80) and *FY 1990* (p. 115).

EQUIPMENT SHORTAGES

Despite these appropriations, which were over and above anything the DoD budget submission provided for the Army Reserve's equipment needs, there were shortages in several critical areas. During the period 1984–1991 the Army Reserve identified specific shortfalls in large categories such as materiel handling equipment, water purification systems, tool sets, test sets, and measuring devices, communications equipment, trucks and other wheeled vehicles, artillery, aircraft, and ambulances as well as in such specialized areas as aircrew survival vests.[64]

64. *Annual Report, RFPB, FY 1984* (p. 4–3); *FY 1985* (pp. 28–29); *FY 1986* (p. 33); *FY 1987* (pp. 86–87); *FY 1988* (p. 110); *FY 1989* (p. 98); *FY 1990,* (p. 114, 116); *FY 1991* (p. 148).

Asst. Sec. Webb, however, bristled at the notion that DoD was neglecting its reserve components. In a heated letter to *Army Times* on March 4, 1985, Webb disputed an earlier headline in the same publication: "Reserve Lacks Equipment to Fight a War, Webb Says." He did not mean that at all, said the assistant secretary. He believed the figure of a $24 billion shortfall in reserve component equipment cited in the article was exaggerated and that the administration was doing great things to correct the shortfall that did exist.[65]

Webb was correct in that the equipment shortfalls were being reduced. By the budget years 1990–91, said Army Reserve Chief Maj. Gen. William F. Ward, the USAR would receive about $4 billion of the $30 billion the Army was budgeted to spend on new equipment. This represented about 13–14 percent of the Army's equipment budget, stated Ward, and "When you add the displaced equipment or the hand-me-downs to it, we'll get about 35 to 40 percent of the Army's equipment budget."[66] The gap between required and on-hand was so great, however, that even at the end of this period the Army Reserve was still considerably short of having the equipment that had been identified as needed for war.

The following table shows the dollar value of wartime requirements of equipment, equipment authorized, and equipment on hand in the Army Reserve and the percentage on-hand versus the wartime requirement.

Table 12-3 Major Items of Equipment Status (USAR), 1983–91
(Millions of Dollars)

	Wartime Requirement	Auth	On-Hand	O–H/WT Req.
1983	6,378	5,173	3,216	50%
1984	6,321	4,392	3,236	51%
1985	6,405	6,206	4,398	69%
1986	6,257	5,801	3,873	62%
1987	6,747	6,160	4,000	59%
1988	7,508	6,801	4,379	58%
1989	9,554	7,940	5,549	58%
1990	10,173	9,147	6,319	62%
1991	12,246	9,845	8,400	69%

Sources: *Reports of the Reserve Forces Policy Board, FY 1984* (p. 4–2), *FY 1985* (p. 28), *FY 1986* (p. 37), *FY 1988* (p. 120), *FY 1990* (p. 109), and *FY 1991* (p. 146).

65. James H. Webb, Jr., "Wrong Implications," letter to the editor, *Army Times*, March 4, 1985, p. 22.

66. Cabell Bruce, "Budget helps Reserve battle lack of gear," *Army Times*, January 30, 1989, p. 24.

Considerable progress was made during these years in closing the equipment gap, but throughout this period the Army Reserve had the lowest percentage of authorized or required equipment on hand of any of the reserve components. The Army National Guard was next, and it consistently had an on-hand to wartime requirements percentage that ranged from several points to as much as 10–15 points higher than that of the Army Reserve, depending upon the year.[67]

READINESS PROBLEMS

The lack of equipment provided the Army Reserve during these years translated directly into problems with readiness. Some of these problems were immediately evident and identifiable, such as a unit readiness report that showed a unit to be non-deployable because of the absence of key pieces of equipment. But other effects of this shortage were more subtle.

Training, for example, was adversely affected when units did not have proper equipment to train on. It was impossible to learn how to repair a piece of equipment that the unit did not possess. The Army understood this problem and established in 1984 a program called Minimum Essential Equipment for Training (MEET). Recognizing that some Reserve units that were fairly low on the priority deployment list would never receive what they required for training purposes, MEET simply bypassed the "First to Fight" system. It worked by having Reserve and Guard commanders identify the ten items of equipment most needed by their units for training purposes. From 1984–1988, MEET provided almost 600 equipment items to units in its reserve components.[68]

While MEET may have been of some utility in assisting units that required a particular piece of equipment in order to train a large percentage of its soldiers, it solved only a small part of the equipment shortage problem. Army Reserve units were chronically short of major equipment items. In FY 1989,

---

67. See citations for Table 7.

68. *Annual Report, RFPB, FY 88*, p. 122; *Annual Report, RFPB, FY 85*, p. 29. One of the equipment items furnished to the Army Reserve under the MEET program was the Deployable Medical Systems (DEPMEDS). This equipment and the training on it proved valuable when these Reservists were sent to Saudi Arabia during Desert Shield/Desert Storm. Statement of Lt. Gen. Frank F. Ledford, Jr., The Surgeon General, United States Army, before the Subcommittee on Defense, Committee on Appropriations, House of Representatives, 102d Congress, 1st Session, March 12, 1991, *Department of Defense Appropriations for 1992, Part 3*, p. 179.

for example, 20 percent of Army Reserve units reported degraded readiness status because of equipment shortages.[69]

CROSS-LEVELLING OF EQUIPMENT

Another way the Army attempted to solve equipment problems within its reserve components was by cross-leveling or equipment transfers. This was accomplished by taking equipment from a reserve unit that met the C–3 (deployable) level of readiness and giving it to a unit that was at C–4 (non-deployable) level because of equipment problems. The trick was to move equipment from the C–3 to the C–4 unit without degrading the capability of the C–3 unit to the point where it became non-deployable.[70] This was a short-term fix at best, as it did nothing to address the core problem of lack of equipment within the reserve components of the Army.

NON-PROCURABILITY

Items that could not be bought despite funds being appropriated for them was also a problem for the Army Reserve. An FY 1986 study identified as "non-procurable" over 500 line items on authorization documents for Army Reserve units. These items could not be obtained for any of several reasons: it was not in production because of obsolescence or lack of a contract to produce the item; it may have been replaced by something else, but the authorization document did not reflect the change; the item was a future year procurement; there simply were not enough of the item to go around; the table of organization and equipment (TOE) was not current with new equipment authorizations.[71] Following two years of work on the authorization documents and substitutions of items that could be procured, the non-procurability problem was reduced by 75 percent.[72]

COMPATIBILITY

Second only to the lack of equipment was the problem of equipment compatibility. This problem took three forms: (1) equipment in a Reserve unit that would not work with counterpart equipment being used in the active component, (2) equipment that was so obsolete that it would result in the

69. *Annual Report, RFPB, FY 89*, p. 98.
70. *Annual Report, RFPB, FY, 87*, pp. 85–86.
71. *Annual Report, RFPB, FY 86*, pp. 44–45.
72. *Annual Report, RFPB, FY 88*, p. 122.

unit's being non-deployable, even if on paper the unit was fully equipped and (3) Reserve maintenance personnel whose mobilization responsibility would require support of active component units with equipment more advanced than that on which they routinely trained.

The first of these problems is exemplified by the analog radio sets in a Reserve unit versus digital sets in the active component. There is some evidence that one reason a general officer command USAR signal unit did not deploy to the Gulf in 1990–91 was this very problem. The members of the unit would have been unfamiliar with the equipment they would have been expected to operate on active duty. This specific example is discussed further in the context of failure to deploy the 335th Signal Command.

An example of the second type of compatibility problem was the obsolete aircraft in some Army Reserve units. According to the Reserve Forces Policy Board in 1990, "The Army Reserve has obsolete and nondeployable U–21 and U–8 airplanes and helicopters, which make many units nondeployable for combat missions."[73]

The third type of compatibility problem required a more complicated approach than simply closing a gap or buying equipment to match an updated TOE. In the late 1980s for example, many of the Reserve maintenance units would support active component armor and mechanized forces with M–1 Abrams tanks and M–2 Bradley Fighting vehicles. Unfortunately, these maintenance units had test, measurement, and diagnostic equipment that was designed to support the M60A3 tanks and M113 armored personnel carriers that were the norm in the reserve components.[74]

The same problem applied with communications equipment, data processing equipment and other areas where the combat service support units of the Army Reserve had a significant maintenance responsibility.[75] The CAPSTONE program, discussed earlier, had a beneficial effect, but it was too limited in both participation and yearly duration to be a total solution.

DESERT SHIELD/DESERT STORM AND DOWNSIZING

One way the Army attempted to solve the equipment problem was through the use of the Department of the Army's

73. *Annual Report, RFPB, FY 90*, p. 116.

74. *Annual Report, RFPB, FY 87*, p. 86.

75. For a discussion of the entire compatibility problem see Maj. Donald B. Skipper and Maj. John T. Fishel, "Equipment Compatibility Problems Denigrate Readiness of Reserves," *Army*, February 1985, pp. 34–40.

Master Priority List (DAMPL) and the Status of Resources and Training System (SORTS), which attempted to measure priority for combat and readiness to perform. Desert Shield/Desert Storm brought out some problems with these measures in that certain units that were high on the DAMPL were not mobilized for the Gulf conflict because their high status was based on another scenario, such as Europe.[76]

There was a "massive amount" of cross-levelling of equipment that went on during Desert Shield/Desert Storm to bring low DAMPL units with equipment shortages up to the point where they could be deployed. The downsizing of the Army that has occurred since that time has also contributed to improvements in the equipment readiness of the Army Reserve, as items were taken from units that were either shrinking or being eliminated and given to other units where the need existed. In conclusion, the Reserve Forces Policy Board concluded that "Presently, Army Reserve early-deploying/roundup units appear to be treated equally with Active component units with reference to equipment redistribution. New equipment procurement and deliveries in fiscal year 1991 have enhanced the Army Reserve unit capabilities and favorably impacted readiness."[77]

MOBILIZATION

The whole purpose of the Army Reserve is to be able to mobilize units and individuals and place them on active duty in support of U.S. national security interests. Mobilization is therefore the final test of whether all the training and equipment dollars have been well spent. Throughout this period (1984–1991) the Army Reserve participated in mobilization exercises, often in conjunction with forces from another of the reserve components. Following is a discussion of a sample of these exercises and some of the lessons learned from them.

EXERCISE POWDER RIVER/MOBEX 85

One of the first of the mobilization tests during this period was Exercise POWDER RIVER/MOBEX 85, which took place from October 10–26, 1984. This exercise was a mobilization and deployment exercise that focused on a multi-theater con-

76. *Annual Report, RFPB, FY 91*, p. 138.
77. *Ibid.*

Specific problems that popped up for the 2053d were spread across the board. The most severe problem occurred in the data processing arena. Both personnel and equipment proved inadequate to the task of inprocessing. The lessons-learned conclusion was that "USAR Reception Stations that will establish operations on FORSCOM installations need organic ADP support."[86] The problem during the exercise was that the 2053d was linked to a computer at Fort Benning via a telephone line and modem. Because Operation POWDER RIVER was going on at the same time, the computer at Fort Benning was being flooded with simulated personnel requests, in addition to the "real" requests generated by the 2053d. Response time became excessively long, and the exercise traffic was eventually shut off. Nevertheless, the exercise demonstrated the antiquated nature of the computer system and proved that under real world mobilization conditions it would be completely inadequate.[87]

The final analysis of the 2053d's ability to manage a reception station and process soldiers onto active duty was that "The unit is fully capable of establishing and operating a Reception Station under mobilization." It would require the addition of only three outside personnel to be fully staffed to accomplish its mission: one E–7 computer operator and two E–5 computer operators. It also would require certain additional organic equipment such as laminators and dog tag stampers. Otherwise, concluded the evaluators, the unit was ready to go.[88]

EXERCISE PROUD EAGLE 90

This exercise, conducted during the period from October 12 through November 2, 1989, was the sixth and longest in a series of MOBEXs that dated back to the 1970s and included such learning experiences as NIFTY NUGGET. It was sponsored by the Joint Chiefs of Staff and was based upon a worldwide scenario that included various levels of mobilization. It was designed to test a number of items including the Worldwide Military Command and Control System (WWMCCS), the future

86. Letter, Department of the Army, Headquarters, U.S. Army Reception Station, Fort Jackson, SC, (ATZJ–RS), to: Headquarters, TRADOC (ATTG–MMP), Date: 30 October 1984, Subject: Evaluation of Exercise Baltimore Express, Annex C, Subject: ADP Support. This is attached to the TRADOC memorandum on the Baltimore Express After-Action Report. Hereinafter cited as "Letter, Evaluation of Exercise Baltimore Express."

87. *Ibid.*, Annex C, Subject: ADP Support.

88. Letter, Evaluation of Exercise Baltimore Express, p. 33.

development of the United States Transportation Command (USTRANSCOM), and mobilization procedures in general.[89]

The exercise began with a modest call-up of reserve personnel, proceeded to and through a 200K call-up, went to partial mobilization, and ultimately reached full mobilization. The exercise pinpointed many flaws in the mobilization planning and execution system, some of which had been revealed—and not corrected—years earlier during Exercise POWDER RIVER 85. Among these revelations was the finding that a partial mobilization did not allow the support necessary for mobilization missions and deployment. The reason was the same as that identified four years earlier: "The authority to implement Mobilization Table of Distribution and Allowances (MOBTDAs) is tied to full mobilization."[90]

Data management problems surfaced repeatedly during the exercise, largely because "Numerous systems are used within and among agencies to monitor and report on various aspects of mobilization and deployment. Most of these systems were developed individually to address a discrete function or situation. As a result, they are not coordinated with one another. Many use different data sources to report similar information, reflect different levels of detail, use differing reporting windows, report unnecessary or redundant information, and the like."[91]

In the personnel arena, the exercise likewise revealed potential problems for mobilization. HQDA, showed the exercise, "does not have a single source of data which provides timely and accurate information for monitoring the posture of expanding forces. The lack of this data," concluded the evaluators, "prohibits timely informed decisions to request increased levels of manpower."[92]

The exercise also pointed out a problem with AMOPS, in that it mobilized units at their currently authorized levels, yet required the units to meet deployment standards. If this is to be the case, said the evaluation, "if these units are to be deployed before declaration of a national emergency for mobi-

---

89. Joint Chiefs of Staff, *Evaluation Report, Exercise PROUD EAGLE 90*, p. I–1; Department of the Army, Office of the Deputy Chief of Staff for Operations and Plans, Memorandum, Maj. Gen. James D. Smith (DAMO–ODO) to various addressees, Subject: Exercise Analysis Report—Exercise PROUD EAGLE 90, p. I–1. Hereinafter cited as "Army Evaluation, Exercise PROUD EAGLE 90."

90. Army Evaluation, Exercise PROUD EAGLE 90, p. I–7.

91. *Ibid.*, p. I–8.

92. *Ibid.*

lization, HQDA must change the guidance to reflect authority to increase the authorized level of organization (ALO) for deploying units in the 200K package."[93] Further, revealed the exercise, "There is conflicting guidance in AMOPS on the structure and authorized fill levels of units deploying in the 200K package."[94]

At the mobilization station level, Exercise PROUD EAGLE 90 showed that we were still a long way from perfection. The nine state-owned mobilization stations, said the evaluators, "have no Standard Army Multicommand Management Information Systems (STAMMIS) processing capability. The semi-active mobilization stations have only a limited STAMMIS support capability."[95] This would not be critical during a partial mobilization, but it could cause significant problems during a condition of full mobilization.

ARPERCEN tested some of its notification procedures during the exercise, in what became a practice-run for the January 1991 call-up of members of the Individual Ready Reserve. "The accession feedback system," concluded the exercise evaluation, "requires that a second return-receipt mailgram be sent to no-shows. This procedure required that addressee-unknown returned mailgrams and individuals granted delay and exemptions be annotated to prevent them from being declared no-shows. Procedures and codes do not exits whereby mobilization stations or ARPERCEN could enter such a code into the accessioning system."[96] Two years later, ARPERCEN had developed such a method.

In short, Exercise PROUD EAGLE 90 did exactly what it was designed to do: it stressed the mobilization system to the point where discrepancies were revealed. Some of these problems were corrected before the system was called upon to perform in real-world situation. Others probably still lie in wait, not to be discovered until there is a full scale mobilization of the reserve components.

SELECTED RESERVE CALL-UP

On October 23–25, 1987, 119 reserve component units—including 20 units in the Army Reserve—responded to a test of the President's authority to call up to 200,000 reservists to active duty. Some 15,000 members of the Reserve and Guard repre-

---

93. *Ibid.*
94. Army Evaluation, Exercise PROUD EAGLE 90, p. II–6.
95. *Ibid.*, p. III–F–1.
96. *Ibid.*, p. III–T–7.

senting 34 states, Puerto Rico and the District of Columbia were notified on October 23 to report to their mobilization stations. Turn-out among Reservists was close to 90 percent, and those who organized and ran the exercise declared it a success.[97]

GOLDEN THRUST '88

In November 1988, 24,000 Army Reserve and Army National Guardsmen from 115 units participated in a massive mobilization exercise that tested the capability of 12 Army installations to serve as mobilization stations for reserve component units destined to go overseas. Unlike other exercises that were centered on one specific fort, post, or training area, Golden Thrust was spread from New England to Virginia at installations throughout the First Army area.[98]

The purpose of the exercise was to stress the mobilization capabilities of the locations to which reserve component personnel would report in the event of a large-scale mobilization. In addition, the individual reserve units undertook their unit-specific annual training once they had in-processed. According to Col. Dudley M. Andres, First Army's Deputy Chief of Staff for Operations, "It was a great learning experience in a realistic, fast-paced, full-scale mobilization—we learned what worked and what didn't."[99]

MOBILIZATION AUTHORITY

All of the recruiting and training and equipment procurement are to no avail if the reserve components cannot be mobilized. As of 1980 the President was limited to bringing 100,000 reservists onto active duty at any one time without declaring a national emergency, and they could serve no longer than 90 days.[100] If he declared a national emergency or if Congress declared war, the President could activate up to 1 million members of the reserve components.[101]

---

97. Bernard J. Adelsberger, "Selected Reserve Call-Up Passes Muster," *Army Times*, November 9, 1987, pp. 14–15; "Selected Reserve Tested in Nationwide Call-Up," *Army Reserve Magazine*, Vol. 34, No. 1 (1988), p. 9.

98. Christine F. Britton, "First Army Units Train in Golden Thrust '88," *Army Reserve Magazine*, Vol. 34, No. 1 (1988), p. 18; Sgt. Joseph P. Satterthwaite, "Operation Golden Thrust '88," *Army Trainer* (Spring 1988), p. 34–35.

99. *Ibid.*, p. 19.

100. 10 United States Code 673b (a) and (c).

101. 10 United States Code 673a. This change had been enacted in 1980 when Public Law 96–584 increased the President's call-up authority from 50,000 to 100,000.

Public Law 99–661, signed by the President on November 14, 1986, increased to 200,000 the number that could be called up absent a declaration of war or national emergency and provided that the President could extend the period of active duty to 180 days.[102] This latter provision became critical during the call-up for Desert Shield, when the Department of Defense decided that 180 days was not long enough to allow certain reserve component units to be given refresher training and shipped to the theater of operations. The units, primarily combat units of the Army National Guard, were not activated until Congress changed the law again and allowed a service period of up to 360 days.

102. Public Law 99–661, November 14, 1986, Section 521 (a) and (b).

13

Changes in Organizational Structure Create the Modern Army Reserve

In 1919 The Adjutant General established an agency to maintain the records of discharged World War I soldiers. The agency grew through the years, moved to St. Louis in 1956, and became the Reserve Components Personnel and Administration Center (RCPAC) in 1971. RCPAC took on responsibility for non-unit members of the Army Reserve and became the place to which IRR and IMA soldiers looked for guidance. Its huge building at 9700 Page Boulevard became almost as familiar to Reservists as the Pentagon was to members of the active component.[1]

RCPAC performed its job well, but throughout the early part of the 1980s, the Office of the Chief, Army Reserve (OCAR) sought ways to enhance its control over the Army Reserve. One way that this was accomplished was through the creation of a "field operating agency" of OCAR known as the Army Reserve Personnel Center (ARPERCEN), activated in St. Louis on February 3, 1984.[2] RCPAC was not immediately replaced when ARPERCEN came into existence, but it was clear that its days were numbered. Nineteen months later, on November 5, 1985, RCPAC was gone, and the majority of its functions were transferred to ARPERCEN. ARPERCEN's responsibilities extended to command and management of the Individual Ready Reserve soldiers as well as members of the Standby and Retired Reserve, which includes soldiers from

1. U.S. Army Reserve Personnel Center Public Affairs Office, "Fact Sheet."

2. Maj. Gen. William R. Berkman, "The Posture of the U.S. Army Reserve," testimony delivered to Congress in March 1984, p. 25.

Army Chief of Staff, Gen. Carl Vuono, and ask him to "get Bill Ward under control."[10]

Vuono apparently did nothing, Palastra left FORSCOM, and the answer was two Army studies: a FORSCOM staff study which looked at the command and control and reporting relationships within the Army Reserve and a Secretary of the Army-directed study. The latter was headed by retired General William R. Richardson and was told to offer recommendations to the Secretary of the Army and the Vice Chief of Staff, Gen. Robert W. RisCassi "concerning which USAR command and control arrangement best supports the Army's ability, both now and into the future, to organize, train, and equip the Army Reserve to achieve Total Army war fighting readiness."[11]

FORSCOM STUDY

The FORSCOM study came in first. It was presented on June 19, 1989, to the FORSCOM commander, who by this time was Gen. Colin Powell.[12] It asserted five "Facts Bearing on the Problem": (1) The USAR has 7% of combat and 48% of combat support and combat service support assets of the Army, (2) USAR units have 39 training days per year for all functions combined, (3) USAR units are "CAPSTONE aligned for wartime planning and training to support specific OPLANs," (4) "Selected U.S. Army Reserve units are required to mobilize and deploy before some active Army units," and (5) "FORSCOM command and control of U.S. Army Reserve forces is consistent with the Goldwater-Nichols Defense Reorganization Act."[13]

Its bottom line conclusion was that "the current USAR command and control system . . . does not need replacing."[14] It did, however, offer four options for possible consideration, all of which seem to have been merely nibbling around the edges of the more radical proposal set forth by the Chief,

10. Topper interview, p. 2; Coker, *The U.S. Army Reserve Command*, pp. 8–11; "USAR Command and Control Study Final Report," August 11, 1989, "Study Charter." Copy in possession of the author.

11. Coker, *The U.S. Army Reserve Command*, pp. 8–11; interview, Kathryn Roe Coker, with Gen. William R. Richardson (USA, Ret.), July 12, 1993, published as part of the USAR Oral History Program Series, *Founders of the USARC* (Atlanta: USARC, 1994), p. v. Hereinafter cited as "Richardson interview."

12. Memorandum, Col. Robert F. Helms, II, Chief, Joint Strategy and Concepts Office, to Commanding General, Forces Command, 19 June 1989, Subject: U.S. Army Reserve Command and Control (USAR C2), copy in possession of the author. Hereinafter cited as "FORSCOM Study Memorandum."

13. *Ibid.*, p. 1.

14. *Ibid.*

Army Reserve and the Congress.[15] The FORSCOM staff recommended Option 3: make some changes in the system to "provide consistency in performing functions for the active Army and the USAR," add full-time USAR positions in the FORSCOM chain of command, and make the CAR a lieutenant general principal on the Army staff with duty as advisor to the Chief of Staff of the Army on Reserve affairs.[16]

Powell accepted the recommendation of the FORSCOM study group and took his case to Gen. Carl Vuono, Chief of Staff of the Army on June 20, 1989.[17] He took his case into other forums as well, including an appearance at the Summer Senior Commander's Conference (SSCC). In his appearance before the SSCC, Powell admitted that "many in the USAR don't trust the AC [active component]. They don't believe that the AC will fulfill its obligations and responsibilities to the USAR. They feel that . . . the AC uses the USAR as bill payers. This view, unfortunately, is shared in some quarters in Congress."[18]

The FORSCOM commander, soon slated to become the Chairman of the Joint Chiefs of Staff, then suggested that "there is a widespread perception in the USAR that the AC considers the Reservist as second class soldier. Unfortunately, there are enough cases where these concerns can be validated that it is tough to make a convincing counter argument."[19]

CONGRESS RESPONDS

Congress, however, did not like what it was hearing from the Army on this subject and used the "foot on the financial windpipe" approach to grab the Army's attention. The House of Representatives did this by proposing to withhold $100 million in Management Headquarters funds in the Operation and Maintenance, Army (OMAR) account "until the Secretary of the Army submitted a plan providing the Chief, Army Reserve command and control authority over the Army Reserve forces."[20] The concerns of the chairman of the Defense Ap-

15. These options are set forth in the previously-referenced FORSCOM Study Memorandum, pp. 8–12. They are also discussed in Coker, *The U.S. Army Reserve Command*, pp. 14–15.

16. FORSCOM Study Memorandum, pp. 12, 10.

17. Coker, *The U.S. Army Reserve Command*, pp. 15–17.

18. Speech Prepared for General Powell's Use at the 6–8 August [1989] Army SSCC, pp. 2–3. Copy in possession of the author.

19. Powell speech to SSCC, p. 3.

20. Quoted in the Conference Report to accompany H.R. 3072, a bill "Making Appropriations for the Department of Defense for the Fiscal Year Ending September 30, 1990, and for other purposes." Hereinafter cited as "Conference Report, FY 1990 Defense Appropriations Bill, November 13, 1989."

clude that "these problems can be solved best within the current command arrangement."[27]

Powell's official response to the final report was transmitted to Lt. Gen. Gordon R. Sullivan, Army Deputy Chief of Staff for Operations and Plans, in an undated letter written about the end of September 1989. "The problems with both the study panel [the Richardson study] and OCAR recommendations is that in their attempt to fix a problem, they recommend substituting nothing for something. Adopting either of these proposals will have the effect of isolating rather than integrating the Army Reserve in the Total Force. The problems are real. There is a structure in place that can solve these problems. It is called DA, FORSCOM, and the CONUSA."[28]

CONGRESS' STUDY

Congress had meanwhile weighed in with its own study report, a thirty page product of the Investigations and Surveys staff of the House Appropriations Committee. It addressed the Congressional interest in having the reserve components provide leadership for the reserves. It pointed out that the Air Force Reserve was commanded by an Air Force Reservist and that the Naval Reserve was commanded by a Naval Reservist. It also focused on particular issues that troubled the Congressional staffers: layering, lack of fulltime support, problems with automatic data processing, and the negative perceptions that Reservists expressed about how the active component viewed them. It also zeroed in on the relative lack of influence the CAR had on the use of funds appropriated for the Army Reserve. There were no clear findings as to desirable command and control for the USAR. In its August 1989 bill, however, the House Appropriations Committee directed that the Army transfer command and control of the Army Reserve to the Chief, Army Reserve.[29]

ARMY RESERVE SUPPORT COMMAND

Secretary of the Army Stone conveyed the Army's position on USAR command and control in a November 6, 1989, letter to

27. Letter, Gen. Colin Powell, Commander in Chief, Forces Command to Gen. William R. Richardson (USA, Ret.), July 21, 1989. Copy in possession of the author.

28. Letter, Gen. Colin Powell, Commander in Chief, Forces Command to Lt. Gen. Gordon R. Sullivan, Deputy Chief of Staff for Operations and Plans, United States Army, undated. Copy in possession of the author.

29. Quoted in Coker, *The U.S. Army Reserve Command*, pp. 12–13; cited in Conference Report, FY 1990 Defense Appropriations Bill.

Chairman Murtha. The Army, said Stone, intends "to set up a new Army Reserve Support Command (ARSC). ARSC will be commanded by a three-star reserve officer who will be responsible for oversight and control of administration for reserve units. Most importantly," informed the Secretary, "this new command will be delegated direct control of funding for all reserve units. The CONUSA will exercise command responsibilities for reserve training, mobilization and deployment." Addressing the FORSCOM connection, Stone explained that the Commanding General of the ARSC "will also be dual-hatted as the Deputy Commanding General FORSCOM to preserve the direct command relationship to the person who has the responsibility for the active component units with which the reserve component units would fight."[30]

Stone's letter may have had some minimal effect on the Congress, because by mid-November 1989 when the conference met on the defense appropriations bill, the legislators had backed away a bit from the hardline House position. There still seemed little doubt, however, as to what they expected ultimately. The conference report provided that "The Secretary of the Army is directed to prepare a plan to increase the role of the Chief, Army Reserve, consistent with the command, planning and management responsibilities of the Chief of the Air Force Reserve and the Chief of the National Guard Bureau."[31]

The conferees decreed that "an initial step" in this process would be to "have the Chief of Army Reserve become a more active partner in control of the fiscal year 1990 funds and to involve him directly in the on-going budget process for fiscal year 1991 and the Program Objective Memorandum process in fiscal year 1992." The conferees also required the Secretary of the Army to submit by March 15, 1990, a report "which delineates what needs to be accomplished in order to provide the Chief of Army Reserve command authority and when the transition should be implemented. The Chief of Army Reserve," the conferees cautioned, "should become an active partner in preparation of this report." The conferees did give the Army some respite by deleting the $100 million penalty that the House appropriators had levied against it.[32]

30. Letter, Secretary of the Army Michael P.W. Stone to Rep. John P. Murtha, Chairman, Defense Appropriations Subcommittee, Committee on Appropriations, United States House of Representatives, November 6, 1989. Copy in possession of the author.

31. Conference Report, FY 1990 Defense Appropriations Bill, November 13, 1989.

32. *Ibid.*

FORSCOM'S PLAN

In an "Eyes Only" message on December 12, 1989, Army Chief of Staff Carl E. Vuono, directed the FORSCOM commander, Gen. Edwin R. Burba, "in coordination with OCAR," to develop "a detailed draft plan to be forwarded to DA within 60 days that would implement the basic guidance provided in Ref A [appropriations conference report] and Ref B [revised diagram of Draft DA concept for USAR C2, dated December 5, 1989]." The message further instructed that the draft plan should:

—describe the U.S. Army Reserve Force (USARF) headquarters structure, responsibilities, functions and resource requirements;
—address the roles, missions, and responsibilities, and number of CONUSAs, functional commands, and ARCOMs;
—address fulltime manning requirements;
—describe the funding process from the CAR to USAR user units;
—address relationships between TRADOC and Reserve training units, meaning the USARF schools;
—address "methodology to improve USAR readiness."[33]

A month later, on January 12, 1990, the FORSCOM commander, Gen. Edwin R. Burba, Jr., informed the Army staff (and through it Gen. Vuono) that "work is in progress along lines directed in reference." Burba suggested severing the CONUSA/ARCOM issue, the TRADOC/USARF school issue, and the USAR readiness issue from the 60 day reporting requirement.[34] Burba's request was promptly approved by Lt. Gen. Gordon Sullivan, the Deputy Chief of Staff of the Army for Operations and Plans,[35] and FORSCOM planning continued apace.

Less than a week later, FORSCOM was ready to consummate its work. On January 18, 1990, FORSCOM hosted an in-process review (IPR) with the Chief, Army Reserve. At this IPR the participants reached a number of decisions that would affect the ultimate shape, size and placement of the new Army

33. Msg., Gen. Carl E. Vuono, Chief of Staff, United States Army, to Gen. Edwin R. Burba, FORSCOM Commander in Chief, dtg: 121430Z Dec 89 (December 12, 1989), Subject: USAR Command and Control. Copy in possession of the author.

34. Msg., Cdr, FORSCOM to various addressees, including Brig. Gen. McCaffrey (ODCSOPS) and Maj. Gen. Ward (CAR), dtg: 121435Z Jan 90 (January 12, 1990), Subject: USAR Command and Control. Copy in possession of the author.

35. Coker, *The U.S. Army Reserve Command*, p. 22.

Reserve command. Following the conclusion of the meeting, the Commander of FORSCOM, Gen. Burba, and the Chief, Army Reserve, Gen. Ward, signed a "Memorandum of Agreement" (MOA) which set forth the decisions made to date.[36]

THE FORSCOM–OCAR MOA

This MOA summarized the results of the January 18 IPR and listed the following agreements:

—The reserve command would be organized as a Major Subordinate Command of FORSCOM;
—FORSCOM would "develop overall policy for the USAR in support of the Total Army;"
—Span of Control Alternative 5,[37] which provided for CONUS corps commanders to be dual-hatted as DCGs of the Army Reserve command and the command itself to be subordinate to FORSCOM, was "selected for further staff development." Alternative 6, which was offered by the CAR, did nothing to the CONUSAs, while also establishing an Army Reserve command under FORSCOM.[38] The MOA stated that this alternative would be "examined and the good aspects of it [would] be factored into the final plan."[39]

The MOA acknowledged that the Chief, Army Reserve did not really like Alternative 5. "The CAR," said the MOA, "emphasized his role in accepting Alternative 5 was one of acceptance—not one of championing the cause. The CAR is supporting the decision by CG FORSCOM, not a major advocate of the proposal."[40]

The FORSCOM–OCAR Memorandum of Agreement was a large step toward the creation of an Army Reserve command, but it was not the final resolution of the controversy. In an explanatory memorandum to the Chief of Staff of the Army, Maj. Gen. Barry R. McCaffrey, Director of Strategy, Plans and Policy on the Army staff, outlined the status of the plan and some of the remaining issues.

---

36. Memorandum of Agreement between Forces Command and Office, Chief, Army Reserve, Subject: United States Army Reserve Command and Control, January 18, 1990, reprinted in Coker, *The U.S. Army Reserve Command*, pp. 243–44. Hereinafter cited as "FORSCOM–OCAR MOA."

37. *Ibid.*, p. 202.

38. *Ibid.*, p. 203.

39. FORSCOM–OCAR MOA, as found in Coker, *The U.S. Army Reserve Command*, p. 243.

40. *Ibid.*, p. 244.

The memorandum emphasized that the Army Reserve Command would be a "Major Subordinate Command" of FORSCOM, "as are Corps, CONUSAs, and Third U.S. Army." It further emphasized that "CAR cannot support any option which threatens the current authorization of LTGs [lieutenant generals] as CONUSA commanders or gives the perception of layering."[41] Alternative 5, the one preferred by FORSCOM, would, in fact, result in both of these circumstances.

The memorandum also included a most significant warning note. One of the staff members on the House Appropriations Committee, Ms. Sandra Gilbert, had been briefed on the plan and "stated that Span of Control Alternative 5 gives the perception of increased layering to the C2 process. Further, Alternative 5 may allow the DCG, USARC to circumvent the CG USARC by his dual-hatted status as CONUSA commander. Gilbert will refer any plan submitted to Congress to the S&I [Surveys and Investigations staff of the House Appropriations Committee] for review/field study."[42]

FORSCOM formally submitted its proposal to HQDA on February 20. In a letter to Chief of Staff Vuono, FORSCOM commander Burba enclosed a "detailed draft plan to establish a U.S. Army Reserve Command (USARC)." He proposed to "stand up a provisional command in July 1990," setting an ambitious schedule for both FORSCOM and Department of the Army Headquarters. He proposed full activation of the USARC a year later, in July 1991.[43]

He said that the recommended command and control relationship for the Army Reserve was "consistent with Congressional language in that the CAR commands USAR organizations assigned to Forces Command and controls resource allocation for these forces." Burba stated that the plan to dual-hat the active component CONUSA deputy commanding generals as USARC DCGs was designed "to assist the CG, USARC in exercising command functions." Concluded Burba: "It is a low-risk approach. . . ."[44] Burba's analysis revealed a singular lack of understanding of the political climate.

41. Information Paper, Maj. Gen. Barry R. McCaffrey, Director of Strategy, Plans, and Policy, to Chief of Staff of the Army, January 29, 1990. Copy in possession of the author.

42. *Ibid.*

43. Letter, Gen. Edwin H. Burba, Jr., Commanding General, Forces Command, to Gen. Carl E. Vuono, Chief of Staff, United States Army, February 20, 1990. Copy in possession of the author.

44. *Ibid.*

REP. MONTGOMERY STEPS IN

Shortly, another influential member of Congress weighed in on the issue. On March 23, 1990, Rep. Gillespie V. (Sonny) Montgomery (D–Miss.), Chairman of the House Committee on Veteran's Affairs and a retired National Guard general officer, sent a letter to the Secretary of the Army.

In his letter Montgomery stated that he had "been apprised of some of the proposals submitted to the Army. I understand the latest proposal from Forces Command activates an Army Reserve Command subordinate to FORSCOM with the reserve units under the operational control of the Army Commanders for everything except administration. This arrangement in effect makes the Army Reserve Command a large headquarters company. This," concluded the lawmaker, "is obviously not in concert with the intent or the law of Congress. . . . It is time for the Army to settle this issue and designate the Chief of the Army Reserve as the commander for all purposes of his component."[45]

ARMY DELAYS

The Army's response was an official delay in letting Congress know what was happening, attributing the requirement for such to "changes in the strategic environment" and not mentioning that FORSCOM had formally submitted its plan for the USAR. A week after Montgomery sent his letter, Stone informed Rep. Murtha that "The impending CFE [Conventional Forces in Europe] agreement, the reality of reduced fiscal resources, and a significant change in the Soviet/Warsaw Pact threat are causing us to reexamine our total force structure. It is obvious," wrote the Secretary, "that the command and control arrangement for the Reserve Component and its relationship to the Active force must also be readdressed." As for the specifics of what the Army was doing toward establishing the Army Reserve command, the Secretary informed Murtha that ". . . the CG, Forscom [*sic*], along with the Chief, Army Reserve, will continue their planning efforts in order that the final solutions can be implemented as soon as possible."[46]

Four members of the Surveys and Investigations staff of the House Appropriations Committee meanwhile requested

---

45. Letter, Rep. G.V. (Sonny) Montgomery to Army Secretary Michael P.W. Stone, March 23, 1990. Copy in possession of the author.

46. Letter, Army Secretary Michael P.W. Stone, to Rep. John P. Murtha, Chairman, Subcommittee on Defense, House Appropriations Committee, March 30, 1990. Copy in possession of the author.

and received a briefing on the status of the reorganization. On March 26, 1990, they met with representatives of the Deputy Chief of Staff for Operations and Plans to discuss such issues as the delay that was apparently to result from the Total Force Policy Study referenced in the letter from Stone to Murtha.[47]

According to the note-taker for the meeting, the "S&I team seems well grounded in basic facts currently affecting USAR C2" and requested three documents from the Army: the Richardson study, a copy of the FORSCOM Plan of Improvements, and a wiring diagram of the current USAR C2 arrangement.[48] It seemed clear that the House Appropriations Committee was not prepared to allow this matter to drop and would be watching closely the Army's actions. It was also clear that the committee was being well-served by a group of staffers who were not the least bit reticent about asking questions. What they did not know, however, was the exact state of play with regard to the FORSCOM plan for the USARC.

FORSCOM PLANNING GROUP

What the Secretary had not told the subcommittee chairman in his letter of March 30 and what the S&I investigators had not learned was that two days before he sent his letter, Forces Command had accelerated its planning for an Army Reserve command, had already submitted its plan to HQDA for coordination and approval, and had established on March 28, 1990, the "Forces Command United States Army Reserve (USARC) Planning Group," with Col. John A. Topper, the senior Army Reserve advisor at FORSCOM, as its chief.[49]

Topper's charge was to work with OCAR and keep the CAR "apprised of your progress." His tasking was quite specific. He was instructed to prepare a Table of Distribution and Allowances (TDA), an Organization and Functions Manual and "other supporting documents in anticipation of HQDA decision to establish a headquarters subordinate to FORSCOM to effect command and control of assigned USAR units."[50]

47. Memorandum for the Record, Maj. Timothy M. Byrne, Functional Monitor (DAMO–SSP), Subject: United States Army Reserve Command and Control (C2), March 26, 1990. Copy in possession of the author.

48. *Ibid.*

49. Memorandum, Maj. Gen. Robert D. Wiegand, Chief of Staff, FORSCOM, to Col. John A. Topper, March 28, 1990, Subject: Establishment of Forces Command United States Army Reserve (USARC) Planning Group. Copy in possession of the author.

50. *Ibid.*

Topper was given additional instructions to "validate functions" of the new command, to "prepare plan for transition to provisional command," and to "prepare plan for phased transfer of functions" from elsewhere into the new Army Reserve command." He was finally admonished to "ensure OCAR is invited to have representatives at all IPRs and is included in all actions worked by the planning group."[51] There was no discussion in the memorandum as to the organizational relationship of the USARC to FORSCOM or to any other commands, such as the CONUSAs. The clear implication was that as far as FORSCOM was concerned, these decisions had already been made, and all that remained was the nuts-and-bolts work like preparing TDAs.

REACTIONS TO THE FORSCOM PLAN

Department of the Army headquarters was meanwhile laying the groundwork for its attempt to sell the plan to the Army Reserve's principal professional group—the Reserve Officers Association (ROA)—and to Congress. It also had substantial resistance to overcome within the Pentagon.

The disapprobation from within the Army staff itself came from several directions. One non-concurrence came from Eric A. Orsini, the Deputy Assistant Secretary of the Army (Logistics). Orsini was a career civil servant whose views commanded great respect within Army circles. A Silver Star winner during the Battle of the Bulge, Orsini knew everyone who mattered and had influence that extended well beyond the bounds of his office. He disapproved of the plan because of the OPCON relationship of CONUSA and MUSARC. "This special/unique relationship," observed Orsini, "does not appear to be necessary, and, in fact, would seem to fragment command responsibility/authority as well as confuse the much needed clarity in establishing an effective Army Reserve chain of command." Orsini went on to suggest that "In this regard, I see no reason why the CONUSA cannot be given a mission to simply support the USARC as required for the TAG [National Guard Adjutant General]."[52]

Orsini's was not the only objection to the proposal from within the Army staff. Maj. Gen. William H. Reno, Director of Program Analysis and Evaluation, also non-concurred, sin-

---

51. *Ibid.*

52. Memorandum, Eric A. Orsini, Deputy Assistant Secretary of the Army (Logistics), to Lt. Gen. Gordon R. Sullivan, Deputy Chief of Staff for Operations and Plans, March 1, 1990. Copy in possession of the author.

gling out several aspects of the plan. He disagreed with the FORSCOM designation of the USARC as a "major subordinate command," believing that "Major Army Subcommand" would be more appropriate. He further disagreed with the recommendation that the USARC be located at Fort McPherson, Ga., and he felt that the staffing proposed for the USARC (500–600 personnel) was excessive.[53]

Most importantly, however, he, like Orsini, zeroed in on the CONUSA issue. "It is not necessary," wrote Reno, "to dual hat the CONUSA DCGs [deputy commanding generals] for regional command and control. . . . The insertion of Active component major generals into a newly established Reserve chain of command," he observed, "only adds a layer." Drawing an analogy with the National Guard, Reno suggested that ". . . this NGB [National Guard Bureau] structure has proven effective. The FORSCOM plan dismisses an effective structure without substantial rationale.[54]

Finally, though not entering a non-concurrence, Maj. Gen. Merle Freitag, Deputy Assistant Secretary of the Army for Army Budget, raised several red flags. Congressional interest, suggested Freitag, centered about two issues. Does it place the Chief, Army Reserve in command of the Army Reserve? And does it eliminate unnecessary command layers? "The plan," he observed, "appears vulnerable to challenge" on both these issues. Furthermore, said Freitag, members of Congress "will also be concerned that the FORSCOM plan places reserve units under the operational control of the CONUSAs for everything except administration."[55] Freitag was most prescient.

The seriousness with which the Army regarded its relationship with ROA is exemplified in the detailed notes prepared for use in a telephone call between the FORSCOM commander and the executive director of ROA, Maj. Gen. Evan L. Hultman (Ret.) The Army had learned from Defense Secretary McNamara's aborted attempt to combine the Army Reserve with the Army National Guard that this was potent lobbying force with considerable clout on Capitol Hill.[56]

53. 1st Endorsement (DACS–DPZ–C) to letter DAMO–SSP/27 Feb 90, Maj. Gen. William H. Reno, Director, Program Analysis and Evaluation, to Deputy Chief of Staff for Operations and Plans, Subject: United States Army Reserve Command (C2), March 5, 1990. Copy in possession of the author.

54. *Ibid.*

55. Memorandum, Maj. Gen. Merle Freitag, Deputy Assistant Secretary of the Army for Army Budget to Deputy Chief of Staff for Operations, Plans,and Training, Subject: United States Army Reserve Command and Control (C2), March 5, 1990. Copy in possession of the author.

56. See the discussion in Chapter 8.

Interestingly, one of the key points that the FORSCOM commander was expected to make to the ROA director was that ROA "cannot place CSA [Chief of Staff of the Army] and Sec Army in position of being rejected by Congress again. All parties must accept less than the optimal to maintain team spirit and unity before Congress." This talk of "team spirit" and need for unity may have been seen as in the best interests of the FORSCOM planners, but it did not convince the leadership at ROA.[57]

STONE MEETS WITH MONTGOMERY AND MURTHA

Once again, the House members weighed into the fray. On April 25 and again on April 30, 1990, Secretary Stone met with Representatives Murtha and Montgomery, the two members most interested in the USAR command and control (C2) issue. At this meeting the three men recognized that the two primary issues were command and control of personnel and control of Army Reserve funding. Stone agreed to give the Army Reserve additional control over USAR funding, but according to the Memorandum for the Record (MFR) prepared on the meeting, he was reluctant to change the C2 situation.[58]

AUTHORIZATION BILL OMITS THE USARC

Rep. Les Aspin (D–Wisc.), Chairman of the Armed Services Committee, introduced the FY 1991 authorization bill for the Department of Defense, and a USAR command and control provision was not in the original text. This omission may have lulled the Army leadership into a false sense of security, but if it did so, this was an erroneous feeling that was not to be long-lived.[59]

PLEDGES OF SUPPORT FROM THE SENATE

According to Topper, the Army worked the other side of Capitol Hill to organize a counter-weight to the House Appropriations Committee effort on the Army Reserve Command. This

57. "Notes for CG Telephone Call with MG Hultman." Copy in possession of the author.

58. Cited in Coker, *The U.S. Army Reserve Command*, p. 39.

59. 101st United States Congress, House of Representatives, H.R. 4739, National Defense Authorization Act for Fiscal Year 1991. The original bill was introduced by House Armed Services Committee Chairman Les Aspin (D–Wisc.) and others on May 8, 1990.

was accomplished by enlisting members of the Senate Armed Services and Appropriations Committees. On the Armed Services Committee the Army received pledges of support from Senators Sam Nunn (D–Ga.), the committee's chairman and from Strom Thurmond (R–SC), a retired Army Reserve general officer, former president of the Reserve Officers Association, and the ranking Republican on the committee.[60]

Appropriators who agreed with the Army's position were Senators Daniel Inouye (D–Hawaii), Chairman of the Appropriations Committee and Ted Stevens (R–Ak.), ranking Republican on the Defense Appropriations Subcommittee. According to Topper, Nunn offered that "We'll see to it in the Senate that it doesn't become a separate command."[61] This was a powerful lineup on the Senate side. It remained to be seen whether it would hold against the strongly-held desires of the House of Representatives.

OCAR RECEIVES FUNDING AUTHORITY

Secretary of the Army Stone meanwhile attempted to fulfill part of the agreement he had reached with Murtha and Montgomery in April. On June 1, 1990, he signed a memorandum to Maj. Gen. Ward, giving him "direct control over the allocation, distribution, and control of funds for the three Army Reserve appropriations [Reserve Personnel, Army (RPA), Operations and Maintenance, Army Reserve (OMAR), and Military Construction, Army Reserve (MCAR)] . . . effective October 1, 1990. This authority includes appropriations sponsorship and the management and control of fuunds directly to the major U.S. Army Reserve commands." Stone told Ward to develop a plan for "allocation, distribution and control of funds" by August 1, 1990.[62]

Stone sent a letter with an identical text to the commander of FORSCOM that same day. The letter directed FORSCOM to "support the Chief, Army Reserve, in the development of the implementation plan and . . . provide the resources necessary to assure smooth transition of Reserve appropriations funds control to the Chief, Army Reserve."[63]

60. Topper interview, p. 18.

61. *Ibid.*

62. Memorandum, Secretary of the Army Michael P.W. Stone to Chief, Army Reserve [Maj. Gen. William F. Ward], Subject: Control of U.S. Army Reserve Funds, Date: June 1, 1990. Copy in possession of the author.

63. Letter, Secretary of the Army Michael P.W. Stone to Gen. Edwin H. Burba, Jr., Commanding General, Forces Command, Date: June 1, 1990. Copy in possession of the author.

Stone also sent letters to Representatives Montgomery and Murtha telling them of his accomplishment.[64]

CONGRESSIONAL REACTION

Stone may have thought that his actions on the budget had defused the situation with Murtha and Montgomery. If so, he was greatly mistaken. Five days later, Montgomery fired a strong letter back to Stone. In its entirety, it read:

> I have received your letter of June 1, 1990, concerning the command and control of the Army Reserve. I am disappointed in what you propose. Jack Murtha and I are under the impression from our April 25 meeting that funding control is the first step toward providing command authority to the Chief of the Army Reserve (CAR). The Army proposal gives funding authority to the CAR, but reserves the decisions on priorities, requirements, training, standards, and readiness to the Forces Command Commander. This in effect makes the CAR the financial bookkeeper for FORSCOM.
>
> A plan for command authority or a separate Army Reserve command is not even mentioned. This still needs to be addressed and resolved.
>
> The proposal of waiting for the Total Force Policy study, the Army management study and the CFE talks has nothing to do with the need for the CAR to command his component. It does not matter if the USAR is 50,000 or 500,000, we still need a command and control system that streamlines the administration, planning, programming, funding, logistical support and the responsibility for training and readiness.
>
> I urge you to end this long debate and take the initiative and designate the Chief of the Army Reserve as the commander of his component with full responsibility for administration and supervision.[65]

Montgomery had sent a copy of his letter to Rep. Murtha, and the following day the Defense Appropriations Subcommittee chairman added his voice to that of the Mississippi Congressman. "I am in total agreement with the position of Congressman Montgomery as expressed in his letter to you, dated June 5, 1990. Therefore, I expect to receive the plan requested in last year's conference report prior to the Committee's markup of the Fiscal Year 1991 Defense Appropriations Bill scheduled for July 1990."[66]

---

64. Cited in Coker, *The U.S. Army Reserve Command*, p. 40.

65. Letter, Rep. Gillespie V. Montgomery to Secretary of the Army Michael P.W. Stone, June 5, 1990. Copy in possession of the author.

66. Letter, Rep. John P. Murtha, Chairman, Defense Subcommittee, House Appropriations Committee, to Army Secretary Michael P.W. Stone, June 6, 1990. Copy in possession of the author.

It was evident that the parties at the April 25 meeting—Montgomery, Murtha, and Stone—had talked past one another. Stone apparently thought that he was going a long way toward meeting the desires of the Congressmen. The Congressmen were just as certain that he had totally misunderstood what had been agreed to at the meeting.

NEW COURSES OF ACTION

The Army's next move was to consider three courses of action (COA). In brief, these were to (1) implement the Secretary's decision on funding, ignoring for the present the issues of Army Reserve command and control, (2) make a commitment to Congress to establish an Army Reserve command, but withhold details on its structure or the time period for implementation, and (3) establish an Army Reserve command.[67]

It is difficult to see just how anyone who had been involved at all in the back-and-forth with the Congress on this issue could have ever thought that courses of action 1 and 2 had any viability. The Army decided to go with COA 1 anyway, while COA 3 was held out as a "fallback position."[68] Furthermore, in a decided departure from its previous manner of working with the Chief, Army Reserve, on issues relating to the USAR, the ODCSOPS briefing slides on this issue "were treated as 'close hold' and not shared with OCAR."[69]

Proceeding as if COA 1 were the answer to its problems, but fearing that it might have to implement COA 3, the Forces Command Planning Group under Topper proceeded to revise the FORSCOM model of a USARC to reflect the latest thinking on the proper organizational structure.[70] It was to little avail, however, as the Chief, Army Reserve objected to the proposal when he was finally briefed on its contents on July 14, 1990.[71]

CAR–FORSCOM MOA ON FUNDING

Despite the early June responses from Montgomery and Murtha on the plan to give the CAR control over Army Reserve funding, the Army went ahead with implementation of the

67. Coker, *The U.S. Army Reserve Command*, p. 42.

68. *Ibid.*

69. *Ibid.*

70. There is a detailed discussion of the changes recommended by the Planning Group, many of which devolved into the minutiae of headquarters organization, in Coker, *The U.S. Army Reserve Command*, pp. 42–43.

71. *Ibid.*, p. 43.

plan set forth in the Secretary's June 1 letter and memorandum. On July 9, 1990, the Chief, Army Reserve signed a Memorandum of Agreement between himself and the Commanding General, Forces Command on the subject of "U.S. Army Reserve Funds Allocation, Distribution and Control—FY 91."[72]

In this MOA, the CAR, Maj. Gen. Ward, and the FORSCOM commander, Gen. Burba, acted as if the Secretary's June 1 letter and memorandum had solved the problems surrounding the Army Reserve. The purpose of the MOA, as stated in paragraph 1, was to "delineate roles and relationships governing the allocation, distribution, and control of U.S. Army Reserve appropriations by the Commanding General, Forces Command . . . and the Chief, Army Reserve."[73] There was no mention of the command and control issue.

GEN. WARD AND THE ARMY RESERVE FORCES POLICY COMMITTEE

The same day on which he signed the MOA (July 9), Ward sent a memorandum to the members of the Army Reserve Forces Policy Committee letting them know the current status of the various issues. He was doing this, he wrote "at the request of DCSOPS, Lt. Gen. Reimer" who was afraid that the Policy Committee members might "feel that the current move toward establishing a USAR command is counterproductive to the Total Army policy that we have all worked so hard to establish and make a reality over the past several years."[74]

Ward indicated in his memorandum that "the once contentious issue of dual hatting the CONUSA DCGs as DCGs of the USAR command has apparently been eliminated."[75] The timing on Ward's announcement to the committee on this critical point was interesting and apparently reflected an agreement he had reached with the USARC Planning Group, headed by Col. Topper. It was not until a week later, on July 18, that Topper was at the point of briefing Gen. Burba and

72. Memorandum of Agreement between the Chief, Army Reserve, Maj. Gen. William F. Ward, and the Commanding General, Forces Command, Gen. Edwin H. Burba, Jr., Subject: U.S. Army Reserve Funds Allocation, Distribution, and Control—FY 91, dated July 9, 1990 (Ward) and July 13, 1990 (Burba). Copy in possession of the author.

73. *Ibid.*

74. Memorandum, Maj. Gen. William F. Ward, Chief, Army Reserve, to Members of the Army Reserve Forces Policy Committee, Subject: USAR Command and Control Issues and Status, date: July 9, 1990. Copy in possession of the author. Hereinafter cited as "Army Reserve Forces Policy Committee memo."

75. *Ibid.*

recommending that this "dual hatting" arrangement be dropped from the FORSCOM plan, a change in the plans to which the FORSCOM commander gave his assent.[76]

Ward also told the Army Reserve Forces Policy Committee that "the last remaining problem is the nature of the USAR command itself, i.e., should it be a SUBMACOM or a major subordinate command of FORSCOM?"[77] This question, of course, had supposedly been answered in the January 18, 1990, MOA between Ward and Burba, which specified that "The USARF will be organized as a Major Subordinate Command."[78] Ward concluded by stating that the question of whether the CAR wears two stars on each shoulder or three "is entirely moot. The sole object of this exercise is, and always has been, to improve USAR readiness and accountability."[79]

USAR PLANNING MEETING

On July 19, 1990, the Army DCSOPS hosted a USAR command and control meeting to develop a plan that would be presented to Congress. The plan that came out of the meeting proposed solutions to several difficult issues. First, the USARC would be a major subordinate command of FORSCOM. Second, the command would be located in Atlanta.[80] Third, the Chief, Army Reserve would be a lieutenant general and triple-hatted as the CAR, Commanding General of the USARC, and Deputy Commanding General of FORSCOM. Fourth, "control of USAR units for operations, mobilization, and training to remain with the CONUSAs."[81] These were the proposals, but there was no certainty that they would stick.

ESTABLISHMENT OF THE USARC

The Army moved rapidly to establish the Army Reserve Command prior to final resolution of the issue in the defense authorization bill, hoping perhaps that doing so would strengthen the hands of its Senate supporters. On October 1, 1990, Gen. Vuono, informed Gen. Burba at Forces Command

76. Coker, *The U.S. Army Reserve Command*, p. 44.

77. Army Reserve Forces Policy Committee memo.

78. MOA, January 18, 1990, printed in full in Coker, *The U.S. Army Reserve Command*, pp. 243–44.

79. Army Reserve Forces Policy Committee memo.

80. There was a considerable lobby in favor of locating the command in St. Louis with ARPERCEN; another group favored the Washington, D.C., area.

81. Coker, *The U.S. Army Reserve Command*, p. 46.

that he and the Secretary of the Army had "approved your plan to establish a United States Army Reserve Command (USARC)."[82]

Burba was directed to "establish a provisional USARC headquarters in the Atlanta area," wrote Vuono. "The mission of this headquarters is to facilitate the establishment of the new USARC as a Major Subordinate Command of FORSCOM. The USARC should become fully operational by 30 September 1992." Burba was informed that Maj. Gen. Ward, would command the USARC. "In this capacity," continued Vuono, "he will ultimately command all U.S. Army Reserve units assigned to FORSCOM, while continuing to serve as my principal staff advisor on the Army Reserves."[83] Maj. Gen. Ward assumed command of the USARC that same day. The new command had at that time a strength of 1 officer, 1 warrant officer, and 4 enlisted personnel.[84]

CONGRESS PASSES A BILL

Congress was at the same time moving rapidly toward a legislative resolution of the command and control issue. As mentioned previously, the House version of the Defense Department authorization bill for FY 1991 (H.R. 4739) had not contained a specific provision on the Army Reserve command when it was introduced. A section providing that the chiefs of the reserve components would be "solely responsible for administering and supervising their respective components," was added in committee, however. This provision was part of the bill that was reported out of the Armed Services Committee on August 3, 1990, and passed the House of Representatives on September 19, just 12 days before the USARC was established by the Army.[85]

The Senate version of the defense authorization bill (S. 2884) contained no comparable provision, reflecting the understanding that the Army apparently had with those certain in-

82. Letter, Gen. Carl E. Vuono, Army Chief of Staff, to Gen. Edwin H. Burba, Jr., Commander, Forces Command, October 1, 1990. Copy found in Coker, *The U.S. Army Reserve Command*, p. 245.

83. *Ibid.*

84. Headquarters, United States Army Reserve Command (Prov), Memorandum for Distribution, Subject: Assumption of Command by Authority of AR 600–20, para 2–3, date: October 1, 1990; Department of the Army, Headquarters, Forces Command, Permanent Orders 183–13, October 1, 1990.

85. Section 1034, which related to the authority of the reserve chiefs, was added to the House bill during committee markup. 101st Congress, House of Representatives, Report No. 101–665, p. 332.

fluential Senators. The bill was reported from committee on July 20 and passed the Senate on September 25.[86] This meant that a conference committee would be convened to work out the differences between the two versions of the defense authorization bill, including the reserve chiefs' authority. Given the pace of the Congress, this conference was likely to meet after the Army's preemptive strike of establishing the Army Reserve Command. The Army could certainly count on its not finishing prior to October 1. The only question was what the conferees would do when presented with the USARC *fait accompli.*

Part of the scenario worked out as anticipated. The conference did not complete its work until after the establishment of the USARC. The members of the committee were in fact quite aware of the Army's actions, but they seem not to have been overly impressed by them. "The conferees are pleased," stated the conference report, "that the Army has initiated actions to establish an Army Reserve Command. The conferees are concerned, however, that command and control relationships between active and reserve forces, which are perceived by many as contributing factors to the relatively low readiness status of the Army Reserve, are not sufficiently changed in the current Army plan to provide actual command and control to the Chief of the Army Reserve. Specifically, the conferees note that the Chief of the Army Reserve should command all non-mobilized reserve units with the exceptions included in the amendment [forces assigned to carry out functions of the Secretary of the Army specified in section 3013 of Title 10, United States Code.]"[87]

As a result of this lack of clear command and control by the Chief, Army Reserve, said the conferees, "the command relationship should evolve during the test period to one that vests administrative and operational control of non-mobilized Army Reserve units in the Chief of the Army Reserve."[88]

The final version of the authorization bill for FY 1991, reflecting the language in the conference report, contained a provision requiring the establishment of an "Army Reserve Command under the command of the Chief, Army Reserve. The Army Reserve command shall be a major subordinate command of Forces Command."[89] Though HQDA may have had prior commitments from certain Senators to oppose the

86. 101st Congress, United States Senate, Report No. 101–384.

87. 101st Congress, House of Representatives, Conference Report No. 101–923, p. 637.

88. *Ibid.*, p. 637–38.

89. Coker, *The U.S. Army Reserve Command,* p. 48; Section 903, Public Law 101–510, National Defense Authorization Act for Fiscal Year 1991.

creation of the command if was not what the Army wanted, by the time the matter reached conference, the Army had decided not to oppose the House position. The conference report was adopted by the House of Representatives on October 24, 1990, and the Senate on October 26. It was signed into law on November 5.[90]

PROVISIONS IN THE LAW

It seemed as if, finally, the deed had been done. There was now a United States Army Reserve Command, and the Chief, Army Reserve was its commander. It was even an organization that had been blessed in statute. The only fly in the ointment, so to speak, was the provision in the Defense Authorization Act that made the USARC's establishment subject to a two year test period.[91]

The law also required the Secretary of the Army to submit semiannual reports to Congress on the progress of the command, and most importantly, it required the Secretary to establish an "independent commission" to assist in "assessing the progress and effectiveness of the United States Army Reserve Command after it has been in existence for a period of one year."[92] To paraphrase Benjamin Franklin's comment at the close of convention that drafted the United States Constitution in 1787, we now had an Army Reserve Command, if we could keep it.

90. *United States Code Congressional and Administrative News, 101st Congress—Second Session, 1990, Vol. 6, Legislative History: Public Laws 101–508 cont'd to 101–588,* (St. Paul, Minn.: West Publishing Co., 1991), p. 2931.

91. Section 903, Public Law 101–510, National Defense Authorization Act for Fiscal Year 1991, November 5, 1990.

92. Section 903(d) and 903(e) of PL 101–510, National Defense Authorization Act for Fiscal Year 1991.

14

The Individual Reservist, 1984–1991, Issues of Numbers, Quality, Equality

INDIVIDUAL READY RESERVE

The Individual Ready Reserve (IRR) is one of the least known—but largest—parts of the Army Reserve. IRR members are for the most part soldiers who still have a portion of their service obligation remaining after they have completed several years of active service. Most of these individuals are in the lower enlisted ranks, and they are a ready source of trained soldiers who can be brought back to active duty and used as individual replacements.[1] Among the problems with the IRR are maintaining the skills of these Reservists, keeping track of their addresses, and having some degree of confidence that they will come when called.

Skepticism as to the readiness of the members of the IRR was widespread in the mid-1980s. James H. Webb, Jr., in his first interview after being named Assistant Secretary of Defense for Reserve Affairs in 1984, singled out the IRR as an area about which he had considerable doubt.

"I have some real problems with the IRR," Webb was quoted as saying. "I don't think we have a real good feel for how many of those people would really show up. Or how many of those that do show up you could count on." Webb went on to state that "from figures I've seen, about 40 percent of the Army IRR are people who left either the Regulars or the

1. The Individual Ready Reserve is a sizable part of the Army Reserve. The Army National Guard also has non-unit soldiers, but they are fewer in number. At the end of FY 1987, for example, the IRR contained 205,900 soldiers; the Inactive National Guard had 10,500. *Annual Report, RFPB*, FY 87, p. 24.

Reserves for nonperformance. We should take a close look at how many of those people would show up and whether you'd want them to show up."[2]

The Reserve Forces Policy Board assessment issued at the end of FY 1984 echoed many of the same concerns, without suggesting that the IRR was filled with soldiers who would be problems if they ever reported for a mobilization. Subsequent boards touched on the IRR as posing potential problems if called upon as a mobilization asset, but not along the same lines as Assistant Secretary Webb.[3] The 1985 board, for example, suggested that "there must be a program to keep skills current, to retain or retrain so as to correct skill imbalances, and to administer the system so that adequate numbers of personnel can be quickly accessed."[4]

There were several directions that one might have gone to address the issues identified by the critics of the time. One way to improve the quality of personnel in the IRR was to offer reenlistment bonuses, which was done beginning in June 1984. These cash bonuses of $750 each were offered in the last four months of the fiscal year and resulted in 2000 reenlistments in the USAR from among soldiers with critical skills.[5] This bonus program continued into the next fiscal year and after, with the Department of the Army deciding which specialties would qualify for the incentive.[6] There was also another significant incentive program instituted during this time period: the Montgomery GI Bill.

The state of readiness of the IRR was of concern to the leadership of the active component, also. The Armor Force Mobilization Readiness Task Force, for example, had much to say about the Individual Ready Reserve in 1985. "While concern about reserve readiness is usually focused on RC units," said the task force, "a substantial portion of the reserve manpower is in the Individual Ready Reserve (IRR) and Individual Mobilization Augmentation (IMA) manpower pools. These individual reservists," it went on to say, "will be called to active duty in the event of mobilization and will fill vacancies in Active Component (AC) as well as RC units, both United States Army Reserve (USAR) and Army National Guard (ARNG). While unit readiness is critical for the success of the

2. Paul Smith, "New Reserve Chief Says IRR Readiness in Doubt," *Army Times*, June 18, 1984, p. 4.

3. *Annual Report, RFPB, FY 84*, pp. 3–3 and 3–4.

4. *Annual Report, RFPB, FY 85*, p. 11.

5. *Annual Report, RFPB, FY 85*, p. 3–3.

6. *Annual Report, RFPB, FY 85*, p. 44.

Armor Force, because of the heavy reliance on individual reservists to fill deploying units, readiness of individual reservists is an important factor."[7]

The task force observed that there were not enough soldiers in the IRR to fill active and reserve component units scheduled for deployment upon full mobilization. The task force recommended that both the quantity and the training of soldiers in the IRR be increased. It noted with some dismay that during FY 1984 only 5 percent of armor enlisted soldiers in the IRR received some form of training, and it further noted that even this small group of approximately 500 individuals did not necessarily receive training that was related to wartime skills.[8]

For armor officers in the IRR, said the task force, the percentage trained during FY 1984 was higher—about 25 percent—but the number was still small, amounting to only 550 officers. The real problem, concluded the task force, lay within the system for training enlisted personnel, as the officer training program was judged to be "basically sound."[9]

The armor task force went on to suggest that IRR soldiers who wanted to participate in two weeks of annual training should be managed separately from those who were in the IRR simply to wait out their service obligation. "Those who participate in training on a regular basis," said the task force, "should be identified as the 'Intensely Managed Group' and trained for critical combat positions which require extensive training to achieve skill level and which have rapid skill decay." These positions, it said, included gunner, vehicle commander, platoon sergeant and operations sergeant among the enlisted soldiers.[10] For officers, the comparable positions would be platoon leader, company/troop commander, battalion/squadron operations officer, and battalion/squadron executive officer.[11] These recommendations were not implemented, primarily because of the additional expense this would have entailed at ARPERCEN. As discussed below, some

7. Department of the Army, Office of the Deputy Chief of Staff for Operations and Plans, Memorandum, DAMO–TRI (Lt. Col. G.G. Perry III, Acting Chief, Institutional Training Division), to Brig. Gen. Corns, Brig. Gen. Drudik, Brig. Gen. Freitag, Brig. Gen. Budge, Brig. Gen. Beavers, Brig. Gen. Dean, Brig. Gen. Mott, and Col. Pickus, Subject: Coordination Papers from the Armor Forces Mobilization Task Force, Date: 29 July 1985, unpaginated. Copy in possession of the author.

8. *Ibid.*

9. *Ibid.*

10. *Ibid.*

11. *Ibid.*

enlisted IRR members with armor specialties were given the opportunity to train with active component units, but they were few in number, and the concept espoused by the task force simply disappeared into the bureaucracy.

IRR AVIATORS

As of 1987 the Individual Ready Reserve contained approximately 4700 Army aviators, qualified in rotary wing, fixed wing, or both. It is hard for even troop unit aviators to receive enough flying time to maintain proficiency, and for those individuals in the IRR, the problem was almost insurmountable. Beginning in FY 1987, the Army initiated what it called the Ready Reserve Aviator Sustainment Training Program. Through this program, IRR aviators were sent through a 19-day refresher course taught by other IRR aviators who were serving on a longer tour of active duty. It was probably not enough to solve the problem entirely, but it was a start.[12]

TRAINING WITH ARMY RESERVE UNITS

Another part of the IRR-improvement program was to have members of the IRR train with units of the Selected Reserve. This was done on an intermittent basis. At Camp Atterbury, Ind., for example, 105 junior grade infantrymen from the IRR volunteered for two weeks of active duty refresher training in what it meant to be an 11B.

These lower-ranking enlisted soldiers came from across the country, arrived at Indianapolis, and were trucked to the camp site. The trainers and support personnel were drawn from five major Army Reserve commands: the 70th Division (Training), 123d Army Reserve Command, 102d Army Reserve Command, 103d Corps Support Command, and the 300th MP Brigade.

The IRR members were given training in first aid, land navigation, radio comms, camouflage, NBC warfare, and forty hours with a variety of weapons ranging from the light anti-tank weapon (LAW) to the M–16 rifle. They also practiced night patrol techniques and completed a land navigation exercise.

The result of the two-week training was over a hundred members of the Individual Ready Reserve who had enhanced their skills as soldiers; seven IRR members who reenlisted; 19 who were promoted; and a number who inquired about joining Army Reserve units. The trainers practiced their skills as

12. *Annual Report, RFPB, FY 87*, p. 95.

well, in areas ranging from the infantry requirements to providing three hot meals a day.[13]

TRAINING WITH THE ACTIVE COMPONENT

Four years later, IRR armor soldiers were given the opportunity to train with the 2d Armored Division at Fort Hood, Tex. The complement of IRR members was only 19 strong, but its significance lay in the fact that these IRR soldiers might well become filler or replacement personnel for the division if it went into combat. During their two weeks at the hot Texas post, the Reservists qualified at the Unit Conduct of Fire Trainer and worked with one of two battalions in the division: the 3/67th or 1/66th Armor. The reason the IRR soldiers had volunteered for this training was their desire to change their MOS from 19E (M–60 tanker) to 19K (M–1 tanker).[14]

Meanwhile, 200 of their IRR counterparts in the medical specialties were also enduring the Texas summertime. These soldiers participated in a five-day field training exercise with 300 medical specialists from the active component. In an attempt to overcome one of the gaps in medical department training—lack of realistic field training—the soldiers devoted two days of their time to a field exercise that taught them combat medical skills. During this training they prepared improvised litters, evacuated injured soldiers from tanks and helicopters, and learned about the Deployable Medical System (DEPMEDS). As with the infantrymen who had trained at Camp Atterbury, several of the IRR soldiers decided to join Reserve units or become Individual Mobilization Augmentees.[15]

IRR MUSTERS

One of the concerns of planners who contemplated use of the Individual Ready Reserve to fulfill the Army's replacement needs during the first 180 days of combat was how to keep track of these soldiers. No one knew for sure whether the addresses on hand were accurate, or whether these former active duty members would come when called. The partial answer to

---

13. Maj. Mark Benezra, "Unit Troops Train IRR Soldiers in Basics," *Army Reserve Magazine*, Vol. 30, No. 1 (1984), pp. 14–15.

14. SSgt. Rich Staley, "IRR Soldiers Train in Texas . . . Tankers at Fort Hood, with 2d Armored Dvision," *Army Reserve Magazine*, Vol. 34, No. 4 (1988), p. 18.

15. MSgt. Curtis R. Palmer, ". . . Medics at Fort Sam Houston," *Army Reserve Magazine*, Vol. 34, No. 4 (1988), pp. 19–20.

this problem was a series of musters and screenings, conducted solely for members of the Individual Ready Reserve.

The idea for such musters originated with Asst. Sec. Webb. The concept was first tested during one-day musters which took place on each of three weekends in September 1985 at three sites. During these musters the reporting soldier underwent a screening which included a physical examination, a common skills test, a personal data update, and a uniform check. As of the end of FY 1985, the plan was to conduct similar musters in January 1986, three more musters during the period February–September 1986, and full implementation in 1987 of a plan for mandatory annual screening, including one day of active duty, for each member of the IRR.[16]

The requirement for the Secretary of Defense to conduct a one-day muster for members of the Individual Ready Reserves of all the reserve components was included in the FY 1986 Department of Defense Authorization Act. The law also required the Secretary to submit to the Congress by February 1, 1986, a report on the muster, including whether the members of the IRR were prepared for duty and whether current call-up procedures were adequate.[17]

The problem was money. The Army estimated that a one-day call-up of all 313,000 members of its IRR would cost $56 million, as each of these soldiers would receive one day's pay for the muster. The total for the entire 478,000 soldiers, sailors, airmen and marines in the various IRRs would amount to something on the order of $61 million.[18] Nevertheless, even without additional funding, the requirement to conduct a muster test was the law, and the Department of Defense complied.

The Army Reserve's musters took place in thirteen cities[19] scattered throughout the country. ARPERCEN sent letters to 30,000 members of the Individual Ready Reserve inviting them to participate in the muster. Of the 30,000 letters sent out, some 3400, or just over 11 percent, were returned as "undeliverable." Almost 6000 Reservists responded and said that they wanted to attend the muster. These individuals were sent a mailgram telling them where to report.[20] The musters were done over a

16. *Annual Report, RFPB, FY 85*, p. 11.

17. Dick Kaufman, "Across the River and up the Hill," *AUSA News*, January 1986, p. 7.

18. *Ibid.*

19. New Haven, Conn.; Springfield, Mass.; Charlotte, N.C.; Pittsburgh, Pa.; Miami, Fla.; St. Petersburg, Fla.; Cincinnati, Oh.; Indianapolis, Ind.; San Antonio, Tex.; Phoenix, Ariz.; Denver, Col.; Oakland, Calif.; and Seattle, Wash.

20. "More on the Musters," *Army Reserve Magazine*, Vol. 33, No. 3 (1986), pp. 11–12.

weekend in January 1986, and Reservists were allowed to choose between Saturday and Sunday. ARPERCEN had set a goal of 5000 Reservists, and this goal was exceeded when 6,678 soldiers showed up, ranging in rank from private to colonel.[21]

Granting that this was a self-selected group of IRR members, the quality of those who reported was higher than had been anticipated. Seventy-eight percent met the Army's weight standards and 81 percent were evaluated as having no medical defects that would prevent overseas deployment. Of the 6600+ soldiers who reported, only 25 were found to be medically disqualified from further service in the Army.[22] All-in-all, the Department of Defense judged this trial muster to have been a success. For the full-scale mandatory muster, however, the department wanted specific additional funding.

Assistant Secretary Webb pushed the idea as part of the DoD legislative package for FY 1987, seeking $61 million from Congress to fund a one-day muster for every member of the IRR. The House Appropriations Committee denied the funding, indicating its concern about the cost of such an endeavor. Cost was an issue with the House committee because of its "considerable doubt" that enough members of the IRR would attend the muster to make it worthwhile, even if it were supposed to be mandatory.[23]

Webb then took his argument to the Senate, where he suggested that the purpose of the exercise was "not to estimate how many will show up for the muster but to initiate long overdue management of this critical mobilization resource."[24] He got some funding, but not all that he had requested, and a large-scale—but still not comprehensive—muster was set for FY 1987.[25]

The FY 1987 muster was a mandatory one, unlike the voluntary screenings of the past, but some Reservists did not understand the distinction. Accordingly, some Reservists did not report for screening as ordered. Those who did not report were sent a letter that informed them that this was indeed a mandatory event and that disciplinary action could be taken against them if they failed to appear as requested.[26] No-shows

21. "PFC for a Day," *The Officer*, Vol. LXII, No. 6 (June 1986), pp. 21–23.

22. *Ibid.*, p. 23.

23. Larry Carney, "DoD Seeks Funding for IRR Muster Test," *Army Times*, September 15, 1986, p. 8.

24. *Ibid.*

25. Paul Smith, "Non-Drilling Reservists Face One-Day Callup," *Army Times*, August 4, 1986, p. 4.

26. *Annual Report, RFPB, FY 87*, p. 45.

were a bigger problem for the Army than for the other services, as the following table demonstrates.

Table 14-1 Individual Ready Reserve Screening Results, FY 1987

	IRR Strength	Number Ordered to be screened	Number Screened & percent	Percent of IRR Screened
Army	287,000	197,000	104,000 (53%)	36%
Navy	78,000	27,000	21,000 (80%)	27%
Marines	45,000	15,000	13,000 (84%)	28%
Air Force	48,000	17,000	14,000 (81%)	29%
DoD Total	459,000	256,000	152,000 (81%)	33%

Source: *Annual Report, Reserve Forces Policy Board, FY 1987*, p. 46.

As with earlier screenings, the FY 1987 experience accomplished several objectives. It allowed verification of addresses of Reservists and subjected them to some testing to determine the level of their military skills. In addition, 26 percent of the screened Reservists showed an interest in joining the Selected Reserve, and as of the end of the fiscal year, some 5,380 had actually received orders transferring them to either a unit or into an IMA billet.[27]

The IRR screening program continued during the next fiscal year (1988), and the results were even more encouraging. The show-rate increased slightly for the Army Reserve and approximately 100,000 of the 180,000 ordered for screening actually showed-up. Compared with the 1986 muster of the 6000+ Reservists, these members of the IRR were in better health. Over 95 percent were found to be medically qualified for deployment, compared with the 1986 rate of 81 percent.[28]

In FY 1989, the Army again conducted a partial screen of its IRR soldiers, reaching only 23% of them—10% less than it had screened during the previous fiscal year. Again, this was a much smaller percentage than was accomplished by the other services, whose IRRs were much smaller than the Army's. The decision to screen such a small percentage of the IRR, despite the supposedly mandatory nature of the requirement was budget driven. Without the required funding, the Army was simply not prepared to call-up every member of the IRR, even for one day. As it was, field grade officers and soldiers who were

27. *Ibid.*, p. 46.
28. *Annual Report, RFPB, FY 88*, pp. 61–62.

within one year of mandatory retirement or expiration of term of service were not included in the screening.[29]

Fiscal Year 1990 saw a continuation of the screening procedures of the previous year, except that it was applied to an even smaller percentage of the force. For the Army Reserve, the percentage screened dropped to 13.1%. The following year, FY 1991, began after the commencement of Operation Desert Shield. Because of the resources, both personnel and monetary, that were devoted to getting Reserve units and individual Reservists onto active duty, the screening of members of the IRR was cancelled after January 1991.[30]

Being a member of the Individual Ready Reserve is sometimes the only choice for a soldier who wants to remain in the Army Reserve, but who cannot find a unit or IMA vacancy. It is difficult to remain competitive for promotion while remaining in the IRR, in part because of the lack of opportunity to perform the two-week active duty tour that allows a Reservist to show his or her capability. With proper planning, an IRR member can often secure a couple of weeks of active duty each year, but this was not a certainty during this period.

At the end of FY 1989, for example, 1100 Reservists who were scheduled for tours had them cancelled at the last minute because of a money shortage on the part of the Army Reserve. Even Reservists who had already received their active duty orders had them cancelled. The cuts in IRR training were necessitated because of a $29 million shortfall in the budget for inactive duty training—weekend drills—for troop program units of the Army Reserve. As a result, some of the lower priority soldiers in the IRR were left without the opportunity for FY 1989 active duty training.[31]

Despite the lack of funding for the musters, or screens, and the lack of active duty training afforded members of the IRR, the worth of this part of the Army Reserve was proven by the call-ups of Desert Shield. There were fewer bad addresses and many fewer no-shows than might have been the case without the musters, and the active component discovered to its surprise and pleasure that these soldiers had not lost their skills entirely. Given more funding, it is conceivable that the results of the January 1991 call-up of members of the Individual Ready Reserve would have been even more impressive than it was.

---

29. *Annual Report, RFPB, FY 88*, p. 59.

30. *Annual Report, RFPB, FY 90*, pp. 65–66; *Annual Report, RFPB, FY 91*, p. 66.

31. Bernard J. Adelsberger, "Budget Crunch Forces Reserves to Scrap Active Tours," *Army Times*, August 7, 1989, p. 3.

INDIVIDUAL MOBILIZATION AUGMENTEES

Individual Mobilization Augmentees (IMAs) are trained soldiers—commissioned officers and enlisted personnel—assigned to a billet in an active component unit, a Defense agency, the Selective Service, or the Federal Emergency Management Agency. These individuals have a service pattern which resembles that of Individual Ready Reservists, in that they are not assigned to Reserve units and do not perform weekend drills. Unlike IRR members, however, they perform two weeks of active duty each year with their assigned organization. Furthermore, they are members of the Selected Reserve and as such are subject to the call-up authority that applies to unit members.

From the inception of the program, Army Reserve IMAs did not have the option of drilling for pay, though IMAs in other reserve components had attended paid drills for a number of years. During the summer of 1988, however, the Army Reserve established a paid IMA program on a trial basis. One hundred IMAs were given orders allowing them to perform twenty-four paid inactive duty drills per year with their agency.[32] (In contrast, troop unit members of the Army Reserve are generally given forty-eight drills per year.)

Table 14-2 Army Reserve Individual Mobilization Augmentees

	Officers	Enlisted
1986		
Authorized	12,281	9,181
Actual	8,515	4,545
1987		
Authorized	8700	4,838
Actual	8,225	4,914
1988		
Authorized	11,304	3,376
Actual	8,816	3,110
1989		
Budgeted	14,655 (combined)	
Actual	14,708 (combined)	
1990		
Budgeted	8,804	2,568
Assigned	10,865	3,300
1991		
Budgeted	10,436	3,602
Assigned	10,899	3,294

Source: *Annual Reports of the Reserve Forces Policy Board for FY 1986* (p. 25), *FY 1987* (p. 46), *FY 1988* (p. 58), *FY 1989* (p. 56), *FY 1990* (p. 50), *FY 1991* (p. 64).

32. "Paid Drills for IMA Soldiers Being Explored," *Army Reserve Magazine*, Vol. 34, No. 4 (1988), p. 4.

As can be seen from this table, the number of enlisted IMAs dropped significantly between fiscal years 1987 and 1988 and then remained relatively constant. Officer IMA billets remained relatively stable through fiscal year 1989, then rose significantly and remained at approximately the same level (10,900) during FYs 1990 and 1991.

The total number of IMA positions identified as "required" reached over 19,000 (officer and enlisted) in FY 1989, but funding constraints prevented these positions from being filled. As it was, fewer than 60% of all Army Reserve IMAs were allowed two weeks of active duty training with their agencies that year. By FY 1990, the number had risen to 80 percent, but in FY 1991 it fell: to 65% for officer IMAs and 75% for enlisted IMAs, despite a Department of Defense Directive (DoD Dir 1235.11) that requires IMAs to perform 12–14 days of annual training each year.[33]

The downturn in annual training for IMAs during FY 1991 was somewhat surprising, as one might have thought that Desert Shield/Desert Storm would have prompted more of these members of the Selected Reserve to train with their agencies. Although a considerable number of IMAs did serve active duty tours of varying lengths, it is possible that the agencies were simply too busy to request that the Reservists join them for two weeks.

WOMEN IN THE ARMY RESERVE

From FY 1980 to the end of FY 1987, the number of women in the reserve components increased by 92 percent. In the Army Reserve the increase in the number of women was even more dramatic. The number of female officers in the Selected Reserve of the USAR stood at 3864 in 1980; seven years later it had reached 9673, a increase of 150.3 percent. Among enlisted personnel the increase was even more significant in raw numbers, though the percentage was not as high: from 25,267 in FY 1980 to 47,813 in FY 1987, an increase of 89.2 percent.[34]

In the IRR, the numbers had likewise jumped. Among officers the number had risen from 2056 to 6630 (222.5% increase), while the enlisted increase was incredible: from 4,688 to 33,271 (609.7%). Compared with the overall strength of the Army Reserve in FY 1987, women comprised 18 percent of the

33. *Annual Report, RFPB, FY 89*, pp. 56–57; *Annual Report, RFPB, FY 90*, pp. 49–50; *Annual Report, RFPB, FY 91*, pp. 64–65.

34. *Annual Report, RFPB, FY 87, p. 57.*

Its popularity was attested to by the fact that during the first two+ years of the program (July 1985–September 1987), over 15,000 members of the Army Reserve, out of 37,000 eligible for the program, had enrolled. At 41.4%, the enrollment percentage for Army Reserve soldiers during this period was higher than that of any other of the reserve components except for the minuscule Coast Guard Reserve, where 500 of 644 eligible had taken advantage of the benefit.[39]

The program was modified during FY 1988 to allow funding for less-than-half time educational pursuit. The Montgomery GI Bill continued to be popular with members of the Army Reserve, as 47.1% of those eligible as of the end of FY 1988 were participating in it.[40]

FY 1990 saw another change in the bill, expanding it to include vocational and flight training in addition to higher education. This change, which had been favored by both the bill's principal sponsor, Rep. Montgomery, and the Reserve Forces Policy Board, was effective as of October 1, 1990. To obtain this benefit, a member of the Army Reserve had to agree to remain in the Selected Reserve for a minimum of six years after that date. Once again, the USAR participation rate increased—to 53% of those eligible (38,152 of 72,023).[41]

The Army Reserve's usage rate for the Montgomery GI Bill went up again during FY 1990, with 58% of those eligible (48,716 of 84,714) choosing to enroll some form of higher or additional education using its benefits. According to the Reserve Forces Policy Board, the Bill was "a highly-effective recruiting and retention incentive."[42]

The following year, FY 1991, the GI Bill enrollment rate for the Army Reserve increased still again. As of September 30, 1991, a fiscal year period which encompassed the entirety of Desert Storm and almost all of Desert Shield, the Army Reserve had enrolled 59,023 of 94,643 eligible (62%). Though this was no longer the highest enrollment percentage among the reserve components—the Marine Corps Reserve was slightly higher at 66%—it was still significantly higher than that of the Army National Guard (46%), the Air Guard (43%) and the Air Force Reserve (30%). This benefit was clearly one that appealed to a large percentage of the Army Reserve, as almost 20 percent of the Selected Reserve was taking advantage of its offering.[43]

39. *Ibid.*, p. 38.

40. *Annual Report, RFPB, FY 88*, p. 52.

41. *Annual Report, RFPB, FY 89*, pp. 44–45; Mowery, "New Rules, Benefits Coming . . .," p. 10.

42. *Annual Report, RFPB, FY 90*, pp. 60–61.

43. *Annual Report, RFPB, FY 91*, p. 73.

COMMISSARY BENEFITS

Members of the Army Reserve and other reserve components had long been eligible to shop in Defense Department commissaries whenever they were on active duty for periods of seventy-two hours or longer. Because of the manner in which reservists generally did their active duty each year—two consecutive weeks—they were forced to engage in gigantic shopping sprees during that limited time period. It was not at all unusual to see a reservist in the commissary line-up four or five shopping carts filled with non-perishable items ranging from baby diapers to canned goods and spend $500 on his purchases in an attempt to maximize the benefit.

This forced binge shopping did not make sense to many who knew of the situation, and proposals were offered through the years to allow reservists to spread their shopping days throughout the year. The Department of Defense did not favor this idea, offering two arguments against the proposal. The one made openly was that increasing reservists' access would necessitate an increase in funding for the commissaries.[44] The argument offered *sub rosa* by a "senior Pentagon manpower official" was that if reservists gained commissary access, "the grocery industry . . . undoubtedly will complain we are taking more customers out of the Safeway and Piggly Wiggly and letting them shop on base." This, he said, "could be the final nail in the coffin for commissaries."[45]

DoD, however, was compelled by Congress, led by Senator J. James Exon (D–Neb.), to experiment with the benefit. The Defense Authorization Act of 1984 directed DoD to test the idea of allowing reservists to spread their commissary shopping privileges throughout the year.[46]

The test was conducted in three regions of the country and resulted in reservists using the commissaries less than the Department of Defense had expected.[47] According to the Reserve Forces Policy Board Report for FY 1985, the commissary test "resulted in minimal impact on the commissary system, but OMB and DoD opposed legislation to 'expand' commissary privileges of Reservists."[48] Despite this opposition, the commissary usage provision was included in the FY 1987 De-

44. Rick Maze, "Few Reservists Seen Using Commissaries," *Army Times*, November 17, 1986, p. 15.

45. Rick Maze, "Reserves Allowed to Choose Shopping Days," *Army Times*, October 27, 1986, p. 17.

46. *Annual Report, RFPB, FY 84*, p. 3–6.

47. "Reserve Commissary Test," *The Officer* (January 1985), p. 13.

48. *Annual Report, RFPB, FY 85*, p. 16.

fense Authorization Bill.[49] Defense Secretary Weinberger, in announcing on March 30, 1987, the new guidelines for spreading the shopping days of reservists, stated that "these actions will create a more meaningful and realistic benefit for our reserve component members and their families, and thereby, will serve as a recruiting and retention incentive."[50]

DoD wrestled with its implementation and foundered for several years over the mechanics of issuing a commissary privilege card to members entitled to one. The Department of Defense eventually decided on the design of such a card and began its use on January 1, 1990. The card, which had to be shown and checked off for each day of commissary shopping, finally provided a system for implementing the statute.[51]

MORALE, WELFARE AND RECREATION (MWR) ACCESS

In partial recognition of the fact that the reserve components had become a significant part of the Total Force and deserved to be treated more like full partners, Congress gave unlimited MWR facilities benefits to members of the reserves in the FY 1991 Defense Authorization Act. Before enactment of this statute, reservists had been restricted to one day of post exchange access for each day of drill, a requirement that was met by showing a leave and earnings statement at the entrance to the PX and having a checker mark off one day. MWR facilities and benefits include post exchange and other recreational facilities such as swimming pools, racquetball courts, weight rooms, gymnasiums, and recreation equipment issuing locations.[52]

GRAY AREA RETIREES

That same bill—the Defense Authorization Act of 1991—also extended benefits to "gray area retirees," those members of the reserve components who retired after twenty or more years of good service, but who had not reached age 60. Before the FY 1991 authorization bill, Reservists received no access to commissaries, post exchanges or other facilities between retirement and age 60. In the law Congress provided

49. *Annual Report, RFPB, FY 87*, p. 60; Sharon B. Young, "Reservists to Have Open Access to Commissaries as of March 30," *Army Times*, February 23, 1987, p. 8.

50. "Using Commissaries," *AUSA News*, Vol. 9, No. 7 (May 1987), p. 6.

51. *Annual Report, RFPB, FY 89*, p. 59.

52. "New law broadens access to support facilities for all Reservists and their families," *Army Reserve Magazine*, Vol. 36, No. 4 (1990) p. 7.

full access to MWR facilities (see above) and limited access to commissaries. Gray area retirees were given the same 12 commissary shopping days as drilling Reservists. Once a Reservist reaches age 60 and begins drawing retirement pay, commissary shopping becomes unlimited, just as if he had retired from the active component.[53]

UNIFORM CODE OF MILITARY JUSTICE (UCMJ)

The final move toward equality between drilling Reservists and members of the active component was in the realm of military justice. When Congress prescribed disciplinary rules for Reservists in 1950, following enactment of the Uniform Code of Military Justice in 1949, "it simply never considered the present amalgamation of the reserve forces into the 'Total Force' concept of today."[54] In the mid-1980s, Reservists were subject to the UCMJ only under certain circumstances, which including active duty and "inactive duty training authorized by written orders which are voluntarily accepted by them [the Reservist] and which specify that they are subject to this chapter."[55] Because of the manner in which the Army administered inactive duty training—a lack of orders being the usual way inactive duty time is performed—Army Reservists on weekend drills did not come under the purview of the federal law.[56]

A move to change the UCMJ was initiated as the result of a member of the Naval Reserve, a sailor named Caputo, who escaped punishment for a crime he had committed while on active duty for training because the law did not provide for jurisdiction to be continued into his subsequent inactive duty (weekend drill) period. Caputo had already been released from active duty when his command decided it wanted to press charges against him.[57] Congress responded to the Caputo case[58] by including a change in the UCMJ as part of the National Defense Authorization Act for FY 1987.

53. "Congress and the Department of Defense fix long-running 'gray area' shortfalls," *Army Reserve Magazine*, Vol. 36, No. 4 (1990), p. 7; "'Gray area' benefits set," *Army Times*, December 31, 1990, p. 6.

54. Maj. Harry L. Williams, Jr., "Reserve Component Jurisdiction: New Powers for the Reserve Component Commander and New Responsibilities for the Reserve Component Judge Advocate," *The Army Lawyer* (July 1987), p. 5. Hereinafter cited as "Williams, 'Reserve Component Jurisdiction.'"

55. 10 United States Code 802, Art. 2 (a)(1) and (3).

56. Williams, "Reserve Component Jurisdiction," p. 5.

57. *Ibid.*, p. 6.

58. *United States* v. *Caputo*, 18 M.J. 259.

This law amended the UCMJ by providing military court martial authority over "Members of the reserve component while on inactive-duty training, but in the case of members of the Army National Guard of the United States or the Air National Guard of the United States only when in Federal service." The law also provided that Reservists could be ordered to active duty involuntarily for the purpose of conducting an Article 32 investigation, being tried by court martial, or being punished under Article 15.[59]

In addition to the application of the jurisdiction of the UCMJ to the inactive duty reservist, the law provided that officers in inactive duty status could administer oaths for the purpose of investigating crimes. This meant that Army Reserve commanders were able to commence investigations against members of their command and take sworn testimony during the course of the investigation. Most importantly, the new legislation provided that a reservist continued to be subject to the UCMJ even after he had left active duty or inactive duty. His status as a reservist was sufficient to provide the necessary jurisdiction for crimes committed while on military duty of any type.[60]

Because of the significance of the law, its implementation was phased in. The first phase, which lasted from July 1, 1987, through June 30, 1988, was designated a training phase. During this period, Reserve commanders received instruction in the law and Reserve judge advocates general were trained in their roles under it. In the second phase, which began July 1, 1988, the change was fully implemented.[61]

A problem immediately arose with respect to how a reservist could be punished under Article 15, for example, when such punishment might usually include such items as restriction to quarters or extra duty. The answer in the implementing instructions was that if such punishment were imposed during inactive duty training (as opposed to its being done while the servicemember was on active duty), the punishment could only be served during regularly scheduled weekend drills. The Reservist could not be required to come in during the week to work off his punishment. The extra duties could, however, be carried over from one weekend drill to another until they were completed.[62]

---

59. Public Law 99–661, National Defense Authorization Act for Fiscal Year 1987, Section 804. Court Martial Jurisdiction over Reserve Members.

60. Williams, "Reserve Component Jurisdiction," p. 7.

61. Ibid.; Michael Detzky, "Military Code of Justice Revised," *Army Times*, January 25, 1988, p. 55.

62. Williams, "Reserve Component Jurisdiction," p. 8.

In extreme cases, a Reservist could even be court martialed for his actions during inactive duty training, though the Reserve commander would have to consult with an active component legal advisor before preferring charges that would require a general court martial. The actual convening authority would be the supporting active component general court martial convening authority. In this instance, the offending soldier would be placed on active duty for the trial. Again, according to the implementing instructions, the active component legal staff would be primarily responsible for conducting the trial, but Reserve legal officers were supposed to be involved as much as possible.[63]

Summary courts martial, however, were left with the Reserve and "may be held entirely within the reserve structure and during inactive duty training periods."[64] This also meant that summary trials could not last past the end of the regularly scheduled drill period and the soldier if convicted could not be held past the end of drill to serve his sentence. He could, however, be required to serve his sentence on subsequent drill weekends.[65]

The usage of this provision in law suggests, however, that its effect has been more symbolic than real. Statistics taken from the monthly reports submitted to the Clerk of Court, U.S. Army Judiciary, by staff judge advocates for commanders with general court martial authority show just how seldom the provisions of this change in law have been applied. Because of the way in which incidents are reported, the figures include both the Army Reserve and the Army National Guard. It is most likely, however, that the numbers are almost exclusively Army Reserve, since National Guard soldiers are not subject to the law while in state status, which is their usual status for weekend drills.

During FY 1990, there were 20 Articles 15 given to members of the Army's reserve components for offenses committed during inactive duty training. For FY 1991, it was 32; for FY 1992, it was 13; for FY 1993, it was 32; and for FY 1994, it was two Articles 15. There were no summary courts martial under this statute during this time, and there was only one example of a Chapter 10 discharge in lieu of trial.[66]

---

63. *Ibid.*

64. *Ibid.*

65. *Ibid.*, pp. 8–9.

66. Interview, Col. James T. Currie, with Mr. William S. Fulton, Jr., Clerk of Court, U.S. Army Judiciary, Washington, D.C., November 8, 1995. Mr. Fulton indicated that even though the figures are for all Army Reserve components, the likelihood is that these are Army Reservists. Notes of the interview are in possession of the author.

Though this change in the military legal system may have been largely symbolic, it still marked a step along the path of the Reservist being accepted as a member of the Total Force.

CONCLUSION

All of the nights and weekends of study, the procurement of equipment, the mobilization exercises and inactive duty drills and years of annual training; the IRR musters and training; the overseas training in Latin America and the Caribbean; the BRIGHT STAR exercises in Egypt and REFORGER exercises in Germany; the attempts to identify problems within the IRR and to beef-up the readiness of the troop units. All of this effort was aimed at one unspecified mobilization that would be for real. No one knew when it would come or even if it would come. Best guesses had it happening in Europe in something connected with the Cold War. When mobilization and war did come, the locale was the Middle East, and the Operations were Desert Shield and Desert Storm. This was the first time that the Army Reserve, as part of the Total Force, would be there when the big show started.

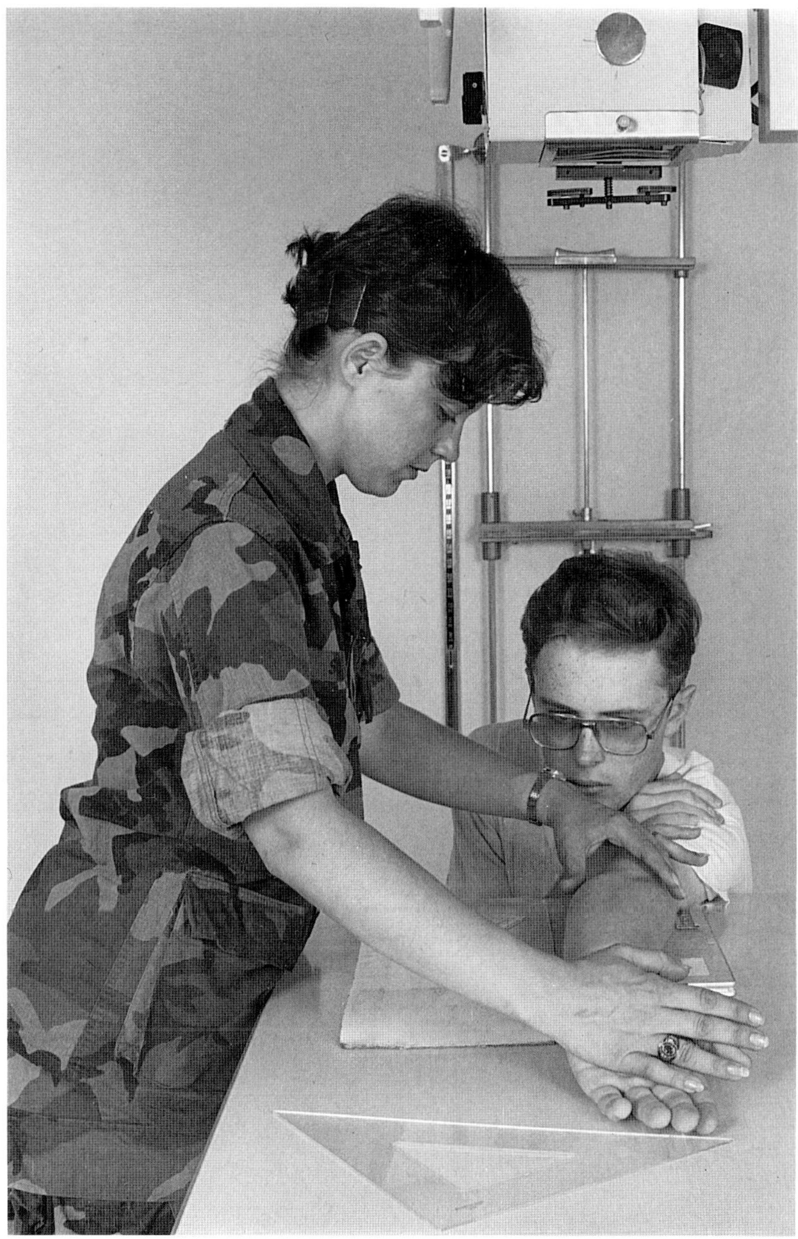

The Army Reserve's Private Cindy L. Sutton positions Private Robert E. Tate for a simulated X-ray during training at the Army's Academy of Health Sciences, Fort Sam Houston, Texas..

In 1994 the Army Reserve participated in REEFEX, a DOD exercise creating artificial reefs off the coast of several states. The Army Reserve was involved in cleaning, preparing, hauling, and loading M–60 tanks, shown here, which were placed in the Gulf of Mexico and other coastal locations.

In December, 1995, members of an Army Reserve Civil Affairs unit undergo training at Fort Bragg, North Carolina, prior to deployment to Bosnia in support of Operation Joint Endeavor.

The Army Reserve is made up of soldiers—men and women who are fully prepared to leave their homes and jobs and go out to defend their country.

In 1992 more than 1,400 Army Reservists helped transport approximately 760 truckloads of cargo over 1,270 miles. This was part of Operation Golden Cargo, a four year Army effort in support of the Department of Defense BRAC (base realignments and closures) program. Here, Reservists are loading disarmed Nike warheads at the Pueblo Army Deport, Colorado. Cargo loaded at Pueblo was hauled to either Salina, Kansas, or McAlester, Oklahoma.

15

Desert Shield/Desert Storm: Assembling the Force

The Total Force concept discussed in Chapter Ten was conceived in part to ensure that the American military would never again be sent into a major conflict without the support of the citizens of the country, as had been done during Vietnam. Prior to Total Force implementation in 1973, the three components of the Army had been more or less mirror images of one another—each of them containing a mix of combat, combat support, and combat service support units, though not equally apportioned. This changed with the Total Force.

By placing much of the combat support and combat service support function in the Army Reserve and many of the reserve combat units in the Army National Guard, the Pentagon's planners had structured an Army that could not fight a lengthy conflict without calling up the reserve components. This concept, which directly affected the U.S. Army Reserve as the "Total Army," had been neither tested nor challenged by the URGENT FURY (Grenada) or JUST CAUSE (Panama) operations. Saddam Hussein's invasion of Kuwait in August 1990, however, was another matter entirely.

OPERATION DESERT SHIELD—THE FIRST WEEKS

After weeks of feinting and threats, Iraqi leader Saddam Hussein sent his forces into Kuwait on August 2, 1990, taking almost immediate control of the small oil-rich Middle Eastern country and threatening Saudi Arabia to the south. President George Bush reacted to this aggression by issuing an Executive Order declaring a national emergency and freezing Iraqi assets in the United States.[1]

The United Nations Security Council reacted by passing a resolution demanding an Iraqi withdrawal from Kuwait and calling upon Iraq and Kuwait to negotiate their differences. On August 6 the Security Council met again and imposed an embargo on all transactions with Iraq, excepting only medical supplies and "humanitarian" foodstuffs. On August 8 President Bush addressed the people of the United States, told the nation that U.S. military forces were being sent to Saudi Arabia, and asserted that "America will stand by our friends. The mission of our troops is wholly defensive. Hopefully, they will not be needed long."[2]

On August 9 the President officially informed the Congressional leadership that a brigade of the U.S. Army's 82d Airborne Division and two squadrons of F–15 fighter aircraft had been sent to Saudi Arabia to deter aggression against that country. Using the language of the War Powers Resolution—though, like every U.S. President since its passage in 1973, never invoking it—President Bush indicated that he did not believe ". . . involvement in hostilities [to be] imminent."[3]

The Joint Staff was simultaneously preparing the paperwork necessary to effect a call-up of the reserve components. A draft prepared by the J–4 staff at the Pentagon proposed the call-up of some 137,000 reservists (88,000 Army, 38,000 Air Force, 8,000 Navy, 3,000 Marines, and 360 Coast Guard), using the President's authority to order up to 200,000 members of the Selected Reserve to active duty. The reserves did not have long to wait. On August 22, President Bush issued an executive order authorizing the Secretaries of Defense and Transporta-

1. Executive Order 12722, 2 Aug 90; U.S. News & World Report, *Triumph without Victory: The Unreported History of the Persian Gulf War* (New York: Random House, 1992), pp. 7–12, 39; hereinafter cited as "USNWR, *Triumph*."

2. Micah L. Sifry and Christopher Cerf, *Gulf War Reader: History, Documents, Opinions* (New York: Random House, 1991), pp. 137–40; "Administration Struggles to Clarify Gulf Objectives," *The Washington Post*, November 15, 1990, p. A28.

3. Letters, President George Bush to Speaker of the House of Representatives Thomas S. Foley, Senate President *pro tempore* Robert C. Byrd, and Senate Republican Leader Robert Dole, August 9, 1990; copies in Desert Shield/Desert Storm files, U.S. Army Center of Military History; hereinafter cited as "DS/DS files, USACMH."

tion (the latter controlled the Coast Guard) to order to active duty units and individual members of the Selected Reserve.[4]

Secretary of Defense Richard Cheney responded the following day with a memorandum to the service secretaries and the Chairman of the Joint Chiefs of Staff. Citing Section 673b of Title 10 of the U.S. Code, the Defense Secretary delegated to the Secretary of the Army the authority to order to active duty up to 25,000 members of the Selected Reserve of the Army "to provide combat support and combat service support." He gave similar authority—without restrictions on military specialties—to the Secretaries of the Navy and the Air Force, though the numbers in each instance were lower than for the Army.[5] This was the first time the 673b authority had been used to order units and individuals of the reserve components to involuntary active duty.[6]

QUESTIONS ABOUT COMMITMENT TO THE TOTAL FORCE

The ink was hardly dry on Secretary Cheney's memorandum directing the activation of reserve component units before members of Congress began asking about the use of these forces in the Gulf. The first of these Congressmen was Rep. Gillespie V. (Sonny) Montgomery (D–Miss.), a retired National Guard general officer and a strong supporter of the reserves.

In a letter dated August 24, 1990, Rep. Montgomery told the Secretary that he had written President Bush on August 15 urging that reserve component units be included in the response to the Gulf crisis. He then suggested to the Secretary that reserve "combat units, along with the support personnel" be included in the call-up. Rep. Montgomery knew quite well that if reserve combat units were omitted from the force mix, most National Guard troops—including the 155th Armored Brigade, Mississippi Army National Guard (MSARNG), which was the Roundout brigade for the 1st Cavalry Division—would never make it to the Gulf.[7]

---

5. Memorandum, Secretary of Defense to the Secretaries of the Military Departments and the Chairman of the Joint Chiefs of Staff, Date: August 23, 1990, Subject: Call of Selected Reserve Units and Personnel to Active Duty; copy in DS/DS files, USACMH.

6. Typescript copy of testimony of Stephen M. Duncan, Assistant Secretary of Defense for Reserve Affairs, before the Subcommittee on Defense, Appropriations Committee, United States House of Representatives, 102d Congress, 1st session, April 16, 1991, p. 6. Copy in possession of the author. Hereinafter cited as "Duncan testimony, April 16, 1991."

7. Letter, Rep. Gillespie V. (Sonny) Montgomery to Secretary of Defense Richard Cheney, August 24, 1990; copy in DS/DS files, USACMH. For a discussion of the Roundout concept, see pp. 254–55.

Rep. Montgomery's concerns were echoed on September 6 when the Chairman of the House Armed Services Committee, Rep. Les Aspin (D–Wisc.), also sent a letter to the Defense Secretary. Aspin's letter, which was co-signed by Montgomery as well as by Reps. Dave McCurdy (D–Okla.) and Beverly Byron (D–Md.), received a response on September 18. In his response the Secretary expressed his full commitment to "the Total Force Policy that provides for the mix of Active, Reserve, and Guard components in the force structure of the U.S. Armed Forces that maximizes the Nation's military capabilities." He then addressed the question of the reserve component combat units. He had excluded them from the call-up, explained Cheney, for two reasons: (1) his military advisors had not told him that they were needed and (2) given the time that would be required for units such as Mississippi's 155th Armored Brigade and the 48th Infantry Brigade (Mechanized), from the Georgia Army National Guard to train up to active component standards, the limitation of 180 days of active duty contained in Title 10, U.S. Code, Section 673b would allow too little time in theater. He did not suggest that the administration could ask Congress to change the 180 day limitation. The Secretary had offered his response, but the matter was far from over as far as these members of Congress were concerned.[8]

Congressional interest on this subject did not end with the secretary's reply of September 18. The issue was, in fact, rejoined on October 15, 1990, when House Armed Services Chairman Aspin, House Armed Services Military Personnel and Compensation Subcommittee Chairwoman Beverly Byron, and House Veteran's Affairs Chairman Montgomery issued a joint statement on the reserve call-up. Entitled "Iraq, Saudi Arabia and the Reserve Components: Missing Lessons for a Future Force Structure," the six page document was a forceful blast at

8. Letter, Secretary of Defense Cheney to Rep. Les Aspin, September 18, 990; copy in DS/DS files, USACMH. The secretary did not address the authority of the President to order up to one million reservists to active duty using his authority under 10 U.S.C. 673 after declaring a national emergency. Andrew Effron, General Counsel to the Senate Armed Services Committee, noted this authority in an interview with the author on December 21, 1993, and recalled a discussion of this very issue with DoD staff at the time of Desert Shield. The volume published by the U.S. Army Center of Military History notes that "the President has the power to use as many as one million reservists for two years simply by declaring a national emergency. That was a step the administration did not want to take in early September." Frank N. Schubert and Theresa L. Kraus, eds., *The Whirlwind War: The United States Army in Operations Desert Shield and Desert Storm* (Washington: U.S. Army Center of Military History, 1995, pp. 82–84. 89–80; hereinafter cited as "Schubert and Kraus, *Whirlwind War.*"

reserve call-up policies in general and at Secretary Cheney's rationale for omitting reserve combat forces in particular.

"Operation Desert Shield has provided the first occasion to observe and evaluate a large scale operational deployment of forces constructed after the adoption of the Total Force policy," wrote the three powerful House members. "To date, it [DoD] has chosen not to do so." Much of the missive addressed the failure of the Department of Defense, and specifically the Department of the Army, to call up combat units of the Army National Guard. But many of its conclusions are equally applicable to the non-combat units of the Army Reserve. Wrote the three House members:

> Authority is available to the President to call the reserves for longer than six months. He would only have to declare a national emergency—as was done to impound Kuwaiti assets in this country—to extend the call up. The announced reserve mobilization of even the support units appears to be quite small in comparison to the overall size of the forces deployed. . . .
>
> Failure to make greater use of reserve units may send a negative and unintentional message about their overall place in the Total Force. The men and women in our National Guard and reserve units work hard to serve their country. The suggestion, unintended or not, that their work is neither fully appreciated or really needed in time of hostilities would have a disastrous influence on morale and performance. The failure to make greater use of reserve units in this crisis raises the broader question of when—and even whether—they would be used in the future."[9]

Cheney had argued that there would not be enough time to mobilize and train reserve component combat units (almost exclusively those of the Army National Guard) during the 180 days of active service allowed under existing law. He was correct, but his argument was undermined by these House Armed Services Committee members less than ten days later.

Addressing one of the specific impediments named by Cheney in his letter of September 18, the conferees on the fiscal year 1991 defense appropriations bill, which was the first suitable legislative vehicle after the exchange between the Defense Secretary and the House Armed Services Committee members, doubled the length of time for which reserve combat units could be called to active duty—from 180 days to 360

9. Reps. Les Aspin, Beverly Byron, and G.V. (Sonny) Montgomery, "Iraq, Saudi Arabia, and the Reserve Components: Missing Lessons for a Future Force Structure," October 15, 1991; copy in DS/DS files, USACMH.

days. In the report on the conference on H.R. 5803, the conferees lauded the Department of Defense:

> for utilizing the authority of 10 United States Code 673b to call up Selected Reserves for Operation Desert Shield. For the last several years, the Congress had been appropriating substantial funds over and above the Department's budget request for the reserve components. Operation Desert Shield appears to be an appropriate time to see whether those additional funds have indeed improved readiness. Therefore, the conferees agree to include language which provides the President authority to call up the Selected Reserve combat units in and around the Arabian Peninsula and Operation Desert Shield for 180 days with an extension for an additional 180 days.[10]

The language of the bill itself reflected the conferees' desire that this extension of authority apply "only to Selected Reserve combat units," meaning that the combat support and combat service support units of the Army Reserve were unaffected. The length of prospective service for these USAR units had never been raised as an issue by the Department of Defense. In the end, the combat units of the National Guard were what mattered to the members of the House of Representatives, and these were the ones that were taken care of in this legislation.[11]

Bowing to the Congressional pressure, the Defense Department did eventually mobilize three National Guard maneuver brigades, but they were promptly sent to the National Training Center at Fort Irwin, Calif., and there they spent the war. At least one National Guard artillery unit—the 142d Field Artillery Brigade, Arkansas Army National Guard—did get into the war and performed admirably. But none of the armored or mechanized infantry units of the National Guard ever made it to the Gulf.[12] Meanwhile, Army Reservists had begun the task of building up the force in the desert.

---

10. United States Congress, House of Representatives, Conference Report to accompany H.R. 5308, "Making Appropriations for the Department of Defense [FY 1991]," 101st Congress, 2d session, Report 101–938, October 24, 1990, p. 143.

11. H.R. 5803, "Making Appropriations for the Department of Defense [FY 1991]," Section 8132, as quoted in Conference Report accompanying H.R. 5803, p. 33.

12. James C. Hyde, "Congress Skeptical That DoD Lives Up to Total Force Policy," *Armed Forces Journal International*, May 1991, p. 8; Brig. Gen. Robert H. Scales, Jr., Director, Desert Storm Study Project, *Certain Victory: United States Army in the Gulf War* (Washington: Office of the Chief of Staff, United States Army, 1993), p. 379; hereinafter cited as "Scales, *Certain Victory*."

VOLUNTEER RESERVISTS ANSWER THE CALL

Many Army Reservists did not wait to see whether they would receive the call to active duty. By August 15 some 200 men and women from the Army Reserve had been placed on active duty in support of the deployment, and by August 22 their numbers had almost doubled, to 392. They were but the first of many thousands of individuals who would volunteer their services during the next few months.[13] Many of these individuals served in the Transportation Terminal Units (TTUs) of the Army's Military Traffic Management Command (MTMC), but others came from across the spectrum of military skills and qualifications.

SHIPPING OUT THE FORCE

Indeed, Reservists assigned to units that came under MTMC were vital to the shipping of materiel to the Gulf. MTMC is the Army component of the U.S. Transportation Command, one of the unified commands, and it depends heavily upon Army Reservists to accomplish its missions at both U.S. and foreign ports. As of August 1, 1990, MTMC's total assigned strength was 720 active duty soldiers, 3,042 civilian employees, 22 Naval Reservists, and 2,132 Army Reservists. As Mason Schaefer points out in his fine work on the command's operations during Desert Shield/Desert Storm, MTMC's reservists do not physically load the ships. Instead, they provide direction to civilian stevedores who do the actual cargo moving.[14]

Army Reservists began volunteering almost at once. There were, however, initial difficulties in persuading the Total Army Personnel Command (PERSCOM) that Army Reserve volunteers could be brought onto active duty to load ships going to Southwest Asia, rather than simply to train and learn how to load ships. This bureaucratic red-tape was sliced

13. Duncan testimony, April 16, 1991, p. 6.

14. John R. Brinkerhoff, *United States Army Reserve in Operation Desert Storm: Port Operations* (Washington: Office of the Chief, Army Reserve, 1991), pp. 4–5; hereinafter cited as "Brinkerhoff, *Port Operations*; Mason Schaefer, *The Military Traffic Management Command's CONUS Port Operations during Operation Desert Shield/Storm, 1990–1991*, typescript prepared by the MTMC History Office, pp. iii–iv; hereinafter cited as "Schaefer, *MTMC*." Schaefer indicates that at one point "the command [MTMC] briefly sent in military stevedores" to North Carolina to help unravel port congestion, but this was not the norm for the operation.

through by then-Army Vice Chief of Staff Gen. Gordon Sullivan, who directed that the Reservists be used.[15]

The first Army Reserve volunteers reported for duty on August 13; others arrived on August 15; and still others reported on the 19th, making a total of 200 volunteer Army Reservists on active duty with MTMC by that date. Some of these volunteers reported to Jacksonville, Fla., where they, some active component soldiers, and a contingent of MTMC civilians operated the port from August 10–27. According to Brinkerhoff, "During that time, they loaded out almost the entire 101st Airborne Division. They worked seven days a week and put in some 20 hour shifts getting the job done." [16]

The Port of Wilmington, N.C., was the deployment point for the XVIIIth Airborne Corps and the 1st Corps Support Command (COSCOM). Volunteer Army Reservists from the 1175th, 1176th, 1182d, and 1189 TTUs reached Wilmington on August 10, one day before the first empty cargo ship arrived in port. On August 12 the first equipment from the deploying Army units—155mm howitzers, trucks, multiple launch rocket systems (MLRS), and High Mobility Multi-purpose Wheeled Vehicles (HMMWV) arrived. By August 14 the make-shift group of Army Reservists had begun to load the *USNS Pollux*. Difficulties inherent in the early stages of an operation that depended upon volunteers for its success were compounded by automation problems and by the tendency of some units of the XVIIIth Airborne Corps to send equipment to the port without waiting for scheduling instructions. The volunteers did a yeoman's job at Wilmington, but they were delighted when the 1176th was mobilized and arrived at the port on August 30. By that time the volunteers had loaded and sent out two ships.[17]

---

15. The argument is recounted in Brinkerhoff, *Port Operations*, pp. 10–11. The controversy involved varying interpretations of what constitutes "training" as opposed to actually doing useful tasks, as does the question of whether the Army could accept reserve volunteers without some sort of presidential declaration.

16. Brinkerhoff, *Port Operations*, pp. 3–9. The initial 200 volunteers came from the following Transportation Terminal Units: 1174th (Fort Totten, N.Y.), 1175th (Pedricktown, N.J.), 1176th (Baltimore, Md.), 1181st (Meridian, Miss.), 1182d (Charleston, S.C.), 1184th (Mobile, Ala.), 1186th (Tampa, Fla.), 1189th (Charleston, S.C.), 1191st (New Orleans, La.), and the 1192d (New Orleans, La.) There were also 11 Individual Mobilization Augmentee volunteers and 3 volunteers from the Individual Ready Reserve.

17. Schaefer, *MTMC*, pp. 33–38, 42.

ACTIVATING UNITS OF THE USAR

Call-up of combat support and combat service support units of the Army Reserve began immediately after the Secretary's guidance was issued to the service chiefs on August 23. On August 25 the Secretary of the Army initiated STOP LOSS, meaning that soldiers in certain critical military specialties were not allowed to leave the Army, even if their twenty years had been completed or their term of enlistment had expired. On September 1 STOP LOSS was applied to the Army's reserve components.[18] Meanwhile, the Secretary of Defense and members of Congress continued their discussions about the use of reserve component combat units, and volunteer Army Reservists worked around the clock loading ships and dispatching them to the Gulf.

BUILDING THE NATIONAL CONSENSUS

The decision to mobilize the reserve components of the U.S. military establishment was an obvious result of the Total Force policy. The way in which the units were distributed geographically, however, suggested more than simply a way to meet the theater commander's requirements. As more Army Reserve and non-combat Army National Guard units—along with reserve units from the other services—were mobilized, observers began to detect a pattern. It seemed to some that every effort was being made to include in the build-up reserve component units from across the nation.

It was clear that the President and his advisors had learned one of the lessons of Vietnam: that you might be able to build support for a war effort by involving as much of the American public in the affair as practicable. The reserve components were a way of doing this, particularly the Army's reserve components, for they were scattered across the country. Furthermore, with the end of the draft many years earlier, every member of these units was a true volunteer.

The observers were correct in their observations. In an interview in June 1992, Gen. Edwin C. Burba, then commander of the U.S. Army Forces Command (FORSCOM), recounted just

---

18. Susan Canedy, James T. Stensvaag, Anne W. Chapman, John L. Romjue, Charles H. Cureton, and Henry O. Malone, Jr. (Editor), *TRADOC Support to Operations Desert Shield and Desert Storm: A Preliminary Study* (Fort Monroe, Va.: Office of the Command Historian, United States Army Training and Doctrine Command, 1992), p. 21. This is an incredibly fine study detailing TRADOC's role in the war. Hereinafter cited as "Canedy *et al.*, TRADOC Support."

how the force was built. According to Burba, the Commander-in-Chief on the scene, Gen. H. Norman Schwarzkopf, specified his needs in terms of divisions and corps, and FORSCOM put the units together to meet those needs.

"Part of the goal," recounted Burba, "was to have no American who did not know someone over there." In effecting this, said Burba, he and the Army leadership in Washington had a conference call each morning at which they considered force mix and geographic dispersion. If there were two units of the same type that were ready to go, recounted Burba, and one was from an area from which no reservists had been called, while the other was from an area where units had already been mobilized, they chose the one from the untouched area. "We really went after geographical diversity," said Burba, commenting further on the "excitement on the part of the American people as we sent the units off to the desert." Burba also admitted that "we can't do it without the reserve components."[19]

TERMINAL TRANSPORTATION UNITS

Volunteer Reservists did a fine job at the MTMC ports, but it was obvious that the Transportation Terminal Units and Deployment Control Units themselves would be needed on active duty as quickly as possible. An exception to the need to mobilize was the 1185th Transportation Terminal Unit (TTU) from Lancaster, Pa., commanded by Col. Donald R. Detterline. The 1185th had been scheduled to perform its annual training in Wilmington, N.C., in early August. When the decision was made to send the 24th Mechanized Infantry Division to Saudi Arabia, the 1185th was sent instead to Savannah, Ga., where it worked from August 12–25 and got the 24th Mech on its way only six days after the division was alerted.

The 1185th was then retained on active duty and went next to Wilmington, N.C., then to Newport News, Va., to Bayonne, N.J., to Sunny Point, N.C., to Rotterdam, The Netherlands, where it helped load VIIth Corps and send it to the Gulf, then to Bayonne again. The 1185th served on active duty until July 23, 1991, and has the distinction of having

19. Interview, Lt. Col. James T. Currie with Gen. Edwin C. Burba, June 29, 1992; notes in the possession of the author.

worked in more ports than any other Transportation Terminal Unit during Desert Shield/Desert Storm.[20]

The 1181st TTU, commanded by Col. Richard G. Simmons, was ordered to active duty on August 27 and reported to the Port of Jacksonville, its previously-assigned mobilization station. Most of the Army Reserve volunteers running the port to that time—primarily members of the 1175th, 1181st, 1182d, 1184th, and 1186th TTUs—went on to other assignments or returned to civilian life. The twenty volunteers from the 1181st simply remained where they were and worked with their fellow unit members. The 1181st worked in Jacksonville throughout the Desert Shield/Desert Storm period, except during November and December, when it went to Antwerp, Belgium. During that two-month period the 1176th out of Baltimore, Md., commanded by Col. Calvin S. Powell, took over Jacksonville. During its months there the 1181st loaded and sent out 58 ships, giving Jacksonville the distinction of being the most active of the MTMC ports.[21]

The Texas ports of Houston and Beaumont also depended upon Army Reservists for their operation. These ports supported the deployment of the heavy units from Fort Hood, Tex., including the 1st Cavalry Regiment, 2d Armored Division, 3d Armored Cavalry Regiment (ACR), III Corps Artillery, 11th Air Defense Brigade, and the 13th Corps Support Command. The 1191st TTU out of New Orleans, commanded by Col. Ulysses S. Hargrove, was responsible for the Port of Houston, while the 1192d, also from New Orleans and commanded by Col. Charles Kelly, operated at Beaumont.[22]

The 1191st was activated on August 27, and from August 30, 1990–January 19, 1991, it loaded 40 ships with 22,500

---

20. "Reserve Forces in Theater," *The Officer* (March 1991), p. 7; "Army Transporters Take Virtual Control of Marine Terminal," *Norfolk Virginian-Pilot*, September 20, 1990, p. 2; U.S. Army Center for Army Lessons Learned (CALL), U.S. Army Combined Arms Command (CAC), Fort Leavenworth, Kans., "Mobilization of the Reserve Components (RC) for Operations Desert Shield and Desert Storm," Newsletter No. 92–2, February 1992, p. v; hereinafter cited as "CALL, Mobilization of Reserve Components;" Brinkerhoff, *Port Operations*, pp. 13–15; Terminal Transportation Units activated during Desert Shield/Desert Storm included the 1176th, 1181st, 1185th (Lancaster, Pa.), 1191st, and the 1192d. Additionally, the 1173d, 1174th, 1182d, and 1184th TTUs worked at U.S. ports during regular annual training periods, but they were not mobilized. The 1302d Port Security Detachment (Orangeburg, N.Y.) and the 4249th PSD (Pocahontas, Ia.) and the 1190th Deployment Control Unit (Baton Rouge, La.) were also activated as part of the MTMC effort.

21. Schaefer, *MTMC*, p. 21; Brinkerhoff, *Port Operations*, pp. 1–3.

22. Brinkerhoff, *Port Operations*, pp. 15–16.

pieces of equipment. During part of this period it worked out of New Orleans, where it loaded Navy Construction Battalions (SeaBees) and shipped them to the Gulf. Houston's hot, humid, climate caused problems with the bar-code labelling system used to mark equipment before it was loaded on the ships, while the heat, humidity and swarms of mosquitoes and gnats tormented the Reservists. In a concession to the climatic conditions, the Reservists were allowed to work "only" thirteen hours per shift.[23]

The 1192d TTU out of New Orleans was also activated on August 27. Some of its members were already in Beaumont, having volunteered for duty there earlier in the month. The 1192d was unusual among the activated TTUs in that it served on active duty for only 54 days, during which time it loaded 15 ships with the equipment of the 3d ACR, the 1st COSCOM, the 11th ADA Bde, and the 1st Bde, 2d Armored Division. MTMC then decided that it did not require its services at Beaumont, and demobilized the unit on October 19. MTMC later determined that it could have used the 1192d at other ports throughout the Desert Shield/Desert Storm period. By the time MTMC headquarters realized that it could use the 1192d, it was too late, as the unit had already been sent home. Once demobilized, it was impractical—not to mention unprecedented—to recall the unit to active duty.[24]

Other ports where Army Reserve Terminal Transfer Units worked included Sunny Point N.C.; Oakland and Long Beach, Calif.; Charleston, S.C.; Savannah, Ga.; and Newport News, Va. These ports had difficulties similar to those experienced elsewhere, and they were all locations where the Army Reservists proved the value of their training and the depth of their dedication.[25]

In addition to the previously-mentioned overseas deployment of the 1185th TTU to Rotterdam, the Army Reserve sent the 1186th TTU to that same Dutch port. The 1181st went to Antwerp, Belgium, and the 1182d TTU did a split annual training in Germany, dividing its time between the ports of Bremerhaven and Bremen.[26]

---

23. Brinkerhoff, *Port Operations*, pp. 15–16; Schaefer, *MTMC*, pp. 56–59.

24. Brinkerhoff, *Port Operations*, p. 16; Schaefer, *MTMC*, pp. 61, 63, 69–70.

25. Brinkerhoff, *Port Operations*, pp. 14–19; Schaefer, *MTMC*, pp. 81–101.

26. Brinkerhoff, *Port Operations*, p. 19.

DEPLOYMENT CONTROL UNITS

Meanwhile, the 1190th Deployment Control Unit was activated and deployed to Stuttgart, Germany, and sent teams throughout Europe. Deployment Control Units (DCUs) are a little-known Army Reserve asset, but they are invaluable when a military unit is preparing to leave its home station and travel overseas. The DCU can offer assistance in preparing for deployment, including how to mark equipment for shipping. There are only three DCUs in the entire Army, and they are all Army Reserve units.[27]

These DCUs are light and fast to deploy, often being on station and prepared to do business within two days of being alerted. They consist of officers and senior NCOs with considerable experience in the nuances of moving equipment by any means available: air, rail, truck, or ship. According to Brinkerhoff, one Army division sent 5,000 pieces of equipment to its port of debarkation without any labels on them. The TTU serving that port—it happened to be the 1181st—had the task of sorting and logging everything before it could be loaded. The division then accepted assistance from the 1190th DCU, began using the LOGMARS labels that are the heart of the automated inventory control system, and the remainder of the deployment went more smoothly. Once word got around about the help rendered by the DCU, commented Brinkerhoff, "support teams from the 1190th were welcomed with open arms by the deploying units."[28]

ARMY RESERVE RAILROAD UNITS

Even the railroad units of the USAR—a unique asset not found in the active component—came into play during Operation Desert Shield. The 1205th Railway Services Unit, for example, commanded by Lt. Col. Robert W. McGuire, sent twelve-member teams of volunteers to Sunny Point, N.C., for 30-day tours of duty during the period from September 4–December 18, 1990. The unit itself was called to active duty on January 15, 1991. Augmented by volunteer Army Reservists from two other USAR railway units, the members of the 1205th replaced 100 ties per day in the marshalling area and the wharf complex. Old and decrepit tracks and equally-antique switching

---

27. Tom R. MacKenzie, "DCU's Help the Army Move," *Army Logistician*, May–June 1991, p. 12.

28. *Ibid.*, p. 19; Brinkerhoff, *Port Operations*, p. 19.

systems caused more than thirty derailments during the first six weeks, all of which fell to the 1205th to repair.[29]

REALISTIC TRAINING PAYS OFF FOR MTMC

Realistic training of the MTMC-affiliated Army Reserve units paid big dividends during the Desert Shield deployment. During the 1960s and early 1970s, Reservists had practiced their skills by moving wooden blocks from one room to another, the blocks representing cargo being loaded onto a ship. For at least ten years, though, Army Reserve annual training had consisted of loading real ships with real cargo, including stowing it and properly securing it for sea passage. When the real thing came along, the Reservists were ready.[30]

One reason for the MTMC success in using Reservists was that the command regarded its Army Reserve members as significant assets. Army Reservists, found one historian, were fully integrated into the command structure in peacetime and "are included in staff meetings, Commanders' conferences, seminars, and other command events as a matter of course. Reservists were given responsible positions in peacetime and expected to deliver the goods [in wartime]. . . . When the time came to support OPERATION DESERT STORM, Reserve officers were . . . treated as full partners."[31]

This partnership between MTMC and its reserve members was a model for the way in which active component soldiers, Department of Defense civilians, and members of the reserve components can work together for the national defense. MTMC's handling of its Reserve soldiers can serve as an example for others, as the cooperation experienced there was not the unanimous experience of Reservists during Desert Shield/Desert Storm.

29. Schaefer, *MTMC*, p. 23.
30. Brinkerhoff, *Port Operations*, pp. 28–29.
31. *Ibid.*, p. 29.

16

Desert Shield/Desert Storm: USAR Troop Units Respond

The port control units (TTUs, DCUs, and railroad units) were joined on active duty before the end of August 1990 by other varieties of Army Reserve units, such as medical, military police (for port security), judge advocate general (preparation for overseas deployment requires lawyers), personnel, garrison (to receive and process those being activated and sent overseas), water distribution, linguists, and public affairs. September picked up the pace of mobilization, as additional adjutant general units, including those that were trained and equipped to operate post offices, joined the ones already called to active duty. More medical units came on board, as did chemical decontamination and defense and smoke generator units, engineer units, and water handlers.[1]

For purposes of this study, the various USAR units called to active duty have been divided into several types: (1) those that dealt with materiel, such as transportation, ordnance, supply, water, and engineers, (2) those that supported the American soldier, including personnel services/adjutant general, finance, judge advocate general, mortuary and casualty matters and training units, (3) those that ministered to the physical and non-physical needs of the soldier such as medical and chaplains, and (4) those that dealt directly with the Iraqis, such as military police, civil affairs, and military intelligence. We have also included in category three the historical

1. Memorandum, AFKC–ACD–TCB, 319th Transportation Brigade (COSCOM), 7 September 1990, Col. John T. Crowe, with later attachment; copy in DS/DS files, USACMH.

and public affairs units, as they, too, centered themselves on the activities and performance of U.S. soldiers and their units.

In addition, we have focused our attention on another area of the Army Reserve: parts that were not used or that were largely ignored in the effort against Iraq, such as infantry, signal, theater logistics management, and general officers. The Individual Ready Reserve (IRR), Individual Mobilization Augmentees (IMA), and the actions at the United States Army Reserve Personnel Center (ARPERCEN) are treated in still another chapter.

A GIANT LOGEX

Desert Shield has sometimes been described as "a giant LOGEX"—meaning the "*log*istical *ex*ercise" that many reserve units have experienced at Fort Pickett, Va.—and in many ways that is exactly what it was. Desert Shield was the "get ready" phase, and the fact that Saddam Hussein allowed months in which to transport and position millions of tons of supplies and hundreds of thousands of troops in nearby staging areas meant that when the war actually began, there would be no materiel shortages affecting the outcome of the conflict. It took the combat service support assets of the Army Reserve to make this happen.

WATER TREATMENT AND SUPPLY UNITS

On September 12 the 79th Quartermaster Company (Water Supply), the first USAR unit ever to mobilize at Fort Benjamin Harrison, passed through the main gate with a military police escort. Under the European scenario used to train the Army since the beginning years of the Cold War, the 79th was of relatively low mobilization priority. There was little need, figured the Army's planners, for water purification and supply units in Europe.

A potential war in the desert gave water a new importance, however, and the 79th suddenly became a priority unit. Unfortunately, the 125-person unit was only 75 strong, a personnel shortage that was quickly remedied by the addition of fifty individuals from elsewhere in the Fourth Army area. Military Occupation Specialty (MOS) qualification was likewise low, with barely 65% of the unit being MOS qualified. This was hardly surprising for a unit that three years earlier had been a petroleum pipeline company.[2]

---

2. Col. Richard B. Crossland, "Historical Report—RCAG—July–December 1990," pp. 4–5. Typescript in possession of the author. This change in mission is not unusual for reserve component units, but it does take a few years for members of the unit to qualify in their new specialties.

Instructors from Army Reserve Forces Schools were quickly put on active duty and directed to conduct a brief qualification course for MOS 77W (Water Treatment Specialist) for the non-qualified members of the 79th. Limited to two weeks, the instructors decided to eliminate half the course—that part which dealt with water purification—in order to concentrate on water supply. At the end of the course, the trainees were awarded the 77W MOS, though they knew only half of what was required. This lack of knowledge later became a problem when the XVIIIth Airborne Corps cross-leveled 77W MOS personnel in Saudi Arabia, only to discover that these newly-trained individuals from the 79th were not fully qualified. As a result of this experience, the Army discontinued the practice of awarding MOSs for shortened courses.[3]

The 13th Quartermaster Detachment (WP) from Great Bend, Kans., did not have the same problem as the 79th, though it had another which was just as severe—its commander was not mobilizable.[4] This small unit—only 15 soldiers authorized and assigned—was placed on alert on August 24, 1990, and reported to Fort Riley, Kans., minus its commander, on September 16.[5]

News media coverage of this unit's activation was disproportionately intense, largely because it was the first Army Reserve unit in the 89th Army Reserve Command (ARCOM) ever to be mobilized. While at Fort Riley the detachment's members went through the standard refresher training, with an emphasis on threats from chemical warfare. The unit members had time to paint their equipment in the desert camouflage colors and to receive an issue of desert pattern battle dress uniforms. They learned that the filtration-type water purification units they were familiar with would remain at Fort Riley, and that their task in the Kuwait Theater of Operations (KTO) would be to operate reverse osmosis water purification units (ROWPUs).[6]

The 13th left Fort Riley on September 30 and reached Half Moon Bay on the Persian Gulf two days later for what

---

3. *Ibid.*, p. 5.

4. This problem can occur in the reserve components because an individual may have a temporary physical profile which prevents his being placed on active duty, but which has no detrimental effect on his or her performance of duty during the monthly inactive duty drills. In some instances a physical condition that is not readily apparent might not be known to the unit commander until it became time to take a physical.

5. *Annual Historical Supplement, Headquarters, 89th U.S. Army Reserve Command, FY 91*, pp. IX–17, IX–18, copy in USACMH; hereinafter cited as "*AHS, 89th ARCOM.*"

6. *Ibid.*, p. IX–18.

has been described as "intensive training on the 150K ROWPU. . . ." On October 26 the unit moved to a location known as Guardian City, about forty kilometers north of Dharan, picked up its own 150K ROWPU, and moved to Sarran, Saudi Arabia, where it supported the 24th Infantry Division (Mechanized). Following additional moves, the unit left Saudi Arabia on April 25, 1991, and returned to Kansas. According to their estimation, they produced some 8 million gallons of potable water during their time in Southwest Asia.[7]

Another Army Reserve quartermaster unit with a specialty in water supply became noted for tragedy, rather than mission accomplishment.

DEATH IN THE DESERT

The 14th Quartermaster Detachment was a sixty-nine member water purification unit from Greensburg, Pa., a small town southeast of Pittsburgh. The 14th was typical of many Army Reserve units, in that its members had grown up in the surrounding towns and villages and knew each other well from years of serving together in the reserves. Their Reserve participation was a combination of patriotic expression, parttime job, and opportunity to socialize.

The 14th was not one of the priority units in the USAR, even with its water purification specialty. It was not mobilized, in fact, until January 1991, and had been in the Gulf for less than two weeks when it achieved unwanted fame. It was the evening of February 25, and one of many Iraqi SCUD missiles had been launched on its way toward the coalition forces assembled in Saudi Arabia.

Patriot missiles had shot down most of the incoming SCUDs. But the Patriots missed this one, and it plunged to earth at 2023 hours, Saudi time, exploding its nearly half-ton warhead inside the Dharan Barracks where members of the 14th and other Army Reservists were sleeping, reading, or playing cards.

Twenty-eight American soldiers were killed in the blast, and another 100 were wounded. (By comparison, a total of only 146 U.S. service members were killed in action during the entire war, including 35 killed by friendly fire. Four hundred sixty-seven were wounded during the war, including 72 from friendly fire).[8]

---

7. *Ibid.*, pp. IX–18, IX–19.

8. Department of Defense, *Final Report to Congress, Conduct of the Persian Gulf War. Pursuant to Title V of the Persian Gulf Supplemental Benefits Act of 1991 (Public Law 102–25), April 1992*, p. 589. Hereinafter cited as "DoD, *Final Report*."

Thirteen of the dead and 43 of the wounded were members of the 14th Quartermaster Detachment, USAR. Only 13 members of the unit were not harmed in the attack. The other soldiers who died in the attack were also Army Reservists, though not from one unit.[9] The 14th suffered the greatest combat loss of any U.S. Army unit since Vietnam, and the percentage of casualties taken by the 14th in the attack—over 80 percent—places it in the tragic first ranks of all American military units in any war.[10]

According to unit administrator Capt. Mary Hughes, as of February 1994 only seven soldiers from January 1991 remained in the 14th. Many of the others, she explained, had retired or left the Army Reserve for medical reasons. The unit itself, however, is prospering. Despite the losses suffered in the desert, three years later the unit was at more than 150 percent of authorized strength, and it was part of the Contingency Force Pool, meaning that its mobilization priority is much higher than in 1991. The sacrifices made by the unit in January 1991 are certainly not forgotten, however, and each year the 14th QM Detachment conducts a memorial ceremony in honor of their fallen comrades.[11]

TRANSPORTATION

"We called every truck company in the reserve structure," said FORSCOM mobilization chief Mike Hamer, "except for those in the National Guard divisions." The Army Reserve is home to a large percentage of the Total Army's transportation assets, and whenever a mobilization the size of Desert Shield/Desert Storm is undertaken, the USAR's truck companies are necessarily among the first units to be called to duty.

---

9. Other Army Reservists killed in the missile attack included 3 from the 475th POL Group HHD, Farrell, Penn., 1 from the 402d QM POL Battalion HHD, Farrell, Penn.; 2 from the 477th Transportation Co, Fort Lee, VA; 2 from Co E, 36th Transportation Bn, Fort Dix, N.J.; and 3 from the 23d Replacement Detachment, AC, Fort Stewart, Ga. Draft manuscript, ANDRULIS Research Corp, *Personnel Service Support*, p. 1–1, citing letter, Ken Tipton, PERSCOM Mortuary and Casualty Affairs, 10 Feb 95.

10. "The Fires of Patriotism and Cold Necessity Put 13 in Harm's Way," *New York Times*, March 4, 1991, p. A12; "Scud Kills Reservists," *The Officer* (March 1991), p. 11; USNWR, *Triumph without Victory*, pp. 328–31; "100 Hour War to Free Kuwait," *Jane's Defence Weekly*, March 9, 1991, p. 326; interview, Lt. Col. James T. Currie with Capt. Mary Hughes, Unit Administrator, 14th QM Detachment, February 22, 1994; notes in possession of the author.

11. Interview, Currie with Capt. Hughes. See also Evelyn D. Harris, "Fallen Soldiers," *Army Reserve Magazine*, Vol. 38, No. 2 (1992), p. 30.

Today's Army runs not just on its stomach, but on POL: petroleum, oil, and lubricants. Army Reserve units were there to transport each of these commodities and to manage the relocation of soldiers and materiel that the final battle plan required.

TRANSPORTERS

The mission of the 623d Transportation Company, a part of the 77th ARCOM in New York City, is to supply bulk petroleum to the user. In this conflict, though, it found itself a carrier of both ammunition and bulk dry cargo. Commanded by Capt. Ely Ramirez, the 623d was alerted on August 18, 1990 and mobilized on October 11. The delay between alert and actual mobilization allowed the 77th ARCOM to fill vacancies in the unit with fully-qualified personnel, so that the unit arrived at its Fort Dix mobilization site with 100 percent of its authorized strength.

Just over a month later, on November 14, the unit left for Saudi Arabia, where it supported the 24th Infantry Division (Mechanized). The unit historian has suggested that the 623d may have been the first Army Reserve unit to cross into Iraq at the beginning of the ground war, but this claim has not been verified.[12]

The 623d remained in place until April 4, 1991. During barely five months in theater it drove over 500,000 miles and delivered some 4.1 million gallons of petroleum products and 10,000 tons of dry cargo, including ammunition. It was altogether a successful deployment.[13]

The 298th Transportation Company from Franklin, Pa., was mobilized on September 20, 1990. It was sent to Saudi Arabia, where its primary mission was to provide bulk fuel support to the U.S. Army's XVIIIth Airborne Corps. During its time in the desert the 298th operated twenty-four hours a day and drove routes that sometimes reached seven hundred miles in length. Its trucks covered an aggregate 1.25 million miles and delivered over 32 million gallons of fuel. Just before the ground war began, the 298th moved 4.5 million gallons of jet fuel to the northern part of the staging area in support of Marine Corps units. The hours were long, said the unit's commander, Capt. Robert Mortimer, "but we had positive attitudes from day one, and it carried us through—the whole way."[14]

---

12. *The 77th Army Reserve Command Goes to War: A History of Unit Involvement in Operations Desert Shield and Desert Storm, 1990–1991*, unpaginated; copy in USACMH files; hereinafter cited as "*77th ARCOM*.".

13. *77th ARCOM*.

14. Jack Gordon, "298th Transportation Company," *Checkerboard* (99th ARCOM quarterly), Vol. 3, No. 2 (Spring 1992), p. 10.

The 619th Transportation Company (Medium-Heavy) of Auburn, Me., hauled ammunition rather than petroleum products. This company, commanded by Capt. Martin Remillard, was activated on October 11 and spent a month in training before deploying to Saudi Arabia, where it was assigned to the 7th Transportation Group. The men and women of the company supported the 82d Airborne Division, the 1st Cavalry Division, and the 101st Airborne Division (Air Assault), among others. They operated sixty M–915 flatbed tractor trailers and other smaller trucks and carried everything from small arms ammunition to Patriot missiles to food, water, and clothing. They also carried bombs for the Air Force. "The bombs were unloaded from our trucks . . . and directly loaded on the aircraft," said 1st Sgt. Gary Arsenault. "Less than two hours later, those bombs were dropped on enemy positions in Kuwait and Iraq." The trucks of the 619th travelled more than 1.7 million miles; drivers averaged some 14,500 miles behind the wheel. The unit returned to the United States on May 16, 1991.[15]

The 129th Transportation Company (Heavy Truck) of Osage, Kans., had the people and equipment required to transport main battle tanks and other heavy tracked vehicles, thus saving wear and tear on the vehicles and fuel and maintenance costs. This 146-member unit, commanded by Capt. Janice N. Ott, was activated on September 25, 1990, and ordered to Fort Riley for pre-deployment processing and training. Arriving in Saudi Arabia on November 25, the 129th immediately began transporting the Army's M1A1 main battle tanks from the ports to the forward deployment areas. The unit moved seven times during its stay in the Middle East, and it worked long hours—often twenty-four hours at a time—in accomplishing its mission. Despite the long hours and hazardous driving conditions that prevailed in much of Saudi Arabia, the unit suffered no serious accidents and incurred no injuries. The 129th left Saudi Arabia in late April 1991 and arrived at Fort Riley on April 25, from which it was released from active duty.[16]

The 842d Quartermaster Company (Petroleum Supply), headquartered in Kansas City, Kans., had the mission of providing temporary storage facilities for both water and petroleum products at the corps and theater level. It was equipped with both 10,000 and 50,000 gallon collapsible storage tanks, forward area refueling equipment, and 5000 gallon tank trucks, together with other equipment necessary for its mission.

15. Terry Brown, "619th Transportation Co. hauls ammunition in Gulf Area," *The Reserve Voice* (newspaper of the 94th ARCOM), Vol. 20, No. 3 (Summer 1991), p. 4.

16. 77th ARCOM, pp. XIII–28 thru XIII–29.

This company, commanded by Capt. Richard A. Gaunt, was mobilized on October 11, 1990, and proceeded to Fort Riley, Kans., where it spent a month getting ready to move to the Gulf. The sixty-six members of the unit left Fort Riley on November 11 and arrived in Dharan, Saudi Arabia, the next day. Initially stationed at Half Moon Bay, the unit was assigned to the 370th Quartermaster Battalion (Water). On December 20, it was reassigned to the 383d Quartermaster Battalion (Petroleum Terminal and Pipeline Operating) and moved to a location near Hafr Al Batin, some 65 kilometers south of the Iraqi border, where it was given the mission of supplying bulk petroleum to the forces of Saudi Arabia, Egypt, and Syria. The unit established facilities capable of storing 200,000 gallons of motor gasoline (MOGAS), 600,000 gallons of Jet A1 aviation fuel, and 1.4 million gallons of diesel fuel.

The 842d was supposed to receive host-nation augmentation to bring it up to a total strength of 189. Because this augmentation did not occur, the unit was assigned an additional 35 active component personnel, some of whom had recently graduated from quartermaster advanced individual training at Fort Lee, Va.

As with many of the Army Reserve units in the KTO, the 842d exceeded the performance norm. During the period it was providing fuel to user units (December 18, 1990–April 23, 1991), it pumped almost 44.5 million gallons of petroleum products. The 842d returned to Fort Riley for outprocessing on June 3, 1991, and its members were released from active duty five days later.[17]

The 475th Quartermaster Group of Farrell, Pa., commanded by Col. John Koshan, operated at a different level of supply from the companies previously mentioned. Two of the group's subordinate units—the 328th Quartermaster Detachment and the 635th Quartermaster Detachment—were activated on September 20. A week later, the group itself was called to active duty, mobilized at Fort Lee, and arrived in Saudi Arabia on October 12. Assigned to U.S. Army Central Command (Forward) at Dharan, Saudi Arabia, the 475th was responsible for command and control of four battalions and their 45 subordinate units, a total of some 5,000 soldiers.[18]

---

17. *Ibid.*, pp. X–44 thru X–47.

18. Jack Gordon, "475th Quartermaster Group," *Checkerboard* (newsletter of the 99th ARCOM), Vol. 3, No. 2 (Spring 1992), pp. 8, 12; Department of the Army, Headquarters, 475th Quartermaster Group, Memorandum for 22d SUPCOM, Subject: 475th Quartermaster Group After Action Report, 7 April 1991, unpaginated. This document is found at Tab E in Part 4A of the *22d SUPCOM After Action Report.* Cited hereinafter as "475th QM Group After Action Report."

The 475th learned from its deployment and offered suggestions for alleviating problems during future conflicts. For one thing, said the unit, the MTOE (Modified Table of Organization and Equipment) is inadequate to the tasks assigned a quartermaster group. "Assets for personnel administration, logistical administration, water management, and Host Nation coordination proved to be inadequate." The unit also felt that the number of medium truck companies in the Army inventory was far too small. If it had not been for the 1200 8,000-gallon tankers furnished by the Saudis, "Fuel re-supply would have limited the overall operation." This quantity of vehicles, said the 475th, was the equivalent of 32 U.S. Army medium truck companies.[19]

The 475th was also dismayed by the lack of adherence to the CAPSTONE affiliation they had established before the war. "Although all elements of our capstone [*sic*] trace were in theater, they were not assigned."[20] This was a common complaint among the Reservists,[21] and it appears to reflect the belief that the CAPSTONE trace was somehow a sacred bond between AC and RC units. The fact that units had trained together and presumably knew each other personally was an advantage that was apparently overlooked in deciding what units to assign where. It wasted, undoubtedly unintentionally, some of the benefits of the CAPSTONE program.

Capt. Barry Stegeman, an active duty Army officer assigned to the 475th, had the following to say about the performance of the headquarters: "This was my first experience working directly with a reserve unit. . . . It's not that I doubted so much that they [Army Reservists] could do the job, but I saw that when it comes down to knowledge and technical expertise, these soldiers are a match for any active duty soldiers in any army."[22]

MOVEMENT CONTROL

The final battle plan of General H. Norman Schwarzkopf involved a massive relocation of forces and supplies. Included in the lift requirement were over 230,000 U.S. and coalition soldiers, 95,000 trucks and other wheeled vehicles, and

19. 475th QM Group After Action Report.

20. *Ibid.*

21. See the same complaint from the 301st Area Support Group at p. 3 of its after action report to the 22d SUPCOM. The report from the 301st is found at Tab D of Part 4A of the 22d SUPCOM After Action Report.

22. Quoted in *ibid.*, p. 12.

12,000 tanks and other tracked armored vehicles. The order to begin the movement was issued on January 17, 1991, and personnel and supplies immediately began a 400–500 mile shift to the west. The unit that managed this undertaking for the command was the 318th Transportation Agency (Movement Control), an Army Reserve unit from New York City.[23]

The 318th, commanded by Col. Peter C. Langenus, was mobilized on September 20, 1990, and reached Saudi Arabia in October. During the entire period of Desert Shield and Desert Storm the 318th was the theater army movement control agency. One of the unit's responsibilities was that of scheduling convoys on Main Supply Route Dodge, the two-lane highway that carried great quantities of everything from ammunition to aviation gasoline from one end of Saudi Arabia to the other. The 318th also validated intratheater airlift requests, a task which required the unit to control the flights of some 120 C–130 aircraft. Finally, the 318th coordinated the daily movement of 71 railroad trains consisting of almost 4000 railcars.[24]

ORDNANCE

The 351st Ordnance Company, headquartered in Romney, W.Va., was activated for desert duty on November 21, 1990. Following mobilization at Fort Pickett, Va., the unit was transported to Saudi Arabia. The company took over and ran Theater Supply Area #4 (TSA #4), described by one author as "the largest ammunition reception, storage and issue point not only in the war . . . and the world, but in all of military history."[25]

There were 120 trailers full of ammunition at the TSA, containing every conceivable type of conventional ordnance, from small arms ammunition to Patriot missiles. The area occupied by this ammo supply point was extensive: fifty square miles near King Khalid Military City. It was naturally enough a target for Saddam Hussein's Scud missiles, and as company commander Capt. Harry Fuller said in a post-war interview, "Junk fell down all over the place" when a Scud was intercepted and destroyed by a Patriot anti-missile missile.[26]

Following the ceasefire with Iraq, the 351st was assigned the duty of caring for almost 6,000 tons of captured enemy

23. Col. Peter C. Langenus, "Moving an Army: Movement Control for Desert Storm," *Military Review*, September 1991, p. 41.

24. *Ibid.*, pp. 41–42, 46, 48, and 51.

25. Jack Gordon, "351st Ordnance Company," *Checkerboard* (publication of the 99th ARCOM), Vol. 3, No. 2 (Spring 1992), p. 19.

26. *Ibid.*

ammunition, everything from rocket propelled grenades to Silkworm (anti-ship) missiles. It was a fascinating and worthwhile mission, said members of the unit, and they would be more than willing to do it again if called upon.[27]

The 395th Ordnance Company, Appleton, Wisc., received its activation notice on November 21, 1990, and reported to Fort McCoy, Wisc., just three days later. It remained at Fort McCoy for some seven weeks—until January 8, 1991—and during this period it was able to MOS-qualify twenty-six unit members, acquire authorized but previously-unavailable equipment, and sharpen skills in everything from shooting to land navigation to communications. A particular morale-builder during this time, suggests the unit's historian, were the passes that practically everyone received on the weekends.[28]

The 395th reached Saudi Arabia on January 10, and on January 17 deployed to King Khalid Military City, where it worked for the next six months. Its sister unit was the 351st Ordnance Company from Rodney, W.Va., and together these two Army Reserve units worked to eliminate the backlog of ammunition which had piled up at KKMC.

The war ended before a small fraction of the ammunition was expended, but that fortunate circumstance created another problem: there was little packaging material for the ammunition, since most of it had been discarded when the ammo was unpacked by the combat units. The 395th and other ordnance companies devoted months to preparing the unexpended ammunition for return to the United States, as well as to removing captured enemy ordnance from Kuwait. The 395th ended its mission in early August 1991, almost exactly a year after Iraq's invasion of Kuwait had started the whole affair. The unit returned to Appleton on August 18, where it enjoyed a welcoming parade. "It was really a great day to be an American," wrote the unit's historian, "and be in the 395th Ordnance Company. The local support for the unit was at an all time high."[29]

---

27. *Ibid.*

28. *Annual Historical Review, 86th U.S. Army Reserve Command, 1 October 1990 to 30 September 1991*; copy in USACMH files; hereinafter cited as *"AHR, 86th ARCOM."* It should be noted that Army Reservists were treated in widely varying fashion upon mobilization. While members of the 395th were allowed to return home on the weekends, members of one of the Army Reserve hospitals mobilized for the conflict were confined to Aberdeen Proving Grounds at night. This restriction applied even to field grade officers.

29. *Ibid.*

Among the mobilized Army Reserve units sent other than to the Persian Gulf was the 295th Ordnance Company (Ammo) (DS) of Hastings, Neb. This 173-person unit, commanded by 1st Lt. Robert E. Echternach, was alerted on January 3, 1991 and reported to its mobilization station, Fort Riley, Kans., on January 6. It departed Fort Riley on January 17 and reported to Darmstadt, Germany, where it was attached to the 15th Ordnance Battalion. The soldiers of the 295th assisted the 60th and 184th Ordnance Companies during the war and closed down seven ammunition supply points and one pre-stock point once the war had ended. Unit members returned to Fort Riley on June 8 and were allowed to go home five days later.[30]

SUPPLY

The 452d General Supply Company, Winthrop, Minn., was called to active duty in 1968 and became one of only thirty-five USAR units to serve in Vietnam. On November 21, 1990, the 452d was called again, this time as one of hundreds of Army Reserve units sent to the Gulf war. As in 1968, the men and women of the 452d answered the call and performed their duties.

After staying in Khobar Towers for a week, the 452d was sent to Log Base Echo, some twenty miles northwest of Hafar al Batin. The unit supplied basic items such as bottled water and meals-ready-to-eat (MREs) to 170,000 soldiers of the VIIth Corps, and remained at this location until May 1, 1991. As it had done in Vietnam some twenty-three years earlier, the 452d was an exceptional unit, the results of which were reflected in its contribution to the Meritorious Unit Commendation received by its higher headquarters, the 13th Supply and Service Battalion.[31]

The 988th Supply Company, headquartered in Dublin, Ga., was activated on September 27, 1990, and was sent to Fort Stewart for training. It remained there until November 10, when it departed for Saudi Arabia, arriving at Camp Jack on November 12. It went to Camp Expo on November 27 and then to King Khalid Military City, where it remained from December 23, 1990, until June 13, 1991. The 988th's mission was repair parts, and its main customers were the XVIIIth Air-

30. *AHS, 89th ARCOM*, pp. XIII–17 thru XIII–18.

31. Letter, Sgt. Pamela J. Kamm, 452d General Supply Company, to Lt. Col. James T. Currie, no date; in possession of the author; Permanent Orders 17–4, United States Army Forces Central Command, 30 January 1992.

borne Corps, VIIth Corps, and the 11th Armored Cavalry Regiment. From June 14–25, 1991, the men and women of the 988th cleaned vehicles and equipment for shipment home. It was during this two week period, wrote SSgt. Adrian Page of the 988th, that members of the unit enjoyed their first indoor showers and bathrooms in over seven months.[32]

The 1012th General Supply (CS) Company of Fremont, Neb., was activated on October 11, 1990, and sent to Fort Riley for pre-deployment training. The unit left Fort Riley a month later and arrived in Saudi Arabia on November 13. The 200-member unit, commanded by Capt. Scott A. Neumiller, was one of many Army Reserve units under the 22d SUPCOM, the Army's main logistical headquarters in Saudi Arabia. The company was split into two parts: one to operate a Class I and bottled water supply point at Log Base Alpha and the other to establish theater supply activities at Log Base Bravo.

The company used stocks from Log Base Bravo to establish forward log bases Echo and Charlie for the 18th Airborne and VIIth Corps. On February 23 the 1012th was given the mission of stocking rear assembly areas for these two corps, and it accomplished the mission without a problem. The unit was also tasked with support of the Kurdish relief efforts, Operations Provide Comfort and Provide Relief. The 1012th departed Saudi Arabia on June 26, some 7½ months after arriving in the Middle East. The unit demobilized at Fort Riley, and the members of the 1012th returned home on July 3, 1991.[33]

ENGINEERS

The active army has a significant engineer capability, but Army Reserve engineering units were nevertheless among those activated for the campaign against Iraq. Before the conflict in the desert ended, there were some 97 engineer units in theater: 57 active component, 20 Army Reserve, and 20 Army National Guard. Two of the Army Reserve units were general officer commands: the 416th Engineer Command, from Chicago. Ill., and the 411th Engineer Brigade, from New York City (Brooklyn). The 416th was one of two engineer command headquarters in the Army Reserve, the other being the 412th in Vicksburg, Miss. Of the engineer personnel strength in theater, there were 19,453 active component soldiers, 1,953 Army Re-

---

32. Letter, SSgt. Ralph J. Page to Lt. Col. James T. Currie, November 5, 1992, in possession of the author.

33. *AHS, 89th ARCOM,* pp. XIII–20 thru XIII–23.

servists—including about half the engineers at echelons above corps—and 2,275 Army National Guardsmen.[34]

The August 1990 answer with regard to the need for engineers in theater, however, had been the same as with other combat support and combat service support elements: we would rather have fighters. Additionally, according to one study of the deployment of the 416th, "Force planners were reluctant to call up the entire Engineer Command headquarters. Constraints on airlift and a desire to avoid too many high level headquarters was part of the basis for this reluctance."[35]

The solution from Maj. Gen. (soon to be Lt. Gen.) William G. "Gus" Pagonis, the Army's logistics commander in Saudi Arabia, was the same as with other such requirements: he put together an *ad hoc* arrangement of forces. Pagonis did this with theater logistics, and he attempted to do it with the engineers by assigning to his 22d SUPCOM headquarters an engineer officer who served as "SUPCOM Staff Engineer, ARCENT (Forward)."[36]

416TH ENGINEERS

This makeshift arrangement did not hold, however, for the theater really needed an engineer command. Over a period of several months, elements of the 416th were called to active duty and deployed to Saudi Arabia, while individual personnel from the 416th had begun reporting for active duty as early as August 11. The first of these was Lt. Col. Ben M. Colcol, who was assigned to U.S. Central Command (CENTCOM) to serve as the ARCENT representative to the CENTCOM Regional Contingency Construction Management Team. Additional 416th personnel followed on August 20, and on October 15 a twenty-five man advanced detachment was sent to Saudi Arabia under the command of Col. Alan J. Berg, Assistant Chief of Staff for

34. 416th Engineer Command, *Command History Report: Operation Desert Storm, 416th Engineer Command, 17 January 1991 Through 1 April 1991*, April 22, 1991, p. 1 and interview with, Col. Phillip W. Carroll, III, ARCENT Engineer, cited in John R. Brinkerhoff, *United States Army Reserve in Operation Desert Storm: Engineer Support at Echelons above Corps: The 416th Engineer Command* (Washington: Office of the Chief, Army Reserve, 1992), pp. 6 and 15; hereinafter cited as *416th Engineer Command History*, and Brinkerhoff, *416th Engineers*.

35. Interview with Col. Carroll, November 29. 1991, cited in Brinkerhoff, *416th Engineers*, pp. 8, 10.

36. Presentation by Col. Robert B. Flowers, 416th Engineer Command, Mar 14, 1992 and telephone interview, Col. Alan J. Berg, 416th Engineer Command, January 14, 1992, both cited in Brinkerhoff, *416th Engineers*, pp. 8–9.

Facilities Management at the 416th. This advanced party was assigned to the 22d SUPCOM, and Col. Berg became, in fact if not in title, the staff engineer for the SUPCOM.[37]

Despite the massive build-up of U.S. forces in theater, it was not at all certain that the 416th headquarters would ever be mobilized. Finally, it became clear that a unit like the 416th was required, and on November 29 the 264-member headquarters—including its two reserve general officers, Maj. Gen. Terrence D. Mulcahy, the Commander, and Brig. Gen. Max L. Schardein, the Deputy Commander—was mobilized. According to one study of the mobilization, the key to having the reserve generals command their unit was the U.S. Army's Chief of Engineers, whose policy was that "if the unit goes, it goes with its commander." Having gotten over the biggest hurdle to full unit mobilization, the 416th arrived in Riyadh on December 11, 1990.[38]

The commander of the 416th, Maj. Gen. Mulcahy, was the senior engineer officer in the theater of operations, and he frequently accompanied Lt. Gen. John J. Yeosock, the ARCENT commander, on his travels. This included sitting in on the weekly meetings with Yeosock's counterpart, Saudi Lt. Gen. Khalid Bin Sultan. Mulcahy functioned in every way as the Army commander's engineer staff officer.[39]

The 416th had five major engineer units under its command: the 411th Engineer Brigade, an Army Reserve unit from Brooklyn, NY; the 30th Engineer Battalion (Topo), an active component unit from Fort Bragg; the 1030th Engineer Battalion, an ARNG unit from Gate City, Va., reported directly to the 416th. The 43d Engineer Battalion (Cbt Hvy), an active component unit from Fort Benning and the 864th Engineer Battalion (Cbt Hvy), another active component unit from Fort Lewis were under the 411th. The engineer tasks within the theater were divided so that construction was assigned to the 411th and its subordinate units; facilities engineering was assigned to the 1030th; and topographic support was the responsibility of the 30th. The 416th kept certain jobs for itself, including "theater army engineer planning and design, real

---

37. *416th Engineer Command History*, p. 49, and interview, Col. Alan J. Berg, 416th Engineer Command, January 14, 1992, cited in Brinkerhoff, *416th Engineers*, pp. 9–11.

38. Interview with Lt. Col. Gordon Quisenberry and Mr. Harry Painton, Office of the Chief of Engineers, December 12, 1991, cited in Brinkerhoff, *416th Engineers*, p. 12; *416th Engineer Command History*, p. 49.

39. Interview with Col. Phillip W. Carroll, III, ARCENT Engineer, November 29, 1991, cited in Brinkerhoff, *416th Engineers*, p. 1.

estate operations, prime power, contracting, and construction materials." It was also responsible for training Saudi engineers in breaching of minefields and other obstacles.[40]

The obstacle-breaching assignment was awarded to a task force commanded by the 416th's deputy commander, Schardein, and included Lt. Col. Merrill W. Watt and Capt. Steven C. Woods of the 416th and Lt. Col. James Bland of ARCENT. With the assistance of the 416th and some other U.S. Army engineers, the Saudis constructed a site that allowed training in the full range of breaching techniques, including mine detection, use of bangalore torpedoes, operation of mine plows, and mine field marking. Two battalions of Saudis were trained by the task force, and according to one study, they acquitted themselves well during the offensive.[41]

The 416th also engaged in planning, engineering, and construction of facilities used by the incredible number of U.S. troops who descended on Saudi Arabia in a relatively short period of time. These facilities included such items as petroleum pipelines and wash racks which were used prior to redeployment to prevent contaminated vehicles from being brought back to the U.S. The 416th also did real estate leasing and contracting for bunking facilities and toilets under the auspices of the Middle/East Africa Projects Office (MEAPO), which was a DoD operation from Winchester, Va. Army Reserve participation under MEAPO was represented by the 308th Real Estate detachment from Bismarck, N.D., commanded by Maj. Thomas M. Senger. This small, sixteen-member unit, operated out of Dharan and managed existing leases.[42]

Largely by default the 416th became the manager of the approval process for new major military construction projects. ARCENT had attempted to perform this mission in its engineer staff section. It simply could not keep up with the flood of requests, so it turned the job over to the 416th, which processed 42 requests worth $278.6 million during the period January 17–March 10, 1991. Projects examined and approved by the

---

40. Brinkerhoff, *416th Engineers*, p. 23; *416th Engineer Command History*, pp. 3–5.

41. Presentation by Lt. Col. Merrill W. Watt, 416th Engineer Command, March 14, 1992, cited in Brinkerhoff, *416th Engineers*, pp. 24–25.

42. *416th Engineer Command History*, pp. 4 and 7; letter, Col. Lee J. Pryor, February 24, 1992; presentation by Tommy R. Hill, Asst. Chief of Real Estate Operations, Savannah District, March 14, 1992; and 308th Engineer Detachment (Real Estate) *Desert Storm After Action Report*, all cited in Brinkerhoff, *416th Engineers*, pp. 25–28.

416th included roads, airfields, helipads, displaced civilian camps, and hazardous waste clean-up.[43]

The 416th was also the control headquarters for Class IV engineer construction materials, which included such necessities as cement, asphalt, sand and gravel, prefabricated shelters, lumber, and concertina wire. The 416th became the controlling headquarters for these items despite resistance from the 20th Engineer Brigade, which had enjoyed a near-monopoly on construction material prior to the arrival of the Reservists. Working closely with the 411th Engineer Brigade, the 416th was able to contract for materials from the Saudis and established a Class IV supply depot at King Khalid Military City. Altogether, the 416th managed a purchase agreement that totalled some $64 million and took delivery of an additional $10 million in engineer equipment paid for by Japan. The 411th contracted for $2 million in rental equipment and $6 million in Class IV supplies.[44]

Today's Army is more environmentally-conscious than ever before. Though environmentalism clearly takes a backseat during actual combat, the aftermath of a war such as Desert Storm results in someone's having to take a look at what we have left behind. The 416th was given the mission in Saudi Arabia. The Reservists had begun working on a theater policy as soon as the advance party from the 416th arrived in theater in October 1990. The 416th drafted the work plan for clean-up within the theater, with the actual work being done by a contractor, Bechtel International Systems, Inc.[45]

Finally, headquarters 416th provided 102 soldiers under Brig. Gen. Schardein for Task Force Freedom, the organization that worked at restoring some semblance of physical order to Kuwait after the liberation. The task force itself was under the command of Maj. Gen. Robert Frix, the Deputy

43. Presentation by Maj. Salvatore M. Cremona, Office of the Chief of Engineers, at 416th Engineer Command, March 15, 1992; "Command Report: Operation Desert Shield RCCM Cell Personnel Activities (1 AUG 90 to 16 JAN 91)" February 9, 1991, all cited in Brinkerhoff, *416th Engineers*, pp. 28–29; *416th Engineer Command History*, pp. 4–7.

44. 411th Engineer Brigade *Unit Historical Report, Operation Desert Storm*, March 25, 1991 and Col. James R. Martin, DCS Logistics, 416th Engineer Command, November 22, 1991 and February 14, 1992, both cited in Brinkerhoff, *416th Engineers*, pp. 31–32.

45. Memorandum, 416th Engineer Command, Subject: "Turn-in of Hazardous Wastes to Approved Collection Points for Operation Desert Storm/ Desert Calm," April 11, 1991, cited in Brinkerhoff, *416th Engineers*, pp. 34–35; Lt. Gen. Henry J. Hatch and Janet McDonnell, "Laying the Groundwork for Theater Operations," *Military Review* (March 1992), p. 10..

Commander and Chief of Staff of ARCENT, and included personnel from the 416th, the 352d Civil Affairs Command (USAR), and other units.[46]

411TH ENGINEERS

The major Army Reserve unit under the 416th was the 411th Engineer Brigade, commanded by Brig. Gen. Richard Storat. The 411th received its activation orders on December 3, 1990, and following three days of mobilization processing at Fort Dix, N.J., sent an advance element to Saudi Arabia. By December 20 the 411th had a tactical operations center established. It was responsible for construction activities, including the EPW camps operated by the Army Reserve's 800th Military Police. The brigade's area of operations encompassed the Eastern Province and half the Central Province of Saudi Arabia, and under its command were two combat heavy engineer battalions, two combat support equipment companies, four construction support companies, and three pipeline companies, totalling over 2,600 soldiers from all three components of the Army.[47]

The 411th, like the 416th, established two command posts: one at Dharan and one at KKMC. The location of these two CPs placed the 411th close to the 22d SUPCOM, which was its main customer. This closeness sometimes created problems for the brigade, as it often received its assignments direct from Pagonis and the 22d SUPCOM at the same time its higher headquarters—the 416th—was receiving varying, and sometimes conflicting, assignments from Yeosock at ARCENT. These conflicts were largely worked out by the ARCENT engineer section, which developed a common set of project priorities.[48]

During its fourteen week deployment to Saudi Arabia, the 411th was able to perform a wide variety of engineering tasks, including some that would have stretched or exceeded the capabilities of almost any engineer unit. In some instances the accomplishment of these jobs was possible only because the members of the command brought to the job skills that

46. *416th Engineer Command History*, pp. 10–11 and memorandum, 416th Engineer Command, "DAST After Action Report with Supplemental Data," March 13, 1991, cited in Brinkerhoff, *416th Engineers*, p. 35.

47. *77th ARCOM*; Col. Anthony R. Kropp, *Engineers Build for Victory in Operation Desert Storm*, unpublished manuscript prepared by the deputy brigade commander, pp. 1–2.

48. 411th Engineer Brigade, *Unit Historical Report* and interview with Col. Phillip W. Carroll, III, November 29, 1991, both cited in Brinkerhoff, *416th Engineers*, p. 36.

they had acquired and honed as civilians, including pipeline construction and construction and maintenance of some of the main supply routes in Saudi Arabia.[49]

The pipeline construction was a particularly massive and vital project and was assigned to Task Force 864 one of the two task forces established by the 411th. TF 864 was commanded by Lt. Col. Robert Griffin, commander of the active component 864th Engineer Bn (Cbt Hvy), and had responsibility for the eastern half of the brigade's area of operation. The pipeline stretched 286 miles and contained 28 pumping stations. The Task Force also constructed a tactical petroleum terminal with a capacity of 3.2 million gallons.[50]

The actual construction work was largely accomplished by two engineer companies, the 808th Engineer Co. (PL), an Army Reserve unit from Pasadena, Calif., commanded by Capt. Robert O. Delley, and the 515th Engineer Co. (PL), an active component unit from Fort Leonard Wood, augmented by personnel from other companies within the battalion. This Inland Petroleum Distribution System (IPDS), which ran along the coast to log bases Bastogne and Alpha, consisted of dual pipelines which carried diesel and JP1–A fuel. By laying the pipe on the surface, rather than burying it, and by putting it in culverts where it crossed a road, the construction progressed at the astonishing rate of eight miles per day, roughly four times the expected rate.[51]

As has been mentioned previously, the 411th was a critical part of the EPW camp construction effort. The arrangement agreed to by ARCENT, the 800th MP Brigade, and the 416th in mid-January 1991 was that the 416th would construct four EPW camps "to austere standards."[52] The 800th would provide 300 soldiers to assist in the construction, would provide all materials and equipment for the camps—including generators and concertina wire—and would lease trailers to

---

49. *77th ARCOM.*

50. Kropp, *Engineers Build for Victory*, pp. 4–5.

51. Presentation, Lt. Col. Brennan, 416th Engineer Command, March 15, 1992, cited in Brinkerhoff, *416th Engineers*, pp. 38–39; *416th Engineer Command History*, p. 7.

52. The meaning of the term "austere" was unclear. The after-action report of the 416th Engineer Command suggested that the term "became an issue in this Theater. Each group had a different meaning associated with this work [meaning the EPW camp construction.] JCS has defined construction categories utilizing initial, temporary, and permanent as categories." *416th Engineer Command History*, p. 40.

be used for EPW processing. The 416th tasked the 411th with upholding its part of the deal.[53]

The 411th, in turn, directed each of its subordinate task forces—the 864th and the 43d—to construct two camps each. According to Col. Phillip W. Carroll, III, the ARCENT Engineer, the engineers—burdened with a myriad of tasks—expected the MPs to do most of the actual construction of the camps; the MPs counted on the engineers to do it. Ultimately, according to Carroll, the MPs did most of the labor, assisted by soldiers from the 411th. The EPW camps required large quantities of Class IV material, including 155 km of electrical cable, 1,500 light fixtures, 19 km of PVC pipe, and 500 km of concertina wire, all of which was procured by the 416th and its subordinate units.[54]

The 411th also provided repair services on the main supply routes in theater, including MSR Dodge, the main road from Dharan west. TF 864 had the eastern 200 kilometers of this MSR, while the TF 43 had the western portion. The task forces performed both maintenance and construction on the MSRs and other roads. In addition, TF 864 also constructed an 8,000′ airstrip and protective berms for Patriot missile batteries.[55]

Task Force 43 was responsible for the western half of the brigade area. This TF was commanded by Lt. Col. Philip Jones of the 43d Engineer Bn (Cbt Hvy), an active component unit. In addition to its role in constructing EPW encampments, TF 43 constructed forward heliports and landing ramps as the battle shifted into Iraq.[56]

Finally, the 411th had a major part in the work of redeploying U.S. forces and equipment to the United States after the cease fire. Soldiers of the 411th disassembled the pipeline they had so laboriously constructed just a few months earlier and prepared it for shipment to the U.S., tore down the temporary structures they and others had erected, and set up a washing facility capable of handling 110 wheeled vehicles at a time.

53. Memorandum of Understanding between 416th Engineer Command and 800th Military Police Brigade, Subject: "Enemy Prisoner of War (EPW) Camp Construction," January 1991, cited in Brinkerhoff, *416th Engineers*, pp. 39–40.

54. Presentation by Maj. Selton J. Sampson and Capt. Patrick A. Porteus, 416th Engineer Command, March 15, 1992 and interview with Col. Phillip W. Carroll, III, both cited in Brinkerhoff, *416th Engineers*, p. 40; *416th Engineer Command History*, p. 8; Kropp, *Engineers Build for Victory*, p. 5.

55. *416th Engineer Command History*, p. 14; Kropp, *Engineers Build for Victory*, p. 5.

56. Kropp, *Engineers Build for Victory*, p. 6.

This latter was an attempt to prevent the introduction of dirt-borne insects and pathogens into the United States or Europe.[57]

FIREFIGHTING

Army Reserve engineer units in theater were also key players in three other types of activities. Firefighting, for example, was the responsibility of nine specially-equipped detachments of engineer troops, four of which came from the Army Reserve. (Four of the others were from the ARNG, while one was an active component unit). The USAR units were the 376th Engineer Detachment (FF) from Granite City, Ill., commanded by Capt. Danny W. Rapert; the 475th Engineer Detachment (FF) from El Dorado, Kans., commanded by Capt. Jerry K. Lucas; the 683d Engineer Detachment (FF) from Pascagoula, Miss., commanded by Capt. Joseph B. Galle; and the 907th Engineer Detachment (FF) from Pullman, Wash., commanded by Capt. Steven K. Janzen.[58]

The 475th and the 907th were assigned to the 20th Engineer Brigade, an active component unit. The 475th was primarily responsible for airfields in the XVIIIth Airborne area, while the 907th, attached to the 27th Engineer Battalion, supported the French 6th Light Armored Division and during the ground war operated from an airfield at As Salman in Western Iraq. The 683d was assigned to the 1030th Engineer Battalion, an ARNG unit from Gate City, Va., and provided firefighting capabilities at Dharan and King Khalid Military City.[59]

WELL DRILLING

Army Reserve units were also responsible for well drilling within the theater, as well as for locating sources of water, which quartermaster units then exploited. Two of the six well drilling units in theater were from the Army Reserve. These were the 322d Engineer Detachment (WD) from Kings Mill, Oh., commanded by Sgt. 1st Class Donald Lunkheimer and the 747th Engineer Detachment (WD) from Missoula, Mont., commanded by Sgt. 1st Class George F. Beatty.[60]

---

57. Letter, Col. Lee J. Pryor, December 24, 1992, cited in Brinkerhoff, *416th Engineers*, p. 46; *416th Engineer Command History*, p. 4; Kropp, *Engineers Build for Victory*, p. 7.

58. *Ibid.*, p. 52.

59. Brinkerhoff, *416th Engineers*, pp. 51–52.

60. Brinkerhoff, *416th Engineers*, p. 54; *416th Engineer Command History*, p. 16.

The 747th reported into Riyadh, Saudi Arabia, on January 11, with their equipment. They quickly discovered, however, that they had neither further orders, nor any assignment. After a few days of waiting for someone in authority to notice them and offer additional instructions, Beatty spotted an engineer unit close by. It was Headquarters, 416th, and after making the presence of himself and his unit known to the Reserve engineer command, the 747th was assigned to the 416th. It was then attached to the 1030th Engineer Battalion. During the period January 17–February 18, 1991, the 747th worked with the 2d Area Support Command at a troop billeting area in Riyadh. Its primary success during this time was its reconditioning of an old well and bringing it into service as a backup for the city water supply. The Army Reserve well drillers were attached to the 926th Engineer Group on February 19 and moved forward with the ground campaign five days later. By the time of the March 3 ceasefire, the 747th was 130 miles into Iraq. On March 6 the unit went into Kuwait and restored two water wells that the Iraqis had damaged, leaving Kuwait and returning to the 926th Engineers on 9 March.[61]

None of the Army's well drilling units—Army Reserve, active component, or National Guard—ever drilled a successful water well inside Saudi Arabia. The reason for this was simple: they were equipped and trained to drill wells only to 600 feet, while the water table in much of the area of operations was 1,200 to 1,500 feet down.[62]

TOPOGRAPHY

Finally, Army Reserve topographic units provided considerable support to the map-making and distribution effort required by a military undertaking the size of Desert Shield/Desert Storm. The 624th Map Distribution Detachment from Granite City, Ill., was a 38-member USAR unit commanded by Sgt. Ervan V. Reeves. It was structured in three detachments, but only one 13-member detachment was mobilized and ordered to active duty on September 10, 1990. It arrived in theater on October 1 and was assigned to the Theater Map depot in Bahrain, a Defense Mapping Agency activity. The other two parts of the 624th were never mobilized, so the unit was aug-

61. 747th Engineer Detachment, *Desert Storm After Action Report*, May 28, 1991, cited in Brinkerhoff, *416th Engineers*, pp. 54–55; *416th Engineer Command History*, pp. 16–17.

62. Brinkerhoff, *416th Engineers*, pp. 54–55.

mented in theater. The 624th worked twelve-hour shifts, seven days a week for six months and contributed significantly to the ability of the Theater Map Depots to distribute some 50 million maps—almost 100 maps for each member of the coalition forces.[63]

Meanwhile, back in the U.S., the 1085th Map Distribution Center from Annapolis, Md., commanded by Capt. David H. Stroup, provided thirty-three volunteers who performed active duty at Fort Gillem, Ga., in support of FORSCOM's map distribution efforts.[64]

These supply, transport, water purification, and engineer units of the Army Reserve were joined in their effort on behalf of the U.S.-led coalition forces by other types of Army Reserve units that demonstrated the value of a trained and ready reserve force.

---

63. *416th Engineer Command History*, p. 59; letter S.Sgt. Ervan V. Reeves, December 19, 1991, cited in Brinkerhoff, *416th Engineers*, p. 63.

64. Interview with James R. Churn, 1085th Map Distribution Center, January 28, 1992, cited in Brinkerhoff, *416th Engineers*, p. 63.

17

Desert Shield/Desert Storm: Looking the Enemy in the Eye

Army Reserve units that were designed to confront the Iraqis directly, whether as prisoners, intelligence targets, objects of propaganda, or displaced persons, were a significant part of the U.S. plan in the Gulf.

MILITARY POLICE

U.S. military planners anticipated victory in the Gulf and believed that military police would be critical to handling the large number of Iraqi prisoners. Army Reserve military police units were among the first to be called to active duty after August 23, 1990.[1] Many of these military police units were assigned to port security duty, both in the United States and overseas. Others, however, were responsible for handling the large numbers of Iraqi prisoners ("EPWs", or Enemy Prisoners of War—not "POWs") encountered by the U.S. and coalition forces as a result of the ground war, as many of the U.S. Army's assets devoted to the EPW problem are in the Army Reserve. The only military police brigade devoted to enemy prisoner of war handling, for example, was an Army Reserve unit.

---

1. The first USAR MP unit in Saudi Arabia was Headquarters and Headquarters Detachment, 160th Military Police Battalion from Tallahassee, Fla. It was placed under the 16th MP Brigade, an active component unit from Fort Bragg. Lt. Col. Jon F. Bilbo, *Enemy Prisoners of War (EPW) Operations during Operation Desert Storm*, p. 24. This was a study project by a student at the U.S. Army War College, Carlisle, Pa., in 1992 and is available through the Defense Technical Information Center.

800TH MP BRIGADE

This unit was the 800th Military Police Brigade (EPW), headquartered in New York City. Commanded by Brig. Gen. Joseph F. Conlon, III, the 800th had an authorized strength of 8,461, though its maximum strength during Desert Storm was about 7,300 personnel.[2] The 800th was activated on December 6, 1990, and following mobilization at Fort Meade, Md., arrived in Saudi Arabia on Christmas Day.[3]

It was assigned to the 22d Support Command (SUPCOM), which was the Army's logistical headquarters in Saudi Arabia established by Maj. Gen. William G. "Gus" Pagonis. According to one student of the operation, "This alignment differs from Army doctrine, which states that MP units to support EPW and U.S. prisoner confinement operations are assigned to the PERSCOM when the latter is formed."[4]

Nevertheless, the assignment seemed to work. With the assistance of the 411th Engineer Brigade, an Army Reserve unit from the same Army Reserve Command (the 77th, from New York City), the 800th established and ran four EPW camp sites, the first enemy prisoner arriving within an hour of the completion of the first compound. Altogether, some 70,000 Iraqi prisoners passed into the hands of the 800th, which then became responsible for their incarceration, feeding, clothing, and general well-being.[5]

The pre-war plan had been to pass captured Iraqis through the U.S.-run camps to enemy prisoner of war facilities set up and run by the Saudis. However, the Saudis were unable to cope with the hordes of Iraqis who turned themselves in to the coalition forces. The temporary U.S. facilities then took on some of the aspects of longer-term imprisonment, with attendant problems of sanitation, food, and shelter. The 800th overcame these problems, worked hand-in-hand with the Saudis, and satisfied the international inspectors who visited the camps on a daily basis.[6]

---

2. Letter, Col. Peter D. Hoffman, Office of the Deputy Chief of Staff for Operations and Plans, June 1, 1992, and *Long Island Newsday*, March 6, 1991, both cited in John R. Brinkerhoff, *United States Army Reserve in Operation Desert Storm: Enemy Prisoner of War Operations: The 800th Military Police Brigade* (Washington: Office of the Chief, Army Reserve, 1992), pp. 7, 14. Hereinafter cited as "Brinkerhoff, *800th MP Brigade*."

3. Bilbo, *Enemy Prisoners of War (EPW) Operations during Operation Desert Storm*, pp. 37–38.

4. *Ibid*., p. 38.

5. Brinkerhoff, *800th MP Brigade*.

6. *77th ARCOM Annual Historical Summary*.

The 800th Military Police Brigade (EPW), did not accomplish these tasks by itself. It was, in fact, a command and control headquarters—the senior command and control headquarters for the EPW effort in the Gulf. Under the brigade headquarters were various types of units required for prisoner processing and control, including military police battalions, guard and processing companies, camp advisory teams, and even a psychological operations battalion. Twenty-nine of the 69 units under the 800th were Army Reserve; the other 40 were Army National Guard.[7]

If there was one type of unit that was most critical to the success of the 800th, it was the EPW Camp units themselves, which actually administered the encampments where the prisoners were held. Four such Army Reserve units operated camps for the 800th: the 301st from Inkster, Mich.; the 401st from Nashville, Tenn.; the 402d from Ashley, Pa.; and the 403d from Omaha, Neb. In addition, the 400th MP Camp from Tallahassee, Fla., performed other missions under the 800th.[8] The 301st and 402d MP Camps were located in the west and formed a unit called "Brooklyn," with the commander of the 402d in charge. The 401st and 403d were in the east and were designated "Bronx." The commander of the 401st was in charge of this duo.[9]

The 301st MP Camp, commanded by Col. Charles S. Johnson, was called to active duty on January 3, 1991, and reported to Fort McCoy, Wisc., four days later. Following the usual three weeks of refresher training, it departed for Saudi Arabia, arriving in theater on January 21. The mission of the 1,615 personnel of the 301st was to construct and operate an EPW camp at Hafr Al Batin, primarily in support of the XVIIIth Airborne Corps.

The 301st operated the camp until May 4, 1991, and processed a total of 23,020 Iraqi prisoners. These prisoners were eventually turned over to Saudi authorities, with the exception of 294 who were directly repatriated. The soldiers of the 301st managed to keep their collective sense of humor despite the adverse conditions. Evidence of this was captured in a sign they erected along Tapline Road: "Welcome to the Hotel 301. . . . We'll leave the light on for you." Attached to the bottom of the carefully-lettered billboard was a large "No Vacancy" sign, which the MPs changed to "For Sale" as they left the area.[10]

---

7. Brinkerhoff, *800th MP Brigade*, p. 18.

8. *Ibid.*, pp. 29–30, 34, 37, 41, 44–45.

9. Bilbo, *Enemy Prisoners of War (EPW) Operations during Operation Desert Storm*, pp. 42–43.

10. Sgt. Eileen M. McChrystal, "Chicago-based MP unit tackles job after job in the desert," *Army Reserve Magazine*, Vol. 38, no. 1 (1992), p. 17.

400TH MP BATTALION

One of the major units under the 301st was the 400th MP Battalion (Enemy Prisoner of War/Counter Intelligence), headquartered at Fort Meade, Md. The 400th, commanded by Lt. Col. Cotton W.S. Bowen, was called to active duty in the fall of 1990, the first large Army Reserve EPW unit to be mobilized. It arrived in theater on December 10 and 11, 1990, and was the only EPW camp unit in the Gulf until the 401st EPW Camp arrived over a month later. The 400th was a new type unit for the Army, designed to process and secure 2,000 prisoners. This meant that it is supposed to be able to do the same thing the standard EPW camps do, but on a smaller scale. The 400th was not tested in its new role in the Gulf, but instead, performed other functions, including scouting for and evaluating possible EPW camp sites.

The 400th MP Battalion was the unit that actually established the camp at Hafr Al Batin, beginning construction on January 21, 1991, and completing its work on January 24. It then turned responsibility for the camp over to the next higher headquarters, the 301st MP Camp.

Army Reserve and Army National Guard units under the 301st, in addition to the 400th MP Battalion, were the 313th MP Prisoner of War Information Center (PWIC), an Army Reserve unit from Delbarton, W.Va. commanded by Lt. Col. George R. Busch, and nine MP companies (three USAR and six ARNG). The Army Reserve units were the 344th MP Co. (Escort Guard), New Haven Conn., commanded by Capt. Anthony V. Serrano; the 361st MP Co. (Guard), North Canton, Oh., commanded by Capt. Robin E. Brown; and the 304th MP Co. (Escort Guard), Bluefield, W.Va., commanded by Capt. Brett Starnes.[11]

401ST MP CAMP

The 401st MP Camp, Nashville, Tenn., was commanded by Col. Larry J. Stovall. It was mobilized on December 9, 1990, and performed its pre-deployment training at Fort Campbell, Ky. It arrived in theater on January 16, 1991, and was assigned the task of constructing and operating a 12,000-capacity EPW camp at As Sarrar, referred to by the Music City soldiers as "Al Opryland." Col. Stovall dispatched a portion of the unit to As Sarrar as soon as the 401st arrived in Saudi Arabia, and this ad-

11. Brinkerhoff, *800th MP Brigade*, pp. 29–30, 38.

vance party began construction of the camp on January 17. Assisted by Army engineers and quartermaster personnel, the 401st completed the first usable concertina wire enclosure on January 20. The remainder of the unit reached the site on January 25, and the pace of construction picked up considerably.

During the three months that it operated the camp, the 401st processed a total of 21,861 EPWs. It was also part of Task Force Rafha, which VIIth Corps set up to care for almost 21,000 displaced civilians, mostly Iraqi refugees, who flooded the area around Rafha Air Base.

Organizationally, the 401st commanded an MP battalion headquarters (the 193d, an ARNG unit from Golden, Colo.), two USAR MP companies: the 358th MP Co (Processing), Decatur, Ill., commanded by 1st Lt. Jeffrey M. Marsh, and the 342d MP Co (Escort Guard), Zanesville, Oh., commanded by Capt. Jeffrey D. Creed; and six Army National Guard MP companies. The 401st turned over control of Al Sarrar to the Saudis on April 21, 1991, left for the U.S. a month later, and was released from active duty on June 3.[12]

402D MP CAMP

The 402d MP Camp from Ashley, Pa., was commanded by Col. Wendell Rich. It was activated on January 3, 1991, and sent to Fort Pickett, Va., for mobilization processing. Arriving in theater on January 31, it got a later start than some of the other units under the 800th. Its main task was to construct and operate an EPW camp for VIIth Corp. Using only its own personnel and assets, the 402d constructed a 12,000 person camp in three weeks, a task which included laying concertina wire, installing lighting, building guard towers, and putting in a sanitation system.

Within a week, the camp held more than its rated capacity of prisoners. Despite difficulties brought on by having too few interpreters and obsolete delousing equipment, the 402d set a Desert Storm record by processing 1,925 EPWs during one particularly hectic 24-hour period. Altogether, the 401st processed 16,277 EPWs. The unit completed its mission by conducting EPW camp-operation training for a Saudi National Guard battalion. On 4 April, the camp was turned over to the Saudis. The 402d remained on station until May 6 in an advisory capacity, redeployed to the States on May 21, and was released from active duty on June 5. Reserve component

12. *Ibid.*, pp. 30–34.

units under the 402d were all from the Army National Guard, including an MP battalion headquarters (the 143d, San Mateo, Calif.) and nine MP companies.[13]

403D MP CAMP

The 403d MP Camp, commanded by Col. Carl D. Novak, was headquartered in Omaha, Neb. It had an assigned strength of some 300 soldiers. It was mobilized at Fort Riley, Kans., on December 10, 1990, and for the next month it prepared for overseas deployment. Among the activities undertaken at Fort Riley was a four-week 95B MOS course for members of the unit who had not completed advanced individual training (AIT) prior to the unit call-up.

Once it arrived in Saudi Arabia on January 15, the 403d was given the task of constructing a camp capable of holding 12,000 enemy prisoners, a mission for which it was not particularly well-suited. (The 403d, like the other MP camps, is designed to operate existing EPW encampments, not build new ones.) Nevertheless, the soldiers of the 403d did their best to build the camp, hindered as they attempted to do so by a lack of engineer support, low priority for essential materials such as concertina wire, and the failure of the unit's own TOE equipment to arrive from Fort Riley.

With assistance from the 864th Engineer Battalion, the MPs completed a site survey and began construction of the camp on January 25. The Reserve unit's efforts were greatly enhanced by the civilian skills of many of its members, including soldiers were trained as electricians, construction workers, carpenters, mechanics, and heavy equipment operators.[14] By February 17 the camp was ready and the first enemy prisoners were accepted. The camp was roughly 0.67 mile on a side and encompassed approximately 300 acres. In all, the 403d received 10,159 prisoners, and by the end of the war it was processing 1,400 prisoners per day—almost three times the brigade's goal of 500 per day. One of the factors that helped the 403d achieve such a high processing rate were the 45 Saudi (all volunteer) and 15 Kuwaiti interpreters who worked with the unit.[15]

---

13. *Ibid.*, pp. 41–44.

14. Bilbo, *Enemy Prisoners of War (EPW) Operations during Operation Desert Storm*, p. 47.

15. *AHS, 89th ARCOM*, pp. XII–1 thru XII–7; Brinkerhoff, *800th MP Brigade*, p. 25.

Other missions for the 403d included security functions in and around Dharan, Saudi Arabia. The first of these involved the mass evacuation of U.S. and Canadian civilians from Saudi Arabia. This operation, which took place during the period January 19–February 6, 1991, was accomplished without incident. A squad from the 257th MP Company (Guard) provided security for the movement of the evacuees from the U.S. Consulate to Dharan Air Base. The 346th MP Co (Escort Guard) provided security for the air base at Dharan from January 9–22, 1991, and the 213th MP Co (Guard) was responsible for VIP security at the 22d SUPCOM headquarters. The 403d departed Saudi on May 16, 1991, and returned to Fort Riley, where it spent a week processing out.[16]

400TH MP CAMP

The 400th MP Camp from Tallahassee, Fla., was commanded by Col. Timothy Kerns. It exemplifies what happened to a reserve unit that was mobilized late in the call-up, though the 400th was mobilized on the same date as the 402d MP Camp. The 400th was activated on January 3 and reported to Fort Stewart, Ga., on January 6. Pre-deployment training for the 400th was shorter than for many other units of its type—only 10 days. Unfortunately, that ten days ended on January 16, the day the air war began. The commencement of the air war changed the unit's priority for transport to the theater.[17]

The 400th reached Saudi Arabia and discovered that the support it was supposed to give to the 1st and 2d Marine Divisions was no longer needed. Furthermore, it could neither construct nor operate an EPW camp, because the unit's equipment—shipped by sea instead of by air, as originally planned—had not arrived in theater. What the soldiers of the 400th brought with them was what they had to work with.[18]

The 400th was reorganized into three task forces, which then took on special missions for the 800th. These missions included setting up and operating a makeshift EPW enclosure for the Marines and providing processing help to the 401st and 403d EPW Camps. The 400th gave up its EPW missions entirely in mid-March and took on other tasks such as customs inspection, area security, and law and order.[19]

---

16. *AHS, 89th ARCOM*, pp. XII–1 thru XII–7; Brinkerhoff, *800th MP Brigade*, pp. 35–36.
17. Brinkerhoff, *800th MP Brigade*, pp. 44–45.
18. *Ibid.*
19. *Ibid.*, p. 47.

The customs inspection duty became the most important one for the 400th, as it performed the job for the entire theater from April 15 to the end of redeployment. Working closely with both the U.S. Customs Service and the U.S. Department of Agriculture, the soldiers of the 400th ferreted out the illegal war souvenirs that GIs attempted to ship home. These prizes ran the gamut from the usual firearms and ammunition to indigenous snakes.[20]

The units under the 400th consisted of a battalion headquarters, the 34th MP Battalion Headquarters, ARNG, from Johnston, Ia.; one Army Reserve company: the 822d MP Company (Guard), Chicago, Ill., Capt. Jeffrey Sacks, commander; and eight Army National Guard companies.[21]

ADVISORY TEAMS; PROCESSING TEAMS

Two other types of Army Reserve units that came under the 800th were the Military Police Camp Advisory Teams and the Military Police Processing Advisory Team. Four of the former arrived in theater at the end of January 1991, just as the number of EPWs was increasing significantly. Their job was to help account for Iraqi prisoners and to advise the Saudis on EPW operations. The Camp Advisory Teams were the 346th from Nashville, Tenn.; the 439th from Omaha, Neb.; the 418th from Tallahassee, Fla.; and the 424th from Ashley, Pa. Another type of Army Reserve unit involved in this effort was the EPW Processing Advisory Team, of which there were three: the 498th from Nashville; the 440th from California; and the 446th from Inkster, Mich.[22]

Not only did the MPs have to construct the camps in which the enemy prisoners lived, they were responsible for guarding these prisoners and supplying them with food and water. Despite the number of reservists assigned to the EPW problem, the typical EPW camp of 500–1,000 prisoners had only three or four MPs per twelve-hour shift. Luckily, most of the Iraqi EPWs seem to have been relieved to have the war over and to have survived it, and to receive regular issues of food and water. They were simply not interested in escaping.[23]

20. *Ibid.*, pp. 47–48.

21. *Ibid.*, p. 46.

22. *Ibid.*, pp. 19–20.

23. The bizarre ways in which Iraqis surrendered are many: to a grounded pilotless reconnaissance vehicle, to individual members of the allied force, to an Italian television crew. These stories only serve to illustrate the fact that these were willing prisoners. "Iraqis Surrender to Italian TV," *New York Times*, February 28, 1991; Brinkerhoff, *800th MP Brigade*, p. 27.

The sheer number of prisoners taken by the coalition posed monumental feeding problems. The dietary rules of the Muslim prisoners were met by supplying U.S. Army rations in some instances, fresh foodstuffs in others. The feeding problem was eventually solved by contracting with a private company for 4.5 million German rations, with the Saudi government paying for the food. The Saudis also contracted for 50,000 sets of clothing for the EPWs, as well as for items such as prayer rugs—something for which the U.S. forces had not planned.[24]

However they came into U.S. hands, and however many prisoners there were, reserve component military police had the responsibility for processing and guarding them. Following established procedures for segregating different types of prisoners from each other, Army Reserve units like the 313th MP Company divided the Iraqis into different groups. Wrote SSgt. Mary Eads of the 313th, "We had the enlisted, non-commissioned officer, the Republican Guard, some civilian pro-Iraq workers . . . and the children." According to Eads, some of the Iraqis handed over to them for processing were as young as ten years old, and many were no more than fourteen or fifteen.[25] The 313th worked twenty-four hours a day processing Iraqi prisoners of war, and by the time the job was done, they had accounted for some 30,000 of the Iraqis who had fallen into U.S. hands.[26]

Despite its overall success, there were some problems with the EPW set-up, notably the failure of the theater logistics command to supply certain items that would have made the job much easier. Specifically, some reservists were told that they did not need to bring their HMMWVs or tactical radios with them, as they would "receive what they needed" after arriving in theater. This seems to have been a promise like "the check is in the mail," for the MPs were never issued the promised items.[27]

Nevertheless, the reserve MPs—both Army Reserve and Army National Guard—under the leadership of the 800th MP Brigade and the EPW Camps, were able to handle the masses

---

24. Brinkerhoff, *800th MP Brigade*, pp. 27–28.

25. It is entirely probable that the youngest of these "prisoners" were erroneously turned over to the MPs. Civilian internees (displaced civilian) were routinely placed in EPW camps, though they should not have been taken there. For a discussion of this problem in the after-action reporting see Bilbo, *Enemy Prisoners of War (EPW) Operations during Operation Desert Storm*, pp. 191–92.

26. Jack Gordon, "313th Military Police Company," *Checkerboard* (publication of the 99th ARCOM), Vol. 3, No. 2 (Spring, 1992), pp. 14–15.

27. Brinkerhoff, *800th MP Brigade*, pp. 62–63.

of Iraqi prisoners with few difficulties. That they could do so with little assistance from the active component was testimony to the maturity, ingenuity, and hard work of these reservists.[28]

The ability of the Reservists to accomplish their tasks despite handicaps was noted by Lt. Gen. Pagonis in his after-action report. "Since all engineer assets were totally committed elsewhere," stated the SUPCOM commander, "the 800th MP Brigade (EPW) actually constructed the EPW Camps they ran. This once again demonstrated the initiative and flexibility of this command."[29] An Army War College student who examined the handling of EPWs in the Gulf War concluded the following:

> Special recognition should be given the 800th Military Police Brigade (PW) whose officers, NCOs, and young soldiers, despite arriving in theater on the end of the Desert Shield deployments, in some cases without their equipment, overcame equipment shortages; transportation, logistical, and medical shortfalls; and apathetic personnel from myriad support agencies; and performed their theater EPW missions in a singularly outstanding manner![30]

Not all Army Reserve military police who became involved in the EPW mission served in the desert. The National Prisoner-of-War Information Center (NPWIC), for example, was staffed and run primarily by Army Reservists. Part V, Article 22 of the Third Geneva Convention requires that information on enemy prisoners be gathered, maintained, and forwarded through the International Committee of the Red Cross to the country from which these prisoners were captured. NPWIC, which is part of the Army's Office of the Deputy Chief of Staff for Operations (ODCSOPS), exists to fulfill that requirement.[31]

According to Col. Robert D. Pidgeon, NPWIC's chief during the Gulf War, the NPWIC was staffed entirely by Army Reserve Individual Mobilization Augmentees (IMAs). The IMAs devoted two week active duty tours to the center during the period from August 1990 to mid–January 1991. On January 16, the NPWIC went to full activation, with a staff of five Army Reserve officers, three Army Reserve NCOs, and one recalled retiree. The center continued to operate throughout the conflict, serving as the U.S. point of contact with the International Com-

28. *Ibid.*, p. 47.

29. Department of the Army, Headquarters, 22d Support Command, Executive Summary to the 22d Support Command After Action Report.

30. Bilbo, *Enemy Prisoners of War (EPW) Operations during Operation Desert Storm*, p. 102.

31. Robert G. Koval, "The National Prisoner-of-War Information Center," *Military Police*, June 1992, pp. 25–28.

mittee of the Red Cross, through which information on EPWs—U.S. and Iraqi—was exchanged by the two countries.[32]

Army Reserve MP units, like the 822d MP Company from Chicago, Ill., performed a variety of functions. Some members of the 822d performed perimeter security duties for U.S. troops billeted in the Khobar Towers area near Dharan, Saudi Arabia. Others were deployed as security for an aviation maintenance point, where, according to SSgt. Phil Roseman, "We would provide armed escorts for truck convoys to pick up crashed or battle damaged helicopters to be brought to the site." A third platoon from the 822d was sent out to do what the members of the 313th had spent their time doing: processing and guarding enemy prisoners. The company was finally brought back together in April 1991, when it was given a three-month task of providing departure services for U.S. troops departing Saudi Arabia.[33]

This was an interesting task, as Army authorities figured that many GIs would attempt to bring home war trophies. Some of these might be allowed, but explosives and weapons were definitely forbidden. As part of the country clearance process, soldiers were briefed on U.S. Department of Agriculture and U.S. Customs regulations about imports into the United States. They then entered an "amnesty box," where contraband could be discarded before they were searched. If there were no problems, they could proceed to the departure area.[34]

MILITARY INTELLIGENCE

The Army Reserve provides much of the augmentation that the Defense Intelligence Agency requires during a conflict. There are fifty-nine strategic intelligence detachments in the USAR, each one specializing in a particular subject or region. Three of these detachments—the 446th Military Intelligence Detachment (Strategic) of Allison Park, Pa.; the 480th MID(S) of Bloomington, Ind.; and the 484th MID(S) from Boston, Mass.—were called to duty for Desert Storm, the first time since 1961 that any of these detachments had been activated.[35]

---

32. Letter, Col. Robert D. Pidgeon to Lt. Col. James T. Currie, August 3, 1992, in possession of the author; Koval, "National Prisoner-of-War Information Center," pp. 27–28; see also, Brinkerhoff, *800th MP Brigade*, p. 13.

33. McChrystal, "Chicago-based MP unit tackles job after job in the desert," pp. 16–17.

34. *Ibid.*, p. 17.

35. John R. Brinkerhoff, *United States Army Reserve in Operation Desert Storm: Strategic Intelligence Support: Military Intelligence Detachments for the Defense Intelligence Agency* (Washington: Chief, Army Reserve, 1991), p. 1. Hereinafter cited as "Brinkerhoff, *Strategic Intelligence*."

The 446th is one of twenty-three Army Reserve strategic intelligence detachments with a CAPSTONE affiliation with the Defense Intelligence Agency. (The other thirty-six detachments are assigned to various CINCs, army schools, and the Army Intelligence command.) Having a mobilization mission with the Defense Intelligence Agency (DIA), the 446th has served with DIA during many annual training periods and specializes in the Middle East. [36]

The unit was activated on December 27, 1990, almost four months after the Iraqi invasion of Kuwait. Since the 446th's mission is to analyze the military strength and capabilities of countries in the Middle East, it seems reasonable to wonder why the 446th was not called to duty much earlier than late December. The story behind its late activation is instructive.[37]

DIA realized quite early that it needed the Reserve augmentation and requested such in August 1990. According to a study done for the Chief, Army Reserve, "DIA admits that there was an internal problem of not understanding how to request these units, and that time was lost in finding the proper channels." By September it had found the proper channels, but to no avail: the Department of the Army disapproved the request. A second DIA request in October was also disapproved by DA. The reason offered for the disapproval was that the Department of the Army was "giving priority to the request of the Theater Commander, and since these detachments were neither on the CINC's list nor slated for movement to the Persian Gulf, they were simply too low to be given any attention." It took a third DIA request—this time directly to the Vice Chief of Staff of the Army—before the approval to activate the units was finally granted.[38] This suggests that at least some parts of the mobilization system do not work as well as they might be expected to work. The lack of stress the activated Reservists would have placed on the Desert Shield logistics train seems to have been ignored by those who denied the initial activation requests.

The 446th finally reported for duty and its members discovered that the full-timers at DIA both welcomed them and accepted their contribution as intelligence professionals. As with the Army Reservists at MTMC, one of the keys to the good relationship between the 446th and the active duty and civil-

---

36. Brinkerhoff, *Strategic Intelligence*, pp. 1–2; Mark L. Geiger, "446th Military Intelligence Detachment," *Checkerboard* (publication of the 99th ARCOM), Vol. 3, No. 2 (Spring 1992), p. 23.

37. Brinkerhoff, *Strategic Intelligence*, pp. 2–3.

38. *Ibid.*, p. 2.

ian analysts at their mobilization site was the latter's knowledge of the Reservists and an appreciation of their ability.

According to Col. David Dragics, who commanded the 446th during this period, one of the greatest compliments the unit received was uttered by one of the full-time DIA analysts: "After a couple weeks, I forgot that your guys were reservists." It was also quite heady, commented Dragics, "to see some of your own analytical work in documents that went to the White House."[39]

The 480th MID(S), commanded by Col. Gary C. Steinhardt, was assigned the mission of preparing transportation and logistics studies on the Middle East. The versatility brought to the intelligence problem by its ten members is not atypical of the Army Reserve and was reflected in their foreign language capabilities: Arabic, French, German, Spanish, and Afrikaans. Once at DIA the 480th was put to work updating a ten-year old study of the highways in one of the countries in the region, a study which had been written originally by the 480th.

The 484th MID(S), commanded by Col. Bernard F. Wilkes, Jr., specializes in counterterrorism. Its ten members reported to DIA on January 3, 1991, and were immediately assigned to the Threat Analysis Section and the National Military Intelligence Center Terrorism Desk, where they worked twelve-hour shifts, seven days a week from January to April.[40]

One of the reasons for the successful experience of these three Army Reserve units was the caliber of the personnel in the units, whether measured by education, seniority, or time with the unit. Of the thirty-one members of the three units discussed above, thirteen had master's degrees and four had doctorates. The average time in service was 16+ years, and the average time with the detachment ranged from 5.8 years in the 446th to 9.3 years in the 480th. Such experience with one unit is scarcely possible in the active component, and only among the DIA civilians would such continuous attention to one region and specialty be found.[41]

Other Army Reserve intelligence units were sent to the Kuwaiti theater, with varying experiences. One of these, the 211th Military Intelligence Company of the 77th ARCOM, went on active duty on August 27, 1990. This was one of the first of the 77th's units to receive the call, and its members reported to Fort Dix, N.J., for a four-week refresher course that

39. Geiger, "446th Military Intelligence Detachment," p. 23.
40. Brinkerhoff, *Strategic Intelligence*, pp. 3–4.
41. *Ibid.*, p. 5.

concentrated on nuclear, biological and chemical (NBC) survival skills, weapons qualification, and MOS training.

The unit was soon sent to Riyadh, Saudi Arabia, where it performed a forty-seven day mission of counter-intelligence support within the theater. The unit did not have much to do, according to its commander, as it was given only "minor and makeshift missions." He attributed this lack of involvement to "Active Component skepticism of the Reserve Component's ability to perform its mission satisfactorily."[42] That may have been the case, or it may simply have been that there was little need for counterintelligence work in the theater at that time.

A totally different—and more positive—experience awaited the members of "C" Detachment, 24th Military Intelligence Battalion. This unit was alerted on January 12, 1991, and ordered to active duty just five days later. Its refresher training at Fort Dix was among the shortest accorded any deploying Army Reserve unit—only nine days—and it departed for Saudi Arabia before the end of January. Attached to the 513th Military Intelligence Brigade, it divided its forty-two personnel between the U.S. Army Forces Central Command (ARCENT) intelligence center and the U.S. Central Command (CENTCOM) Joint Imagery Production Center. In this latter operation the detachment's members operated experimental electronic imagery dissemination systems, performed imagery exploitation, and helped Army engineers update tactical maps of the Kuwait Theater of Operations. In one of the fine examples of reserve-active component cooperation, the unit's historian states that "C Detachment personnel had little difficulty integrating with the Total Force. . . ." The detachment left the theater of operations on March 21, 1991, and was returned to reserve status on April 1.[43]

CIVIL AFFAIRS

In 1991 almost all of the civil affairs personnel of the U.S. Army were (and still are as of 1996) in the Army Reserve, with the 172 active component soldiers greatly outnumbered by 4,650 Army Reservists. There is only one active duty civil affairs battalion—the 96th CA Bn at Fort Bragg. So it is almost always necessary to call upon the Army Reserve civil affairs specialists when there is a need for such activities. Desert Shield/Desert Storm would prove no exception.

---

42. *77th ARCOM.*
43. *Ibid.*

Army planners realized that civil affairs units should be on the list of early deployments to Saudi Arabia, but the CINC, Schwarzkopf, put his foot down and vetoed their deployment. According to one account of the decision process at Central Command headquarters, Schwarzkopf only wanted units "that could kill tanks." Civil affairs units did not perform this mission, so they were not in the initial wave of USAR units activated and deployed.[44] Another factor, identified by Gen. Wayne Downing, Commander of the U.S. Army's Special Operations Command, was that Schwarzkopf and his staff were not as comfortable with what civil affairs could do for them as were personnel in other commands. Said Downing, "A great gulf of knowledge existed there, and I think there are some lessons learned that we need to implement."[45]

A further reason for the failure to request early deployment of the reserve civil affairs units may have been a miscalculation on the part of the first civil affairs personnel on the scene. According to remarks delivered by Col. Lawrence C. Blount at the Fort Bragg civil affairs symposium in October 1991, part of the delay in calling up the Reserves lay with the 96th Civil Affairs Battalion. This unit had been deployed to Saudi Arabia in August 1990. The 96th's analysis, according to Blount, who served in CENTCOM headquarters during the conflict, "was that there wasn't much of a Civil Affairs mission" in the theater.[46]

By late fall, however, it became obvious that the liberation of Kuwait—and not just the defense of Saudi Arabia—would be the U.S. mission, and it was evident that civil affairs units would be required in theater.[47] On December 5 CENTCOM requested the call-up and deployment of all USAR civil affairs units. By the time the ground war against Iraq began on February 24, 1991, some 16 Army Reserve civil affairs units

44. Office of the Assistant Secretary of Defense for Special Operations and Low-Intensity Conflict, *Civil Affairs Gulf War Symposium—Read Ahead Documents*, pp. 41, 44; hereinafter cited as "OASD, SOLIC, *Civil Affairs*."

45. "Remarks by General Wayne Downing, Commander, U.S. Army Special Operations Command, for the Civil Affairs Symposium, October 26, 1991," in *Civil Affairs in the Persian Gulf War: A Symposium. Proceedings. October 25–27, 1991, U.S. Army JFK Special Warfare Center and School, Fort Bragg, North Carolina*, p. 59. Hereinafter cited as "*Civil Affairs Symposium Proceedings*."

46. "Civil-Military Operations during Operation Desert Shield/Storm from a USCENTCOM Perspective. Remarks Prepared by Col. Lawrence C. Blount," in *Civil Affairs Symposium Proceedings*, p. 229.

47. Blount, "Civil-Military Operations" in *Civil Affairs Symposium Proceedings*, p. 229.

had been activated and deployed to Saudi Arabia. Total civil affairs assets in theater at that time consisted of 136 active component members and 1,924 Army Reserve soldiers. This activation and deployment had not occurred, however, without considerable difficulties.[48]

VALIDATION AND PROCESSING

Civil affairs soldiers are part of the special operations forces (SOF) community, and they need to meet SOF standards for fitness. In coordination with FORSCOM, TRADOC, and HQDA, Brig. Gen. Joseph C. Hurteau, Commander of the USAR Special Operations Command (USARSOC), decided that the way to validate the preparedness Army Reservist civil affairs specialists was to have them mobilize at one location, and that location would be Fort Bragg, N.C.—home of the Army's special forces.[49]

This decision caused difficulty with the deploying units that had pre-positioned equipment elsewhere, and it caused problems for Fort Bragg, which had not anticipated a training requirement for the additional Reservists. With assistance from 56 members of the 351st Civil Affairs Command, which performed annual training at Fort Bragg to help with the SOF validation process, the testing and re-testing was eventually completed.[50]

Hurteau was determined that the Army Reservists would be as capable of taking care of themselves on the battlefield as any active component soldier, so each Reservist was tested in five areas: physical fitness, weapons qualification, basic soldier skills, specialty skills and leadership, and unit readiness.

Members of the Army Reserve had been taking the standard active Army physical fitness test since October 1983, when the USAR abandoned the 4-mile walk as the test of Reserve fitness.[51] These Reservists took the standard Army phys-

48. *Ibid.*, pp. 46–48.

49. *Ibid.*, p. 51; *Civil Affairs Symposium Proceedings*, p. 255. The one exception to the Fort Bragg mobilization was the use of Fort Meade, Md., for the 352d Civil Affairs Command.

50. John R. Brinkerhoff, *United States Army Reserve in Operation Desert Storm: Civil Affairs in the War with Iraq* (Washington: Office of the Chief, Army Reserve, 1991), p. 24; hereinafter cited as "Brinkerhoff, *Civil Affairs*;" Department of the Army, Headquarters, United States Army Civil Affairs and Psychological Operations Command (Airborne), "Civil Affairs Support to Operation Desert Storm," *Civil Affairs Symposium Proceedings*, p. 255.

51. Maj. Gen. William R. Berkman, "The Posture of the U.S. Army Reserve," testimony delivered before Congress, March 1984, pp. 31–32.

ical fitness test, the APFT, but Hurteau set a passing score of 70 points out of 100 points possible in each category (push-ups, sit-ups, and two-mile run) instead of 60. For a thirty year old Reservist this meant 48 push-ups, instead of 38; 52 sit-ups, instead of 42; and a two-mile run in 16:18, rather than 17:18. There was some doubt as to Hurteau's authority to increase the required scores, but his increases stood, nevertheless. In addition, the Reservists were required to complete a 10 kilometer road march in two hours, wearing BDUs and full combat gear, carrying a total of one-third of their body weight counting weapon and pack. Weapons qualification was accomplished on the automated range at Fort Bragg, and refresher training in basic soldier skills such as defense against chemical and biological warfare, was done on an individual basis.[52]

Even as soldiers were being tested in their particular specialty, the units and their commanders were themselves given a thorough review. As a result of this validation process, some eighty-five percent of the Reservists who reported to Fort Bragg were given a green light for deployment. The 276 unit members who did not meet the deployment standards were replaced by qualified Army Reservists from non-deploying CA units elsewhere in the force structure and by volunteers from the Individual Ready Reserve.[53]

The length of time consumed by the testing and validation process—some two weeks in most cases—meant that the supported active component units had already moved into their combat locations by the time the Reservists arrived in theater. This, in turn, meant that there was little time to get acquainted and establish good working relationships before the commencement of the ground war. This lack of familiarity may have led to some of the subsequent problems with misuse or lack of use of the civil affairs assets.[54]

EQUIPMENT SHORTAGES

Despite the funding given to the Army's reserve components in recent years, there are many areas where the reserves are not up to the level of the active component. Certain equipment shortages, for example, threatened to reduce the effectiveness of the civil affairs Reserve units.

The Army Reservists, for example, deployed in woodland (green, black, and brown) pattern BDUs, and they stood

---

52. DA Form 705 (May 1987); OASD, SOLIC, *Civil Affairs*, pp. 53–55.
53. OASD, SOLIC, *Civil Affairs*, pp. 53–55; Brinkerhoff, *Civil Affairs*, p. 27.
54. See Brinkerhoff, *Civil Affairs*, pp. 30–31.

out among the troops clad in desert camouflage. As one Reservist explained, "If anyone asks, we could just stand together and pretend we are an oasis." Joking aside, when the Reservists were supporting and working with a unit that wore the desert uniform, they felt very conspicuous and were instantly marked as late-arrivals and as Reservists. In many instances, they received their desert camouflage BDUs as they prepared to leave the theater.[55]

Likewise, the Army Reservists deployed with the weapons they had at their Reserve centers, and these were often the .45 caliber pistol and the M16A1 rifle, rather than the 9mm pistol and the M16A2 model. The Reservists' weapons were not the ones used by the active component, and the ammunition was different. Additionally, few Army Reserve units were equipped with the HMMWV, and the civil affairs Reservists were no exception. The Reservists were instead saddled with CUCVs, a somewhat-militarized version of the Chevrolet Blazer. Once in theater, the civil affairs teams discovered that the CUCVs simply could not keep up with the combat units they were supporting.[56]

Radios, too, were a problem for the Reservists, in that they had too few standard ones, and they had no secure voice communications. The 360th CA Brigade, for example, was responsible for supporting the XVIIIth Airborne Corps, but it had no means of communicating directly with the civil affairs companies supporting the divisions under the corps. Makeshift, jury-rigged, and off-the-shelf commercial communications gear got them through the problem, but the solution was far from ideal.[57]

Neither did the civil affairs units have the latest navigation equipment, such as the global positioning receivers that could instantly fix a location within a few yards. The Reservists were instead forced to rely upon compasses for desert navigation, and they experienced considerable difficulties in doing so.[58]

Finally, the Reserve civil affairs units did not even have all of their mission-essential gear, such as public address systems. These are absolutely vital if one is to broadcast surrender messages to the enemy, but there was such a shortage, that

55. *Ibid.*, p. 27.

56. *Ibid.*, pp. 27–28; "Experiences of the 450th Civil Affairs Company during the Persian Gulf War, and Lessons Learned," *Civil Affairs Symposium Proceedings*, p. 589.

57. Brinkerhoff, *Civil Affairs*, p. 28.

58. *Ibid.*

some of the units were issued Sony "boom boxes" with dual audio cassettes as a replacement for the standard equipment.[59]

COMMAND AND CONTROL

According to one of the studies of civil affairs operations during the Gulf War,

> The primary role of CA in Operation DESERT STORM was to support the combat elements of U.S. and coalition forces. CA units exist primarily for this purpose. The CA units help combat commanders to avoid problems due to local civilians, and they did this job well during their time in the desert. CA operations, however, were hampered by lack of overall direction and coherence. The doctrinal organization for combat support for CA calls for a theater-wide command which exercises some degree of influence over all functional activities within the theater. This was not achieved for CA during Operation DESERT STORM.[60]

There was, in fact, no theater-level civil affairs command during the Gulf War, despite doctrinal suggestions that such an arrangement would be the appropriate one. The ARCENT G–5, Col. James T. Kerr, realized that civil affairs was not going to be organized according to the book and decided on an ad hoc arrangement for the CA units—much as the logistical units were placed in an ad hoc organization under Pagonis.

Kerr decided that civil affairs command and control would be at corps level, rather than at the higher theater level. The two civil affairs brigades and their subordinate units were therefore attached to XVIIIth Airborne Corps and VIIth Corps. The brigades commanded the civil affairs companies, which were assigned direct support missions for the divisions. Additionally, the 304th Civil Affairs Company was attached to the 22d SUPCOM, and the 403d Civil Affairs Company was attached to the Marine Expeditionary Force. The active component 96th Civil Affairs Battalion assumed responsibility for civil affairs support to units outside the two designated corps.[61]

360TH CA BRIGADE

Col. Miller J. Love commanded the 360th Civil Affairs Brigade, of Columbia, S.C., which supported the XVIIIth Airborne

59. All of these equipment shortages are described in OASD, SOLIC, *Civil Affairs*, pp. 56–57 and in Brinkerhoff, *Civil Affairs*, pp. 27–29.
60. OASD, SOLIC, *Civil Affairs*, p. 61.
61. *Ibid*.

Corps. This brigade was the CAPSTONE civil affairs unit for the corps, meaning that it had worked extensively with the active duty headquarters prior to the beginning of Desert Shield. The familiarity bred by the CAPSTONE relationship resulted in much greater integration of the 360th into the Corps and suggests the value of the CAPSTONE concept. Assignment of the brigade headquarters and the companies to the various elements of the corps was as follows:

360th CA Bde HQ	Corps HQ
450th CA Co	82d Airborne Div
489th CA Co	101st Airborne Div (Air Assault)
422d CA Co	24th Inf Div
413th CA Co	1st Cav Div
407th CA Co	COSCOM

According to the authors of the civil affairs symposium materials, operations in support of XVIIIth Airborne Corps "were very successful. The Corps wanted a lot of CA help, and they were willing to provide vehicles, radios, and other equipment to their CA units."[62]

450TH CA COMPANY

The 450th CA Company from Riverdale, Md., performed one of the most remarkable feats of any civil affairs unit in the conflict. President George Bush's announcement that offensive operations against Iraqi units would cease on February 27 had come at a most inopportune time for Col. Glynn Hale, commander of the 3d Brigade, 82d Airborne Division. Hale wanted to seize Tallil airbase in southern Iraq, but the cessation order left him with few choices. He thereupon turned to the commander of the 450th CA Company, Lt. Col. King F. Davis, Jr., and established Task Force PSYOP, to which he gave the mission of capturing Tallil without violating the ceasefire. This JTF consisted of the 354th, a detachment from the 4th PsyOps Group, and some Kuwaiti interpreters.[63]

The Task Force moved surreptitiously into Tallil and seized the airport control tower. It then opened up on the Iraqis with loudspeakers. Though the initial Iraqi reaction was to fire on the Task Force members, clearer thinking led them

62. *Ibid.*, p. 63; "360th Civil Affairs Brigade Narrative, Operation Desert Shield/Desert Storm," *Civil Affairs Symposium Proceedings*, pp. 385–94.

63. "Experiences of the 450th Civil Affairs Company during the Persian Gulf War, and Lessons Learned," *Civil Affairs Symposium Proceedings*, p. 580.

either to surrender (which 52 did) or flee (which 100 did). Task Force PSYOP took complete control of the airbase, capturing in one swoop—and without firing a single weapon—some twenty Iraqi jet aircraft, five attack helicopters, and tons of ammunition and other supplies.[64]

354TH CA BRIGADE

The 354th Civil Affairs Brigade was a replacement for the 308th Civil Affairs Group, which was not activated because of "low readiness scores." The 354th, commanded by Col. Robert H. Beahm, supported VII Corps during Operation Desert Storm and then went on to participate in Operation Provide Comfort, the Kurdish relief effort. The 354th had not been CAPSTONE to the VII Corps, and the active duty units in the corps were not familiar with what civil affairs could do for them. As a result, "Civil affairs operations in support of VII Corps were only moderately successful. The VII Corps units did not provide their supporting CA units with vehicles, radios, or other equipment and supplies. In some cases, the CA units were allowed to take only 30%–40% of their people along on the movement into Iraq." Organization in support of the VII Corps was as follows:

354th CA Bde HQ	VII Corps HQ
418th CA Co	1st Inf Div
401st CA Co	1st Arm Div
404th CA Co	3d Arm Div
414th CA Co	COSCOM[65]

304TH CA GROUP

The 304th Civil Affairs Group, from Philadelphia, Pa., was commanded by Col. Robert J. Mitkus. This unit had participated in numerous exercises in the Middle East, and was mobilized at its home station in late December 1990. Most aspects of the mobilization went as expected, but the necessity of loading the 304th's 2½ ton trucks onto flatbed trailers for transport to Fort Bragg revealed an unexpected problem: the unit had no loading ramps that could support a truck of this

64. *Ibid.*, p. 581.

65. OASD, SOLIC, *Civil Affairs*, p. 64; "354th Civil Affairs Brigade, Operations Desert Storm and Provide Comfort," *Civil Affairs Symposium Proceedings*, pp. 347–48.

size. The required ramps were eventually located, however, and the unit proceeded to North Carolina.[66]

Part of the inprocessing at Fort Bragg, as mentioned previously, was a determination of deployability. In the case of this unit, 13 individuals—including the group's command sergeant major and its operations sergeant—were found to be undeployable for medical reasons. Added to members who had been declared non-deployable while at home station, the 304th lost almost 20 percent of its assigned personnel before departing for Saudi Arabia.[67]

The 304th reached Saudi Arabia on January 20 and 21, 1991, and was assigned to provide civil affairs support to the 22d SUPCOM.[68] The 304th worked on laundry, shower, and mail facilities with the Saudis, as well as on ramp space for coalition aircraft and warehouse space for everything from medical supplies to captured enemy weapons. The 304th assisted with the redeployment of U.S. units after the end of the war and finally left Saudi Arabia on May 10, leaving behind a 16-member group of volunteers. The majority of the unit reached Fort Bragg on May 11, devoted eight days to outprocessing, and returned to Philadelphia. [69]

Civil affairs units like the 304th and the 354th performed a variety of functions for the combat and logistical units they supported. Such activities included coordination and negotiation with local and Red Crescent officials, managing host nation support, locating sources of drinking water, interviewing Iraqi prisoners of war, diverting dislocated civilians so they

66. "Synopsis of the Mobilization and Deployment of the 304th Civil Affairs Group in Support of Operations Desert Shield/Desert Storm (27 Dec '90—3 Jun '91)," *Civil Affairs Symposium Proceedings*, p. 399.

67. *Ibid.*, pp. 399–400. This impresses the author as an unusually large percentage for any Army Reserve unit. In each unit in which the author has served, there are always a few individuals who are capable of doing their jobs and contributing to the unit in peacetime, but who would never be sent overseas, particularly in wartime. According to testimony given to Congress, "Less than one percent of the drilling Reservists and Guardsmen (Selected Reserve) called to active service were sent home because of physical or mental disability." Answer to question for the record submitted by Christopher Jehn, Assistant Secretary of Defense for Force Management and Personnel, testifying before the Subcommittee on Defense, Appropriations Committee, United States House of Representatives, 102d Congress, 1st session, *Department of Defense Appropriations for 1992, Part 3*, p. 310.

68. *Ibid.*, p. 395.

69. Brinkerhoff, *Civil Affairs*, pp. 37–38; "Synopsis of the Mobilization and Deployment of the 304th Civil Affairs Group in Support of Operations Desert Shield/Desert Storm (27 Dec '90—3 Jun '91," *Civil Affairs Symposium Proceedings*, pp. 412–13.

would not be in the way of U.S. combat operations, inspecting food and water, and persuading Iraqi soldiers to surrender. While certain of these activities—such as the care and feeding of displaced civilians—falls under the heading of "classic" civil affairs operations, some others clearly did not. The CA specialists did them, however, because they needed to be done and because they possessed the skills to do them.[70]

KUWAIT TASK FORCE

The Kuwait Task Force (KTF) was also staffed with individuals from the Army Reserve civil affairs community, specifically the 352d Civil Affairs Command and the 354th Civil Affairs Brigade. The idea for the Kuwait Task Force began with the Kuwaitis themselves, who foresaw a need for assistance in rebuilding their country once the Iraqis were evicted from it.[71]

Money was clearly no limitation for the Kuwaiti government; availability of technical assistance was the limiting factor. A Washington-based task force from the emir's government learned of the abilities of the Army's civil affairs units in September 1990—months before the liberation of their country from its Iraqi invaders—and immediately asked for a briefing on civil affairs capabilities.[72]

The October 4, 1990, briefing for the Kuwaitis was also attended by Edward Gnehm, newly-designated U.S. ambassador to Kuwait, and by Lt. Gen. Thomas W. Kelly, the J–3 on the Joint Staff. Following the briefing, the Kuwaitis formally requested U.S. government assistance in the forthcoming reconstruction of their country. This request set in motion the process which led through the twists and turns of the DoD bureaucracy, to the Deputies Committee of the National Security Council, and finally to a November 22, 1990, message from the Chairman of the Joint Chiefs of Staff to the Chief of Staff of the Army and Commander, Special Operations Command to activate elements of the 352d Civil Affairs Command to form the Kuwait Task Force.

The task force came into existence on December 1, when 38 Army Reservists from the 352d Civil Affairs Command and 18 Army Reservists from the 354th Civil Affairs Brigade reported for duty and were in-processed at Fort Meade, Md.

70. OASD, SOLIC, *Civil Affairs*, pp. 65–70.

71. "The Kuwait Task Force," *Civil Affairs Symposium Proceedings*, pp. 263–64.

72. *Ibid.*, p. 263.

The Task Force went through a rocky start when its commander, Brig. Gen. Howard T. Mooney (Commander of the 352d Civil Affairs Command), was ordered to active duty, then immediately released. The reasons for this change in plans have not been adequately explained, and the author's efforts to solve the mystery have been unsuccessful.[73] Mooney was replaced as commander of the KTF by the 352d's Deputy Chief of Staff for Operations, Col. Randall Elliott.[74]

The KTF worked closely with members of the Kuwaiti government, in the areas of public safety, public health, public works and utilities, transportation, communications, and public welfare. The Task Force sent daily reports to CENTCOM on its work, and CENTCOM was represented on the Steering Group Committee, a sub-unit of the National Security Council's Deputies Committee, which provided guidance to the rebuilding effort. There was, however, no actual liaison officer from CENTCOM, though the command was invited to have someone work with the Task Force.[75]

As with other Army Reserve civil affairs soldiers, the members of the KTF were required to pass the SOF physical qualification standards. All but one of the reservists assigned was able to do, and the task force—now 63 in number—departed for Saudi Arabia on January 29, 1991. Upon arrival, its initial efforts were directed at assisting the Kuwaiti government contract for services to be performed after the Iraqis were driven out. The members of the Task Force helped the Kuwaitis arrive at specifications for work to be done, reviewed contracts, and advised on the merits of the proposals made by the prospective contractors. The Kuwait Task Force remained in country until May 1991, at which time it disbanded and returned to the U.S. It eventually assisted the Kuwaiti government in issuing some 271 contracts worth $685 million.[76]

One of these contracting areas was oilwell firefighting, and in this arena the KTF showed the value of the widespread experience of the members of the Army Reserve. Maj. Tom

---

73. Discussions with some of the individuals involved in the decision have only led to contradictory assertions, none of which are supported by adequate documentation.

74. According to Brinkerhoff, the Vice Chief of Staff of the Army, Gen. Gordon Sullivan, ordered Mooney off of active duty because his activation had not been blessed by the Army Chief of Staff. See Brinkerhoff, *Civil Affairs*, p. 47.

75. OASD, SOLIC, *Civil Affairs*, pp. 77, 74, 79.

76. *Ibid.*, pp. 77, 80–81; "Kuwait Task Force," *Civil Affairs Symposium Proceedings*, pp. 265–67.

Wilson, one of the soldiers in the task force, was a senior official of Hunt Oil. Wilson knew the oil well fire fighters in the United States, and he was one of those who helped the Kuwaiti government address the problem.[77]

COMBINED CIVIL AFFAIRS TASK FORCE (CCATF)

The idea of forming the Combined Civil Affairs Task Force (CCATF) originated within the ARCENT G–5 with the realization that there would be a significant relief effort once Kuwait was liberated. This effort resulted in the establishment on February 14, 1991, of the CCATF, with Brig. Gen. Howard T. Mooney, commander of the 352d Civil Affairs Command, as its leader. The CCATF consisted of Mooney's 352d Civil Affairs Command (−), the 431st CA Company of Little Rock, Ark., the 432d CA Company of Green Bay, Wisc., and the Kuwait Task Force. Parts of the active component 96th CA Bn were placed in direct support.[78]

The primary function of the CCATF was to assist the Kuwaiti government provide for the immediate, short-term needs of its citizens, and in this endeavor the CCATF was quite successful. It arranged for food, water, and medical supplies and worked with the Kuwaitis to provide transportation to deliver the items as they were purchased.[79] In addition, most of the work of the Kuwait Task Force ultimately came under the control of the CCATF.[80]

CIVIL AFFAIRS CONCLUSION

It is apparent that the civil affairs work of the Army Reservists, to include the Kuwait Task Force, was a success story. It is also apparent from reading the extensive materials put together by the Reserve civil affairs community for its post-war symposium at Fort Bragg, that there is a certain amount of resentment among the Reservists at the way the active component treated them. The failure to allow the reserve civil affairs

77. "Kuwait Task Force," *Civil Affairs Symposium Proceedings*, p. 269.

78. Brinkerhoff, *Civil Affairs*, pp. 53–54; "Combined Civil Affairs Task Force," *Civil Affairs Symposium Proceedings*, pp. 294–95.

79. *Ibid.*; "Combined Civil Affairs Task Force, Operations Desert Shield/Storm, After Action Report," *Civil Affairs Symposium Proceedings*, pp. 284–315.

80. "Combined Civil Affairs Task Force," *Civil Affairs Symposium Proceedings*, pp. 297.

general officers, particularly generals Hurteau and Mooney, to perform active duty without considerable machinations, and the poor use of reserve civil affairs assets by some of the active army commanders both point to a "we versus them" problem that needs to be addressed by all concerned.[81]

81. It should be noted that after being removed from command of the Kuwait Task Force, Brig. Gen. Mooney remained commander of the 352d Civil Affairs Command. In this capacity he was placed on various forms of active duty, including annual training and active duty for special work (ADSW), until he was finally ordered to active duty with the remaining members of the 352d on January 25, 1991, to command the Combined Civil Affairs Task Force. Even then, says the report, "it took . . . special pressure . . . by the Joint Staff and OSD . . . to get General Mooney on active duty." OASD, SOLIC, *Civil Affairs*, p. 79.

18

Desert Shield/Desert Storm: Working with U.S. Soldiers

PERSONNEL SERVICES

Personnel, postal, and data processing units were a vital part of Desert Shield/Desert Storm. Additional reserve personnel support of the active component units deployed to Saudi Arabia was not generally required because these units had their own personnel support, and personnel actions in wartime are not much different from peacetime operations. There were exceptions, however. One of these was the 425th Personnel Services Company, an Army Reserve unit from Indianapolis, Ind., that was mobilized in support of XVIII Corps and assigned to the 18th Personnel Group.[1]

The 425th was not employed as a unit, but was broken up, and its members were used as fillers for other units. Among the soldiers of the 425th, some 26 were trained as truck drivers and were used to transport soldiers from the airport; 25–30 were sent to KKMC to work casualties; still others were sent to Dharan as fork lift operators to help move the massive amounts of mail that poured into the theater. In short, the 425th lost its unit identity, and the company commander and first sergeant had a most difficult time maintaining contact with their soldiers.[2]

There was considerable dissension within the unit and complaints of favoritism by the unit's leadership. Problems escalated to the point where the 123d ARCOM sent an inves-

1. "Personnel Services," Chapter 3 of ANDRULIS Research Corporation's draft manuscript *Personnel Service Support*, p. 3–7. Manuscript prepared for the Chiefs, Army Reserve.

2. *Ibid.*

tigative team, and after the unit returned to Indianapolis, there was further investigation. As a result, the commander, XO, sergeant major and first sergeant were relieved.[3]

Though most of the deploying active component units required little Army Reserve augmentation in the personnel services area, this was not the case at echelons above corps nor with one of the Army Reserve major commands that was deployed to Saudi Arabia. The 10th Personnel Command, Provisional, for example, depended upon the 324th AG Personnel & Administration Battalion from Livingston, Ala., the 344th AG Data Processing Unit from Fort Belvoir, Va., the 701st AG Company, Personnel Services, from Ada, Okla., and the 815th AG Company, Personnel Services, from Orangeburg, S.C.[4]

The 10th PERSCOM was the theater's personnel command. It was organized with a nucleus of active component soldiers, augmented with large numbers of personnel from the Army Reserve. Of its 476 members, 18 were from the Third Army AG section, 150 were from the 701st Personnel Services Company, 100 were USAR filler personnel, an additional 100 were active component fillers, 46 came from the 324th Personnel & Administration Batttalion, and 22 others were USAR troop unit personnel. The 815th PSC operated the theater's personnel locator and performed certain casualty operations. The 351st Postal Company was theater locator for misdirected mail, and the 344th DPU operated the personnel data base.[5] The 344th was cited by Lt. Gen. Yeosock for its "development of casualty accounting and reporting software, supporting operation of an intertheater personal computer/remote job entry data transmission facility and a substantial amount of programming."[6] (Another data processing unit that deployed to Southwest Asia was the 324th Data Processing Unit from New Bedford, Mass.)[7]

Seven other Army Reserve personnel service companies were mobilized for DS/DS but never left the U.S. These include the 244th AG Personnel Service Company (PSC) D from Fort Douglas, Utah, the 389th AG PSC C from Starkville, Miss., the 408th AG PSC E from Fort Totten, N.Y., the 430th AG

3. *Ibid.*, pp. 3–8 through 3–9.

4. *Ibid.*, p. 3–9.

5. *Ibid.*, p. 3–13.

6. Citation awarded by U.S. Army Forces Central Command, hanging in the J.S. Mosby USAR Center, Fort Belvoir, Va.

7. John R. Brinkerhoff, *United States Army Reserve in Operation Desert Storm: The Signal Support Dilemma: The 335th Signal Command* (Washington: Office of the Chief, Army Reserve, 1992), pp. 31; hereinafter cited as "Brinkerhoff, *Signal Support.*"

(PSC) C from Wichita, Kans., the 461st AG (PSC) F from East Point Ga., the 478th AG (PSC) D from Chicago, Ill., and the 678th AG (PSC) D from Nashville, Tenn. These and other units that were never officially mobilized for DS/DS played vital roles in the Desert Shield/Desert Storm success.[8]

For example, members of the 430th AG Personnel Service Company performed what was termed "an extended AT" at Fort Riley, beginning on December 15, 1990. In less than six weeks these individuals helped process 11,000 soldiers of the 1st Infantry Division for deployment to Saudi Arabia. The 430th itself was mobilized on January 25 and joined its unit members at Fort Riley. While at Fort Riley the 430th manned the Reserve Deployment Support Unit and out-processed returning Army Reserve personnel.[9]

The 678th Personnel Service Company was alerted in November, but only 50 of the unit were placed on active duty at that time. These 50 soldiers were sent to Fort Bragg, where they joined what remained of the 572d Personnel Service Company, an active component outfit. The 572d (augmented) was attached to the 18th Personnel and Administration Battalion's Rear Detachment, the commander of which departed shortly for maternity leave. The commander of the 678th, Maj. Bill Banks, was then named Rear Detachment commander. On February 15, 1991, the other members of the 678th were mobilized and joined their fellow unit members at Fort Bragg.[10]

RECEPTION AND REPLACEMENT CENTERS

As part of the plan for augmenting the force in Southwest Asia, the Army called-up thousands of members of the Individual Ready Reserve (IRR). The story of the IRR call-up is recounted in Chapter 21. What is related here is the story of the Army Reserve units that were mobilized to assist with this call-up.

First, the Army Reserve furnished reception battalions that were mobilized to process and assign incoming trainees at the training centers. Five of these reception battalions were part of the training divisions or maneuver training commands, while two others were separate units. The 1018th AG Reception Battalion (AGRB) was part of the 78th Training Division, the 3398th AGRB was from the 108th Training Division, the 4073d AGRB was from the 95th Training Divison, and the

8. "Personnel Services," *Personnel Service Support*, p. 3–14.
9. *AHS, 89th ARCOM*, pp. X–57 thru X–58.
10. "Personnel Services," *Personnel Service Support*, p. 3–15.

5089th AGRB from the 70th Training Division, and the 100th AGRB, which was part of the 100th Maneuver Training Command. In addition, there were two AG reception battalions—the 387th, which worked at Fort Leonard Wood, Mo., and the 402d, which worked at Fort Sill, Okla.—that were stand-alone units, not part of either training divisions or maneuver training commands.[11]

The work of these reception battalions was augmented by the efforts of the replacement battalions, which also came from the Army Reserve. One of these, the 387th AG Replacement Battalion, reported to Fort Leonard Wood, Mo., on January 26, 1991. Its job was to process Army Reservists from the Individual Ready Reserve (IRR) who had reported to Fort Leonard Wood for refresher training prior to overseas deployment. The 387th performed this mission for some 1,200 IRR soldiers on their way to Southwest Asia. When the soldier stream was reversed, the 387th out-processed 2,400 soldiers who passed through the post on their return from active service during Desert Shield/Desert Storm. The 387th received the Superior Unit award for its efforts.[12]

The 381st Replacement Battalion, another Army Reserve unit, was activated on January 22, 1991, and reported to Fort Sill, Okla., on January 25. This unit, commanded by Lt. Col. Gary Mann, was completely integrated into the adjutant general section at Fort Sill and worked on both replacements for Desert Storm and on the usual active component replacement soldiers passing through Fort Sill. According to the unit administrator, the Reservists and soldiers of the active component worked well together without noticeable difficulties.[13]

These IRR soldiers required refresher training and this is where the Army Reserve training divisions performed their mission. All of the Army's training divisions are in the Army Reserve force structure, so it was not surprising that some of these units were activated for Desert Shield/Desert Storm. Indeed, parts of the 70th, 78th, 80th, 84th, 85th, 98th, and 100th Divisions were activated during the course of DS/DS and sent to stateside posts ranging from Fort Benning, Ga., to Fort Dix, N.J. In most instances these soldiers provided training for members of the Individual Ready Reserve who had been called to active duty; in some cases the war ended before the

11. "Personnel Replacement Operations," Chapter 7 of ANDRULIS Research Corporation's draft study entitled *Personnel Service Support*, p. 7–12.

12. *Ibid.*, p. 7–13.

13. *Ibid.*

trainers could properly begin their work at the posts to which they were assigned.[14]

CONUS REPLACEMENT CENTERS

Finally, the Army established three CONUS Replacement Centers (CRCs) that processed the soldiers who were trained and validated at the reception and training stations and sent them off to the theater of war. These CRCs, which handled only individual replacements, and not units that were moving overseas, were established at Fort Benning, Ga., Fort Jackson, S.C., and Fort Knox, Ky. The CRC at Fort Benning was the place through which passed individuals in the rank of colonel and above, some civilians, aviators, and medical personnel. It was also the CRC of choice for combat arms replacements. Fort Jackson was the CRC designated for female soldiers and civilians. And Fort Knox took overflow loads from Forts Benning and Jackson. All of the units that operated the CRCs were from the Army Reserve.[15]

The Fort Benning CRC was operated by the 347th AG Battalion HHD, Personnel & Administration, from Marion, Ill. The 347th was mobilized on December 27, 1990, and reached Fort Benning three days later. Following thirty days of training, the Reservists took over the CRC from the active component personnel who had been operating it. At its most active, the 347th commanded five Army Reserve replacement companies: the 415th from Bell, Calif.; the 235th from Redmond, Wa.; the 403d from Punxatawny, Pa.; the 412th from Pascagoula, Miss.,; and the 813th from Gordo, Ala. It also commanded an active component provisional replacement company that had been put together at Fort Benning.[16]

The mission of the 347th and the companies under its command was to schedule and coordinate the processing of the soldiers who passed through Fort Benning on the way to an Aerial Port of Embarkation (APOE), which for Fort Benning was Charleston Air Force Base, S.C. The Reservists assigned to this mission handled 1,000–1,200 replacements per week, providing such services to them as scheduling medical and dental ap-

14. Information Paper, DAAR–FMF, Lt. Col Fritz, February 9, 1991, Subject: USAR Training Units Activated for Desert Storm, copy in DS/DS files, USACMH; Capt. Loren J. Dathe, "3d Bde, 70th Division (Training) Mobilization Narrative." Copy in possession of the author.

15. "Personnel Replacement Operations," *Personnel Service Support*, p. 7–14.

16. *Ibid.*, pp. 7–14 and 7–15.

pointments and issuing clothing and equipment. The Reservists at Fort Benning reported excellent cooperation with the active component commander and soldiers with whom they worked. The 347th remained on active duty until long after the war had ended, returning to its home in Marion, Ill., on May 15.[17]

The 326th AG Battalion HHD, Personnel & Administration, from Fort Benjamin Harrison, Ind., was under the command of Lt. Col. Timothy R. Love. It was mobilized on December 27, 1990, reported to Fort Knox, Ky., on December 30, and took over operation of the Fort Knox CRC the next day. The 326th commanded five replacement companies: the 221st from Lake Charles, La.; the 413th from Forest Park, Ill.; the 800th from Tulsa, Okla.; the 801st from Antlers, Okla.; and the 978th from Oak Ridge, Tenn.[18]

Processing activities at Fort Knox were similar to those at Fort Benning. The Fort Knox experience was normally a four-day one. Day one was devoted to issuing protective masks and organizational clothing and equipment; day two saw the soldiers testing masks, undergoing NBC training and zeroing weapons; day three was packing and shipping of hold baggage and receiving a myriad of briefings, including familiarization with Saudi customs and the Geneva Convention; day four was devoted to drawing weapons and being transported to the airield for the journey to Southwest Asia. During their four months or so at Fort Knox the members of the 326th and its subordinate units processed a total of 4212 replacement soldiers.[19]

The Reservists running the CRC's encountered a number of difficulties in accomplishing what should have been the fairly routine task of verifying the Soldier Readiness Program status of the individual[20] and issuing items needed for combat. The first problem was that many soldiers reached the CRC without having completed the checklist. That meant that the Reservists running the CRC had to assist the soldier in making the necessary financial, legal, and other arrangements. In addition, there were shortages of required equipment at the replacement centers. Body armor, for example, was in very short supply, as were protective masks and certain weapons such as the squad automatic weapon (SAW). The TRADOC study of

17. *Ibid.*, pp. 7–17 and 7–18.

18. *Ibid.*, pp. 7–18 and 7–15.

19. *Ibid.*, p. 7–18 and 7–20.

20. The Soldier Readiness Program (SRP) was the new term for the more familiar Preparation for Overseas Replacement (POR). It involved verification of the existence of a will, power of attorney, dental record and immunizations, and family care plan if necessary.

mobilization points out that these problems—which partly stemmed from disagreements about funding—would have been much more easily solved if President Bush had declared a full mobilization. "With the declaration of full mobilization, a host of legalities and constraints would have been removed or ceased; mobilization short of full required more expedients."[21]

One of the other significant problems at the CONUS Replacement Centers was that there were certain ambiguities in the chain of command. According to the official TRADOC history, "Those personnel who were actually operating the replacement centers had no idea who was in charge above them as each higher headquarters—the Department of the Army, the Personnel Command, the Forces Command, TRADOC, and the Health Services Command—acted as if it was. All three replacement centers reported receiving guidance from each headquarters, all authoritative and all conflicting."[22]

REPLACEMENT OPERATIONS IN SWA

Replacement soldiers entering Saudi Arabia likewise required managing as they were moved to their ultimate unit of assignment. These activities were under the control of personnel groups: the 3d Personnel Group for echelons above corps, the 7th AG HHD Personnel Group for VII Corps, and the 18th Personnel Group for XVIII Corps. Under the 3d Personnel Group, an active component headquarters from Fort Hood, Tex., was the 386th AG HHD Personnel & Administration Battalion, an Army Reserve unit from Starkville, Miss. The 386th was given the EAC personnel replacement mission and had under its command four personnel replacement companies: three from the active component, and one Army Reserve unit, the 875th AG Replacement Company from Fort Dodge, Iowa.[23]

The 386th had a challenging assignment, as it was neither trained nor configured as a replacement battalion headquarters. It also faced the challenge of having been deployed at 80% of authorized strength and never reached full strength its entire time in theater. The 386th had been activated on November 28, 1990, and arrived at Camp Shelby, Miss., on December 9 for its pre-deployment training and processing. It only devoted ten days to this phase of its active duty assignment and arrived in Saudi Arabia on December 21.[24]

---

21. Canedy *et al., TRADOC Support*, pp. 35–36.
22. *Ibid.*, pp. 32–33.
23. *Ibid.*, p. 7–21.
24. *Ibid.*, pp. 7–22 and 7–23.

The 386th and its subordinate replacement companies were responsible for taking care of incoming units and individuals until they were shipped out to their assigned headquarters duty station. For units, this meant telling the gaining headquarters that they had arrived and arranging transportation to the assigned location. The battalion and its companies met individual replacements, in-processed them, arranged for orders, fed and housed them, and set up transportation to take them to their assigned unit.[25]

The 194th Replacement Company, an Army Reserve unit from Lake Charles, La., was activated on December 7, 1990, and arrived in Saudi Arabia later that month. It was soon assigned to the 7th Personnel Command of VII Corps and was placed in charge of processing all individual replacements for the Corps. During the period January 29–February 28, 1991, the 194th handled some 5,200 corps replacements.[26] It was released from active duty in Lake Charles on May 7, 1991.

The 18th Personnel Group was the personnel headquarters under XVIII Corps. Its replacements were handled by two companies: the active component 19th from Fort Bragg and the 460th AG Replacement Company, a USAR unit from Florence, S.C. The 19th was augmented by several dozen soldiers from the 425th Personnel Service Company, an Army Reserve unit from Indianapolis, Ind., that had been assigned to XVIII Corps.[27]

Altogether, the Army Reserve personnel units played vital roles in the processing of individual soldiers and units that were sent to Southwest Asia. They were also part of the reception operation at the receiving end, handling both reserve and active component personnel. Though there were some misunderstandings between active and reserve troops, this part of DS/DS seems to have been relatively free of the friction that characterized other areas.

POSTAL SERVICES

One of the keys to the morale of any United States military force deployed abroad is the prompt delivery of the mail. Within the Army, the postal service is a responsibility of the Adjutant General Corps and the soldiers working in that specialty. At the time of Desert Shield, the active component of the Army contained

25. *Ibid.*, pp. 7–23 and 7–24.
26. *Ibid.*, p. 7–26 and 7–27.
27. *Ibid.*, pp. 7–21, 7–25, and 7–26.

12 postal companies, all of them of the direct support(DS)type. Ten of these companies were so committed to forces in either Europe or Korea that they could not be deployed to Southwest Asia. This meant that if the mail were to be delivered to soldiers mobilized and sent to the Persian Gulf region, reserve component postal companies would have to be called up.[28]

ARMY RESERVE POSTAL COMPANIES

Of the 18 postal companies in the reserve components in 1990—16 in the USAR and 2 in the ARNG—12 were mobilized. Eleven of these were sent to Southwest Asia, and 1—the 329th AG Company GS Postal, from Fort Snelling, Minn.—was sent to Fort Dix, N.J.[29] Nine of the companies sent to SWA were from the USAR, where they, the two active component postal companies, and the two companies from the Army National Guard, handled the mail.[30]

Included in the unprecedented volume of mail sent to the Gulf—approximately 1.88 pounds per day per soldier—were the millions of "Any Soldier" letters and parcels that began arriving almost as soon as the first troops deployed overseas. Minimal restrictions on the size and weight of packages that could be sent to those serving in Southwest Asia also increased the parcel flow.[31] There were also problems with units that changed Army Post Office (APO) numbers as they moved about the theater. Each unit was assigned an APO number as it initially deployed. It should have kept this same number throughout their time overseas, but some of them did not do so. Some units apparently thought that when they were reassigned they should adopt the APO of the parent headquarters. This confused mail delivery and caused tremendous problems in getting mail to the troops in a timely fashion.[32]

---

28. "Military Postal Service," Chapter 5 of the ANDRULIS Research Corporation's draft study, *Personnel Service Support*, pp. 5–3 and 5–5.

29. *Ibid.*, pp. 5–5, 5–8 and 5–9.

30. *Ibid.*, p. 5–9 and 5–23. The USAR direct support postal companies mobilized and sent to Southwest Asia were the 300th from Chicago, Ill., the 312th from Charlotte, N.C, the 320th from Cincinnati, Oh., the 336th from Muscle Shoals, Ala., the 341st from Athens, Ga., the 351st from Tallahassee, Fla., the 834th from Coral Gables, Fla., the 755th from Texarkana, Tex., and the 795th from Richards-Gebaur AFB, Mo.

31. *Ibid.*, pp. 5–8 and 5–10.

32. *Ibid.*, p. 5–21.

Indeed, the problems of mail delivery became so acute that there was a Congressional hearing on the issue.[33] The immense quantities of mail sent to and from the Persian Gulf region simply overwhelmed the Army postal system, despite the best efforts of the postal companies there.

The 834th Postal Company, from Coral Gables, Fla., was commanded by Capt. David D. Meek. It was assigned to one of the hubs of the entire theater mail distribution system: the entry point at Dharan. The members of the 834th, who worked this location with assistance from one other postal company, were responsible for sorting the mailbags by APOs and directing them to the proper unit. The quantity of mail that arrived at this location was huge: 250,000 pounds in one day was not unusual. A mail-sorting backlog developed, and the situation became so critical as Christmas approached that 100 additional soldiers were pressed into service as mail handlers, augmenting the 50 members of the 834th. With this additional soldier-power, the backlog disappeared.[34]

Postal support for VII Corps was provided by four postal companies: one from the active component and three from the Army Reserve. The three Army Reserve units that handled the mail for VII Corps were the 795th from Richards-Gebaur AFB, Mo., under the command of 1st Lt. Elizabeth Richardson; the 312th from Charlotte, N.C., under the command of Capt. Phillip R. McChesney, and the 341st from Athens, Ga.[35]

The 795th handled mostly outgoing mail for the 1st and 3d Armored Divisions and operated out of Al Jubayl and King Fahd International Airport. The 312th supported the 1st Infantry Division from near Log Base Alpha. And the 341st, which also operated from Log Base Alpha, provided mail service to the COSCOM and the Corps artillery. None of these were large units, as the three companies combined only had a strength of 222 soldiers.[36]

The 341st also performed *ad hoc* missions in mail delivery. On one such occasion in January 1991, the 341st was involved in a one-time use of CH–47 Chinook helicopters to deliver 4 tons of mail to the soldiers of the 2d Armored Cavalry Regiment. After an initial problem with pallets that were too

33. United States Congress, House of Representatives, Committee on Post Office and Civil Service, *Free Mailing Privileges for the Armed Forces Deployed in the Persian Gulf* (September 12, 1990) and *Examine Mail Service to the Persian Gulf* (February 20, 1990).

34. "Military Postal Service," *Personnel Service Support*, pp. 5–18 and 5–20.

35. *Ibid.*, p. 5–19.

36. *Ibid.*, pp. 5–19 and 5–17.

large to fit into the Chinooks, the mail was broken down into individual bags and heaped on board. Reports that reached the 341st indicated that the Cav troopers were delighted with the delivery and greatly appreciated their first mail in many days.[37]

The XVIII Airborne Corps was provided postal support by a combination of one active component postal company, one company from the Army National Guard (the 1015th from Lafayette, Ind.) and two companies from the Army Reserve. These companies were the 336th from Muscle Shoals, Ala., and the 300th from Chicago. The 336th supported the COSCOM, while the 300th provided mail delivery services to the 24th Mechanized Infantry Division.[38]

Operating the mail system at the highest organizational levels—echelons above corps (EAC)—was the 351st Postal Company from Tallahassee, Fla. This unit arrived in theater in October 1990 and was assigned to the ARCENT Personnel Command. It operated the theater locator system, processed casualty mail, and dealt with mail that had somehow been misdirected or misaddressed. The 755th Postal Company from Texarkana, Tex., and the 834th Postal Company from Coral Gables, Fla., also provided services at EAC.[39]

The 329th Postal Company from Fort Snelling, Minn., was the one Army Reserve postal unit that was mobilized but not sent to Southwest Asia. The 329th was activated on December 6, 1990, and sent to the location at which much of the mail for the Persian Gulf was consolidated before it was shipped overseas: Fort Dix, N.J. The 329th, under the command of Capt. Richard Hedberg, had a strength of 152 soldiers, only half of whom had been with the unit when it was mobilized. Forty of the unit's members had been assigned to it as a result of cross-leveling from other Army Reserve units, while 34 others were members of the Individual Ready Reserve and the active component who had been assigned after the unit reached New Jersey. [40]

The 329th was not alone at the mail-handling facility at McGuire Air Force Base (Fort Dix), as it worked with two Air Force Reserve Aerial Port Squadrons that had been similarly mobilized. The 329th and its cohorts worked seven days a week, twenty-four hours a day and moved 200 tons of mail each day, shipping it out to Dharan, Al Jubayal or King Khalid Military City.[41]

---

37. 2nd. Lt. John R. Heil, "USAR postal units get first 'air mail' to the Cav," *Army Reserve Magazine*, Vol. 38, No. 1 (1992), p. 15.

38. "Military Postal Service," *Personnel Service Support*, p. 5–17.

39. *Ibid*., p. 5–11.

40. *Ibid*., p. 5–13 and 5–14.

41. *Ibid*., pp. 5–12 and 5–13.

Mail handling was not all that the 329th was called upon to do during its time at Fort Dix, and the other responsibilities heaped upon it led to some difficult times. The 329th was assigned to the Special Troops Battalion at Fort Dix, which was part of the U.S. Army Garrison there. The battalion commander decided that the members of the 329th were troops just like the others under his command, and that they should therefore be required to undertake the same training activities of all the other parts of the battalion. These activities included such events as the battalion run, physical fitness and Nuclear-Biological-Chemical (NBC) training, weekly NCO meetings, and post details. While it was nice to be treated "just like the active component soldiers," these Army Reservists were not, in fact, "just like the actives." They were working twelve hour shifts, every day of the week, unlike the military police, maintenance, and transportation units that comprised the other parts of the Special Troops Battalion.[42]

These were not the only problems encountered by the Reservists. Housing for the 329th was substandard, consisting of unrenovated World War II barracks in the area where basic trainees marched and ran throughout the day, chanting and yelling. For soldiers who had just worked a twelve-hour night shift and who were in desperate need of sleep, these were trying conditions. This situation persisted for some five weeks until the Fort Dix commander moved the troops into barracks away from the basic trainee area.[43]

The Military Postal Service Agency made several attempts to relieve the 329th from these non-mission-related duties with no success. Word soon reached the the 88th Army Reserve Command (ARCOM), parent headquarters of the 329th, and it, too, attempted to affect the situation. The ARCOM sent Lt. Col. Richard Pletcher to Fort Dix to make an assessment of the situation. According to Pletcher, the battalion commander seemed surprised that the ARCOM would concern itself with these Army Reservists, since they were now on active duty. According to the battalion commander, the members of the 329th were not performing to his standards, and he was not asking them to do more than he was requiring of any other unit under his command. The fact is that the 329th *was* doing more than the other members of his command, though they were doing it for a different com-

42. Interview with Maj. Richard Hedberg, March 20, 1995, cited in *ibid.*, p. 5–14.

43. *Ibid.*, p. 5–14.

mander: Col. Rick Delaney, the man who ran the postal facility at McGuire Air Force Base. The conflict with the special troops battalion commander's expectations was never satisfactorily resolved, and the Reservists remained on duty, twelve hours per day, seven days a week, and caught all the other details in addition. When the 329th finally completed its tour of duty, it was awarded the Superior Unit Award, having done its job and done it well.[44]

JUDGE ADVOCATE GENERAL (JAG)

The first Army Reserve unit mobilized for Desert Shield was the 46th Judge Advocate General Detachment (International Law Team) from Boston, Mass. This unit was quickly sent to Saudi Arabia, where it served as the legal staff for the 22d Support Command. These lawyers and legal specialists were but the first of many Army Reserve legal profesionals who were called to active duty for the effort against Saddam Hussein. Before the conflict came to an end, over 180 Army Reserve lawyers had served on active duty in support of the war effort, and many of these individuals had served in Southwest Asia.[45]

Most of the Army Reserve lawyers served at stateside locations where Reservists and others were preparing for overseas deployment. This was necessary because soldiers cannot be sent overseas without a certain amount of legal processing. As Col. Ray Ruppert, who served as the CENTCOM Staff Judge Advocate during Desert Storm, said in an interview, "The Reserve JAGs were invaluable to the Army during this period in supporting the posts, camps and stations. They provided legal assistance to the individual soldiers who were deploying to Southwest Asia by drawing up wills and powers of

44. Interviews with members of the 329th and with Lt. Col. Pletcher, cited in *ibid.*, p. 5–15.

45. Army Reserve JAG detachments mobilized for DS/DS and sent to Southwest Asia in addition to the 46th included the 173d JAG Legal Services Team, Birmingham, Ala.; 187th JAG Det Criminal Trial Team, Columbia, S.C.; 199th JAG Det International Law Team, St. Petersburg, Fla.; and the 207th JAG Det Contract Law Team, Washington, D.C.; JAG units mobilized and retained in the U.S. were the 127th JAG Det Legal Services Team, Morgantown, W.Va.; 181st JAG Det Legal Services Team, Columbia, S.C.; 188th JAG Det Legal Services Team, Memphis, Tenn.; 204th JAG Det Criminal Defense Team, Greensboro, N.C.; 205th JAG Det Legal Servixces Team, Garner, N.C.; 208th JAG Det International Law Team, Washington, D.C.; and the 218th JAG Det Legal Services Team, Bismarck, N.D. "JAGC Operations," Chapter 9 of ANDRULIS Research Corporation's draft manuscript *Personnel Service Support*, prepared for the Chief, Army Reserve, pp. 9–2 through 9–3, 9–9.

attorney, supplementing—and sometimes replacing—the active duty lawyers assigned there [mobilization stations]."[46]

Many of the Army Reserve JAG detachments that remained in the U.S. performed exactly as Col. Ruppert described: they joined their active component counterparts and assisted where ever they were needed. The 188th JAG Detachment (Legal Services Team) from Memphis, Tenn., acquired a new commander—Maj. Joseph S. Daniel—one day, mobilized the next, and drove to Fort Knox, Ky., three days later. They left Fort Knox 100 days later, having provided legal assistance to thousands of soldiers who processed through the post.[47]

Other legal assistance was rendered by units like the 127th JAG Detachment from Morgantown, W.Va., which was activated on January 25, 1991, to assist with the legal preparation of members of the Individual Ready Reserve who were being called to active duty. The 127th did its work at Fort Leonard Wood, Mo., and devoted most of its efforts to preparing wills, powers of attorney, and other legal documents. [48]

Other Army Reserve legal personnel were like the members of the 113th JAG Detachment (Military Law Center) of Wichita, Kans., which pulled its 1991 annual training at Fort Hood, Tex., and operated the III Corps Legal Office in the absence of most of the active Army legal personnel. Or they performed as did the 119th JAG Detachment of Omaha, Neb., which functioned in much the same way during its annual training at Fort Bliss, Tex. Or they were like the 111th JAG Detachment, also of Omaha, which did its annual training at Fort Leavenworth, Kans., and assisted the soldiers there. [49]

One special type of Army Reserve JAG unit was called to active duty during the conflict, and this was the international law detachment. One of these detachments, the 199th out of St. Petersburg, Fla., commanded by Lt. Col. Lee A. Haworth, was mobilized on January 15, 1991, and sent to Southwest Asia to collect evidence to be used in proceedings against Saddam

46. Interview, Lt. Col. James T. Currie with Colonel Ruppert, January 12, 1994; notes in possession of the author. For a good discussion of the process of providing legal assistance to deploying soldiers—active and reserve—see Maj. Gregory M. Huckabee, "Legal Assistance for Those Who Go in Harm's Way," *Military Review* (April 1991), pp. 33–38.

47. "JAGC Operations," *Personnel Service Support*, pp. 9–31 through 9–32.

48. Bruce Kish and Mark L. Geiger, "127th Judge Advocate General Detachment," *Checkerboard* (publication of the 99th ARCOM), Vol. 3, No. 2 (Spring 1992), p. 32.

49. *AHS, 89th ARCOM*, pp. XV–1 to XV–6.

Hussein and other Iraqis for war crimes. It completed its mission and left Saudi Arabia on April 28.[50]

The other international law detachment, the 208th from Washington, D.C., was commanded by Lt. Col. James G. Hergen. It was assigned to the Office of the Judge Advocate General, U.S. Army. The 208th functioned as the War Crimes Documentation Center and collected information from U.S. government sources, the news media, and private citizens about atrocities committed by the Iraqis. The 208th demobilized on April 28, 1991, though a few of its personnel continued to work on the war crimes documentation and report writing until the end of the year.[51]

In addition, numerous Army Reserve lawyers and other legal personnel gave of their time to assist units that were being shipped to Saudi Arabia. And volunteers from the 213th Military Law Center, stationed in Chamblee, Ga., and other Army Reserve JAG detachments went to Europe to assist VII Corps lawyers prepare its soldiers for deployment to Southwest Asia.[52]

HISTORY

The chief historian for the European Theater during World War II has been quoted as saying that "History is the last thing we care about during operations and the first thing we want afterwards. Then it is too late."[53] This truism was partially corrected during the Gulf War by the presence of both active and reserve component historians who worked directly with the Army units in Saudi Arabia and attempted to document the problems and successes of the operation. The first military historians in Saudi Arabia came from the active side of the house, but they were soon joined by military history detachments from both the Army Reserve and the Army National Guard.[54]

A total of eight military history detachments were sent to Southwest Asia: 1 active component, 4 Army Reserve, and 3 Army National Guard. Of the USAR units, the 50th Military History Detachment (MHD) of Bozeman, Mont., was assigned to VII Corps, as was the 326th MHD of Columbus, Oh. The

50. "JAGC Operations," *Personnel Service Support*, pp. 9–27 through 9–28.

51. *Ibid.*, pp. 9–26 through 9–27; DoD, *Final Report,* p. 622.

52. "JAGC Operations," *Personnel Service Support*, pp. 9–14 through 9–17.

53. Col. William A. Ganoe, quoted in Billy A. Arthur, "Clio in Desert Shield and Desert Storm," *Army History: The Professional Bulletin of Army History* (Spring 1991), p. 13.

54. *Ibid.*

317th MHD from Atlanta, Ga., was assigned to XVIII Corps, and the 90th MHD from San Antonio, Tex., was assigned to cover the 22d SUPCOM.[55]

The 322d MHD from Tuscaloosa, Ala., was the first Army Reserve historical unit to be mobilized for Desert Shield/Desert Storm. The 322d was assigned to Second Army Headquarters at Fort Gillem, Ga., where it devoted many of its efforts to the mobilization experience of reserve units.[56]

The work of these history detachments was augmented by historians—some of whom were Army Reservists—assigned to the deploying units themselves. For example, Dr. Richard W. Stewart, was the civilian command historian of the U.S. Army Special Operations Command. Dr. Stewart became "Major Stewart," went on active duty for forty-five days, and ended the war in Kuwait City. [57]

Additionally, some Individual Mobilization Augmentee (IMA) historians were ordered to active duty to perform historical documentation functions. One such individual, Lt. Col. Richard D. Adamczyk, was attached to the Army's Deputy Chief of Staff for Personnel, where he conducted oral history interviews and collected documents of historical significance. Two IMAs, Colonels Charles A. Endress and Arthur Samuel, were mobilized and assigned to positions at the Army's Center of Military History (USACMH), where they concentrated on the mobilization and deployment of reserve component units. A third IMA, Lt. Col. Carolyn M. Feller, also worked at USACMH, filling the position of Army Nurse Corps Historian.[58]

The Army's Center of Military History also dispatched a three-man team of Army Reservists to the KTO to obtain artifacts for Army museums. These three soldiers, experienced in museum operations, were tasked with collecting "representative examples of American, allied, and captured enemy material of all types, ranging from weapon systems to camp equipment and personal equipment and clothing." They devoted six months to the mission and returned over 18,000 separate items to the United States, many of which are on display.[59]

Little of this narrative about the Army Reserve's role in Desert Shield/Desert Storm could have been written without the unit historians who compiled much of the raw data and

55. "Military History," *Personnel Service Support*, p. 11–8.
56. Arthur, "Clio in Desert Shield and Desert Storm," p. 15.
57. *Ibid.*, pp. 14–15.
58. *Ibid.*, p. 16.
59. Canedy *et al.*, *TRADOC Support*, p. 80.

analysis on which it is based. Many of these nameless individuals are amateurs, in the finest sense of the word, who compile unit histories and submit the annual historical summaries as an addiitonal duty. Few of these are professionally trained historians, as are the members of the 101st Military History Detachment, of Omaha, Neb., who compiled the exhaustive history of the 89th ARCOM.

The 101st, commanded by Maj. Michael R. Howland, was mobilized on January 25, 1991, and sent to Fort Sam Houston, Tex., where it supported the Fifth U.S. Army. During some five months of active duty the three members of the 101st completed the Fifth Army FY 1990 Historical Supplement, conducted over 150 oral history interviews, and prepared plans that allowed Fifth Army to capture a record of its involvement in the Gulf area. The detachment was demobilized on June 30. Two of the unit's members volunteered for six more weeks of ADSW at home station to allow them to complete work on a special project, a monograph entitled *Mobilization: A History of Fifth Army Support for Operation Desert Shield/Desert Storm.*[60]

The 51st Military History Detachment from San Francisco, Calif., commanded by Maj. John H. King, was ordered to active duty on February 26, 1991. This two-member unit was assigned to the U.S. Army Center of Military History and devoted many months to inventorying records shipped from Southwest Asia. They also researched and wrote part of the Army's official history of the operation and eventually went to Fort McPherson, Ga., where they inventoried and organized the Desert Shield/Desert Storm records of FORSCOM and Third Army. This unit was not demobilized until December 8, 1991.[61]

PUBLIC AFFAIRS

Anyone who watched the daily news coverage of Desert Storm quickly understood why commentators referred to this as the first "CNN war." Journalists were there in strength, video images of precision strikes were breathtaking, and the carefully-controlled broadcasts from USCENTCOM headquarters undoubtedly helped create the overwhelming support for the war.[62] None of this coverage happened without the in-

60. *AHS, 89th ARCOM,* pp. XIII–10 thru XIII–12.

61. "Military History," Chapter 11 of ANDRULIS Research Corporation's draft manuscript *Personnel Service Support,* pp. 11–5 through 11–6.

62. Everette E. Dennis *et al.*, *The Media at War: The Press and the Persian Gulf Conflict* (New York: Gannett Foundation Media Center, 1991), p.1.

(with one small exception), and to mobilize Army Reserve finance units to backfill within the U.S. for the active component units that had been deployed overseas.[71]

In making this decision, Army leadership decided against using the 336th Theater Finance Command, an Army Reserve unit from Lake Charles, La., that was designed to perform a central funding and finance and accounting policy mission that was not a part of the tasking given the two active component finance groups that served in Saudi Arabia. The two finance groups were thereupon compelled to assume the mission of the finance command. It has not been determined whether they were able to assume these additional missions without neglecting any of their other responsibilites.[72]

The one USAR finance unit that was mobilized and deployed to Southwest Asia was the 338th Finance Support Unit from Fort Buchanan, Puerto Rico. The 338th, commanded by Lt. Col. Juan R. Gonzalez, left for Saudi Arabia on February 6, 1991, arriving with no fanfare and no idea what it would be doing. As it developed, the 80-person strong 338th worked with the members of the 18th Finance Group providing financial support to units in Dharan and elsewhere. Gradually, the Reservists took over the entire finance mission in Dharan. In so doing, the 338th formed mobile finance support teams and went to some 60 locations outside Dharan. The 338th redeployed to Puerto Rico in three increments: one in July 1991, one in August, and the final group of five unit members in October. In recognition of its hard work the 338th was awarded the Meritorious Unit Commendation.[73]

The finance units that were mobilized as CONUS backfill do not have unit commendations of which to boast, but they have the satisfaction of knowing that they served and did their duty under what were often trying circumstances. Of the reserve component finance units mobilized for stateside duty during Desert Shield/Desert Storm, four each were from the Army Reserve and the Army National Guard.[74]

One of the Army Reserve finance units that remained in the U.S. for the duration of the conflict was the 368th Finance Support Unit, commanded by Lt. Col. Douglas Winkley. The 368th, from Wichita, Kans., was mobilized reasonably early—on November 24 1990—and assigned to Fort Riley. The members of the 368th worked with the few active component fi-

71. *Ibid.*, p. 4–7.
72. *Ibid.*, p. 4–9
73. *Ibid.*, p. 4–10.
74. *Ibid.*, p. 4–12.

nance specialists who remained at Fort Riley and performed all the duties one might expect of soldiers there.[75]

The 376th Finance Support Unit from Wausau, Wisc., was commanded by Lt. Col. Henry Rueden and was activated two months later than the 368th—on January 25, 1991. It was ordered to report to Fort Sheridan, Ill., and after a short period of training, the unit was split into three parts. Sixteen unit members were sent to Fort Dix, N.J., 30 went to Fort Leonard Wood, Mo., and the balance of the unit—42 soldiers—remained at Fort Sheridan.[76]

The unit members who went to Forts Dix and Leonard Wood were integrated into the finance operations at those posts, just as the members of the 368th had been at Fort Riley. Unit members who remained at Fort Sheridan, however, became, in the words of one study, "almost permanent detail soldiers."[77] The members of the unit that had gone to Fort Dix were demobilized on September 21, while unit members at Forts Leonard Wood and Sheridan were sent back to Wausau for demobilization on July 15.[78]

Of the other Army Reserve finance units mobilized during this period, the 412th Finance Support Unit from Fort Wayne, Ind., was sent to to provide augmentation at Fort Knox, Ky., while the 453d Finance Support Unit from Annville, Penn., went to Fort Stewart, Ga. During the demobilization phase, the 325th Finance Support Unit of Columbis, Oh., provided additional assistance to the active component finance personnel at Fort McPherson, Ga.[79]

CASUALTY AND MORTUARY

For those soldiers who did not survive the deployment to Southwest Asia and the subsequent war against Iraq unscathed, it became necessary for the Army's casualty and mortuary system to step in. Despite early predictions to the contrary, the war against Iraq was as close to a bloodless operation as any force the size of the one assembled for Desert Shield/Desert Storm is ever likely to experience. As mentioned above, there were only 146 servicemembers killed during the war, with another 476 wounded.[80] This does not include the non-battle injuries and deaths from events such as

75. *Ibid.*, p. 4–12 and 4–13.
76. *Ibid.*, p. 4–13.
77. *Ibid.*, pp. 4–13 and 4–14.
78. *Ibid.*, p. 4–13.
79. *Ibid.*, p. 4–12.
80. DoD, *Final Report*, p. 589.

traffic accidents, which totalled only 120.[81] Altogether, the total number of bodies that passed through the U.S.-operated mortuary system and were evacuated from the theater was relatively small: only 302.[82]

Given the small number of Army personnel trained to take care of deceased soldiers, this small number of KIA (killed-in-action) was readily cared for. A larger number could have exceeded the Army's capabilities in this area.

Army graves registration capacity in 1990 was concentrated in the Army Reserve, but it was not high priority, and the units assigned this task were not well-staffed. Of the five graves registration companies in the Army structure in 1990, four were in the Army Reserve, while one was an active component unit. The one battalion headquarters was Army Reserve. All of these units were understrength, ranging from 90 percent strength in the active unit and one of the USAR companies down to barely one-third strength (101 authorized, 36 assigned) for a USAR company. Perhaps more critically, the number of assigned personnel carrying the 57F military occupation specialty (mortuary specialist) was also well below authorization. Altogether, the Army had only about 300 57Fs, about half the number prescribed for a two-corps operation.[83]

The first graves registration company to deploy to Southwest Asia was the 54th Quartermaster Company, the active component unit stationed at Fort Lee, Va. This unit's advance party arrived in September 1990, and the remainder of the unit arrived soon after. The first Army Reserve graves registration unit to reach Saudi Arabia was the 311th Quartermaster Graves Registration Company from Aguadilla, Puerto Rico. It arrived on October 19, 1990, to be joined on December 19 by the 689th QM Graves Registration Company of Oakland, Calif., on February 1, 1991; by the 630th QM Graves Registration Company from New Orleans, La. The 246th QM Battalion, Graves Registration, also a USAR unit, arrived in theater on January 2, 1991, and assumed command of the graves registration companies.[84]

---

81. "Mortuary and Casualty Affairs," Chapter 6 of ANDRULIS Research Corporation's draft study on *Personnel Service Support* during Desert Shield/Desert Storm, p. 6–27.

82. *Ibid.*, p. 6–16.

83. *Ibid.*, p. 6–7 and 6–8.

84. *Ibid.*, p. 6–11. According to the ANDRULIS study, the commander of the 246th QM Battalion was relieved of his position three weeks after the unit arrived in Saudi Arabia "for disciplinary problems not related to the professional work of the battalion." He was succeeded by Lt. Col. Thomas A. Rexrode, the active component head of the Mortuary Affairs Center in Saudi Arabia (p. 6–32).

The tasks assigned the graves registration companies were similar, but there were variations as to how they were fulfilled. The 689th, commanded by 1st Lt. William Gordon established and operated the facility at KKMC airfield through which remains were processed and sent to the mortuary at Dover Air Force Base, Del. The 630th, as indicated above, did not arrive in theater until February 1, 1991, just prior to the commencement of the ground war. It also operated a collection point at KKMC and ran the night shift at the KKMC mortuary. A dozen of its personnel were sent to Dharan to assist in the Air Force mortuary there.[85]

The 311th, which was attached to the 2d COSCOM, VII Corps, set up mobile collection points in forward areas. The members of the 311th were divided into 17 teams, each of which was equipped with a HMMWV and a trailer and placed in direct support of one of the brigades. These teams went with the brigades when they moved into Iraq, quite a change of pace from the sandbag-filling and similar activities that had occupied much of the time of the members of the 311th for the first three months after their arrival in country.[86]

What the members of these units did with the bodies of deceased Americans and a few allies was quite special and was handled with both dignity and professionalism. The remains were first fingerprinted and a tentative identification was made. Amazingly, given the few American soldiers killed during the conflict, even this latter task was not without its difficulties. Personal effects were removed from the body, and these were shipped to the next-of-kin. The remains were then prepared for shipment. This in itself was sometimes challenging, as soldiers killed on the battlefield often carried with them ammunition and pyrotechnics, both of which had to removed prior to shipment. The remains were then placed in what are today called "human remains pouches"—the new term for "body bags"—placed into a refrigerated van, and transported to aircraft for shipment back to Dover.[87]

The graves registration teams were also confronted with the necessity of dealing with hundreds of Iraqi bodies. In these instances, the teams established folders for bodies, just as they did with the bodies of Americans. Rather than being shipped, however, the Iraqis were buried in temporary—sometimes mass—graves, the locations of which were reported to Saudi and Kuwaiti authorities.[88]

It should be pointed out that the Army Reserve also played a significant role in other parts of the mortuary and ca-

85. *Ibid.*, p. 6–12.
86. *Ibid.*
87. *Ibid.*, pp. 6–10 and 6–11.
88. *Ibid.*, pp. 6–15 and 6–16.

sualty system. As the Department of Defense anticipated the requirement for casualty handling prior to the beginning of the war, it became evident that the number of personnel devoted to this activity would have to be increased. The Army part of that increase was concentrated in three areas: Dover Air Force Base and the mortuary there, the Personal Effects Depot at Fort Dix, N.J., and the Casualty and Memorial Affairs Operations Center (CMAOC) in Alexandria, Va.[89]

The Army Reserve's personnel contribution at Dover consisted of 10 IMAs and 50 other Army Reservists, both IRR and Selected Reserve. An additional 35 Army Reservists worked at Fort Dix, and it is safe to say that the CMAOC in Alexandria would have found it almost impossible to function without its Army Reserve soldiers. Of the 397 personnel assigned to this operation during Desert Shield/Desert Storm, 275 were from the USAR. This total included 10 IMAs and 265 members of the Individual Ready Reserve. This compares with a pre-war CMAOC strength of 85.[90]

After the end of the ground war the 246th became a redeployment center at KKMC for the 40,000 soldiers of the VII Corps, feeding and housing soldiers for several days as they awaited airlift out of the theater. In this capacity the 246th had under it a number of units of both the Army Reserve and the Army National Guard.[91]

CROSS-LEVELING

Hundreds of Army Reserve units across the country were selected for mobilization, and there were often personnel vacancies in the units being called up. Early in the process, individual troop unit members were culled out by grade and MOS and were added involuntarily to units that were going on active duty. According to a Department of Defense study,

> This expedient, which was used in combat, CS, and CSS, as well as medical units, had a less than desirable effect on morale and cohesiveness. This policy may have long-term detrimental effects on retention. An alternative to involuntarily cross-leveling must be developed for future contingencies. Options might include manning Reserve units to full wartime strength levels, developing a more flexible reserve force structure, or making earlier use of the Individual Ready Reserve, which exists to fill unit vacancies and to provide casualty replacements.[92]

89. *Ibid.*, pp. 6–18 and 6–21.
90. *Ibid.*
91. *Ibid.*, p. 6–13.
92. DoD, *Final Report*, pp. 468–69.

19

Desert Shield/Desert Storm: Medics and Chaplains—Caring for Body and Soul

A very large percentage of the U.S. Army's medical assets reside in the Army Reserve, ranging from small specialized detachments to large hospitals.[1] Preliminary estimates that the U.S. and its coalition partners would suffer high casualty rates during combat action against Iraq led the Army to include medical units in the initial reserve call-up, and the number of Army Reserve medical units mobilized increased over the next few months. In addition to the prospects for battlefield casualties, another factor that had a great impact on medical planning—and the call-up of reserve medical assets—was that of dependent care.

Pre-war planning scenarios had assumed that in the event of war—and this was generally a European war that was anticipated—Army medical assets would be diverted to troop care, leaving dependent care to the private sector. This scenario was not realized, for on August 9, 1990, Gen. Carl Vuono, Chief of Staff of the Army, decided that Army medical facilities would continue dependent treatment as before. This had great significance for members of the Army Reserve, for many of them were now to be used as fillers in active component hospitals in both Europe and the U.S.[2]

---

1. For medical brigades, the USAR furnished 50% of the total Army force structure; for medical groups, it was 65%; for hospitals, 59%. *Annual Report, Reserve Forces Policy Board, FY 1992* (Washington: OSD, 1993), p. 15.

2. Interview with Lt. Col. Ralph E. Bradford, Chief, Military Personnel Division, U.S. Army Health Services Command, October 13, 1992, cited in John R. Brinkerhoff, *United States Army Reserve in Operation Desert Storm: Reservists of the Army Medical Department* (Washington: Office of the Chief, Army Reserve, 1993), p. 15; hereinafter cited as "Brinkerhoff, *Medical*."

Ultimately, 18,988 Army Reserve medical personnel were mobilized, with 8,273 sent to Southwest Asia, 3,096 going to Europe, and 7,619 remaining stateside. A total of 74 Army Reserve medical units were sent to Southwest Asia, and the Army Reserve provided 37% of the medical personnel in the theater of operations, more than either the active component (35%) or the Army National Guard (28%).[3]

The United States General Accounting Office conducted a study of the deployment of medical units of all types—active and reserve component—during the Gulf War and concluded that there were some problems in the way the system operated. Many of the GAO findings—such as the non-deployability of medical doctors who had not completed their officer basic training or the lack of field training for members of medical units—were applicable across the board. Other GAO findings, however, related specifically to the Army Reserve.

The GAO found, for example, that some of the medical skills in the specialized teams simply did not match. Since most of these teams were from the USAR (16 out of 21), the problem lay mostly within the Army Reserve. According to the GAO, an Army Reserve thoracic surgical team, for example, that mobilized at Fort Carson, Colo., was found to have no thoracic surgeons among its complement. The person filling one of the two thoracic surgeon positions in the team was a gynecologist, who knew that he was not qualified for the position to which he was assigned. According to the report, "The only chest he had opened was in medical school and belonged to a goat."[4] There is no suggestion from the GAO that this was a common problem within the USAR medical units generally, and it should not be taken here as an indictment of the qualifications of the overwhelming number of USAR medical personnel who were called up for Desert Shield/Desert Storm, but it was a problem.

The following chart shows the types and component of medical units deployed to the Persian Gulf during Desert Shield/Desert Storm:[5]

3. Brinkerhoff, *Medical*, p. 33.

4. United States General Accounting Office, *Operation Desert Storm: Full Army Medical Capability Not Achieved*, Report No. GAO/NSIAD–92–175 (August 1992), p. 25. The problem was remedied by assigning a qualified surgeon to the team.

5. *Ibid.*, p. 12.

Table 19–1 Medical Units Deployed to the Persian Gulf

Type of Unit	Active	USAR	ARNG	Total
Hospital	16	17	11	44
Evacuation	16	11	8	35
Logistics	10	9	1	20
Area support	14	0	7	21
Command and control	9	7	7	23
Combat stress	1	2	0	3
Preventive medicine	11	3	0	14
Veterinary services	3	6	0	9
Dental	5	0	0	5
Surgical Teams	4	16	1	21
Laboratory	0	3	0	3
Total	89	74	35	198

The mobilization of Army Reserve medical units began in August 1990, when six USAR hospitals and two dental detachments with a total assigned strength of over 1,000 reservists were called up. The early call-ups included the 1207th U.S. Army Hospital (USAH), a 100-bed unit from Tuskegee, Ala.; the 3271st USAH, a 300-bed unit from Charleston, S.C.; the 3273d USAH, a 300-bed unit, from Greenville, S.C.; and three 1,000-bed units: the 3274th from Durham, N.C.; the 4005th from Houston, Tex., and the 3297th from Chamblee, Ga.[6]

According to John R. Brinkerhoff, a retired Army colonel who has studied and written more about the Army Reserve's mobilization during Desert Shield and Desert Storm than any other individual, "There were many problems between AC [active component] and RC [reserve component] military personnel in the AMEDD [Army Medical Department]—probably more than in other functional areas of the Army, and certainly more than in other areas covered in this series of historical case studies on the Army Reserve in DESERT STORM." Stated Brinkerhoff, "The evidence for AC–RC antagonism is anecdotal but massive. . . ."[7] The case of the 3297th U.S. Army Hospital illustrates some of the frustrations and problems associated with the mobilization of Army Reserve medical units.

3297TH U.S. ARMY HOSPITAL

The pre-war mobilization mission of the 3297th was that of filling the mobilization table of distribution and allowances

6. Brinkerhoff, *Medical*, p. 21.
7. *Ibid.*, p. 78 and fn 171 on p. 106.

(TDA) at an Army hospital at Fort Gordon, Ga. The problem for the Reservists, however, was that this was not the way it worked out. In the first place, the entire hospital unit was not mobilized. Of the 900 members of the 3297th, two-thirds were called up, and these individuals were placed in what is called a "derivative unit identification code" (UIC), meaning that they immediately lost their identity as members of the 3297th. When they reported to Fort Gordon, many of them were told that they were not going to serve there, but would be reassigned as fillers to hospitals elsewhere in the Army system. In the end, 500 members of the 3297th served at 42 different medical facilities in the U.S., including Fort Gordon, and 15 unit members were sent to Southwest Asia as individual fillers.

The explanation for this dissolution of unit identity was offered by the Army Surgeon General in March 1991 testimony before Congress. ". . . Our need," said Lt. Gen. Frank F. Ledford, Jr., "was for individuals to replace the active component members who were preparing to or had deployed. To meet that need we called up our augmentation hospitals. . . . To avoid activating any unneeded personnel, we only activated portions of those hospitals."[8]

To further add to the frustration of the Reservists, they were housed in substandard quarters: medical corps colonels and lieutenant colonels placed in open bay barracks that are not satisfactory for new recruits, much less for senior Army officers. Though the housing situation was eventually corrected, the scattering of unit members and failure to remain deployed to Fort Gordon left a bad taste in the mouths of the Reservists. According to Brinkerhoff, many of the senior officers in the unit—the colonels and lieutenant colonels—left the Army Reserve shortly after the end of the conflict.[9]

PROBLEMS IN THE AMEDD

Problems of CONUS deployment were matched by the difficulties encountered by Army Reserve units sent to Southwest Asia. First of all, there were questions of rank and hierarchy. The ARCENT (U.S. Army Central Command) surgeon and commander of the 3d Medical Command, Col. Demetrios Tsoulos, was outranked by the commander of the Army Re-

8. Statement of Lt. Gen. Frank F. Ledford, Jr., Surgeon General, United States Army, before the Defense Subcommittee, Committee on Appropriations, United States House of Representatives, March 12, 1991. *Department of Defense Appropriations for 1992, Part 3*, 102d Congress, 1st session, p. 171.

9. *Ibid.*, pp. 1–3.

serve's 332d Medical Brigade, Brig. Gen. Michael D. Strong. Strong was not placed in charge, however, because Tsoulos did not believe that the personnel of the 332d were an experienced and capable enough staff, a charge with which Strong and his staff disagreed.[10]

General officer/commander pecking order disputes are of such byzantine complexity that one might never hope to unravel them. At lower levels within the officer corps, however, even more egregious disruptions of rank structure prevailed, with active component officers placed in positions where they were supervising Army Reserve officers several grades their superior. There are stories, for example, of Army Reserve medical doctor colonels being assigned to work for the active component medical doctor lieutenant colonels without problems developing therefrom, though one has to wonder how the Reservists actually felt about the situation. More disturbing, however, were the reports of Army Reserve lieutenant colonels being supervised by active component lieutenants, a situation that would never be allowed in a pure active component environment.[11]

WORKING WITH THE SAUDIS

Problems between active and reserve component officers were nothing, however, compared with the difficulties encountered by those Army Reserve medical units and personnel assigned to Saudi-run medical facilities. These included the 50th General Hospital, assigned to Riyadh al Kharj Military Hospital (MODA), and the 316th Station Hospital from Harrisburg, Pa., and the 382d Field Hospital, from Augusta, Ga., assigned to the King Fahd NG Hospital.[12]

Patient care at Saudi hospitals was conducted according to a memorandum of understanding (MOU) between the U.S. and Saudi governments. Under one MOU, for example, U.S.

---

10. Interview with Col. Tsoulos, December 14, 1992, cited in *ibid.*, fn 106 and 107. The discussion of the problems with the 332d Medical Bde are found in *ibid.*, pp. 50–52. A fine discussion of the significance of not establishing a MEDCOM in Southwest Asia is found in Lt. Col. Gerald A. Palmer, *Army Medical Department Issues from Operation Desert Shield*, an unpublished paper written at the United States Army War College in 1991. It is available through the Defense Technical Information Center.

11. Brinkerhoff, *Medical*, p. 80.

12. Lt. Col. Bernard J. Horak, Col. Richard J. Williams and William H. Borton, "Preparations for War in a Saudi Arabian Host Nation Hospital," *Military Medicine*, Vol. 157 (July 1992), p. 342.

medical personnel were "forced to sign contracts to work at the King Faisal Research Hospital in Saudi Arabia." Additionally, they were compelled to wear civilian clothes, rather than their uniforms. As a result of this latter condition, stated a group of Army nurses at a lessons-learned conference, they "lost military identity and the comfort and safety that provided."[13]

At King Fahd National Guard Hospital, on the other hand, U.S. military personnel wore "clothing as appropriate to the KFNGH department," with military rank and branch insignia worn on the lapel or over the lab coat pocket. Commanders and administrative personnel in the hospital wore BDUs.[14]

Saudi law and customs did create some problems for the U.S. medical personnel. X-rays, for example, could not be taken during afternoon prayers, and male nurses could not care for female patients.[15]

The Saudis found certain common U.S. customs to be objectionable, such as male and female staff having lunch together or socializing after work. They also objected to having a female nurse "talking at length to a male patient."[16] At KFNGH, U.S. Army commanders issued "stern reminders" to U.S. personnel on these matters, warning them about displeasing the Saudis by their conduct.[17] The Army nurses felt so strongly about the difficulties encountered at the Saudi hospitals that one of their recommendations was "Do not use Host Nation fixed facility."[18]

---

13. Office of the Surgeon General, "After Action Report for Operation Desert Shield/Storm Army Nursing Lessons Learned Conference, 9–10 July 1991," dated August 23, 1991, unpaginated, "Issue: Use of Host Nation Support Facilities." Copy in possession of the author.

14. Horak, Williams, and Borton, "Preparations for War in a Saudi Arabian Host Nation Hospital," p. 343.

15. Office of the Surgeon General, "After Action Report for Operation Desert Shield/Storm Army Nursing Lessons Learned Conference, 9–10 July 1991." Issue:

16. Horak, Williams, and Borton, "Preparations for War in a Saudi Arabian Host Nation Hospital," p. 344.

17. Horak, Williams, and Borton, "Preparations for War in a Saudi Arabian Host Nation Hospital," p. 344; Office of the Surgeon General, "After Action Report for Operation Desert Shield/Storm Army Nursing Lessons Learned Conference, 9–10 July 1991."

18. Office of the Surgeon General, "After Action Report for Operation Desert Shield/Storm Army Nursing Lessons Learned Conference, 9–10 July 1991." For a more positive view, see Capt. Frederick E. Ludwig II, Lt. Col. Bernard J. Horak, Cdr. Mark R. Wallace, and Cdr. Martin K. Deafenbaugh, "Rapid Host Nation Medical Deployment," *Military Medicine*, Vol. 157 (November 1992), pp. 598–601.

ATTRITION

The financial hardships suffered by self-employed professionals in the Army Reserve has received a fair degree of attention. Many of these individuals were members of the medical department, particularly medical doctors and dentists. Not only were these practitioners compelled to abandon their practices for months, thereby incurring the sometimes-permanent loss of patients they had served for years, but they were often required to continue to pay significant malpractice premiums. In some instances, physicians who were making $4,000 per month as military officers were paying $5,000 per month in malpractice premiums. Such a situation necessarily led to disenchantment with the notion of serving their country as a reserve commissioned officer. The result was a dramatic increase in voluntary separations from the Army Reserve at the end of Desert Storm.[19]

An extreme example of the hardship experienced by some of these medical personnel was the case of Dr. (Lt. Col.) John Roane. Roane, a periodontal specialist in Houston, Tex., was called to active duty for eight months during Desert Shield/Desert Storm. Given three days notice of his call-up, Roane did not even have time to properly prepare his practice for his absence. Though the protection afforded Reservists under the Soldiers' and Sailors' Civil Relief Act was of some benefit, said Roane, "all my creditors came for me like wolves."[20]

Roane ended up hiring a lawyer to try to gain some relief from his creditors, a move that cost him $20,000. Ulti-

---

19. U.S. Army Health Services Command, "A Survey of Army Medical Department Reserve Personnel Mobilized in Support of Operation DESERT STORM," cited in Brinkerhoff, *Medical*, fn 186, p. 107. See also Grant Willis, "The backfill blues," *Air Force Times*, December 16, 1991, p. 14. A Reserve optometrist quoted in William Matthews, "Financial protection loses in White House," *Army Times*, May 9, 1994, p. 26, said that "Among doctors, 75 percent lost money during the Persian Gulf War." In its own survey, the Navy found an even greater percentage of Naval Reserve doctors who lost money during call-up. According to their figures, which may or may not reflect the experience of Army Reservists, general surgeons reported losses of $72,000; anesthesiologists lost $84,000; family practitioners lost $52,000; orthopedic surgeons lost $104,000, and dentists lost $32,000. In terms of percentage of income they lost, 21% reported income losses of 50% or more; 9.3% lost 40%; 22% lost 30%; 23.8% lost 20%; and 13.1% lost income of 10%. On the other end, 4.2% reported income gains of 10% and 6.6% gained 20% or more. Survey results cited in Patrick Pexton, "Gulf recall proved costly for some docs," *Navy Times*, April 26, 1993, p. 8.

20. Soraya S. Nelson, "Doctors pay high price for deployment," *Army Times*, October 18, 1993, p. 19.

mately, said Roane, bill collectors ruined his credit rating, and he could not obtain a loan to restart his practice. "Now I just work out of [referring dentists'] offices. I wander around like a gypsy and probably will never have my own office again."[21]

Comparing fiscal years 1990 and 1991, the differences in numbers of resignations are significant. In FY 90, 28 reserve officers resigned from the Dental Corps; in FY 91 the number was 115. Among Medical Corps officers (physicians), the comparable figures were 99 and 435.[22] Though these numbers represent only a small percentage of the Army Reserve's medical strength, they are enough to suggest a problem that warrants examination.

AMBULANCE UNITS

September 1990 call-ups included three ambulance units—two air evacuation and one wheeled ambulance unit, with others of this type being called throughout the build-up. USAR aeromedical evacuation units called up during Desert Shield/Desert Storm were the 273d Helicopter Ambulance Detachment from Conroe, Tex.; the 316th Helicopter Ambulance Detachment from Elyria, Oh.; and the 321st Helicopter Ambulance Detachment from Salt Lake City, Utah.[23]

The 316th, commanded by Maj. Ernest Hollo, Jr., arrived in Dharan on January 6, 1991, and then spent two weeks waiting for equipment and supplies. After some shuffling around, it was finally assigned to the 217th Medical Battalion, an ARNG unit from Colorado. Because the 316th had brought a considerable quantity of supplies with it from home station, it was able to operate effectively with little in-theater support—which seemed not to be forthcoming anyway. The 316th and the 273d were part of the unit that moved with the battalion task force into Iraq with the Forward Area Support Team of the 1st Cavalry Division on February 27, 1991. Task Force 217, which included the 321st, moved into Kuwait with elements of the 2d Armored Cavalry Regiment on March 1, 1991, remaining there until March 5.[24]

The 477th Medical Company (Ambulance) was commanded by Capt. Richard Kuznia. This unit, from Duluth,

21. *Ibid.*

22. Brinkerhoff, *Medical*, p. 82.

23. Memorandum, AFKC–ACD–TCB, 319th Transportation Brigade (COSCOM), September 7, 1990, Col. John T. Crowe, with later attachment, copy in DS/DS files, USACMH; Brinkerhoff, *Medical*, pp. 45–48.

24. Brinkerhoff, *Medical*, pp. 45–46.

Minn., was mobilized on November 21, 1990 and reached Saudi Arabia on January 12, 1991. Its ambulances consisted of 22 HMMWVs and 12 CUCVs, and it was issued additional ambulances in country. The 477th was assigned to the 803d Medical Group, an Army Reserve unit from Boston, Mass. The 477th was in Southwest Asia for almost five months, and during this period it transported over 8,000 patients, most of them Iraqi prisoners and displaced civilians.[25]

803D MEDICAL GROUP

The 803d Medical Group, headquartered in Boston, Mass., went from mobilization at Fort Devens to arrival in Saudi Arabia in only seventeen days. The 803d, commanded by Col. Richard H. Kennedy, was assigned to the 3d Medical Command and provided echelons above corps support to the VII and XVIII Corps.[26]

The 803d commanded 11 other units, operating out of Log Base Bravo. Among the major units under the Boston Reservists were the 251st Evacuation Hospital from Columbia, S.C., which helped manage a Saudi hospital. Other evac hospitals under the 803d were the 114th from San Antonio, Tex., and the 350th from Canton, Oh. These two hospitals did not have the luxury of working in an established, fixed hospital, but created their own facilities with Deployable Medical Systems (DEPMEDS) sets that had been shipped into Saudi Arabia.[27]

345TH COMBAT SUPPORT HOSPITAL

An Army Reserve Combat Support Hospital (CSH) that had an unusual experience during Desert Storm was the 345th, from Jacksonville, Fla. The 345th, commanded by Col. John E. Butler, reached Saudi Arabia on January 14, 1991, and was assigned to the 127th Medical group, an ARNG unit from Kentucky. In late January the 345th moved to a forward assembly area, where it was reconfigured into a Mobile Army Surgical Hospital (MASH). It then lost 70 of its personnel to other units and received 30 in return.[28]

As the 345th MASH, it was reassigned to the 341st Medical Group. On February 21 and 22, the 345th went into Iraq

---

25. *Ibid.*, p. 48.

26. Ro Chamberlin, "Boston medics provide 'echeolns-above-corps' support," *Army Reserve Magazine*, Vol. 38, No. 1 (1992), p. 14.

27. *Ibid.*, pp. 14–16.

28. Brinkerhoff, *Medical*, pp. 46–47.

behind the 3d Armored Division, remaining in its vehicles to follow the advance further. It then moved into the Iraq-Kuwait border area, then back into Saudi Arabia. It had remained loaded on its trucks and other vehicles throughout the ground war. It certainly functioned as the "M" part of MASH, if not totally as the "SH."[29]

MEDICAL DETACHMENTS

In addition to hospitals and company-sized units, the Army Reserve also furnished 21 medical detachments to the Southwest Asia theater: 1 anesthesiology, 3 laboratory, 3 maxillofacial surgery, 5 neurosurgical, 3 orthopedic surgery, 3 general surgery, 1 thoracic surgery, and 2 psychiatric. These detachments are small—sometimes no more than four or five personnel assigned—and specialized.[30]

DENTAL DETS

There were also Army Reserve dental detachments mobilized for the conflict, though none were sent to Southwest Asia. Instead, three USAR dental detachments—the 300th from Bellmore, N.Y.; the 308th from Fort Sheridan, Ill.; and the 919th from Aurora, Colo.—were sent to Europe, where they filled in for active component units that had been sent from Germany to Southwest Asia.

In addition, 17 Army Reserve dental detachments were mobilized and dispatched to installations in the U.S., where their primary function was to provide dental services to activated Reservists. This augmentation of the dental capability at the active component mobilization sites was necessary because of the terrible dental condition among deploying Reservists. While only 17% of active component soldiers examined were ineligible for deployment until they had received dental care, some 52% of reserve component soldiers fit into this category.[31]

---

29. *Ibid.*

30. *Ibid.*, pp. 42–43.

31. These detachments were the 1204th from Flushing, N.Y.; the 1205th from Utica, N.Y.; the 1206th from Dover, N.J.; the 2287th from Rockville, Md.; the 2288th from Sharonville, Oh.; the 3295th from Niagara Falls, N.Y.; the 3298th from Brooklyn, N.Y.; the 3299th from Chamblee, Ga.; the 3342d from Miami, Fla.; the 3346th from Fort Knox, Ky.; the 4005th from Houston, Tex.; the 5504th from Springfield, Mo.; the 5505th from Fort Benjamin Harrison, Ind.; the 5506th from St. Louis, Mo.; the 5507th from Madison, Wisc.; the 6254th from Phoenix, Ariz.; and the 6255th from Tacoma, Wash.; cited in *ibid.*, pp. 58, 56.

BLOOD UNITS

A final type of Army Reserve health care unit mobilized for Desert Shield/Desert Storm was ones concerned with blood supply. These units, which range from blood collecting, to processing, to distribution, were a vital part of the total medical picture. Seven USAR blood collecting detachments were mobilized, with five of these remaining in the U.S. and two being sent to Europe. Of the three Army Reserve blood processing detachments mobilized, one remained stateside, one went to Europe, and one went to Southwest Asia. Both of the Army Reserve blood distribution detachments were sent to Southwest Asia, as was the one Army Reserve Blood Bank Company, the 379th from Folsom, Pa. Each of these detachments has no more than ten or twelve soldiers assigned. The blood bank company is even smaller: it is a six person unit designed as command and control for a field blood program.[32]

MEDICAL LOGISTICS

The medical logistics organization in theater also depended upon Army Reserve units for a significant part of its assets. At the U.S. Army Medical Materiel Center Saudi Arabia (USAMMCSA), the 402d Inventory Control Detachment from Chester, Pa., the 484th Inventory Control Detachment from Kalamazoo, Mich., were complemented by the 220th Medical Maintenance Detachment of Madison, Wisc. At echelons above corps level, the 145th MEDSOM Battalion served the Army's needs, while the 482d Medical detachment worked under VII Corps. The inventory control detachments assisted with control of medical logistics in the theater, while the 220th Medical Maintenance Detachment, an eight-member unit commanded by Sgt. 1st Class Ray Beutler, was responsible for oxygen cylinder and regulator supply.[33]

PSYCHIATRIC DETACHMENTS

Two Army Reserve psychiatric detachments also deployed to Southwest Asia. These units, the 467th from Madison, Wisc.,

32. *Ibid.*, pp. 60–61. The blood collecting dets were the 334th from Perrine, Fla.; the 353d from Fort Bliss, Tex.; the 355th from Fort Hamilton, N.Y.; the 371st from Weirton, W.Va.; the 375th from Fort Benjamin Harrison, Ind.; the 324th from Chester, Pa.; and the 325th from Mesquite, Tex. The blood processing dets were the 392d from Fort Hamilton, N.Y.; the 548th from Madison, Wisc., and the 448th from Des Moines, Iowa. The blood distribution dets were the 387th from Brooklyn, N.Y. and the 605th from Des Moines, Iowa.

33. *Ibid.*, pp. 63–66.

and the 531st from Baltimore, Md., were authorized 48 personnel, including 17 officers and 31 enlisted personnel. They were supposed to be staffed with 7 psychiatrists, 1 psychologist, 6 social workers, and 2 psychiatric nurses, but the units were chronically short of psychiatrists. Some vacancies were filled before the units left for Saudi Arabia, while others were not. In the case of the 531st, the detachment commander was initially undeployable because he had not completed the officer basic course. (This was a common problem with Army Reserve medical officers and is mentioned in the "lessons learned" sections of numerous reports, including those from the Army Center for Lessons Learned at Leavenworth and the ARPERCEN lessons learned documents).[34]

The 467th, commanded by Lt. Col. Virginia Sincavan, was mobilized on November 21, 1991, and reached Riyadh on December 13. It had only one psychiatrist when mobilized, so its vacancies were filled by the National AMEDD Augmentation Detachment (NAAD). It worked with the 50th General Hospital, a USAR unit from Fort Lawton, Wash., and took patients from units near Riyadh. As the ground war loomed, the 467th was divided into four teams, and its personnel were placed well-forward in the theater. Even after the end of the war a seven-member team remained behind to offer combat stress treatment to those who remained in the theater awaiting re-deployment. This final team returned to the U.S. on May 27, 1991.[35]

The 531st, meanwhile, was assigned in support of VII Corps. Like its counterpart, the 531st was divided into teams, with one team supporting each division within the corps and a fifth team at the corps itself.[36]

82D FIELD HOSPITAL

Sometimes an Army Reserve unit that was not itself mobilized proved significant in the Desert Shield/Desert Storm endeavor. This was the case with the 82d Field Hospital of Omaha, Neb., commanded by Col. Joseph Bertinetti. With an assigned strength of over 475 personnel, including two dozen

34. *Ibid.*, pp. 66–68. Some relief was granted the Army in the National Defense Authorization Act for Fiscal Year 1994. Section 511 provided that "A period of basic training (or equivalent training) shorter than 12 weeks may be established by the Secretary concerned for members of the armed forces who have been credentialed in a medical profession or occupation and are serving in a health care occupational specialty. . . ."

35. *Ibid.*

36. *Ibid.*

medical doctors and ninety nurses, the 82d is staffed and equipped to provide temporary care for up to 400 patients. One hundred forty-seven members of the 82d were involuntarily called to active duty on December 20, and 6 additional unit members volunteered for active service.

These individuals were scattered to some thirty units or stations, the largest numbers going to the 410th Evac Hospital (20), the 217th Evac Hospital (17), and the 44th Evac Hospital (12). In addition, 17 unit members were involuntarily called to active duty on January 31, 1991, and sent to Fort Hood, Tex. In total, over one-third of the unit was called to active duty during Desert Shield/Desert Storm, and many of them were sent to Southwest Asia.[37]

VETERINARY UNITS

Not all Army Reserve medical units treat people. The 356th Medical Detachment, a unit in the 77th ARCOM, specializes in veterinary medicine. The members of a unit like the 356th are as likely—perhaps even more likely—to inspect food and food handling procedures as to be called upon to give rabies shots to a working dog like one used to patrol fence perimeters.

The 356th was mobilized in December 1990 and reported to Fort Meade, Md., where it received the standard refresher training in chemical warfare defense. It reported into the Southwest Asia Theater of Operations on January 11, 1991, and remained there until April 13. Its thirty-five soldiers were spread throughout the region and inspected food supplies, including live animals that would become food for American military personnel.[38]

The job of these detachments was vital to the health and well-being of the American soldiers in the theater because of the considerable quantities of fresh food that was served. By mid-January 1991 some 300 food purveyors throughout Saudi Arabia, the UAE, Qatar, Oman, and Bahrain had been subjected to U.S. veterinary inspections, and seventy-five percent of the suppliers were approved as sources for food for U.S. troops.[39]

---

37. *AHS, 89th ARCOM*, pp. XI–3 thru XI–7.

38. *77th ARCOM*; other Army Reserve veterinary services detachments that were called up and sent to Southwest Asia were the 320th from Chicago, Ill.; the 358th from Opelika, Ala.; the 422d from Rockville, Md.; the 423d from Chicago, Ill.; the 449th Veterinary Detachment (Small Animal) from Ames, Ia.; and the 888th Veterinary Detachment (Small Animal) from Lexington, Ky.

39. Brinkerhoff, *Medical*, pp. 71–72.

PREVENTIVE MEDICINE

Preventive medicine was also in part an Army Reserve responsibility. The 12th Preventive Medicine Detachment from Beloit, Wisc., was mobilized on November 24 at Fort McCoy and reached Saudi Arabia on December 10. Its sixty-five personnel did water quality testing at local bottling plants, checked sanitation at EPW camps, and tested air quality both at vehicle painting shops and near the burning oil wells of Kuwait.

The 983d Medical Detachment from Fort Snelling, Minn., was commanded by Lt. Col. William J. Phillipsen. Its nine members arrived in Saudi Arabia on December 12, 1990, and spent most of their time in Saudi at Khobar Village, Dharan. This unit had the decidedly unglamorous—but extremely necessary—job of inspecting mess halls, latrines, showers, water supply points, and anywhere else that might be a source of disease for U.S. troops. It also conducted field sanitation classes for representatives of eighty-four troop units. and sprayed for insects and rodents. Though it cannot be absolutely ascribed to the efforts of the these Army Reserve units and their active component colleagues—there were no ARNG preventive medicine units in theater—the disease/non-battle injury (DNBI) daily rate of patients admitted to hospitals per 1,000 soldiers for Desert Shield (0.34) and Desert Storm (0.40) compares most favorably with Vietnam's 0.89 and the Korean War's 1.67. [40]

44TH GENERAL HOSPITAL

Most of the Army Reserve medical units mobilized for Desert Shield/Desert Storm were sent to Southwest Asia, but some were not. One of these units was the 44th General Hospital (1,000-bed), headquartered in Madison and Menasha, Wisc. This hospital was alerted on December 4, 1990, and during the remainder of the month its vacancies were filled with qualified personnel from the 452d and 801st General Hospitals. As a result, when it was actually mobilized on January 9, 1991, it was at 96 percent strength.

Following mobilization at Fort McCoy, Wisc., the unit was sent to Germany, where its members were divided among fourteen sites in Germany, one in Italy, and one in Turkey. This fragmentation, not surprisingly, caused morale problems within the unit and made it very difficult for the hospital commander, Col. Steven W. Babcock, to maintain control of his soldiers. The Reservists began immediately to prepare for the influx of casualties that was expected as a result of the war, but, of course, the casualties never came.

40. *Ibid.*, pp. 77–78.

The unit's historian relates that "unit personnel were given commensurate responsibilities with those of the active component," a statement which suggests that professionalism and mutual respect can go a long way toward overcoming reserve component/active component rivalries and misunderstandings. Redeployment of unit members stateside began at the end of April 1991, with demobilization for most of the unit accomplished at Fort McCoy on May 6. Some 160 hospital personnel were retained in Europe to fill in for active army members who had not yet returned from Southwest Asia. These individuals returned to Fort McCoy by the end of June, thus completing the mission of the hospital.[41]

NURSES OF THE 365TH EVAC

For many Reservists, the call to active duty was both a surprise and a challenge. Three nurses from the 365th Evacuation Hospital in Niagara Falls, N.Y., for example, had only recently returned from completing the Command and General Staff College course at Dover, Del., when Desert Shield began. During the fall of 1990 they drilled and trained and wondered whether their unit would be mobilized. The 365th was not included among the first medical units called up, but in the late fall the unit was alerted for mobilization and was called to active duty a few days later. These nurses, like Army Reservists across the country, suddenly faced the prospect of leaving their spouses and their children—in some cases their grandchildren—and going off to the desert.

As one of them, Maj. Jo Wood, put it, "We were upset at first because the mobilization meant disruption of our lives, and of the lives of our families. But then we got to thinking about it, and we all decided that if American soldiers were going to get hurt, they needed the best possible medical care—and that is us." Major Wood and the other members of the 365th were initially sent to Aberdeen Proving Grounds, Md., where they were housed in old barracks and bused to Walter Reed Army Medical center each day for refresher training. Following their training, the 365th was sent to Oman, where they waited for the casualties that never came.[42]

---

41. *AHR, 86th ARCOM*, pp. 42–43

42. Interview, Lt. Col. James T. Currie with Maj. Jo Wood, December 11, 1990; the author arranged for several of these nurses to join him for lunch in the Senators' Dining Room in the U.S. Capitol. They appeared in their BDUs and were a big hit with the dining room crowd. Senators John Glenn (D–Oh.) and William Cohen (R–Me.) came over and were introduced to the group. It was quite an experience, said the nurses.

This group of nurses was typical of the Army Reservists who went when they were called. On the day of the desert war ceasefire (February 28, 1991), Maj. Wood wrote the following: "Being here has truly been a wonderful experience in so many ways. Living in our warehouse home and learning to live so simply has made me re-evaluate what the important things are in life. It also makes me appreciate what America is all about."[43] The 365th treated a few minor injuries and suffered none themselves. They were among the lucky ones.

CHAPLAINS

These chapters are largely devoted to *units* of the USAR that were mobilized for Desert Shield/Desert Storm, and chaplains do not fit into this category. They deserve special mention in this history, however, because they are assigned to major units of the USAR and have a significant role to play whenever large numbers of Reservists are mobilized. In addition to the troop program unit chaplains, there is a significant requirement for augmentation when hundreds of reserve units are mobilized and tens of thousands of individual reservists are called to active duty.

One of the problems with the Desert Shield/Desert Storm call-up was a shortage of chaplains. Chaplains are a vital part of the family support network as soldiers are sent overseas, and there simply were not enough active duty chaplains to meet the needs of the Army. The commander of the Army's Training and Doctrine Command (TRADOC), Gen. John W. Foss, determined early in the mobilization effort that he would not ask for reservists to be called to active duty to support base operations, a category that included the chaplains.[44]

Active component units that deployed overseas took their chaplains with them, leaving many installations with too few chaplains to do the required work. Fort Benning, for example, was left with only two Catholic chaplains, Fort Bliss had one, and Fort Story, Va., operated with one chaplain on the post.[45] There was desperate need for augmentation.

When it became apparent that there was to be a large-scale mobilization of Army Reserve units, the United States Army Reserve Personnel Center's (ARPERCEN) Chaplain's Office was quickly tasked with identifying the individuals

---

43. Letter, Maj Jo Wood, in possession of the author.
44. Canedy *et al., TRADOC Support*, p. 77.
45. *Ibid.*

needed for this augmentation. Chaplains are an unusual group within the Army, however, in that they have to be endorsed, or recognized, by their denomination in order to serve as a chaplain. If for some reason they lose that endorsement, they are no longer qualified to serve as a chaplain. These rules are clear and are understood by those involved in the program.

What ARPERCEN discovered, however, was that "neither the Army nor the denominations were carefully monitoring the endorsement of Reserve Component chaplains." This situation did not extend to the active component, but it was magnified with regard to chaplains in the Retired Reserve who were still considered mobilization assets. In addition, early in the build-up some chaplains were actually pulled from their units and sent to Europe on active duty assignments. When their Reserve units were later mobilized, these chaplains were not reassigned to be with the Rservists with whom they had long served.

To fill the need, chaplains were called from the Individual Ready Reserve (IRR), from troop units, and even from among the retirees. According to the chief of the chaplain's office at ARPERCEN, these retired chaplains proved a significant source of strength for the program. Of those contacted and asked to voluntarily come onto active duty, some 76 percent agreed to do so.[46]

Of the 1,300-plus chaplains in the Army Reserve at the time of Desert Shield, 346 were ultimately placed on active duty. As mentioned above, some of these were from Army Reserve units that were later mobilized; others went with their units. Two hundred twelve Reserve chaplains served at CONUS installations, often as replacements for active component chaplains who had been sent elsewhere, while 104 went to Southwest Asia and 30 went to Germany.[47]

Policies governing the USAR chaplains in Southwest Asia were not established by the Army Reserve. USAR chaplains followed the rules and guidance issued at Headquarters, Department of the Army for all chaplains in the theater of operations. These rules were not always applauded by the Reservists to whom the chaplains were ministering. The Chicago-based 416th Engineer Command, USAR, for example, included some

---

46. U.S. Army Reserve Personnel Center (ARPERCEN), *Desert Shield/Desert Storm: A History*, p. C13–14; interview, Lt. Col. James T. Currie with Chaplain Bruns, ARPERCEN, June 23, 1992; notes in possession of the author.

47. "Chaplains," chapter 8 of *Personnel Service Support*, draft manuscript, ANDRULIS Research Corporation, 1995, pp. 8–3 through 8–5, 8–8.

hicles, 103,124 wheeled vehicles, 1,224 aircraft, and 26,062 forty-foot shipping containers to the United States.[14]

Pagonis, though not effusive in his praise of the 21st TAACOM (which had functioned under his 22d SUPCOM), described Jones as "energetic and dedicated" and noted that the 21st TAACOM "ably held down the fort during much of the redeployment phase." Jones spoke later of the sixteen-hour days his troops put in, and said that "I imagine some of them will never want to see an Army cot, a uniform, or a tent the rest of their lives. "There was," he said, "never a more dedicated, educated group in the military, and I think they completely validated the reserve's role in a volunteer Army."[15]

INFANTRY: 3/87TH

There were few combat units in the Army Reserve in 1990. One Army Reserve infantry unit, the 3d Battalion, 87th Infantry, was activated for Desert Shield/Desert Storm, but it got no closer to the fray than Germany. It was one of forty-seven reserve component units deployed there during the build-up.

Some of these reserve units were sent to Germany in direct support of operations in the desert, but others like the 3/87th were sent overseas to provide security in the areas vacated by active component troops that were transferred from Europe to the Southwest Asia theater. Germany had long been a place where terrorist activities might occur at any time, and the war against Saddam Hussein was thought to be a likely catalyst for such. The 3/87th was specifically tasked with guarding the Frankfurt area.[16]

The 3/87th was headquartered at Fort Carson, Colo., with Company A in Pueblo, and Companies B and C in Denver. Its commander at the time of Desert Shield was Lt. Col. Dean F. O'Neil, a former Vietnam War rifle platoon leader who had been with the unit since June 1989. In the spring of

14. *AHS, 123d ARCOM.*

15. *Ibid*; Pagonis, *Moving Mountains*, p. 136.

16. John R. Brinkerhoff, *United States Army Reserve in Operation Desert Storm: Countering the Terrorist Threat: The 3d Battalion, 87th Infantry* (Washington: Office of the Chief, Army Reserve, 1993), pp. 2–4; hereinafter cited as "Brinkerhoff, *3/87th*." There were 121 terrorist incidents directed against U.S. interests worldwide during this period, but none was of such a nature as to require the dispatch of U.S. troops. Testimony of Gen. Carl W. Stiner, Commander-in-Chief, U.S. Special Operations Command, May 9, 1991, to Defense Subcommittee, Appropriations Committee, United States House of Representatives, 102d Congress, 1st session, *Department of Defense Appropriations for 1992, Part 2*, p. 236.

1990 the unit had been evaluated by a team from the 193d Light Infantry Brigade—to which the 3/87th had a CAPSTONE assignment—and was judged "a truly competent sister battalion." Annual training 1990, conducted from August 5–17 at Fort Carson, resulted in a mixed set of ratings, with most areas needing improvement and some, including ability to operate in a nuclear, biological, and chemical environment, rated "U," for unsatisfactory.[17]

The unit was called to active duty on January 17, with 594 personnel (out of 780 assigned) actually reporting with the unit. The strength shortage was partially remedied when the Army Reserve Personnel Center in St. Louis (ARPERCEN) assigned 114 enlisted IRR volunteers to the unit.

While at Fort Carson the unit devoted five days to in-processing, ten to training, two to preparation for overseas movement, and three to preparing for deployment. Training included sessions on the "Uniform Code of Military Justice, subversion, and the threat." The unit received mission-specific training on such items as the nature of NATO and how to handle civil disturbances, as well as individual training in NBC defense, communications and first aid. Bayonet drills were offered as a way to instill "the fighting spirit" in the soldiers of the 3/87th, and everyone took the standard Army physical fitness test. Much time was devoted to range firing.[18]

Many members of the unit did accept the fact that they would be sent to Germany and not to Saudi Arabia, despite every attempt to convince them that this was indeed the case. The IRR soldiers who had volunteered for active duty and received an assignment to the 3/87th were particularly upset, as they did not feel that they had come out of the IRR and back onto active duty for any reason other than to go fight the Iraqis. The desire for a combat assignment manifested itself in the unit's request that it be allowed to deploy to Germany with its full complement of weapons, including machine guns, mortars, and TOWs. FORSCOM, however, directed that only individual weapons be taken.[19]

The unit and its active component evaluators differed as to the readiness of the unit to undertake an active duty mission. Readiness Group Denver, commanded by Col. James E. Record, was responsible for validation of the ability of the unit to perform its assigned mission, and the Readiness Group sim-

17. *Ibid.*, pp. 8, 6, 11.
18. *Ibid.*, pp. 15–16.
19. *Ibid.*, p. 18.

ply did not believe the unit to be very capable. According to a November 1992 memorandum from the Readiness Group, "the only way they [the 3/87th] could have been validated for deployment was if they did not have to go into combat."[20] The Readiness Group did not feel that the battalion was capable of performing at any level above that of the platoon, an observation that members of the unit were quick to dispute.

Mirroring other active component-reserve component controversies about who was ready to fight and who was not, the dispute over the 3/87th deteriorated into rumor, innuendo, and hard feelings all around. According to the battalion chaplain, he and another member of the 3/87th were told by an officer from the Readiness Group that their unit "would never go to Saudi Arabia" because the Army would not allow reserve component combat units to look good.[21] Correctly understood and reported or not—and one active component Army historian who read this chapter in draft form questioned whether any active duty officer would make such a statement—it is an accurate reflection of the tension that has existed between active and reserve components, particularly in the combat arms.[22]

Soon enough, the pre-deployment training at Fort Carson was completed, and the unit left for Germany, where it was placed under the 18th MP Brigade, an active component unit. Relations with the 18th were strained, to say the least. There was a feeling among the soldiers in the 3/87th that these active component MPs did not regard them as equals, while the Reservists thought that they as infantrymen were clearly superior to any military police.

Despite the rocky beginning, the tutelage of the MPs seems to have improved the ability of the Reserve infantrymen to perform their mission, though there were continuing controversies between the 3/87th and the 18th in seemingly unimportant—but terribly symbolic—requirements levied on the Reservists by the

20. Quoted in Brinkerhoff, *3/87th*, p. 19.

21. Telephone interview with Chaplain Richard T. Leever, October 21, 1992, quoted in *ibid.*, p. 19.

22. In his position as a faculty member at one of the senior service ("war") colleges, the author has heard many members of the active component of the Army disparage the ability and training of the reserves. These individuals are almost invariably officers who have never worked directly with the reserve components. Conversely, Army officers who have seen the reserve components in action, including many who worked closely with Army Reserve units during Desert Shield/Desert Storm have been almost unanimous in their praise of their reserve component colleagues. Interestingly, active duty Air Force officers never have anything but complimentary comments about their reserve component counterparts.

active component headquarters. These requirements ranged the gamut from a requirement to wear rubber boots while on guard duty to the daily counting of ammunition.[23]

The actual assignment given the men of the 3/87th, assumed on March 1, 1991, was to "Conduct force protection operations in the Frankfurt area; one company remains at Ray Barracks, conducts unit training, and on order, executes security reaction force mission within USAREUR." In other words, the Reservists provided security for the area, both by standing fixed guard mount and by active patrolling. The primary threat, as indicated earlier, was thought to be from Iraqi-sponsored terrorists. Germany was like other areas of the world during this period, however: there were no incidents unequivocably attributable to Iraq. The 3/87th completed its mission in good fashion and after eighty-four days in Germany returned to Fort Carson on May 1 for out-processing.[24]

The time at Fort Carson saw some of the same tensions resurface between the battalion and the Readiness Group, and especially between battalion commander O'Neil and Readiness Group commander Record. Personality conflicts surfaced between the two men once again, and Record eventually got O'Neil relieved from command, with treatment of the IRR assignees to the 3/87th largely the catalyst.

Part of the conflict between the two men arose from O'Neil's allowing soldiers from the Denver and Pueblo companies to go home at night, over the objection of Record, while not affording the same privilege to the IRR members of the command.[25]

The story of the 3/87th is not one of glory in the desert, as is the case with most of the units chronicled in this narrative. It is illustrative, however, because it shows the breadth of missions that the Army Reserve can be called upon to perform, and to perform successfully.[26] It is also an example, as is the case with other stories told in these pages, that so much of what a unit does and how it is perceived by others is personality-dependent.

---

23. *Ibid.*, pp. 20–30.

24. *Ibid.*, pp. 28–29, 32.

25. *Ibid.*, p. 32.

26. V Corps recognized the quality of the mission performance of the 3/87th as follows: "3/87th IN Bn has performed its mission in an outstanding manner and served as an excellent representative of the Reserve Components. Their professionalism is commendable, and the soldiers, civilian employees, and family members of the V (U.S.) Corps greatly appreciate their efforts and contributions to security in USAREUR during DESERT STORM." Quoted in Brinkerhoff, *3/87th*, p. 34.

SIGNAL

Among the significant non-players during Desert Shield/ Desert Storm were the reserve component signal units, in contrast to reserve component units of other types. Some 23% of the Army personnel in the Southwest Asia Theater were from the reserve components, and reserve units of various types provided a significant percentage of the total Army assets in theater. For example, 73% of military police, 19% of psychological operations personnel, and even 5% of the soldiers doing military intelligence were from the reserve components. Reserve signal units, however, provided only 0.6% of the total assets used in theater.[27]

335TH SIGNAL COMMAND

For some observers, one of the greatest surprises of the signal unit non-deployment was the failure to mobilize the 335th Theater Signal Command, USAR, from Atlanta, Ga. Commanded by Maj. Gen. John R. McWaters, the 335th was the signal support headquarters for the Third U.S. Army—the Army component of the U.S. Central Command. The 335th had a CAPSTONE trace which reflected its potential command of two signal brigades: the 11th, an active component unit from Fort Huachuca, Ariz., and the 228th, an ARNG unit from Spartanburg, S.C. The 335th had also been working since 1986 to develop plans on the Southwest Asia mission in support of Third Army. In this context it had participated in various BRIGHT STAR, GALLANT EAGLE, GALLANT KNIGHT, and BLUE FLAG exercises. When the war began, the 335th assumed it would be called to duty.[28]

The decision not to mobilize the 335th is in many ways analogous to that taken with respect to the 377th TAACOM. The decision about the 335th, however, seems to have revolved more around personality clashes than about unit capabilities—on its face a poor way to make mobilization decisions.

According to one study of the decisionmaking process, Maj. Gen. McWaters was a primary cause of the clash. On August 11 Reserve general McWaters visited Third Army headquarters at Fort McPherson and suggested to the leadership there that the G–6 of Third Army, Col. James C. Cannon, be replaced with his own man, Col. Gene Neelly. The presumed reason for this suggestion was that Cannon, who had taken

27. Brinkerhoff, *335th Signal,* p. 1.
28. *Ibid.*, pp. 17–18.

over as G–6 barely a month earlier, had gone on personal leave at a time when everything was breaking in Kuwait. It was absolutely none of McWaters' business what leave Cannon took, and McWaters had no right to suggest the removal of Cannon, but he did so anyway. In so doing he further alienated the active component command and led to the release from duty of the fifteen AGR officers—including Col. Neelly—who had been serving with the Third Army G–6.[29]

The personality of McWaters may have played a significant role in the non-deployment decision for the 335th, but, on the other hand, it may have simply been an irritant. One of the reasons offered for the decision not to call the 335th and its subordinate Reserve units was that they were not equipped with the latest digital equipment and were not trained to operate such. Furthermore, there was thought to be no need for the type of theater signal command represented by the 335th. The recommendation that the 335th not be used was made to Yeosock by Cannon, the man whom McWaters wanted to have replaced.[30]

According to Yeosock, personalities had nothing to do with the decision not to mobilize the 335th. He simply did not need another headquarters in theater. So he created an *ad hoc* arrangement called the 6th Signal Command, a lean headquarters that functioned as the 335th might have done. The new headquarters operated under the ARCENT G–6.

This led to a tit-for-tat contest in which the Army's needs were subordinated to ego and personality clash. When the commander of the Army Information Systems Command sought to augment the new headquarters with fifteen soldiers from the 335th, McWaters refused to release the Reservists, declaring that the 335th was not a "replacement pool" for the active component and that "if anyone from the 335th was to go, the flag would go also."[31]

In the end, neither the 335th nor its subordinate units were mobilized. In fact, only one reserve component signal

---

29. This was apparently not the first time that McWaters had gotten into a tiff with active component general officers. As a result of an earlier run-in, the Deputy Third Army Commander, Maj. Gen. William H. Riley, had declared McWaters *persona non grata* and had vowed that he would personally escort him from the building if he ever showed up again. On August 11, however, Riley was not present. See Brinkerhoff, *Signal Command*, pp 20–21.

30. *Ibid.*, p. 23. This, of course, raises the question of why a major Reserve unit would be saddled with equipment that was so outdated as to be useless during a war and why the members of the unit would not be trained in how to operate current Army equipment.

31. *Ibid.*, p. 27.

unit—the 653d Signal Company (Light Tropo) from the Army National Guard—was mobilized and made a part of the 6th Signal Command. Further, a total of only four Army Reserve signal units were mobilized for Desert Shield/Desert Storm. The 2361st Signal Detachment from Akron, Oh., and the 2369th Signal Detachment from Chattanooga, Tenn., were called up and assigned to support duties at Fort McCoy, Wisc. The 858th CS Detachment (Crypto Support) of St. Louis, Mo., and the 884th CS Detachment (Crypto Support) of San Marcos, Tex., were mobilized and sent to the Southwest Asia theater of operations.[32]

Various reasons are offered for the failure to use the 335th. Having examined them, it seems most likely to have been a combination of the continuing lack of confidence in reserve component general officers, coupled with the particularly abrasive personality of the Army Reserve general in question in this instance, compounded by a lack of modern equipment in the reserve unit, together with the good job done by the active component colonel placed in charge of theater signal operations. Any one of these factors might have been enough to derail the deployment of the 335th. Together, they were more than sufficient. What this analysis does not explain, however, is the Army's failure to call company and detachment size signal units from the reserve components, as was done with the logistical units that served with the 22d SUPCOM. For that omission, no conclusions are offered.

PROBLEMS OF THE DEPLOYMENT: ARMY RESERVE GENERALS

There is within the Army Reserve community a belief that few reserve general officers were called to active duty during Desert Shield/Desert Storm. Many Reservists are convinced that there was a conspiracy on the part of the active component to keep reserve general officers from commanding units on active duty. The story is as follows.

In August 1990 there were 120 general officers in the Army Reserve: 73 brigadiers and 47 major generals. Five Army Reserve general officers (like the Chief and Deputy Chief, Army Reserve) were serving extended active duty tours, while other Army Reserve generals commanded ARCOMs—Army Reserve Commands that are themselves not mobilization assets. According to a study conducted for the Chief, Army Reserve, 10 of the 84 general officers assigned to troop units were called to active duty with their units. Seven of these

32. *Ibid.*, pp. 30–32.

were deployed to Southwest Asia. Of the 47 Army Reserve major generals, only one—the commander of the 416th Engineer Command—was called to active duty with his unit.[33]

Of the 31 Army Reserve general officers assigned to Individual Mobilization Augmentee (IMA) positions, only one, Maj. Gen. Max Baratz, then assigned as Deputy Commanding General of FORSCOM, was activated. According to the Army Reserve study, "The case of General Baratz is all the more exceptional because General Baratz simply reported for duty without waiting to be ordered, went to work, and after some delay was finally legalized in his status."[34]

The failure to call the Army Reserve IMA generals to active duty is all the more remarkable because the Desert Shield/Desert Storm mobilization seems precisely the sort of contingency for which the IMA program is designed. Although "each general staff section of the Army Staff had a Reserve general IMA, and each Army major command had one or more Reserve generals as IMAs, none of them were called to active duty to help out. . . ."[35]

So, was there a conspiracy on the part of the active component? Rumors of such abound, but neither the author of this study nor the historians at the U.S. Army Center of Military History ever found evidence of such.

The troop units of the USAR, important as they were, were only part of the contribution that the Army Reserve made to Desert Shield/Desert Storm. Less familiar than the troop unit personnel are those Reservists who serve in the Individual Ready Reserve (IRR), as Individual Mobilization Augmentees (IMAs), or as members of the Active Guard and Reserve (AGR) program. There were also retired Reservists who returned to active duty and served during the build-up and the war, as well as civilians who work for the Army Reserve. These individuals, the contributions they made, and the problems they encountered, are detailed in the following chapter.

33. John R. Brinkerhoff, *United States Army Reserve in Operation Desert Storm: Individual Manpower Mobilization: The Army Reserve Personnel Center* (Washington: Office of the Chief, Army Reserve, 1992). Hereinafter cited as "Brinkerhoff, *Individual Manpower Mobilization*," p. 34.

34. *Ibid.*, p. 35.

35. *Ibid.*

Army Reservists driving and refueling equipment during Fuertes Caminos '89, a road building operation in Honduras.

Female soldier ascending stairs to tower is Specialist Angela County, former Individual Ready Reservist. She was one of 41 Army Reservists activated in a battalion that deployed to the Sinai Peacekeeping Operations in Egypt.

Army Reservists at work in Saudi Arabia during Operation Desert Shield in 1990. Ultimately, more than 90,000 Army Reservists were activated in support of Operations Desert Shield/Desert Storm.

The Army Reserve provides a large percentage of the total Army's combat service support assets. This USAR member is just one of the thousands of such soldiers.

Members of the 926th Combat Engineer Battalion doing construction during CARIB '95, a humanitarian effort in the Bahamas.

21

Desert Shield/Desert Storm: ARPERCEN and the IRR

The troop unit members of the Army Reserve received most of the recognition and publicity for their contribution to the Desert Shield/Desert Storm effort. These Reservists, however, were but part of the Army Reserve story. A minority, but significant, percentage of the Army Reservists involved in this Total Army effort were members of the Individual Ready Reserve (IRR), a pre-trained group of men and women who are used as individual replacements in both reserve and active component units.

The Army's Individual Ready Reserve consisted in late 1990 of some 290,000 individuals. About eighty percent of these soldiers were in the grade of E–4 and below, and some forty percent of IRR members were men and women who had completed only a portion of the eight year service obligation that they incurred when they enlisted in the Army.[1]

For example, an enlistee who served four years on active duty would have a four year IRR requirement, during which time they would be available for recall to active duty; a three year active duty hitch would mean a five year IRR membership. The remaining sixty percent of the IRR consists of men and women—officers and enlisted personnel—who have satisfied their service obligation but want to maintain

1. Prior to July 1984 the obligation was only six years. Office of the Assistant Secretary of Defense, Reserve Affairs, Memorandum for OASD (PA)/DPL (Desert Storm Cell), Subject: Public Affairs Guidance—Presidential Authority to Call Units and Personnel of the Ready reserve to Active Duty, January 18, 1991.

an Army affiliation and contribute to the strength of the country's reserve components.[2]

STRENGTH OF THE IRR

The following chart indicates the enlisted strength and specialties that the Individual Ready Reserve contained during the Desert Shield/Desert Storm time frame. The numbers in this chart are from the DCSPER 46 report for May 1991, but the figures for the fall of 1990 and early 1991 would be quite similar:

Table 21-1 Enlisted IRR—Distribution by Career Management Field (CMF)

CMF	Number	CMF	Number
11 Infantry	33,224	71 Admin	18,851
12 CBT Engr	11,075	74 ADP	903
13 Field Arty	18,222	76 Sup & Svc	20,365
16 AD Arty	3,351	77 Petro & Water	3,956
18 Sp Ops	245	79 Recr & Reenlist	494
19 Armor	11,501	81 Top & Engr	479
23 AD Sys Maint	491	88 Transportation	13,651
25 Visual Info	395	91 Medical	22,220
27 L CPT & AV Sys Maint	862	93 Avn Opns	921
29 Sig Maint	2,993	94 Food Svc	9,177
31 Sig Ops	21,227	95 Mil Police	12,355
33 EW/Int Sys Maint	366	96 Mil Intel	1,788
46 Public Aff	243	97 Band	591
51 Gen Engr	7,615	98 Sig IN/EW Ops	2,080
54 Chem	2,479		
55 Ammo	1,863	Spec Duty	214
63 Mech Maint	29,863	Untrained	15,338
67 Aircraft Maint	6,269	CMF Unknown	2,357
		CMD Sgts Major	951
Total			278,975

ROLE OF THE IRR

The build-up of U.S. troop strength throughout the fall of 1990 was largely accomplished without resorting to the IRR. As Army planners anticipated the commencement of combat operations in January 1991, however, there were certain shortages in the force structure that seemed appropriate for

2. Memorandum for Correspondents No. 043–M, 20 January 1991, Desert Storm #11, ARPERCEN.

fill by members of this part of the Army Reserve. Among these were water purification specialists, military police, fuel handlers, truck drivers, medical personnel, and—ominously enough—graves registration specialists.[3]

Even the manpower pool of the IRR could not supply enough graves registration personnel to satisfy the Army's projected needs. The answer was to train more specialists, so the Quartermaster School at Fort Lee, Va., put on a class in January 1991 to train IRR members in this unpleasant—but necessary—task. Of the 63 soldiers who began the 57F course, 28 completed it and received the MOS designation. A requirement was also levied on ARPERCEN for 1,500 additional truck drivers (88M MOS), a shortfall which was remedied by establishing special training courses at Fort Dix, N.J.

Finally, a requirement for water treatment specialists (77W) was also met through additional MOS-producing courses, though in the case of the 77Ws, the shortened nature of the course led to some in-theater problems, such as those already mentioned in connection with the 79th Quartermaster Company (Water Supply). Of course, the soldiers of the 79th were troop unit members, while these water specialists were IRR, but the incompleteness of the short course caused the same types of problems.[4]

As can be seen from the previous chart, the IRR offered significant mobilization assets in the fall of 1990. ARPERCEN's planners began therefore to anticipate the Army's needs, even before the tasking was made. Linguists, for example, were a logical shortfall for the Army, so ARPERCEN used a data base search to identify Reservists who might prove helpful in the Gulf. The requirement for Arab linguists was easy to foresee, and the records branch at ARPERCEN was able to screen records and identify individuals who had once enjoyed a proficiency in that language. Records, however, do not offer any indication of current linguistic ability. ARPERCEN solved this problem by having the Defense Language Institute in Monterey, Calif., conduct over-the-telephone language tests of the reservists.[5]

---

3. Interview, Lt. Col. James T. Currie, with Charles V. Nahlik, Chief, Mobilization Plans and Operations Branch, ARPERCEN, June 23, 1992. Notes in possession of the author.

4. U.S. Army Reserve Personnel Center (ARPERCEN), *Desert Shield/ Desert Storm: A History*, pp. A2, C10; hereinafter cited as "ARPERCEN *History*."

5. Interview, Lt. Col. James T. Currie, with Maj. Michael Antonelli, ARPERCEN, June 23, 1992; notes in possession of the author. Ironically, the "logical" need of the Army for Arab linguists never materialized. Though ARPERCEN identified twenty-seven individuals with Arab language skills, none of them were called to active duty.

PARTIAL MOBILIZATION

On January 18, 1991, the day following the commencement of the air war in the Gulf, President George Bush signed Executive Order 12743 authorizing a "partial mobilization" in support of the war effort. In this executive order the President cited his authority under the United States Code, Title 10, Section 673, to order "any unit, and any member not assigned to a unit, in the Ready Reserve to active duty (other than for training) for not more than 24 consecutive months. . . ." Presidential press spokesman Marlin Fitzwater added that "this step is necessary to support the continued operations of U.S. forces in Operation Desert Storm. This authority will enable reservists to remain on active duty for longer than 180 days and will also permit the call to active duty of personnel in excess of the 200,000 previously authorized."[6]

This legally-significant step had not been taken until then, despite the call-up of tens of thousands of reservists. At this point the involuntary call-up of individual reservists began. ARPERCEN immediately increased its operational tempo and within a period of ten days sent out two batches of mailgrams.

On January 21 ARPERCEN sent 20,102 Western Union Mailgrams to enlisted soldiers in the IRR—87 percent in grades E–4 and below—ordering them to report for active duty within ten days. This package, designated "A–1," was followed on January 29 by a much smaller Package A–2, consisting of 101 officers, 28 warrant officers, and 689 enlisted soldiers. The commissioned officers were all captains and lieutenants. Altogether, some 20,920 IRR soldiers were ordered to involuntary active duty. (See Appendix H for an example of these mailgrams).[7]

Of the 20,000+ Army Reservists to whom mailgrams were sent, only about 300 had shown up at their designated mobilization sites by January 30—one day before the due date for Package A–1. There were reports of panic at the Department of the Army level, and questions of "Would the reservists report?" There was even dispute within the Army Staff about the decision to use the IRR, with some experts estimating that no more than 50 percent of the individual Army Re-

---

6. Quoted in *Weekly Compilation of Presidential Documents*, Monday, January 21, 1991, Volume 27, Number 3, pp. 59–61.

7. Ross G. Pickus, "Pride in Performance," *The Officer*, October 1991, p. 12; ARPERCEN *History*, p. C7; Brinkerhoff, *Individual Manpower Mobilization*, pp. 24–25.

servists would show up when ordered. The "traditional IRR show rate planning factor" was 70 percent, a figure derived from exercises and the earlier call-ups for Korea and the Berlin Crisis. But no one knew for sure how the Army Reservists of today would respond to an involuntary call-up.[8]

But respond they did. And some of them reported in style. According to one story, four enlisted Army Reservists arrived at Fort Jackson, S.C., at 11:45 p.m. on January 31—in a stretch limousine. They had beaten the reporting deadline by a mere fifteen minutes, and it was apparent to all who saw them that these men had been having quite a party. By February 2, some 14,422 Army Reservists had reported to their mobilization sites, and 17,310 eventually did so. The reasons why the other 3,610 reservists did not report as ordered were many and varied, though many of the no-shows are directly attributable to bad addresses, and consequently, to undeliverable mailgrams.[9]

Table 21-2 MOSs of Certain IRR Members/Enlisted IMAs Activated for Desert Shield/Desert Storm

MOS	Specialty	Number Called to Active Duty
11B	Infantry	3,100
13B	Cannon Crewmember	1,793
91A	Medical Specialist	1,774
88M	Motor Transport Operator	1,297
63B	Light Wheel Vehicle Mech	1,137
12B	Combat Engineer	1,114
19K	M1 Armor Crewman	749
77F	Petroleum Supply Spec	690
11M	Fighting Vehicle Infantryman	660
76Y	Unit Supply Specialist	627
76C	Equip Records & Parts Spec	627
11C	Indirect Fire Infantryman	623
19D	Cavalry Scout	590
11H	Heavy Anti-Armor Weapons Inf	519
76V	Material Storage & Handling Sp	402
13F	Fire Support Specialist	385
63T	Bradley Fighting Veh Sys Mech	383
16S	Stinger Crewmember	302

8. Scales, *Certain Victory* p. 136; Brinkerhoff, *Individual Manpower Mobilization*, p. 28.

9. Briefing Slide, "IRR Reporting Status (Cumulative), ARPERCEN Enlisted Personnel Management Directorate;" Briefing Slide, "Problem: Resolve No-Show Issue," in ODCSPER Mobilization Briefing to JSSUMP Working Group, May 8, 1991; copies of both in DS/DS files, USACMH; ARPERCEN, *History*, p. F.

Table 21-2 MOSs of Certain IRR Members/Enlisted IMAs Activated for Desert Shield/Desert Storm—Continued

MOS	Specialty	Number Called to Active Duty
19E	M48–M60 Armor Crewman	290
76P	Material Control & Acct Spec	277
63H	Track Vehicle Repairer	265
63W	Wheel Vehicle Repairer	257
13E	Cannon Fire Direction Spec	224
63S	Heavy Wheel Vehicle Mech	202
55B	Ammunition Specialist	201
52C	Utilities Equipment Repairer	166
71L	Administrative Specialist	154
91C	Practical Nurse	152
67N	Utility Helicopter Repairer	151
63D	Field Arty System Mech	145
67V	Observ/Scout Heli Repairer	143
63E	M1 Abrams Tank System Mech	134
91B	Medical NCO	129
63Y	Track Vehicle Mech	118
63J	QM/Chem Equip Repairer	112
88N	Traffic Management Coordinator	106
91D	Operating Room Spec	106
67T	Tac/Transport Heli Repairer	104
45K	Tank Turret Repairer	102
67U	Medium Helicopter Repairer	96
Total		20,406

This chart includes 87.5% of the 23,324 enlisted soldiers ordered to active duty: 20,291 IRR, 424 IMAs, and 2,109 TTADs, with data as of March 20, 1991.

Source: Briefing Chart, ARPERCEN Enlisted Personnel Management Directorate, May 6, 1991, in ARPERCEN files.

MAILGRAM CONFUSION

The mailgrams themselves are an interesting story (see Appendix H). The first page of the mailgram is the order to active duty. The second page is a warrant which directs a common carrier (bus, train, or airline) to issue a ticket to the soldier whose name appears on the order and the warrant. The problem was that this system, which had been in place since 1982 and which had been "discussed in conferences and written into essentially all mobilization plans," was abandoned at precisely the time it was needed.

This abandoning of the common carrier warrant system was effected by the Army's Deputy Chief of Staff for Logistics and the Military Traffic Management Command, which decided that the warrant portion of the mailgram would not be honored. ARPERCEN was not notified of this change until after the 20,000+ mailgrams had already been sent out. This was part of the reason for the delayed reporting, concluded ARPERCEN, because of the confusion it created with the common carriers. The Reserve Personnel Center resolved the problem by establishing a travel hotline, by tasking a travel agency to have airline tickets waiting for the mobilized soldier at the airport, and by contracting for bus service between airports and mobilization stations.[10] Part of the problem was undoubtedly caused by the partial nature of the mobilization; part of it was undoubtedly caused by one portion of a huge bureaucracy failing to talk with another part.

DELAYS AND EXEMPTIONS

As the fall build-up in the Gulf continued and swelled in intensity, it seemed obvious to most observers that some members of the Individual Ready Reserve would eventually be called to active duty. Nevertheless, some Reservists were simply not prepared when their mailgram arrived, and a small percentage of the mailgram addressees contacted ARPERCEN and asked for delays of four to six days beyond their January 31 reporting date to allow them to get their personal affairs in order.

Maj. Gen. William F. Ward, Jr., the Chief, Army Reserve, quickly established the atmosphere in which the ARPERCEN delay and exemption boards would operate. In a memorandum of January 24, 1991, Ward pointed out that the Reserve Personnel Center's jurisdiction applied only prior to a soldier's reporting to his mobilization site. For cases that were within the board's jurisdiction, wrote the OCAR chief, "I expect that you will exercise that authority, judiciously resolving individual cases in a manner that both supports the needs of the Army and compassionately recognizes the circumstances of the individuals involved. . . . Where there is a question," he continued, "you are to favor the individual soldier and grant up to a 30-day delay to allow the affected individual sufficient time to gather documentation and submit it to you for your timely adjudication prior to his/her adjusted reporting date." Concluded Ward, "While we must fully support Operation Desert Storm, our support procedures must be

10. Arpercen, *History*, p. C26.

demonstrably fair and reasonable. In short, the Army must have a human face."[11]

In accordance with the spirit of Ward's memorandum, ARPERCEN granted almost 88 percent of the requests for delay (694 of 791). Another 948 reservists requested total exemption from the call-up. The ARPERCEN board that considered these requests used in-house personnel and retirees who had been recalled to active duty to work on personnel matters.

Ward's memorandum, as well as the provisions of AR 601–25, provided guidance to the board, which eventually granted exemptions in 760 of the 948 cases (80 percent). The largest number of exemptions were granted for hardship (398), medical problems (134), and dependency (94). Many of the hardship and dependency exemptions were granted to soldiers who had been released from active duty within the previous few months for precisely the reasons for which they now sought the exemption from active service. Likewise, many of the medical disqualifications were of individuals who had been discharged for medical cause from the active component only a few months earlier.[12]

The procedures established by ARPERCEN for soldiers who sought a delay or exemption seem quite reasonable. Once the request was received at ARPERCEN, it was forwarded to the personnel management officer or personnel management NCO of the soldier concerned. This individual determined the nature of the request and referred the action to the board for consideration. Board recommendations were forwarded to the staff judge advocate for review, after which they were sent to the ARPERCEN commander for final action.

A denial of the request could be appealed to the commander of PERSCOM, but the soldier was required to report

11. Memorandum, DAAR–ZXP, Maj. Gen. William F. Ward, Jr. to Commander, ARPERCEN, January 24, 1991, Subject: Delays, Deferrals, Exemptions, and Separations from Active Duty for Individual Ready Reserve (IRR) Members Called to Active Duty in Support of Operation Desert Storm; copy in ARPERCEN files.

12. Interview, Lt. Col. James T. Currie with Capt. Acie Angel, ARPERCEN, June 23, 1992; notes in possession of the author; ARPERCEN, *History*, p. E7; CALL, "Mobilization of the Reserve Components," p. 3; Col. Rodney S. Nishimura, Director, Mobilization Operations and Training, ARPERCEN, to Chief, Army Reserve, July 30, 1991, Subject: U.S. Army Reserve Personnel Center (ARPERCEN) Desert Storm/Shield Lessons Learned, Title: "Exclusion Policies;" hereinafter cited as "Memorandum, Nishimura, ARPERCEN Lessons Learned, Title: (name)."

for active duty while the appeal was being considered. Business hardship was not a reason for exemption.[13]

FINANCIAL HARDSHIPS

Some Army Reservists received a financial boon from their active duty service, and others were aided financially by the provisions of the Soldiers' and Sailors' Civil Relief Act, which offered deferment for some debts and reduced interest rates on others. Other Army Reservists, however—troop unit members, IRR soldiers, and Individual Mobilization Augmentees (IMAs)—suffered considerable financial hardship when they were ordered to active duty.

The Military Personnel and Compensation Subcommittee of the House Armed Services Committee conducted a hearing on April 18, 1991, in which many examples of the financial hardships caused by the extended reserve mobilization were entered into the record. The individual Reservist, found the Congressmen, was often caught by surprise at the extent of financial loss that he would suffer if called to active duty.[14]

Medical doctors were particularly affected by the reduction in their income as a result of being called to active duty. Many of these highly-paid professionals were suddenly drawing pay at the captain or major rate, and even a lieutenant colonel or colonel on active duty does not make nearly the income of a medical doctor in private practice.[15]

It is also apparent, however, that the hardships caused by reserve mobilization extend beyond those encountered by the reservists themselves. In many of the small communities where Army Reserve units are located, for example, the absence of key personnel from the town—the local medical doctor, the village dentist, the nurses from the community hospital, even the national sales manager for a local manu-

13. Information Paper, DARP–MOP, Major Knox, ARPERCEN, January 1991, Subject: Delays, exemptions, AWOLs, and revocations during mobilization; in ARPERCEN files. The financial hardships endured by medical professionals have already been discussed.

14. United States House of Representatives, Military Personnel and Compensation Subcommittee, Committee on Armed Services, 102d Congress, 1st session, H.A.S.C. No. 102–20 (April 18, 1991), *Redeployment of Reserves from Operation Desert Storm*; hereinafter cited as "House of Representatives, *Redeployment*."

15. Brinkerhoff, *Individual Manpower Mobilization*, p. 29 and *Medical*, p. 83. For additional, specific information on the financial hardships suffered by medical personnel see Chapter Nineteen.

facturing establishment—has financial and societal implications far beyond those which touch the individual reservist.[16]

One of the complaints aired by the reservists was that they were not released from active duty once the conflict with Iraq had ended. Reservists did not like being retained in the KTO for other chores, or being sent to places like Kurdistan or Turkey for missions that had little, if anything, to do with Desert Shield and Desert Storm.[17]

American soldiers—volunteers and draftees alike—offered the same complaint following World War II, with the result that there was a massive and dramatic drawdown in military strength even as the Army was suggesting in 1945 that soldiers be retained on active duty as occupiers of Germany and Japan. There is an obvious conflict of perceptions as to the business and duty of the reserves, and it has yet to be sorted out at the DoD level.[18]

SINGLE PARENTS/DUAL MILITARY SERVICE PARENTS

The area that attracted more media attention and a greater percentage of the 237 congressional inquiries at ARPERCEN than any other was the activation of single parents and husbands and wives who were both in the military. Many of these individuals were in the group that applied for delay or exemption.

The rules that govern Army Reservists are quite simple: if you want to be a member of the USAR and you are a single parent, or if both parents are in the military, then you are supposed to have a family support plan in place. Such a plan means that the Reservist has worked out care arrangements for minor children in the event of mobilization or call to active duty.

Most single-parent Reservists have had to make such arrangements for the annual period of active duty training common to unit members and IMAs, but it quickly became evident that some of these same individuals had never considered the possibility that they might be ordered to active duty for an extended period of time.

A couple who might well have fallen into the complainer category, but did not do so, were Sergeants Dennis and Norah Bowers. They were both ordered to active duty with the 79th

16. House of Representatives, *Redeployment.*

17. For additional information on demobilization problems, see Chapter 22.

18. See Chapter 22.

Quartermaster Company of Marion, Oh., when this unit was mobilized in mid-September 1990. The Bowers family, both of whom had served on active duty prior to joining the Army Reserve, went with it. Their three children stayed with their grandparents—a family care plan that worked to perfection. According to the Bowers, they realized the potential difficulty posed by unit mobilization when they decided to join the 79th, but they joined anyway. The attitude expressed by Sgt. Dennis Bowers was typical of the overwhelming percentage of Army Reservists: "It's a way of life you choose when you raise your right hand. You don't look forward to it [family separation], but you can't look away from it."[19]

The Bowers family may not have been completely typical, however. According to ARPERCEN, "Family support plans of many reservists were found to be inadequate or missing entirely." Failure of some Army Reservists to plan adequately for unit or individual mobilization remains one of the achilles heels of the Army Reserve.[20]

NEW MOTHERS

Female Army Reserve soldiers who had recently given birth were also the subject of considerable news media and Congressional attention. This situation was different from the single parent/dual military parent phenomenon, but it provided its own difficulty for the mobilization deferment/exemption boards.

Photographs of new mothers—and Army Reservists—like Carolynne Zales and Faith Stewart appeared in newspapers throughout the country. Their babies were born shortly after they had received orders to report for active duty. "I'm going to fight like crazy so I can come home to my baby," said Zales, referring not to the fight against Saddam Hussein, but to the fight against going onto active duty at all. Stewart opined that "It's outrageous to separate a mother and a new baby."[21]

The plight of the new mothers was not ignored by ARPERCEN, which automatically gave a six week deferment from active duty following the birth of a child. Female soldiers who were pregnant would still have to report for active duty, but they would not be sent overseas. Neither of these policies

19. Jim Allen, "Desert Shield was a 'family affair' for some," *Army Reserve Magazine*, Vol. 36, No. 4 (1990), p. 21.

20. Memorandum, Nishimura, ARPERCEN Lessons Learned, Title: "Single Parent/Dual Military Family."

21. Bethany Kandel, "Military: New duty for new mothers," *USA Today*, February 7, 1991, p. 7.

was enough to satisfy members of Congress, a significant number of whom called ARPERCEN on behalf of their constituents. New mothers, like anyone else ordered to active duty, could apply for a delay or an exemption, but motherhood alone was not a reason to be exempted from active service or overseas deployment.[22]

It was apparent that some of the individuals who volunteered for military service—including the two soldiers quoted above—had not thought through the implications of their enlistment. According to the newspaper story, "For Zales and Stewart, volunteering for the Army was a matter of economics; it enabled them to go to college. They say they never imagined being sent to war and didn't foresee being separated from their children."[23]

Fortunately for the Army, there seem to have been few soldiers in the "I volunteered, but I never thought they would take me seriously" category. The total numbers of complainers in this category was quite small. According to Christopher Jehn, the Assistant Secretary of Defense for Management and Personnel, the number amounted to "one or two each" in the Reserve and Guard.[24]

One group that did consider seriously the whole question of single parents, dual military service parents and new mothers was the Military Personnel and Compensation Subcommittee of the House Armed Services Committee. Though legislation ranging from "exempt all single parents from combat service" to "give them six months exemption after childbirth" was introduced in the Congress, no statute resulted. The Department of Defense was given numerous and conflicting per-

22. Interview, Lt. Col. James T. Currie with Ms. Gladys Maeser, ARPERCEN Public Affairs Office, June 23, 1992; notes in possession of the author. In August 1991, the Department of Defense issued a new policy, applicable to active and reserve component personnel alike, which provided that mothers of newborns would not be assigned away from home for a period of four months after childbirth. The period could be waived by the servicemember. Cited in testimony of Stephen M. Duncan, Assistant Secretary of Defense for Reserve Affairs, before the Subcommittee on Defense, Appropriations Committee, United States Senate, 102d Congress, 2d session, March 19, 1992, p. 16 of typescript in possession of the author.

23. Kandel, "Military: New duty for new mothers."

24. Testimony of Christopher Jehn, Assistant Secretary of Defense for Management and Personnel, March 20, 1991, before the Defense Subcommittee, House Appropriations Committee, *Department of Defense Appropriations for 1992, Part 3,* p. 303. 102d Congress, 1st session, United States House of Representatives.

sonal opinions by members of Congress, but in the end, the issue was left to another day and another mobilization.[25]

IN-PROCESSING: ACTIVE DUTY ONCE AGAIN

There are no definitive studies of what happened to the individual Reservists who reported for active duty during the period of Desert Shield/Desert Storm. Unlike units that retained their identity even after they were mobilized, the individual member of the Army Reserve—with the exception of some Individual Mobilization Augmentees who will be discussed later—was quickly lost in the maelstrom of the active Army.

One problem with the way the individual reservist was ordered to active duty was that the mobilization system then in place (MOBPERS) was ignored when it came to filling personnel requirements. This system "allowed mobilization planners of each mobilization processing station staff element to plan for the reception, housing, accessioning, and supplying the needs of mobilized unit or individual personnel." Because this system was not used, the entire process did not go as smoothly as it might have.[26]

According to Charles V. Nahlik, mobilization planner at the reserve personnel center, the ad hoc system used by ARPERCEN resulted in such anomalies as Army Reservists from the Fort Polk, La., area being sent to Fort Knox, Ky., for mobilization, rather than reporting to the post nearest them, which was also receiving mobilized reservists. According to the ARPERCEN lessons learned report, the procedures used for Desert Storm had the following drawbacks:

(1) Negated the mobilization plans that had been developed and tested since 1980;
(2) Overburdened the receiving installations;
(3) Caused needless travel by mobilized reservists;
(4) Required the last-minute development and transmission of data to mobilization stations;
(5) Required mobilization staffs to use untested procedures for data collection on mobilized reservists.[27]

---

25. United States House of Representatives, Hearing before the Military Personnel and Compensation Subcommittee of the Committee on Armed Services, 102d Congress, 1st session, February 19, 1991, H.A.S.C. No. 102–5, *Parenting Issues of Operation Desert Storm.* See also Julia M. Klein, "Some aren't ready for reserve call," *Philadelphia Inquirer*, February 10, 1991, p. 3E.

26. Memorandum, Nishimura, ARPERCEN Lessons Learned, Title: "Fill Requirements for Individual Ready Reserve."

27. *Ibid.*

Just as noteworthy as the institutional problems of ARPERCEN, however, were the experiences of the individual Reservists who reported to mobilization sites strung across the country.

One such group of 2,600 IRR soldiers arrived at Fort Lee, Va., home of the Army's Quartermaster School, on January 31, 1991. The reporting deadline was midnight on the 31st, and the majority of the mobilized Reservists did not report until shortly before that time. The newly-activated soldiers were taken to a large Quonset hut field house where they spent the next few hours in-processing.[28]

Processing continued throughout the night, and the Reservists caught naps on the floor of the field house or stretched out on the bleachers as they waited their turn. By the next morning these men and women were now fully part of the active army again, and they reported to their new company for additional—and in some cases refresher—training. To help until the military pay system caught up with soldier needs, each reservist was given a $250 cash advance against their first paycheck. In addition, there were a fair number of individuals for whom the activation had been a wrenching experience, and they had the opportunity to talk with a chaplain about their situation.[29]

The primary problems at Fort Lee seem to have been the long lines and the wasted time, largely brought about by the fact that the IRR members did not report until the last possible minute. There were the usual soldier gripes about "hurry up and wait," but there seem to have been no serious problems with the in-processing.[30]

According to Lt. Col. John Rousellot of the Combined Arms Support Command at Fort Lee, "Most IRR soldiers that are being in-processed have a good attitude. While some are irritated by the wait, most realize that Fort Lee is processing a great number of soldiers in a short time. They are appreciative of the support and help given by the many personnel that are conducting the operation." Among the personnel who helped with the in-processing was a group of Army Reservists, the 408th Personnel service Company of Queens,

---

28. "Mobilizing Individual Ready Reservists," *Army Logistician*, May–June 1991, pp. 22–25.

29. *Ibid.*

30. It should be pointed out that one of the problems encountered by some Army Reservists was that if they reported before the "not later than" date specified in their orders, they were not paid for the extra days. This is recounted in Brinkerhoff, *Individual Manpower Mobilization*, p. 26.

N.Y., a unit that had been activated to take care of their fellow members of the USAR.[31]

OTHER PROBLEMS OF MOBILIZATION

There were common difficulties or problems at most of the mobilization sites. Both Army Forces Command (FORSCOM) and Army Training and Doctrine Command (TRADOC) posts were used for mobilization of individual Reservists. According to one of the principal mobilization planners at ARPERCEN, the TRADOC sites "were better organized to provide training to the new accessions [Reservists]," presumably because that was a task that they performed on a routine basis.[32]

Common problems at both FORSCOM and TRADOC sites ranged from major to minor. One major problem was that ARPERCEN had no data system capable of tracking either individual reservists (IRR) or individual mobilization augmentees (IMA) once they were placed on active duty. There was a system that could have worked at the total mobilization level, but since this effort was far less than total, it was useless. Once the Army Reservists reached their active duty mobilization post, they were lost, so far as ARPERCEN was concerned. Tracking was made doubly difficult because the mobilized IRR members were used to fill vacancies in both active component units and reserve units.[33]

Another problem was caused by the decision to ship the records of mobilized Reservists to the mobilization stations to which they were assigned. This decision, made at Department of the Army level, contradicted ARPERCEN's mobilization plans, Army Regulations, and FORSCOM mobilization plans. As with other decisions (such as the mailgram travel warrants) that changed standing plans and procedures, this change may not have been thought through at the DA level. When the order was given to ARPERCEN to ship the records, they were shipped. The problem occurred because the records were shipped to the twenty-two planned mobilization sites. When the number of such sites was reduced to nine, records were floating around at thirteen sites with no Reservists attached to them. Some of these records never found the soldier to whom they belonged, and as of the date of the ARPERCEN history

31. "Mobilizing Individual Ready Reservists," pp. 22–25.
32. Interview, Currie with Nahlik, June 23, 1992;.
33. ARPERCEN, *History*, p. C21; interview, Currie with Nahlik,.

(May 1992), some of the records had still not found their way back to the reserve personnel center.[34]

RECRUITS OR VETERANS?

There was also difficulty with the way in which some installation commanders treated the Reservists. It is not uncommon for basic trainees to have certain restrictions placed on them until they reach a certain phase of their training. At some of the active installations to which the mobilized Reservists were sent, however, these soldiers—none of whom was a basic trainee—were treated as if they had just entered the Army for the first time. The Army Center for Lessons Learned reported that "Some RT–12s[35] were treated as recruit trainees. In some cases RT–12s were not allowed to use rec centers, make telephone calls, watch television, or read newspapers during free time. At some posts RT–12s were escorted everywhere, and were not allowed to keep appointments made to resolve personal problems."[36]

OTHER PROBLEMS

Likewise, check cashing was a problem for the IRR soldiers because they largely banked out-of-state and were not permanent party on the post. In addition, some soldiers received only a partial issue of clothing—particularly short in Class A and Class B—and were told that they would receive additional clothing at their next post. This was often not the case.[37]

---

34. ARPERCEN, *History*, pp. 2–3. The decision to change the number of mobilization sites was not without its advantages, however. The Chief of Staff of the Army, Gen. Carl Vuono, wanted to ensure that each combat soldier called up from the IRR was truly prepared before being sent to Southwest Asia. He therefore directed that TRADOC certify the individual as being "combat ready" before he was deployed. This meant that infantry personnel were sent to Fort Benning, armor soldiers to Fort Knox, and combat engineers to Fort Leonard Wood. It also meant that the effort did not require 22 mobilization sites. Cited in Brinkerhoff, *Individual Manpower Mobilization*, pp. 23–24.

35. An "RT–12" was a soldier who had received training on active duty within the previous twelve months.

36. Memorandum (ATZL–CTL (350), Colonel Huey B. Scott, Director, Center for Army Lessons Learned (CALL), Leavenworth, Kans., to various addressees, Subject: Interim Report on Lessons Learned from RT–12 Call Up, February 15, 1991.

37. "Class A" is the complete green uniform, consisting of trousers, shirt, black necktie, jacket ("blouse" in Army language), and hat. "Class B" is the same uniform minus the blouse. Brinkerhoff, *Individual Manpower Mobilization*, pp. 27–28.

A minor problem, though it may not have seemed minor to the individuals involved, occurred at Forts Benning and Jackson (and possibly at other posts as well). According to one observer, "soldiers are reporting in with too much baggage. In some cases, soldiers needed to ship three or four boxes of personal belongings back home. Shipment is at government expense. Also, the extra time and work required to make all this happen is a real strain on the CRC [CONUS Replacement Centers] staff." Part of the problem of excess baggage was undoubtedly brought about because the mailgrams did not specify what the individual was to take with them to the reporting station. As an observer at Fort Benning indicated, "A standard list of items to bring to the CRC does not exist."[38]

Another problem was caused by soldiers who reported to the mobilization sites with medical or personal difficulties that warranted an immediate dismissal and return to civilian life. These problems often occurred among the RT–12 IRR soldiers who had been released from active duty for the precise problem which continued to eliminate them from active service. This complaint surfaced time and again during the mobilization. According to the Center for Army Lessons Learned, "Activating personnel without screening their records, and discharging them within a few days, costs the government thousands of dollars in travel expenses, active duty pay and allowances, and administrative costs."[39]

ARPERCEN planners believed that some of the problems of unqualified soldiers being issued active duty orders and then having to apply for an exemption could have been avoided if they had been allowed to go through the records of those being proposed for call-up and done an "edit check" on them. This would presumably have identified some of the obviously-disqualified and would have resulted in no mailgram being sent to them. The Army Judge Advocate General denied that option to ARPERCEN, however, on the grounds of fairness.[40]

It is apparent that individual Reservists in the category of "not suitable for active duty" were among those who applied to ARPERCEN for exemption; it is equally clear that others who did not apply for exemption should never have been called up. As of February 2, 1991, 280 Army Reservists who

38. Memorandum, ATSG–DTU (310–2g), From: Capt. Roger S. Billings, To: Director, Directorate of Training and Doctrine, Adjutant General School, January 25, 1991, Subject: Visit to CONUS Replacement Centers. Document in possession of the author.

39. CALL, "Mobilization of the Reserve Components," p. 3.

40. Brinkerhoff, *Individual Manpower Mobilization*, p. 29.

reported to their mobilization site were released from active duty and sent home. The largest number of these (101) was for weight, with 90 more dismissed for unspecified medical problems. Another 79 were released for "compassionate" reasons, and the remaining few were released for reasons ranging from lack of physical fitness (1) to drug abuse (1) to erroneous enrollment (1). Of the thousands of IRR members who reported for active duty, the number disqualified from further active service was not large.[41]

As a general observation, the difficulties at the mobilization sites did not do significant damage to the success of the mobilization, though they were of considerable aggravation to the soldiers affected. There were lesser difficulties, however, that form the basis for lessons learned. ARPERCEN itself compiled over 220 such, the U.S. Army Center for Lessons Learned issued other findings, and still others were compiled at Army level. Despite some difficulties in the Individual Ready Reserve mobilization experience, however, it can be stated unequivocally that it was a success.

The call-up was especially gratifying to the Army Reservists who had been telling their active component counterparts about the high quality of the soldiers in the USAR. Army Staff planners, for example, had projected that the newly-activated reservists would require "weeks of training" before becoming proficient enough to send to active component units. In some instances they required only "a few days." As the Army's own study expressed it, "Some IRR Abrams and Bradley crews who had served with units in Germany assembled at stations there and qualified after a single live-fire battle run on the demanding training tables at Grafenwohr."[42]

ARMY RESERVE VOLUNTEERS

The August 22, 1990, reserve call-up, discussed in Chapter Fifteen, did not envision or allow the involuntary call-up of members of the Individual Ready Reserve as part of the Desert Shield operation. The Department of the Army announced, however, that volunteer Army Reservists, including members of the IRR and the retired reserve, would be accepted for active service. (Some of these volunteers have already been discussed in connection with the MTMC-operated

41. ARPERCEN Briefing, DAPE–MO, February 2, 1991, "IRR Statistics—Reason Sent Home," copy in ARPERCEN files.

42. Scales, *Certain Victory*, p. 136.

ports of debarkation.) At that point the staff at ARPERCEN began to field thousands of telephone calls from interested Reservists. During the next five months some 12,000 IRR and IMA (Individual Mobilization Augmentee) members of the Army Reserve volunteered for active duty.[43]

INDIVIDUAL MOBILIZATION AUGMENTEES (IMAS)

Besides the IRR soldiers, the other non-troop unit members of the Army Reserve are the Individual Mobilization Augmentees (IMAs), who are similar to the men and women of the IRR in that for the most part they do not drill on a monthly basis. Instead, they have a mobilization assignment with an active Army unit or a Department of the Army or other organization to which they would report in the event of a national emergency or other call-up.[44]

One of the problems that arose early in Desert Shield was that some Department of the Army agencies were not exactly sure how to effect the call-up of their IMA assets. According to Lt. Col. Gerald Rosenbaum, Individual Mobilization Augmentation Division Chief at ARPERCEN, "The process of ordering an IMA to active duty under the Presidential 200K Call-Up and Partial Mobilization is unclear to the IMA agencies. Project officers at the agencies are under the assumption that they have authority to call up their IMAs based on the Presidential announcement. ARPERCEN had to explain the procedure of going through ODCSOPS [Office of the Deputy Chief of Staff of the Army for Operations] for approval on numerous occasions." In addition, wrote Rosenbaum, not all Department of the Army agencies had access to the Army Mobilization Operations Planning Systems (AMOPS) document that would have explained proper IMA call-up procedures.[45]

Despite these difficulties, some 2,364 of the 14,189 Army Reserve IMAs at the time of Desert Shield/Desert Storm were called to active duty during this period, a 17 percent utilization rate. Of these, 1,559 were called up under the involun-

---

43. "ARPERCEN's Role in Desert Shield/Desert Storm Mobilization," information paper issued by the command; Ross G. Pickus, "Pride in Performance," *The Officer*, October 1991, p. 11.

44. As of 1988 there have been IMAs who drill for pay with an active headquarters, but they are few in number. IMAs can also drill with active headquarters or units in a "points only" status. Brinkerhoff, *Individual Manpower Mobilization*, p. 48.

45. Memorandum, Nishimura, ARPERCEN Lessons Learned, Title: "IMA Call-Up Procedures;" ARPERCEN, *History*, p. 2.

tary 10 U.S.C. 673b authority, and 805 volunteered for Temporary Tours of Active Duty (TTAD) of various lengths.[46]

As of the commencement of Desert Shield, the 14,189 Army IMAs were distributed by grade as indicated in the following table.

Table 21-3 Army IMA Strength and Rank as of 30 June 1990

Rank	Number	Rank	Number
General	31	Sergeant Major	143
Colonel	824	Master Sergeant	515
Lt. Colonel	2,875	Sgt. First Class	871
Major	3.360	Staff Sergeant	820
Captain	2,382	Sergeant	845
Lieutenant	913	Specialist and PFC	50
Total	10,385		3,244
Total			13,629

Source: Brinkerhoff, *Individual Manpower Mobilization*, p. 5.

Despite what one might assume, the call-up of IMAs was neither front-loaded to the beginning of Desert Shield, nor spread evenly throughout the Desert Shield/Desert Storm period. On the contrary, only 113 IMAs were activated during Desert Shield, and 1,283—54 percent of those called to active duty, including those on TTAD—were not brought in until the war was over.[47]

QUALITY OF IMAS

In January 1992 ARPERCEN sent out questionnaires to agencies to which Individual Mobilization Augmentees had been assigned during Desert Shield/Desert Storm and to the IMAs themselves. The responses to these questionnaires offer some opportunities for a quality assessment of the IMA population on active duty during this period and insights into problems encountered and jobs performed. Some specific findings of the supervisors' survey:

—84 percent of the respondents indicated that their IMAs were "adequately trained to perform their specific wartime duties," while 16 percent felt they were not.

46. Brinkerhoff, *Individual Manpower Mobilization*, p. 6.
47. Brinkerhoff, *Ibid.*, pp. 6–7.

—70 percent rated the IMA performance as "very good," 22 percent as "good," and 8 percent as "fair" or "poor."
—95 percent felt the IMA contributed to the mission; 5 percent did not.

Perhaps more importantly, the survey's respondents pointed out problems that the individual IMAs had encountered after being brought onto active duty. The short period allowed before reporting to active duty—as little as seventy-two hours in some instances—was specifically mentioned by 18 percent of supervisors responding to the survey. Some fifty percent of the IMAs themselves stated that they had been given less than seven days to report for active duty. This short reporting time caused significant problems for some of the medical doctor IMAs who were mobilized. As one of them put it, "I had a particular hardship finding someone to care for patients I had operated on (major surgery), and to find another surgeon to perform surgery that I had scheduled. I had three patients in ICU [intensive care unit] when I was given 48 hours to report." Pay was singled out by 16 percent of the respondents as having been a problem for the IMAs who worked for them, while 27 percent of the IMAs themselves indicated that they had waited more than thirty days before receiving their first paycheck.

IMAs often performed critical jobs during the call-up, including one lieutenant colonel who worked as a shift chief in the mobilization cell in the Army Operations Center in the Pentagon. Others served as team chief for the Headquarters, Department of the Army Crisis Action Team, as manager of the U.S. Army Security and Intelligence Command's briefings for senior Army officials, as members of the Kuwait Infrastructure Recovery Program, and on the Crisis Response Cell at Special Forces Command. IMAs were men and women of many talents, and they served well during this time in every theater of war, in combat, combat support, and combat service support jobs.

As with the troop unit members, however, they also brought problems with them, especially those soldiers who were self-employed. As one survey respondent put it, "A few that owned their own business or were self-employed had to continue to invest time in that business so that it did not collapse in their absence." In this respect IMAs who remained stateside were better able to continue to monitor their businesses than were the professionals and self-employed IMAs and troop unit members who were sent to Southwest Asia and had to abandon their businesses for months. As previously mentioned, a business hardship exemption was not allowed under the PERSCOM rules, and many of the men and women who served in the KTO suffered severe financial penalties for their active duty service. As one IMA put it in his survey response, "I am currently facing bankruptcy" and as another indicated, "I had to close my private business and cancel appointments."[48]

THE IMA CALL-UP: SUCCESS OR NOT?

The study done for the Chief, Army Reserve, by the ANDRULIS Research Corporation gave a mixed review to the IMA program as it functioned during Desert Shield/Desert Storm. On the one hand, the 2,300 IMAs did provide much-needed augmentation for active component headquarters and units. On the other hand, it is apparent that the system did not work as it was designed to do. Only a small percentage of IMAs were ever called to duty to work with the active unit to which they were assigned. This then suggests the obvious question: If they were not called during this mobilization, when would they ever be called?

Moreover, IMAs cost more money than IRR members, because they are guaranteed an active duty tour each year, while the IRR soldiers are not. In the words of the OCAR study, "One of the inescapable conclusions is that most jobs that were filled by IMAs could have been filled by members of the IRR or by recalled retirees." There is, therefore, ". . . a real . . . question as to why the Army should pay for an IMA to fill a need that could be met by a less expensive form of pretrained individual manpower."[49]

ACTIVE GUARD AND RESERVE (AGR)

The only other military members of the Army Reserve not previously mentioned (other than members of the Standby Reserve, which did not figure in this mobilization) consists of reservists who are on active duty as part of the Active Guard and Reserve (AGR) program. These AGR soldiers are part of the Selected Reserve assigned as full-time members of an Army Reserve troop unit or as staff at the Department of the Army or other headquarters levels.

48. All comments and data taken from results of the IMA "Supervisor's Survey" and "Soldier Survey" sent out by ARPERCEN in January 1992.

49. Brinkerhoff, *Individual Manpower Mobilization*, pp. 19–20

AGRs are active duty Reservists, and at the time of Desert Shield/Desert Storm, there were 7,746 of them serving with troop units of the Army Reserve and at Army headquarters. These individuals generally did whatever their units did during the conflict: remained at their Reserve center and went to regular monthly training assemblies, reported to a stateside active duty post, or went overseas. The OCAR study suggested that "during the manpower mobilization the Army regarded these soldiers as individual replacements instead of unit members." This is borne out by the decision to separate some AGR soldiers from their Reserve units and assign them elsewhere. Altogether, 1,283 AGR soldiers went with their units when the unit was mobilized or were assigned to serve with active Army units or another Army Reserve unit. A total of 617 AGR soldiers deployed to Southwest Asia.[50]

ARMY RESERVE RETIREES

In addition to the USAR's Selected Reserve (troop unit members, IMAs, and AGRs) and Individual Ready Reserve, there is a sizable number of soldiers (in 1990 it was over 550,000) in the Retired Reserve. Of this number, some 230,000 are under the age of sixty and are likeliest to be mobilization assets. In the 1970s, it became DoD policy that these individuals would be subject to recall in the event of a national emergency.

After the Secretary of the Army announced on September 12, 1990, that certain retiree volunteers would be accepted for active duty, more than 10,000 members of the Retired Reserve—primarily non-commissioned officers—called ARPERCEN and offered their services. Of these volunteers, 1,250 were eventually recalled. Some of these individuals went to the KTO, but the overwhelming majority of them served in assignments in the United States, including 150 retired medical personnel who served at Army hospitals. In addition, for the first time ever, a few retirees were recalled to active duty involuntarily. An Army-wide

50. Brinkerhoff, *Individual Manpower Mobilization*, pp. 37–38. It should also be noted that there are thousands of civilian employees of the Army Reserve in addition to the military members. Many of these individuals worked hundreds of extra hours as a result of Desert Shield and Desert Storm. Some of this overtime was compensated, but many a weekend and night was given to the effort by these Department of the Army civilians without financial remuneration. Scattered throughout the ARPERCEN history are references to the overtime worked by the civilian employees of the center.

shortage of medical and aviation personnel led to the involuntary recall of 131 soldiers with specialties in these two areas.[51]

ARPERCEN found it a real challenge to handle the avalanche of retired volunteers, since the computer support available to track such individuals is geared to a full mobilization effort. Desert Shield and Desert Storm were accomplished at a considerably lower level of mobilization, and ARPERCEN resorted to using inexperienced personnel with personal computers to track volunteer retirees. There were also problems with allotments, in that the Army pay system failed to pick up the new status of the reservist and to transfer and continue any allotment the retiree had taken from his pay. In some instances retired pay continued at the same time the servicemember was receiving active duty pay. This caused problems for the servicemember when the system discovered its error, which it eventually did.[52]

In addition, according to the action officer at ARPERCEN who was responsible for the retiree recall effort, Army regulations then in effect (specifically AR 601–10) were inadequate to the task of bringing retirees onto active duty for extended periods of time. Neither this particular regulation nor any other applicable Army regulations offered proper guidance to the individuals working the problem at ARPERCEN. Finally, at the end of their active duty period, retirees were entitled to have their retired pay recalculated on the basis of their additional active duty service, though there was some question at ARPERCEN as to exactly how this should be accomplished.[53]

DISCIPLINARY PROBLEMS

As with the Army Reserve units that were mobilized for duty in Vietnam in 1968, the Army Reserve units and individuals called-up for Desert Shield and Desert Storm in 1990 and 1991

51. ARPERCEN, *History*, pp. A1, C25, E2. Interestingly, there were more volunteers from the retired pool (10,486) than from the younger pool of IRR and troop unit members (7,200). The author is not prepared to speculate as to the cause of this phenomenon. "ARPERCEN's Role in Desert Shield/Desert Storm Mobilization," information paper issued by the command; Memorandum, Nishimura, ARPERCEN Lessons Learned, Executive Summary; Brinkerhoff, *Individual Manpower Mobilization*, p. 30.

52. Memorandum, Nishimura, ARPERCEN Lessons Learned, Titles: "Retiree Recall-Administrative Processing," "Retiree Recall—Automation," and "Retiree Recall—Finance Processing."

53. Memorandum, Nishimura, ARPERCEN Lessons Learned, Titles: "Retiree Recall—Regulatory Guidance" and "Retiree Recall—Recomputation of Retired Pay."

posed few disciplinary problems. In addition, there were no mass protests against going to war this time, as there were with some Army Reserve units in the 1960s. This is not to suggest that there were not individual Army Reservists who protested the U.S. effort in the Gulf by refusing to live up to their obligation. There were some, but they were few in number.

Army Reservists who were punished for failure to report to active duty made news precisely because there were so few of them. According to press accounts, an Illinois Army Reservist, Spec. Stephanie Atkinson, refused to report for duty when her unit was mobilized, claiming to be a conscientious objector.

Atkinson was not granted conscientious objector status, but instead was given a discharge under "other than honorable conditions." According to her attorney, Atkinson was the first Army Reservist to refuse the order to report for active duty during Desert Shield.[54]

CAPT. HUET-VAUGHN

More celebrated was the case of medical doctor Yolanda Huet-Vaughn. Huet-Vaughn practiced medicine in Kansas City, Kans., serving at the same time as a captain in the Army Reserve, a member of a hospital unit. When mobilization came in the fall of 1990, Huet-Vaughn was ordered to active duty with her unit. She refused to report as directed, stating during her court martial that "My intent at that time was to bring to the public the issues about the catastrophic consequences of the war which resulted, and that it was preventable."[55]

She was convicted of "desertion with intent to avoid hazardous duty and shirk important service" and sentenced to 2½ years in prison. The court martial convening authority reduced her confinement to fifteen months, of which she served eight months. She then became a cause celebre for pacifists and others opposed to the Gulf war. The Army saw her simply as an officer who refused to uphold her oath and do her duty.[56]

---

54. "Reservist Refuses to Go to Gulf," *Washington Times*, November 12, 1990, p. 2.

55. Associated Press, "Army Doctor Sentenced in Desertion Case," *The Washington Post*, August 10, 1991, p. A5.

56. Associated Press, "Army Doctor Sentenced in Desertion Case;" "Army Court Asked to Nullify Conviction in Gulf Desertion," *The Washington Post*, February 24, 1993, p. A6; "Around the Nation," *The Washington Post*, November 3, 1993, p. A7; Colman McCarthy, "Anti-War Doctor Under Fire," *The Washington Post*, Health Magazine, November 30, 1993, p. 6.

The Kansas State Board of Healing Arts, the official body which decides for the State of Kansas whether an individual is allowed to practice medicine there, considered whether to revoke Huet-Vaughn's license. The charge against her was that she had been convicted of a felony, and the Board decided that it had "investigated the complaint and has determined that there are reasonable grounds to believe that Yolanda M. Huet-Vaughn, M.D. . . . has committed an act or acts in violation of of the Kansas Healing Arts Act."[57]

In November 1993 her desertion conviction was set aside by the Army Court of Military Review.[58] In response, the Kansas Board for the Healing Arts suspended its disciplinary proceeding against Huet-Vaughn "without prejudice," meaning that it could be resurrected at any time.[59] Huet-Vaughn's troubles were not over, however, as the Army appealed the dismissal of the conviction against her. On September 28, 1995, the U.S. Court of Appeals for the Armed Forces decided against Huet-Vaughn, confirming her original conviction and sentence.[60] The only remaining legal avenue for Huet-Vaughn was a potential appeal to the United States Supreme Court. It remained to be seen what the Kansas Board would do to her medical license.

IRR NO SHOWS

In addition to the specific disciplinary cases mentioned above, ARPERCEN attempted to identify soldiers who had ignored the mailgram orders of January 21 and 29, 1991. A certain number of the 20,000+ individuals to whom the mailgrams were sent had simply not responded. Some of these were caused by bad addresses in the files, but others were not. On May 24, 1991, the Reserve Center sent a second mailgram to 719 of these soldiers. Four hundred five of these mailgrams were returned to ARPERCEN as "undeliverable," but of the remaining 314—which presumably reached their intended recipient—80 were referred to the U.S. Army Deserter Information Point for further action as being Absent without

57. Petition to Revoke, Suspend, or Limit Licensure, Case No. 92–00142, in the matter of Yolanda M. Huet-Vaughn, M.D., April 7, 1992. Copy in possession of the author.

58. *United States* v. *Yolanda M. Huet-Vaughn*, 43 M.J. 105 (1995)

59. Order of Dismissal without Prejudice, Case No. 92–00142, In the Matter of Yolanda M. Huet-Vaughn, M.D., July 5, 1994. Copy in possession of the author.

60. *U.S.* v. *Huet-Vaughn*, 43 M.J. 105 (1995)

Leave (AWOL). Of the 80, 57 were eventually cleared, 12 were caught and given administrative discharges from the Army, and 11 were still missing as of mid-1992.[61]

CONSCIENTIOUS OBJECTORS

Soldiers—active or reserve—who develop a religious or, in certain cases, philosophical objection to war, are entitled to assert a claim as a conscientious objector and request discharge from the Army. Some individuals do not make a "CO" claim until they actually face the possibility of going to war. Such was the case with fifteen IRR soldiers who were ordered to active duty in January 1991. An Exemption Review Board at ARPERCEN considered the applications for CO status lodged by these individuals and rejected all of them.[62]

CONCLUSION

The individual Reservists who volunteered or were called involuntarily to active duty during Desert Shield and Desert Storm provided invaluable augmentation to the active Army and the Army Reserve units to which they were assigned. The difficulties encountered in locating them, providing refresher training, and assigning them to units was minor compared with the skills they brought with them. These are individuals in whom the country has a considerable investment, and they were then and are now a national asset.

That there were a few—we might emphasize *very few*—of these individuals who refused to live up their obligation does not detract in any way from the thousands who reported as ordered. The individual Reservist mobilization system may not have worked exactly as planned, but it did work. Desert Shield/Desert Storm provided a much-needed opportunity to test the resolve of the members of the IRR and the IMAs, and they passed the test with close to a perfect score.

61. ARPERCEN, *History*, p. C11; Brinkerhoff, *Individual Manpower Mobilization*, p. 26.

62. ARPERCEN, *History*, p. E7; Memorandum, Nishimura, ARPERCEN Lessons Learned, Title: "Conscientious Objector (CO) Applications."

22

After the Storm, 1991–1994

The bloom of victory from Desert Storm had barely faded before the Army Reserve was hit by attempts to reduce its size. Testifying before the Congress on September 25, 1991, Chairman of the Joint Chiefs of Staff Gen. Colin L. Powell addressed the issue of cutting the reserve components of the various military services. After discussing the philosophy of the proposed cuts as they applied to the Air Force, Navy and Marine Corps, he turned to the Army.

"The Army," he told the House Appropriations Subcommittee on Defense, ". . . is the most controversial one." The problem engendered by the Army, said Powell, was that "for the decade of the eighties, the Army kept its active end strength relatively constant. In the same period, the reserves [meaning Army Reserve and Army National Guard] grew from roughly 575,000 to roughly 776,000—a significant increase in the size of the Reserves during the Reagan years."[1]

As a result of this build-up in the Army's reserve components, suggested Powell, and the drawdown that had already occurred in the active component, there was now a disparity between the reserve force structure and what he called "the reality of our needs."[2] He loved the reserves, said the Chairman, because we "couldn't operate our force right now

---

1. Testimony of Gen. Colin L. Powell, Chairman of the Joint Chiefs of Staff, before the Subcommittee on Defense, Committee on Appropriations, United States House of Representatives, 102d Congress, 1st session, *Department of Defense Appropriations for 1992, Part 8*, p. 38. Hereinafter cited as "Powell testimony, FY 1992 Appropriations Bill."

2. *Ibid.*

without the Reserves." But the Army simply had no need for such a robust reserve force structure and could not afford to pay for a force structure that was predicated upon the requirement to fight a war in Europe, a requirement that the Pentagon's strategic planners believed was unlikely.[3]

Powell was then asked what the Army would do if Congress refused to allow the Reserve Component reductions it sought. "How would these personnel be utilized?" asked Rep. Norman D. Dicks (D–Wash.) Directing his answer to the types of units that were most likely to be found in the Army Reserve, Powell said that "They would be in the structure, and they would have no specific missions," meaning that these units would not be tied to a specific war plan and would not be CAPSTONE to an active component higher echelon. "They would train to—a transportation company that had no specific mission would train as a transportation company but wouldn't be allotted to a particular contingency plan."[4]

This philosophical justification for the Reserve Component reduction was based upon the assumption that Reserve units that were tied to particular war plans, regions, missions, and CAPSTONE traces would be used in those capacities when war came and that as those traces lessened through a reduction in the size of the active component, the reserves should be reduced accordingly. As has been demonstrated earlier in this volume (Chapter 20), the sanctity of such war plans and traces was often not the case during Desert Shield and Desert Storm.

Indeed, what this author found when researching the question of how and why particular Army Reserve units had been called up for duty overseas was that CAPSTONE trace had not been a significant factor. Truck companies were called because truck companies were needed; water purification units were called because water purification units were needed. The readiness of the units was a factor, but geographical balance seems to have been more of a determinant than was the "specific mission" assignment referred to by the Chairman.

The Department of Defense also addressed the issue of the reserve component drawdown in its answers to questions-for-the-record submitted by the House subcommittee. According to the Defense Department, the reason why the reserves seemed to be disproportionately targeted for cuts fol-

3. *Ibid.*, pp. 38, 52.
4. *Ibid.*, p. 55.

lowing Desert Shield/Desert Storm was that they had been spared previously.

The Army's active component was reduced by 68,000 soldiers and two divisions during FY 1990–91, said DoD, but "associated reductions of reserve forces which supported those divisions . . . were denied by Congress, and the Army Reserve Component end strength has been frozen at the fiscal year 1989 end strength for 2 years. . . . The need to 'catch up' with active reductions already executed accounts for the large Reserve reductions in fiscal years 1992 and 1993." The answer volunteered that "no attempt was made to circumvent Congress," which had forbidden the reductions during FY 1991.[5]

It seemed clear from Powell's statements and testimony and from the earlier testimony of Christopher Jehn, Assistant Secretary of Defense for Force Management and Personnel,[6] that the Department of Defense was determined to reduce the size of all the Reserve Components, with the Army Reserve taking a larger share of the planned reductions than the other Reserve Components. From a Selected Reserve[7] FY 1990 end strength of 310,000, the USAR was programmed by the Army to drop to 282,700 in FY 1992 and to 254,500 in FY 1993, a reduction of 55,500 soldiers (17.9%).[8]

By FY 1996, testified Jehn, "both active duty and reserve military end strength will be about twenty percent lower than in FY 1990."[9] Calculating from Jehn's figures, assuming that the reductions had been spread equally among the reserve components, this would have translated into a fairly steep reduction in the size of the Selected Reserve of the USAR to 248,000 soldiers at the end of FY 1996. The Army's plans in 1991 called for such reductions. Congress, however, had other ideas about the proper size of the Army Reserve.

---

5. Subcommittee on Defense, Committee on Appropriations, United States House of Representatives, 102d Congress, 1st session, *Department of Defense Appropriations for 1992, Part 8*, p. 75.

6. Christopher Jehn appeared before the Defense Appropriations Subcommittee of the Committee on Appropriations, United States House of Representatives, 102d Congress, 1st session, on March 20, 1991. His statement and testimony are found on pages 264–334 of *Department of Defense Appropriations for 1992*. Hereinafter cited as "Jehn testimony, FY 1992 Appropriations Bill."

7. The Selected Reserve is comprised of troop unit members, Individual Mobilization Augmentees (IMAs), and members of the Active Guard and Reserve (AGR) program.

8. Jehn testimony, FY 1992 Appropriations Bill, p. 267.

9. *Ibid.*, p. 268.

For FY 1993 the Army proposed an Army Reserve end strength of 257,500. Congress, however, refused to allow the USAR to drop so low and set an end strength of 296,230 in the combined FY 1992/1993 authorization act.[10] Because this was a two year authorization, Congress revisited the issue the following year and passed a separate authorization act for fiscal year 1993. In setting the FY 1993 end strength for the Army Reserve it apparently listened to the entreaties of the Army and reduced the USAR to 279,615.[11] For FY 1994, Congress established an Army Reserve end strength of 260,000.[12]

The assigned strength of the Army Reserve was very close to these prescribed authorized end strengths, ranging from 98.6 percent in FY 1993 to 99.9 percent for FY 1994.[13] Though the Army Reserve was being reduced in size during these years, it was doing so much more gradually than Headquarters, Department of the Army wished. This would soon enough be remedied.[14] Meanwhile, there were other issues that confronted the Army Reserve during the four years after the end of Desert Storm in 1991.

---

10. National Defense Authorization Act for Fiscal Years 1992 and 1993, Section 411, Public Law 102–190, December 5, 1991.

11. National Defense Authorization Act for Fiscal Year 1993, Section 411, Public Law 102–484, October 23, 1992.

12. National Defense Authorization Act for Fiscal Year 1994, Section 411, Public Law 103–160, November 30, 1993.

13. Office of the Secretary of Defense, *Reserve Component Programs, Fiscal Year 1993: Report of the Reserve Forces Policy Board* (Washington: OSD, 1994), p. 57; hereinafter cited as "*Annual Report, RFPB, FY 1993*;" Office of the Secretary of Defense, *Reserve Component Programs: FY 1994 Report of the Reserve Forces Policy Board* (Washington: OSD, 1995), p. 37; hereinafter cited as "*Annual Report, RFPB, FY 1994*."

14. For additional information on Army Reserve strength reductions see Sgt. Bruce D. Junkmann, USAR, "All-Out Effort Pays off," *The Officer*, December 1992, pp. 12–13; William Matthews, "Reserves smiling in time of change," *Army Times*, January 4, 1993, p. 25; William Matthews, "Reserve lobby launches blitz," *Army Times*, February 1, 1993, p. 19; "Reserve drawdown gains steam," *Army Times*, June 21, 1993, p. 2; Katherine McIntire, "33,000 to be cut: Reserve takes biggest hit; soldiers will miss out on separation bonuses," *Army Times*, April 12, 1993, p. 20; Rick Maze, "Political clout shields Guard, Reserve from cuts," *Army Times*, October 18, 1993, p. 19; Katherine McIntire, "New cuts promise a year of turmoil," *Army Times*, January 3, 1994, p. 30; William Matthews, "Drawdown may cut jobs, training," *Army Times*, January 10, 1994, p. 20; Bernard Adelsberger, "Leaders: Keep drawdowns on schedule," *Army Times*, March 14, 1994, p. 3; William Matthews and Katherine McIntire Peters, "Reserve cuts 'old news' to those facing unit ax," *Army Times*, March 14, 1994, p. 3; Paulette V. Walker, "About 30,000 Reserve, Guard positions slated for closure," *Army Times*, November 28, 1994, p. 8; Maj. Gen. Max Baratz, "Creating the future Reserve," *Army Reserve Magazine*, Vol. 40, No. 2 (1994), p. 4.

DEMOBILIZATION

"It is clear to me," said Stephen M. Duncan, Assistant Secretary of Defense for Reserve Affairs in testimony before Congress in 1992, "that similar attention [to that paid to mobilizing the reserve components] must now be given to the process of demobilization."[15] It is clear that the Reservists who went to the Gulf were no different from their counterparts from wars past. For the most part, they went gladly, served proudly, and wanted to go home when it was over.

An active component commander of a combat service support battalion, for example, commented about the quality of the Army Reserve soldiers who served under him. The Reservists were a truck unit with 5,000 gallon tankers. "They did a superb job," said the commander. "Without them, we would not have been able to accomplish our mission. . . . Once the conflict was over, then they became very antsy to start leaving. And they developed a morale problem. . . . "[16]

The problem with Reservists wanting to return home once the fighting had ended, said Duncan, was "the result of insufficient understanding by Reserve families and employers of the precise nature of the missions which were being performed by the Reserve components."[17] Duncan went on to say that the operational needs of the field commanders would have to be the primary determinant in the release of reservists from active duty.

According to Duncan, many reserve units were sent home after active component units had departed the theater of operations. Part of the reason for this order of departure was basic fairness, he said: those who arrived first in theater went home first.[18] But the more important reason lay in the nature of many of the Army Reserve units that served in the conflict. "Transportation units, maintenance units, port operations, medical units, and units with other logistical skills . . .

15. Testimony of Stephen M. Duncan, Assistant Secretary of Defense for Reserve Affairs before the Subcommittee on Manpower, Personnel, and Compensation, Armed Services Committee, United States House of Representatives, 102d Congress, 2d session, May 1, 1992, p. 19. Hereinafter cited as "Duncan testimony, May 1, 1992."

16. Interview with an active component lieutenant colonel who commanded a combat service support battalion during the war. The interview is in the files of the U.S. Army center of Military History. Because the interviewee has not signed a release form, he cannot be cited by name.

17. *Ibid.*

18. There were exceptions to the "first in, first out" rule, and some of these exceptions were Reserve units. See David Evans, "Reservists may stay in gulf until '92," *Chicago Tribune*, April 26, 1991, p. 5.

were precisely the type of units that were required to engage in the huge task of preparing hundreds of shiploads of cargo for redeployment from Saudi Arabia to the United States."[19]

At the least, concluded Duncan, in future deployments we need to offer a realistic date for redeployment, even if that date is "disappointingly late because of operational requirements."[20] What Duncan was doing, whether he realized it at the time or not, was beginning the ongoing debate about the roles and missions of the Army's reserve components, especially the Army Reserve. There will be much more about this topic later in this chapter.

The Congress soon offered its own views on the question of demobilization of the reserve components. Though it was but the "sense of Congress," the legislative branch found that "the Department of Defense . . . was not sufficiently sensitive to the sacrifices made by reservists called or ordered to active duty in connection with the Persian Gulf conflict . . . and did not give adequate priority to the demobilization of reserve forces. . . . It is the sense of Congress that the Secretary of Defense should examine the deployment policy used during the Persian Gulf conflict with a view toward developing a policy for future contingencies that would expedite the return of reserve units activated or deployed during the contingency at the earliest opportunity consistent with mission requirements."[21]

EQUIPMENT RETURN AND REPAIR

At least as early as March 1991, the re-deployment of equipment from Saudi Arabia to the United States began in earnest. In one example, Fifth Army, headquartered at Fort Sam Houston, Texas, faced the task of recovering 5,300 pieces of equipment shipped overseas with 111 different Army Reserve and Army National Guard units.[22]

There were significant problems associated with recovering the equipment and returning it to the reserve units to whom it belonged. One of the problems was that equipment was sent to the Saudi ports and loaded onto ships without regard for unit integrity. The pieces of equipment were simply put onto the

19. *Ibid.*, p. 20.

20. *Ibid.*, p. 22.

21. Section 555, Public Law 102–190, December 5, 1991, National Defense Authorization Act for Fiscal Years 1992 and 1993.

22. Lt. Col. Ed Peschke, USAR and Lt. Col. Walter R. Schumm, USAR, "Returning Reserve Component Equipment," *Army Logistician* (July–August 1993), pp. 32–33.

ships in whatever fashion they would best fit. Accordingly, the equipment that belonged to any one Reserve unit might come in on different ships and arrive at different ports.[23]

For example, twelve pieces of equipment were returned from overseas to the 601st Transportation Detachment, USAR. This equipment arrived at six different ports on nine ships during the period from July 1991 through January 1992. Other units with more equipment had even larger problems: one unit had to track equipment that came in on 24 different ships.[24]

Further problems were created by what was termed "nesting." This occurred when a truck from one unit arrived with a generator from another unit in its cargo bed, towing a trailer from a third unit. It took careful coordination and inspection, much of which was done by Army Reservists who remained on active duty long after the end of Desert Storm, to make this process work as well as it did.[25]

Once the equipment was returned to the unit it was often necessary to effect repairs on it. This process often took from 10–12 months, and validation of equipment status took additional months. The authors who studied this process as it took place in Fifth Army singled out the 89th U.S. Army Reserve Command (ARCOM) for particular praise during the validation stage. "This command," said the authors, "validated its units at a much more rapid rate than other commands. . . ."[26]

At the other end of the country, many miles from the heat of the Southwestern United States and Fifth Army, Fort McCoy, Wisc., was given the mission of inventorying, inspecting, repairing and returning to the owners some 5,700 pieces of equipment. This operation, dubbed "Desert Fix," began in June 1991 and continued through the first half of 1992.[27]

The work at Fort McCoy was accomplished by a mixed group of soldiers representing all of the Army's components. The largest group, however, consisted of the 280 Army Reservists (out of a total workforce of 615). These Reservists, all volunteers, worked alongside Army civilians, National Guard soldiers, and active component members in repairing 4,800 vehicles and other rolling stock, 400 containers of field equipment, and 900 miscellaneous items.[28]

---

23. *Ibid.*, p. 32.
24. *Ibid.*, p. 33.
25. *Ibid.*, p. 34.
26. *Ibid.*
27. "Operation Desert Fix: After the 'hot war' in Iraq, it was a 'cold war' at Ft. McCoy," *Army Reserve Magazine*, Vol. 38, No. 2 (1992), p. 18.
28. *Ibid.*, pp. 18–19.

The work of the Army Reserve in Saudi Arabia and elsewhere in the Gulf in preparing equipment for shipment back to the United States, and then in receiving it at the ports and in some instances making repairs on it before it was returned to the using units, was the final act of Desert Shield and Desert Storm. What remained ahead was in some ways a more difficult task: determining exactly what role the USAR would play in the future defense posture of the country.

ROLES AND MISSIONS

There was irony in the decision to make significant cuts in the strength of the Army Reserve. The cuts were being taken at precisely the time when the Army Reserve was being called upon to assume more responsibility for national security than ever before.

One of the first discussions of the nature of the Army Reserve mission in the post-Desert Storm era was prepared by retired FORSCOM commander Gen. Robert W. Sennewald. In a June 1991 article in *Army* magazine, Sennewald sang the praises of the Reserve contribution to the victory in the Gulf. He concluded, however, by suggesting that "the predominant European orientation of many of the Army's RC units needs to be changed, and the units must be better prepared to deploy to an immature theater. . . ."[29]

In a comment that reflected his understanding of what such a deployment strategy would require, Sennewald concluded by suggesting that "this may mean that RC units must be more robust in terms of people and equipment and deploy with a higher readiness posture. Established command relationships that dictated exclusive theater orientations," he warned, perhaps taking a shot at the CAPSTONE program, "should be reviewed."[30]

The next year saw a thinkpiece from Rep. G.V. (Sonny) Montgomery (D–Miss.)[31] and a report from the Congressional General Accounting Office (GAO) that offered some ideas about the proper role of the Army's Reserve Components.[32]

---

29. Gen. Robert W. Sennewald (USA, Ret.), "Fine Tuning Reserve Forces in the Wake of Desert Storm," *Army* (June 1991), p. 17.

30. *Ibid.*

31. Rep. G.V. Montgomery, "Greater Reliance on Reserve is Essential," *The Officer* (May 1992), pp. 23–26).

32. General Accounting Office, *Army Force Structure: Future Reserve Roles Shaped by New Strategy, Base Force Mandates and the Gulf War*, December 15, 1992 (Washington: GAO, 1992). See also the analysis of this report in Jim Tice, "Hill investigators urge look at larger role for reserves," *Army Times*, February 8, 1993, p. 8.

One of the first administration responses to the debate over the role of the Army Reserve came in a May 1993 interview with Deborah R. Lee, Assistant Secretary of Defense for Reserve Affairs.

In this interview the assistant secretary responded to a question from Lt. Col. James M. Nielsen, then editor of *Army Reserve Magazine*, about the ability of the Army Reserve to respond quickly to crises. "You have just touched upon a key area—accessibility of the reserve components," said Lee, who went on the explain that the Department of Defense supported a change in law to give the Secretary of Defense the authority to call up to 25,000 Selected Reservists to active duty without declaring a national emergency. "We've also requested a change," she said, "to allow us to keep reservists on board for two 180-day periods."[33]

Lee also spoke of her vision of an Army Reserve that would provide more support to the active component in the area of base operations and training, that would work on problems at home through the administration's "Rebuild America" program, to include providing medical care to communities in the U.S., and that would work overseas on the military-to-military contact program with the former Warsaw Pact countries.[34]

In short, Lee revealed in 1993 a vision of an Army Reserve that was better supported, better equipped, better trained, and in a higher state of readiness than ever before. In return, she envisioned Army Reserve missions well beyond anything done routinely before that time and saw the call-up authority to be requested for the Secretary of Defense to be a necessary concomitant to these increases in the roles and missions of the Army Reserve. It was an expansive view of the Army Reserve of the future.

Assistant Secretary Lee's vision of an enhanced role for the Army Reserve preceded only slightly the release of the results of the "Bottom-Up Review" (BUR) conducted under the auspices of Secretary of Defense Les Aspin. This study concluded that the Army would have to depend upon the combat power of the Army National Guard if it were to be able to fight and win two wars simultaneously. In contrast to the attention given the Army Reserve by Assistant Secretary Lee,

---

33. Lt. Col. James M. Nielsen, "The Nation's Number One Reservist: Deborah R. Lee," *Army Reserve Magazine*, Vol. 39, No. 3 (1993), p. 13. The 360-day authority spoken of was granted by Congress during Desert Shield/Desert Storm, but the law that allowed this extended duty was an *ad hoc* arrangement for this one conflict.

34. *Ibid.*

however, the Bottom-Up Review barely mentioned the USAR. "There is not sufficient detail concerning the Army Reserve for us to have any thoughts one way or the other," was how Lt. Col. Art House phrased the official DCAR reaction.[35]

Despite this lack of attention to the Army Reserve in the BUR, it soon became evident that the Defense Department was planning to call upon the expertise of the USAR more often than ever. As the active component is reduced in size, said Army Chief of Staff Gen. Gordon Sullivan said in a speech to the National Guard Association, the Army will rely more on its reserve forces. These forces, said Sullivan, "must be prepared to deploy promptly to operations ranging from combat to humanitarian assistance."[36]

"With crises erupting around the globe," wrote one observer, "operating tempos climbing, and stress on the troops and their families mounting, the Pentagon plans to look to the reserves for relief."[37] It was evident that defense officials—particularly those in the Army—were by 1994 looking at the reserves as a source of relief for the tasks that until now had been performed almost solely by the active component. Following a visit to Europe, Secretary of Defense William Perry suggested that he planned "to make greater use of Reserve and Guard forces for contingency operations in Europe."[38]

It is not clear that this comment by the Secretary was greeted with any particular alarm within the Reserve community, nor did it seem to have made much of an impression on Reservists themselves. Once again, the irony of the situation was that the Army Reserve—which would be the reserve component called upon most frequently for non-combat operations—had seen a considerable diminution in size since the days of the Cold War, even in comparison with the Army

35. William Matthews, "Bottom-up Review calls for 15 'enhanced readiness' brigades," *Army Times*, September 13, 1993, p. 20.

36. William Matthews, "Future holds bigger role for reserves, Sullivan says," *Army Times*, September 12, 1994, p. 20.

37. William Matthews, "Larger Reserve role means longer drills, overseas rotations," *Army Times*, October 24, 1994, p. 26. As of June 1992, 8% percent of the Army Reserve's units were designated as Force Activity Designator (FAD) I or II. This meant that they were expected to be able to deploy immediately. An additional 38% were FAD III, meaning deployment within 30 days. By contrast, 71% of the active component units were FAD I or II and 25% were FAD III. For the Army National Guard, the comparable figures were 5% at FAD I or II and 28% at FAD III. General Accounting Office, *Reserve Forces: Aspects of the Army's Equipping Strategy Hamper Reserve Readiness*, GAO/NSIAD–93–11 (February 1993), p. 31. Hereinafter cited as "GAO, *Army's Equipping Strategy*."

38. *Ibid.*

National Guard. Unit flags were being furled throughout the Army Reserve, and the number of Selected Reservists was on a downward trend.

Perry followed his comments by including $25 million in the FY 1996 budget proposal to pay for overseas deployments of reserve forces. According to the Defense Secretary, "We are developing more and more ways of using [reservists] to relieve the too-high personnel tempo of some of our deployed units."[39]

This again was a new concept for use of the Reserve Components. Traditionally, meaning since colonial times, reservists—citizen soldiers—had been called to serve only during periods when the nation was endangered or U.S. national interests were significantly threatened. This new concept for reserve deployments was coupled to little more than a desire to provide relief for the active component, which was being stretched further than its capabilities could apparently handle.

Assistant Secretary Lee suggested that the Reservists could accomplish these expanded missions through "more creative or flexible use of the time already allotted for training," but others were skeptical of the demands being placed upon parttime soldiers.[40]

Gen. George Joulwan, Commander-in-Chief of the European Command, told the Senate Armed Services Committee that he believed that there were difficulties when Reservists were asked to spend too much time away from their jobs and families. Employers, particularly, are upset when Reservists take too much time away from their jobs to perform military duties, said the CINC. Though there are legal protections, said an official of the Reserve Officers Association, "There is a genuine fear that employers will find ways to fire" Reservists who miss too much work.[41]

Indeed, the Reserve Forces Policy Board reported that during FY 1993, the National Committee for Employer Support of the Guard and Reserve (NCESGR) had experienced a four-fold increase in employer complaints about "excessive duty" of reservists as compared with FY 1989. These complaints represented eight percent of the problems handled by NCESGR.[42]

---

39. William Matthews, "Perry pledges $25 million for reserve missions," *Army Times*, February 20, 1995, p. 22.

40. William Matthews, "Pentagon says expanded role won't engulf reserves, kin," *Army Times*, March 6, 1995, p. 33.

41. *Ibid.*

42. *Annual Report, RFPB, FY 93.* p. 71.

ROA's Executive Director, Maj. Gen. Roger Sandler (USAR, Ret.), a former Chief of the Army Reserve, said that the reserve association had recently gone on record as opposing the too-frequent call-ups of reservists. Besides the problems with absences from work, Reserve units need time to conduct their collective training. This training is generally accomplished during the two-week annual training period, which the Department of Defense would use instead to furnish relief for active forces.[43]

As this was being written (December 1995), the question of alternative annual training tours used as relief for active component forces was on hold, though some Army Reserve units were undertaking what was termed "extended annual training."[44] It was clear, however, that there had been a sea change in the way in which senior officials of the Defense Department were looking at the Army's reserve components. There may have been lingering questions about how ready reserve combat units would be on M-Day, but there seemed little doubt that the units of the Army Reserve were regarded as worthy to take the place of active component soldiers in performing the types of missions that the post-Cold War era seemed to produce in greatest abundance.

Missions that called for individual volunteers from the USAR were not thought to be a problem, but involuntary use of an entire Reserve unit was another matter indeed. The difficulty that the Defense Department confronted in attempting to make this change in call-up and deployment philosophy was that the law was not written to facilitate such. The answer, said the Defense Department, was to give the Secretary of Defense a certain limited authority for call-ups.

THE 25K CALL-UP AUTHORITY

One of the keys to the Clinton administration's plan for reservists was to call them to active duty more routinely than in the past. This could be done, of course, under what is called the "673b" authority of the President, but such authority has been used only once—during Desert Storm.[45] It was clear

43. William Matthews, "Too much of a good thing? Reservists getting leery about expanding active-duty tours," *Army Times*, March 27, 1995, p. 22.

44. *Annual Report, RFPB, FY 94*, p. 74.

45. This refers to 10 United States Code 673b. Under this provision the President can call-up 200,000 members of the Selected Reserve without declaring a national emergency.

from the statements coming from the Assistant Secretary of Defense for Reserve Affairs that the administration wanted more flexibility in this matter, to include the ability to call up reserve units involuntarily. The answer, said the Department of Defense, was to change the law and give the Secretary of Defense the authority to do a limited call-up, on the order of 25,000 reservists.[46]

In her interview with *Army Reserve Magazine* in May 1993, Assistant Secretary Lee said that the Pentagon had asked Congress for two new powers for the Secretary of Defense: the "25K call-up" authority that would allow the Secretary to order up to 25,000 Selected Reservists to active duty involuntarily without declaring a national emergency and the authority to retain these reservists on active duty for up to 360 days. Lee was optimistic in assessing the chances for the legislation. "The Senate has adopted as part of its authorization bill the 25,000 authority. The House has adopted as part of its version the 180/180 authority." She acknowledged the work that had to be done by DoD to convince each house to accept the other's provisions. "Hopefully," she concluded, "we may just get both."[47]

What happened was that they got neither. The members of the Congressional conference committee were apparently unconvinced by the arguments put forward by the Defense Department hierarchy. These arguments confirmed that what was being proposed was a significant departure from past practices, and the members were not sure of the wisdom of such a move. Relying upon volunteers had been the past answer to the need for reserve capabilities, Lee had told the conferees, "but this is not always as effective as it could be, particularly where unit capabilities are required."[48]

According to an unnamed Senate staffer cited on the topic, the conferees were concerned that giving this call-up authority to the Secretary of Defense would result in more frequent call-ups, and this would harm both recruiting and retention.[49]

The Department of Defense did not allow the issue to die with its first rejection by the Congress, however. By March of 1994 the request for Secretarial call-up authority had been presented once again to the Congress. The aim of the legislation,

46. This proposal did not originate with the Clinton administration. The Reserve Forces Policy Board made just such a recommendation in its report for FY 1992. *Annual Report, RFPB, FY 92*, p. 86.

47. Nielsen, "The Nation's Number One Reservist: Deborah R. Lee," p. 13.

48. William Matthews, "Aspin denied call-up power," *Army Times*, December 6, 1993, p. 24.

49. *Ibid.*

said Assistant Secretary Lee, was the "mobility people," meaning the Army Reservists who perform jobs for organizations such as the Military Traffic Management Command. If war comes, Lee was quoted as saying, among the first people needed are "the people who get everyone else out the door." [50]

By June, the Defense Department was saying that even if it were given this enhanced authority, it would be unlikely to use it "except in genuine emergencies." Expressing the same arguments used three months earlier, Lee said that the Reservists called to duty would be used "for priming the transportation and mobilization pipeline." [51]

Negatively, there were reports of reserve discontent over the prospect of more frequent call-ups. Some of those expressing their opinions felt that "giving the defense secretary call-up authority will greatly increase their chances of being ordered to active duty, altering the traditional expectation that the reserves are to be called only in dire emergencies." [52] The answer from Assistant Secretary Lee was that "the people that I talk to, by and large, are very gung-ho" about the prospects of being called to active duty." [53]

In 1994 it was looking quite good for Secretarial call-up authority. Unlike 1993, the House Armed Services Committee included the 25,000 call-up authority in its version of the Defense Authorization Bill. The provision was opposed by the Non-Commissioned Officers Association, but it was endorsed by the Reserve Officers Association, the National Guard Association, the Adjutants General Association, the Marine Corps Reserve Officers Association, and others.[54] There were caveats expressed, however, even by some who endorsed the provision. Adm. Phillip Smith (Ret.), legislative director of the Naval Reserve Association, suggested that the Secretary of Defense should not be given a carte blanche in this area. The Secretary should not have the authority to call up reservists "at any time for any purpose," said Smith.[55]

By the end of June, it was evident that the call-up plan was not going anywhere in the Senate, despite the fact that it

50. William Matthews, "Pentagon asks expanded call-up authority, again," *Army Times*, March 2, 1994, p. 24.

51. William Matthews, "Call-ups more likely," *Army Times*, June 6, 1994, p. 20.

52. *Ibid.*

53. *Ibid.*

54. William Matthews, "Call-ups: Loosening the leash," *Army Times*, May 23, 1994, p. 22.

55. *Ibid.*

had endorsed such only a few months earlier. The Senate Armed Services Committee had taken a harder stand than simply not accepting the Pentagon proposal. Senator Dan Coats (R–Ind.) offered an amendment, accepted by the Armed Services Committee, that specifically forbade the Secretary of Defense from exercising any type of call-up authority. The primary concern for the members of the Senate committee was that an unelected official—the Secretary of Defense—would be able to call reservists to duty. That authority, said Coats, had to remain with the President.[56]

The Senators also professed to see some contradictions between the assertion that there would be no adverse effects on either recruiting or retention if call-ups became more frequent and the Defense Department's request for both mobilization insurance for reservists and tax credits for employers. As one Senate staffer was quoted as saying, "If there would be no effect [on recruiting and retention], then why do they need mobilization insurance and tax credits?"[57]

The House of Representatives was prepared to give the Defense Department more nearly what it wanted. The House version of the authorization bill provided that the Secretary could exercise 25K call-up authority, but only if granted by the President for each instance in which he wanted to use it. The burden in this case would clearly remain with the President to decide on the occasions when the authority might be used.[58]

Confronted with Senate recalcitrance and House ambivalence, the Defense Department resorted to a bit of a threat. If you do not grant us the authority to call up the reserves as we wish, suggested Assistant Secretary Lee, there might be additional cuts in Reserve Component strength. "We simply can't afford to keep force structure that we may not use," she said, adding that if the Secretary were granted such powers, they would be used "judiciously and only for major operations." For what she described as "lesser conflicts" and "peace operations," only volunteers would be used.[59]

---

56. William Matthews, "Call-up plan hits snag in Senate," *Army Times*, June 27, 1994, p. 20.

57. *Ibid.* The Congress need not have worried about the idea of income protection insurance for Reservists and tax breaks for employers. The White House rejected the DoD proposal as being "too costly." See William Matthews, "Financial protection loses in White House," *Army Times*, May 9, 1994, p. 26.

58. William Matthews, "Pentagon insists on call-up authority," *Army Times*, July 18, 1994, p. 26.

59. *Ibid.*

There were obvious contradictions in the messages being sent to Congress and the reserve community on this issue. If involuntary call-ups by the Secretary of Defense were to be reserved for "major operations," there would seem little reason why the Presidential call-up authority in 10 U.S.C. 673b would not suffice, obviating the need for Secretarial authority. On the other hand, if volunteers alone were to be used for "lesser conflicts" and "peace operations," then again there would seem to be little need for additional call-up authority.

Neither the Senate nor the House bought the Defense Department's case for Secretarial call-up authority. For the second year in a row, the conferees on the defense authorization bill rejected the proposal for enhanced call-up authority. They did, however, agree to allow reservists to be called to involuntary active duty for up to 270 days, splitting the difference between the House's 360 days and the Senate's limit of a 180 day call-up.[60] In February 1995, Assistant Secretary Lee admitted that the Defense Department had "given up trying to get call-up authority for the Secretary." She said that DoD would instead develop "streamlined internal procedures" to allow more expeditious call-ups.[61]

THE ARMY RESERVE-ARMY NATIONAL GUARD UNIT SWAP

More critical for the Army Reserve in the long term was the agreement reached among Army Reserve, Army National Guard, and active Army leaders, with input from several of the reserve component professional associations, in December 1993. This arrangement, dubbed the "Offsite Agreement," set the structure for what the Army Reserve would look like at the end of the millennium.[62]

Under this agreement, which was announced by Defense Secretary Aspin, Army Chief of Staff Gen. Gordon Sullivan, and the chiefs of the Army's reserve components at a December 10, 1993, press conference, the Army Reserve would transfer some 14,000 positions to the National Guard. These would be primarily combat arms and aviation positions, in-

60. William Matthews, "Call-up power remains with President," *Army Times*, August 22, 1994, p. 22; United States House of Representatives, 103d Congress, 2d session, Report No. 103–701, *National Defense Authorization Act for Fiscal Year 1995*, Conference Report to accompany S. 2182 (August 12, 1994), Subtitle B, "Reserve Component Matters," Section 511.

61. William Matthews, "Income insurance advances; $50 nets $5,000," *Army Times*, February 22, 1995, p. 22.

62. "Army Reserve faces major restructuring of Forces," *Army Reserve Magazine*, Vol. 39, No. 4, (1993/94), p. 5.

cluding 4,400 rotary wing aviator positions. In return, the USAR would receive from the Guard about 10,000 positions in the combat support and combat service support areas, specifically including medical, signal, military police, and transportation. The aviator positions were referred to as a "migration" of positions, rather than a "swap," since the Army Reserve received nothing in return for them.[63]

The benefit to the Army Reserve from this agreement was that it received 58 Contingency Force Pool units from the Army National Guard. The USAR retained two AH–64 attack helicopter battalions, three CH–47 transport helicopter companies, and all its fixed wing aviation assets.[64]

The Army Reserve, which had been scheduled to drop steadily from its FY 1990 strength of 299,000 (Selected Reserve only) to 260,000 in FY 1994, took a significant hit in the Offsite Agreement. Under this agreement, by the end of FY 1999 the USAR would be reduced by 91,000 soldiers (30%), to a Selected Reserve strength of 208,000. The Army National Guard, by comparison, would be reduced by 70,000, a 16% reduction from its FY 1990 level.[65]

In reality, it was more significant than it appeared. The units that would be "swapped" between the two components would not actually be swapped. What would happen was that drawdown of particular unit types would be played against the "swap" agreement. "The Army does not now plan to actually transfer specific units and individuals between the two components [Army Reserve and National Guard]," concluded the Congressional Research Service's senior specialist on reserve component issues. "Rather, as the military drawdown proceeds, units in some categories would be drawn down disproportionately in the Army Guard and others in the Army Reserve."[66]

The case of the Army Reserve's 12th Special Forces Group is illustrative. The agreement meant that the USAR group would simply fade away, as had been planned previously for the 11th Special Forces Group of the Army Reserve. The National Guard, on the other hand, would be allowed to retain both of its Special Forces Groups, rather than having one of them disappear as planned.[67]

---

63. Katherine McIntire, "Army Reserve, Guard to swap units," *Army Times*, December 20, 1993, p. 3; Robert L. Goldich, *Army Reserve Component Reforms and the Bottom-Up Review: Issues for Congress* (CRS Report for Congress), May 10, 1994, p. CRS–4; *Annual Report, RFPB, FY 94*, pp. 11–12.

64. *RFPB Report, FY 1994*, p. 12.

65. Goldich, *Army Reserve Component Reforms*, p. CRS–3.

66. *Ibid.*, p. CRS–4.

67. *Ibid.*, p. CRS–4.

According to Army Vice Chief of Staff Gen. James H. Binford Peay, III, "There was very little difference in the readiness [of Special Forces units] between the two components. Two of the groups were going to come out anyway. It's just how you decide which component kept them. The people around the table, the U.S. Army Reserve, the Army National Guard, concurred in that particular approach."[68]

The agreement was lauded by the Chief of the Army Reserve, Maj. Gen. Roger W. Sandler. "These were not easy negotiations," said Sandler. "The units we are getting will continue our focus on our core competencies, and are a significant step toward keeping all the Army Reserve in the war fight."[69] Not unsurprisingly, it appeared to many observers that the National Guard had bested the Army Reserve in the negotiations. Though the agreement was supported by ROA, which had been a party to it, other organizations and prominent individuals disagreed with it.

The Army Reserve Association, speaking through its president, Maj. Gen. James Mukoyama (USAR), suggested that the agreement was not a good one for the Army Reserve. The Special Operations Council likewise opposed it for what it did to the Army Reserve's special forces groups.[70]

Mukoyama later reported what he interpreted as a career threat from TRADOC chief of staff Maj. Gen. John P. Herrling. According to Mukoyama, Herrling suggested, that "his services would no longer be required" at the Training and Doctrine Command if he broke with the Army on the issue. When asked about this allegation, Herrling said that he had told the Reserve general that he (Mukoyama) was "putting the commanding general [of TRADOC] in a very tough situation," adding that he hoped Mukoyama had not drawn "any conclusion that this might adversely affect him."[71]

The most vociferous opposition to the deal, however, came from two retired general officers who had been a part of the Army Reserve for many years. Brig. Gen. Harry J. Mott, III (Ret.) served as Deputy Chief of the Army Reserve from 1983–87 and as acting Chief, Army Reserve from August to December 1986. General Mott's criticism centered about the

68. "Peay: Force overhaul is 'success story,'" *Army Times*, May 30, 1994, p. 26.

69. "Army Reserve faces major restructuring of forces," p. 5.

70. Katherine McIntire, "Reserve Special Forces: Going, going. . .," *Army Times*, May 16, 1994, p. 27.

71. Barton Gellman, "Pentagon Plan Would Cut Reserve," *The Washington Post*, December 11, 1993, p. 1.

fear that this agreement marked the beginning of the end for senior level Army Reserve commands. Mott suggested that the result would be a reduction of the USAR to "company and battalion-size units. The general officer commands will slowly disappear," said Mott, who felt quite clearly that this agreement resulted from an active component plot to "get rid of the Army Reserve as a cohesive force."[72]

Less confrontational, but just as troubled, was Maj. Gen. William F. Ward (Ret.), who served as Chief, Army Reserve from 1986–1991. Ward questioned the purported costs of the agreement, which he said were cited as somewhere between $135 million and $235 million. He also questioned the supposed neutral effect the agreement would have on readiness. How does that comport, he asked, with what has been estimated to be a three to eight year time frame before National Guard aviation units would achieve the readiness currently enjoyed by Army Reserve aviators? He was unpersuaded, said Ward, that this swap agreement was anything other than a "politically expedient way of downsizing the Army, [and] saving Active strength and National Guard overstructure at the expense of the Army Reserve."[73]

The National Guard seemed to embrace the plan wholeheartedly, to the degree that it began to recruit Army Reserve aviators into the Guard even before the order to execute the plan had been given. According to an unidentified Army Reserve "aviation official," the Guard had gone directly to members of Army Reserve aviation units and attempted to persuade them to leave the Army Reserve and join the Guard. "We are not going to take the Reserve structure and inactivate it and then grow from ground zero the facilities, people, and aviation units," said Maj. Gen John D'Araujo, Jr., director of the Army National Guard. "Where they have newer aircraft, we will migrate those aircraft to those [Guard] units and wash out the old. If we have newer aircraft, we will we will turn in the Army Reserve aircraft."[74]

On the subject of the aviators themselves, D'Araujo was equally pragmatic. "I want to dispel the notion that we are slamming the door on qualified Army Reservists. We'd be crazy to do it because they've got a lot of good quality aviators." He

---

72. Harry J. Mott III, "Reserve brass missing during restructuring," *Army Times*, March 7, 1994, p. 33.

73. William F. Ward, "Just the facts, please, General, just the facts," *Army Times*, March 14, 1994, p. 29.

74. Katherine McIntire, "Guard pushes for Reserve transfers," *Army Times*, April 11, 1994, p. 18.

was referring specifically, however, to younger aviators, said D'Araujo. "We will encourage moving some of the older guys out and taking some of the younger qualified aviators. . . ."[75]

The older, more senior aviators in the Army Reserve might have more trouble finding a home in the Guard. Even within the Army Reserve it is hard for a field grade officer to move from one unit to another. To transfer from the Army Reserve into the Army National Guard at the field grade level was even more difficult. Nevertheless, the Offsite Agreement appeared to be an accomplished fact. In the House Report on the Defense Authorization Act for FY 1995, the Armed Services Committee recognized "the historic implications of the offsite agreement between the Army, the Army National Guard, and the Army Reserve. The committee has some reservations about readiness and is concerned about the Agreement's near term costs." The committee did not attempt to undo the agreement legislatively.[76]

ARMY RESERVE ORGANIZATION

The changes engendered by the offsite agreement were but a part of the structural changes that occurred in the Army Reserve during this period. Just as significant, perhaps, was the plan put forward by Army Reserve Chief Maj. Gen. Max Baratz to realign the Army Reserve's command and control structure along regional lines. The regions—to be designated Regional Support Commands (RSCs)—would coincide with the Standard Federal Region boundaries used by all federal agencies including the Federal Emergency Management Agency (FEMA), with which the Army Reserve seemed to be doing more business in the 1990s.[77]

The reorganization was extremely ambitious, in that it would transform ten Army Reserve Commands (ARCOMs) into Regional Support Commands (RSC). These ARCOMs were the 63d, 77th, 88th, 89th, 94th, 96th, 99th, 121st (redesignated the 81st RSC), 122d (redesignated the 90th RSC), and the 124th. In those RSCs that contained more than 20,000 Reservists, Regional Support Groups would be established, which would be centered on former ARCOMs. These included the 90th, the 120th (redesignated the 81st RSC), and

75. *Ibid.*

76. 103d Congress, 2d session, United States House of Representatives, House Report No. 103–499, May 10, 1994, to accompany H.R. 4301, p. 235.

77. "New shape of Army Reserve supports new missions," *Army Reserve Magazine*, Vol. 40, no. 2 (1994), p. 5.

the 123d (redesignated the 88th RSC). ARCOMs that would disappear entirely were the 79th, 81st, 83d, 86th, 97th, 102d, and 125th, although the lineage and colors of the 81st would be retained for their historical significance. Of the 5,000 drilling positions in the twenty ARCOMs as they existed in 1994, approximately 2,000 would be eliminated.[78]

Hardly had the reorganization plan been announced than members of Congress weighed in with objections. The particular Congressmen were all from Missouri, and they objected to the part of the reorganization that would eliminate the ARCOM in St. Louis while making the 89th ARCOM in Wichita, Kans., the headquarters for the Regional Support Command.[79]

Philosophically, the three Congressmen—Reps. Richard Gephardt (D–Mo.), William Clay (D–Mo.) and James Talent (R–Mo.)—questioned the basis for alignment with FEMA regions. "The Army Reserve's first priority is to serve the federal Army; it is the National Guard that has primary responsibility for providing assistance to those domestic agencies which deal with crises such as floods, earthquakes, and hurricanes," wrote the Congressmen.[80] It was nevertheless true that during the 1990s, as never before, the Army Reserve had been engaged in relief efforts following natural disasters, and this realignment was meant to make the USAR better able to respond to such.

The members requested and received a hearing on the issue, but it made no difference. On January 4, 1995, the Army announced its agreement with the plan and told the Army Reserve that it could proceed. This was done despite a last-minute letter from Rep. Floyd Spence, soon to be Chairman of the House National Security (formerly Armed Services) Committee asking that the implementation be delayed.[81]

CHANGES IN ARMY SCHOOL STRUCTURE

Planning began in 1992 for a complete reorganization of the Army's schools structure, which was described by one observer as a "ganglion of 63 active Army, 83 National Guard and 111 Army Reserve teaching institutions. . . ."[82] This reor-

---

78. *Ibid.*, pp. 5–6.

79. Katherine McIntire Peters, "Restructuring plan blasted," *Army Times*, November 28, 1994, p. 14.

80. *Ibid.*

81. Katherine McIntire Peters, "Army gives nod to closing of seven ARCOMs," *Army Times*, January 16, 1995, p. 22.

82. Jim Tice, "Army moves to single school system," *Army Times*, April 4, 1994, p. 24.

ganization was planned by the Army's Training and Doctrine Command (TRADOC), which came up with a new agency, the Total Army School System Coordinating Activity, to effect the changes.[83]

The overall plan called for nine regional training divisions and five exercise divisions. The biggest change for the 81 Army Reserve schools is that they would now come under the training divisions, rather than under Army Reserve Commands (ARCOMs). The training divisions would be subordinate to the CONUSAs and the Army Reserve Command (USARC).[84] The first of the training divisions, the 108th headquartered in Charlotte, N.C., was scheduled to be fully operational in October 1997. It was to control soldiers in Florida, Georgia, South Carolina, and North Carolina.[85]

The stated advantage of this new structure was that it would eliminate duplication among the schools and provide better training for the individual soldier. In addition, said an Army Reserve spokesman, "We're going to see more current information being taught." Furthermore, said Maj. Gen. Carl Ernst, Deputy Chief of Staff for Training at TRADOC, the reorganization would ultimately lead to "a more uniform adherence to [training and educational] standards."[86]

UNITED STATES ARMY RESERVE COMMAND (USARC)

The final organizational issue confronting the Army Reserve during this period was the continuing story of the United States Army Reserve Command (USARC). The USARC was provisionally established by the Army on October 1, 1990, and achieved FORSCOM Major Subordinate Command status on October 1, 1991. Meanwhile, Congress changed the span of control of the USARC by removing Army Reserve special operations forces from its command.[87]

On October 1, 1992, the USARC took over command of all Army Reserve units except special operations forces (as specified in the law) and those outside the United States. In

83. *Ibid.*

84. Katherine McIntire Peters, "Soldier training changes for a changed world," *Army Times*, December 19, 1994, p. 20.

85. *Ibid.*

86. Tice, "Army moves to single school system;" see also Katherine McIntire, "Active, reserve components test training together," *Army Times*, June 13, 1994, p. 29.

87. *U.S. Army Reserve Command Independent Commission, Final Report, October 1992*, Section III, p. 1; Section 704 (a)(7), Public Law 102–25, April 6, 1991. Hereinafter cited as "*Independent Commission Report.*"

doing so it accepted the command and control of 48 Major U.S. Army Reserve Commands (MUSARCs) from the Continental Armies (CONUSAs).[88]

Establishment of the USARC meant that the Chief, Army Reserve was "triple-hatted," with additional hats as Commanding General of the USARC and Deputy Commanding General (Reserve Affairs) of FORSCOM. It also set up an unusual rating chain for MUSARC commanders. These individuals were now rated by the DCG, USARC (a major general), intermediate rated by one of the CONUSA CGs (a lieutenant general), and senior rated by the CG USARC (a major general).[89]

The Army Reserve Command assumed responsibility for all day-to-day activities related to personnel, logistics, resource management, information management, and engineering. Operations, mobilization, and deployment remained the responsibility of FORSCOM and the CONUSAs. Training was split between the USARC and the CONUSAs, with the Army Reserve Command providing training guidance and resources and the CONUSAs responsible for training support and readiness evaluation.[90]

As part of the legislation that statutorily established the USARC (Section 903, National Defense Authorization Act for FY 1991), Congress prescribed the creation of an independent commission to assess the progress and effectiveness of the new Army Reserve Command. That commission was chartered by the Secretary of the Army on December 19, 1991, and it reported to the Secretary on October 15, 1992.[91] Its membership consisted of a mix of serving and retired active component and Army Reserve general officers, a former member of Congress, and a member of DoD's Senior Executive Service.[92]

After months of study, the commission recommended that not later than 1995 the USARC should become a major command "along the lines of the AFRES [Air Force Reserve] model with full command and control responsibility of all USAR units (with the exception of SOF) [special operations forces]. . . ."[93] It specifically recommended that the USARC assume responsibility for training and operations and that FORSCOM be responsi-

88. *Independent Commission Report*, Section III, p. 1.

89. *Ibid.*, Section III, p. 2.

90. Col. Frank A. Edens (USAR, Ret.), "Major Command or Major Subordinate Command Is Question for Army Reserve," *The Officer* (December 1992), pp. 35–37.

91. *Independent Commission Report*, Section I, p. 1.

92. *Ibid.*, p. 3.

93. *Ibid.*, Section III, p. 18.

ble for mobilization and deployment. It also addressed the old question of the proper rank for the USARC CG: it thought lieutenant general would be appropriate given the enormous span of control exercised by this individual.[94]

The recommendations of the commission did not reach receptive ears in the Army hierarchy. The primary issue over the next two years would be the effort to make the Army Reserve Command truly an independent command, and not simply a sub-unit of FORSCOM.

The goal of having an independent Army Reserve Command—that is, one that reported directly to the Chief of Staff of the Army—remained illusory. Reps. G.V. (Sonny) Montgomery and Greg Laughlin introduced a bill calling for such (H.R. 1827) in 1993.[95] This bill was not passed independently, but its key provisions were incorporated as Section 921 of the House version of the defense authorization act for fiscal year 1994. This provision required that the Army Reserve Command become "an independent command reporting directly to the Chief of Staff of the Army."[96]

The Senate version of the defense authorization bill had no similar provision, and the Senate receded to the House in conference. The Senate, however, insisted on an amendment "making the Army Reserve Command a separate Army command that is commanded by the Chief of the Army Reserve, substituting the Commander-in-Chief of the United States Atlantic Command (CINCUSA) for the Commander-in-Chief of the Forces Command (CINCFOR). . . ."[97]

This was a startling development for the USARC. The House and the Senate adopted the conference report, and the provision pulling the Army Reserve Command out from under FORSCOM and putting it under the Atlantic Command became Section 941 of the National Defense Authorization Act for Fiscal Year 1994.[98] So what happened to the USARC? Nothing. Despite the law and the amendment to the Defense Au-

94. *Ibid.*, Section III, pp. 18–19.

95. Col. Frank Edens (USAR, Ret.), "MACOM Status '93 Goal," *The Officer* (June 1993), p. 22.

96. 103d Congress, 1st session, House Report No. 103–200, July 30, 1993, to accompany H.R. 2401, National Defense Authorization Act for Fiscal Year 1994, p. 318.

97. 103d Congress, 1st session, House Conference Report No. 103–357, November 10, 1993, to accompany H.R. 2401, National Defense Authorization Act for Fiscal Year 1994, , p. 704.

98. Section 941, Public Law 103–160, November 30, 1993, National Defense Authorization Act for Fiscal Year 1994.

thorization Act for Fiscal Year 1991, the USARC never left FORSCOM. The explanation was that since FORSCOM was the Army component of the Atlantic Command, the Army complied with the law even though the Army Reserve Command never moved. The issue of the USARC as a separate command, separate and reporting directly to the Chief of Staff of the Army, was not resolved.

This issue came up again during the nomination hearings for General John Shalikashvili, who was picked to become Chairman of the Joint Chiefs of Staff. Shalikashvili told the Armed Services Committee that the move toward separate reserve commands worried him. He felt that it might make the combatant commanders less confident of Reserve component readiness and hence less willing to use them in a crisis situation.[99]

The House version of the FY 1995 defense authorization bill attempted once more to resolve the issue. Section 902 of H.R. 4301 provided that the USARC would be an independent command, "whose commander reports directly to the Army Chief of Staff."[100] The Senate version of the defense authorization contained no similar provision, and the House gave in to the Senate during the conference on the two bills.[101] There was no change in status for the USARC as 1994 ended.

Even into 1995 the issue of independence for the USARC was not closed, however. Rep. Greg Laughlin (D–Tex.), an Army Reserve colonel and the primary proponent of the independent command, continued to push for the USARC to enjoy the same status within the Army as other major commands, such as Forces Command.[102]

---

99. Rick Maze, "Shali voices concerns on separate commands," *Army Times*, October 4, 1993, p. 24.

100. 103d Congress, 2d session, House of Representatives, Section 902, House Report No. 103–499 to accompany H.R. 4301, May 10, 1994, p. 269.

101. 103d Congress, 2d session, House of Representatives, House Conference Report No. 103–701, to accompany S. 2182, August 12, 1994, p. 739.

102. Katherine McIntire Peters, "Reaching for the stars," *Army Times*, March 6, 1995, p. 32.

searched in archives in both the United States and the former Soviet Union (FSU) and traveled through the FSU states seeking information about missing Americans.[12]

Finally, Army Reservists were very much involved in an operation called "RETROEUR," or Retrograde Europe. This exercise involved Army Reserve ordnance and aviation maintenance companies, as well as engineers and other combat support units. Army Reservists began to take part in RETROEUR in 1992, with the number of Reservists and Reserve units increasing each year. In 1994 over 30 units and 4,720 Reservists took part in the operation, a 55 percent increase over FY 1993. RETROEUR was an outgrowth of the end of the Cold War and the need to return some of the enormous quantities of materiel to the United States. By its close, over 1 million short tons of equipment—including over 11,000 vehicles—would be returned to the United States. All of this materiel had to be cleaned, inspected, and often repaired before it was crated and shipped. Much of this work was accomplished by the Army Reserve, including volunteer Reservists who traveled to Europe for 139 day tours.[13]

More conventional overseas training, that is, training without another product resulting, also took place across the border. Exercise Nordic Shield II was held at Gagetown, New Brunswick, Canada, in the summer of 1992. The exercise involved 4,500 Army Reservists and small contingents from other services and components who simulated the defense of Iceland. Primary participants were the 187th Infantry Brigade (Fort Devens, Mass.) and the 167th Support Group (Manchester, N.H.) Part of the exercise involved lanes training, discussed earlier in this chapter in conjunction with Bold Shift.[14]

DOMESTIC TRAINING

Army Reserve units also took part in numerous domestic training exercises during this period. One of these, "Operation Golden Cargo," was a five-year exercise that originated as a way to train Army units that moved equipment and sup-

12. Maj. Elizabeth Checchia, "Task Force Russia," *Army Reserve Magazine*, Vol. 40, No. 1 (1993), pp. 10–11.

13. Katherine McIntire Peters, "Reservists retrieve Cold War surplus," *Army Times*, July 18, 1994, p. 27; Lt. Col. Arthur E. House, "Final days of the Cold War," *Army Reserve Magazine*, Vol. 40, No. 1 (1994), pp. 14–15.

14. Steve Harding, "Northern Warriors," *Army Reserve Magazine*, Vol. 38, No. 4 (1992/93), pp. 16–21; Master Sgt. Terry Brown, "Army Reserve fuelers complete tank missions," *The Reserve Voice* (94th Army Reserve Command) (Spring 1993), p. 3.

plies and at the same time save the Army a considerable amount of money. The primary cargo hauled during this exercise was ammunition, tons of ammunition. The ammo was being relocated as a result of base realignment and closure activities. Using the Army Reserve as prime movers, along with soldiers from the active component and the Army National Guard, as well as DA civilians, saved the Army hundreds of thousands of dollars. At the same time, it provided unparalleled training opportunities for the soldiers involved.[15]

DOMESTIC RELIEF MISSIONS

The domestic disaster relief mission has historically belonged to the National Guard. "Calling out the Guard" has been the state governor's response to crises ranging from prison riots to floods. During the 1990s, however, the Army Reserve began to be regarded as a force that could serve the community during times of natural disaster.

In late August 1992, Hurricane Andrew slashed through south Florida, leaving 100 square miles destroyed and more than 200,000 people homeless. A few weeks later, Pacific hurricane Iniki hit the Hawaiian island of Kauai, killing several people and causing an estimated $1 billion in damage. In both instances, the Army Reserve was used to provide relief. In Florida hundreds of Reservists showed up to help. All were volunteers, for their units were not themselves activated for the disaster relief effort. Reservists performed debris clearing work, transported supplies, and provided meals and shelter for the homeless. In addition to the unit members, forty-five Army Reserve Individual Mobilization Augmentees (IMAs) were called up by the Army Corps of Engineers to work in both Florida and Hawaii.[16]

---

15. "'Golden Cargo' Supports Moves," *Army Logistician*, July–August 1993, p. 47; Pam Briola, "'We got us a Golden Cargo convoy," *Army Reserve Magazine*, Vol. 38, No. 2 (1992), pp. 24–25; letter, James R. Klugh, Deputy Under Secretary of Defense (Logistics) to Senator John C. Danforth, August 25, 1993; copy in possession of the author.

16. SSgt. Greg Deiml, SSgt. Donald Dunn, Maj. Annie Simmons, Lt. Col. Paul Adams, and ARNEWS, "Disaster," *Army Reserve Magazine*, Vol. 38, No. 3 (1992), pp. 14–17; Lt. Col. Robert Wilson and Maj. Don Kester, "IMAs touch the people of Florida, Hawaii," *Army Reserve Magazine*, Vol. 38, No. 3 (1992), p. 17. *Army Reserve Magazine*, Vol. 38, No.3 (1992), p. 15, lists the 46 Army Reserve units from which volunteers came to assist in the hurricane relief work. For a particularly comprehensive story about the contributions of Reservists from one ARCOM, see Master Sgt. Terry Brown, "Reservists help hurricane survivors recover, rebuild," *The Reserve Voice* (94th ARCOM) (Spring 1993), pp. 1, 4–5.

Of fourteen missions assigned to the Corps of Engineers by the Federal Emergency Management Agency (FEMA), twelve were directed by Army Reserve IMAs. One of the IMA soldiers, Maj. Michael Pickard, was in charge of temporary housing, while another IMA, Maj. Rex Holman, was the debris clearance director. It was also IMAs who labored in the relief effort in Hawaii, which was not as extensive as in Florida.[17]

Army Reservists also responded when the Missouri River ranged over its banks during the great flood of 1993. Answering a call from the Army Corps of Engineers were the Chinook helicopters of Company C, 2d Battalion, 158th Aviation Regiment from Olathe, Kans. The Army Reserve aviators helped the Corps by transporting and dropping huge boulders into breaches in a levee.[18]

In addition to hurricanes and floods, Army Reservists also fought fires. One of these occurred on August 10, 1993, in Tampa Bay, when a large ocean-going ship collided with two barges, both of which were carrying large quantities of fuel. The resulting fire blocked Tampa Bay's Mullet Key shipping channel, but Tampa's firefighters were unable to reach the blaze. A call quickly went out to the 231st Transportation Company, a medium boat unit in nearby St. Petersburg. The 231st responded within three hours with four Landing Craft Marines (LCMs) and sixteen soldiers to operate them. These Reserve volunteers loaded fire fighting equipment onto the boats and maneuvered close enough to the inferno to allow the firefighters to extinguish it.[19]

Finally, under DoD's civil-military cooperation program, Army Reservists were involved in projects ranging from inoculating schoolchildren to depositing tanks in the ocean to make artificial fishing reefs. The former project took Army Reserve medical personnel into both inner cities and rural areas of the United States to provide health care to those in need. Analogous to the MEDRETEs conducted overseas, these exercises represented a change in emphasis for the Army Reserve,

17. Wilson and Kester, "IMAs touch the people of Florida, Hawaii," p. 17.

18. Frank Tucker, "missouri boulderbombers," *Army Reserve Magazine*, Vol. 39, No. 3 (1993), p. 15.

19. Elaine McGee, "Fire!" *Army Reserve Magazine*, Vol. 39, No. 4 (1993/94), pp. 12–13. Army Reserve aviators from A Company, 6th Battalion, 158th Aviation Regiment also battled a fire in a Washington state forest in August 1994. See 1st Lt. John Klinkam, "What in the Blazes!" *Army Reserve Magazine*," Vol. 40, No. 3 (1994), p. 25.

the logical outgrowth of a decade of expansion of the definition of an appropriate Reserve mission.[20]

The reef-building exercise was in many ways even more innovative. Also operating under the aegis of the Office of Civil-Military Cooperation, Reservists from the 310th Theater Army Area Command at Fort Belvoir, Va., commanded a joint task force that took obsolete M–60 tanks from Anniston Army Depot, Ala., pulled the engines and transmissions, steam cleaned them to specifications established by the Environmental Protection Agency, and placed them in the water off Gulf and Atlantic coast states to create artificial fishing reefs.[21]

The project was useful training for the Reservists, who worked with members of the Air Force Reserve, Naval Reserve, and Army National Guard, as well as with the Coast Guard, the states in whose waters the tanks were placed, and various federal agencies. REEFEX 94, as the operation was designated, was lauded by Vice President Al Gore, who wrote that it "links a healthy environment and a healthy economy."[22]

OVERSEAS MISSIONS

"War training giving way to real missions" read the headline in a January 2, 1995, issue of *Army Times*.[23] To members of the Army Reserve, the recognition that they were now doing more "real missions," was long overdue. Just in the three years after Desert Storm, there had been the Kurdish relief effort (Provide Comfort), the Bangladesh relief effort (Sea Angel), the Somali excursion (Restore Hope), the Cuban operation in Panama (Safe Haven), and, finally, the Haiti operation (Uphold Democracy).

OPERATION PROVIDE COMFORT

Following the war against Iraq, Saddam Hussein launched a series of attacks against Kurds who had risen against his regime. The Kurds, numbering in the hundreds of thousands, fled into the mountains of northern Iraq along the border with

---

20. William Matthews, "Reserves get larger role in battle on domestic ills," *Army Times*, July 25, 1994, p. 22.

21. Lt. Col. James T. Currie, "Fish tanks," *Army Reserve Magazine*, Vol. 40, No. 3 (1994) pp. 15–17.

22. See *REEFEX: A Special Edition of the Gray Ghost*, October 1994, command publication of the 310th TAACOM, Fort Belvoir, Va., inside front cover.

23. William Matthews, "War training giving way to real missions," *Army Times*, January 2, 1995, p. 34.

Turkey. By April 6, 1991, the first U.S. military unit moved in to assist the Kurds and to attempt to prevent massive starvation.[24]

The 354th Civil Affairs Brigade was the only such brigade on active duty at this time, so it was chosen by the JCS to be the on-the-ground civil affairs headquarters. It took several weeks, however, before the 354th and its subordinate companies arrived in Turkey. It was joined there by elements from the active component 96th Civil Affairs Battalion from Fort Bragg. The Coalition Combined Task Force Civil Affairs Command consisted of 447 persons and was commanded by Brig. Gen. Don Campbell. The 354th Civil Affairs Brigade, commanded by Col. Robert H. Beahm, was attached to Task Force Bravo in Zakho, Iraq. In addition, a Civilian Agencies Task Force commanded by Col. Edward F. Dandar, the Deputy Brigade Commander, deployed teams to Turkey and northern Iraq to support the efforts of the United Nations High Commissioner for Refugees and the non-governmental organizations that were involved in the relief effort.[25]

The mission of all of these organizations was to prevent the starvation of some 360,000–760,000 Iraqi Kurds who had revolted against Saddam Hussein and had consequently been driven from their homes. Organizationally, the 354th Civil Affairs Brigade had under it the 418th, 431st, and 432d Civil Affairs Companies. For almost six weeks the brigade and the associated companies moved, housed, clothed, and fed hundreds of thousands of Kurdish refugees. The 431st Civil Affairs Company moved into Dahak, Iraq, to assist private organizations in the resettlement efforts in that city. By June 1991 the mission had been completed, and the civil affairs soldiers, who had worked alongside the active component special forces and psychological operations units, were able to return home.[26]

One of the parts of Provide Comfort that was not as directly involved with assisting the refugees played itself out on a computer terminal, rather than at the back of a truck filled with relief supplies. Two Army Reserve officers, Capt. Mark Wolfenberger and 1st Lt. Angela Blevins, developed a soft-

---

24. "354th Civil Affairs Brigade's Participation in Operation Provide Comfort," *Civil Affairs Symposium Proceedings*, p. 349.

25. *Ibid.*, p. 350.

26. Col. Robert H. Beahm, "354th Civil Affairs Brigade, Operations Desert Storm and Provide Comfort," *Civil Affairs Symposium Proceedings*, p. 348; Dr. Richard W. Stewart, Director, History and Museums, U.S. Army Special Operations Command, untitled and undated paper on Army Civil Affairs in the Gulf war; hereinafter cited as "Stewart paper." Copy in possession of the author.

ware program that allowed the tracking of these relief supplies. The program, called the Disaster Assistance Logistics Information System (DALIS) provided the tool required to maintain an accurate inventory of the supplies that poured into the area. One of the keys to the software was that it was user-friendly and was developed quickly—in less than three weeks—at minimal cost to the government.[27]

OPERATION SEA ANGEL

In May 1991, soldiers from the 351st Civil Affairs Command, USAR, joined active component soldiers and marines to assist in humanitarian relief efforts in Bangladesh. A cyclone—a Pacific hurricane—had hit the country on April 29 and 30 and killed as many as 100,000 people. It left millions of others stranded on disease-ridden islands in the Ganges and Brahmaputra River delta areas. The Reservists from the 351st were soon joined by other soldiers from the 364th Civil Affairs Brigade, the 322d Civil Affairs Group, and the 402d and 413th Civil Affairs Companies. The operation ended in late May and all U.S. soldiers and marines had returned home by June 3.[28]

OPERATION RESTORE HOPE

It is hard to say exactly why the United States went into Somalia, except that there were pictures of starving children on the television news each evening, and national leaders decided that the United States military could help the volunteer organizations distribute the food and other supplies. The 352d Civil Affairs Command from Riverdale, Md., began planning for the mission in August 1992, long before any decision to send U.S. forces had been made. It was the 96th Civil Affairs Battalion (Airborne) from Fort Bragg, the one active component civil affairs unit in the Army's inventory, however, that got the initial call.[29]

The 96th reported in late 1992, and it remained the only CA asset in country until October 1993. At that time volunteers from the 352d began arriving in Somalia, where they worked beside their active component counterparts. By De-

---

27. Capt. Cynthia Crosson, "DALIS: Designed for Disasters," *Army Reserve Magazine*, Vol. 38, No. 3 (1992), pp. 18–19; briefing on Provide Comfort, U.S. Army Special Operations Command. Copy in possession of the author.

28. Stewart paper.

29. Katherine McIntire, "'Would have been ready' for Somalia," *Army Times*, June 14, 1993, p. 30.

cember, the 96th CA Battalion had departed, and the civil affairs mission had been taken over by the Army Reservists.[30] These soldiers proved their worth in many situations.

In one instance, U.S. convoys were regularly taking sniper fire from one particular neighborhood. One way of handling the matter would have been to cordon off the area and do a house-to-house search, a plan that might well have provoked a violent confrontation with the Somalis. Instead, an Army Reserve civil affairs team went into the area and persuaded the village elders to turn over the sniper to the U.S. forces.[31]

711TH POSTAL COMPANY

Postal operations was another aspect of the Somalia operation that involved the Army Reserve. There were thousands of U.S. troops in Somalia following the initial deployment in December 1992. These troops required mail delivery services, and the first postal unit on the scene was the active component 129th AG Company (Direct Support)(Postal). This unit served until February 1993, at which time it was relieved by the 711th AG Company (General Support) (Postal), an Army Reserve unit.[32]

The way in which the 711th received the mission was unique. FORSCOM tasked the USARC to come up with an Army Reserve postal unit, and the USARC passed the tasking to the 81st ARCOM, headquartered in Atlanta, suggesting that the 351st Postal Company (GS Postal) from Coral Gables, Fla., would be the appropriate unit. The 351st, however, was on annual training in Korea and was unavailable. The 81st recommended that the 834th Postal Company be tasked to provide soldiers for the mission. After several false starts, including a misunderstanding as to whether the 834th had been asked to volunteer as a unit, a provisional postal company—the 711th—was established.[33]

The call then went out for soldiers with postal experience, and 250 Army Reservists came forward. All of these were troop program unit members, and the final make-up of the 711th was 5 officers and 43 enlisted personnel, who came

30. Maj. Randy Pullen, "Return from Somalia," *Army Reserve Magazine*, Vol. 40, no. 2 (1994), pp. 12–13.

31. *Ibid.*, p. 13.

32. John R. Brinkerhoff and Stanley A. Horowitz, *Case Studies in Reserve Component Volunteerism: The 711th Postal Company in Operation Restore Hope* (Alexandria, Va.: Institute for Defense Analyses, 1995), pp. 1–2. Hereinafter cited as "Brinkerhoff and Horowitz, *711th Postal Company*."

33. *Ibid.*, pp. 5–6.

from 17 different Army Reserve units. Volunteers were neither solicited nor accepted from the Individual Ready Reserve, nor were volunteers accepted from units in the Contingency Force Pool.[34]

These Reservists from across the country were placed on a Temporary Tour of Active Duty (TTAD) of 179 days. They assembled at Fort Bragg, N.C., shortly after Christmas 1992 and proceeded to put together a functioning postal unit. The unit's commander was Capt. Tamara Dozier. One of the difficulties was that in addition to assembling personnel, the unit had to acquire the equipment it would need in Somalia.[35] All of this was done with reasonable speed, and the unit arrived in Somalia on January 14, 1993.[36]

On February 1 the 711th took over from the 129th and operated the entire mail system in Somalia, including the two post offices at Bela Dogle and Kismayu. The two outposts were staffed by seven soldiers from the 129th who had remained behind when the balance of their unit departed.[37]

The mail volume in Somalia did not approach that of Desert Shield/Desert Storm, and the 711th found itself with more soldiers than were required. By the end of March, it was reduced to only 19 members, the others having redeployed to Fort Bragg. Among those who returned to Fort Bragg was Capt. Dozier. 1st. Lt. Lee J. Perkins then assumed command of the unit. The 711th served in Somalia until June 1993, at which time it was replaced by the active component 43d AG Detachment (GS Postal).[38]

Evaluations of the performance of the 711th are mixed. There was criticism of the unit at the Department of the Army level, and an Army Inspector General investigation in Somalia looked into allegations of poor mail handling and delivery, among other issues.[39] Other sources suggest that any problems the 711th might have experienced in Somalia were "systemic," and not attributable to the unit itself. Individuals in positions higher in the postal arena than the 711th, such as the DA Staff Postal Officer, the G–1 of the 10th Mountain Division, and the commander of JTF Support Command, felt that

34. *Ibid.*, p. 7.

35. Lt. Col. Jim Nielsen, "Moving the mail in Mogadishu," *Army Reserve Magazine*, Vol. 38, No. 4 (1992/93), p. 13; Brinkerhoff and Horowitz, *711th Postal Company*, p. 8..

36. Brinkerhoff and Horowitz, *711th Postal Company*, p. 11.

37. *Ibid.*, p. 11.

38. *Ibid.*, 11–13, 2.

39. *Ibid.*, p. 16, 13.

the 711th did a good job. Indeed, Lt. Col. Mike Hardesty, the 10th Mountain Division G–1, felt that the "RC unit could run circles around the AC unit," meaning the 129th.[40]

What an analysis of this case suggests is that it is very difficult to throw together a unit from volunteers and have it succeed. The 711th had very little time to establish any sort of mission cohesion before it was deployed, and it showed when the unit hit the ground in Somalia. Though the use of provisional units is not unusual within the active component, it is clear that more thought should be devoted as to how to go about doing so, including the necessity for training and time to achieve unit cohesion. The Reservists of the 711th did their jobs despite these handicaps, but a bit more planning could have made their task much easier.[41]

CUBANS IN PANAMA

Cubans began fleeing their country in ever greater numbers in 1993 and 1994, and almost before the United States realized what was happening, the refugee camp at Guantanamo, Cuba, was filled to capacity. After casting about for alternatives other than bringing the refugees into the United States, the United States persuaded Panama to allow the establishment of a camp at Empire Range, near the Panama Canal. Active component soldiers operated the camp itself, but it was Army Reserve civil affairs specialists who were the primary contact between the Cubans and the American authorities.[42]

The Panamanian camp, run as part of what was called Operation Safe Haven, was designed to accommodate up to 10,000 Cubans, who were flown into Howard Air Force Base, Panama, from Guantanamo. The Cubans were housed in four tent cities built on a former U.S. range. Each city consisted of ten blocks of eighteen tents each, with each tent holding fifteen people. A civil affairs specialist assigned to each block was given the task of getting to know the Cubans and assisting them in making the best of their condition.[43]

---

40. *Ibid.*, p. 18.

41. Nine members of the 324th Data Processing Unit, USAR, also went to Somalia, where they worked at providing logistics automation for the relief effort. See Master Sgt. Terry Brown, "324th DPU personnel help speed relief supplies to Somalia," *The Reserve Voice* (94th Army Reserve Command) (Spring 1993), pp. 1, 7.

42. Katherine McIntire Peters, "Empire Range is Safe Haven for Cubans," *Army Times*, October 17, 1994, p. 32.

43. *Ibid.*

OPERATION UPHOLD DEMOCRACY

It was a curious name for an operation in Haiti, for as far as can be determined, Haiti had never had a democratic government to be upheld. It was, nevertheless, "Uphold Democracy," and the Army Reserve played a key part in its execution.

The operation itself involved an unopposed landing in Port-au-Prince, Haiti, by soldiers from the U.S. 10th Mountain Division. Once it was clear that one of the major tasks of Uphold Democracy would be that of preparing the country for the transition to democracy under the leadership of the elected president, Bertrand Aristide, it was clear that Army Reserve participation would be required. President Clinton accordingly authorized a ninety-day call-up of members of the Selected Reserve. As this was translated by the Defense Department, the Secretary of the Army was authorized to call up 800 members of the Selected Reserve.[44]

The Army Reservists mobilized on September 19, 1994, were civil affairs and psychological operations (psyops) specialists and transporters from nine different units.[45] Their mission was to "support civil institutions in Haiti and serve as liaisons between military personnel and civil authorities—once civil authorities are recognized as legitimate."[46] These Reservists were followed shortly by other members of the Army Reserve, including additional psyops and civil affairs units.[47]

---

44. "President calls up Army Reservists," *Army Reserve Magazine*, Vol. 40, No. 3 (1994), p. 7. See also Executive Order 12927, September 15, 1994, "Ordering the Selected Reserve of the Armed Forces to Active Duty;" Memorandum, Deputy Secretary of Defense to Secretaries of the Military Departments and Chairman, Joint Chiefs of Staff, Subject: Additional Call-up of Selected Reserve Units and Personnel to Active Duty, October 14, 1994. Copy in possession of the author. Hereinafter cited as "Deputy Secretary of Defense Memorandum on Call-up of Selected Reserve."

45. Assistant Secretary of Defense for Public Affairs, Memorandum for Correspondents, No. 247–M, September 17, 1993. Copy in possession of the author. The USAR units called up were the 361st Civil Affairs Bde Support Element, Pensacola, Fla.; 458th Transportation Detachment, Belleville, Ill.; 305th Psychological Operations Bn Support Element, Arlington, Ill.; 15th Psychological Operations Bn Support Element, Fort Thomas, Ky.; 450th Civil Affairs Bn Support Element, Riverdale, Md.; 422d Civil Affairs Bn Support Element, Greensboro, N.C.; 2d Psychological Operations Support Group Element, Cleveland, Oh.; 358th Civil Affairs Bde, King of Prussia, Pa.; and 360th Civil Affairs Bde, Columbia, S.C.

46. Katherine McIntire Peters, "Reservists to focus on civil affairs," *Army Times*, October 3, 1994, p. 14.

47. *Ibid.* These Reservists were from the 416th Civil Affairs Bn, King of Prussia, Pa.; 478th Civil Affairs Bn, Coral Gables, Fla.; 350th Psychological Operations Co, Cleveland, Oh.; 245th Psychological Operations Co, Dallas, Tex.; 246th Psychological Operations Co, Blacklick, Oh.; and 362d Psychological Operations Co, Fayetteville, Ark.

Calling up the Army Reserve psyops units was almost a necessity, as 75 percent of the Army's assets (33 out of 44 units) were found in the USAR.[48] These psychological operations soldiers were given the mission of broadcasting messages to the Haitian people to insure that they understood U.S. intentions and policies.[49]

In addition to the civil affairs and psyops units, other Army Reservists supported Operation Uphold Democracy without going to Haiti itself, some without even being mobilized. The 458th Transportation Detachment from Belleville, Ill., a 34-soldier air terminal control team, was sent to Fort Bragg. It reached the North Carolina post 48 hours after it was mobilized and worked there coordinating the clearance of personnel and cargo at five locations from Fort Bragg to the Port of Jacksonville.[50]

The 1179th Deployment Support Brigade from Fort Hamilton, N.Y., sent a nine-member detachment to Fort Drum to assist the 10th Mountain Division with its deployment. Two other teams from the 1179th went to Fort Bragg to help the XVIIIth Airborne Corps with its deployment. The 1190th Deployment Support Brigade from Baton Rouge, La., sent a team to Fort Huachuca, Ariz., to assist with the movement of equipment from there to Haiti; and the 1185th Transportation Terminal Brigade from Lancaster, Pa., placed thirty-three of its members on active duty for training (ADT) to help the Military Traffic Management Command's 1303d Major Port Command with its cargo handling work.[51]

Some of these Reservists, and others called up in the following months, were activated under the authority granted by the Deputy Secretary of Defense to the service secretaries on October 14, 1994. This authority allowed the Secretary of the Army to call an additional 3,200 members of the Selected Reserve to active duty, bringing the total to 4,000. None of these soldiers, stated the Deputy Secretary, were to be retained on active duty for more than 180 days.[52]

---

48. *Annual Report, RFPB, FY 1994*, p. 13.

49. "President calls up Army Reservists," p. 7. For the story of how members of the 246th Psychological Operations Company, Columbus, Oh., helped a Haitian orphanage obtain much-needed food supplies despite a washed-out bridge, see Lt. Col. Bill Maddox, "A Helping Hand in Haiti," *Soldiers*, May 1995, pp. 41–42.

50. *Ibid.*

51. *Ibid.*

52. Deputy Secretary of Defense Memorandum on Call-up of Selected Reserve.

By the Spring of 1995, Army Reserve soldiers were still being deployed to Haiti, their numbers having increased from the initial deployment of 160. Joining their civil affairs colleagues in April 1995 were fifteen Army Reserve lawyers and judges, whose skills would be directed at the restoration of Haiti's legal system, a task which was described as "perhaps the most difficult task for Haiti to accomplish if it is ever to become a true democracy."[53]

It was clear that given the incredible poverty of the country, the lack of a large middle class, and the history of political and other violence, the odds against a successful Haitian democracy were long. Regardless of the outcome, however, it is certain that the contributions of the Army Reserve to whatever success the effort enjoyed were substantial.[54]

SINAI PEACEKEEPING

Another overseas mission for the Army Reserve involved only a small number of Reservists, but it was important because it marked a first for the USAR. This "first" was participation in a United Nations peacekeeping force in the Sinai, called the Multinational Force and Observers. The plan was to send a mixed battalion on rotation as the U.S. contingent, the battalion to consist of 80 percent reserve component personnel. Some 400 of these soldiers would come from the 29th Infantry Division, a National Guard unit from Virginia and Maryland, but 41 of the peacekeepers were Army Reservists from the Individual Ready Reserve.[55] These reserve component volunteers went to the Sinai, did their duty, and returned home without incident. The active component commander in the

53. Katherine McIntire Peters, "Haiti's professional help," *Army Times*, April 24, 1995, p. 14.

54. Army Reserve civil affairs personnel figured prominently in most of these overseas deployments. Additional information on the civil affairs community during these years can be found in SSgt. Keith Butler, "Uncivil Affairs," *Army Reserve Magazine*, Vol. 39, No. 2 (1993), pp. 24–25; Katherine McIntire, "All dressed up, hard to find anywhere to go," *Army Times*, June 14, 1993, p. 30; Katherine McIntire, "Unit status upgraded," *Army Times*, January 17, 1994, p. 23; Peters, "Reservists to focus on civil affairs," p. 14.

55. Katherine McIntire Peters, "Volunteers sought for Sinai duty," *Army Times*, March 28, 1994, p. 23; *Ibid.*, "Reserves to stay busy," *Army Times*, January 2, 1995, p. 34.

Sinai reported that they were the equivalent of any soldiers who had served there.[56]

One question that remained unanswered was whether these Reservists and others who were called up for extended periods of active service would suffer in their civilian jobs as a result.

JOB PROTECTION

A 1991 Supreme Court case (*King* v. *St. Vincent's Hospital*)[57] seemed to indicate that there was no limitation on the frequency and duration of active duty that a reservist might perform and still retain rights to his job.[58] The reality, however, was that in the 1990s employers became more skeptical of the time off that reservists were requesting for their military duties.

Even reservists returning from the much-acclaimed war in the Gulf in 1991 often found that they had been left behind on the promotion ladder by their contemporaries who had not served. Despite the law being on their side, many reservists discovered that enforcing their rights was more difficult than it should have been. According to statistics maintained by the U.S. Department of Labor, over 2,200 returning reservists went to the United States government for assistance in claiming the job that was rightfully theirs.[59]

Late in 1994 Congress enacted a new version of the Veterans Re-employment Rights Act, updating the 1940s era statute. This law provided members of the Reserve Components with several benefits. First, the Department of Justice was required to either furnish lawyers or pay fees to private attorneys when a reservist was faced with the necessity of pursuing legal action as a result of their military service. In addition, the new law increased from four years to five the length of time that a reservist could be away from his civilian

56. Conversation reported to the author by Robert M. Walker, Assistant Secretary of the Army for Installations, Logistics, and Environment, December 5, 1995. See also William Matthews, "'Redesign' likely for threatened units," *Army Times*, December 11, 1995, p. 20.

57. 502 U.S. 215

58. Col. Nick Dawson, "Supreme Court decision supports reserve training," *Army Reserve Magazine*, Vol. 38, No. 1 (1992), pp. 8–9.

59. William Matthews, "Employer ire stymies citizen-soldiers," *Army Times*, April 18, 1994, p. 20. See also, William Matthews, "Reservist duty stints riling employers," *Army Times*, December 13, 1993, p. 22.

job for military service. It also forbade employers from refusing to hire reservists because they might be going off on military duty.[60]

Of course, there was only so much legal protection that could be extended to members of the Reserve components. Any employer who desired to do so could probably make up a reason to terminate or fail to hire a member of the reserves without the reservist being able to prove that his or her military status was the reason. It remained to be seen whether the increasing frequency of reserve call-ups and deployments would lead to more complaints from reservists or more disgruntlement from employers.

MOBILIZATION EXERCISES

These three years also found the Army Reserve engaged in mobilization exercises in addition to the real-life call-ups described above.

Two of these were Exercise Optimal Focus '93 and its counterpart in 1994. Optimal Focus '93 took place on January 8 of that year when 8000 Army Reserve and Army National Guard soldiers were ordered to report to their reserve centers and armories. The idea behind the exercise was to determine to what extent the Army's reserve components would be able to assemble their units on short notice. During the exercise the reserve units took all the actions they would take if it were a genuine mobilization, "short of driving out the front gate," said FORSCOM liaison officer Lt. Col. Dennis Drake.[61]

Optimal Focus '94 involved fewer soldiers—just 3,000 this time—but it was designed to test once again the deployment readiness of the reserves. What these exercises demonstrated was that the Reserves could locate and bring together their unit members on short notice and be prepared to move out if given the order to do so.[62]

60. William Matthews, "Reservists win expanded job protection under new law," *Army Times*, October 31, 1994, p. 25; Public Law 103–353, October 13, 1994, Uniformed Services Employment and Reemployment Rights Act of 1994, 103d Congress, 2d session; "What are my reemployment rights?" *Army Reserve Magazine*, Vol. 41, No. 1 (1995), pp. 17–19, is a useful summary of the law.

61. Katherine McIntire, "Reservists answer call in crisis mobilization drill," *Army Times*, February 1, 1993, p. 18.

62. Sgt. 1st Class Marty Martin, "Focus on Mobilization," *Army Reserve Magazine*, Vol. 40, No. 2 (1994), pp. 14–15.

INDIVIDUAL READY RESERVE

The Individual Ready Reserve (IRR) has no mandated maximum end strength, its size being highly dependent upon the number of soldiers leaving the active component. As such, it grew dramatically after FY 1990. At that time (September 30, 1990) the IRR stood at 477,262 soldiers. It increased steadily to 595,501 a year later, to 743,004 at the end of FY 1992, and to a peak of 784,210 at the end of FY 1993. It declined slightly to 783,514 during the next year, but the overall increase from FY 1990–FY 1994 was an impressive 64.2 percent.[63]

Most of these individuals were lower ranking enlisted personnel whose career path included very little participation in Army training during their time in the IRR. They were in the IRR because that is where soldiers were sent to fulfill the portion of their eight-year service obligation that remained after completing active duty. There were sporadic training opportunities for a few members of the IRR,[64] but for the most part these soldiers had only the skills they had brought with them when they left active duty.

Screening of the IRR continued during this period, but it seemed to lose some of the urgency it had enjoyed earlier. These screenings were now accomplished either through the mail or by having the Reservist report to a Reserve center. In FY 1994, for example, the Army Reserve screened 12,560 soldiers out of a total IRR strength of 412,235, for a 3 percent rate. This was a much smaller percentage of screening that was the case with the other federal reserve components, some of which (USNR and USCGR) conducted their screenings by means of a mail survey. Nevertheless, the screenings were considered a valuable means of checking addresses and testing mobilization procedures.[65]

At the end of 1994 the IRR was a robust part of the Army Reserve, larger than it had been since 1973 and much healthier than it had been in the late 1970s when it bottomed out at less than 200,000. Questions yet remained about just how prepared its members were to go to war, but the example of Desert Shield/Desert Storm had demonstrated that at least the younger and newer IRR soldiers would come if called and could perform their assigned tasks with minimal refresher training.

---

63. *Annual Report, RFPB, FY 94* p. 38.

64. SSgt. Dorothy Young, "The IRR Attacks!" *Army Reserve Magazine*, Vol. 38, No. 4 (1992/93), p. 27; Capt. Thomas Cummings, "Putting the IRR into ROTC," *Army Reserve Magazine*, Vol. 39, No. 4 (1993/94), pp. 14–15.

65. *Annual Report, RFPB, FY 1994*, p. 55.

INDIVIDUAL MOBILIZATION AUGMENTEES (IMAS)

The IMA program continued as a robust part of the Army Reserve during these years. The following table shows the number of Army IMAs during the period 1992–94.

Table 23-1 Army Individual Mobilization Augmentees

	Officer		Enlisted	
	Budgeted/ Auth	Assigned	Budgeted/ Auth	Assigned
1992	10,597	10,597	3,203	3,203
1993	13,000	10,155	4,645	2,913
1994	9,738	10,039	3,262	2,970

Source: *Annual Report, Reserve Forces Policy Board, FY 92* (p. 54), *FY 93* (p. 77), *FY 94* (p. 42).

In FY 1994, there were 967 Army Reserve IMAs who drilled for pay: 60 were eligible to do 48 drills, the same as unit members; 17 could do 36 drills; and 890 could drill 24 times during the year. The vast majority of the IMAs, however—some 12,042—were in a non-drilling category.[66] According to the Reserve Forces Policy Board, the IMA program continued to be "a cost-effective way of retaining personnel with skills to meet wartime and contingency requirements."[67]

BENEFITS

Recognizing both the increasing role the Reserve Components were playing in national defense and the eroded power of the $50,000 Servicemen's Group Life Insurance (SGLI), Congress increased the amount of the insurance to $100,000 in April 1991.[68] It was increased to $200,000 coverage very shortly thereafter, in October 1992.[69]

Problems having to do with earned leave were also addressed by Congress. Reservists deployed on contingency operations earned leave during their active duty tour, just as did members of the active component. The problem from the

66. *Annual Report, RFPB, FY 94*, p. 43.

67. *Ibid.*, p. 40.

68. Section 336, Public Law 102–25, April 6, 1991, Persian Gulf Conflict Supplemental Authorization and Personnel Benefits Act of 1991, 102d Congress, 1st session.

69. Section 210, Public Law 102–568, October 29, 1992, Veterans' Benefits Act of 1992.

viewpoint of the reservist, however, was that his/her active duty might end before they were given the opportunity to take this leave. If they had previously served on active duty and been paid for sixty days of leave when they left, they were out of luck: the leave was theirs and they had earned it, but they could not be paid for it and they could not take it. There was no "terminal leave" for reservists, such as members of the active component took as they neared retirement.

The National Defense Authorization Act for 1992 and 1993, however, corrected this inequity. It provided that Reservists, retired Reserve, and retired active component soldiers called to active duty in support of a contingency operation could be paid for their leave when they left active duty, regardless of whether they had previously been paid for sixty days of leave.[70]

MONTGOMERY GI BILL

The Montgomery GI Bill continued to have an attraction for members of the Army Reserve. During FY 1992 the Army Reserve enrolled 71.2 percent (68,533) of the 96,316 eligible for the program. The following year the comparable figures were 80 percent (78,156) of the 97,400 eligibles. The Army Reserve's enrollment rate was significantly higher than that of the other reserve components, with the exception of the much smaller Marine Corps Reserve, which consistently enrolled the highest percentage.[71] What this suggests is that enlisted soldiers in the Army Reserve were highly motivated to improve themselves educationally.

The benefit to the Army Reserve from this high rate of enrollment was that each soldier participating in the program was required to serve at least six years in the Selected Reserve. "An analysis of available data," stated the Reserve Forces Policy Board, "indicates that the Montgomery GI Bill-Selected Reserve plays a particularly important role with respect to retention, especially for the first six years of a Reservist's military affiliation."[72] Though there were undoubtedly other factors that affected reenlistment in the USAR, the Army Reserve's

70. "Reservists Accrue Excess Leave if on Active Duty to Support a Contingency," *CARNOTES*, Vol. VIII, No. III (May–June 1992), p. 1; Section 637, Public Law 102–190, December 5, 1991, National Defense Authorization Act for Fiscal Years 1992 and 1993, 102d Congress, 1st session.

71. *Annual Report, RFPB, FY 92*, p. 59; *Annual Report, RFPB, FY 93*, p. 79; *Annual Report, RFPB, FY 94*, p. 51.

72. *Annual Report, RFPB, FY 94*, p. 51.

overall retention rate from 1985 to 1993 increased from 39 percent to 91 percent.[73]

Monthly payments for reservists using the Bill increased periodically, but the most notable change was an increase in its coverage. In the Defense Authorization Act for FY 1994, Congress finally approved post-graduate education for those using the Montgomery GI Bill.[74] The effect of this change on retention was uncertain.

SEPARATION BENEFITS

The deactivation of Army Reserve units and the overall reduction in size of the USAR led invariably to Army Reservists being forced out of the troop unit program. These soldiers were in many instances career Reservists who had not yet completed 20 years toward retirement. They were suddenly faced with the prospect of transferring to the IRR and scrambling for enough points to have a "good year" and progress toward retirement or of throwing away all the years they had served in the active component or the reserves.

Congress, however, realized the inequity in this situation and passed legislation that would allow benefits to those who were separated involuntarily from the Selected Reserve (troop program unit and IMAs). The benefits were available to Reservists who were separated between October 1, 1991, and September 30, 1999, and who had served at least one year in the Selected Reserve as of the date of their separation.[75] If these Reservists were offered a position in another unit within what was called "reasonable commuting distance" (defined as 50 miles or 90 minutes of travel time), they would not qualify for the benefits if they rejected the position.[76] The exact nature of the benefits depended upon how many years he or she had toward retirement.

---

73. *Annual Report, RFPB, FY 93*, p. 79.

74. William Matthews, "'Sonny': A sunny year for benefits," *Army Times*, October 25, 1993, p. 21; Section 518, Public Law 103–160, November 30, 1993, National Defense Authorization Act for Fiscal Year 1994, 103d Congress, 1st session. See also "GI Bill benefits OK'd for graduate studies," *Army Reserve Magazine*, Vol. 40, No. 2 (1994), pp. 6–7.

75. Section 4411, Public Law 102–484, October 23, 1992, National Defense Authorization Act for Fiscal Year 1993, 102d Congress, 2d session; Subtitle F, Sections 561–562, Public Law 103–160, National Defense Authorization Act for Fiscal Year 1994, November 30, 1993, 103d Congress, 1st session; Katherine McIntire Peters, "Bonuses, benefits for Guard, Reserve drawdown victims," *Army Times*, February 27, 1995, p. 22.

76. Maj. Tom Vance, "Transition Benefits: Whatcha gonna get when they come for you . . .," *Army Reserve Magazine*, Vol. 39, No. 3 (1993), pp. 16–17.

For Reservists with less than six years of service, the benefits included the Montgomery GI Bill, and PX and commissary privileges for two years. Reservists with six to fifteen years toward retirement received the above benefits, plus separation pay.[77] Reservists with more than fifteen, but less than twenty years of service who transferred to the Retired Reserve were also eligible for retirement pay at age sixty in addition to all the benefits listed above. Reservists with twenty or more years toward retirement received Special Separation Pay[78] and would be eligible to receive their earned reserve retirement pay when they reached age sixty.[79]

RESERVE OFFICERS PERSONNEL MANAGEMENT ACT (ROPMA)

Legislation that would change the way in which reserve officers were promoted and careers managed was first introduced into the Congress in the mid-1980s. The House of Representatives finally passed the legislation at the end of the 102d Congress in 1992, but the Senate did not act on the measure that year.[80] It was reintroduced in the following Congress, with Rep. Ike Skelton (D–Mo.) as its prime sponsor.[81]

Though it worked its way through the House of Representatives as separate legislation, the House forced the hand of the Senate—which had failed to pass similar legislation in the past—by incorporating it into the Defense Authorization Bill. When the conferees met on the defense bill for FY 1995, the House insisted on having its way on this measure and the Senate receded on the ROPMA provision of the bill, insisting, however, that the bill not go into effect until October 1, 1996.[82] As a result, ROPMA was enacted into law on October 5, 1994, as Title XVI of the National Defense Authorization Act

77. The formula for figuring such was as follows: 15% X years of service (total retirement points divided by 360) X daily base pay amount X 62.

78. Determined as follows: annual base pay X 5% + 0.5% for each year of service over 20, not to exceed 10% total. Reservists separated because of unit inactivation, relocation, or reorganization received five such payments, or payments until they reached age sixty and began receiving retirement pay. Reservists in drilling units separated for other reasons and IMAs received one payment.

79. Vance, "Transition Benefits," pp. 16–17; William Matthews, "Pays, benefits to ease separation shock," *Army Times*, December 12, 1994, p. 24.

80. *Annual Report, RFPB, FY 1992*, p. 61.

81. Rick Maze, "Officer personnel bill resurrected in House," *Army Times*, April 5, 1993, p. 14.

82. 103d Congress, 2d session, House Conference Report No. 103–701, August 12, 1994, to accompany S. 2182, p. 776.

for Fiscal Year 1995.[83] It was scheduled to go into effect on October 1, 1996.[84]

ROPMA was designed to parallel—though not to duplicate—the Defense Officer Personnel Management Act (DOPMA), which was passed in 1980 and applied to active component officers. As such, it changed substantially the way in which the careers of reserve officers were managed.

Promotions were one significant change under ROPMA. For one thing, promotion selections for officers being considered for the rank of captain or above were now to be made on the basis of the "best qualified" officers, rather than those who were "fully qualified," as in the past.[85] As in the law that ROPMA replaced, officers twice considered unfavorably for promotions below the rank of colonel would be removed from active status.[86]

Additionally, for the first time, the Secretary of the Army (in the case of Army Reserve officers) could establish "below the zone" promotion considerations if he wished to do, recognizing that some particularly outstanding officers ought to be allowed to move ahead of their peers in the promotion lists. The Secretary could also establish competitive categories such as might be used for chaplains and medical corps officers.[87]

Other features of ROPMA included the establishment of a "Reserve active-status list," (RASL) which would list troop program officers, members of the IRR, IMAs, and AGRs in the order of their rank. Officers must be on the RASL to be considered for promotion.[88]

In a change from the existing law, ROPMA allowed an officer who was selected for promotion to decline the promotion for up to three years, compared with one year under the then-existing law.[89] Declining a promotion may sound strange to an outsider, but for the Army Reserve officer this is a common nightmare. Unlike the active component officer who only has to wait for his number to come up on the promotion list, the Reserve officer must also locate a position of the grade to which he or she has been selected. Failing this,

83. Title XVI ("Reserve Officer Personnel Management Act"), Public Law 103–337, October 5, 1994, National Defense Authorization Act for Fiscal Year 1995.

84. Public Law 103–337, Section XVI, Subtitle F (Section 1691).

85. Section 14108(a), Title XVI, PL 103–337.

86. Section 14501(a)(2) and Sections 14504(a), 14505, and 14506 of Title XVI, PL 103–337.

87. Section 14301(d) and Section 14302, Title XVI, PL 103–337.

88. Sections 14003 and 14004, Title XVI, PL 103–337.

89. Section 14312, Title XVI, PL 103–337.

the officer can transfer to the IRR and secure the promotion, but in doing so he loses the benefits of troop unit service, including payment for weekend drills.

ROPMA was the first new and comprehensive reserve officer management statute since passage of the Reserve Officer Personnel Act of 1954 (ROPA), which is discussed in Chapter Six of this volume.[90]

BEYOND ROPMA

There were also other changes for Army Reserve officers seeking promotions to higher grades. Beginning October 1, 1994, for example, captains were required to have completed the Combined Arms and Services Staff School (CAS^3) before they could be promoted to major.[91]

For more junior officers there was a statutorily-imposed provision that might cause problems for some members of the USAR. Congress included a provision in the Defense Authorization Act for Fiscal Year 1994 specifying that after September 30, 1995, all reserve component officers must possess a baccalaureate degree before they could be promoted to the rank of captain (O–3) or above.[92] At the end of FY 1993, 89 percent of USAR officers possessed a college degree, but given the number of officers in the Army Reserve at that time (51,718), there were almost 5,700 Army Reserve officers who did not have a bachelor's degree.[93]

FULL-TIME SUPPORT (FTS)

Full-time support continued to be a shortfall for the Army Reserve during the years 1992–94. For FY 1992 the Army Re-

90. For additional information on ROPMA, see William Matthews, "Promoting the 'best,'" *Army Times*, June 6, 1994, p. 18; Katherine McIntire Peters, "'Best' officers will win under Reserve promotion law," *Army Times*, August 29, 1994, p. 22; "ROPMA overhauls officer management system: Appointments, promotions, tenure and separation of Army Reserve officers will be affected," *Army Reserve Magazine*, Vol. 40, No. 3 (1994), pp. 5–6; *Annual Report, RFPB, FY 1994*, pp. 46–47.

91. Katherine McIntire Peters, "CAS3 needed for gold leaf," *Army Times*, January 2, 1995, p. 35.

92. Section 523, Public Law 102–190, National Defense Authorization Act for Fiscal Years 1992 and 1993, December 5, 1991. This law was modified slightly to change the requirement from graduation from "an accredited educational institution" to graduation from "a qualifying educational institution" in Section 519, Public Law 103–337, October 5, 1994, National Defense Authorization Act for Fiscal Year 1995.

93. *Annual Report, RFPB, FY 93*, pp. 81, 62.

serve had a 71 percent fill rate for its authorized full-time positions. This compared favorably with the Army National Guard's fill rate of 70 percent, but it did not tell the entire story.[94] The Army Reserve lagged far behind the ARNG in the ratio of Selected Reserve members to FTS. The ratio for the USAR was 13.9:1; for the ARNG it was 7.9:1.[95]

For FY 1993 the picture was even worse. The percentage of fill of authorized FTS positions had dropped to 63 percent for the Army Reserve, while its ratio of Selected Reserve strength to FTS had risen slightly 13.6:1. The actual number of full-time support personnel assigned to the Army Reserve, however, dropped from 23,128 to 20,595.[96]

During Fiscal Year 1994 the Army Reserve was forced to fight more than the benign neglect of Headquarters, Department of the Army. In its effort to "reinvent government," the Clinton administration proposed to cut the Army's reserve components civilian technician strength by 4,000 and the full time support for the other reserve components by 6,000.[97]

In addition, Defense Secretary William J. Perry ordered an across-the-board reduction in DoD civilian personnel strength of 4 percent by the year 2001. In a speech to the Adjutants General Association on January 30, 1995, the defense secretary admitted that he had ordered the cuts, but stated that the technician reductions were "not what I had in mind." Perry said that he had told Assistant Secretary for Reserve Affairs Deborah Lee to develop a plan to shield technicians from the cuts he had mandated.[98]

Regardless of how these threatened reductions might play out in the years ahead, FY 1994 found the Army Reserve barely holding its own in the full-time support arena. The ratio of Selected Reserve to full-timers improved slightly to 12.8:1 simply because of the reduction in number of Reservists. The actual number of FTS personnel declined by 213, to 20,382.[99] It did not appear that the full-time support picture for the Army Reserve was improving, even as the requirements levied upon its units were increasing exponentially.

94. *Annual Report, RFPB, FY 92*, p. 51.

95. Computed from figures on pp. 35 and 51, *Annual Report, RFPB, FY 92*.

96. *Annual Report, RFPB, FY 93*, pp. 57 and 70.

97. William Matthews, "Plan to cut technicians seen threat to readiness," *Army Times*, September 19, 1994, p. 23.

98. William Matthews, "Perry pledges effort to save technicians' jobs," *Army Times*, February 13, 1995, p. 22.

99. *Annual Report, RFPB, FY 94*, pp. 37 and 41.

equipment included automatic switchboards and tactical radio equipment. According to the Reserve Forces Policy Board report, "Overall readiness is degraded because obsolete and incompatible Reserve equipment does not integrate with modern Active Army systems."[109]

NATIONAL GUARD AND RESERVE EQUIPMENT APPROPRIATIONS (NGREA)

Congress responded, as it had done for many years, by including separate equipment appropriations for the National Guard and Reserve above the amount proposed in the President's budget. The following chart shows the amount of such appropriations for the Army Reserve and Army National Guard during the period FY 1992–95.

Table 23-3 Army Reserve Component Equipment Funding
National Guard & Reserve Equipment Appropriations (NGREA)
(Millions of Dollars)

	Army Reserve	Army National Guard
1992	104	344
1993	32	399
1994	194	126
1995	69	89
Total	399	958

Source: *Annual Report, Reserve Forces Policy Board, FY 94* (p. 87)

Despite these appropriations and the continuing transfer of equipment from both reserve and active component units that were deactivating, the Army Reserve was still short of meeting its wartime equipment requirements.

Table 23-4 Major Items of Equipment Status (USAR), 1992–95
(Millions of Dollars)

	Wartime Requirement	Auth	On-Hand	O–H/WT Req.
1992	10,879	9,320	7,126	76%
1993	7,892	7,232	6,025	83%
1994	6,523	—	5,722	88%

Sources: *Annual Reports, Reserve Forces Policy Board, FY 1993* (p. 127), *FY 94* (p. 93)

109. *Ibid.*, p. 116.

Though the USAR appeared to be getting well in terms of equipment shortages and wartime requirements, what was happening was actually a changing of the reporting methodology, rather than a dramatic equipment get-well. Beginning with FY 1994, the reporting was of "combat essential" equipment, which was a sub-set of the "major items" of equipment previously reported.[110]

Even at the end of FY 1994, the Army Reserve reported continuing shortages of C–12 aircraft, communications systems (radio and telephone equipment), tactical wheeled vehicles (HMMWVs), and 10-ton, 5-ton, and 2½-ton trucks. Added to the list in 1994 were night vision goggles and NBC equipment.[111] In short, most of the equipment items that the Army Reserve lacked in 1991 were still missing in 1994.

A report from the General Accounting Office in 1993 compared the status of required items of equipment for the active component, Army National Guard, and Army Reserve. As of April 30, 1992, the active component had 89 percent of its required equipment, the Army National Guard was at 79 percent, and the Army Reserve brought up the rear with only 59 percent.[112]

Despite the increases in equipment status in the Army Reserve since that time, some of the 1992 GAO findings still had great relevance for the Army Reserve. For example, the congressional investigators noted that the Army's "First to fight-First to be equipped" philosophy shortchanged the combat support and combat service support units, many of which are in the Army Reserve.[113]

What this meant for the Army Reserve, found the investigators, was that active component units at Force Activity Designator (FAD) level III (which was where 38 percent of the Army Reserve's units were listed in June 1992) were generally better equipped than were Army Reserve units with the same FAD.[114]

On the plus side for the USAR, the GAO found that "A limited number of combat and combat support units in the reserves have been given a high priority for equipment because they have been designated part of the Army's contingency

110. *Annual Report, RFPB, FY 94*, p. 93.
111. *Ibid.*, p. 94.
112. GAO, *Army's Equipping Strategy*, p. 17.
113. *Ibid.*, p. 30.
114. *Ibid.*, p. 31.

force." On the downside, however, the investigators continued by stating that ". . . Some combat forces outside this early deploying force have been given higher equipping priorities in the DAMPL [Department of the Army Master Priority List] than some support forces in the contingency force."[115]

Even the downsizing of the active component did not help the Army Reserve eliminate its equipment shortages.[116] According to Brig. Gen. Thomas Kilmartin, Deputy Chief of the Army Reserve, "Traditionally, the equipment we're short is the same equipment the active component is short." Deactivating active component units therefore did little to alleviate the USAR equipment shortage.

A June 1994 report of the Defense Science Board Task Force on Readiness confirmed Kilmartin's statement. "Of particular concern," said the task force, "is the Army Reserve, which because of the nature of its role, has many high-priority support units that suffer readiness decrements because they lack low-visibility equipment (water purification, medical, laundry, decontamination, etc.) on which to train and operate." The task force noted that excess equipment from Europe has been combat equipment, while the Army Reserve has need of non-combat items.[117]

None of these negative comments about the equipment status of the Army Reserve mean that there were no improvements in equipment readiness during these years. Even considering the statistical comparison difficulties brought about by the change in reporting methodology, as previously mentioned, it was evident that the percentage of fill of essential equipment items increased. Moreover, the Army Reserve received some big-ticket items like new utility landing craft and ocean-going tugboats that vastly increased its capability in certain areas.[118] Moreover, if redistribution of equipment within the USAR were to take place as downsizing occurred, the overall equipment posture of the USAR would certainly improve.

---

115. *Ibid.*, p. 34. For a summary of the GAO report, see Katherine McIntire, "Equipment shortages may harm reserve effectiveness," *Army Times*, April 5, 1993, p. 14.

116. "Reserve picks up pieces of active component's loss," *Army Times*, February 21, 1994, p. 22.

117. Katherine McIntire Peters, "Less training, less gear—less ready?" *Army Times*, August 8, 1994, p. 24.

118. CWO James Bundgaard, "State-of-Art Ships Join Army Reserve," *Army Reserve Magazine*, Vol. 39, No. 2 (1993), p. 25; Michael P.W. Stone and General Gordon R. Sullivan, *Strategic Force, Strategic Vision for the 1990s and Beyond. A Statement on the Posture of the United States Army, Fiscal Year 1993* (Washington: GPO, 1993), p. 48.

RESERVE COMPONENT AUTOMATION SYSTEM (RCAS)

In 1979 the Army began its attempts to field an automated information system for the Army Reserve and Army National Guard. The first of these systems was called the Continental Army Management Information System, which was suspended in 1985. It was replaced by the Reserve Component Automation program, which lasted until 1987. At that time the Department of Defense began planning for what became known as the Reserve Component Automation System (RCAS). Funding for this latter system, in contrast to the previous two attempts, came from reserve component appropriations which Congress set aside specifically for RCAS. The program was managed by the Chief of the National Guard Bureau and was expected to cost up to $2 billion by the time it was fully installed in 1999.[119]

RCAS consists of hardware, software, and technical assistance and was designed to be installed in 4700 Army Reserve Centers and National Guard Armories.[120] The contract for RCAS was awarded in October 1991, ending four years of development effort. The awardee was Boeing Computer Services, with Computer Sciences Corporation (CSC) the runner-up and loser. CSC immediately protested the award, but the General Accounting Office upheld the original contract decision.[121]

CONCLUSION

It is fitting to end this chapter and this revised edition of the history of the Army Reserve by discussing a major effort toward automation and information management. It is evident that the "information revolution" as it is often called will influence the Army Reserve as it does the other parts of the national defense structure. The citizen soldiers of the Army Reserve have come a long way from their origins in colonial America, to their first real appearance as federal reservists following the Spanish-

119. General Accounting Office, *Army Acquisition: Contract for the Reserve Component Automation System*, GAO/NSIAD–93–5 (November 1992), pp. 1–2. Hereinafter cited as "GAO, *RCAS*;" *Prepared Statement of the Assistant Secretary of Defense for Reserve Affairs, Honorable Stephen M. Duncan, Hearing before the Subcommittee on Manpower, Personnel, and Compensation, House Armed Services Committee, May 1, 1992*, p. 17. Copy in possession of the author. Hereinafter cited as "*Duncan, RCAS*."

120. Lt. Col. Arthur M. House, "RCAS! Is it here at last?" *Army Reserve Magazine*, Vol. 39, No. 2 (1993), p. 13.

121. GAO, *RCAS*, pp. 2–3.

American War, to their performance in Desert Storm and subsequent real-world mission deployments.

The Army Reserve is no longer a mirror image of either the active component of the Army or of the Army National Guard. By the mid-1990s it had been stripped almost entirely of any vestige of combat forces and had become almost 100 percent combat support and combat service support soldiers.

Ironically, this change meant that the Army Reserve was probably going to be called upon more frequently than ever it had been, and as it became smaller, it would have to become smarter and more technologically advanced.

It seemed clear to many observers, including this author, that the strategic vision for the Army Reserve had to include a leaner, better educated, more technologically prepared and better trained force than it had been in the past. The preparation, training, and real-world missions of the years 1992–1994 were a large step toward that goal.

Conclusion

The last thirteen years (1983–1995) have been critical ones in the history of the Army Reserve. From minimal participation in Urgent Fury (Grenada) and Just Cause (Panama), the USAR has assumed an increasingly important role in the defense forces of the nation. It is not going too far to suggest that so totally has the Army come to depend upon the Army Reserve, that Desert Shield and Desert Storm would not have been possible without it. This realization is discomfiting to some in the active component, to some in the civilian leadership of our government, and even to some Army Reservists.

On one level Desert Shield proved that a good way to get the American people behind a military endeavor is to call up the reserves. On another level, mobilizing the reserves is more than just a military action. As strategists have realized since at least World War I, mobilization is itself a powerful political statement and signal for the other side, one not to be taken lightly.

So we have ourselves on the horns of a dilemma. Calling upon the reserves may well mobilize national will; but calling upon the reserves may send more of a signal than we want to send. The Army has put itself into a position, however, where it almost has to call on the reserves if it is to use more than its immediate reaction forces or if it plans to be engaged for longer than a few months.

Military analysts still debate the full extent of the victory in the desert, as the allied coalition allowed Saddam Hussein to remain in power. But at least one unchallenged winner emerged from the desert war, and that was the United States Army Reserve.

As recounted earlier, Army Reserve volunteers were there from the beginning of Desert Shield to get the equipment and the troops on their way to the Gulf. Troop program members of the Army Reserve were among the first reservists called to duty, and they performed magnificently under conditions that would have stretched the capabilities of the finest active component soldiers in the force. Individual reservists—officers and enlisted alike—volunteered and were sent involuntarily, but they went and did their duty. As the HHC Commander at ARPERCEN remembered, the most common question posed in the early days of the mobilization was "How do I get to go?"[1]

As in Vietnam, Army Reservists in the Gulf were the source of very few disciplinary problems, and there were few Reservists who did not report when ordered, even if they understood that this indeterminate period of active duty could be financially devastating to them.

Were there problems? Certainly. Did the Total Force concept work? Yes, it did. Did it work precisely as planned and anticipated? No, it did not. "Total Force" was embraced and uttered so many times by the nation's senior civilian and military leadership that it took on the characteristic of a mantra. But as the nation draws down its military forces and active and reserve components compete for scarce funding, the careful observer can see in the Desert Shield/Desert Storm experience some signs that the fabric of Total Force is stretched thin at some of its seams.

With the exception of general officer commands, disputes on call-up at the DoD-congressional level are of little consequence to the Army Reserve. Most of the argument has centered about the capability of reserve combat units to function immediately at the same level as active component units of the same type. The Army Reserve had few such combat units in 1990, and it has been restructured to lose virtually all of them. What is critical to the USAR is the acceptance of combat support and combat service support units by the active component, and here the record is much better, though still mixed.

A report by the General Accounting Office issued in December 1992 suggested that

> Experiences from the Gulf war also showed that the Army had difficulty providing some types of support forces, especially during the operation's earlier phases. The Army was unable to do so because it was heavily reliant on the reserves for some types of support forces, and it took a few

1. Interview, Lt. Col. James T. Currie with Maj. John G. Kramb, ARPERCEN, June 22, 1992. Notes in possession of the author.

weeks to implement the President's reserve call-up. . . . Reacting to this experience, the Army has decided to substitute active support forces for some reserves in the earliest deploying elements of its contingency force. While reserves would provide 40 percent of the support forces intended for the entire 5-division contingency force, only 7 percent of the support forces that would deploy within the first 30 days are reserve forces. Plans call for the remaining reserve forces to deploy between 30 and 75 days."[2]

Total Force? The political answer from the Department of Defense is that the policy worked as it was supposed to work during Desert Shield/Desert Storm. Indeed, the mobilization of the reserve components was still underway in December 1990—and the IRR had yet to be tapped—when the Secretary of Defense's special study group pronounced the Total Force Policy "a great success."[3]

Many members of Army Reserve units that were not mobilized for Desert Shield/Desert Storm, however, have a different view of the extent to which the policy worked. The 377th TAACOM has already been discussed at length, and this is probably the most blatant example in the Army Reserve of the CAPSTONE trace being ignored as the reserve components were mobilized. And there were others besides the Louisiana TAACOM that have been mentioned previously.

Despite the role that the Army Reserve played in the desert war, many Army Reservists had a sense of betrayal in the way it played out for them. They had trained for years, and when the big show came, they were not invited. It may sound perfectly insane to an outsider that anyone would want to go to war, but at some point in almost every soldier's career, he or she would like to see whether they have what it takes in this ultimate of tests. Some of these individuals were given the opportunity to go onto active duty after the war was over, but their attitude was often like that of a senior Reservist who expressed to the author his feelings about such an offer: "I did not want to be the one pushing the broom at the end of the elephant parade."

Total Force? Many reservists believe that the force structure may be in place, but that mistrust of the reserves by the active component looms as large as ever. Every Army Reservist today is a true volunteer, just like every member of the active

2. United States General Accounting Office, *Report to the Chairman, Subcommittee on Military Personnel and Compensation, Committee on Armed Services, House of Representatives, Army Force Structure: Future Reserve Roles Shaped by New Strategy, Base Force, and Gulf War*, Report No. GAO/NSIAD–93–80 (December 1992), p. 23

3. Office of the Secretary, Department of Defense, *Total Force Policy Study Group, Final Report*, p. 1.

component. There are none of those "draft-motivated volunteers" so common to Reserve units in the 1960s and early 1970s. Yes, these men and women get paid for going to drills, but anyone who has served in an Army Reserve unit in the last decade knows that a Reservist typically gives much more time to his or her unit than they get paid for. The days of "weekend warriors" and "good old boys" sitting around the Reserve center swapping lies about how great they used to be are long gone.

Today's Army Reservist finds every weekend drill a whirlwind of mandatory training and preparation for mission accomplishment. They are every bit as professional and as dedicated as the members of the active component—perhaps more so in some ways because they are freely giving their weekends and week nights to train and administer their units, and this is neither their career nor their full-time employment.

One of the official Army histories of the recent conflict in the desert explains as well as any document just why the Army Reserve was able to succeed in accomplishing missions they had no business succeeding at, such as constructing Enemy Prisoner of War camps with minimal outside assistance. "The greatest practical leverage to be gained from the Reserves," wrote the Desert Storm Special Study Group, "will come from Reservists who perform tasks in war similar to those they practice daily in peace. . . . Years of practical experience as a plumber and heavy equipment operator could not be replicated by an 18-year-old engineer soldier just out of high school and advanced individual training at Fort Leonard Wood."[4]

But regardless of force structure changes or active distrust of or lack of confidence in the reserves, there will always be other reasons to call up Army Reserve units early in a crisis. In a message to Generals John Galvin and Gordon Sullivan, General Crosbie Saint, Commander-in-Chief of U.S. Army Forces in Europe, offered an interesting observation on the reserve call-up for Desert Shield/Desert Storm. Mused Saint,

> The early decision to call up the reserves [meaning Army Reserve forces], while probably motivated by necessity, turned out to be a major catalyst in consolidating American public opinion firmly behind our strategy in the Gulf. The size of the call up meant that everyone had players from their state. The moral ascendancy that U.S. troops had when they knew their country was behind them cannot be discounted.[5]

---

4. Scales, *Certain Victory*, p. 379.

5. Message, General Saint, personal for General Galvin, General Sullivan, Subject: Thoughts on the Victory in Desert Storm; DTG: P260800Z Mar 91. Copy in DS/DS files, USACMH.

This message brings to mind the statements of Gen. Edwin Burba, the FORSCOM commander quoted earlier in this work. Burba told the author that the leadership of the Army used the reserves as a way to ensure that every American knew someone in the Gulf. Saint's comment also suggests one of the criteria then-Secretary of Defense Caspar Weinberger proposed in 1984 to determine whether to commit U.S. forces to combat. These six "Weinberger Tests" have not been elevated to the level of either dogma or doctrine, but they are studied at the war colleges and have undoubted effect on the thinking of many individuals at senior levels in the Army.

Paraphrased, Weinberger's criterion number five is that troops should not be committed to action without the support of the American people. Calling up the reserves, as General Saint observed and as General Burba said was behind some of the mobilization decisions, is one way to gain such support. As this author suggested in 1983 when he was writing about the Vietnam mobilization in Chapter Nine of this book, "Once a national consensus is reached . . . and the Congress and the President agree on U.S. objectives, the Army Reserve should be ready and able to do its part." As in Vietnam, but at an immensely higher level of activity, the Army Reserve was once again tested and found ready and able to do its part. Its soldiers proved in the desert, as they had done in the jungle, that they are indeed, "twice the citizen."

As mentioned in the conclusion to Chapter Twenty-three, this dedication will undoubtedly be tested severely in the years ahead. As this is being written (December 1995), Army Reserve units and individuals have been called to active duty for deployment to Bosnia. They were called because the Army really had few choices. What we are seeing today is the Total Force policy so completely consummated that the Army finds it impossible to send even a modest contingent—20,000 soldiers in the case of Bosnia—to a hotspot overseas without relying on the Army Reserve. This dependence on the Reserve is both challenging and daunting. The next few years should demonstrate whether this confidence is misplaced or overdone. The early years of the twenty-first century should help the nation determine whether being "Twice the citizen" is enough for the coming age.

Appendix A

Chiefs of the Army Reserve[1]

* MAJ. D. F. THOMPSON, Chief of Reserve Section, G–2, June 12–July 1, 1923.

* MAJ. WALTER O. BOSWELL, Chief of Reserve Section, G–2, July 2, 1923–july 31, 1924.

* COL. DOUGLAS POTTS, Chief of Reserve Branch, G–2, August 1, 1924–December 30, 1925.

* LT. COL. J. C. PEGRAM, Chief of Reserve Branch, G–2, December 31, 1925–August 14,1926.

* COL STANLEY H. FORD, Chief of Reserve Branch, G–2, October 1, 1926–February 10, 1927.

* COL. DAVID L. STONE, Executive for Reserve Affairs, March 5, 1927–June 30, 1930.

* BRIG. GEN. CHARLES D. HERRON, Executive for Reserve Affairs, Jul;y 1, 1930–June 30, 1935.

* BRIG. GEN. EDWIN S. HARTSHORN, Executive for Reserve Affairs, July 1, 1935–September 15, 1938.

* BRIG. GEN. CHARLES E. THOMPSON, Executive for Reserve Affairs, September 16, 1938–June 9, 1940.

1. Memo, War Department General Staff, G–2 to Col. Hartshorn, June 27,1 935, RG 319, Entry 343, Box 97; War Department Order, AG 008 O.R.C. (6–11–41), dated June 16, 1941, RG 319, Entry 343, Box 104; memorandum, (with additions in pen) The Adjutant General to Executive for Reserve Affairs, May 1, 1941, Subject: Data re Tenure of Office of Executives for REserve Affairs, RG 319, Entry 343, Box 104; James E. Hewes, Jr., From Root to McNamara: Army Organization and Administration, 1900–1963 (Washington: Center of Military History, United States Army, 1975), p. 400; Files of the Chief, Army Reserve, the pentagon.

*** Performed function in addition to other duties.**

* BRIG. GEN. JOHN H. HESTER, Executive for Reserve Affairs, June 21, 1940–March 23, 1941.

* BRIG. GEN. FRANK E. LOWE, Executive for Reserve and R.O.T.C. Affairs, June 5, 1941–August 10, 1942.

* BRIG. GEN. EDWARD W. SMITH, Executive for Reserve and R.O.T.C. Affairs, September 16, 1942–October 14, 1945.

* EDWARD S. BRES, Executive for Reserve and R.O.T.C. Affairs, October 15, 1945–November 30, 1947.

* BRIG. GEN. WENDELL WESTOVER, Executive for Reserve and R.O.T.C. Affairs, December 1, 1947–November 14, 1949.

* MAJ. GEN. JAMES B. CRESS, Executive for Reserve and R.O.T.C. Affairs, January 1, 1950–January 31, 1951.

* BRIG. GEN. HUGH M. MILTON, Executive for Reserve and R.O.T.C. Affairs, February 24, 1951–November 18, 1953.

* BRIG. GEN. HUGH M. MILTON, Executive for Reserve and R.O.T.C. Affairs, February 24, 1951–November 18, 1953.

* BRIG. GEN. PHILLIP F. LINDEMAN, Executive for Reserve and R.O.T.C. Affairs, November 1953–December 6, 1954, and Chief, Army Reserve and R.O.T.C. Affairs, December 7, 1954–July 31, 1957.

* MAJ. GEN. RALPH A. PALLADINO, Chief, Army Reserve and R.O.T.C. Affairs, August 1, 1957–May 31, 1959.

* MAJ. GEN. FREDERICK M. WARREN, Chief, Army Reserve and R.O.T.C. Affairs, September 1, 1959–February 12, 1963, and Chief, Army Reserve, February 1;3, 1963–August 31, 1963.

* MAJ. GEN. W. J. SUTTON, Chief, Army Reserve, September 1, 1963–May 31, 1971.

* MAJ. GEN. J. MILNOR ROBERTS, Chief, Army Reserve, June 1, 1975–May 31, 1979.

* MAJ. GEN.WILLIAM R. BERKMAN, Chief, Army Reserve, June 1, 1979–July 31, 1986.

* MAJ. GEN. HARRY J. MOTT, III, Acting Chief, Army Reserve, August 1, 1986–November 30, 1986.

* MAJ. GEN. WILLIAM F. WARD, JR., Chief, Army Reserve, December 1, 1986–July 31, 1991.

* MAJ. GEN. ROGER W. SANDLER, Chief, Army Reserve, August 31, 1991–January 31, 1994.

* MAJ. GEN. MAX BARATZ, CHIEF, Army Reserve, February 1, 1994–present.

NOTE: BRIG. GEN. JOHN MCAULEY PALMER is sometimes regarded as the "Father of the Army Reserve" Though his influence on the evolution of the Army Reserve cannot be over-emphasized, Palmer was never in an official position within the Army Reserve structure.

Appendix **B**

Army Reserve (Organized Reserve Corps) Appropriations

Army Reserve Appropriations (in millions of dollars)

Fiscal Year	Army Reserve Appropriation	Total Army (War Dept.) Appropriation	% Army Reserve
1917	$ 11.5	$ 2,864.4	0.4
1918	10.3	5,730.9	0.2
1919	7.0	1,406.3	0.5
1920	4.2	1,622.0	0.3
1921	3.4	1.118.1	0.3
1922	3.9	457.8	0.9
1923	4.9	397.1	1.2
1924	7.3	357.0	2.0
1925	9.4	371.0	2.5
1926	10.3	364.1	2.8
1927	10.4	369.1	2.8
1928	9.6	401.0	2.4
1929	11.1	425.9	2.6
1930	11.5	464.9	2.5
1931	13.4	486.1	2.8
1932	13.3	476.3	2.8
1933	13.0	434.6	3.0
1934	12.3	408.6	3.0
1935	8.4	488.0	1.7
1936	12.8	618.6	2.1
1937	15.4	628.1	2.5
1938	16.2	644.3	2.5
1939	18.3	695.3	2.6
1940	20.5	907.2	2.3
1941	136.5	3,939.0	4.1
1942	7.6	14,325.6	0.01
1943	5.5	42,525.6	0.01

Army Reserve Appropriations (in millions of dollars)—Continued

Fiscal Year	Army Reserve Appropriation	Total Army (War Dept.) Appropriation	% Army Reserve
1944	$ 2.1	$49,438.3	<0.01
1945	(*)	50,490.1	<0.01
1946	(*)	27,986.8	<0.01
1947	72.8	9,172.1	0.8
1948	92.9	7,698.6	1.2
1949	143.2	7,862.4	1.9
1950	140.0	5,789.5	2.4
1951	154.9	8,635.9	1.8
1952	132.8	17,452.8	0.6
1953	123.1	17,054.3	0.9
1954	121.5	13,515.4	0.9
1955	133.9	9,450.4	1.8
1956	211.3	9,274.3	2.3
1957	344.0	9,704.8	3.5
1958	339.6	9,775.9	3.5
1959	314.8	10,284.1	3.1
1960	349.8	10,294.0	3.4
1961	321.5	11,102.6	2.9
1962	309.9	12,425.9	2.5
1963	313.7	11,499.0	2.7
1964	3.5.3	12,050.0	2.5
1965	346.6	13,999.3	2.5
1966	344.6	20,919.1	1.6
1967	415.1	24,810	1.7
1968	397.4	25,290	1.6
1969	400.4	26,684	1.5

*Organized Reserve Corps funding was only $200.00 each for the years 1945 and 1946.

Fiscal Year	RPA	OMAR	MCAR	USAR Total	Army Total	% Army Reserve
1970	$ 338.7	$129.3	$10.0	$ 478.0	$23,580	2.0
1971	374.5	140.7	10.0	525.2	20,300	2.6
1972	431.5	171.3	33.5	636.3	22,480	2.8
1973	461.6	203.0	39.2	702.8	21,820	3.2
1974	465.5	253.9	40.7	760.1	21,650	3.5
1975	489.9	284.0	43.7	817.6	21,580	3.8
1976	478.8	323.5	50.3	852.6	24,040	3.5
1977	479.8	364.7	53.8	898.3	26,810	3.4
1978	532.6	391.5	50.5	974.6	28,770	3.3
1979	566.8	420.3	37.1	1,024.2	31,570	3.2
1980	659.3	440.4	30.0	1,102.7	34,580	3.2

Army Reserve Appropriations (in millions of dollars)—Continued

Fiscal Year	RPA	OMAR	MCAR	USAR Total	Army Total	% Army Reserve
1981	$ 865.5	$520.7	$43.2	$1,429.4	$44,030	3.2
1982	1,071.0	666.0	65.0	1,802.0	53,040	3.4
1983	1,247.0	705.0	42.0	1,994.0	57,220	3.5
1984	1,322.0	691.6	54.2	2,067.8	61,516	3.4
1985	1,966.6	731.4	68.6	2,766.6	72,760	3.8
1986	2,149.1	740.9	56.1	2,947.0	73,770	4.0
1987	2,110.0	769.2	86.6	2,965.8	75,241	3.9
1988	2,222.9	859.4	95.0	3,177.3	76,346	4.2
1989	2,240.8	810.7	85.8	3,137.3	78,562	4.0
1990	2,199.2	868.0	99.1	3,166.3	79,131	4.0
1991	2,178.8	942.5	77.4	3,198.7	92,498	3.5
1992	2,314.1	1,017.9	110.4	3,442.4	74,653	4.6
1993	2,182.2	1,037.2	42.2	3,261.6	66,737	4.9
1994	2,146.9	1,072.7	99.5	3,319.1	63,123	5.3
1995	2,174.1	1,239.8	57.4	3,471.3	63,956	5.4

RPA Reserve Personnel, Army
OMAR Operations, Maintenance, Army Reserve
MCAR Military Construction, Army Reserve

Note: There were apparently no separate appropriations for the Medical Reserve Corps and the Organized Reserve during the years 1908–1916. During the years 1917–1969 the figures given for the Army Reserve appropriation include funds for the Officers' Reserve Corps, the Enlisted Reserve Corps, the Reserve Officers' Training Corps, and the Citizens' Military Training Camps.

Sources: Chart 10, *OSD Project 80 Report, Part VII (Reserve Components)*, pp. VII–B–24 and VII–B–25; Russell F. Weigley, *History of the United States Army* (New York and London: Macmillan Publishing Co., Inc. and Collier Macmillan Publishers, 1967), p. 561; *Annual Historical Supplement, Department of the Army* (various years); *Annual Report of the Secretary of the Army* (various years); and from files of the Comptroller Division, Office of the Chief, Army Reserve.

It should be understood that other figures purporting to represent the same information are available from other sources. Budget figures may vary substantially, depending upon whether one is talking about appropriations, total obligation authority, or actual spending for a given year.

Appendix C

Army Reserve Units Mobilized in 1968[1]

Unit	Home Station
277th MI Det	Phoenix, Ariz.
*978th Army Postal Unit (Type U)	Ft. Smith, Ark.
*HHC 336th Ord Bn (Ammo) (DS)	Little Rock, Ark.
*231st Trans Co., Fltg Cft (SRF)	St. Petersburg, Fla.
*319th Trans Co. (Light Truck)	Augusta, Ga.
*413th Fin Sec (Disbursing)	Atlanta, Ga.
100th Bn, 442d Inf	Ft. DeRussy, Hawaii
*482d Med Det (Equip Maint)	Aurora, Ill.
724th Trans Co. (Medium Trk Petr)	Forest Park, Ill.
890th Trans Co. (Medium Trk Cargo)	Ft. Wayne, Ind.
*1011th Sup & Svc Co. (DS) (–)	Independence and Emporia, Kans.
*842d QM Co. (Petr Dep)	Kansas City, Kans.
*950th Army Postal Unit (Type F)	Lexington, Ky.
*472d Med Det (Amb) (SRF)	Rockville, Md.
*HQ & Main Spt. Co., 513th Maint Bn (DS)	Boston, Mass.
241st MI Det	Boston, Mass.
*424th Pers Svc Co. (Type B)	Livonia, Mich.
*452d Gen Spt Co (–)	Worthington & Winthrop, Minn.
*173d Petr Co. (Oper) (Type B)	Greenwood, Miss.
*172d Trans Co. (Med Trk Cargo)	Omaha, Neb.
*295th Ord Co. (DS/GS) (SRF)	Hastings, Grand Island & New York, Neb.
*1018th Sup & Svc Co. (DS)	Schenectady, N.Y.
*448th Army Postal Unit (Type Z)	Garden City, N.Y.

1. "Army Reserve Units Respond to Call-Up," *Army Reserve Magazine,* (May 1968), pp. 6–7; News Release, Office of the Assistant Secretary of Defense (Public Affairs), January 23, 1969, Subject: "Final Army Reserve Component Unit Arrives in Vietnam."

Unit	Home Station
*237th Maint. Co. (DS)	Ft. Hamilton, N.Y.
*316th Med Det (Blood Dist)	New York, N.Y.
*74th Field Hosp	New York, N.Y.
203d Trans Co. (Light Truck)	Garden City, N.Y.
*312th Evac Hosp (Semi-mobile)	Winston-Salem, N.C.
*1002d Sup & Svc Co. (DS)	Cleveland, Ohio
*311th Field Hosp	Sharonville, Ohio
*630th Trans Co. (Med Truck Cargo)	Washington, Penn.
*357th Trans Co. (Aircraft Maint) (DS)	Greencastle, Penn.
*305th Med Det (Ortho)	Philadelphia, Penn.
*378th Med Det (Neurosurgical)	Memphis, Tenn.
*238th Maint Co. (DS)	San Antonio, Tex.
*HHC, 259th QM Bn (Petr)	Pleasant Grove, Utah
304th Med Det (Equip Maint) (SRF)	Richmond, Va.
*313th Med Det (Surg)	Richmond, Va.
*889th Med Det (Surg)	Richmond, Va.
*737th Trans Co. (Med Truck Petr)	Yakima, Wash.
*377th Light Maint Co. (DS)	Manitowoc, Wisc.
*826th Ord Co. (Ammo) (DS/GS) (–)	Madison & Baraboo, Wisc.

Units identified by an asterisk were deployed to Vietnam. The other Army Reserve units were assigned to the Strategic Army Forces (STRAF).

NARRATIVE HISTORIES OF CERTAIN USAR UNITS IN VIETNAM

HHC, 336th Ordnance Battalion (Ammo) (DS)—Little Rock, Arkansas

Following its activation on May 13, 1968, this unit went to Fort Carson, Colorado, where it underwent four months of intensive training. The unit was augmented by an Explosive Ordnance Disposal Unit upon its arrival at Fort Carson. The training ended on September 25, 1968, when HHC, 336th Ord Bn was deployed to Vietnam. The unit was assigned to Da Nang, where the men of the unit constructed their own buildings for billeting and operational functions. The battalion supplied Class V (ammunition) for all Army units in the I Corps area, and it received the Meritorious Unit Commendation for its performance on duty.[2]

2. Letter, Cdr, HHC 336th Ordnance Battalion (Ammo) (DS/GS) to Lewis C. Brodsky, Chief of Public Affairs, OCAR, January 15, 1983, Subject: "336th Ordnance Battalion Historical Information," OCAR Historical Files; General Orders No. 783, Headquarters, United States Army Vietnam, March 30, 1970, "Award of the Meritorious Unit Commendation."

319th Transportation Co. (Light Trucks)—Augusta, Georgia

The 319th was mobilized on May 13, 1968, and convoyed to Fort Lee, Virginia. Upon arrival at Fort Lee the unit TOE was reorganized from 55–17F to 55–17G; it was further reorganized on May 25 when it gave up one truck platoon. The "G" series reorganization resulted in an equipment change from 2½ ton "slush box" trucks to 5 ton multifuel trucks, but the unit met the challenge and was fully prepared when it arrived in Vietnam on September 26, 1968.[3]

While in Vietnam the 319th achieved an enviable record while operating from "TC Hill," Long Binh. The unit drove a total of 1,073,641 miles and hauled 92,375 tons of supplies. It supported the 1st Infantry Division, the 1st Air Cavalry, the 9th Infantry Division, the 25th Infantry Division, the 199th Light Infantry Brigade, the 11th Armored Cavalry Regiment, the Royal Thai Volunteer Force, and the 1st Australian Task Force. The 319th had anything but a boring tour in Vietnam, for its convoys were ambushed on seven occasions.[4]

The men of the 319th had gone to Vietnam, they stated proudly in a Public Information Release, without "unfavorable Congressional Inquiries or Court Injunctions . . . initiated . . . prior to or after arrival in Vietnam." Once in Vietnam, however, they were subject to something described by the unit as "one of the most demoralizing [situations] the unit faced." This was the "infusion" policy initiated by the Army for Reserve units in Vietnam. Infusion was accomplished by pulling men out of the Reserve units and sticking them into similar units elsewhere, while simultaneously putting non-unit personnel into the Reserve unit. "The infusion policy," stated the 319th, "severely hampers the unit morale, efficiency, and esprit." The reasons given for the infusion policy were two: (1) to prevent a local tragedy in the event of severe casualties and (2) to reduce the effects of having an entire unit pull-out at once. One of the real strengths of the Army Reserve, however, is the esprit de corps and the sense of unit integrity and teamwork that is

3. Letter, Cdr, 319th Transportation Company (LT) (5T) to Cdr, 544th S&S Bn (GS) (FWD), September 10, 1968, Subject: "Operational Report of the 319th Transportation Company (LT) (5T) for Period Ending 26 August 1968 (RCS CSFOR-65 (R–1)), copy in OCAR Historical Files.

4. Public Information Release, 319th Transportation Company (LT) (5T), July 31, 1969, copy in OCAR Historical Files

built up over the years, and infusion was not conducive to these qualities. The 319th, like many other Reserve Component units, was out "to overcome the stigma of the citizen soldier fighting the professional man's war."[5] It definitely overcame that stigma, but infusion did not help the process.

The 319th received a Meritorious Unit Citation for its work in Vietnam, and individual unit members received 2 Bronze Star Medals with "V", 8 other Bronze Stars, 3 Army Commendation Medals with "V", 62 other ARCOMs, and 3 Purple Heart Medals.[6] The members of the unit received a rousing welcome when they came home from Vietnam, too, for more than 300 wives, children, parents, and friends were on hand when the unit landed in Augusta.[7]

HQ and Main Spt Co, 513th Maintenance Bn (DS)—
Boston, Massachusetts

The 513th Maintenance Battalion, as already related, was a hot-bed of opposition to the Vietnam mobilization. Despite the protests that had accompanied the departure of the 513th for Vietnam in October 1968, however, there was no protest from the unit after that time. "We supported 77 tactical units and worked seven days a week. Once we got out of the United States the morale was good. We had a job to do," said the commander of the 513th, Lt. Col. Eugene Martinez.[8]

In Vietnam the 513th was assigned to the 26th General Support Group at Phu Bai and provided maintenance services to non-divisional units in the supported area, which reached north from the Hai Van Pass to LZ Nancy and from Laos to the sea. The battalion participated in four campaigns while in Vietnam and returned to Boston in October 1969, almost a year after it had left the United States.

5. Public Information Release, 319th Transportation Company (LT) (5T), July 31, 1969, copy in OCAR Historical Files. Letter, Commander, 81st US Army Reserve Command, to Commanding General, Third US Army, March 4, 1970, Subject: "After Action/Lessons Learned Report—319th Transportation Company (Lt Trk), WSZ0AA, for Period 11 April 1968 through 19 September 1969, RCS CS FOR-65 (RZ)," copy in OCAR Historical Files.

6. "Citations Go To 319th at Ceremony," *The Augusta Chronicle,* August 20, 1969, copies of both in OCAR Historical Files.

7. "Army Reservists Welcomed Home from Vietnam Tour" *The State,* August 15, 1969, Section C, p. 1, copy in OCAR Historical Files.

8. "Boston Unit Returns from Viet," *Sunday Herald-Traveler,* October 5, 1969.

Upon its return the members received a tremendous welcome from some 450 relatives and friends.[9]

452d General Spt Co—Worthington and Winthrop, Minnesota

The 452d spent four months at Fort Riley, Kansas, training and preparing for deployment to Vietnam. In Vietnam the unit was stationed at Da Nang, where it operated Class II (Individual equipment, general supplies) and Class IV (construction materials) supply sites. After a month in Da Nang the Class I (rations) Platoon moved to Phu Bai and operated the subsistence supply point there. The 452d left Vietnam in August 1969 and returned to Fort Riley.[10]

172d Transportation Co (Medium Truck Cargo)—Omaha, Nebraska

After four months of training at Fort Lewis, Washington, the 172d left for Vietnam and arrived at Cam Ranh Bay on October 10, 1968, with its trucks and other equipment. The unit became fully operational within seven days and began running convoys to the Central Highlands. Convoy destinations were Ban Me Thuot (154 miles one-way; two day round-trip), Bao Loc (169 miles one-way; four day round-trip), and Dalat (119 miles one-way; two day round trip). During the period from October 10, 1968, to August 18, 1969, the 172d participated in thirty-six convoy operations, hauling 79,977 tons a total of 659,051 miles. There were no incidences of AWOL during the time the 172d was in Vietnam, a total of only twenty-four punishments under Article 15 of the Uniform Code of Military Justice, and only two court martial convictions. Both of the latter were men who had been assigned to the 172d as a result of the Army's infusion program. No original member of the unit was ever court martialed.[11]

---

9. Unsigned memorandum, HQ, 513th Maintenance Battalion (DS), December 9, 1968, Subject: "Summary of Unit History 5 Jan 66 to 31 Nov 68," copy in OCAR Historical Files; Department of the Army Lineage and Honors, Headquarters and Headquarters Detachment, 513th Maintenance Battalion, copy in OCAR Historical Files; "Boston Unit Returns from Viet," *Sunday Herald-Traveler*, October 5, 1969.

10. Unit History, 452d General Supply Co. (GS), copy in OCAR Historical Files.

11. Letter, Lt. Col. Edward Honor, Cdr, 36th Transportation Battalion (Truck) to Cdr, US Army Support Command, August 18, 1969, Subject: "Nomination for Meritorious Unit Commendation," copy in OCAR Historical Files.

The 172d was the only unit in the 36th Transportation Battalion to receive a Meritorious Unit Commendation. According to Lt. Col. Edward Honor, the 36th Bn Cdr,

> The Unit's enthusiasm was immediately apparent. In many instances, drivers made twice as many runs per shift as compared with regular drivers from other units. The unit was determined to prove itself . . . . The unit passed its Annual General Inspection (AGI) with a rating of excellent. It also passed its CMMI with a rating of satisfactory and the best overall score in the battalion. The Inspector General made a point of praising the unit for its high caliber of administration in the orderly and supply rooms. This can be attributed, in part, to the mature attitude of most of the reservists in the unit as well as in the innate ability of the high caliber individuals called to duty.[12]

The men of the 172d sent word from Vietnam that they did not want any parades when they returned home, and that they wanted to be treated "like guys returning with lunch buckets after a hard day's work." Their families and friends would not accept the idea of an austere homecoming, however, and the 172d was greeted with a full-fledged ceremony, complete with the Strategic Air Command's band.[13]

237th Maintenance Co (DS)—Fort Hamilton, New York

The 237th Maintenance Company (DS) performed its pre-Vietnam training at Fort Meade, Maryland, though individual members of the unit were sent to Army service schools at Forts Dix, Gordon, Monmouth, Belvoir, and Lee. The 237th reached Vietnam on October 21 and 22, 1968, and was assigned to provide maintenance support to the 108th Artillery Group and electronics maintenance support to the Third Marine Division. Company Headquarters with service and evacuation sections soon moved to Quang Tri, and the electronics, maintenance, and armament sections moved to Dong Ha. These locations were within a few miles of the De-Militarized Zone (DMZ), and the unit came under enemy fire on numerous occasions.[14]

---

12. *Ibid.*, letter, SSG Armand K. Gibbons, Unit Historian, 172d Transportation Co. to Office of the Chief, Army Reserve, December 24, 1982, in OCAR Historical Files.

13. "Like It or Not, 172d Greeted as Heroes," *Sunday World-Herald*, October 5, 1969, p. 1.

14. Letter, 1Lt. George H. Wills, Cdr., 237th Maintenance Co and CW4 Louis E. Lorenzo, Unit Historian, 237th Maintenance Co, to

The 237th was responsible for all armament, electronics, and motor maintenance support in the area from Quang Tri north to the DMZ, east to the South China Sea, and west to the Laotian border. Unit personnel constructed their own air conditioned repair shop to assist in their electronics repair work and each day sent repair teams to remote fire bases. Tube changes on 175 mm guns and 8 inch howitzers, repair of hydraulic leaks, welding of cracked spades, and similar repair operations were all routinely accomplished with the weapon in firing position. This procedure minimized down-time and resulted in maximum availability of the weapon.[15]

The 237th Maintenance Company distinguished itself as one of the top outfits of its type in Vietnam, and it was awarded the Meritorious Unit Commendation for its fine work. Unit personnel received 5 Bronze Star Medals, one Air Medal, and 7 Army Commendation Medals.[16] The 237th was greeted with an elaborate welcoming ceremony upon its return from Vietnam, and John V. Lindsay, Mayor of New York City, sent the unit a letter of congratulations and thanks.[17]

316th Medical Detachment (Blood Distribution)—New York, New York

This unit was organized in January 1968 and mobilized in May of the same year. The 316th moved to Vietnam in October 1968 and was attached to the 9th Medical Laboratory. Personnel from this unit were widely dispersed throughout Vietnam, where they did an outstanding job of blood distribution. This particular Army Reserve unit was unusual in that it had no officers authorized. The 316th, like all of the units in the 77th US Army Reserve Command, received an elaborate welcome home upon its return from Vietnam. The ceremony for the 316th was combined with that of the 74th Field Hospital, also a 77th ARCOM unit.[18]

OCAR Public Affairs Office, January 28, 1983, Subject: "Historical Information," in OCAR Historical Files.

15. *Ibid.*

16. General Orders No. 288, HQ, US Army Vietnam, February 1, 1970; "Awards and Decorations," in "Historical Information," 237th Maintenance Company, copies of both in OCAR Historical Files.

17. *Welcome Home Ceremony, 237th Maintenance Company* and letter, Mayor John V. Lindsay, October 10, 1969, copies of both in OCAR Historical Files.

18. *Welcoming Home Ceremony for 74th Field Hospital and 316th Medical Detachment,* copy in OCAR Historical Files.

74th Field Hospital—New York, New York,

Members of the 74th Field Hospital were among the individuals who participated in court action in an attempt to avoid being sent to Vietnam. Nevertheless, the entire unit was shipped to Southeast Asia, where its primary mission was caring for wounded prisoners of war. The 74th was stationed at Long Binh, where it was the only prisoner of war hospital in the III Corps and IV Corps Tactical Zones.[19]

The 74th met every medical challenge that came its way, from high velocity wounds of the chest to amputations to grafts of the femoral vein. The one problem it never could overcome, however, was the excessive temperature of the wards. There were days when ward temperatures reached 118°F and weeks when they did not go below 90°F at any time of the day or night. Nevertheless, the quality of care given by this Army Reserve unit was impressively high. A Swiss representative of the International Red Cross visited the 74th and remarked that the level of professional medical treatment given the prisoners was "equal to and perhaps even better than" that given civilians in many Western nations.[20]

While in Vietnam the 74th, as Army units have done in every war, "adopted" a local orphanage as its own civic action project. In addition to providing medical support to the Tan Lap Orphanage, the men and women of the 74th Field Hospital contributed money and school supplies to the orphans.[21] The men and women of the 74th were not ignored when they returned from Vietnam, either, for the 77th ARCOM staged an impressive ceremony to welcome them back to New York.[22]

312th Evacuation Hospital (Semi-mobile)—Winston-Salem, North Carolina

In April 1968 Sue Walker was working as Assistant Director of Nurses in a civilian hospital in Winston-Salem, North

19. Letter, Maj. Gen. Victor J. Mc Laughlin, Cdr, US Army Quartermaster Center and Fort Lee to Maj. Joseph P. Cillo, Cdr, 74th Field Hospital, October 14, 1968, Subject: "Letter of Commendation," copy in OCAR Historical Files; "Welcoming Home Ceremony for 74th Field Hospital and 316th Medical Detachment."

20. "Welcoming Home Ceremony for 74th Field Hospital and 316th Medical Detachment."

21. *Ibid.*

22. *Ibid.*

Carolina, when a friend called to tell her that her Army Reserve unit was being called up for Vietnam. Lt. Col. Walker checked with her unit commander, but he had not heard the news. The 313-member hospital unit was mobilized in 1968, however, and after three months training at Fort Benning, it was off to Southeast Asia. The 312th was based at Chu Lai, on the South China Sea coast, and it provided medical support to US and allied forces in the Northern I Corps Tactical Zone.[23]

The unit arrived while Chu Lai was under rocket attack, but this did not deter the men and women of the 312th and its attached units (889th Medical Detachment, USAR; 378th Medical Detachment, USAR; and 305th Medical Detachment, USAR) from taking over existing hospital facilities without any disruption in patient care. After only one month the 312th had expanded the hospital's capacity from 120 beds to 400 beds. On several occasions when the hospital came under direct, heavy fire, the hospital's personnel refused to take cover and continued to provide medical services to the massive number of wounded. The men and women of the 312th also participated in numerous civic action programs in which they provided surgical instruction and consultation to local Vietnamese health care centers.[24]

Lt. Col. Walker also spoke of the Army's infusion program, which she said they referred to in Vietnam as the "confusion" program. "They seemed to take our best quality personnel," said Walker, "and send us ones who were not so good." It hurt morale in the 312th, said the Chief Nurse, to have friends and co-workers, with whom a real team spirit had been developed, transferred to some other unit in Vietnam.[25]

The 312th received the Meritorious Unit Commendation for its performance of duty in Vietnam. When the members of the 312th returned to Winston-Salem, however, it was anything but a warm homecoming. There was a brief official ceremony, recalled Lt. Col. Walker, but when the ceremony was over "we were afraid to wear our uniforms. It

---

23. "At 48 She Answered Call to Vietnam War," *Messenger* (Madison, NC), March 30, 1983; General Orders No. 206, HQ, United States Army, Vietnam, January 24, 1970; copies in OCAR Historical Files.

24. *Ibid.*

25. Interview of Lt. Col. Sue Walker (USAR-Ret.) by Maj. James T. Currie, June 27, 1983, notes in OCAR Historical Files.

dividual members of the unit. The quality of personnel in the 259th was exemplified by the fact that members of the battalion won the 1st Logistical Command's Soldier of the Month competition three times in a row. The 259th received a Meritorious Unit Commendation for its service in Vietnam.[31]

173d Petroleum Company (Oper)—Greenwood, Mississippi

Personnel from this unit were among the Army Reservists who filed suit to prevent their being sent to Vietnam. The suit, as previously discussed, was unsuccessful, and the unit went to Southeast Asia on schedule. The company was headquartered at Phu Bai and operated pipelines between Phu Bai and Camp Evans and the Phu Bai Tank Farm. The company operated a pump station in Hue and one at Camp Evans.[32]

842d QM Co (Petr Dep)—Kansas City, Kansas

This unit operated the pipeline from Camp Evans to Quang Tri and one from Quang Tri to Dong Ha. It also operated a 59,000 barrel tank farm at Quang Tri and line-hauled bulk fuel to combat bases as far south as Camp Evans and northwest to Camp Vandergrift near Khe Sanh.[33]

737th Transportation Co (Med Truck Petr)—Yakima, Washington

The 737th was mentioned in Chapter Nine in connection with the fine send-off it received from citizens in the Yakima area. After several months of training at Fort Lewis, Washington, the unit left for Vietnam in September. The unit with its equipment landed at Da Nang and transferred to Quang Tri, where it immediately began convoy operations. The 737th supported the 1st Air Cavalry Division (Airmobile) with POL (petroleum, oil, and lubricants) for two months, after which the 101st Airborne Division moved

---

31. *Ibid.;* General Orders No. 205, Headquarters, United States Army Vietnam, January 24, 1970; *The Northern Log,* March 15, 1969, p. 5; copies in OCAR Historical Files.

32. "Historical Supplement, HHC, 259th Quartermaster Battalion (Petroleum)," p. 5, copy in OCAR Historical Files.

33. *Ibid.*

in. On January 6, 1969, the Company, minus the 3d Platoon, was moved to Chu Lai and assigned to the 57th Transportation Battalion. The 3d Platoon remained in Phu Bai until the unit returned to the US in August 1969.[34]

The 737th received the Meritorious Unit Commendation, and individual unit members won one Bronze Star Medal with "V", 6 other Bronze Star Medals, and 2 Purple Hearts. Upon returning to Yakima, the men of the 737th were given a "welcome home" ceremony by a crowd of 1000 people. Yakima Mayor Jack Larson proclaimed a day of honor for the returnees, and everyone dined on roast beef dinners.[35]

377th Light Maintenance Co (DS)—Manitowoc, Wisconsin

The 377th began calendar year 1968 as the 377th Ordnance Company (DAS). It was redesignated the 377th Light Maintenance Co (DS) on January 31, 1968, and in April it was notified that it was going to be mobilized. The post-mobilization training period at Fort Riley was not without problems. The 377th was first placed under a supply and service battalion, but it did not receive adequate training in this arrangement. On July 15, therefore, the unit was put under a maintenance battalion, and the quality and type of its training immediately improved. The change and confusion at Fort Riley resulted, however, in the 377th having the longest time between mobilization and arrival in Vietnam—seven months—of any Army Reserve unit.[36]

In Vietnam the 377th was assigned to the 69th Maintenance Battalion (GS), US Army Support Command, Cam Ranh Bay. The unit provided direct support maintenance to sixty-seven units of the 1st Logistical Command in the II Corps area. The unit's primary repair responsibilities were in the area of wheeled and tracked vehicles, towed and self-propelled artillery, small arms, refrigeration equipment, office machines, and chemical equipment. The 377th was awarded the Meritorious Unit Commendation for its service

---

34. "Unit History of Mobilization," 737th Transportation Company (MDM TRK) (PTRL), copy in OCAR Historical Files.

35. General Orders No. 408, HQ, U.S. Army Vietnam, February 4, 1971; "Unit History of Mobilization;" "Long, long trail ends—737th home," *Yakima Herald-Republic,* August 14, 1969, p. 1; copies in OCAR Historical Files.

36. 377th Light Maintenance Company (DS), "Unit History—1968," copy in OCAR Historical Files.

in Vietnam, and individuals in the unit were awarded 7 Bronze Star Medals and 34 Army Commendation Medals.[37]

826th Ord Co (Ammo) (DS/GS) (–)—Madison and Baraboo, Wisconsin

The 826th performed five months of post-mobilization training at Fort Knox, Kentucky from May 16, 1968, to October 13, 1968. Upon arriving in Vietnam the company was assigned to the 3d Ordnance Battalion (Ammo), Long Binh Ammunition Supply Depot. After a short period of orientation, the 826th took over Sub-Depots I and III at Long Binh and worked a two-shift, twenty-four hour day. The unit established a ten-month record of 450,000 short tons of ammunition lifted, as well as a twelve-hour lift record of 2250 short tons. The United States Army Support Command, Saigon, awarded the 826th its Certificate of Achievement. Personnel of the 826th received 14 Bronze Star Medals with "V", 12 other Bronze Star Medals, 2 Army Commendation Medals with "V", 58 other ARCOMs, and one Purple Heart. The unit left Vietnam for Fort Riley, Kansas, on October 2, 1969.[38]

---

37. "Unit History (Annual Supplement) 377th Light Maintenance Company (DS), 1969;" General Orders No. 752, Headquarters, United States Army Vietnam, March 25, 1970; copies in OCAR Historical Files.

38. "826th Ordnance Company (Ammo) (DS/GS) Annual Historical Supplement (1968)," "Annual Historical Supplement, 1969" and copy of Certificate of Achievement, all in OCAR Historical Files.

Appendix **D**

Post-Vietnam Emergency Use of the Army Reserve

In the fourteen years since the last Army Reserve unit returned from Vietnam, units of the USAR have been used during at least four emergencies, none of which were directly related to national defense. These four occasions were the following: (1) the Postal Strike of March 1970, (2) Tropical Storm Agnes, June 1973, (3) the Vietnamese refugee influx of 1975, and (4) the Cuban refugee operations in 1980. Each of these episodes was unique, and each one of them provided mobilization, training, and perhaps command experience for individuals involved.

1. *Postal Strike*—Operation Graphic Hand

On March 17, 1970, postal employees in New York City began a wildcat strike that soon spread to cities in nine other states. A Federal judge's injunction was ignored in New York City, as was President Richard M. Nixon's March 21 plea to the strikers. On March 23, Nixon declared that a "national emergency" existed as a result of the strike and thereafter some 28,100 Army personnel were ordered to duty in New York City. Army Reservists comprised almost exactly half (14,000) of the force, while the National Guard (11,600), the active Army, and other reserve components supplied the remainder.

The 77th Army Reserve Command, a major USAR headquarters, was mobilized on March 24 to provide com-

1. *History, First United States Army, Annual Supplement, Calendar Year 1970*, p. 66; see also *Ibid.*, pp. 43–66.

mand and control of particular USAR units, as well as certain Marine Corps Reserve and Navy Reserve units. Other USAR commands involved in the operation were the 11th Special Forces Group, 301st Support Brigade, 411th Engineer Brigade, 353d Civil Affairs Area (A) and 818th Hospital Center.

Military personnel served in the New York City Post Office until June 30, providing what were described as "essential postal services," including certain mail collection and processing activities, limited deliveries, and limited window service. Postmaster General Winston M. Blount was lavish in his praise for the job done by the Reservists and others during Operation Graphic Hand. The Reservists themselves seemed to have few complaints about being called to duty, the biggest gripe centering about the cold "C" rations they were served at noon. The exercise was generally considered a successful use of Reserve Component forces in an unusual situation, and according to the official First United States Army History, it "appeared to justify the conclusion that the military forces, both active and reserve, are prepared on very short notice to perform any conceivable assigned mission."

2. *Tropical Storm Agnes*—Operation Noah II

Tropical Storm Agnes, which originated off the Yucatan Peninsula in the Gulf of Mexico in mid-June 1972, reached the Virginia coast on the afternoon of June 21. The storm took the scenic route up the Virginia and Maryland coasts, causing rainfalls of one inch per hour. It passed Delaware and New Jersey, swept through New York City, and then looped back down through Pennsylvania on what might be called a "Honeymooners Tour" of the Poconos and Williamsport. Agnes then visited Niagara Falls and followed the St. Lawrence River to the ocean.

The greatest damage was in central Pennsylvania, where residential property losses were estimated at $570 million, and industrial, commercial, and public property damage was placed at $2 billion. From June 22 to September 15, 1972, a total of 28 Army Reserve units with 1466 men took part in disaster relief efforts in Pennsylvania and adjoining states.

---

2. Col. John F. McElhenny, *After Action Report: Tropical Storm Agnes–Operation Noah II*; Col George H. Russell, DCSOT to various addressees, Subject: "After-Action Report—Tropical Storm Agnes."

Joining the unit members were some 3000 individual Army Reservists.

Seventeen USAR units served in Pennsylvania, performing such tasks as cleaning debris from streams and rivers, building bridges, transporting food and water, and providing medical and law enforcement support. Most of the work of disaster assistance fell naturally to the National Guards of the states concerned, but the Army Reserve also played a vital and well-appreciated role.

3. *Vietnamese Refugees*—Project New Arrivals

With the collapse of the South Vietnamese government in the spring of 1975, the United States was soon on the receiving end of what appeared to be a nearly-inexhaustible stream of refugees. The United States Army Forces Command (FORSCOM) was soon given responsibility for the refugee operations at Fort Chaffee, Arkansas, and Fort Indiantown Gap, Pennsylvania. Active Army personnel did most of the work with the refugees, but in the civil affairs area the Army Reserve had to become involved. The 96th Civil Affairs Battalion was the only such unit in the active Army, so FORSCOM sought volunteers from USAR personnel who were qualified civil affairs specialists.

Thirty volunteer Army Reservists at Fort Chaffee were organized into the Directorate of Civil Military Affairs, while the twenty-five USAR members at Fort Indiantown Gap comprised the Civil Affairs Support Battalion (Composite/Provisional). According to a story that appeared in *Army Reserve Magazine,* USAR personnel "set up English, American customs, and history classes. Several WACs are giving classes on the women's liberation movement and how it differs from the traditional role of the Vietnamese woman."

Finally, it should be pointed out that the operations at Fort Chaffee and Indiantown Gap were funded under Army Reserve Operation and Maintenance (OMAR) appropriations. This was apparently the only source of flexible funding available to the Army at the time, though one would be hard-pressed to show how the refugee operations were of di-

3. Frank W. Pew, *The Role of the U.S. Army Forces Command in Project New Arrivals: Reception and Care of Refugees from Vietnam* (Fort McPherson, Georgia: Historical office, Office of the Chief of Staff, U.S. Army Forces Command, 1981), pp. 20–21, 173-75, 212; "The New Arrivals," *Army Reserve Magazine* (November-December 1975), pp. 16–18

rect benefit to more than the few Army Reservists who volunteered for duty.

4. *Cuban Refugees*

Barely four years after the Vietnamese refugee camps at Forts Chaffee and Indiantown Gap were emptied and closed, the Army had to reopen them, plus Fort McCoy, Wisconsin, to take care of thousands of refugees from Fidel Castro's Cuba.

Army Reserve units, which operated under FORSCOM, were involved in refugee operations from the beginning. At Fort Chaffee, Arkansas, the 369th Station Hospital, a USAR unit from Puerto Rico, was particularly effective because its members were Spanish-speaking. Three Army Reserve Military Police units from Indiana—the 222d MP Co, 396th MP Co, and 496th MP Co—were also used at Chaffee.

At Fort McCoy, Army Reservists from the 432d Civil Affairs Group worked with the refugees, as did members of the 432d PSYOP Battalion, USAR.

More Army Reservists served at Fort Indiantown Gap than anywhere else. Army Reserve Civil Affairs units in the First Army area were especially active at the "Gap," spending their two weeks of annual training, plus many weekend drills, working with the refugees there.

According to the after action report on activities at the Gap, "The performance of individual Reservists ranged from outstanding to unsatisfactory. For the first months of the operation, Reserve Civil Affairs personnel augmented by Reservists from other branches ran the seven alien compounds. . . . Generally speaking, their performance was more than satisfactory . . . . The most serious drawback to the use of Reservists was the necessity for changing Area Commanders every two weeks . . . ."

4. Jean R. Moenk, Frank W. Pew, and Maj. Charles Bishop, *Annual Historical Review, United States Army Forces Command, United States Army Forces, Readiness Command, 1 October 1980–30 September 1981 (RCS CSHIS–6 (R–3)) (U)* (Fort McPherson, Georgia: Historical Office, Office of the Chief of Staff, U.S. Army Forces Command, 1981), pp. 342–54; "First Army Reservists Find Themselves 'Doing Real Thing' at Fort Indiantown Gap," *The Officer,* August 1980, p. 12; *Task Force, Fort Indiantown Gap After Action Report*, Vol II, p. 3.

Appendix E

Strength of the Army Reserve (Medical Reserve Corps, Organized Reserve) Prior to World War II

End of Fiscal Year	Med. Res. Corps	Army Reserve[1]		
1909	364			
1910	420			
1911	922			
1912	1105			
1913	1205	8		
1314	1254	16		
1915	1426	17		
1916	1903	27	4621[2]	
		ORC	ERC	Total
1917	4855	21,543	35,000	61,398
1918	20,855	86,262	80,000	187,117
1919		45,573	none	45,573
1920		68,232	none	68,232
1921		66,905	1	66,906
1922		67,390	480	67,870
1923		76,923	1557	78,480
1924		81,706	3400	85,106
1925		95,154	5115	100,269
1926		103,829	5775	109,604
1927		110,014	5735	115,749
1928		114,824	5464	120,288
1929		112,757	5192	117,949
1930		113,523	4721	118,244

	Active ORC	Inactive ORC	ERC	Total
1931	80,399	27.811	4837	113,047
1932	83,808	31,028	4872	119,709
1933	86,338	33,147	5028	124,513
1934	88,107	26,250	4646	119,003
1935	91,955	20,635	4323	116,913
1936	95,619	19,550	3897	119,066
1937	96,545	14,624	3189	114,358
1938	100,116	18,796	2998	121,910
1939	104,575	12,144	3054	119,773
1940	104,228	12,408	3233	119,869
1941	110,931	22,028	2149	135,108[3]

[1] Created by the Army Appropriation Act of August 24, 1912.

[2] Consists of individuals furloughed to the reserve from the Regular Army under the provisions of the Army Appropriation Act of August 24, 1912.

[3] Includes 57,309 Officers' Reserve Corps members on extended active duty.

ORC Officers' Reserve Corps of the Organized Reserve
ERC Enlisted Reserve Corps of the Organized Reserve

All figures are taken from the reports of the Secretary of War, The Adjutant General, and The Surgeon General for the appropriate years.

Appendix F

Strength of the Army Reserve (Organized Reserve Corps) after World War II

End of Fiscal Year	Paid Drill	IRR	Total Ready Reserve	Standby Total	Retired Reserve	Total Army Reserve
1946	none					none
1947 (Dec. 31)	none					729,289
1948	none					752,271
1949	196,427					588,972
1949 (Dec. 31)	245,585					580,459
1950	186,541					613,526
1951	154,816					278,327
1952	135,003					340,580
1953	117,323					798,026
1953 (Dec. 31)	127,613		883,820	23,463	38,320	945,603
1954	136,918					1,108,967
1954 (Dec. 31)	153,932		1,290,833	9,828	43,584	1,344,245
1955	163,137		1,593,419			1,648,626
1955 (Dec. 31)	173,196			8,209		
1956	197,340		1,917,250			1,975,559
1956 (Dec. 31)	225,345					1,814,333
1957	260,377		1,008,438			1,839,474
1958	272,683		955,462			2,034,598
1959	314,173		1,008,837			2,282,550
1960	301,081		1,024,549			2,217,472
1961	301,796		1,028,168	772,543	93,036	1,893,747
1962	261,456	580,034	841,490	496,762	107,649	1,445,901
1963	284,182	382,899	667,081	293,283	132,470	1,092,834
1964	268,524	453,485	722,089	255,592	154,180	1,131,782
1965	261,680	456,758	718,438	233,916	176,212	1,128,566

End of Fiscal Year	Paid Drill	IRR	Total Ready Reserve	Standby Total	Retired Reserve	Total Army Reserve
1966	250,794	546,845	797,819	233,683	190,663	1,222,165
1967	261,957	444,204	706,161	312,503	199,320	1,217,984
1968	244,239	629,237	873,476	230,875	230,879	1,335,230
1969	261,322	818,471	1,079,793	262,000		1,304,000
1970	257,490	931,715	1,192,453	344,000		1,386,000
1971	262,299	991,039	1,254,338	335,000		1,605,000
1972	235,192	1,059,064	1,294,256	382,215	327,189	2,003,660
1973	235,499	757,675	993,174	415,268	344,457	1,752,989
1974	239,715	532,575	772,290	340,481	357,591	1,470,362
1975	225,057	355,099	580,156	282,696	365,489	1,228,341
1976	191,919	217,621	409,540	184,478	376,037	970,055
1977	189,420	149,427	338,847	152,784	386,368	877,999
1978	185,753	168,607	354,360	82,677	391,304	828,341
1979	189,990	201,783	391,773	30,544	400,825	823,142
1980	195,146	215,810	410,946	19,047	413,431	843,784
1981	225,003	212,925	437,928	5,014	449,406	893,348
1982	256,659	218,991	475,650	357	464,634	940,641
1983 (Jan 31)	256,379	223,904	480,283	614	466,936	947,833
1984	275,062	276,651	551,713	244	602,096	1,154,053
1985	292,080	301,825	593,905	266	*342,100	936,271
1986	309,709	300,919	610,527	318	615,527	1,226,372
1987	313,638	287,459	601,097	391	618,913	1,220,401
1988	312,825	292,857	605,682	430	628,422	1,234,534
1989	319,244	274,588	593,832	632	642,364	1,236,828
1990	310,071	284,248	594,319	788	648,966	1,244,073
1991	309,681	359,074	668,755	1,189	661,809	1,331,753
1992	302,850	418,592	721,442	1,047	610,401	1,332,890
1993	275,900	438,036	713,938	921	633,618	1,348,475
1994	259,856	412,235	672,091	1,145	655,519	1,328,755
1995	241,300	376,790	618,090	1,128	683,723	1,302,941

*In 1985 the Department of Defense did not count certain Gray Area reservists in their total Retired category.

Strength figures in this appendix are based upon the reports of the Secretary of Defense. Because the reports varied in format from year to year, there are some unavoidable gaps in the chart. There was no paid drill in the Organized Reserve Corps prior to FY 1949. The ORC did not exist at all in 1946, and figures for 1947 reflect only the most tenuous of military connection for the members of the Corps.

Appendix **G**

Army Reservists on Active Duty—1948–1982 (excluding active duty for training)

End of Fiscal Year	Number	End of Fiscal Year	Number
1948	39,090	1966	74,373
1949	54,149	1967	100,115
1950	44,107	1968	127,513
1951	205,338	1969	134,025
1952	118,444	1970	121,575
1953	115,119	1971	102,592
1954	107,791	1972	71,905
1955	102,688	1973	66,507
1956	106,016	1974	55,798
1957	124,779	1975	53,373
1958	104,773	1976	51,432
1959	74,976	1977	51,636
1960	63,018	1978	52,307
1961	58,762	1979	52,924
1962	128,884	1980	53,078
1963	64,897	1981	53,252
1964	67,976	1982	49,071
1965	68,808		

Source: *Department of Defense Selected Manpower Statistics, Fiscal Year 1982*, pages 199 and 200.

Appendix H

Western Union Mailgram

This is a facsimile of a mailgram sent to members of the Individual Ready Reserve on January 20, 1991.

ARPERCEN, DARP-MOP-P
9700 PAGE BLVD.
ST. LOUIS, MO 63132-5200

0-070202U020 01/20/91 ICS PH09658 MLTN
02014 MLTN VA 01/20/91 JN01899

DARP-MOP-P PERSCOM MOB ASSET A
[redacted]
34[redacted]ANVILL
TR[redacted]40

PURSUANT TO PRESIDENTIAL EXECUTIVE ORDER OF JANUARY 18, 1991:
YOU ARE ORDERED TO ACTIVE DUTY FOR THE PERIOD INDICATED BELOW. YOU ARE RELIEVED FROM YOUR PRESENT RESERVE COMPONENT STATUS. PROCEED FROM YOUR CURRENT LOCATION IN SUFFICIENT TIME TO REPORT ON THE DATE SPECIFIED.
REPORT TO: MIL PERS DIV BLDG T-20 UIC: W7XC56 7XC56
WALTER REED ARMY MEDICAL CENTER
WASHINGTON DC 20012 REPORTING DATE: 31 JAN 91

ACTIVE DUTY COMMITMENT: NOT TO EXCEED 12 CONSECUTIVE MONTHS
ORDER NUMBER: M-12-256988 DATE PREPARED: 20 JAN 91
PURPOSE: MOBILIZATION COMPONENT: INDIVIDUAL READY RESERVE
AUTH: 10 USC 673 MOS/SSI: 91A10
FORMAT: 172 GRADE: SP4 PEBD: 870219
SSN: [redacted] MDC: 1AE1 DOR: 900901

ADDITIONAL INSTRUCTIONS: REPORT ON DATE INDICATED. A DETERMINATION TO DE LAY OR EXEMPT YOU FROM SERVING ON ACTIVE DUTY WILL BE MADE AFTER YOU REPORT AS DIRECTED. FAILURE TO REPORT WILL BE CONSIDERED ABSENCE WITHOUT LEAVE (AWOL) AND MAY SUBJECT YOU TO UCMJ ACTION UNDER TITLE 10 USC 886. BRING WITH YOU: ALL SERVICEABLE UNIFORMS; PROOF OF MARRIAGE; BIRTH CER-TIFICATES OF CHILDREN; DOCTOR'S STATEMENT FOR CHILDREN OVER 21 INCAPABLE OF SELF SUPPORT; COURT ORDERS GOVERNING LEGAL CUSTODY;ILLEGITIMATE CHIL-DREN OR CHILD SUPPORT; YOUR IMMUNIZATION RECORDS; DD214; ID CARD & TAGS. TRANSPORTATION OF DEPENDENTS & HOUSEHOLD GOODS IS NOT AUTHORIZED. THE ENCLOSED TRAVEL WARRANT SHOULD BE USED TO OBTAIN TRANSPORTATION. TRAVEL BY PRIVATELY OWNED VEHICLE IS NOT AUTHORIZED. LEAVE COPIES OF THIS WITH YOUR DEPENDENT/ NEXT OF KIN. FAMILY ASST. HOTLINE 1-800-874-8451.

BY ORDER OF THE SECRETARY OF THE ARMY:

****
* ARPERCEN *
* OFFICIAL *
****

THOMAS J. KILMARTIN
BRIGADIER GENERAL, USA
COMMANDING

Western Union Mailgram®

DEPARTMENT OF DEFENSE
MILITARY EMERGENCY TRAVEL WARRANT

DATE PREPARED: 20 JAN 91
ORDER NO: M-12-256988

INFO FOR CARRIER AGENTS: CERTIFIED AS ESSENTIAL TRAVEL. UPON PRESENTATION OF THE MOBILIZATION ORDER, WITH MILITARY EMERGENCY TRAVEL WARRANT ATTACHED, & UPON VERIFICATION OF TRAVELER'S IDENTITY, THIS WARRANT AUTHORIZES YOU TO ISSUE A BUS, TRAIN, OR PLANE COACH TICKET TO THE PERSON NAMED BELOW FROM YOUR LOCATION TO OR TOWARD THE DESIGNATED DESTINATION. THROUGH TICKETING IS REQUESTED WHENEVER POSSIBLE. DO NOT HONOR EXPIRED OR ALTERED WARRANTS. WARRANT EXPIRES 30 DAYS FROM REPORTING DATE SHOWN ON THE ORDER. PLEASE COMPLETE APPROPRIATE SECTION BELOW & RETAIN FIRST OR SECOND CARRIER RECEIPT.

TRAVELER: MA[redacted]ER SSN: [redacted] RANK: SP4 U.S. ARMY

FROM: T[redacted]0

DESTINATION: WALTER REED ARMY MEDICAL CENTER WASHINGTON DC

FIRST CARRIER'S NAME: ....
TICKET NO: ....TICKET VALUE: ....
FROM: ....TO: ....

SECOND CARRIER'S NAME: ....
TICKET NO: ....TICKET VALUE: ....
FROM: ....TO: ....

**** TRAVELER: RETAIN ABOVE SECTION FOR FILING WITH TRAVEL VOUCHER *****
****
****************** SECOND CARRIER AGENT DETACH HERE ******************
DOD MILITARY EMERGENCY TRAVEL WARRANT
CARRIER SUPPORT DOCUMENT FOR TICKETING & BILLING ORDER NO: M-12-256988
TRAVELER: M[redacted]ER SSN: [redacted]8 RANK: SP4 U.S. ARMY
SECOND CARRIER'S NAME: ....
TICKET NO: ....TICKET VALUE: ....
SEND BILL TO: USAFAC ATTN:FINCH,INDIANAPOLIS,IN 42649 FISCAL DATA: 1AE1

SIGNATURE OF TRAVELER: ....
SECOND CARRIER AGENT: FOLLOW ABOVE DIRECTIONS & RETAIN THIS SECTION
****
******************* FIRST CARRIER AGENT DETACH HERE ******************
DOD MILITARY EMERGENCY TRAVEL WARRANT
CARRIER SUPPORT DOCUMENT FOR TICKETING & BILLING ORDER NO: M-12-256988
TRAVELER: M[redacted]ER SSN: 5[redacted]8 RANK: SP4 U.S. ARMY
FIRST CARRIER'S NAME: ....
TICKET NO: ....TICKET VALUE: ....
SEND BILL TO: USAFAC ATTN:FINCH,INDIANAPOLIS,IN 42649 FISCAL DATA: 1AE1

SIGNATURE OF TRAVELER: ....
FIRST CARRIER AGENT: FOLLOW ABOVE DIRECTIONS & RETAIN THIS SECTION
16:37 EST

MGMCOMP MGM

Select Bibliography

MANUSCRIPT SOURCES

National Archives of the United States, Washington, D.C.
Record Group 319—Records of the Army Staff (Records of the Executive for Reserve and ROTC Affairs; Records of the Chief, Army Reserve [1922–1954])
Record Group 407—Records of the Adjutant General, United States Army
Washington National Records Center, Suitland, Md.
Record Group 319—Records of the Army Staff (Records of the Cief, Army Reserve)
National Archives and Records Center, National Personnel Records Center, St. Louis, Mo. (Personnel Records of Individual Reservists)
Desert Shield/Desert Storm Files, U.S. Army Center of Military History, Washington, D.C.
Oral History Interview Files, U.S. Army Center of Military History, Washington, D.C.
United States Army Reserve Personnel Center (ARPERCEN) Files, St. Louis, Mo.

NOTE: Copies of all documents designated as "in possession of the author" have been placed in the files of the Command Historian, United States Army Reserve Command (USARC), Atlanta, Ga.

INTERVIEWS

Capt. Acie Angel, ARPERCEN, by Lt. Col. James T. Currie, June 23, 1992. Notes in possession of the author.

Maj. Michael Antonelli, ARPERCEN, by Lt. Col. James T. Currie, June 23, 1992. Notes in possession of the author.

Col. Milton Barall (USAR-Ret.) by Maj. James T. Currie, February 4, 1983.

Col. A.S. Behrman (USAR-Ret.) by Maj. James T. Currre, April 11, 1983.

Gen. Edwin C. Burba, FORSCOM, by Lt. Col. James T. Currie, June 29, 1992. Notes in possession of the author.

Capt. Kenneth Carson (USAR-Ret.) by Maj. James T. Currie, April 1, 1983.

Col. Richard B. Crossland, U.S. Army Soldier Support Center, by Col. Arthur R. Samuel and Dr. Stephen E. Bower, April 3 and July 2–3, 1991. Published as typescript "End of-Tour Oral History Interview. In possession of the author.

Desert Shield/Desert Storm Oral History Interviews, U.S. Army Center of Military History.

Lt. Col. D.Y. Dunn (USAR-Ret.) by Lt. Col. Richard B. Crossland, April 23, 1983.

Andrew Effron, Counsel, United States Senate, Committee on Armed Services, by Lt. Col. James T. Currie, December 21, 1993. Notes in possession of the author.

William S. Fulton, Jr. Clerk of Court, U.S. Army Judiciary by Lt. Col. James T. Currie, November 8, 1995. Notes in possession of the author.

Col. Frank B. Gregory (AUS-Ret.) by Maj. James T. Currie, July 27, 1983.

Mike Hamer, FORSCOM, by Lt. Col. James T. Currie, June 29, 1992. Notes in possession of the author.

Capt. Mary Hughes by Lt. Col. James T. Currie, February 22, 1994. Notes in possession of the author.

Maj. John G. Kramb, ARPERCEN, by Lt. Col. James T. Currie, June 22, 1992. Notes in possession of the author.

Gladys Maeser, ARPERCEN, by Lt. Col. James T. Currie, June 23, 1992. Notes in possession of the author.

Charles V. Nahlik, ARPERCEN, by Lt. Col. James T. Currie, June 23, 1992. Notes in possession of the author.

Gen. William R. Richardson by Kathryn Roe Coker, July 12, 1993. Published in *Founders of the USARC.* Atlanta: USARC. 1994.

Col. Ray Ruppert by Lt. Col. James T. Currie, January 12, 1994. Notes in possession of the author.

Col. John A. Topper by Kathryn Roe Coker, June 16, 1993. Published in *Founders of the USARC*. Atlanta: USARC, 1994.

Col. John A. Topper, FORSCOM, by Lt. Col. James T. Currie, June 29–30, 1992. Notes in possession of the author.

Hon. Robert M. Walker, Assistant Secretary of the Army for Installations, Logistics, and Environment, by Col. James T. Currie, December 5, 1995. Notes in possession of the author.

Lt. Col. Sue Walker (USAR-Ret.) by Maj. James T. Currie, June 27, 1983.

Maj. Jo Wood by Lt. Col. James T. Currie, December 11, 1990. Notes in possession of the author.

LETTERS TO THE AUTHOR

Dr. Walter B. Edgar, Professor of History and Director, Institute for Southern Studies, University of South Carolina, to Lt. Col. James T. Currie, July 21, 1992. Letter in possession of the author.

Harold Gallman, 412th Engineer Command, to Lt. Col. James T. Currie, December 16, 1993. Letter in possession of the author.

Sgt. Pamela J. Kamm, 452nd General Supply Co., to Lt. Col. James T. Currie, no date. Letter in possession of the author.

Maj. Michael E. Long, 360th Civil Affairs Brigade, to Lt. Col. James T. Currie, July 9, 1992. Letter in possession of the author.

Sgt. 1st. Class Dominick Merced, AMEDDC&S, to Col. James T. Currie, October 2, 1995. Letter in possession of the author.

Lt. Col. Mike Moose to Lt. Col. James T. Currie, April 24, 1994. Letter in possession of the author.

SSgt. Ralph J. Page, 998th Supply Co., to Lt. Col. James T. Currie, November 5, 1992. Letter in possession of the author.

Col. Walter D. Pidgeon to Lt. Col. James T. Currie, August 3, 1992. Letter in possession of the author.

Dr. Richard W. Stewart, Special Operations Command, to Lt. Col. James T. Currie. Letter in possession of the author.

Maj. Jo Wood, 365th Evacuation Hospital, to Lt. Col. James T. Currie, February 28, 1991. Letter in possession of the author.

COMPTROLLER GENERAL (GENERAL ACCOUNTING OFFICE) REPORTS

Army Acquisition: Contract for the Reserve Component Automation System. (Report No. GAO/NSIAD–93–5, November 1992).

The Army's Ability to Mobilize and Use Retirees as Planned Is Doubtful. (Report No. FPCD–83–6, 1982).

Army Force Structure: Future Reserve Roles Shaped by New Strategy, Base Force Mandates, and the Gulf War. (December 15, 1992).

Can the Army and Air Force Reserve Support the Active Forces Effectively? (Report No. LCD–79–404, 1979).

Critical Manpower Problems Restrict the Use of National Guard and Reserve Forces. (Report No. FPCD–79–71, dated 20 August 1979).

Operation Desert Storm: Full Army Medical Capability Not Achieved. (Report No. GAO/NSIAD–92–175, August 1992).

Personnel Problems May Hamper Army's Individual Ready Reserve in Wartime. (Report No. FPCD–83–12).

Report to the Chairman, Subcommittee on Military Personnel and Compensation, Committee on Armed Services, House of Representatives. Army Force Structure: Future Reserve Roles Shaped by New Strategy, Base Force, and Gulf War. (Report No. GAO/NSIAD–93–80, December 1992).

Reserve Forces: Aspects of the Army's Equipping Strategy Hamper Reserve Readiness. (Report No. GAO/NSIAD–93–11, February 1993).

CONGRESSIONAL HEARINGS, PRINTS, AND PUBLIC LAWS

Conference Report No. 101–345. *To Accompany H.R. 3072, Making Appropriations for the Department of Defense for the Fiscal Year Ending September 30, 1990, and for other purposes.* United States House of Representatives, 101st Congress, 1st session.

Conference Report No. 101–923. *To Accompany the Department of Defense Authorization Act for Fiscal Year 1991.* United States House of Representatives, 101st Congress.

Conference Report No. 101–938. *To accompany H.R. 5308, a bill Making Appropriations for the Department of Defense [FY 1991].* United States House of Representatives, 101st Congress, 2d session.

Conference Report No. 103–357. *To Accompany H.R. 2401, National Defense Authorization Act for Fiscal Year 1994.* United States House of Representatives, 103d Congress, 1st session.

Conference Report 103–701. *To Accompany S. 2182, National Defense Authorization Act for Fiscal Year 1995.* United States House of Representatives, 103d Congress, 2d session.

Conference Report. *To Accompany H.R. 3072, a bill Making Appropriations for the Department of Defense for the Fiscal Year Ending September 30, 1990, and for other purposes.*

Department of Defense Appropriations for 1992, Part 2. United States House of Representatives, Defense Subcommittee, Committee on Appropriations, 102d Congress, 1st session.

Department of Defense Appropriations for 1992, Part 3. United States House of Representatives, Defense Subcommittee, Committee on Appropriations, 102d Congress, 1st session.

Department of Defense Appropriations for 1992, Part 8. United States House of Representatives, Defense Subcommittee, Committee on Appropriations, 102d Congress, 1st session.

Examine Mail Service to the Persian Gulf. United States House of Representatives, Committee on Post Office and Civil Service, 101st Congress, 2d session.

Free Mailing Privileges for the Armed Forces Deployed in the Persian Gulf. United States House of Representatives, Committee on Post Office and Civil Service, 101st Congress, 2d session.

Hearings before the Committee on Armed Services. House of Representatives, 83d Congress, 1st session, Pursuant to H.R. 122, Reserve Officers Personnel Act.

H.A.S.C. Report No. 102–20. *Redeployment of Reserves from Operation Desert Storm.* United States House of Representatives. Hearing before the Military Personnel and Compensation Subcommittee, Committee on Armed Services, 102d Congress, 1st session, April 18, 1991.

H.A.S.C. Report No. 102–34. *Reserve Demobilization Problems.* United States House of Representatives, Committee on Armed Services, 102d Congress, 1st session, December 30, 1991.

H.R. 4739, National Defense Authorization Act for Fiscal Year 1991, 101st Congress.

House Report No. 103–200. *National Defense Authorization Act for Fiscal Year 1994.* United States House of Representatives, 103d Congress, 1st session.

House Report No. 103–499. *National Defense Authorization Act for Fiscal Year 1995.* United States House of Representatives, 103d Congress, 2d session.

Merger of the Army Reserve Components. Subcommittee No. 2, Committee on Armed Services, United States House of Representatives. Washington: GPO, 1965.

National Defense Authorization Act for Fiscal Year 1987, Public Law 99–661.

National Defense Authorization Act, Fiscal Year 1991, Title III, Operations and Maintenance. Hearings on H.R. 4739. United States House of Representatives, Readiness Subcommittee, House Armed Services Committee, 101st Congress, 2d session.

National Defense Authorization Act for Fiscal Year 1991, Public Law 101–510.

National Defense Authorization Act for Fiscal Years 1992 and 1993. Public Law 102–190.

National Defense Authorization Act for Fiscal Year 1993. Public Law 102–484.

National Defense Authorization Act for Fiscal Year 1994. Public Law 103–160.

Persian Gulf Conflict Supplemental Authorization and Personnel Benefits Act of 1991. Public Law 102–25.

Report No. 101–384, Department of Defense Authorization Act for Fiscal Year 1991. United States Senate, 101st Congress.

Report No. 101–665, Department of Defense Authorization Act for Fiscal Year 1991. United States House of Representatives, 101st Congress.

Report No. 102–5. *Parenting Issues of Operation Desert Storm.* United States House of Representatives, Subcommittee on Military Personnel and Compensation, Committee on Armed Services, 102d Congress, 1st session.

Report No. 103–200. *To Accompany H.R. 2401, National DefenseAuthorization Act for Fiscal Year 1994.* United States House of Representatives, 103d Congress, 1st session.

Report No. 103–499. *To Accompany H.R. 4301, May 10, 1994.* United States House of Representatives, 103d Congress, 2d session.

Report No. 103–701. *National Defense Authorization Act for Fiscal Year 1995.* United States House of Representatives, 103d Congress, 2d session.

Report of Subcommittee No. 3 on Military Posture. Committee on Armed Services, United States House of Representatives, 87th Congress. Washington: GPO, 1962.

Reserve Officer Personnel Management Act. Title XVI of Public Law 103–337, National Defense Authorization Act for Fiscal Year 1995.

Uniformed Services Employment and Reemployment Rights Act of 1994. Public Law 103–353.

United States-Vietnam Relations, 1945–1967. Twelve Volumes. Printed for the use of the House Committee on

Armed Services. Washington: GPO, 1971. "The Pentagon Papers."

Veterans' Benefits Act of 1992. Public Law 102–568.

BOOKS AND MONOGRAPHS

A Chronological History of Our Reserve Components. Compiled by an *ad hoc* group from OCMH, NGB, CORC, and OCAR, 19 Nov 1965, at the request of Lt. Col. John P. Parker, Projects Division, DC & A, Office of the Chief of Staff, Army. (Copy in CMH Files).

Adkins, Mark (Maj.) *Urgent Fury: The Battle for Grenada.* Lexington, Mass: Lexington Books, 1989.

Ambrose, Stephen E. *Upton and the Army.* Baton Rouge: Louisiana State University Press, 1964.

ANDRULIS Research Corporation. *Personnel Service Support.* Unpublished manuscript prepared for the Chief, Army Reserve.

Association of the United States Army. *A Status Report on the Army National Guard and the United States Army Reserve.* Arlington: AUSA, 1980.

Baskir, Lawrence M. and Strauss, William A. *Chance and Circumstance: The Draft, the War, and the Vietnam Generation.* New York: Alfred A. Knopf, 1978.

Berger, Carl. *Broadcasts and Bayonets.* San Rafael, Calif: Presidio Press, 1976.

Bilbo, Jon F. (Lt. Col.) *Enemy Prisoners of War (EPW) Operations during Operation Desert Storm.* Unpublished typescript prepared at the U.S. Army War College. Available through the Defense Technical Information Center.

Bradley, Omar N. (Gen. of the Army) and Blair, Clay. *A General's Life: An Autobiography.* New York: Simon and Schuster, 1983.

Brayton, Abbot A. *Military Mobilization and International Politics.* Unpublished Ph.D. dissertation, University of Arizona, 1971.

Brinkerhoff, John R. *United States Army Reserve in Operation Desert Storm: Civil Affairs in the War with Iraq.* Washington: Office of the Chief, Army Reserve, 1991.

———. *United States Army Reserve in Operation Desert Storm: The Case of the Unit That Was not Called: The 377th Theater Army Area Command.* Washington: Office of the Chief, Army Reserve, 1991.

———. *United States Army Reserve in Operation Desert Storm: Countering the Terrorist Threat: The 3d Battal-*

Endicott, John E. and Stafford, Roy W. (eds.). *American Defense Policy.* 4th Ed. Baltimore: The Johns Hopkins University Press, 1977.

Examples of How the CAPSTONE Trace Was Broken. Typescript manuscript in the Desert Shield/Desert Storm files of the U.S. Army Center of Military History.

1st COSCOM. *1st COSCOM Public Affairs—After Action Report, Operation Desert Shield/Operation Desert Storm.* Unpaginated and unpublished typescript report. Copy in possession of the author.

Fishel, John T. *The Fog of Peace: Planning and Executing the Restoration of Panama.* Carlisle, Pa.: Strategic Studies Institute, U.S. Army War College, 1992.

416th Engineer Command. *Command History Report: Operation Desert Storm, 416th Engineer Command, 17 January 1991 Through 1 April 1991.* Typescript. Copy in U.S. Army Center of Military History.

Galloway, Eilene. *History of the United States Military Policy on Reserve Forces, 1775-1957.* Washington: GPO, 1957. Prepared for use of the Committees on Armed Services.

Gerard, Francis R. (Maj. Gen.). *A Long-Range Look at the Future of the Army and Air National Guard.* Washington: National Guard Bureau, 1982.

Goldich, Robert L. *Army Reserve Component Reforms and the Bottom-Up Review: Issues for Congress.* Congressional Research Service Report, May 10, 1994.

Goodpaster, Andrew J. (Gen.). *Toward a Consensus on Military Service.* New York: Pergamon Press, 1982.

Gray, Gordon (Chairman). *Reserve Forces for National Security.* Washington: Department of Defense, 1948. This is the "Gray Board Report."

Hagood, Johnson (Maj. Gen.). *Can We Defend America?* Garden City. NY: Doubleday, Doran & Co., 1937.

Halberstam, David. *The Best and the Brightest.* New York: Random House. 1969, 1971, 1972.

Harrison, Gordon A. *United States Army in World War II. The European Theater of Operations. Cross-Channel Attack.* Washington: Office of the Chief of Military History, Department of the Army, 1951.

Heinl, Robert D., Jr. *Dictionary of Military and Naval Quotations.* Annapolis: Naval Institute, 1966.

Hewes, James E., Jr. *From Root to McNamara: Army Organization and Administration.* Special Studies Series. Washington: Center of Military History, United States Army, 1975.

Higham, Robin (ed.). *A Guide to the Sources of United States Military History.* Hamden, Conn.: Archon Books, 1975.

Holley, I.B., Jr. *General John M. Palmer, Citizen Soldiers, and the Army of Democracy.* Westport, Conn. and London: Greenwood Press, 1982.

Johnson, Lyndon Baines. *The Vantage Point: Perspectives of the Presidency, 1963–1969.* New York, Chicago, and San Francisco: Holt, Rinehart, and Winston, 1971.

Joint Chiefs of Staff. *The History of the Joint Chiefs of Staff. The Joint Chiefs of Staff and the War in Vietnam, 1960–1968, Part II.* Historical Division, Joint Secretariat, Joint Chiefs of Staff. This is an unpublished study that is currently classified TOP SECRET.

Kauffmann, William W. *The McNamara Strategy.* New York: Harper and Row, 1964.

Kriedberg, Marvin A. (Lt. Col.) and Henry, Merton G. (1st. Lt.). *History of Military Mobilization in the United States Army, 1775–1945.* Washington: Department of the Army, 1955. (DA Pam 20–212).

Kropp, Anthony R. (Col.) *Engineers Build for Victory in Operation Desert Storm.* Unpaginated and unpublished manuscript in possession of the author.

Lee, Gus C. and Parker, Geoffrey Y. *Ending the Draft: The Story of the All Volunteer Force.* Alexandria, Va: Human Resources Research Organization, 1977.

Lenahan, Rod. *Operation JUST CAUSE: The U.S. Intervention in Panama.* Washington: National Defense University Press, 1995.

Levantrosser, William F. (Col., USAR). *Congress and the Citizen Soldier: Legislative Policy-making for the Federal Armed Forces Reserve.* Colimbus, Ohio: Ohio State University Press. 1967.

Lynch, Charles M., *et al. The Medical Department of the United States Army in the World War.* Washington: GPO, 1923.

Marshall, George C. (Gen. of the Army). *The Winning of the War in Europe and the Pacific.* Washington: War Department, 1945.

Matloff, Maurice (Gen. ed.). *American Military History.* Washington: Office of the Chief of Military History, United States Army, 1969.

Meditz, Sandra W. and Hanratty, Dennis M. (eds.) *Panama: A Country Study.* Washington: GPO, 1989.

O'Connor, Raymond G. (ed.). *American Defense Policy in Perspective: From Colonial Times to the Present.* New York: John Wiley & Sons, Inc., 1965.

Office of the Chief of Military History, Department of the Army. *Historical Résumé, Division Force Structure, Active and Reserve, 1935–1963.* Copy in CMH Files.

Office of the Chief of Military History, Department of the Army. *Problems Encountered in Bringing Units up to Strength and Condition of Readiness for Korea.* Copy on microfilm, CMH.

123d U.S. Army Reserve Command. *Annual Historical Summary, 123d U.S. Army Reserve Command, FY 1991.* Typescript. Copy in U.S. Army Center of Military History.

Order of Battle, United States Army, World War II, European Theater of Operations, Divisions. Paris: United States Army, 1945. Copy in Army Library, The Pentagon.

Pagonis, William G. (Lt. Gen.) with Cruikshank, Jeffrey L. *Moving Mountains: Lessons in Leadership and Logistics from the Gulf War.* Boston: Harvard Business School Press, 1992.

Palmer, Gerald A. (Lt. Col.) *Army Medical Department Issues from Operation Desert Shield.* Unpublished typescript available through the Defense Technical Information Center.

Palmer, John McAuley (Brig. Gen.). *America in Arms.* New Haven: Yale University Press, 1941.

Palmer, Robert R., Wiley. Bell I., and Keast, William R. *United States Army in World War II. The Army Ground Forces. The Procurement and Training of Ground Combat Troops.* Washington: Historical Division, Department of the Army, 1948.

Pate, Robert I. *U.S. Army Reserve Components—Peacetime Assessment and Management to Meet Mobilization Requirements.* Unpublished Paper, U.S. Army War College. Copy in Army Library, The Pentagon.

Perry, Ralph Barton. *The Plattsburg Movement.* New York: Dutton, 1921.

Pew, Frank W. *The Role of the U.S. Army Forces Command in Project New Arrivals: Reception and Care of Refugees from Vietnam.* Fort McPherson. Ga.: U.S. Army Forces Command, 1981.

Powicke, Michael. *Military Obligation in Medieval England: A Study in Liberty & Duty.* Oxford: Clarendon Press, 1962.

Public Papers of the Presidents of the United States. Lyndon B. Johnson. Containing the Public Messages, Speeches, and Statements of the President, 1965, II. Washington: GPO, 1966.

Public Papers of the Presidents of the United States. Lyndon B. Johnson. Containing the Public Messages, Speeches, and Statements of the President, 1968–69. I. Washington: GPO, 1970.

Riker, William H. *Soldiers of the States: The Role of the National Guard in American Democracy.* Washington: Public Affairs Press, 1957.

Risch, Erna. *Special Studies. Supplying Washington's Army.* Washington: Center of Military History, United States Army, 1981.

Salmond, John A. *The Civilian Conservation Corps, 1933–1945: A New Deal Case Study.* Durham: Duke University Press, 1967.

Sarnoff, David (Brig. Gen.). *Final Report to the Congress, National Security Training Commission.* Washington: GPO, 1957.

Scales, Robert H., Jr. (Brig. Gen.) *Certain Victory: United States Army in the Gulf War.* Washington: Office of the Chief of Staff, United States Army, 1993.

Schaefer, Mason. *The Military Traffic Management Command's CONUS Port Operations during Operation Desert Shield/Storm, 1990–91.* Typescript. Washington: MTMC History Office, 1991.

Schnabel, James F. *United States Army in the Korean War. Policy and Direction: The First Year.* Washington: Office of the Chief of Military History, United States Army, 1972.

Schnabel, James F. and Watson, Robert J. *The History of the Joint Chiefs of Staff. The Joint Chiefs of Staff and National Policy. Volume III—The Korean War, Part I.* Unpublished.

Schubert, Frank N. and Kraus, Theresa (eds.) *The Whirlwind War: The United States Army in Operations Desert Shield and Desert Storm.* Washington: U.S. Army Center of Military History, 1994.

77th U.S. Army Reserve Command. *The 77th Army Reserve Command Goes to War: A History of Unit Involvement in Operations Desert Shield and Desert Storm, 1990–91.* Unpaginated typescript. Copy in U.S. Army Center of Military History.

77th ARCOM. *Welcoming Home Ceremony for 74th Field Hospital and 316th Medical Detachment.* Copy in OCAR Historical File.

77th ARCOM. *Welcome Home Ceremony, 237th Field Maintenance Company.* Copy in OCAR Historical File.

Sharpe, A.C. (Lt. Col.). *Making a Soldier.* Cleveland: The Acme Publishing Co., 1908.

Sherry, Michael S. *Preparing for the Next War: American Plans for Postwar Defense, 1941–45.* New Haven and London: Yale University Press. 1977.

Sifry, Micah L. and Cerf, Christopher. *Gulf War Reader: History, Documents, Opinions.* New York: Random House, 1991.

Sparrow, John C. (Maj.). *History of Personnel Demobilization in the United States Army.* Office of the Chief of Military History, United States Army, 1951.

Spector, Ronald H. (Lt. Col.) *U.S. Marines in Grenada.* Washington: Headquarters, U.S. Marine Corps, 1987.

Stebbins, Richard P. *The United States in World Affairs, 1961.* New York: Harper & Brothers, 1962.

Stillwaugh, Elva (Maj.). *Personnel Policies in the Korean Conflict.* Unpublished manuscript, microfilm, CMH.

Taylor, Maxwell D. (Gen.). *The Uncertain Trumpet.* New York: Harper & Brothers, 1960.

Taylor, William J. *et al. Defense Manpower Planning: Issues for the 1980s.* New York: Pergamon Press, 1981.

310th Theater Army Area Command (Fort Belvoir, Va.) *REEFEX: A Special Edition of the Gray Ghost.* Published by the 310th TAACOM, October 1994.

377th Theater Army Area Command (New Orleans, La.) *377th TAACOM Orientation Booklet.*

Treadwell, Mattie E. *United States Army in World War II. Special Studies. The Women's Army Corps.* Washington: Office of the Chief of Military History, Department of the Army, 1954.

Trewhitt, Henry L. *McNamara.* New York: Harper & Row, 1971.

U.S. Army Reserve Personnel Center (ARPERCEN). *Desert Shield/Desert Storm: A History.* St. Louis: ARPERCEN. Undated (1992?).

U.S. News & World Report. *Triumph without Victory: The Unreported History of the Persian Gulf War.* New York: Random House, 1992.

Upton, Emory (Maj. Gen.). *The Military Policy of the United States.* Washington: GPO, 1916.

Watson, Mark Skinner. *United States Army in World War II. The War Department. Chief of Staff: Prewar Plans and Preparations.* Washington: Historical Division, United States Army, 1950.

Weekly Compilation of Presidential Documents, Vol. 27, No. 3, January 21, 1991.

Weigley, Russell F. *History of the United States Army.* New York and London: Macmillan Publishing Co., Inc. and Collier Macmillan Publishers, 1967.

———. *Towards an American Army: Military Thought from Washington to Marshall.* Westport, Conn.: Greenwood Press, 1962.

Weinberger, Caspar W. (Chairman). *A Report to the President on the Status and Prospects of the All-Volunteer Force.* Washington, 1982. Military Manpower Task Force.

Westmoreland, William C. (Gen.). *A Soldier Reports.* Garden City, NY: Doubleday and Company, Inc., 1976.

Whisker, James B. *The Citizen Soldier and U.S. Military Policy.* North River Press, 1979.

Wood, Leonard (Maj. Gen.). *Our Military History, Its Facts and Fallacies.* Chicago: Reilly and Britton, 1916.

Wright, Robert K., Jr. *Army Lineage Series. The Continental Army.* Washington: Center of Military History, 1983.

———. (ed.). *The American Military: Readings in the History of the Military in American Society.* Reading, Mass.: Addison-Wesley Publishing Co., 1969.

Zurcher, Louis A. and Harris-Jenkins, Gwyn (eds.). *Supplementary Militias, Auxiliaries.* Beverly Hills, Calif.: Sage Publications, 1978.

ARTICLES

"Action Shifts to Ecuador for 'Abriendo Rutas.'" *Army Reserve Magazine*, Vol. 33, No. 3 (1987), p. 25.

Adams, David (Sgt.) "Comforting the Island of Comoros." *Army Reserve Magazine*, Vol. 40, No. 1, (1993), pp. 22–23.

Adams, Paul (Lt. Col.), "Bolivian Smiles." *Army Reserve Magazine*, Vol. 40, No. 1 (1993), pp. 24–25.

"Address by Senator Margaret Chase Smith to the 29th National Convention, Reserve Officers Association." *The Reserve Officer*, August 1955, pp. 12–13, 19.

Adelsberger, Bernard J., "Budget Crunch Forces Reserves to Scrap Active Duty Tours." *Army Times*, August 7, 1989, p. 3.

———. "Selected Reserve Call-Up Passes Muster." *Army Times*, November 9, 1987, pp. 14–15.

———. "Leaders: Keep drawdowns on schedule." *Army Times*, March 14, 1994, p. 3.

"Administration Struggles to Clarify Gulf Objectives." *The Washington Post*, November 15, 1990, p. A28.

"AGF Initiates Reserve Training Mobilization in Six Army Areas." *The Reserve Officer*, August 1946, pp. 7–9, 30–31.

Allen, Jim. "Desert Shield was 'family affair' for some." *Army Reserve Magazine*, Vol. 36, No. 4 (1990), p. 21.

"Army Court Asked to Nullify Conviction in Gulf Desertion." *The Washington Post*, February 24, 1993, p. A6.

"Army Reserve faces major restructuring of Forces." *Army Reserve Magazine*, Vol. 39, No. 4 (1993/94), p. 5.

"Army Reservists Welcomed Home from Vietnam Tour." *The State* (Columbia, SC). August 15, 1969.

"Army Transporters Take Virtual Control of Marine Terminal." *Norfolk Virginia-Pilot*, September 20, 1990, p. 2.

"Army Trims Command Structure." *CARNotes*, July–August 1983, p.1.

"Army's Revision of Reserve Units and Guard Begins." *New York Times*, December 5, 1962, pp. 1, 25.

ARNEWS, "U.S., Honduran Engineers Work Together in Latest Road-Building Exercise." *Army Reserve Magazine*, Vol. 34, No. 1 (1988), p. 25.

"Around the Nation." *The Washington Post*, November 3, 1993, p. A7.

Arthur, Billy A. "Clio in Desert Shield and Desert Storm." *Army History: The Professional Bulletin of Army History*, Spring 1991, p. 13.

Associated Press. "Army Doctor Sentenced in Desertion Case." *The Washington Post*, August 10, 1991, p. A5.

"At 48 She Answered Call to Vietnam War." *Messenger* (Madison, NC). March 30, 1983.

"Awards for Vietnam Service." *Army Reserve Magazine*, January 1970, p. 7.

Baratz, Max (Maj. Gen.). "Creating the future Reserve." *Army Reserve Magazine*, Vol. 40, No. 2 (1994), p. 4.

Barnes, Rudolph C. (Maj.) "Grenada Revisited." *The Officer*, July 1985, pp. 14–17.

Beecher, William. "Pentagon to Cut Use of Draftees in Fast Build-Ups. *New York Times*, September 9, 1970, p. 1.

"The Big Slice." *The National Guardsman*, May 1962, pp. 6–7.

Benezra, Mark (Maj.) "Unit Troops Train Soldiers in Basics." *Army Reserve Magazine*, Vol. 30, No. 1 (1984), pp. 14–15.

"Bold Shift Maintains War-fighting Edge of Active Army and USAR Units, Improves Training Initiatives and Advances Total Army Cohesion." *CARNOTES*, May–June 1992, p. 3.

Boldt, David R. "Reserve: Force or Farce?" *The Washington Post*, September 4, 1972, p. 1.

Bolinger, Donna. "Grenada: The Mission Continues." *The Voice*, June 1984, p. 3.

"Boston Reservists Fight Viet Duty." *Boston Herald-Traveler*, October 4, 1968, p. 1.

"Boston Unit Returns from Viet." *Sunday Herald-Traveler* (Boston). October 5, 1969, p. 1.

Bottin, Robert R., Jr. (Maj.), and Fowler, Jimmy E. (Maj.) "Reserve Engineer Command: Helping Latin America." *Engineer*, November 1992, p. 6.

Bottin, Robert R., Jr. (Maj.) "412th Engineers Train in Central and SouthAmerica," *Open Channels*, Spring 1991, pp. 12–13.

Briggs, O.D. (Cdr.), and Rowley, Doug (Sgt.) "USAR Artillery Unit Trains with Navy Attack Fighters." *Army Reserve Magazine*, Vol. 34, No. 1 (1988), pp. 16–17.

Briola, Pam. "We got us a Golden Cargo convoy." *Ar ny Reserve Magazine*, Vol. 38, No. 2 (1992), pp. 24–25.

Britton, Christine F. "First Army Units Train in Golden Thrust '88." *Army Reserve Magazine*, Vol. 34, No. 1 (1988), p. 18.

Brodsky, Lew and Miller, Tim. "Grenada: USAR Takes on Vital Schools Mission." *Army Reserve Magazine*, Vol. 31, No. 3 (1985), p. 145.

Brown, Terry (Master Sgt.) "324th DPU personnel help speed relief supplies to Somalia." *The Reserve Voice*, Spring 1993, pp. 1, 7.

———. "Army Reserve fuelers complete tank missions." *The Reserve Voice*, Spring 1993, p. 3.

———. "Focus of training changes as result of Persian Gulf War." *The Reserve Voice*, Spring 1993, p. 1.

———. "Reservists help hurricane survivors recover, rebuild." *The Reserve Voice*, Spring 1993, pp. 1, 4–5.

———. "Infantrymen outsmart opposition in Nordic Shield II." *The Reserve Voice*, Spring 1993, p. 7.

———. "619th Transportation Co. hauls ammunition in Gulf Area." *The Reserve Voice*, Vol. 20, No. 3 (Summer 1991), p. 4.

"Building the Strength of the Army Reserve." *Army Reservist*, November 1963, pp. 3–4.

Bundgard, James (CWO). "State-of-the-Art Ships Join Army Reserve." *Army Reserve Magazine*, Vol. 39, No. 2 (1993), p. 25.

Butler, Keith (SSgt.) "Uncivil Affairs." *Army Reserve Magazine*, Vol. 39, No. 2 (1993), pp. 24–25.

———. "Cobra Gold." *Army Reserve Magazine*, Vol. 39, No. 3 (1993), pp. 18–19.

Cabell, Bruce. "Budget helps Reserve battle lack of gear." *Army Times*, January 30, 1989, p. 24.

Carney, Larry. "FORSCOM Told to Increase Command's Control." *Army Times*, May 2, 1983, p. 3.

———. "DoD Seeks Funding for IRR Muster Test." *Army Times*, September 15, 1986, p. 8.

———. "Hill Panel Wants to Fill Some AGR Slots." *Army Times*, August 4, 1986, p. 42.

———. "Reserve Strength in Europe to Increase to 4000." *Army Times*, August 5, 1985, p. 25.

———. "20 Reservists Serving in Grenada." *Army Times*, December 19, 1983, p. 37.

Chamberlin, Ro. "Boston Medics provide 'echelons-above-corps' support." *Army Reserve Magazine*, Vol. 38, No. 1 (1992), p. 14.

Checcia, Elizabeth (Maj.) "Task Force Russia." *Army Reserve Magazine*, Vol. 40, No. 1 (1993), pp. 10–11.

"Choices Available to Fulfill Enlisted Service Obligation." *Army Information Digest,* February 1956, pp. 36–37.

"Citations Go to 319th at Ceremony." *The Augusta* [Georgia] *Chronicle,* August 20, 1969.

Colby, Elbridge. "Elihu Root and the National Guard." *Military Affairs,* Spring 1959, pp. 28–34, 20.

Conder, Terry L. (Sgt.) "Reserve Signallers Take Part in Natural Team IV." *Army Reserve Magazine*, Vol. 34, No. 4 (1988), p. 21.

"Congress and the Department of Defense fix long-running 'gray area' shortfalls." *Army Reserve Magazine*, Vol. 36, No. 4 (1990), p. 7.

Covington, Benjamin W., III (Col.) "Reserves and Active Army: Mission is theSame, Challenges Different." *Army* (July 1988), pp. 39–42.

Cox, Frank (SSgt.) "USAR-Europe Unique." *The Officer*, (March 1985), pp. 21–24.

Crossland, Richard B. (Maj.). "RDJTF: Can It Get There Without the USAR." *Army Reserve Magazine,* Spring 1982, pp. 8–10.

———. "Suppose the Balloon Goes Up: Then What?" *Army Reserve Magazine,* Winter 1981, pp. 24–27.

Crossland, Richard B. (Col.) "Historical Report—RCAG—July–December 1990." Typescript in possession of the author.

Crosson, Cynthia (Capt.) "DALIS: Designed for disasters." *Army Reserve Magazine*, Vol. 38, No. 3 (1992), pp. 18–19.

Cummings, Thomas (Capt.) "Putting the IRR into ROTC." *Army Reserve Magazine*, Vol. 39, No. 4 (1993/94), pp. 14–15.

Currie, James T. "Fish Tanks." *Army Reserve Magazine*, Vol. 40, No. 3 (1994), pp. 15–17.

Darwin, Joyce (SSgt.) "*Fuertes Caminos* '88." *Army Reserve Magazine*, Vol. 34, No. 3 (1988), pp. 14–17.

Dawson, Nick (Col.) "Supreme Court decision supports reserve training." *Army Reserve Magazine*, Vol. 38, No. 1 (1992), pp. 8–9.

Deiml, Greg (SSgt.); Dunn, Donald (SSgt.); Simmons, Annie (Maj.); Adams, Paul (Lt. Col.); and ARNEWS. "Disaster." *Army Reserve Magazine*, Vol. 38, No. 3 (1992), pp. 14–17.

Detzky, Michael. "Military Code of Justice Revised." *Army Times*, January 25, 1988, p. 55.

"Dissidents in Uniform: Supreme Court Rejects Challenge." *Boston Herald-Traveler*, October 8, 1968, p. 1.

Dove, Diane. "Costa Abajo '86." *Army Reserve Magazine*, Vol. 32, No. 4 (1986), pp. 23–26.

Edens, Frank A. (Col.) "MACOM Status '93 Goal." *The Officer*, June 1993, p. 22.

———. "Major Command or Major Subordinate Command Is Question for Army Reserve." *The Officer*, December 1992, pp. 35–37.

"Eisenhower, Dwight D. (Gen.). "The Reserve Component and Our Future Security." *The Reserve Officer*, July 1946. pp. 9–10.

"European ARCOM gets first general officer." *Army Reserve Magazine*, Vol. 36, No. 3 (1990), p. 7.

Evans, David. "Reservists may stay in gulf until '92." *Chicago Tribune*, April26, 1991, p. 5.

"Exercise Reveals Defense Problems." *Pentagram News*, July 31, 1980, pp. 1–4.

Fenstermacher, Willard B. (Lt. Col.) "CAPSTONE Relationship Put to Test in Grenada." *The Officer*, February 1984, pp. 21–24.

Fialka John J. "The Pentagon's Exercise Proud Spirit: Little Cause for Pride." *Parameters: Journal of the US Army War College*, Vol. XI, No. 1. pp. 38–41.

———. "U.S. Again Fails Test of Ability to Mobilize." *Washington Star*, December 21. 1980, pp. A–1 and 6.

"Fight Is Brewing on Reserve Role." *New York Times*, December 17, 1961, p. 17.

"The Fires of Patriotism and Cold Necessity Put 13 in Harm's Way." *New York Times*, March 4, 1991, p. A12.

"First Army Reservists Find Themselves 'Doing Real Thing' at Fort Indiantown Gap." *The Officer*, August 1980, p. 12.

Fonseca, Ernesto (Maj.) and Garcia, Luis M. (Lt. Col.) "It's Back to School for 448th Engineers." *Army Reserve Magazine*, Vol. 33, No. 3 (1987), p. 18.

"FORSCOM chief discusses the future of the Army Reserve and the Bold Shift initiative in an exclusive interview." *Army Reserve Magazine* Vol. 38, No. 2 (1992), p. 13.

Freed, Ann (Capt.). "Exercise Orchid Sage 1989: USAR Holds One of the Largest Medical Exercises Ever." *Army Reserve Magazine*, Vol. 36, No. 1 (1990), p. 16.

———. "Reserves get larger role in battle on domestic ills." *Army Times*, July 25, 1994, p. 22.

———. "Reserves smiling in time of change." *Army Times*, January 4, 1993, p. 25.

———. "Reservist duty stints riling employers." *Army Times*, December 13, 1993, p. 22.

———. "Reservists win expanded job protection under new law." *Army Times*, October 31, 1994, p. 25.

———. "Too much of a good thing? Reservists getting leery about expanding active duty tours." *Army Times*, March 27, 1995, p. 22.

———. "War training gives way to real missions." *Army Times*, January 2, 1995, p. 34.

Matthews, William, and Peters, Katherine McIntire. "Reserve cuts 'old news' to those facing unit ax." *Army Times*, March 14, 1993, p. 3.

Maze, Rick. "Few Reservists Seen Using Commissaries." *Army Times*, November 17, 1986, p. 15.

———. "Officer personnel bill resurrected in House." *Army Times*, April 5, 1993, p. 14.

———. "Political clout shields Guard, Reserve from cuts." *Army Times*, October18, 1993, p. 19.

———. "Reserves Allowed to Choose Shopping Days." *Army Times*, October 27, 1986, p. 17.

———. "Shali voices concerns on separate commands." *Army Times* October 4, 1993, p. 24.

McCarthy, Colman. "Anti-War Doctor Under Fire." *The Washington Post* Health Magazine, November 30, 1993, p. 6

McChrystal, Eileen (Sgt.) "Chicago-based MP unit tackles job after job in the desert." *Army Reserve Magazine*, Vol. 38, No. 1 (1992), p. 17.

———. "Taming the Devil Hill." *Army Reserve Magazine*, Vol. 39, No. 4 (1993/94), p. 22.

McGee, Elaine. "Fire." *Army Reserve Magazine*, Vol. 39, No. 4 (1993/94), pp. 12–13.

McGurl, Michael L. (Capt.) "Medical Support Vital in Rugged Desert Climate." *Army Reserve Magazine*, Vol. 34, No. 1 (1988), p. 20.

McIntire, Katherine. See "Peters, Katherine McIntire."

Meier, Ed (Pvt.) "The Supporting Cast: It Takes More than Engineers to Build a Road." *Army Reserve Magazine*, Vol. 33, No. 2 (1987), p. 16.

"Mobilizing Individual Ready Reservists." *Army Logistician*, May–June 1991, pp. 22–25.

Montgomery, Gillespie V. (Rep.) "Greater Reliance on Reserve is Essential." *The Officer* (May 1992), pp. 23–26.

Moore, Bruce R. (Capt.) "Reservists Pave Way in Costa Rica." *Engineer Update*, July 1991, p. 11.

Moore, Kenneth (Capt.) "First Person Reflections on Panama." *Army Reserve Magazine*, Vol. 33, No. 1 (1986), pp. 18–19.

Moore, Linda (1st Lt.) "Guyana." *Army Reserve Magazine*, Vol. 39, No. 2 (1993), pp. 10–11.

"More on the Musters." *Army Reserve Magazine*, Vol. 33, No. 3 (1986), pp. 11–12.

Moss, Raymond L. (Col.) "Promoting democracy in Latin America." *Army Reserve Magazine*, Vol. 40, No. 3 (1994), pp. 20–21.

"Most in Congress Relieved by the President's Course." *New York Times*, July 29, 1965, p. 1.

Mott, Harry J. III (Brig. Gen.), "Reserve brass missing during restructuring." *Army Times*, March 7, 1994, p. 33.

Mowery, Jerry L. R. (Lt. Col.) "New Rules, Benefits Coming for Montgomery GI Bill." *Army Reserve Magazine*, Vol. 34, No. 4 (1988), p. 10.

Nelson, Soraya S. "Doctors pay high price for deployment." *Army Times*, October 18, 1993, p. 19.

"The New Arrivals." *Army Reserve Magazine*, November–December 1975, pp. 16–18.

"The New GI Bill—Yours to Use." *Army Reserve Magazine*, Vol. 33, No. 1 (1986), pp. 26–27.

"New law broadens access to support facilities for all Reservists and their families." *Army Reserve Magazine*, Vol. 36 , No. 4 (1990), p. 7.

"New shape of Army Reserve supports new missions." *Army Reserve Magazine*, Vol. 40, No. 2 (1994), p. 5.

Nielsen, James M. (Lt. Col.) "Moving the mail in Mogadishu." *Army Reserve Magazine*, Vol. 38, No. 4 (1992/93), p. 13.

———. "The Nation's Number One Reservist: Deborah R. Lee." *Army Reserve Magazine*, Vol. 39, No. 3 (1993), p. 13.

"Noted Doctors Join Army Medical Corps." *New York Times*, November 30, 1908.

Olsen, Dave (Sgt.) "Blazing Trails Medics Make a Difference." *Army Reserve Magazine*, Vol. 33, No. 2 (1987), p. 18.

"On a political map which seems to change its face daily, it's time to think about making a Bold Shift." *Army Reserve Magazine*, Vol. 38, No. 2 (1992), p. 12.

"Operation Desert Fix: After the 'hot war' in Iraq, it was a 'cold war' at Fort McCoy." *Army Reserve Magazine*, Vol. 38, No., 2 (1992), p. 18.

Pace, Frank, Jr. "The Reserve Forces of the Army." *The Reserve Officer*, March 1952, pp. 6–8, 22–23.

"Paid Drills for IMA Soldiers Being Explored." *Army Reserve Magazine*, Vol. 34, No. 4 (1988), p. 4.

Palmer, Curtis R. (Master Sgt.) ". . . Medics at Fort Sam Houston." *Army Reserve Magazine*, Vol. 34, No. 4 (1988), pp. 19–20.

"Peay: Force overhaul is 'success story.'" *Army Times*, May 30, 1994, p. 26.

Peerenboom, Maury. "U.S. Army Reserve Terminals Move Cargo for Bright Star '87." *Army Reserve Magazine*, Vol. 33, No. 4 (1987), p. 11.

Peers, William R. (Lt. Gen.). "New Priorities for Guard, Reserve," *Army,* October 1971, pp. 71–77.

"Pentagon Maps Cut in Army's Reserves." *New York Times,* December 3, 1961, pp. 1, 11.

Peschke, Ed (Lt. Col.) and Schumm, Walter R. (Lt. Col.) "Returning Reserve Component Equipment." *Army Logistician,* July–August 1993, pp. 32–33.

Peters, Katherine McIntire. "Active, reserve components test training together." *Army Times*, June 13, 1994, p. 29.

———. "All dressed up, hard to find anywhere to go." *Army Times*, June 14, 1993, p. 30.

———. "Army gives nod to closing of seven ARCOMs." *Army Times*, January 16, 1995, p. 22.

———. "Army Reserve, Guard to swap units." *Army Times*, December 20, 1993, p. 3.

———."'Best' officers will win under Reserve promotion law." *Army Times*, August 29, 1994, p. 22.

———. "Bonuses, benefits for Guard, Reserve drawdown victims." *Army Times*, February 27, 1995, p. 22.

———. "CAS3 needed for gold leaf." *Army Times*, January 2, 1995, p. 35.

———. "Empire Range is Safe Haven for Cubans." *Army Times*, October 17, 1994, p. 32.

———. "Equipment shortages may harm reserve effectiveness." *Army Times*, April 5, 1993, p. 14.

———. "Guard pushes for Reserve transfers." *Army Times*, April 11, 1994, p. 18.

———. "Haiti's professional help." *Army Times*, April 24, 1995, p. 14.

———. "Less training, less gear—less ready?" *Army Times*, August 8, 1994, p. 24.

———. "New cuts promise a year of turmoil. " *Army Times*, January 3, 1994, p. 30.

———. "Reaching for the stars." *Army Times,* March 6, 1995, p. 32.

———. "Reserve Special Forces: Going, going. . . ." *Army Times* May 16, 1994, p. 27.

———. "Reserves to stay busy." *Army Times*, January 2, 1995, p. 34.

———. "Reservists answer call in crisis mobilization drill." *Army Times*, February 1, 1993, p. 18.

———. "Reservists retrieve Cold War surplus." *Army Times*, July 18, 1994, p. 27.

———. "Reservists to focus on civil affairs." *Army Times*, October 3, 1994, p. 14.

———. "Restructuring plan blasted." *Army Times*, November 28, 1994, p. 14.

———. "Soldier training changes for a changed world." *Army Times*, December 19, 1994, p. 20.

———. "33,000 to be cut: Reserve takes biggest hit; soldiers will miss out on separation bonuses." *Army Times*, April 12, 1993, p. 20.

———. "Unit status upgraded." *Army Times*, January 17, 1994, p. 23.

———. "'Would have been ready' for Somalia." *Army Times*, June 14, 1993, p. 30.

Pexton, Patrick. "Gulf recall proved costly for some docs." *Navy Times*, April 26, 1993, p. 8.

"PFC for a Day." *The Officer*, Vol. LXII, No. 6 (June 1986), pp. 21–23.

Pickus, Ross, G. "Pride in Performance." *The Officer*, October 1991, p. 11.

"Plan to Shift Reservists Faces a Fight at Capitol." *New York Times*, December 11, 1964.

"Positions open to Reserve women." *Army Times*, August 15, 1994, p. 2.

Pratt, Robert (Capt). "Mobilization: No Straight A Report Card." *Army Reserve Magazine*, Summer 1983, pp. 22-23.

Pratt, Robert (Maj.) "Honduras: Reservists Practice Medicine in the Third World." *Army Reserve Magazine*, Vol. 32, No. 1 (1986), p. 20.

"President calls up Army Reservists." *Army Reserve Magazine*, Vol. 40, No. 3 (1994), p. 7.

"President Eisenhower's Reserve Statement." *The Reserve Officer*, August 1955, p. 2.

"Puerto Rican Reservists Assist Isolated Islanders." *Army Reserve Magazine*, Vol. 33, No. 4 (1987), p. 15.

Pullen, Randy (Maj.) "Return from Somalia." *Army Reserve Magazine*, Vol. 40, No. 2 (1994), pp. 12–12.

"Reorganization Planned." *CARNotes*, January–February 1983, pp. 1 and 6.

"Reserve and Guard Hassle." *Army-Navy-Air Force Register*, January 13, 1962, p. 14.

"Reserve Commissary Test." *The Officer* (January 1985), p. 13.

"Reserve Drop Fight on Revision." *New York Times,* December 6, 1962, p. 25.

"Reserve Forces in Theater." *The Officer,* March 1991, p. 7.

"Reserve Officers Accuse Pentagon of Call-Up Libel." *New York Times,* December 22, 1961, pp. 1, 11.

"Reserve picks up pieces of active component's loss." *Army Times,* February 21, 1994, p. 22.

"Reserves Facing Ten-Division Cut." *New York Times,* December 14, 1961, p. 1.

"Reserves, Guard Get Buildup Role." *The Washington Post,* September 9, 1970, p. 1.

"Reservist Refuses to Go to Gulf." *Washington Times,* November 12, 1990, p. 2.

"Reservists Accrue Excess Leave if on Active Duty to Support a Contingency." *CARNOTES,* Vol. VIII, No. III (May–June 1992), p. 1.

Reston, James, Jr. "A Bigger Role for the Reserves and Guard." *New York Times,* September 13, 1970, Sec. 4, p. 16.

"ROPMA overhauls officer management system: Appointments, promotions, tenure and separation of Army Reserve officers will be affected." *Army Reserve Magazine,* Vol. 40, No. 3 (1994), pp. 5–6.

Rozman, Thomas R. (Lt. Col.) "'90s Reserve Roles Mandate Bold New Training Initiatives." *Army,* November 1992, pp. 14–20.

Satterthwaite, Joseph P. (Sgt.) "Operation Golden Thrust '88." *Army Trainer,* Spring 1988, pp. 34–35.

"Scud Kills Reservists." *The Officer* (March 1991), p. 11.

Seigle, Greg, "Reserves best Pentagon on force cuts." *Army Times,* January 4, 1993, p. 24.

———. "Training shifts into high gear." *Army Times,* February 1, 1993, p. 18.

"Selected Reserve Tested in Nationwide Call-Up." *Army Reserve Magazine,* Vol. 34, No. 1 (1988), p. 9.

"Senate Preparedness Committee Blasts Merger." *The Officer,* June 1966, pp. 5–6.

Sennewald, Robert W. (Gen.) "Fine Tuning Reserve Forces in the Wake of Desert Storm." *Army,* June 1991, p. 17.

"737th earns proud sendoff from Yakima." *Yakima* [Washington] *Herald-Republic,* May 15, 1968.

"737th Mobilizes at Center." *Yakima* [Washington] *Herald-Republic,* May 14, 1968.

Sharp, Benjamin F., Jr. (Col.) and Skipper, Donald B. (Maj.). "The Reserve Component Dilemma: Mission Versus Time." *Military Review,* November 1984, pp. 63–79.

Skipper, Donald B. (Maj.) and Fishel, John T. (Maj.) "Equipment Compatibility Problems Denigrate Readiness of Reserves." *Army,* February 1985, pp. 34–40.

Smith, Dan and Peoples, Bill. "Kiribati's a Long Way from the Great Smokies," *Army Reserve Magazine,* Vol. 36, No. 3 (1990), pp. 8–10.

Smith, Paul. "New Reserve Chief Says IRR Readiness in Doubt." *Army Times,* June 18, 1984, p. 4.

———. "Non-Drilling Reservists Face One Day Callup." *Army Times,* August 4, 1986, p. 4

———. "Reserve Training Troubles May Force Missions on Army." *Army Times,* June 23, 1986, p. 3

Smith, Terence J. (Col.). "The Army's Role in the Success of the CCC." *The Retired Officer,* July 1983, pp. 30–34.

Staley, Rich (SSgt.) "IRR Soldiers Train in Texas . . . Tankers at Fort Hood, with 2nd Armored Division." *Army Reserve Magazine,* Vol. 34, No. 4 (1988), p. 18.

Stewart, Richard W. Untitled and undated paper on Army civil affairs during the Gulf War. Copy in possession of the author.

Sullivan, Will (SSgt.) "Army Reserve Interpreters Essential to Success." *Army Reserve Magazine,* Vol. 33, No. 2 (1987), p. 27.

Tabb, Elizabeth. "CAPSTONE—A Peacetime Partnership Pays Off." *Army Reserve Magazine,* Vol. 30, No. 2 (1984), p. 24.

"Ted Pleads for Boston Reservists." *Boston Herald-Traveler,* Ocrober 8, 1968, p. 1.

"Thunder Over Utah." *Army Reserve Magazine,* Vol. 34, No. 4 (1988), p. 14.

Tice, Jim. "Army moves to single school system." *Army Times,* April 4, 1994, p. 24.

———. "Hill investigators urge look at larger role for reserves."*Army Times,* February 8, 1993, p. 8.

Tucker, Frank. "Missouri boulderbombers." *Army Reserve Magazine,* Vol. 39, No. 3 (1993), p. 15.

"U.S. Crisis Reports Major Gains in Ability to Mobilize." *New York Times,* December 12, 1982.

"Using Commissaries." *AUSA News,* Vol. 9, No. 7 (May 1987), p. 6.

Vance, Tom (Maj.) "Transition Benefits: Whatcha gonna get when they come for you. . . ." *Army Reserve Magazine,* Vol. 39, No. 3 (1993), pp. 16–17.

Vaughan, Harry H. (Maj. Gen.). "National Guard and Reserve Must Be Unified." *The Reserve Officer,* October 1947, pp. 4–5.

Walker, Paulette V. "About 30,000 Reserve, Guard positions slated for closure." *Army Times* November 28, 1994, p. 8.

Walsh, Ellard A. "One Federal Force? No." *The Reserve Officer,* June 1949, pp. 6–7, 23.

Ward, William F. (Maj. Gen.). "Because It Works for All." *The Officer*, (December 1990), p. 16.

———. "Just the facts, please, General, just the facts." *Army Times*, March 14, 1994, p. 29.

Webb, James H., Jr. "Wrong Implications." *Army Times*, March 4, 1985, p. 22.

Welton, Courtenay S., II (Lt. Col.). "Army Reservists Serve in Panama Operation." *Army Reserve Magazine*, Vol. 36, No. 2 (1990), pp. 10–11.

"What are my reemployment rights?" *Army Reserve Magazine*, Vol. 41, No. 1 (1995), pp. 17–19.

"Where Are They Now? Activated Reservists Just Waiting Around." *Wall Street Journal*, March 15, 1968, p. 1.

Whichard, W.K. "Administering the Reserves." *The Reserve Officer*, December 1946, pp. 13, 30.

Williams, Harry L., Jr. (Maj.) "Reserve Component Jurisdiction: New Powers for the Reserve Component Commander and New Responsibilities for the Reserve Component Judge Advocate." *The Army Lawyer*, July 1987, p. 5.

Williams, John D. (Maj.). "Public Affairs Aspects of the 1968 Reserve Mobilization." *Air University Review, Air Force Review*, November–December 1971, pp. 59–67.

Willis, Grant. "The backfill blues." *Air Force Times*, December 16, 1991, p. 14.

Wilson, Robert (Lt. Col.) and Kester, Don (Maj.) "IMAs touch the people of Florida, Hawaii." *Army Reserve Magazine*, Vol. 38, No. 3 (1992), p. 17.

Young, Sharon B. "Reservists to Have Open Access to Commissaries as of March 30." *Army Times*, February 23, 1987, p. 8.

Young, Dorothy (SSgt.) "The IRR Attacks!" *Army Reserve Magazine*, Vol. 38, No. 4 (1992/93), p. 27.

"Your Association Wins Promotions for Officers Reverting to Inactive Status." *The Reserve Officer*, November 1945, pp. 4–5.

Zabecki, David T. (Maj.) "Why Doesn't One Army Concept Reach Reservists in Europe". *Army*, (November 1986), p. 14.

Zimmer, Mark (Capt.) "*Fuertes Caminos* '89." *Army Reserve Magazine*, Vol. 35, No. 2 (1989), pp. 22–25.

DEPARTMENT OF DEFENSE AND DEPARTMENT OF THE ARMY REPORTS, STUDIES, AND DOCUMENTS

Altmann, R.G., Director. *Reserve Compensation System Study, Reserve Compensation Study Group*. Washington: Department of Defense. 1978.

Army Reserve Technician Study. Fort McPherson, Ga.: U.S. Army Forces Command, 1976.

The Army Study of the Guard and Reserve Forces, Final Report. Washington: Department of the Army, 1972.

Berkman, William J. (Maj. Gen.) *The Posture of the U.S. Army Reserve* (March 1984).

Briggs, C.F. (Brig. Gen.). *Final Report, 1980 Reduction of Administrative Workload at the Reserve Component Unit Level*. RCCC Task Force. Washington: Department of Defense, 1980.

Civil Affairs in the Gulf War: A Symposium. Proceedings. October 25–27, 1991, U.S. Army JFK Special Warfare Center and School, Fort Bragg, North Carolina. Cited as "*Civil Affairs Symposium*."

Cocke, Carl E. (Compiler) and Morgan, Marilee S. (ed.). *Department of the Army Historical Summary, Fiscal Year 1985*. Washington: Center of Military History, United States Army, 1989.

Conti, Louis J., Chairman. *The Reserve Forces of the 1990s*. Washington: Reserve Forces Policy Board, 1980.

Department of Defense. *Annual Report of the Reserve Forces Policy Board, Fiscal Year 1984*. Washington: OSD, 1985.

———. *Annual Report of the Reserve Forces Policy Board, Fiscal Year 1985*. Washington: OSD, 1986.

———. *Annual Report of the Reserve Forces Policy Board, Fiscal Year 1986*. Washington: OSD, 1987.

———. *Reserve Component Programs, Fiscal Year 1987: Annual Report of the Reserve Forces Policy Board*. Washington: OSD, 1988.

———. *Reserve Component Programs, Fiscal Year 1988: Annual Report of the Reserve Forces Policy Board*. Washington: OSD, 1989.

———. *Annual Report of the Reserve Forces Policy Board, Fiscal Year 1989*. Washington: OSD, 1990.

———. *Reserve Component Programs, Fiscal Year 1990: Annual Report of the Reserve Forces Policy Board*. Washington: OSD, 1991.

———. *Reserve Component Programs, Fiscal Year 1991: Annual Report of the Reserve Forces Policy Board*. Washington: OSD, 1992.

———. *Annual Report, Reserve Forces Policy Board, Fiscal Year 1992*. Washington: OSD: 1993.

———. *Annual Report, Reserve Forces Policy Board, Fiscal Year 1993*. Washington: OSD, 1994.

———. *Annual Report, Reserve Forces Policy Board, Fiscal Year 1994*. Washington: OSD, 1995.

———. *Final Report to Congress, Conduct of the Persian Gulf War, Pursuant to Title V of the Persian Gulf Supplemental Authorization and Personnel Benefits Act of 1991 (Public Law 102–25), April 1992.* Washington: 1992.

Department of Defense. *Manpower Requirements Report, FY 1984.* Washington, 1983.

Department of Defense, Total Force Policy Study Group. *Total Force Policy Report to the Congress, December 1990.*

Department of the Army, Office of the Surgeon General. "After Action Report for Operation Desert Shield/Storm Army Nursing Lessons Learned Conference, 9–10 July 1991." Dated August 23, 1991. Unpaginated. Copy in possession of the author.

Department of the Army. *Army Reserve Forces Policy Committee, Annual Report 1985.* Washington: Office of the Secretary of the Army, 1986.

———. *Headquarters, 22nd Support Command, After Action Report.* Copy in Pentagon Library.

———. Office of the Deputy Chief of Staff for Operations and Plans. *Exercise Analysis Report—Exercise PROUD EAGLE 90 (U).* Copy in possession of the author.

———. *U.S. Army Reserve Command Independent Commission, Final Report, October 1992.* Cited as "*Independent Commission Report.*"

Duncan, Stephen M. (Asst. Secretary of Defense for Reserve Affairs). *Prepared Statement of the Assistant Secretary of Defense for Reserve Affairs, Honorable Stephen M. Duncan, Hearing before the subcommittee on Manpower, Personnel, and Compensation, House Armed Services Committee, May 1, 1992.* Typescript of testimony concerning the Reserve Component Automation System. Cited as "Duncan, *RCAS.*" Typescript in possession of the author.

———. *Testimony before the Subcommittee on Defense, Appropriations Committee, United States House of Representatives, 102d Congress, 1st session, April 16, 1991.* Typescript in possession of the author.

———. *Testimony before the Readiness Subcommittee, House Armed Services Committee, on H.R. 4739, National Defense Authorization Act for Fiscal Year 1991, Title III, Operations and Maintenance.* Cited as "Duncan statement, FY 1991 Defense Authorization Act."

Gates, Thomas S., Jr., Chairman. *The Report of the President's Commission on an All-Volunteer Armed Force.* Washington, 1970.

Gessert, Robert A. *et al. Problems of Implementing Reserve Components—Active Component Augmentation/Affiliation* (SECRET). McLean, Va.: General Research Corp., 1974.

Hackett, Robert (Lt. Gen.). *Reserve Realignment Staff Simplification.* Washington: Headquarters, Department of the Army, 1965.

Hampton, David R. *Society and the Army Reserve.* Carlisle Barracks, Pa.: Army War College, 1973.

Joint Chiefs of Staff. *Evaluation Report, Exercise PROUD EAGLE 90(U).* Copy in Joint Staff Historical Office.

Lee, Gus C. and Parker, Geoffrey Y. *Ending the Draft: The Story of the All Volunteer Force.* Alexandria, Va.: Human Resources Research Organization, 1977.

McElhenny, John F. (Col.). *After Action Report: Tropical Storm Agnes—Operation Noah II.* Harrisburg, Pa.: U.S. Army Corps of Engineers, Susquehanna District, North Atlantic Division, 1972.

Odegard, Donald C. (Col.). *Non-Mobilization and Mobilization in the Vietnam War.* Carlisle Barracks, Pa.: Strategic Studies Institute, U.S. Army War College, 1980.

Office of the Assistant Secretary of Defense for Special Operations and Low-Intensity Conflict. *Civil Affairs Gulf War Symposium—Read Ahead Documents.* Cited as "OASD, SOLIC, *Civil Affairs.*"

Office of Reserve Components. *Resource Allocations to Reserve Components.* Washington: Headquarters, Department of the Army, 1969.

OSD Project 80: Study of the Functions, Organization, and Procedures for the Department of the Army. Washington: Department of the Army, 1961.

Parker, David S. (Maj. Gen.), Chairman. *Report of the Special Review Panel on Department of the Army Organization.* Washington: Headquarters, Department of the Army, 1971.

Report of the Study of Full-time Training and Administration of the Selected Reserve. Washington: 1978.

Reserve Component Attitude Study, 1981 Tracking Study. Philadelphia: Associates for Research in Behavior, Inc., 1982.

Stone, Michael P.W. (Secretary of the Army) and Sullivan, Gordon R. (Chief of Staff of the Army). *Strategic Force, Strategic Vision for the 1990s and Beyond. A Statement on the Posture of the United States Army, Fiscal Year 1993.* Washington: GPO, 1993.

Stroud, Ansel M. (Brig. Gen.), Director. *Study of the Full Time Personnel Requirements of the Reserve Components.* Washington: Department of the Army, 1977.

U.S. Army Audit Agency. *Report of Audit: U.S Army Reserve Activities* (No. MW 70), 3 April 1970.

United States Defense Manpower Commission. *The Total Force and Its Manpower Requirements, Including Overviews of Each Service.* Washington: GPO, 1976.

White, John P. *Report on Full-time Training and Administration of the Selected Reserve.* Washington: Department of Defense, 1978.

Wilson, Dwight L. (Maj. Gen.), Chairman. *Army Command and Control Study—82 (ACCS—82).* Washington: Headquarters, Department of the Army, 1979.

The Authors

COLONEL JAMES T. CURRIE is a military historian and public affairs officer. He received his B.A. degree *Summa cum Laude* from the University of Mississippi and his M.A. and Ph.D. degrees from the University of Virginia. He has been a college professor and was the first Historian for the United States Department of Education and the first Associate Historian for the United States House of Representatives. He was a legislative assistant to United States Senator Lloyd M. Bentsen, Jr., and was a Professional Staff Member for the United States Senate Select Committee on Intelligence. He is currently Professor of Political Science at the Industrial College of the Armed Forces, where students have twice named him "Educator of the Year." He is also host and moderator of the television program "America's Army," sponsored by the Association of the United States Army. His articles have been published in *Prologue: The Journal of the National Archives, The Journal of Negro History, The Journal of Mississippi History, American Education, Military Review, Parameters: Army War College Quarterly* and elsewhere. He is the author of three books, including *Enclave: Vicksburg and Her Plantations, 1863–1870* (1980) and *The United States House of Representatives* (1988). He received the Charles Thomson Prize from the National Archives and the Southern Historical Association. Currie served almost four years on active duty with the Army. His Reserve career has included assignments with troop units and with the U.S. Army Center of Military History. His current assignment is with the Secretary of the Army's Office of Legislative Liaison. His awards include the Meritorious Service Medal with Oak Leaf Cluster and the Parachutist Badge.

COLONEL RICHARD B. CROSSLAND (1942–1991) described himself in the first edition of this book as a "professional Reservist, with over twenty years of service in the three Army components." After enlisting in the Delaware Army National Guard, he was commissioned in 1965 and served as a Guard officer until he was called to active duty in late 1966. He served in the active Army in field artillery, infantry, and intelligence until he became a full-time Reservist in 1975. He served in Vietnam and was wounded twice. He was a a graduate of the Army's Command and General Staff College and the Advanced Public Affairs Course at the University of South Carolina. He had a B.A. degree from the University of Delaware and did graduate work in journalism and political science. Following his assignment to OCAR, during which he co-authored the first edition of *Twice the Citizen*, he was assigned to the Army's Training and Doctrine Command (TRADOC). He completed his career as the Senior Army Reserve Advisor at the U.S. Army Soldier Support Center at Fort Benjamin Harrison. His awards included the Legion of Merit, Bronze Star Medal, Meritorious Service Medal, Air Medal, Army Commendation Medal, Purple Heart with Oak Leaf Cluster, Combat Infantryman Badge, and the Vietnamese Cross of Gallantry.

Index

MILITARY UNIT INDEX

1st Armored Division, 71, 254
1st Brigade, 2d Armored Division, 379, 380
1st Cavalry Division, 371, 389, 464
1st Cavalry Regiment, 379
1st Corps Support Command, 276, 379, 380
1st Infantry Division, 71, 435
1st Regiment of United States Volunteer Cavalry, 10
2d Area Support Command, 404
2d Armored Cavalry Regiment, 442–443
2d Armored Division, 71, 104, 347, 379
2d Army, 62
2d Battalion, 158th Aviation Regiment, 554
2d Hospital Center (Forward), 297
3d Armored Cavalry Regiment, 379
3d Armored Division, 466
3d Army, 484
3d Army AG section, 434
3d Army Time-Phased Force Deployment List, 475
3d Battalion, 87th Infantry, 480–483
3d Medical Command, 460
3d Personnel Group, 439
4th Infantry Division, 71
5th Army, 526, 527
6th Theater Signal Command, 485
7th AG HHD Personnel Group, 439
7th Army Reserve Command, 298
7th Personnel Command, 440
7th Transportation Command, 476
7th Transportation Group, 389
8th Army, 107
8th Battalion, 40th Armor, 254
8th Medical Brigade, 293
8th Medical Brigade (Forward), 297
10th Mountain Division, 559–560, 561
10th Personnel Command, 434
11th Air Defense Brigade, 379
11th Armored Cavalry Regiment, 395
11th Special Forces Group, 537
11th Theater Signal Command, 484
12th Preventive Medicine Detachment, 470
12th Special Forces Group, 114, 537
13th Corps Support Command, 379
13th Quartermaster Detachment (WP), 385–386
13th Supply and Service Battalion, 394
14th Quartermaster Detachment, 386
15th Ordnance Battalion, 394
18th FA Battalion, 107
18th Finance Group, 452
18th MP Brigade, 482
18th Personnel and Administration Battalion, 435
18th Personnel Group, 433, 439, 440
20th Engineer Brigade, 399, 450
21st Support Command, 477–478
21st Theater Signal Command, 479–480
22d Support Command, 408, 445
24th Infantry Division, 386, 388
24th Mechanized Infantry Division, 443
24th Military Intelligence Battalion, 420
25th Infantry Division, 255
27th Engineer Battalion, 403
29th Infantry Division, 563
29th Infantry Division v, 71
30th Engineer Battalion (Topo), 397
32d Infantry Division, 138

34th Infantry Division (National Guard), 71
34th MP Battalion Headquarters, 414
37th Infantry Division (National Guard), 71
43d AG Detachment (General Support) (Postal), 559
43d Engineer Battalion (Cbt Hvy), 397, 402
44th Evacuation Hospital, 273, 469
44th General Hospital, 470–471
44th Medical Brigade, 451
46th Judge Advocate General Detachment (International Lawm Team), 445
48th Infantry Brigade (Mechanized), 372
49th Armored Division, 138, 145
50th General Hospital, 461, 468
50th Military History Detachment, 447
51st Military History Detachment, 449
54th Quartermaster Company, 454
60th Ordnance Company, 394
61st Battalion, 62
63d Regional Support Command, 540
70th Training Division, 346, 436
76th Division (Training), 292
77th Army Reserve Command, 293
77th Regional Support Command, 540
78th Training Division, 435, 436
79th Army Reserve Command, 541
79th Quartermaster Company (Water Supply), 384, 495
80th Division Logistics Group, 292
80th Training Division, 436
81st Army Reserve Command, 541, 558
82d Airborne Division, 200, 370, 389
82d Field Hospital, 468–469
83d Army Reserve Command, 541
84th Training Division, 436
85th Training Division, 436
86th Army Reserve Command, 541
88th Regional Support Command, 540
89th Army Reserve Command, 385, 527
89th MP Brigade, 475
89th Regional Support Command, 540
90th Infantry Division, 71
90th Military History Detachment, 448
90th Regional Support Group, 540
94th Regional Support Command, 540
95th Training Division, 435
96th Civil Affairs Battalion, 279, 420, 421, 425, 556, 557
96th Regional Support Command, 540
97th Army Reserve Command, 541
98th Infantry Division, 89–90
98th Training Division, 436
99th Regional Support Command, 540
100th AG Reception Battalion, 436
100th Battalion, 442d Infantry, 254–255
100th Maneuver Training Command, 436
100th Training Division, 137, 436
101st Airborne Division (Air Assault), 389
101st Military History Detachment, 449
101st Signal Battalion, 138
102d Army Reserve Command, 346, 541
103d Corps Support Command, 346
108th Training Division, 435
111th JAG Detachment, 446
113th JAG Detachment (Military Law Center), 446
114th Evacuation Hospital, 465
119th JAG Detachment, 446
120th Regional Support Group, 540
121st Regional Support Command, 540
122d Regional Support Command, 540
123d Army Reserve Command, 346
123d Regional Support Group, 541
124th Regional Support Command, 540
125th Army Reserve Command, 541
127th JAG Detachment, 446
129th AG Company (Direct Support) (Postal), 558
129th Transportation Company (Heavy Truck), 389
142d Field Artillery Brigade, 374
143d Transportation Command, 476
145th MEDSOM Battalion, 467
149th Judge Advocate General Detachment, 270
155th Armored Brigade (National Guard), 371, 372
155th Supply and Service Battalion, 291
167th Support Group, 552
180th Transportation Company, 291
184th Ordnance Company, 394
187th Infantry Brigade, 552
188th JAG Detachment (Legal Services Team), 446
193d Light Infantry Brigade, 481
194th Replacement Company, 440
199th JAG Detachment, 446–447
205th Support Battalion, 551
208th JAG Detachment, 447
209th Broadcast Public Affairs Detachment, 450
211th Military Intelligence Company, 419–420
213th Military Law Center, 447
213th MP Company (Guard), 413
217th Evacuation Hospital, 469
217th Medical Battalion, 464
220th Medical Maintenance Detachment, 467
220th MP Brigade, 475
221st Replacement Company, 438
228th Theater Signal Command, 484
231st Transportation Company, Fltg Cft, 207, 554
235th Replacement Company, 437
240th port Company, 108
241st General Hospital, 293
244th AG Personnel Service Company, 434
246th Quartermaster Battalion, Graves Registration, 454, 456

251st Evacuation Hospital, 465
257th MP Company (Guard), 413
273d Helicopter Ambulance Detachment, 464
295th Ordnance Company (Ammo) (DS), 394
298th Transportation Company, 388
300th Dental Detachment, 466
300th MP Brigade, 346
300th Postal Company, 443
301st MP Camp, 409, 410
304th Civil Affairs Company, 425
304th Civil Affairs Group, 268, 427–429
304th MP Company (Escort Guard), 410
305th Field Hospital, 276
308th Civil Affairs Group, 282
308th Dental Detachment, 466
308th QM Salvage Co., 113
308th Real Estate Detachment, 398
310th Theater Army Area Command, 297, 555
310th Theater Signal Command, 479
311th Quartermaster Graves Registration Company, 454, 455
312th Postal Company, 442
313th MP Company, 415
313th MP Prisoner of War Information Center, 410
314th Public Affairs Detachment (Press Camp Headquarters), 450
316th Helicopter Ambulance Detachment, 464
316th Station Hospital, 461
317th Military History Detachment, 448
318th Transportation Agency (Movement Control), 392
319th Mobile Public Affairs Detachment, 450–451
320th Evacuation Hospital, 293
321st Helicopter Ambulance Detachment, 464
322d Civil Affairs Group, 557
322d Engineer Detachment (WD), 403
322d Military History Detachment, 448
324th Data Processing Unit, 434
324th Personnel & Administration Battalion, 434
325th Finance Support Unit, 453
326th AG Battalion HHD, Personnel & Administration, 438
326th Military History Detachment, 447
328th Quartermaster Detachment, 390–391
329th AG Company GS Postal, 441, 443–445
331st General Hospital, 293
332d Medical Brigade, 295, 461
335th Data Processing Unit, 291
335th Theater Signal Command, 308, 476–479, 484–486
336th Postal Company, 443
336th Theater Finance Command, 452
337th Dental Detachment, 273
338th Finance Support Unit, 452
341st Medical Group, 465
341st Postal Company, 442–443
342d MP Company (Escort Guard), 411
343d Rear Tactical Operations Center, 298
344th Data Processing Unit, 434
344th MP Company (Escort Guard), 410
345th Combat Support Hospital, 465–466
345th Mobile Public Affairs Detachment, 450
346th Camp Advisory Team, 414
346th MP Company (Escort Guard), 413
346th Transportation Battalion, 272
347th AG Battalion HHD, Personnel & Administration, 437–438
350th Evacuation Hospital, 465
351st Civil Affairs Command, 422–423, 557
351st Ordnance Company, 392, 393
351st Postal Company, 434, 443, 558
352d Civil Affairs Command, 429, 431, 557
354th Civil Affairs Brigade, 282, 427, 429, 556
356th Medical Detachment, 469
356th Public Affairs Detachment, 292
358th Civil Affairs Brigade, 268, 270
358th MP Company (Processing), 411
358th Public Affairs Detachment, 291
360th Civil Affairs Brigade, 268, 269, 270, 424, 425–426
361st Civil Affairs Brigade, 278, 280, 295–296
361st MP Company (Guard), 410
362d Public Affairs Detachment, 292
364th Civil Affairs Brigade, 557
365th Evacuation Hospital, 471–472
368th Finance Support Unit, 452–453
369th Station Hospital, 272
370th Quartermaster Battalion (Water), 390
375th Chemical Co., 185
376th Engineer Detachment (FF), 403
376th Finance Support Unit, 453
377th Combat Support Hospital, 292
377th Military Police Company, 272–273
377th Theater Army Area Command, 583
377th Theater Signal Command, 479
379th Blood Bank Company, 467
381st Replacement Battalion, 436
382d Field Hospital, 461
383d Quartermaster Battalion (Petroleum Terminal and Pipeline Operating), 390
386th AG HHD Personnel & Administration Battalion, 439–440
387th AG Reception Battalion, 436
387th AG Replacement Battalion, 436
389th AG Personnel Service Company, 434
394th QM Recovery and Disposition Co., 112
395th Ordnance Company, 393
399th port Construction Co., 272
400th MP Battalion (Enemy Prisoner of War/Counter Intelligence), 410

ALPHABETICAL SUBJECT INDEX

Abrams, Chief of Staff Gen. Creighton W., 225
"Abriendo Rutas" project, 275–276
ACSFOR. See Assistant Chief of Staff for Force Development
Active Guard and Reserve, 219–220, 222, 229, 277–278, 300–301, 302–303, 487
  Desert Shield/Desert Storm role, 514–515
Adamczyk, Lt. Col. Richard D., 448
Additional Training Assemblies, 290
Adjutant General Corps, 440
Adjutants General Association, 534
Advisory Board of University Presidents for the National Reserve Corps, 25
Advisory Commission on an All-Volunteer Armed Force, 212–213
Aerial Port of Embarkation, 437
Affiliation Bonuses, 239
Affiliation program, 254–255, 256
Afghanistan, Soviet invasion of, 263
Agency for International Development, 269–270
AGR. See Active Guard and Reserve
Ailes, Secretary of the Army Stephen, 164, 169, 170
Air Medal, 207
Aircrew Flight Training Periods, 290
Al Jubayl, Saudi Arabia, 442, 443
Albrook Air Force Base, 283
All-Volunteer Force. See also Total Force manpower problems, 231–232
Ambulance units, Desert Shield/Desert Storm role, 464–465
AMEDD. See Army Medical Department
American Military History, 4
AMOPS. See Army Mobilization and Operations Planning System
Andres, Col. Dudley M., 315
ANDRULIS Research Corporation, 514
Annual General Inspection, 257, 258
Annual Training, 257
Appleton, WI, 393
ARCOM. See Army Reserve Command
Area Maintenance Support Activities, 250
Aristide, Bertrand, 561
ARMCs. See Army Readiness and Mobilization Commands
Armed Forces Reserve Act of 1952, 100–101, 123, 162, 197
Armor Force Mobilization Readiness Task Force, 344–346
ARMRs. See Army Readiness and Mobilization Regions
Army Appropriations Act of 1912, 23
Army Center for Lessons Learned, 468, 474, 508, 509, 510
Army Center of Military History, 448
Army Command and Control Study—82, 227
Army Commendation Medal, 207
Army Court of Military Review, 518
Army Family Life Communication Lines, 236
Army Medical Department, 459, 460–461
Army Medical Materiel Center Saudi Arabia, 467
Army Mobilization and Operations Planning System, 262, 310–311, 313–314, 511
Army Nurse Corps, 93, 242
  promotion, 118
Army Nurse Corps Historian, 448
Army Readiness and Mobilization Commands, 227
Army Readiness and Mobilization Regions, 261
Army Readiness Regions, 225–226
Army Reserve. See also Army Reserve structure changes; Desert Shield/Desert Storm; specific components and missions; Women in the Reserve active duty for training, 123–124
  Affiliation Bonuses, 239
  Affiliation program, 254–255, 256
  benefits increase, 235–242, 567–570
  Berlin crisis and, 133–148
  Bolivia role, 551
  budget, 116, 151, 212, 245, 325
  CAPSTONE, 255–256, 258, 268, 270, 278, 294–296, 295–296, 391, 418, 426, 475–476, 481, 484, 522, 583
  changeover from manual to machine-processed records, 139–140
  civil affairs specialists, 268, 269–270, 275–276, 278–284, 420–432
  command and control revisions, 228–229
  Comoros role, 551
  competition with National Guard, 124
  Costa Rica role, 274
  data management problems, 313
  discontent during Berlin crisis, 140–142
  domestic relief missions, 553–555
  Ecuador role, 275–276
  educational assistance, 238
  Eisenhower administration and, 115–132
  El Salvador role, 551
  end strength, 176, 183
  enlistment bonuses, 238, 344
  equipment cross-levelling, 307, 309
  equipment problems, 134, 138–139, 146, 163, 204, 211, 232, 245–250, 265, 303–309, 423–425, 438, 485, 575–576
  European Reservists, 297–298
  force structure planning, 163–164
  FORSCOM emphasis on realistic training, 256–258

Fuertes Caminos exercises in Honduras, 272–274, 275, 551
full-time support, 300–302, 572–573
funding for, 173, 303
Grenada role, 268–271
Guatemala role, 274, 551
Guyana role, 551
inadequacy of facilities, 251–253
Iranian crisis role, 263–265
IRR training with Reserve units, 346–347
job protection, 564–565
Kennedy's reorganization efforts, 150–154
Korea role, 298
maintenance improvement, 250
manpower problems, 134, 139, 146, 234–235, 247
materiel readiness and technician support, 127–129
McNamara's reorganization efforts, 133–134, 149–184, 200
medals and awards during Vietnam War, 207
membership problems, 124–127
merger with National Guard proposal, 164–176, 211
minority recruiting, 244–245
mobilization ability, 259–262, 581
mobilization authority, 315–316
mobilization exercises, 309–315
modification of command structure, 177–179
MOS qualification, 288–289
Mutual Support Program, 254–256
non-participation problem, 125
organizational structure chart, 546
overseas training increase, 270–271
paid drill strength in 1984, 287
as part of Total Force, 287–316
Peck Plan for reorganization, 154–160
Pentomic divisional structure, 129–130, 149
promotion issues, 115, 117–118, 570–572
readiness problems, 306–307
real-world missions, 549–580
realignment plans, 156, 160, 161–162
recruiting and retention branch, 234
reduction in size issue, 521–524
reenlistment rates, 574
REP-63, 162
Reserve Forces Bill of Rights and Vitalization Act, 179–183
risk analysis technique and, 164
road-building exercises in Panama, 271–272
ROAD structure, 149, 151, 154, 160
Roundout program, 254–255, 256, 550
separation benefits, 569–570
split-training option, 237–238
Table of Organization and Equipment, 128, 138–139, 204
ten-division plan, 151–152
ten point improvement program, 214
Thailand role, 551
three brigade plan, 178, 179
Vietnam War and, 101, 193–210, 211, 232–234, 585
Army Reserve Association, 538
Army Reserve Blood Bank Company, 467
Army Reserve Command, 134, 149, 179, 224, 542–545
Army Reserve Forces Policy Committee, 299
Army Reserve Personnel Center, 229, 317, 318
Desert Shield/Desert Storm role, 493–519
Army Reserve structure changes
Army considers new courses of action, 336
Army Reserve Support Command, 324–325
Army's delay in letting Congress know what was happening, 329–330
bill establishing an Army Reserve Command subject to a two-year test period, 339–341, 542
CAR-FORSCOM memorandum of agreement on funding, 336–337
Chief, Army Reserve's plan, 319–320
Congress's reaction to Stone's letters, 335–336
Congress's response to the FORSCOM study, 321–322
Congress's study, 324
Department of Defense authorization bill, 333
FORSCOM-OCAR memorandum of agreement, 327–328
FORSCOM plan, 326–327
FORSCOM plan reactions, 331–333
FORSCOM planning group, 330–331
FORSCOM study, 320–321
Gen. Ward and the Army Reserve Forces Policy Committee, 337–338
Montgomery's role, 329
OCAR receives funding authority, 334–335
pledges of support from the Senate, 333–334
Richardson study, 322–324
Stone's meeting with Montgomery and Murtha, 333
United States Army Reserve Command, 318–319
USAR planning meeting, 338
USARC establishment, 338–339
Army Reserve Support Command, 325
Army Reserve Support Operation Center, 318
Army Reserve Technician Program, 128–129
Army Reserve Technicians, 218n
Army Training and Evaluation Programs, 256
Army Training Test, 253, 256
ARPERCEN. See Army Reserve Personnel Center
ARRs. See Army Readiness Regions
Arsenault, 1st Sgt. Gary, 389
ART Study, 218

As Salman, Iraq, 403
As Sarrar, Saudi Arabia, 410, 411
Aspin, Les, 333, 372–373, 529–530, 536
Assistant Chief of Staff for Force Development, 199
Assistant Chief of Staff for Reserve Component, 130
Assize of Arms, 2
Association of the United States Army, 211, 247–248, 263
Atkinson, Spec. Stephanie, 517
Atomic bomb, U.S. monopoly of, 81–83
Aviators, 346

Babcock, Col. Steven, 470
Baker, Secretary of War Newton D., 30
Baldwin, Hanson W., 142, 155
Baltimore Express, 311–312
Bangladesh, relief efforts, 555, 557
Banks, Maj. Bill, 435
Baratz, Maj. Gen. Max, 487, 540
Baskir, Lawrence M., 196–197
Bates, Rep. William H., 172
Bautz, Maj. Gen. Edward, Jr., 233n
Bay of Pigs, 135
Beahm, Col. Robert H., 427, 556
Beatty, Sgt. 1st Class George F., 403, 404
Beaumond, TX, 379
Bechtel International Systems, Inc., 399
Belsky, PFC Marvin, 138
Berg, Col. Alan J., 396–397
Bergquist, Deputy Assistant Secretary of the Army Kenneth P., 228
Berkman, Maj. Gen. William R., 222, 238–239, 245, 264, 317n
Berlin crisis
  background, 135–136
  call-up problems, 138–140
  demobilization, 144–146
  discontent among Reservists, 140–142
  length of, 133
  mobilization, 136–138, 146–147
  reorganization plans for Army Reserve, 133–134
  Reserve Officers Association and, 142–144
Berlin Wall construction, 137
Bertinetti, Col. Joseph, 468
Beutler, Sgt. 1st Class Ray, 467
Billings, Dr. Frank, 18n
Bin Sultan, Lt. Gen. Khalid, 397
Blacks
  active recruiting of, 244
  segregation of, 44–45
Bland, Lt. Col. James, 398
Blazing Trails exercises, 272–274, 275
Blevins, 1st Lt. Angela, 556–557
BLIND LOGIC, 279
Blood units, Desert Shield/Desert Storm role, 467
Blount, Col. Lawrence C., 421
BLUE FLAG, 484
BLUE SPOON, 277, 278–279
Boeing Computer Services, 579
Bold Shift, 549–550, 552
Boldt, David R., 216
Bolivia, MEDRETE exercises, 276, 551
Bosnia, 585
"Bottom-Up Review," 529–530
Bowen, Col. Cotton W.S., 410
Bowers, Sgts. Dennis and Norah, 502–503
Boyer, Col. Charles M., 82, 119
Bradford, Lt. Col. Ralph E., 457n
Breckenridge, Secretary of War Henry, 26
Bres, Brig. Gen. Edward S., 49, 66, 92
Briggs report, 258n
BRIGHT STAR, 294–295, 362, 476, 484
Brinkerhoff, John R., 376, 459
Brodsky, Lewis C., 206
Bronze Star, 207
Brooke, Sen. Edward, 205
Brown, Capt. Robin E., 410
Brucker, Secretary of the Army Wilber M., 130
Bryan, Dr. [first name?], 18n
Bull, Dr. William T., 18n
Bull, Lt. Henry T., 24
Burba, Gen. Edwin, Jr., 326, 327, 328, 337–339, 377–378, 549–550, 585
Burgess, Carter, 122–123
Busch, Lt. Col. George R., 410
Bush, George, 279
  cease fire announcement, 426
  freezing of Iraqi assets, 370
  national emergency declaration, 370
  partial mobilization order, 496
  Selected Reserve call-up, 370–371
Bushnell, John, 284
Byrd, Sen. Robert C., 370n
Byrnes, Secretary of State James F., 95
Byrnes Committee, 95
Byron, Beverly, 372–373

Cadre system, 216–220
Calhoun, John C., 7–8, 21, 216
Camp Expo, Saudi Arabia, 394
Camp Jack, Saudi Arabia, 394
Camp Powder Horn, 274
Camp Shelby, MI, 259n
Campbell, Brig. Gen. Don, 556
Campbell, Maj. Gen. Boniface, 119–120
Cannon, Col. James C., 484–485
Cano Blanco Road project, 274–275
CAPSTONE program, 255–256, 258, 268, 270, 278, 294–296, 391, 418, 426, 475–476, 481, 484, 522, 583

CAR. See Chief, Army Reserve
Carlton, Col. John T., 160, 171
Carr, Lt. Col. James, 282
Carroll, Col. Phillip W., III, 402
Carter, Jimmy, Iranian crisis and, 263
CAS3. See Combined Arms and Services Staff School
CASP. See Civilian Acquired Skills Program
Casualty and Memorial Affairs Operations Center, 456
CATF. See Civil Affairs Task Force
CCATF. See Combined Civil Affairs Task Force
CCC. See Civilian Conservation Corps
Certificates of Achievement, 207
Chaplains, Desert Shield/Desert Storm role, 472–474, 506
Chapman, James P., 75
Chappell, Rep. Bill, Jr., 318–319
Charleston, SC, 380
Cheney, Secretary of Defense Richard, 371, 372, 373
Chief, Army Reserve, 182, 199, 225, 227–228, 229, 247, 250, 543
  DIA requests for units, 418
  efforts to increase authority over USAR, 318, 319–320, 323, 326, 337
  IMA call-up study, 514, 515
  study of general officers conducted for, 486
Chief, Army Reserve and ROTC Affairs, 130
Chief, National Guard Bureau, 199
Chief, Office of Reserve Components, 161
Circular No. 347, 79–80, 81
Cisneros, Maj. Gen. Marc, 284
The Citizen Soldiers, 29
Citizens' Military Training Camps
  benefits to members, 52
  commissioning of officers, 38
  Organized Reserve officers as instructors, 42–43
  statutory authority from the National Defense Act of 1920, 39
Civil affairs specialists, 268, 269–270
  Desert Shield/Desert Storm role, 420–432
  Ecuador role, 275–276
  Haiti role, 561–563
  Panama role, 278–284, 560
Civil Affairs Task Force, 282, 283
Civil War, 9–10, 19
Civilian Acquired Skills Program, 237, 243
Civilian Agencies Task Force, 556
Civilian Conservation Corps
  establishment, 43
  Officers' Reserve Corps work with, 44–45
  Civilian training
  adult camps, 26–27
  camps for college students, 24–25
Clark, Grenville, 26–27, 29
Clay, Rep. William, 541
Clifford, Clark, 201
Clifford, John G., 29
Clinton, Bill, Selected Reserve call-up, 561, 562
Clinton administration, plan for Reservists, 532
CMTC. See Citizens' Military Training Camps
CNGB. See Chief, National Guard Bureau
Coakley, Robert W., 4–5, 147
Coalition Combined Task Force Civil Affairs Command, 556
Coats, Sen. Dan, 535
Colcol, Lt. Col. Ben M., 396
Collins, Rep. Ross A., 47
Colonial America, 2–5
Combat Support Hospitals, 465–466
Combat Support to the Army, 176
Combined Arms and Services Staff School, 572
Combined Civil Affairs Task Force, 431
Commissary benefits for Reservists, 357–358
Committee on Civilian Components, 90
Comoros, 551
Computer Sciences Corporation, 579
CONARCs. See Continental Army Commands
Congress. See also specific members; specific pieces of legislation
  Army Reserve and National Guard merger hearings, 169–173
  Army Reserve Command and, 542–545
  Army Reserve creation, 23
  Army Reserve organization disputes, 149–184
  Army Reserve reorganization and, 133
  Army Reserve structure changes role, 321–322, 324,
  329–330, 333–336, 339–341
  attitude toward greater defense preparedness after Hitler's invasion of Europe, 64
authorization for five Reserve officers for General Staff duty, 220–221
authorization for militia during Civil War, 9
authorization for women in the ORC, 93–94
call-up and new mothers, 503–504
call-up authority for the Secretary of Defense, 533–536, 582
  clarification of the status of the National Guard, 20
  criticism of Army command and control system, 227
  demobilization after Desert Shield/Desert Storm, 526
  earned leave for Reservists, 567–568
  equipment appropriations, 576–578
  equipment shortages funding, 304
  first peace-time conscription, 64
  full-time manning for Reserve units, 300
  General Staff Corps creation, 14
  hearings on reducing the Army Reserve, 521–524
  intervention during Eisenhower administration, 130–132

Investigations and Surveys staff, 324, 329
isolationist sentiment, 63
job protection efforts for Reservists, 564–565
mail delivery problems hearings, 442
morale, welfare and recreation access for Reservists, 358
Presidential authority to call up Organized Reserve and
National Guard to active service during World War II, 64
pressure on Army to eliminate one level of the Reserve's management structure, 229
proposal to expand the standing army after World War I, 33
Regional Support Commands and, 541
removal of geographical restriction on use of Reservists, 67
restrictions on military training of police, 284
separation benefits for Reservists, 569–570
standing army and, 3
status of ORC training, 47
Vietnam War mobilization and, 205–206
War of 1812 and, 7
Congressional Research Service, 537
Conlon, Brig. Gen. Joseph F., III, 408
Conscientious objectors, 517, 519
Constitution, Congressional power to raise and support armies, 6
Continental Army Commands, 221
concern about quality of officers assigned as advisors, 223
Mutual Support Program, 254
reorganization of, 224
Continental Army Management Information "System, 579
Continental Army proposal of Garrison, 25–26, 27
Contingency Force Pool, 550
CONUS Replacement Centers, 437–439, 509
Copeland, Sen. Royal S., 47
Correspondence courses, 50
"Costa Abajo '86" exercise, 271
Costa Rica, Army Reserve role, 274
COSTAR. See Combat Support to the Army
Courts martial. See Uniform Code of Military Justice
Creed, Capt. Jeffrey D., 411
Cuba, refugee camp in Panama, 560
Cuban Expeditionary Force, 10
Cuban Freedom Fighters, 135

DALIS. See Disaster Assistance Logistics Information System
Dandar, Col. Edward F., 556
Daniel, Maj. Joseph S., 446
D'Araujo, Maj. Gen. John, Jr., 539–540
Davis, Jefferson, 9
Davis, Lt. Col. King F., Jr., 426
Davis, Secretary of War Dwight F., 42
DCSPER. See Deputy Chief of Staff for Personnel
Dearborn, Maj. Gen. Henry, 7
Decker, Army Chief of Staff Gen. George H., 144–145
Decker, Maj. Paul, 269
Defense Finance and Accounting Service, 451
Defense Intelligence Agency, 417, 418–419
Defense Language Institute, 495
Defense Mapping Agency, 404
Defense Officer Personnel Management Act, 571
Defense Science Board Task Force on Readiness, 578
Delaney, Col. Rick, 445
Dental Officers' Reserve Corps, 20, 464, 466
Department of Agriculture, 414, 417
Department of Defense
appropriations bills, 173, 197, 228, 304
call-up authority for the Secretary of Defense, 533–536, 582
casualty handling, 456
civil-military cooperation program, 554–555
commissary benefits for Reservists and, 357
criticism of Army command and control system, 227
equipment and manpower shortages of reserves, 147
"First to Fight, First to Equip" policy, 303, 306
full-time manning for Reserve units, 300
Guard and Reserve paid drill strength reduction, 154
inactive duty pay issue, 91–92
McNamara's reorganization, 133, 142–143
merger merits, 170–171
National Guard mobilization, 374
RCAS and, 579
reserve component drawdown issue, 522–523
Retired Reserve call-ups, 515
return of materiel from Desert Shield/Desert Storm back to the United States, 479–480
single parents, dual military parents, and new mothers issue, 504–505
Department of Defense Authorization Act, 348
Department of Justice, 564–565
Department of Labor, 564
Department of the Army
Crisis Action Team, 513
Master Priority List, 255, 308–309
Deployable Medical Systems, 293, 347, 465
Deployment Control Units, 378, 381
DEPMEDS. See Deployable Medical Systems
Deputy Chief of Staff for Personnel, 222
Dern, Secretary of War George H., 47–48
The Desert Dragon, 451
"Desert Fix" operation, 527

Desert Shield/Desert Storm
Active Guard and Reserve role, 514–515, 581–585
assembling the force
activating units of the USAR, 377
building the national consensus, 377–378
Deployment Control Units, 381
the first weeks, 369–371
questions about commitment to the Total Force, 371–374
railroad units, 381–382
realistic training pays off for MTMC, 382
shipping out the force, 375–376
Terminal Transportation Units, 378–380
volunteer Reservists answer the call, 375
CAPSTONE and, 296
chaplains, 472–474, 506
confronting the enemy
battle souvenirs, 414, 417
civil affairs units, 420–432
command and control, 425
customs inspection duties, 414, 417
evacuation of U.S. and Canadian civilians, 413
feeding Muslim prisoners, 415
foreign language abilities, 419
Kuwait Task Force, 429–431
military intelligence, 417–420
Military Police, 407–417
oil well firefighting, 430–431
problems with the EPW set-up, 415
tactical maps of the Kuwaiti Theater, 420
disciplinary problems, 516–517, 582
equipment problems, 308–309
Individual Ready Reserve role
baggage problems, 509
call-up of Reservists "not suitable for active duty," 509–510
Capt. Huet-Vaughn case, 517–518
check cashing problems, 508
clothing issue problems, 508
conscientious objectors, 517, 519
delays and exemptions, 499–501
description of role, 494–495
description of the IRR, 493–494
dual military service parents, 502–503
financial hardships, 501–502
in-processing problems, 505–507
Individual Mobilization Augmentees, 511–514
IRR musters and, 351
mailgram confusion, 496, 498–499
new mothers, 503–505
no shows, 518–519
partial mobilization, 496–498
records shipping problems, 507–508
Reserve volunteers, 510–511
single parents, 502–503
strength of the IRR, 494
tracking problems, 507
treatment of individuals, 508
medical units
ambulance units, 464–465
attrition, 463–464
blood units, 467
combat support hospitals, 465–466
dental detachments, 466
field hospital example, 468–469
GAO study of, 458
general hospitals, 470–471
medical detachments, 466
medical logistics, 467
nurses of the 365th Evacuation Hospital, 471–472
preventive medicine, 470
problems between AC and Reserve personnel, 459–460
problems in the AMEDD, 460–461
psychiatric detachments, 467–468
types and components of, 458–459
unit identity loss, 460
veterinary units, 469
working with the Saudis, 461–462
number of killed-in-action, 454
personnel support
casualty and mortuary services, 453–456
CONUS Replacement Centers, 437–439, 509
cross-levelling, 456
finance support units, 451–453
history detachments, 447–449
Judge Advocate General units, 445–447
personnel services, 433–435
postal services, 440–445
public affairs units, 449–451
reception and replacement centers, 435–437
replacement operations in Southwest Asia, 439–440
post-war period
Army Reserve-Army National Guard swap, 536–540
Army Reserve Command, 542–547
Army school structure changes, 541–542
authority for 25K call-up, 532–536
demobilization, 525–526
equipment return and repair, 526–528
organizational changes, 540–541
reduction in size of Reserve, 521–524
Reserve roles and missions, 528–532
Reserve Retiree role, 515–516
Reserve units excluded from deployment
CAPSTONE and, 475–476, 481, 484
Infantry: 3/87th, 480–483

Reserve Generals and problems of the deployment, 486–487
signal units, 484–486
TAACOMs, 476–480
USAR troop units respond
engineer units, 395–403
firefighting units, 403
Iraqi SCUD missile attack on Dharan Barracks, 386–387
MOS qualification and, 384–385
movement control, 391–392
operation as giant LOGEX, 384
ordnance units, 392–394
supply units, 394–395
topography units, 404–405
transportation units, 387–388
transporter units, 388–391
types of units, 383–384
water treatment and supply units, 384–386
well drilling efforts, 403–404
Desert Storm Special Study Group, 584
Detterline, Col. Donald R., 378
Dharan, Saudi Arabia, 390, 398, 400, 403, 413, 417, 433, 442, 443, 464, 470
Dharan Barracks, SCUD missile attack on, 386
Diaz, Porfirio, 27
Dick, Rep. Charles W., 13
Dick Act, 13–15, 20
Dicks, Rep. Norman D., 522
Disaster Assistance Logistics Information System, 556–557
Disaster relief missions, 553–555
Doctors. See Medical Reserve Corps
DoD. See Department of Defense
Dole, Sen. Robert, 370n
Donohue, Brig. Gen. Francis, 293–294
Donovan, Maj. Gen. William J. "Wild Bill," 71
photo, 105
Doolittle, Gen. James H., 71
Douglas, Justice William O., 206
Dover Air Force Base, DE, 455, 456
Doverspike, Lt. Col. Jay W., 91
Downing, Gen. Wayne, 421
Dozier, Capt. Tamara, 559
Dragics, Col. David, 419
Drake, Lt. Col. Dennis, 565
Draper, Army Under Secretary William H., 89
Drinker, Henry, 25, 29
Du Picq, Ardant, 208
Duncan, Assistant Secretary of Defense Stephen M., 525–526
Dunn, Lt. Col. D.Y., photo, 192
duPont, Sen. Henry A., 29

Eads, SSgt. Mary, 415
Easterday, SSgt. Dennis, 283
Echternach, 1st Lt. Robert, 394
Ecuador, road-building project, 275–276
Education. See Training
Education benefits, 238, 355–356, 568–569
Eisenhower, Dwight D., 47, 102
fiscal conservatism, 116, 132, 150
plan for improved reserve system, 120–124
Eisenhower administration
Army Reserve reorganization, 129–130
congressional intervention, 130–132
massive retaliation policy, 116, 149
materiel readiness and technician support, 127–129
Reserve Forces Act of 1955, 120–124
Reserve Officer Personnel Act of 1952, 116–120
USAR membership problems, 124–127
El Salvador, MEDRETE exercise, 551
ELABORATE MAZE, 277
Elliott, Col. Randall, 430
Endress, Col. Charles A., 448
Enemy Prisoners of War, camp construction, 401–402, 584
Engineer, Signal and Quartermaster Corps, 30
Engineer units
Desert Shield/Desert Storm role, 395–403
Enlisted Reserve Corps
creation of, 29, 30
elimination of, 100
growth during World War I, 31
post-World War II strength, 85
purpose of, 30
EPW Processing Advisory Team, 414
EPWs. See Enemy Prisoners of War
Ernst, Maj. Gen. Carl, 542
ERRA. See Executive for Reserve and ROTC Affairs
European Reservists, 297–298
Executive for Reserve and ROTC Affairs, 97–98, 130
increased importance of, 77–78
Exemption Review Board, ARPERCEN, 519
Exercise Kindle Liberty '87, 272
Exercise Optimal Focus '93, 565
Exercise Optimal Focus '94, 565
Exon, Sen. J. James, 357
Expansible army, 7–8, 21, 216
Expeditious Discharge Program, 241
Extension courses, 51

Federal Emergency Management Agency, 540, 554
Felix, SP5 Jesus Peres, photo, 114
Feller, Lt. Col. Carolyn M., 448
Field hospitals, Desert Shield/Desert Storm role, 468–469
Finance support units, Desert Shield/Desert Storm role, 451–453

Financial hardships, Desert Shield/Desert Storm IRRs and, 501–502
Firefighting units, Desert Shield/Desert Storm and, 403
FIREX '88, 291
First Training Regiment, 26
Fishel, John T., 278, 284–285
FISSURES, 277
Fitzwater, Marlin, 496
Flemming, Arthur, 120–121
Florida, relief efforts in, 553–554
Foley, Rep. Thomas S., 370n
Forces Command Mobilization and Deployment Planning System, 310–311
FORMDEPS. See Forces Command Mobilization and Deployment Planning System
Forrestal, Secretary of Defense James, 90
FORSCOM. See U.S. Army Forces Command
Fort A.P. Hill, VA, 550
Fort Benning, GA, 436, 437, 509
Fort Bragg, NC, 422, 428, 431, 435, 559, 562
Fort Campbell, KY, 292, 410, 550
Fort Carson, CO, 480, 481, 482, 483
Fort Dix, NJ, 400, 420, 436, 441, 443, 550
Fort Gillem, GA, 448
Fort Hood, TX, 347, 379, 469
Fort Huachuca, AZ, 562
Fort Indiantown Gap, PA, 251, 282
Fort Irwin, CA, 374
Fort Jackson, SC, 437, 509
Fort Knox, KY, 437, 438
Fort Lee, VA, 495, 506
Fort Leonard Wood, MO, 436
Fort McCoy, WI, 393, 409, 470, 471, 527
Fort McPherson, GA, 332
Fort Meade, MD, 205, 408, 429
Fort Pickett, VA, 251, 384, 411
Fort Riley, KA, 385, 389, 390, 394, 395, 412, 435, 452
Fort Sam Houston, TX, 526
Fort Sill, OK, 436
Fort Stewart, GA, 394, 413
Foss, Gen. John W., 472
Freitag, Maj. Gen. Merle, 332
French and Indian War, 3
Frix, Maj. Gen. Robert, 399–400
Frost, Col. W.R., 68
Fuller, Capt. Harry, 392
Funk, Sgt. 1st Class Gordon, 269

Gagetown, New Brunswick, Canada, 550, 552
GALLANT EAGLE, 484
GALLANT KNIGHT, 484
Galle, Capt. Joseph B., 403
Galvin, Gen. John, 584
Gann, Brig. Gen. Benard, 279, 282
Garrison, Secretary of War Lindley M., 24, 25–26, 27, 29
Gates, Thomas S., Jr., 212–213
Gaunt, Capt. Richard A., 390
General Accounting Office
  Army's reliance on Reserves report, 582–583
  criticism of Army command and control system, 227
  criticism of Retiree Recall Program, 242
  RCAS and, 579
  role of Army Reserve components, 528
  SRIP program report, 239n
  status of required equipment, 577–578
  study of deployment of medical units, 458
General hospitals, Desert Shield/Desert Storm role, 470–471
General Officers Conference, 319
General Staff Committees on Army National Guard and Army Reserve Policy, 156
General Staff Corps, creation of, 14
Geneva Convention, 416, 438
Gephardt, Rep. Richard, 541
Germany, Reserve units deployed to during Desert Shield/Desert Storm, 481, 482, 483
Gettysburg, PA, 24
Gilbert, Sandra, 328
Gilpatric, Deputy Defense Secretary Roswell L., 155
Ginn, Maj. Gen. Louis H., III, 299n
Glaspy, Capt. Ruth, photo, 187
Gnehm, Edward, 429
GOLDEN THRUST '88, 315
Goldwater-Nichols Defense Reorganization Act, 320
Gordon, 1st Lt. William, 455
Gore, Al, 555
Gorgei, Maj. Frank, 282
Grand Army of the Republic, 9
"Grand Payload," 261–262
Grant, Ulysses S., 10
Graves registration, Desert Shield/Desert Storm and, 454, 495
Gray, Army Assistant Secretary Gordon, 90
Gray Board Report, 90, 94
Grenada
  Army Reserve role, 268–271
  internal politics, 267
  invasion of, 267–268, 581
  school rehabilitation, 269
  textbook shortage, 270
Guatemala
  Army Reserve role, 274
  MEDRETE exercise, 551
Gulf of Tonkin Resolution, 209
Gulf War. See Desert Shield/Desert Storm
Guyana, MEDRETE exercise, 551

Ecuador role, 275
Log Base Alpha, 395, 401, 442
Log Base Bastogne, 401
Log Base Bravo, 465
Log Base Charlie, 395
Log Base Echo, 394, 395
Logan, John A., 11
LOGEX description of Desert Shield/Desert Storm, 384
Long Beach, CA, 380
Long Binh, Vietnam, photo, 189
Love, Col. Miller J., 425
Love, Lt. Col. Timothy R., 438
Lowe, Brig. Gen. Frank E., 51, 65, 66, 77
Lucas, Capt. Jerry K., 403
Lunkheimer, Sgt. 1st Class Donald, 403
Lusitania sinking, 26

Maas, Maj. Gen. Melvin, 117, 119
MacArthur, Gen. Douglas, 96
Mail delivery. See Postal services
Mailgrams sent to IRR members, 496, 498–499
Main Supply Route Dodge, 392
Maneuver Area Commands, 226
Mann, Lt. Col. Gary, 436
Mann, Rep. James R., 17–18
March, Army Chief of Staff Peyton C., 33, 34
Marine Corps Reserve Officers Association, 534
Marsh, lst Lt. Jeffrey M., 411
Marsh, Secretary of the Army John O., 248–249, 318–319
Marshall, Brig. Gen. S.L.A., 168
Marshall, Gen. George C., 59, 68, 75, 79, 83
Massachusetts Bay Colony, 2
Mayo, Dr. Charles H., photo, 55
Mayo, Dr. William J., photo, 55
McAuliffe, Lt. Gen. Anthony C., 98
McCaffrey, Maj. Gen. Barry R., 327
McChesney, Capt. Phillip R., 442
McCosh, Dr. Andrew J., 18n
McCurdy, Rep. Dave, 372
McGuire, George, 270
McGuire, Lt. Col. Robert W., 381
McNamara, Secretary of Defense Robert S.
Berlin crisis and, 133–145
equipment problems of Reserves, 245
neglect of the Army Reserve, 246
relations with Congress, 165–167
reorganization of Army Reserve, 149–184
Vietnam War mobilization and, 193, 199, 200, 201
McQuiston, Rear Adm. I.M., 100
McWaters, Maj. Gen. John R., 484–485
MEAPO. See Middle East/Africa Projects Office
Medical Reserve Corps, 14, 17–20, 29
Medical Service Corps, 242
Desert Shield/Desert Storm role, 457–472
Medical Specialist Service Corps, 242
MEDRETEs exercises, 273, 276, 551
Meek, Capt. David D., 442
MEET. See Minimum Essential Equipment for Training
Meritorious Unit Citation, 207
Meritorious Unit Commendation, 394, 452
Mexico
U.S. involvement in internal affairs of, 27–28
war with, 8–9
Meyer, Army Chief of Staff Gen. Edward, 229–230, 247, 249
Middle East/Africa Projects Office, 398
Military Construction Army Reserve, 251
Military history detachments, Desert Shield/Desert Storm role, 447–449
Military intelligence, Desert Shield/Desert Storm role, 417–420
Military Manpower Task Force Report to the President on the Status and Prospects of the All-Volunteer Force, 242
Military Occupation Specialty qualification, 288–289, 384–385
Military Personnel and Compensation Subcommittee, 501, 504
Military Police, Desert Shield/Desert Storm role, 407–417
Military Police Camp Advisory Teams, 414
Military Police Processing Advisory Team, 414
The Military Policy of the United States, 11, 20
Military Postal Service Agency, 444
Military Traffic Management Command, 295, 562
Desert Shield/Desert Storm role, 375–376, 382
Military Training Camps Association, 12, 24, 27
Militia Act of 1792, 6, 8, 9
Miller, SP5 Willard M., 141
Milton, Brig. Gen. Hugh M., 98
Minimum Essential Equipment for Training, 306–307
Minorities, active recruiting of, 244
"Minute Man" badge, 52
Missouri River flood, 554
Mitkus, Col. Robert J., 427
Miyamura, Sgt. Hiroshi H., photo, 106
Moats, Col. Bruce E., Jr., 275–276
MOBEX 76, 260, 310
MOBEX 78, 259n, 260–261, 310
MOBEX 80, 261, 310
MOBEX 83, 261, 310
Mobile Army Surgical Hospitals, 465–466
Mobilization: A History of Fifth Army Support for Operation
Desert Shield/Desert Storm, 449
Mobilization Designee program, 263
Mobilization Personnel Processing System, 262

Mobilization Tables of Distribution and Allowances, 310, 313
MOBPERS. See Mobilization Personnel Processing System
Montgomery, Rep. Gillespie V. (Sonny), 329, 333, 334–336, 355, 356, 528, 544
  Desert Shield/Desert Storm role, 371, 372–373
Montgomery GI Bill, 355–356, 568–569
Mooney, Brig. Gen. Howard, 430, 431, 432n
Moose, Maj. Mike, 450, 451
Morale, welfare and recreation access, 358
Morse, Ted, 269
Mortimer, Capt. Robert, 388
Mortuary services, Desert Shield/Desert Storm and, 453–456
MOS qualification. See Military Occupation Specialty qualification
Mott, Brig. Gen. Harry J., III (Ret.), 538–539
Movement control in Desert Shield/Desert Storm, 391–392
MPs. See Military Police
MTCA. See Military Training Camps Association
MTMC. See Military Traffic Management Command
Mukoyama, Maj. Gen. James, 538
Mulcahy, Maj. Gen. Terrence D., 397
Mullet Key, FL, fire, 554
Multinational Force and Observers, 563–564
Murtha, Rep. John P., 319, 322, 325, 329, 330, 333, 334–336
Musters and screening for the IRR, 347–352
Mutual Support Program, 252, 254–256
MWR access. See Morale, welfare and recreation access

Nahlik, Charles V., 505
National AMEDD Augmentation Detachment, 468
National Committee for Employer Support of the Guard and Reserve, 531
National Defense Act of 1916, 14, 19, 27, 28–30, 123, 217, 220–221
National Defense Act of 1920, 23, 34, 39, 118, 123
National Defense Authorization Act, 248, 357, 359, 534, 543, 544, 568, 569, 570–571, 572
  gray area retirees and, 358–359
National Defense Transportation Award, 207
National Guard, 9, 573
  Army Reserve-National Guard unit swap, 536–540
  attendance at Regular Army schools, 14
  benefits to members, 52
  Berlin crisis and, 137–138
  Bolivia role, 276
  budget appropriations for, 130
  clarification of the status of, 20
  Comoros mission, 551
  compensation for duty, 48, 91
  competition with Army Reserve, 124
  competition with Organized Reserve Corps, 86–87
  Desert Shield/Desert Storm role, 372, 374, 377, 387, 395, 396, 403, 409, 410, 411, 412, 414, 415, 443, 447, 452
  end strength, 173, 176
  equipment problems, 306
  exemption from the draft and, 94
  Exercise Optimal Focus '93 and, 565
  funding for, 173
  Garrison's Continental Army proposal, 25–26
  Korean conflict call-up, 96
  manpower problems, 139
  merger with Army Reserve proposal, 164–176, 211
  mobilization exercises, 315
  National Defense Act of 1916 provisions, 29
  Operation Golden Cargo role, 553
  performance in the Philippines, 10
  proposal for unification with Organized Reserve, 90–91
  Regular Army officers' attitude toward, 10
  road-building exercises in Panama, 271–272
  Sinai peacekeeping efforts, 563–564
  Spanish-American War and, 10
  ten point improvement program, 214
  training exercises, 293–294, 295, 297
  two weeks of active duty benefit, 45
  Uniform Code of Military Justice and, 360
  women in, 354
  World War II call-up, 64
  National Guard and Reserve Equipment Appropriations, 304, 576–578
National Guard Association, 91, 530, 534
  opposition to reorganization plans, 158
National Military Establishment creation, 90
National Military Intelligence Center Terrorism Desk, 419
National Prisoner-of-War Information Center, 416
National Reserve Plan, 120–124
National Security Act of 1947, 90
National Security Council, 430
National Training Center, Fort Irwin, CA, 374
Nedzi, Rep. Lucien N., 172
Neelly, Col. Gene, 484–485
Neumiller, Capt. Scott A., 395
New Deal, 43
Newport News, VA, 380
NGREA. See National Guard and Reserve Equipment Appropriations
Nielsen, Lt. Col. James M., 529
"Nifty Nugget," 259n, 260–261, 310, 312
Nixon, Richard M.
  draft reform and volunteer military policies, 212–213

Vietnamization policy, 214
Non-Commissioned Officers Association, 534
Nordic Shield II, 550, 552
Noriega, Gen. Manuel Antonio, 271, 276–277, 279, 296
Novak, Col. Carl D., 412
Nunn, Sen. Sam, 334

Oakland, CA, 380
O'Brien, Lt. Col. Bill, 269
OCAR. See Office of the Chief, Army Reserve
Ochalek, Maj. Larry, 270
Office of Civil-Military Cooperation, 555
Office of Reserve Components, 161, 199
Office of the Chief, Army Reserve, 317
Officers Personnel Act of 1947, 117–118
Officers' Reserve Corps
  active duty training, 40–41
  age as factor in denial of active service, 65
  buildup after World War I, 37–40
  call-up during World War II, 64–72
  Civilian Conservation Corps work, 44–45
  compensation for duty, 48, 91
  Congress's removal of geographical restriction on use of Reservists, 67
  desire for active duty assignments, 69–70
  discharge and reappointment in the grade formerly held, 76
  elimination of, 100
  establishment, 29
  executive operations, 77–78
  growth of, 31, 67, 68–69, 72–75
  inactive duty training pay, 49, 91
  merger of Medical Reserve Corps into, 19, 30
  National Defense Act of 1920 and, 34–35
  post-World War II strength, 85
  preparing for mobilization, 52–54
  rewarding membership, 51–52
  segregation of black members, 44–45
  training, 40–51
  war-time policies, 75–77
  years of service ribbons, 51–52
Onaway Eagle, 292–293
O'Neil, Lt. Col. Dean F., 480, 481, 483
"Open Roads" project, 275–276
Operation Cobra Gold '93, 551
Operation Golden Cargo, 552–553
Operation Provide Comfort, 395, 427, 450, 555–557
Operation Provide Relief, 395
Operation Restore Hope, 557–558
Operation Safe Haven, 560
Operation Sea Angel, 557
Operation Uphold Democracy, 561–563
Operational Readiness Evaluation, 550
ORC. See Office of Reserve Components; Officers' Reserve Corps
Orchid Sage training exercise, 293–294
Ordnance units, Desert Shield/Desert Storm role, 392–394
Organization and Functions Manual, 330
Organization of Eastern Caribbean States, 267
"The Organization of the Land Forces of the United States," 15
Organized Reserve Corps. See also Army Reserve
  activation of first post-war units, 87–88
  benefits to members, 52
  competition with National Guard, 86–87
  exemption from the draft, 94
  Korean conflict service, 96–100
  lack of financial support from the President and Congress, 88–89
  lack of growth between the wars, 53
  medical officer recruitment problem, 84–85
  non-disability retirement pay, 92
  number decorated for heroism during World War II, 71
  officers as instructors for CMTCs, 42–43
  post-World War II rebuilding, 83–90
  proposal for unification with National Guard, 90–91
  rebuilding after World War II, 83–90
  renaming, 100
  Roosevelt's order into active duty, 67–68
  terminal leave promotions, 81–83
  women in, 93–94
  World War II call-up, 64
Orsini, Eric A., 331
Oso Grande, 274
Ott, Capt. Janice N., 389
Overseas training, 270–271, 289, 296–297, 550–552. See also specific exercises and operations

Pace, Secretary of the Army Frank, 96, 98
Pacific Grove, CA, 24
Pacifists, 517, 519
Pagonis, Lt. Gen. William G. "Gus," 396, 400, 408, 416, 476–478, 480
Palastra, Gen. Joe, 319–320
Palmer, Brig. Gen. John McAuley, 14–15, 20–24
  post-war service, 79–80
  structure for post-war Reserve components, 77
  testimony before Committee on Military Affairs, 33–34
  unofficial position in the Reserve Office, 37
  Palmer, Gen. Bruce, 254
  Palmer plan, 22–24
  Panama
  "Costa Abajo '86" exercise, 271
  Cuban refugees in, 560

Displaced Civilian Community, 283
JUST CAUSE, 271, 276–279, 296
Operation BLUE SPOON, 277, 278–279
Operation PROMOTE LIBERTY, 279–285
prison upgrades, 282
professional law enforcement, 283–284
relief efforts, 555
road-building exercises, 271–272
seizure of U.S. dependent schoolchildren, 279
solid waste removal, 282–283
Temporary Tour of Active Duty length, 278, 280
Panama Defense Forces, 279
Park, Dr. Roswell, 18n
Parker, Capt. John, 52
Parker, Lt. Col. A.H., 117
Patterson, Under Secretary of War Robert P., 65
Paz, Lt. Robert, 279
Peay, Army Vice Chief of Staff Gen. James H. Binford, III, 538
Peck Plan for reorganization, 154–160
Perkins, 1st Lt. Lee J., 559
Perry, Secretary of Defense William, 530–531, 573
PERSCOM. See Total Army Personnel Command
Pershing, Gen. John J., 27, 34, 35, 37
Persian Gulf War. See Desert Shield/Desert Storm
Personal Effects Depot, 456
Philbin, Deputy Assistant Secretary of Defense Edward J., 248
Philippine Scouts, 29–30
Phillips, Capt. E.H., 84
Phillipsen, Lt. Col. William J., 470
Physicians. See Medical Reserve Corps
Pickard, Maj. Michael, 554
Pidgeon, Col. Robert D., 416–417
Pike, Charles B., 43
Pipeline construction
Desert Shield/Desert Storm and, 401
in Ecuador, 275
Plattsburg, NY, training camps, 26, 29
Plattsburg Manual, 30
Pletcher, Lt. Col. Richard, 444
Police Force Liaison Division, 283–284
Polk, James K., 8
Port of Wilmington, NC, 376
Post Exchange privileges, 236, 237, 358
Post-World War II period
Armed Forces Reserve Act of 1952, 100–101
defense establishment changes, 90–93
Korean conflict, 95–100, 102
military budget cutbacks, 81
planning for, 79–81
rebuilding of ORC, 83–90
selective service and reserve organization, 94–95
terminal leave promotions, 81–83
women in the Reserves, 93–94
Postal services
Desert Shield/Desert Storm and, 440–445
in Somalia, 558–560
POWDER RIVER/MOBEX 85, 309–311, 313
Powell, Col. Calvin S., 379
Powell, Gen. Colin, 320, 321, 323–324, 521–522, 523
Presidential 200K Call-Up and Partial Mobilization, 511
Presidential mobilization authority, 315–316, 532–533
Presidential Unit Citation, 207
Prisoners of war. See Enemy Prisoners of War
Program Objective Memorandum, 265
PROMOTE LIBERTY, 279–285
Promotion issues, 570–572
PROUD EAGLE 90, 312–314
"Proud Spirit," 261, 310
Pruett, Maj. Rick, 283
Psychiatric detachments, Desert Shield/Desert Storm role, 467–468
Psychological operations specialists, 426–427, 561–563
Public affairs units, Desert Shield/Desert Storm role, 449–451
Public Law 74–67, 52
Public Law 80–810, 92
Public Law 90–168. See Reserve Forces Bill of Rights and Vitalization Act
Public Law 93–292, 236
Public Law 95–79, 238
Public Law 95–397, 236
Public Law 96–584, 263
Public Law 99–661, 316
Purple Heart, 207
Putnam, Maj. Gen. George W., Jr., 224

Quartermaster School, Fort Lee, VA, 495, 506

Radbill, Maj. Mike, 269
Radford, Adm. Arthur, 122
Rafha Air Base, Saudi Arabia, 411
Railroad units, 381–382
Ramirez, Capt. Ely, 388
Rapert, Capt. Danny W., 403
Rapid Deployment Force-Army, 263
Rapid Deployment Joint Task Force, 212, 261, 263, 264–265
RAR. See Regular Army Reserve
Rathbone, Col. John V., 91
RC Cop plan, 284
RCAS. See Reserve Component Automation System
RCPAC. See Reserve Components Personnel and Administration
Center
RDJTF. See Rapid Deployment Joint Task Force

Readiness Assistance Regions, 225
Readiness Group Denver, 481–482
Readiness Groups, 225–226
Readiness Management Assemblies, 290
Ready Reserve, 100, 101, 123, 124, 125–126, 162, 221, 231
Berlin crisis and, 136–137, 146–147
Ready Reserve Aviator Sustainment Training Program, 346
Ready Reserve Mobilization Reinforcement Pool, 161, 175
Ready Reserve Reinforcement Pool, 151, 154
Reagan, Ronald
defense build-up, 290
Montgomery GI Bill and, 355
Reagan Administration, 228
"Rebuild America" program, 529
Record, Col. James E., 481–482, 483
Red Crescent, 428–429
Reef-building exercise, 554–555
REEFEX 94, 554–555
Reeves, Sgt. Ervan V., 404
REFORGER, 294–295, 362
Regional Support Commands, 540–541
Regular Army
pre-World War II expansion, 64
rejection of ROTC increasing production of lieutenants, 73–74
Regular Army Instruction Camps, 29
Regular Army Reserve, World War I and, 31
Reilly, Surgeon General R.M. Reilly, 18
Reimer, Lt. Gen, 337
Reinforcement Training Units, 173
Reinforcing Reserve, 161
Relief supply tracking software, 556–557
Religion. See Chaplains
Remillard, Capt. Martin, 389
Reno, Maj. Gen. William H., 331–332
Reorganization Objective Army Division, 129–130
REP–63. See Reserve Enlistment Program-1963
Replacement operations, Desert Shield/Desert Storm and, 437–440
Report of the Secretary of War for 1899, 12
"Report on the Organization of the Land Forces of the United States," 20, 25
"Report on the Reduction of the Army," 7
Research Analysis Corporation
mobilization study, 148
Reserve active-status list, 571
Reserve Compensation System Study, 232
Reserve Component Automation System, 579
Reserve Component Commanders Handbook for Mobilization, 262
Reserve Components Personnel and Administration Center, 317
Reserve Enlistment Program-1963, 162, 204, 252
Reserve Forces Act of 1955, 120–124, 125, 132
Reserve Forces Bill of Rights and Vitalization Act, 179–183, 318
Reserve Forces Policy Board, 101, 124, 126, 127, 128, 181, 290, 300, 301, 303, 309, 344, 356, 357, 531, 568, 575
Reserve Forces Policy Committee, 318
Reserve Militia, creation of, 13–14
Reserve Officer Personnel Act, 132, 572
Reserve Officers Association, 49, 264, 331, 534
Army Reserve budget lobbying, 130, 132
dispute with McNamara, 142–144, 211
opposition to McNamara's reorganization plans, 155–156, 158, 159–160
opposition to merger of Army Reserve with National Guard, 167–169, 171, 211
Reserve Officer Personnel Act and, 117
years of service ribbons, 51–52
Reserve Officers Personnel Management Act, 570–572
Reserve Officers Training Corps
benefits to members, 52
establishment, 29
female membership, 243
growth during World War I, 31–32
new officer source for the ORC, 38
Reserve Personnel Center, 499
Resor, Secretary of the Army Stanley R., 177, 181–182, 205–206
Retired Reserve, 100, 162, 241, 262, 317, 473, 570
Desert Shield/Desert Storm role, 515–516
Retirement Act, 76
RETROEUR, 552
Reverse osmosis water purification units, 385
Revolutionary War, 3–5
RFA. See Reserve Forces Act of 1955
RFD–A. See Rapid Deployment Force-Army
RGs. See Readiness Groups
Rich, Col. Wendell, 411
Rich, Lt. Gen. C.W.G., 177
Richardson, Gen. William R., 211, 292–293, 320, 322–324
Richardson, 1st Lt. Elizabeth, 442
Rickenbacker, Capt. Edward V. "Eddie," 31n
photo, 56
Ricotilli, Maj. Gen. John, 292
Ridgway, Gen. Matthew, 122
Riker, William H., 9
RisCassi, Gen. Robert W., 320
Rivers, Rep. L. Mendel, 169
Riyadh, Saudi Arabia, 404, 420
Riyadh al Kharj Military Hospital, Saudi Arabia, 461
ROAD. See Reorganization Objective Army Division
Road-building exercises
in Honduras, 272–274

in Panama, 271–272
Roane, Dr. (Lt. Col.) John, 463–464
Roosevelt, Brig. Gen. Theodore, Jr., 26, 27, 71–72
photo, 103
Roosevelt, Franklin D., 43, 49, 67
authorization of increase in the Regular Army after Hitler's invasion of Poland, 63
Roosevelt, Theodore, Rough Riders and, 10
Root, Elihu, 11–13, 26, 29
ROPA. See Reserve Officer Personnel Act
ROPMA. See Reserve Officers Personnel Management Act
Rosellini, Gov. Albert D., 159–160
Roseman, SSgt. Phil, 417
Rosenbaum, Lt. Col. Gerald, 511
Ross, Lt. Gen. Jimmy D., 477
ROTC. See Reserve Officers Training Corps
Rough Riders, 10
Roundout program, 254–255, 256, 550
Rousellot, Lt. Col. John, 506
Royal Thai Army, 551
Royall, Army Secretary Kenneth C., 95
RRMRP. See Ready Reserve Mobilization Reinforcement Pool
Rueden, Lt. Col. Henry, 453
Runge, Assistant Secretary of Defense Carlisle P., 151
Ruppert, Col. Ray, 445–446
Russell, Sen. Richard B., 172, 178, 197
Russell Amendment, 197–198

Saddam Hussein, 369–370, 555–556
Saint, Gen. Crosbie, 584, 585
Samuel, Col. Arthur, 448
Sandler, Maj. Gen. Roger, 532, 538
Saudi Arabia. See also Desert Shield/Desert Storm; specific locations by name
medical units working with Saudis, 461–462
objections to some U.S. customs, 462
water treatment, 385
Saudi National Guard, 411
Savannah, GA, 380
Schaefer, Mason, 375
Schardein, Brig. Gen. Max L., 397, 398, 399
Schwarzkopf, Gen. H. Norman, 378, 391–392, 421, 478
Section 5 committees. See General Staff Committees on Army
National Guard and Army Reserve Policy
Selected Reserve, 173–174, 183, 202, 287, 288, 297, 314–315,
346, 350, 352, 355, 523, 569, 573
Clinton's call-up, 561, 562
Montgomery GI Bill and, 568
Selected Reserve Incentive Program, 238–239
Selective Service Act of 1948, 94
Senger, Maj. Thomas, 398
Sennewald, Gen. Robert W., 292, 528
Separation benefits, 569–570
Serrano, Capt. Anthony V., 410
Servicemen's Group Life Insurance, 236, 567
Sharp, Col. Benjamin F., 289–290
Sheppard, Morris, 65
Sherman, William T., 10
Sica, Col. Carl G., 297
Signal units, Desert Shield/Desert Storm role, 479–480, 484–486
Silver Star, 207
Simmons, Col. Richard G., 379
Sinai peacekeeping efforts, 563–564
Sincavan, Lt. Col. Virginia, 468
Skelton, Rep. Ike, 570
Skipper, Maj. Donald B., 289–290
Smith, Adm. Phillip (Ret.), 534
Smith, Brig. Gen. Edward, 69–70, 75, 76, 84, 92
Smyser, Capt. James S., photo, 56
Society of the National Reserve Corps of the United States, 25
Soldier Readiness Program, 438
Soldiers' and Sailors' Civil Relief Act, 463, 501
Somalia, relief efforts, 555, 557–560
Souchin, Dr. [first name?], 18n
Soviet Union
Berlin crisis, 135–136
invasion of Afghanistan, 263
post-war ambitions, 80–81
POWs and MIAs investigation, 551–552
Spanish-American War, 10
Special Active Duty for Training tours, 292
Special Forces Command, Crisis Response Cell, 513
Special Operations Council, 538
Spence, Rep. Floyd, 541
SRIP. See Selected Reserve Incentive Program
St. Petersburg, FL, 207
Stahr, Secretary of the Army Elvis J., Jr., 137–138, 141–142, 152–154
Standard Army Multicommand Management Information Systems, 314
Standby Reserve, 100, 101, 125, 162, 231, 240, 317
Starnes, Capt. Brett, 410
State governors, opposition to National Guard cutbacks, 158–159
"Statement of a Proper Military Policy for the United States," 25
Status of Resources and Training System, 309
Statute of Winchester, 2
STEADFAST program, 221, 256
Stebbins, Horace C., 43
Stegeman, Capt. Barry, 391
Steinhardt, Col. Gary C., 419

Stennis, Sen. John, 169
Stevens, Secretary of the Army Robert T., 122
  photo, 111
Stevens, Sen. Ted, 334
Stewart, Dr. Richard W., 448
Stewart, Faith, 503
Stimson, Secretary of War Henry L., 21–22, 23, 29, 72–73, 74
Stone, Col. David L., 36
Stone, Secretary of the Army Michael P.W., 322, 324–325, 329, 333, 334–336
STOP LOSS, 377
Storat, Brig. Gen. Richard, 400
Stovall, Col. Larry J., 410–411
STRAF. See Strategic Reserve Army Forces
Strategic Army Forces, 202
Strategic Reserve Army Forces, 137
Strauss, William A., 196–197
Strong, Brig. Gen. Michael D., 461
Stroud Study, 219
Stroup, Capt. David H., 405
Sullivan, Lt. Gen. Gordon R., 324, 326, 376, 530, 536, 584
Summer Senior Commander's Conference, 321
Sunny Point, NC, 380
Superior Unit Award, 436, 445
Supply units, Desert Shield/Desert Storm role, 394–395
Supreme Court, Army Reserve job protection case, 564
Survivor Benefit Plan, 235–236
Sutton, Maj. Gen. William J., 182, 242

TAACOMs. See Theater Army Area Commands
Table of Distribution and Allowances, 330
Table of Organization and Equipment, 128, 137–138, 176, 204, 307
Talent, Rep. James, 541
Tallil Airbase, Kuwait, 426–427
Tampa Bay, FL, fire, 554
TAPDB-R. See Total Army Personnel Data Base-Reserve
Task Force 43, 402
Task Force 217, 464
Task Force 864, 401, 402
Task Force 1169, 275
Task Force Bravo, 556
Task Force Freedom, 399–400
Task Force PSYOP, 426–427
Task Force Rafha, 411
Task Force Russia, 551–552
Taylor, Gen. Maxwell D., 133
Technician Conversion Test, 219–220
Technician program as a cadre, 217–220
Terminal leave promotion issue, 81–83
Tet Offensive, 198–199
Thailand, Operation Cobra Gold '93, 551
Theater Army Area Commands, Desert Shield/Desert Storm role, 476–480
Theater Map depots, 404
Theater Supply Area #4, Saudi Arabia, 392
Thompson, Brig. Gen. Charles F., 35, 49–50
Thompson, Lt. Gen. Richard H., 249
Thurman, Gen. Maxwell R., 282
Thurmond, Sen. Strom, 119, 130, 169, 334
Topographic units, Desert Shield/Desert Storm and, 404–405
Topper, Col. John A., 319, 330–331, 333–334, 336, 337–338, 478
Torney, Surgeon General George H., 18, 19
Total Army concept, 134, 212. See also Total Force
Total Army Personnel Command, 375
Total Army Personnel Data Base-Reserve, 281–282
Total Army School System Coordinating Activity, 542
Total Force, 5. See also All-Volunteer Force; Total Army concept
  Army Reserve advisor quality and, 222–230
  Army Reserve as part of, 287–316, 582–585
  Desert Shield/Desert Storm and, 371–374, 375, 377, 582–585
  economic issues, 214–216
  full-time support to the Army Reserve, 220–222, 300–302
  mobilization ability of Reserves and, 259–262, 581
  Operation PROMOTE LIBERTY and, 285
  opposition to, 215–217
  public announcement of, 212
  technicians as a cadre, 217–220
Trainee Discharge Program, 241
Training. See also specific missions
  Annual Training, 257
  Army Training and Evaluation Programs, 256
  Army Training Test, 253, 256
  basic training delays, 252–253
  basic unit training, 253
  Berlin crisis and, 140
  correspondence courses, 50
  cost of, 41
  domestic, 552–553
  extension courses, 50
  facilities for, 212, 232–233, 251–253
  FORSCOM emphasis on realistic training, 256–258
  funding for, 42, 47
  inactive duty training, 299–300
  lanes training, 550
  night training, 258
  Officers' Reserve Corps training between World Wars I and II, 40–51
  overseas training, 270–271, 289, 296–297, 550–552

Panama National Police, 283–284
post-war training opportunities, 89
realistic training emphasis, 256–258
Special Active Duty for Training tours, 292
split-training option, 237–238
three week annual training, 298–299
training detractors, 290–291
training dilemma, 289–290
training exercise examples, 291–295
training readiness factors, 290–291
"20 Hour Course," 283–284
universal military training, 80, 84, 94
Vietnam War and, 204–205
vocational and flight training, 356
Transportation companies, Desert Shield/Desert Storm role, 388–391
Transportation Terminal Units. See also Transportation
companies; Truck companies
Desert Shield/Desert Storm role, 375, 378–380
Treaty of Paris, 5
Truck companies, Desert Shield/Desert Storm role, 387–388
Truman, Harry S.
desire for effective Army reserve organization, 94–95
Korean conflict call-up of Reservists, 96
as ORC member, 46
photo, 59
setting of pattern for military spending, 81
support for unification of Organized Reserve and National Guard, 90, 91
Tsoulos, Col. Demetrios, 460–461
TTUs. See Transportation Terminal Units
Turkey, 556
Twaddle, Brig. Gen. Harry L., 65–66, 74

UCMJ. See Uniform Code of Military Justice
UMT. See Universal military training
The Uncertain Trumpet, 133
Uniform Code of Military Justice
Caputo case, 359
Individual Ready Reserve and, 359–362
training sessions in, 481
Unit Cross of Gallantry (Vietnam), 207
United Nations High Commissioner for Refugees, 556
United Nations Security Council, 370
United States Army Missile and Munitions Center and School, 299–300
United States Army Reserve Command, dispute over establishment of, 317–341
United States Transportation Command, 312–313
Universal military training, 80, 84, 94
Universal Military Training and Service Act, 197–198
Upton, Emory, 10–11, 20
URGENT FURY operation, 267–268, 581
U.S. Army Center of Military History, 487
U.S. Army Deserter Information Point, 518
U.S. Army Forces Command
Army Reserve structure changes role, 320–321, 326–328,
330–333, 334, 336–339
ARR modification, 227
ART Study, 218
emphasis on realistic training, 256–258
Intensified Management Force List, 264
IRR mobilization and, 507–508
personnel strength, 248
plans to convert Senior Staff Administrative Assistant positions to full-time colonel positions, 220
U.S. Army Reserve-Europe, 297
U.S. Army Security and Intelligence Command, 513
U.S. Customs Service, 414, 417
USAID. See Agency for International Development
U.S.S. Pueblo incident, 198

Van Fleet, Gen. James A., 142
Vance, Deputy Secretary of Defense Cyrus R., 172
VanCise, Col. Philip S., 69
Vanik, Rep. Charles A., 205
Variable Housing Allowance, 236
Vaughan, Maj. Gen. Harry, 86–87, 90
Vecchiarello, Maj. Frank, 269
Veterans Re-employment Rights Act, 564–565
Veterinary Officers' Reserve Corps, 19
Veterinary units, Desert Shield/Desert Storm role, 469
Vietnam War
increased troops in, 172
Johnson's 1965 decision on, 193–197
Johnson's original decision not to use Reservists, 193–197
mobilization planning, 199–202
popularity of the Army Reserve for draft-age men, 126
portrayal as limited war, 196, 197
POWs and MIAs investigation, 551
Reserves mobilization, 202–206
Reserves role, 101, 208–210, 211, 232–234, 585
Reservists' experience during, 206–208, 209
Russell Amendment and, 197–198
supply unit role, 394
Tet Offensive, 198–199
training problems, 174
U.S.S. Pueblo incident and, 198
Villa, Francisco "Pancho," 27–28
Vinson, Rep. Carl, 143
The Volunteer Soldier of America, 11
Vuono, Gen. Carl, 320, 321, 326, 328, 338–339, 457

WACs. See Women's Army Corps
Wadsworth, Sen. James J., 33, 34
War Department
  active duty training tours to Regular Army and National Guard officers, 66
  age as factor in denial of active service for ORC members, 65
  "cautious demobilization" after defeat of Japan, 80
  Circular No. 347, 79–80, 81
  commissioning of ORC officers for five years, 73
  establishment, 6
  percentage of Organized Reserve officers by rank in 1944, 70–71
  Reserve Officers' Section, 35–37
  suspension of ROTC camps, 74
  years of service ribbons for ORC, 52
War Department General Order No. 38, 26
War of 1812, 7
War Powers Resolution, 370
War with Mexico, 8–9
Ward, Maj. Gen. William, 305, 319, 327, 334, 338–339, 499, 539
Warren, Maj. Gen. Frederick M., 134
Washington, George
  French and Indian War and, 3
  Regular Army and militia recommendations, 5–6
Water treatment and supply units, Desert Shield/Desert Storm
  role, 384–386, 495
Watt, Lt. Col. Merrill W., 398
Webb, James H., Jr., 288, 305, 343–344, 348, 349
Webb, Sgt. 1st Class Raymond G. "Buddy," 269
Weeks, Secretary of War John W., 37, 50
Weigley, Russell F., 2, 3, 11, 27
Weinberger, Secretary of Defense Caspar W., 303, 358, 585
Weinberger Tests for committing U.S. forces to combat, 585
Well drilling efforts, Desert Shield/Desert Storm and, 403–404
Westmoreland, Gen. William C., 172, 194, 199, 216, 217
Westover, Brig. Gen. Wendell, 88
Wheeler, Gen. Earl C., 194, 195, 200, 201
White, Deputy Secretary of Defense John P., 218–219
White, Maj. Gen. W.G., 76
Wickersham, Attorney General George W., 23
Wiggins, Col. Porter P., 68
Wilkes, Col. Bernard F., Jr., 419
Williams, Maj. Harry L., Jr., 359n
Wilson, Maj. Tom, 431
Wilson, Secretary of Defense Charles E., 115, 122
Wilson, Woodrow, 28
Winkley, Lt. Col. Douglas, 452
Woerner, Gen. Fred, 279
Wolfenberger, Capt. Mark, 556–557
Women in the National Guard, 354
Women in the Reserve
  combat restriction, 94
  first woman to take command of an Army Transportation
  Unit, photo, 187
  inclusion of, 93–94
  increase in numbers, 242–244, 353–354, 574–575
  promotion procedures, 118
  six-year military obligation, 240
Women's Armed Services Integration Act of 1948, 93, 242
Women's Army Corps, 93, 242
  promotion, 118
Women's Medical Specialist Corps, 93
  promotion, 118
Wood, Maj. Gen. Leonard, 12, 21, 23–24, 26, 27, 29, 39
Wood, Maj. Jo, 471, 472
Woodring, Secretary of War Harry H., 49
Woods, Capt. Steven C., 398
Woolnough, Gen. James L., 254
World War I, 30–32
  demobilization after, 33
World War I to World War II
  Congressional attitude toward expanded standing army, 33
  demobilization, 33
  National Defense Act of 1920, 34–35
  Officers' Reserve Corps buildup, 37–40
  preparing for mobilization, 52–54
  Reserve Office establishment, 35–37
  rewards for the Officers' Reserve Corps, 51–52
  training the Officers' Reserve Corps, 40–51
World War II. See also Post-World War II period
  calling-up the ORC, 64–72
  executive operations, 77–78
  financial cost of winning, 81
  Hitler's invasion of Europe, 63–64
  increasing the ORC, 72–75
  POWs and MIAs investigation, 551
  war-time policies, 75–77
Worldwide Military Command and Control System, 312–313
Wyeth, Dr. [first name?], 18n

Yakima, WA, 203–204, 209
Yeosock, Lt. Gen. John J., 397, 400, 434, 477, 478, 485

Zales, Carolynne, 503
Zinni, Col. Gabriel, 268

☆ U.S. GOVERNMENT PRINTING OFFICE: 1997 401–023

UNITED STATES